A
CONFLICT-OF-LAWS
ANTHOLOGY

ANDERSON'S
Law School Publications

Administrative Law Anthology
Thomas O. Sargentich

Administrative Law: Cases and Materials
Daniel J. Gifford

Alternative Dispute Resolution: Strategies for Law and Business
E. Wendy Trachte-Huber and Stephen K. Huber

An Admiralty Law Anthology
Robert M. Jarvis

Analytic Jurisprudence Anthology
Anthony D'Amato

An Antitrust Anthology
Andrew I. Gavil

Appellate Advocacy: Principles and Practice: Cases and Materials, Second Edition
Ursula Bentele and Eve Cary

Basic Accounting Principles for Lawyers: With Present Value and Expected Value
C. Steven Bradford and Gary A. Ames

A Capital Punishment Anthology (and Electronic Caselaw Appendix)
Victor L. Streib

Cases and Problems in Criminal Law, Third Edition
Myron Moskovitz

The Citation Workbook
Maria L. Ciampi, Rivka Widerman, and Vicki Lutz

Civil Procedure: Cases, Materials, and Questions
Richard D. Freer and Wendy C. Perdue

Commercial Transactions: Problems and Materials
Louis F. Del Duca, Egon Guttman, Alphonse M. Squillante, Fred H. Miller, and Peter Winship
    Vol. 1: Secured Transactions Under the UCC
    Vol. 2: Sales Under the UCC and the CISG
    Vol. 3: Negotiable Instruments Under the UCC and the CIBN

Communications Law: Media, Entertainment, and Regulation
Donald E. Lively, Allen S. Hammond, IV, Blake D. Morant, and Russell L. Weaver

A Conflict-of-Laws Anthology
Gene R. Shreve

A Constitutional Law Anthology
Michael J. Glennon

Constitutional Conflicts, Part I
Derrick A. Bell, Jr.

Constitutional Law: Cases, History, and Dialogues
Donald E. Lively, Phoebe A. Haddon, Dorothy E. Roberts, and Russell L. Weaver

The Constitutional Law of the European Union
James D. Dinnage and John F. Murphy

The Constitutional Law of the European Union: Documentary Supplement
James D. Dinnage and John F. Murphy

Constitutional Torts
Sheldon H. Nahmod, Michael L. Wells, and Thomas A. Eaton

Contracts
Contemporary Cases, Comments, and Problems
Michael L. Closen, Richard M. Perlmutter, and Jeffrey D. Wittenberg

A Contracts Anthology, Second Edition
Peter Linzer

A Corporate Law Anthology
Franklin A. Gevurtz

Corporate and White Collar Crime: An Anthology
Leonard Orland

A Criminal Law Anthology
Arnold H. Loewy

Criminal Law: Cases and Materials
Arnold H. Loewy

A Criminal Procedure Anthology
Silas J. Wasserstrom and Christie L. Snyder

Criminal Procedure: Arrest and Investigation
Arnold H. Loewy and Arthur B. LaFrance

Criminal Procedure: Trial and Sentencing
Arthur B. LaFrance and Arnold H. Loewy

Economic Regulation: Cases and Materials
Richard J. Pierce, Jr.

Elements of Law
Eva H. Hanks, Michael E. Herz, and Steven S. Nemerson

Ending It: Dispute Resolution in America
Descriptions, Examples, Cases and Questions
Susan M. Leeson and Bryan M. Johnston

Environmental Law, Second Edition
Jackson B. Battle, Robert L. Fischman, Maxine I. Lipeles, and Mark S. Squillace
    Vol. 1: Environmental Decisionmaking: NEPA and the Endangered Species Act
    Vol. 2: Water Pollution
    Vol. 3: Air Pollution
    Vol. 4: Hazardous Waste

An Environmental Law Anthology
Robert L. Fischman, Maxine I. Lipeles, and Mark S. Squillace

Environmental Protection and Justice
Readings and Commentary on Environmental Law and Practice
Kenneth A. Manaster

An Evidence Anthology
Edward J. Imwinkelried and Glen Weissenberger

Federal Evidence Courtroom Manual
Glen Weissenberger

Federal Income Tax Anthology
Paul L. Caron, Karen C. Burke, and Grayson M.P. McCouch

Federal Rules of Evidence, 1996-97 Edition
Rules, Legislative History, Commentary and Authority
Glen Weissenberger

Federal Rules of Evidence Handbook, 1996-97 Edition
Publisher's Staff

First Amendment Anthology
Donald E. Lively, Dorothy E. Roberts, and Russell L. Weaver

International Environmental Law Anthology
Anthony D'Amato and Kirsten Engel

International Human Rights: Law, Policy and Process, Second Edition
Frank C. Newman and David Weissbrodt

Selected International Human Rights Instruments and Bibliography For Research on International Human Rights Law, Second Edition
Frank C. Newman and David Weissbrodt

International Intellectual Property Anthology
Anthony D'Amato and Doris Estelle Long

International Law Anthology
Anthony D'Amato

International Law Coursebook
Anthony D'Amato

Introduction to The Study of Law: Cases and Materials
John Makdisi

Judicial Externships: The Clinic Inside The Courthouse
Rebecca A. Cochran

Justice and the Legal System
A Coursebook
Anthony D'Amato and Arthur J. Jacobson

The Law of Disability Discrimination
Ruth Colker

ADA Handbook
Statutes, Regulations and Related Materials
Publisher's Staff

The Law of Modern Payment Systems and Notes
Fred H. Miller and Alvin C. Harrell

Lawyers and Fundamental Moral Responsibility
Daniel R. Coquillette

Microeconomic Predicates to Law and Economics
Mark Seidenfeld

Patients, Psychiatrists and Lawyers Law and the Mental Health System, Second Edition
Raymond L. Spring, Roy B. Lacoursiere, M.D., and Glen Weissenberger

Principles of Evidence, Third Edition
Irving Younger, Michael Goldsmith, and David A. Sonenshein

Problems and Simulations in Evidence, Second Edition
Thomas F. Guernsey

A Products Liability Anthology
Anita Bernstein

Professional Responsibility Anthology
Thomas B. Metzloff

A Property Anthology
Richard H. Chused

Public Choice and Public Law: Readings and Commentary
Maxwell L. Stearns

Preventive Law: Materials on a Non Adversarial Legal Process
Robert M. Hardaway

The Regulation of Banking
Cases and Materials on Depository Institutions and Their Regulators
Michael P. Malloy

Science in Evidence
David H. Kaye

A Section 1983 Civil Rights Anthology
Sheldon H. Nahmod

Sports Law: Cases and Materials, Third Edition
Ray L. Yasser, James R. McCurdy, and C. Peter Goplerud

A Torts Anthology
Lawrence C. Levine, Julie A. Davies, and Edward J. Kionka

Trial Practice
Lawrence A. Dubin and Thomas F. Guernsey

Trial Practice And Case Files
Edward R. Stein and Lawrence A. Dubin

Trial Practice and Case Files with *Video* Presentation
Edward R. Stein and Lawrence A. Dubin

Unincorporated Business Entities
Larry E. Ribstein

FORTHCOMING PUBLICATIONS

A Civil Procedure Anthology
David I. Levine, Donald L. Doernberg, and Melissa L. Nelken

A Clinical Law Anthology
Alex J. Hurder, Frank S. Bloch, Susan L. Brooks, and Susan L. Kay

A Constitutional Law Anthology, Second Edition
Donald E. Lively, Michael J. Glennon, Phoebe A. Haddon, Dorothy E. Roberts, and Russell L. Weaver

American Legal Systems: A Resource and Reference Guide
Toni M. Fine

Antitrust Law: Cases and Materials
Daniel J. Gifford and Leo J. Raskind

A Property Law Anthology, Second Edition
Richard H. Chused

Citation Workbook, Second Edition
Maria L. Ciampi, Rivka Widerman, and Vicki Lutz

Constitutional Conflicts, Part II
Derrick A. Bell, Jr.

Contract Law and Practice: Cases and Materials
Michael L. Closen, Gerald E. Berendt, Doris Estelle Long, Marie A. Monahan, Robert J. Nye, and John H. Scheid

European Union Law Anthology
Anthony D'Amato and Karen V. Kole

Family Law Anthology
Frances E. Olsen

Law and Economics: An Anthology
Kenneth G. Dau-Schmidt and Thomas S. Ulen

A
CONFLICT-OF-LAWS
ANTHOLOGY

By GENE R. SHREVE
Richard S. Melvin Professor of Law
Indiana University School of Law — Bloomington

ANDERSON PUBLISHING CO.
CINCINNATI, OHIO

A CONFLICT-OF-LAWS ANTHOLOGY
BY GENE R. SHREVE

Anderson Publishing Co.
2035 Reading Road / Cincinnati, Ohio 45202
800-582-7295 / e-mail andpubco@aol.com / Fax 513-562-5430

ISBN: 0-87084-800-3

TO MAURY HOLLAND, IN FRIENDSHIP AND GRATITUDE

Contents

Introduction

The terms "conflict of laws," "conflicts law," and "choice of law" appear interchangeably in this anthology. They describe law that attempts to provide an intelligible and principled basis for choosing a substantive rule (perhaps tort or contract) over the competing rule of another place. Rules compete when their application would lead to conflicting results and when the relation of each place to the controversy is such that it is plausible for the rule of either place to govern. Conflicts law must legitimate the choice. It must explain why rejection of one law in favor of another is right.

A conflicts anthology is especially useful for two reasons. First, of all important legal subjects, conflict of laws may be the most demanding in theory and complex in application. It is not an overstatement to suggest that conflict of laws must be understood thoroughly to be understood at all. To that end, the selections in this anthology offer numerous opportunities for reflection and insight. Second, conflicts writers have actually shaped a great deal of conflicts law. Frequently, American courts expressly incorporate conflicts scholarship in their opinions. It is impossible to understand the law made in such cases without a grounding in conflicts scholarship. To that end, the anthology provides an introduction to the traditions, themes and main arguments in the conflicts literature.

This anthology is designed either to supplement course materials in the basic law school course in conflict of laws, or to guide advanced study and research, or merely to serve as a reference work for those interested in conflicts law and theory. The selections appearing in the book represent the best in conflicts writing. While these selections capture important ideas of the authors, space limitations prevent me from including as much textual material as I would have liked. I have also been forced to exclude a great many of the footnotes accompanying excerpted material in its original setting. Whenever the opportunity presents itself, readers should seek out and read the originals in their entirety.

Space limitations also prevent me from presenting the work of as many authors as I would have wished. Reference to many other useful books and articles appears in comments throughout the book, in a survey of literature on additional topics in Chapter Eleven, and in an extensive bibliography of conflicts writing in Chapter Twelve.

I am grateful for the support extended by the Anderson Foundation through creation of the Richard S. Melvin Professorship and for the encouragement of Dean Alfred C. Aman of the Indiana University—Bloomington School of Law. I wish to thank research assistants Jill Sears (Class of 1997), who helped in setting up the project, and Marla Wagner (Class of 1998), who provided tireless and invaluable assistance thereafter.

Note on Editing and Citation

The table of contents contains citations for each of the selections in the anthology. Citations also accompany the selections as they appear. The latter include references to the pages in the original from which the selection is drawn. Additions to the text or the footnotes required by the edit appear in brackets: [insertion]. The signal * * * appearing within a paragraph indicates that a portion of the paragraph has been deleted. The signal * * * centered below a paragraph indicates the deletion of one or more intervening paragraphs not exceeding one page. The signal * * * * * centered below a paragraph indicates the deletion of more than one page of intervening material. Most footnotes that accompanied the text have been deleted without elision marks. Footnotes that are included retain their original numbering.

The large bibliography appearing as Chapter Twelve is arranged alphabetically by author. When an author has multiple listings, they are arranged chronologically. This bibliography makes it possible for me to use in my "Comments" throughout the book a short form of citation that is standard in academic writing. To illustrate, the short-form citation, "Beale 1909: p. 5," refers to page 5 of the work appearing in the bibliography as "BEALE, Joseph H. (1909) *What Law Governs the Validity of a Contract,* 23 HARV. L. REV. 1."

In addition, portions of the bibliography dealing with additional conflicts topics are reproduced in full under a series of headings in Chapter Eleven.

CHAPTER ONE

An Overview—Themes Animating
Conflict of Laws

This anthology stresses four themes that animate conflicts law and commentary: multilateralism, unilateralism, substantivism, and party expectations. The goal of *multilateralism* is conflicts law uniformly defined and administered throughout a community of jurisdictions—to produce the same choice-of-law result wherever the case is decided. This is sometimes called a territorial or jurisdiction-selecting approach. On the other hand, *unilateralism* measures a law's applicability not by a jurisdiction-selecting rule but by asking whether the case at hand is one that particular law is designed to govern. This inquiry is about the spatial reach of substantive rules. *Substantivism* represents the idea that conflicts judges should whenever possible choose the best available substantive law. Finally, the *party expectations* theme rests on the assumption that chosen law should not disturb the reasonable expectations of a litigant.

In the following excerpt, the author elaborates on the meaning and influence of each of these themes.

Gene R. Shreve, *Choice of Law and the Forgiving Constitution*, 71 IND. L.J. 271, 281-287 (1996)*

* * * * *

Conflicts law is usually common law, therefore, one can expect to find in judicial opinions a good deal of conflicts theory and policy. As in any common law sphere, decisions creating or adjusting conflicts doctrine aspire to a measure of principled elaboration: careful balancing of social interests and concern for reasoned delineation and continuity in law. Policies enlisted in conflicts opinions to meet the demands of principled elaboration usually support one of three approaches. These are the substantive, multilateral, and unilateral approaches to choice of law. In addition, courts and commentators periodically express concern that chosen law not unreasonably disturb the expectations of a party.

A. The Substantive Approach

The single-minded policy of the substantive approach is that there is a preferable result for a particular type of case (e.g., plaintiffs should win product liability cases). Conflicts law should

---

*   Reprinted with permission.

not obstruct this outcome. It should, if anything, facilitate it. The substantive approach can take one of two forms. One makes the choice-of-law issue disappear. This may happen because the sovereign making substantive law is so powerful that conflicting law from an inferior source must give way. The relation of federal to state substantive law is the most important example. Or a group of coequal sovereigns may all adopt the same substantive rule as their local law. The other substantive approach, necessary when coequal sovereigns have conflicting laws, is to authorize substantive preference within the choice-of-law scheme. An example used by a number of courts is the fifth and last of Professor Robert Leflar's "Choice-influencing Considerations," termed "Application of the better rule of law."[76]

Neither multilateralism nor unilateralism share with the substantive approach the concern over the innate justice of chosen law. Both are concerned instead with selection of the correct sovereign, or law source. These two conflicts approaches have coexisted since medieval times. Our leading conflicts historian writes that this "is remarkable because unilateralism and multilateralism proceed from different assumptions, focus on different questions, and are bound to yield different conclusions."[78]

B. Multilateralism

Multilateralism strives for uniform results in choice of law. To the multilateralist judge, the possible sources of chosen law are sovereigns, or jurisdictions, that make up a kind of legal community. Each type of case has its own conflicts rule, administrable throughout that legal community. For example, the requirement that the tort law of the place of injury should govern is a multilateral rule. Ideally, each member of this community of jurisdictions would use the common conflicts rule, and uniform choice-of-law results would exist in fact. If so, the high-minded suppositions of interjurisdictional order and comity attending the earliest conceptions of multilateralism in this country would be vindicated. To many multilateralists, however, that perfect or even substantial interjurisdictional cooperation is unnecessary to justify their approach. They have contended that multilateralism in any event advances policies of antidiscrimination. And many have used vested rights analysis to maintain that multilateralism leads to the only valid source of law.

Multilateralism dominated choice of law in this country during the 19th century and for the first half of the 20th century. Published in 1834, Joseph Story's strongly multilateralist *Commentaries on the Conflict of Laws* was quite influential in the United States and abroad. No less committed to multilateralism, Professor Joseph Beale extended the movement through his scholarship and through his leadership in the creation of the original *Restatement of the Law of Conflict of Laws*, published one hundred years after Story's treatise. Resistance materialized, however, to the uncompromising multilateralism of Story and Beale. It may be found in commentary beginning in the 1920's and in judicial decisions somewhat later.

Shortly after mid-century, the choice-of-law revolution began in earnest. Particularly in torts and contract cases, American jurisdictions began rejecting multilateralism in rapid succession. Today, the original *Restatement* enjoys widespread acceptance in only a few jurisdictions. Multilateralism may assume new forms in the future and regain some of its prior

---

[76]   Robert A. Leflar, *Choice-Influencing Considerations in Conflicts Law*, 41 N.Y.U. L. Rev. 267, 295-303 (1966).* * *

[78]   Friedrich K. Juenger, *A Page of History*, 35 MERCER L. REV. 419, 427 (1983).* * *

importance. For the time being, however, courts are most receptive to multilateralism when the approach is softened and blended with unilateral, and at times substantive, policies.

C. Unilateralism

Unilateralism shares with multilateralism the idea that choice of law should search for the appropriate sovereign (law source) rather than for the best law. Yet unilateralism shares with the substantive approach a keen interest in the content of the laws vying for application. A unilateralist would see no contradiction here. She does not examine each of the conflicting laws to determine (as a substantivist would) which best promotes justice. Rather, she examines them to determine whether each, upon closer study, is truly applicable. A law is truly applicable to a unilateralist only if the case at hand is one of the cases that the law was designed to govern. If so, then the sovereign creating that law may be said to be interested in having it applied. Interest analysis is the linchpin for conflicts unilateralism in the United States.

Unilateralists are not particularly opposed to the idea of uniformity in choice of law. They simply do not share the multilateralist belief that uniformity is of central importance. Unilateralists would maintain that, in at least some cases, interest analysis leads to a different and better result than that provided by multilateralism. Consider an example. Following the facts of a famous case,[97] let us assume that passenger plaintiff and driver defendant, both residents of State A, travel together to State B, where defendant loses control of his car and negligently injures plaintiff. Assume further that the tort law of the place of the plaintiff's and the defendant's residence makes defendant liable to plaintiff, but the law of the place of injury does not.

The multilateral conflicts rule directs the court in this and other personal injury cases to apply the rule of decision of the place of the injury, State B. If, however, the purpose of State A's pro-recovery law was to compensate victims and the purpose of State B's anti-recovery law was to keep insurance rates down in State B, only State A will be interested in having its tort law applied. The policy of compensation accounting for the existence of State A's pro-recovery law would be implicated because plaintiff is a citizen of State A and could, in the absence of compensation, become a ward of State A. But the cost-conscious policy accounting for State B's anti-recovery law would not be implicated, because recovery by plaintiff would affect insurance rates of State A, rather than those of State B. Through interest analysis, the unilateralist judge chooses the law of State A, concluding that State A is the only sovereign genuinely interested in having its law applied.

Much of the credit for launching unilateralism in this country goes to Brainerd Currie, the principal creator of interest analysis. Professor Currie distinguished cases where only one sovereign was interested in having its law applied (he termed them "false" conflicts) from those where both sovereigns were interested ("true" conflicts). Not all of Currie's unconventional ideas were successful. Some were either stillborn or frayed over time. His greatest accomplishment was to establish through his false conflict principle a formidable argument for departing from multilateral choice of law. Ten years ago, Professor John Kozyris wrote that "interest analysis . . . has dominated the conflicts agenda for the last quarter century and deconstructed traditional conflicts in most states."[104] At the same time, unilateralist policies of interest analysis are now most likely to appear interspersed with those of multilateralism and substantivism.

---

[97]   Babcock v. Jackson, 191 N.E.2d 279 (N.Y. 1963).* * *

[104]   P. John Kozyris, *Foreword*, OHIO STATE Symposium, *supra* note 100, at 457.

D. Party Expectations as to Chosen Law

Taken together, the three conflicts approaches just considered encompass most of the conflicts policies in use today. Yet the following important principle may be difficult to locate within either a substantive, multilateralist, or unilateralist approach. A party may be protected from the choice of unfavorable law if the party reasonably and to his detriment relied on the application of favorable law. The policy justifying this—variously termed party expectations, avoidance of unfair surprise, or foreseeability—is well accepted in conflicts theory.

The availability of this policy is likely to turn on idiosyncracies of fact, such as whether a party actually relied on the application of favorable law, or whether that reliance was reasonable. While courts often discount the expectations factor in tort cases, it can figure there. The policy comes to bear more frequently in other areas, like contract cases, where the parties are more likely to have expectations about choice of law prior to the controversy.

The expectations policy does not seem within the substantive tradition in choice of law because it has little if anything to do with the innate quality of the law upon which a party reasonably relies. Uniformity sought by multilateralism, if actually achieved, might enhance foreseeability in choice of law and correspondingly reduce possibilities for unfair surprise. However, the multilateralist predilection for stern and categorical conflicts rules is ill suited to administer a policy as supple and case variable as expectations. Unilateralism, while a method-centered and case-variable approach, shares classic multilateralism's focus on sovereigns as a source of law. To unilateralism, preoccupied with interest analysis, concern about expectations of the parties would be something of a distraction.

In the end, whether a policy protecting reasonable expectations exists within one of the tripartite categories or separately may not be terribly important. We have already noted that substantive, multilateral, and unilateral approaches have fragmented, and policies attributable to each have become interspersed. The additional presence of an expectations policy simply bears out the eclectic trend in modern conflicts theory.

Comments

1. Multilateralism, unilateralism, substantivism, and party expectations—the four themes presented in this Chapter—matter to our conflicts law only because that law rejects what at first blush might seem to be the most basic and obvious response to a conflicts problem: absolute *lex fori* (invariable forum favoritism). Students beginning their conflicts course may imagine this to be the law. That is, they may assume that each American court always applies its local law, even in cases with interstate or international contacts. This would be an easy rule to administer, and it can be found in some of the conflicts law of ages past (Hay 1991: pp. 293-294;[1] North & Fawcett 1992: p. 23; Juenger 1993: p. 23). Conflicts study soon makes clear, however, that such an approach would foster rampant forum shopping, substantive chaos, and pernicious acts of judicial localism. Because invariable forum favoritism lacks the properties of justice and order demanded of any law, it is not a choice-of-law option.

2. We are therefore presented with numerous questions concerning the form American conflicts law does or should take. There are questions about purpose. "Are

---

[1]   Full citations appear in the bibliography, Chapter Twelve.

choice-of-law rules a consequence of noble altruism, are they compelled by international law, or can they be justified by purely pragmatic considerations?" Juenger 1993: p. 45. There are also questions about the instrumental capacity of conflicts law to achieve any given purpose. Is a particular conflicts rule intelligible in application, does it achieve its intended result, does it facilitate (or at least not obstruct) the operation of other rules of law?

3.   Discussion of these and other important questions is impossible without reference to a scheme of values: norms by which we can identify conflicts law as good or bad. This is why the four themes animate conflicts law and why they are central to a study of our subject. Separately, they present systematic (and to an extent competing) visions of good conflicts law. Together, they pose a comprehensive array of choice-of-law values and illuminate the depth and sophistication of American conflict of laws.

4.   These themes reappear throughout the book. Chapter Two explores the European roots of multilateralism, unilateralism and substantivism. Chapters Three and Four treat the development of multilateralism in the United States. Chapters Five and Six similarly treat unilateralism. Justified expectations and substantivism in choice of law are the focus of Chapter Seven. Chapters Seven and Eight address the interplay of the four themes in contemporary conflicts law and commentary. Chapter Nine reveals how these themes serve as points of departure in a variety of proposals for reforming conflicts law. The four themes reappear in writing on choice of law and the Constitution in Chapter Ten.

CHAPTER TWO

Historic Divisions—Multilateral and Unilateral Approaches to Choice of Law in Europe

In this portion of his path-breaking study, Professor Friedrich Juenger traces the history of European conflicts law and theory from the ninth century. The developments that occupy this historical narrative are interesting in themselves. Perhaps more important, this discussion will enable us to view in broader perspective issues in American conflicts law that we will subsequently encounter.

Friedrich K. Juenger, CHOICE OF LAW AND MULTISTATE JUSTICE 10-27, 32-42 (Boston: Nijhoff 1993)*

* * * * *

2. THE ORIGIN OF THE CONFLICT OF LAWS

(a) The Personal Laws of the Middle Ages

The first strides toward a choice-of-law system were made in darker ages. The Germanic tribes that destroyed the Roman Empire brought along their own laws, but did not eradicate those of the peoples they conquered. Consequently, once the invaders settled in formerly Roman territories, they lived together with people whose legal relations were governed by entirely different rules. As St. Agobar, Archbishop of Lyon, wrote to Louis the Pious in 817, "it often happens that five men, each under a different law, may be found walking or sitting together."[41]

Such legal diversity posed conflicts questions. Which law should govern the marriage of a Lombard with a Roman, or the contract of a Visigoth with a Hispano-Roman? Apparently, rules of considerable complexity were developed to deal with interpersonal choice-of-law problems. Eventually, however, imaginative legal minds found a more elegant solution. The professio iuris, a declaration originally meant to evidence the parties' ethnicity, could be employed in a fictitious manner: by professing to belong to a particular ethnic group, a party could in effect stipulate the law it wished to govern. By condoning this practice, the courts implicitly recognized the principle of party autonomy.

---

*   Reprinted with permission.
41   1 F. VON SAVIGNY, GESCHICHTE DES ROMISCHEN RECHTS IM MITTELALTER 116 (2nd ed. 1834).

(b) The Italian School

The true beginning of the conflict of laws, as we know it, had to await the revival of Roman law in the twelfth century, when scholars began to study and teach Justinian's Code. The political realities of Upper Italy, where these efforts began, explain the glossators' and commentators' interest in the subject. The Italian city-states in which Roman law was taught were independent entities, each having its own judiciary and its own local laws. Since these *statuta* differed from one another they posed choice-of-law issues. For instance, if a citizen of Modena sued a citizen of Bologna on a contract made in Pisa, the judge had to ponder which of the three potentially applicable laws should furnish the rule of decision. The medieval scholars who expounded the *Corpus Juris* were convinced that the answer to this question had to be found in the Code; no matter that neither the classical Roman lawyers nor Justinian's compilers had given the problem much thought.

Distorting history, the glossators attached the choice-of-law problem to a passage in the first title of the *Codex*. Its heading - "About the most exalted Trinity and the Catholic faith that no one shall dare publicly oppose" - indicates that this title is concerned with religion, rather than with conflicts problems. The same is true of the opening lines of the title's first law, which may be translated as follows: "We want all peoples which are subject to Our reign of mercy to live in the religion that according to religious tradition the Divine Apostle Peter gave to the Romans. . . ." With scholastic acumen the glossators deduced from this statement that because even the Roman Emperor could legislate only for his subjects, the power of Italian city-states must be similarly limited. As Accursius explained in a gloss on the *lex cunctos populos*: "If a person from Bologna makes a contract in Modena he may not be adjudged according to the statutes of Modena, to which he is not subject, because as it [the Codex] says: 'which [are subject to] Our mercy.'"[47]

This reasoning is, of course, preposterous. As so many later authors remind us, the *lex cunctos populos* had simply nothing to do with choice of law. And why, in any event, should medieval scholars, who earned their fame and fortunes by elaborating a new European common law from Justinian's old code, choose to dabble in the conflict of laws? It seems inconsistent to expound, on the one hand, a *ratio scripta* of universal application and, on the other, to explore a subject that presupposes the existence of divergent laws. The explanation for this paradox lies in the setting in which these jurists worked. Living in medieval university towns, they were astutely aware of the political importance local law and government had for city-states that cherished their legal autonomy. Inevitably, these realities directed the scholars' attention to the problem of whether a local *statutum* could and should be applied to foreign facts. By finding a fixed place for the choice-of-law problem in the *Corpus Juris,* where it never belonged, they achieved a dual objective: to legitimize the existing diversity of laws in Northern Italy, and to make the conflict of laws a subject worthy of academic pursuit.

Once scholars assumed that multistate problems require a choice among competing local laws, they not only lost sight of the fact that the Romans had dealt with multistate transactions more directly by creating a *ius gentium*, but they faced the question what principle should govern the selection. A glossator called Magister Aldricus, whom Neumeyer believed to be the founder of our discipline, gave a simple answer: he favored application of that law which is better and more useful. This advice, if heeded, might have inspired the development of a new *ius gentium*. Aldricus' suggestion describes what the *praetor peregrinus* had in effect been doing, namely to choose from various rules the one which best accommodates the demands of justice. Consistently applied, his prescription would have produced a substantive body of law. Con-

---

[47]   47 CODE J. 1.1.1.

sensus on those rules of decision that are to be preferred as "better and more useful" would eliminate the choice-of-law problem, for only those rules and no others could claim application to multistate transactions.

Aldricus' successors in Northern Italy and Southern France, however, preferred to tackle the problem in a conceptualist rather than a teleological fashion. Instead of looking for substantive solutions, they theorized about the spatial reach of local law. The wording of the *lex cunctos populos,* which speaks of "peoples subject to" the Emperor's command, implied that the personal link between a state and its citizens is decisive. Thus the laws of a political unit would apply to the unit's subjects (wherever they may be) but not foreigners. The walls ringing medieval cities, however, served as a reminder that there may be territorial as well as personal limits to legal rules. Accordingly, scholars began to discuss whether local *statuta* could be applied extraterritorially to citizens abroad, and whether foreign citizens within the forum's territory were bound by its laws. By viewing the problem in this fashion, the glossators hit upon what has since been called "unilateralist" choice-of-law rules that are geared to divining the scope of application of substantive rules of decision.

These medieval jurists, however, also invented multilateralism, a very different approach that interposes between legal transactions and substantive law "jurisdiction-selecting" choice-of-law rules. For example, Italian glossators and their French colleagues coined the maxim *locus regit actum.* The also debated whether contracts are governed by the law at the place of execution or of performance. Rights in property, they concluded, are controlled by the law prevailing at its situs. Both of these basic approaches to choice of law are intermingled in Bartolus' famous commentary on the *lex cunctos populos*, which contains multilateral rules as well as discussions about the spatial reach of law. The statutory choice-of-law rules of the *Siete Partidas,* which Alfonse the Wise published in 1265, half a century before Bartolus was born, are similarly eclectic.

The coexistence of these two methods in early conflicts literature is remarkable. Unilateralism and multilateralism proceed from different assumptions, focus on different questions, and yield different conclusions. In fact some writers believe in an evolutionary process, by virtue of which the conflict of laws progressed from the unilateral approach to a multilateral one. There is indeed some historical support for this proposition, in that unilateralism may be considered to be the older of the two approaches. While the *mos italicus* did produce some multilateral rules, for obvious reasons its basic thrust was unilateralist. Having linked the choice-of-law problem to the *lex cunctos populos,* the glossators could not avoid the question whom the forum's *statutum* binds, namely only subjects or also foreigners within its territory. Hence their speculations focused on the reach of substantive rules, which is the essence of unilateralism, and they began to ponder whether there might not be different kinds of laws: some of a personal nature that would govern citizens wherever they are, and others that, being territorial, apply to all persons and things within the state.

The search for criteria that would determine the spatial dimension of laws preoccupied scholars for centuries. Alas, the results of their attempts to find a basis for distinguishing between personal and territorial (or "real") statutes were disappointing. A famous example illustrates how eminent jurists can be led astray by an ill-conceived quest. The great Bartolus wrestled with that distinction in the context of the *quaestio Anglica,* the question whether the English rule of primogeniture applies to property in Italy. Blithely disregarding possible differences between Italian *statuta* and English common law rules, he took the position that the wording of the "statute" may determine its reach. Thus, if English law should provide that "the possessions of deceased persons shall pass to the firstborn," the *lex rei sitae* would apply. If the rule were to read "the firstborn shall succeed," the answer might turn on whether or not the deceased was English, because the "statute" would then be personal rather than real. Later writers mocked Bartolus' reliance on the mere "shell of words," but the criteria propounded by his successors, the "statutists," were no better. Ultimately, some scholars realized that even such broad categories as "personal" and "real" might not capture all of life's and law's realities, and added a third category of "mixed" statutes. That merely complicated matters further. * * * For centuries, useless disputes raged about how particular laws should be characterized, until conflicts scholars realized that the statutists' taxonomic obsession was a sure indication of unilateralism's failings.

In hindsight, much of what the glossators and commentators wrote may indeed appear ludicrous. Yet, we should not lose sight of the remarkable accomplishments of those who first discussed conflicts problems in Upper Italy and southern France. These medieval scholars conceived highly original methods, about which the Greeks and Romans had never thought, to resolve multistate problems by making a principled selection among competing local rules. Not only did these jurists invent both unilateralism and multilateralism, but some of them used teleology as a choice-influencing factor. Thus, Aldricus premised the choice between competing substantive rules on a comparison of their respective merits and others, like Bartolus, distinguished between "favorable" and "odious" statutes. The fundamental ideas found in Bartolus' brief commentary still hold sway. The current "crisis" in the conflict of laws boils down to a dispute about the relative merits of the various methods he employed. In other words, Bartolus' eclecticism anticipated, by several centuries, the "pluralism of methods" or "mishmash approach" that prevails today.

Of course, the early scholars had the advantage of a broader intellectual perspective than today's conflicts experts, most of whom have been trained to believe that a choice among competing rules is the only way to deal with multistate problems. Bartolus and his predecessors were, after all, engaged primarily in teaching a supranational Roman and canon law. Choice-of-law problems could arise only when the *ius commune* had to give way to local statutes, and many issues posed by multistate transactions were controlled by a superlaw that eliminated the need for choice. Moreover, upper Italy was not merely the birthplace of a continental European common law. Its flourishing trade and commerce also promoted the development of a law merchant, a process that has been described as "a rebirth of the old *jus gentium* of the Mediterranean." The *lex mercatoria,* which Maitland called the "'private international law' of the Middle Ages," offered supranational solutions to what have since become choice-of-law problems. In other words, when conflicts rules were first conceived, law was still cosmopolitan. The existence of overarching principles and institutions made the particularistic tendencies implicit in such rules more bearable than in our statist and positivist times.

(c) The French School

Italian scholarship declined after Baldus, who outlived Bartolus by some 40 years. There was little movement in the field until leadership in the conflict of laws shifted to France in the sixteenth century. (French scholars had, of course, made important contributions all along. Indeed, it may be more appropriate to refer to the initial phase of conflicts scholarship as the French-Italian school, rather than the *mos italicus,* except that this label would confuse these earlier efforts with the *mos gallicus* that now developed.) In sixteenth-century France, as in thirteenth-century Italy, there were good reasons to ponder conflicts questions. Even after the French kings had established the crown's supremacy, the law varied from province to province, and there was a basic split between the Germanic *coutumes* of Northern France and the *droit ecrit* that prevailed south of the Loire Valley. In fact, the potential for conflicts problems was even greater than in Upper Italy, since in France feudalism lingered on much longer and the grip of Roman law was more tenuous.

Although he wrote almost 200 years after Bartolus, the French scholar Dumoulin arguably still belongs to the Italian school. Like his Italian predecessors, he attached his principal conflicts publication to the *lex cunctos populos,* and much of what he wrote could already be found in Bartolus' commentary. Dumoulin did, however, render a distinct contribution to our discipline by strongly emphasizing party autonomy. Of course, he did not invent the idea that those who enter into an agreement may stipulate the law that governs their bargain. Whether or not the *professio iuris* can be considered their direct precursor, choice-of-law clauses had been used as early as the Middle Ages. Yet, by focusing attention on the parties' power over choice of law at a time when conflicts scholars were preoccupied with the classification of statutes, Dumoulin drew attention to the fact that there are elements that do not fit the mold of an analysis geared to the reach of local laws. Moreover, he added a new ingredient to our discipline by stretching the principle of party autonomy to encompass situations in which the parties had failed to designate the applicable law. Dumoulin's fiction of a "tacit agreement" laid the foundation for the English "proper law" approach, which in turn inspired such current formulae as the "closest connection" and the "most-significant-relationship."

Like Dumoulin, d'Argentre, the other major sixteenth-century conflicts author, still wrote in Latin. But he derided the Italian school's "scholastic writers" and broke with the custom of attaching the conflict of laws to the *lex cunctos populos.* Choosing to present his ideas in a commentary on the *coutume* of Brittany, d'Argentre anticipated the idea that conflicts rules are creatures of local, rather than universal, law. The same forum bias informs his method of classifying legal rules. D'Argentre recognized only a limited number of personal laws, and he added the category of "mixed" statutes, which he contended should be treated like real ones. This classificatory scheme elevated territorialism to the position of a fundamental principle. By reducing the personal law idea to a mere exception, he increased the scope of the *lex rei sitae* and diminished the domain of domiciliary law.

During the sixteenth century the main component of wealth was still realty, and disputes about marital property and the succession to immovables constituted the bulk of legal business. Since such cases were generally adjudicated by the courts at the property's location, d'Argentre's system favored the application of the *lex fori.* This territorialist penchant may explain his polemics against Dumoulin's notion of a "tacit contract," which serves to accord foreign law a greater sway. The two French jurists thus represent opposing conceptions, one favoring a cosmopolitan approach to multistate transactions, the other a forum-centered methodology. D'Argentre's implicit assumption that courts should normally apply their own law, whereas foreign rules of decision are relevant only in exceptional cases, anticipates a mode of thinking that later surfaced in the writing of Wachter and recent American authors.

Guy de Coquille, who discussed conflicts problems in his commentary on the *coutume* of Nivernais, also deserves mention. Since he wrote in the vernacular rather than in Latin, the distinction between French *"coutumes"* and Italian *"statuta"* was apparent to him, and it may have directed his attention to an important difference between the spawning ground of conflicts law and the France of his days. De Coquille noted that in Italy a shared *ius commune* furnished the rule of decision, unless it was displaced by the *statutum* of one or the other city-state, whereas France lacked such an overlaw. In other words, he grasped the essential difference between the legal environment in which Bartolus wrote and that of coordinate jurisdictions bereft of an overarching common law. This distinction still matters today. Conflicts approaches developed in federal systems, such as the United States, whose component states share a common legal tradition, may not work in Europe, where national codifications destroyed the unity that the reception of Roman-law once provided.

De Coquille also gave a surprisingly modern twist to statutist learning. He argued that the classification of laws as personal or real should not depend "on the mere shell of words, but on

. . . the presumed and apparent purpose of those who have enacted the statute or custom."[97] In effect, he suggested that the reach of a rule of decision ought to depend on its purpose (or the intent of the legislator), rather than on its wording, as Bartolus had argued, or on some arbitrary classification. The idea that it is possible to deduce the scope of a rule from the purpose or "policy" behind it reappears in later centuries, and it has become the central idea of modern American conflict analysis.

(d) Dutch Authors

In the seventeenth century the Netherlands assumed the position of leadership in the conflict of laws. Surprisingly, given his vast learning and his interest in international matters, the great Grouches paid scant attention to our discipline: his famous *Law of War and Peace* contains but two brief statements about contract choice of law. One wonders why he had so little to say about conflicts, especially since his home country provided an ideal setting for exploring that field. The Netherlands were organized as independent provinces, but they had also become one of the major trading nations of the world. The combination of extensive foreign commerce and political decentralization engendered conflicts problems of both the internal and the international variety, which soon attracted the scholars' attention.

The conflicts literature of the Netherlands' Golden Age is marked by an inner tension. Although its outlook was cosmopolitan, it had to wrestle with the idea of territorial sovereignty, which Bodin had developed in the preceding century and Grotius had further elaborated. This tension may explain why Dutch jurists spoke of "conflict of laws" (*conflictus legum*), a term suggesting that choice-of-law problems are caused by the clash of sovereign commands. It also serves to explain the Dutch scholars' preoccupation with the question of why courts apply foreign law. The Italians never had an occasion to ponder that question, because they believed that a choice among different *statuta* was compelled by Justinian's Code. The French did not consider it either, because to them the application of foreign law was a necessary consequence of inherent limitations on the reach of the forum's substantive rules. Neither French nor Italian authors had therefore viewed the choice-of-law problem as calling for the resolution of a "conflict" between competing laws. But once scholars began to think about sovereign prerogatives, they were pressed to explain why the supremacy each state enjoys within its borders does not require judges to apply forum law in all cases.

The scholars' responses to this question varied. Rodenburg, who apparently coined the phrase "conflict of laws," attempted to reconcile the application of foreign law with the idea of sovereignty by postulating a superlaw derived from the "very nature and necessity" of the case, which bestowed extraterritorial effect upon local rules.[103] Paul Voet introduced the notion of "*comitas*," a term he borrowed from Justinian's Digests. As Paul's son, Johannes Voet, explained, that notion reflects a principle rooted in enlightened self-interest and convenience. Ulrich Huber made comity the touchstone of his theory. Unlike Rodenburg and the two Voets, who still remained within the framework of statutist tradition, Huber eschewed the classification of laws as personal, real and mixed. Instead, he attempted to deduce a conflicts system directly from the twin ideas of sovereignty and comity.

The first chapter of Huber's ten-page dissertation "*De conflictu legum diversarum in diversis imperiis*" is entitled "Origin and use of the question, forensic indeed, but belonging to international rather than civil law." In his words,

---

[97]   1 A. LAINE, [INTRODUCTION AU DROIT INTERNATIONAL PRIVE] 303 [(1888)].

[103]   [M. GUTZWILLER, GESCHECHTE DES INTERNATIONALPRIVATRECHTS] 132-33 [(1977)].

the solution of the problem must be derived not exclusively from the civil law, but from convenience and the tacit consent of nations. Although the laws of one nation can have no force directly with another, yet nothing could be more inconvenient to commerce and to international usage than that transactions valid by the law of one place should be rendered of no effect elsewhere on account of a difference in the law.[110]

As this quotation and the title heading indicate, Huber assumed that comity has roots in international law. However, he did not believe that the obligation to apply foreign law is absolute. Rather, according to the last of his three famous axioms, a sovereign may refuse to recognize "rights acquired" abroad if they would prejudice the forum's "power or rights." Thus Huber's short essay rendered five distinct contributions to the conflict of laws. It heralded the demise of statutist theory, anchored the discipline in international law, emphasized decisional harmony, anticipated the vested rights doctrine, and introduced the public policy reservation.

Huber's attempt to reconcile sovereignty and the exigencies of multistate transactions is less than convincing. The nebulous notion of comity, his *deus ex machina,* has been criticized harshly. The postulate of decisional harmony remains illusory as long as each forum is free to avoid the application of foreign law by invoking its public policy. The vested rights doctrine, according to which courts do not apply foreign law, but merely enforce rights created abroad, is sheer sophistry.

It is only fair, however, to point out that throughout the ages conflicts scholars have relied on similar question-begging propositions to reconcile the irreconcilable, that is to say the territorial limits of sovereignty and the free flow of multistate transactions. And for all of its deficiencies, it is difficult to overestimate Huber's contribution. As has been said of his essay: "It is all printed in five quarto pages. In the whole history of law there are probably no five pages which have been so often quoted, and possibly so much read. They are distinguished by clearness, practical judgment and a total absence of pedantry." Indeed, Huber's *De conflictu legum* has had "a greater influence upon the development of the Conflict of Laws in England and the United States than any other work."[115]

3. THE ENGLISH DEVIATION

(a) The Common Law Courts

England's unitary legal system was not as fertile a ground for conflicts problems as continental Europe's legal checkerboard. The common law was the work product of powerful central courts that had gained supremacy over feudal and local tribunals. Like the royal judges' jurisdiction, it extended throughout the entire realm. Unlike in Italy, France and the Netherlands, internal conflicts problems could therefore not arise. Englishmen, citizens of a major seafaring power, did, of course, travel to foreign shores. There they acquired property, entered into contracts and suffered injuries. But unless commercial or admiralty courts took jurisdiction, disputes arising out of such foreign transactions could not be adjudicated in England. Common law judges were unable to try them because juries had to be drawn from the vicinage, the neighborhood where the events that prompted the controversy had happened. Since jurors from foreign countries could not be impaneled, the common law courts had to dismiss cases requiring the determination of facts that had materialized beyond the realm. Plaintiffs were therefore left

---

[110]   [E. LORENZEN, SELECTED ARTICLES ON THE CONFLICT OF LAWS] 164-65 [(1947)].

[115]   E. LORENZEN, *supra* note [110], at 136.

to seek redress abroad, which may explain the great liberality with which English courts have traditionally enforced foreign country judgments.

To remedy the obvious injustice of withholding relief in cases with foreign elements, English lawyers ultimately resorted to a typical common law ruse. A tort plaintiff who had been maimed in Brussels, for instance, would aver that that city was situated in England, and the courts accepted such fictitious allegations so that the case could be tried before an English jury. As a judge deciding an action on an instrument dated in Hamburg, Germany, said in 1625:

> [W]e shall take it that Hamburg is in London in order to maintain the action which otherwise would be outside our jurisdiction. And while in truth we know the date to be at Hamburg beyond the sea, as judges we do not take notice that it is beyond the sea.[120]

As late as 1774 a plaintiff had to allege that he had been falsely imprisoned on the island of Minorca, "at London . . . in the parish of St. Mary le Bow, in the ward of Cheap." When the defendant dared object to this geographical folly, Lord Mansfield observed that he "was embarrassed a great while to find out whether the counsel for the plaintiff really meant to make a question of it," and pointed out that "the law has . . . invented a fiction . . . for the furtherance of justice; and . . . a fiction of law shall never be contradicted."[123]

(b) Maritime and Commercial Courts

Since jurisdiction in England necessarily implied application of forum law, there was no need for choice-of-law rules. But what happened in common law courts does not tell the full story of how that country dealt with multinational problems. The common law, which was developed to meet the needs of a feudal society, was not attuned to the legal problems posed by international transactions. To cope with those, special courts, as formerly in Greece and Rome, were granted jurisdiction to deal with commercial and maritime cases. These tribunals did not apply the common law; they relied on rules of decision believed to be of universal application. English commercial courts applied a common European *lex mercatoria,* and admiralty judges drew on sources widely scattered over time and space, such as the ancient sea law of Rhodes, the *Consolat de Mar,* the *Roles d'Oleron* and the Laws of Wisby. It is no accident that English judges referred to this special body of rules as the "law of nations" or "*ius gentium.*" Not only did the commercial and admiralty courts, like the *praetor peregrinus,* rely on the comparative method to elaborate new rules, but there are historical links between these two branches of English law and the Roman *ius gentium.* * * *

Obviously, there is no room for choice-of-law rules in a legal system that, transcending national boundaries, governs multistate transactions directly. Unlike the common law, maritime law was by its very nature applicable worldwide. Accordingly, at the time when common law judges still refused to hear international cases, suitors often proceeded in admiralty, even if the subject-matter was not strictly maritime in nature. Only after accepting the fiction that foreign facts happened in England could the common law courts decide disputes involving foreign facts. By that time they had also assumed the power to deal with commercial cases and begun to encroach on the jurisdiction of the admiralty courts. For a while, the judges still treated the

---

[120]   "[N]ous doiomus entend Hamburgh d'estre diens London, p. mainteyn l'action, quia aliter serroit hors de nostre jurisdic. Et si en verity nous sciamus le date d'estre al Hamburgh ouster le mere, vnc come Judges ne prisamus notice q est ouster le mere." Ward's Case. 82 Eng. Rep. 245, 246 (K.B. 1625).

[123]   [Mostyn v. Fabrigas, 98 Eng. Rep. 1021, 1022, 1030-31 (K.B. 1775)].

law merchant as a separate body of rules, a custom distinct from the common law. But around the turn of the eighteenth century they dispensed with the need to allege and prove mercantile rules. By treating these rules as law rather than mere custom, the courts incorporated the *lex mercatoria* into the common law. Thus, as in Rome, the English *"ius civile"* ultimately absorbed a *ius gentium* and, as a consequence, was enriched and improved.

(c) English Conflicts Law

Once the English courts nationalized what had been regarded as a supranational law, they faced a novel problem. Should they continue to apply the *lex fori* to transactions that were international in nature, or should they, in appropriate situations, also look to foreign law? Sir Edward Simpson's opinion in *Scrimshire v. Scrimshire*, a case decided in 1752, answered these questions. Holding that a marriage of British citizens and domiciliaries celebrated in France was void because it failed to comply with French form requirements, he said:

> Why may not this Court then take notice of foreign laws, there being nothing illegal in doing it? . . . I may infer that it is the consent of all nations that it is the jus gentium, that the solemnities of different nations with respect to marriage should be observed, and that contracts of this kind are to be determined by the laws of the country where they are made . . . The jus gentium is the law of every country, and is obligatory on the subjects of every country. Every country takes notice of it; and this Court observing that law . . . cannot be said to determine English rights by the laws of France, but by the laws of England, of which the jus gentium is part.
>
> * * *
>
> [A]s the law of England takes notice of the law of nations in commercial and maritime affairs; because all countries are interested in those questions; and as all countries are equally interested to have matrimonial questions determined by the laws of the country where they are had . . . ; I am of opinion that this is the jus gentium of which this and all courts are to take notice.[136]

The judge's use of the term "jus gentium" to connote the conflict of laws reveals a remarkable change not only in language, but in legal theory. It substitutes supranational choice-of-law rules for a universal law. But where should English courts find such rules, considering that none had been developed in England? The opinion in *Scrimshire* suggests where to look for authority: Sir Edward found the *lex loci celebrationis* rule in the works of continental European writers, of whom he most prominently cites Johannes Voet.

Scrimshire thus adumbrates the "civilization" of English conflicts law. The Treaty of Union of 1707, which preserved the Scottish legal system, facilitated this process. Since Scotland is a civil law jurisdiction some of whose institutions differ markedly from those of England, intra-British choice-of-law problems soon arose. Moreover, many Scottish jurists had studied on the Continent, particularly in the Netherlands, and were therefore familiar with civilian conflicts literature, which was frequently cited in Scottish cases. Indeed, the first book to discuss the conflict of laws in English was published by Henry Home (Lord Kames), a Scottish judge who wrote about the subject in the statutist manner. Lord Mansfield, another Scot,

---

[136]   [161 Eng. Rep.] 790-91 [(Consist. 1752)].

also did comparative research. Knowing Latin, he could read the continental authorities and his landmark opinion in *Robinson v. Bland*[142] cites a number of them.

* * *

Thus, once the English courts abandoned the earlier practice of resorting to forum law or special substantive rules in deciding multistate transactions, they filled the void with civilian learning. In Westlake's words, there was a "reception in England of continental maxims on topics of private international law."[147] The most influential purveyor of such maxims was doubtless Huber, whose influence is still felt today. His idea of selecting the law of the place the "parties had in mind" to govern their contract, which Mansfield endorsed in *Robinson v. Bland*, still lingers on in the English "proper law" doctrine. Westlake, who pointed out that Mansfield's statement is ambiguous and that tacit expectations belong to the realm of fiction, later objectified Huber's formula and advocated application of the law with which the transaction has "the most real connection." But even nowadays English courts, on occasion, still rely on Huber's subjective test.

Huber's statement about the enforcement of "rights acquired within" a foreign territory proved to be even more influential. Elevating this off-hand remark to the status of an Anglo-American dogma, T. E. Holland said that "what really happens when a law seems to obtain an extra-territorial effect, is rather that rights created and defined by foreign law obtain recognition by the domestic tribunal."[155] As he added in a footnote, he assumed "the foundation of the whole topic . . . to be that of 'vested rights'; a doctrine . . . well stated by Huber."[156] From him, his friend Dicey picked up that doctrine and made it the cornerstone of an influential treatise. Through Dicey, Huber's idea drifted to the United States, where Joseph Beale used it as the theoretical basis of the first Restatement of Conflict of Laws.

* * * * *

5. Two German Authors

Shortly after the publication of Story's *Commentaries,* two German scholars rendered important doctrinal contributions to our discipline.

During 1841 and 1842 Carl Georg von Wachter published a lengthy article, spread over four issues of a German law review, which contains some of the most incisive criticism of conflicts theories ever voiced. Wachter was an iconoclast. He debunked statutist learning, exposed the vested rights theory's circular reasoning and disparaged the comity doctrine. Regrettably, he failed to deal with Story, even though he must have learned about the *Commentaries* through a review published in a German journal which Wachter's article cites. Such indifference to the single most important work extant at the time may seem strange, but Wachter apparently lacked linguistic abilities.

* * *

---

[142]   97 Eng. Rep. 717 (K.B. 1760).

[147]   J. Westlake, A Treatise on Private International Law 10 (N. Betwich 6th ed. 1922).

[155]   T. Holland, The Elements of Jurisprudence 418 (11th ed. 1910).

[156]   *Id.* at 418 n.2.

Wachter was a legal positivist. He believed that in deciding the question which law governs a legal relationship the judge should look, "no doubt to the laws to which he is subject, i.e., the laws that govern in his state."[207] Wachter's ethnocentric belief in the primacy of forum law was rooted in the assumption that a judge is but an instrumentality ("*Organ*") of the legislative will. According to the first of Wachter's three "Guiding Principles," courts must follow, first of all, any provisions of the *lex fori* that expressly designate the applicable law. Absent such a directive, a judge faced with a conflicts problem should examine whether forum law, according to its "spirit," must be interpreted to claim application to the case irrespective of foreign elements. Finally, if such an analysis leaves any doubt as to the applicable law, the judge should resolve it in favor of the *lex fori*.

Wachter's principles anticipate the forum-centered approaches of such modern unilateralists as Currie and Ehrenzweig. Like Ehrenzweig, Wachter recognized a limited number of "true" conflicts norms. Thus he believed in the existence of customary choice-of-law rules, such as the application of situs law to immovables and the law of decedent's last domicile to matters of succession. He also acknowledged, up to a point, the principle of party autonomy. But the basic ingredient of Wachter's contribution was a proposition that later cropped up in Ehrenzweig's "*lex-fori* approach,"[217] and which Currie formulated as follows: "Normally, even in cases involving foreign factors, a court should as a matter of course look to the law of the forum as the source of the rule of decision."[218]

Like Currie, Wachter emphasized local "policies" and "interests" and argued that notions of comity, fairness and convenience, as well as multistate interests in the security of transactions, are irrelevant in deciding conflicts cases. Both of them believed that a judge who resorts to such considerations usurps the legislative function, and both assumed that conflicts problems call for the interpretation of local rules of decision to determine their reach in the light of forum policies. Not surprisingly, such twentieth-century unilateralists who, like Ehrenzweig and Sperduti, had read Wachter's work, found it singularly modern and attractive. But the influence of Wachter's ideas on European conflicts law proved to be minimal because his compatriot Savigny soon overshadowed him.

(b) Savigny

Friedrich Carl von Savigny, whose conflicts classic was published in 1849 as volume eight of his *System of Current Roman Law,* advocated an approach diametrically opposed to Wachter's forum-centered methodology. Upon its publication Savigny was in his seventies, and there is little to indicate that he had given much thought to the conflict of laws earlier on in his long career as a scholar, law teacher and administrator. Because he could draw on Wachter's article and Story's treatise, he was able to complete the volume within a fairly short span of time. The manner in which Savigny treated the subject also helped. He was a theoretician, and the flavor of his discourse is even more dogmatic and abstract than that of Wachter's essay. While the first edition of Story's *Commentaries* referred to more than 500 decisions, Savigny cited a mere dozen, and he usually preferred to rely on hypothetical cases rather than court reports to illustrate a point. In his preface, Savigny said that "the doctrine here presented, as compared to others, should be understood as inchoate, as imperfect."[230] That was far too

---

[207]   Wachter, [*Uber die Collision der Privatrechtsgesetze verschiedener Staaten* (pt 1),] 24 AcP [230,] 237 [(1841)].

[217]   1 A. Ehrenzweig, [Private International Law 54,] 92-93 [(1967)].

[218]   B. Currie, [Selected Essays on the Conflict of Laws] 183 [(1963)].

[230]   [8] F. von Savigny, [System des Heutigen Romischen Rechts] iii [(1849)].

modest a statement, for no one has ever put the deductive method to better use in building a perfect conflicts edifice. Noting that no country had enacted comprehensive legislation on choice of law, so that the field was left to legal theory, he proposed to deal with it "scientifically" by constructing a system that would yield rules of universal application. (The claim to universality may explain why Savigny - like his medieval predecessors - dealt with the conflict of laws in the context of a larger work on Roman law even though, as he admitted, the Romans had precious little to offer on the subject.)

Savigny said that it is possible to pose the choice-of-law question in either of two ways: "What is the scope of legal rules?" or "What relationships do they control?" According to him, "both ways of looking at the question differ only in the point of departure."[235] In other words, Savigny apparently considered unilateralism and multilateralism to be but opposite sides of the same coin. Later on in his book, however, he only discussed multilateral rules, except that he did recognize what he called "strictly positive, mandatory laws." By this he meant rules of decision that express a moral, political, or economic policy strong enough to resist displacement by foreign law, and which are therefore not susceptible to the multilateral approach. As examples he mentioned the prohibitions against polygamy and the acquisition of realty by Jews. Savigny considered such "mandatory laws" to be "anomalous" and believed that they would vanish as time went on.

Putting this peculiar group of rules to one side, he proposed to resolve normal choice-of-law problems by allocating each legal relationship to the territory to which it "belongs," to which it is "subjected," or in which it has its "seat." This guiding principle, according to Savigny, is compelled by the needs of an "international legal community of nations dealing with one another." He argued that the existence of such a community, and the common advantage nations and individuals derive from an increasing flow of multistate transactions, call for reciprocity in dealing with legal relationships. As a corollary to the equality of citizens and foreigners, legal relationships should be treated in the same way, irrespective of the forum that adjudicates them. In other words, Savigny's basic objective was to achieve uniformity of result or, to put it negatively, the prevention of forum shopping. Consequently, he rejected the statutists' unilateralist approaches and the primacy of forum law Wachter had advocated. He also took issue with Wachter's view on the role of judges in conflicts cases, pointing out that the lack of comprehensive legislation on the subject implied a large measure of judicial freedom, and that there is no evidence to show that states jealously insist on asserting their legislative prerogatives in multistate cases.

Savigny called his seat theory a mere "formal principle." To give it substance, he proposed to link persons and legal relationships with a given territory by focusing on certain kinds of contacts. First of all, he selected domicile as the most appropriate nexus to control a person's legal capacity, rejecting the national law principle that had surfaced in the French Civil Code. He then proceeded to divide legal relationships into several broad groups for the purpose of determining which of the four possible connecting factors enumerated (domicile, situs, place of transaction and place of litigation) is best suited to each. To that end, Savigny developed a classification system geared to major private law categories (property, obligations, decedents' estates, family law). All that remained to be done was to find for each of these conceptual pigeonholes the appropriate contact to localize any given legal relationship in the territory to which it belongs "according to its peculiar nature."

The choice-of-law rules and principles Savigny derived from this classificatory scheme, such as the maxim *locus regit actum*, the principle of party autonomy and the situs rule, were

---

[235]   F. VON SAVIGNY, *supra* note 230, at 3.* * *

hardly novel; they had been known since Bartolus' time. Savigny's fame as a conflicts thinker is therefore not attributable to the superior quality of any specific choice-of-law rules he devised. In fact, a number of them are clearly inferior to those Story had proffered. Rather, what counts is Savigny's doctrinal contribution. His seat theory has been called "epochal" and the legacy he left to the conflict of laws a "Copernican revolution."

Some, however, have questioned the originality of Savigny's approach. It is, of course, true that Story and Wachter had already laid to rest what remained of statutist doctrines. Also, his own research is surely paltry in comparison to theirs. The idea that deference to foreign laws reflects the enlightened self-interest of nations engaged in mutually beneficial trade and commerce is implicit in Huber's and Story's notion of comity, a concept Savigny accepted, albeit with certain reservations. Twenty-one years before Savigny wrote about the "international legal community of nations that deal with one another," Livermore had compared the nations of the civilized world to "one great society composed of so many families between whom it is necessary to maintain peace and friendly intercourse." The same thought already underlies the various turns of phrase Grotius used to describe the essential unity of mankind. Similarly, the fiction of a "voluntary submission" of a person to a sovereign, on which Savigny so often relies, can be traced back to Huber and Grotius. Savigny's refutation of the vested rights theory as circular merely restates what Wachter had said earlier, and Wachter had also coined the equally question-begging "seat" metaphor. Finally, the hypothesis that choice of law deals with the control over legal relationships had been propounded by Mittermaier almost twenty years before the publication of Savigny's book.

What, then, was Savigny's principal contribution to the conflict of laws? Apart from organizing the ideas he had gleaned from others in a tidy fashion, he managed to elucidate a principle that had at best been implicit in Story's *Commentaries,* namely that choice-of-law rules should serve the objective of guaranteeing uniform results. Thus, Savigny advanced a pragmatic consideration, rather than mere doctrinal musings, in support of multilateralism. Again, he did not invent the idea of "decisional harmony," as civilians usually call it. Medieval maxims already propounded that different fora should not apply different laws to the same transaction and Huber had made the same point. Nor did the multilateralist approach to choice of law originate with Savigny. Multilateral rules had existed since the Middle Ages, and Huber's comity theory reflected multilateralist thinking. Story had already linked broad categories of legal transactions with a given territory by means of connecting factors and, to that end, classified legal relationships in a systematic and comprehensive fashion. Savigny, however, was the first to explicate a cogent and coherent rationale for neutral, even-handed conflicts rules that accord foreign law the same importance as the *lex fori.* He introduced a categorical conflicts imperative by proposing that conflicts rules should be evaluated in the light of their suitability for inclusion in an international choice-of-law convention acceptable to all nations. Thus, he laid the methodological foundation for multilateralism on which others could build.

The logical symmetry of Savigny's system, his cosmopolitan outlook, and the elegant manner in which he presented the subject matter may explain why his ideas became the conventional wisdom for generations of conflicts scholars. His book was translated into several languages, including English, and has been cited as authority in common law cases. His notion of a "seat" of legal relationships inspired Westlake's formulation of the proper law approach, which, in turn, spawned such concepts as the "closest connection" and the "most significant relationship" that currently enjoy considerable popularity. Standard English and French conflicts treaties emphasize the continuing importance of Savignian doctrine.

Nor was the effect of Savigny's doctrinal efforts limited to the province of scholarship. In the nineteenth century, some German courts let his views prevail over statutory provisions, and in this century his teachings helped transform the unilateral conflicts provisions found in the original Introductory Act to the German Civil Code into a system of multilateral rules. Even socialist conflicts law owes more to the great Romanist than to his "*disciple ingrat*" Karl Marx. To be sure, the acceptance of Savigny's views has never been unanimous. But until this day multilateralism continues to occupy a commanding position, which had not been squarely challenged until the American "conflicts revolution." Outside the United States, Savigny's doctrine still dominates, despite the fact that several European scholars, sufficiently disenchanted with mechanical jurisprudence, have mounted an all-out attack on his conceptual edifice.

6. MANCINI

To complete the story of the conflict of laws' evolution up to modern times, one more author must be mentioned. In 1851, two years after the publication of Savigny's treatise, the Italian patriot, lawyer, statesman and professor Pasquale Stanislao Mancini gave an inaugural address at the University of Turin entitled "Nationality as the Basis of International Law." As that title suggests, Mancini attributed fundamental importance to the ties of allegiance that link individuals to their home countries. As a member of a parliamentary commission that drafted the conflicts rules of the Introductory Provisions of the 1865 Italian Civil Code, he saw to it that the national law principle and other ideas he espoused were enacted into positive law. Mancini's basic premises were that private law is primarily personal, *i.e.*, intended for citizens rather than for a territory, but that citizens and aliens should be entitled to equal treatment. Proceeding from Savigny's idea of a community of nations, he argued that each country should promote legal equality by, on the one hand, respecting the alien's *lex patriae*, and, on the other, permitting the parties to choose the law they wish to govern their transactions. According to Mancini, the personal law principle and party autonomy ought to yield to the territoriality principle only with respect to matters that touch upon public policy, sovereignty and rights in real estate.

Again, the idea of using a person's citizenship rather than his domicile to link him to a given territory was not new. That connecting factor appeared in the conflicts provisions of the French Civil Code, whence it drifted into other European codes, notably those of Belgium and the Netherlands. The great Savigny, however, had strongly endorsed the domiciliary nexus and rejected the connecting factor of citizenship, so that it was left to Mancini to bestow legitimacy on a principle his illustrious predecessor had found wanting. In that Mancini was eminently successful. His principle was ultimately adopted by most European countries as well as in Latin America, Africa and Asia. Nor are Mancini's achievements limited to the advocacy of the *lex patriae* and the codification of Italian conflicts law. Whereas Savigny had talked about the possibility of choice-of-law conventions without endorsing them, Mancini actively promoted the adoption of multilateral conflicts treaties and participated in international projects pursuing that aim. He realized that if states and nations are left to their own devices, their conflicts laws will drift apart rather than converge, as Savigny had assumed. Mancini also attacked the comity doctrine, rigorously defended the equality of forum and foreign law, and focused attention on the notion of public policy, which Savigny's discussion of "strictly positive laws" had failed to address in a satisfactory manner.

As a practical matter, however, none of Mancini's contributions proved to be as consequential as his fervent advocacy of the *lex patriae*. Savigny's multilateralist system and his rejection of Wachter's forum preference opened the door to foreign rules of decision. Mancini's national law principle opened it even wider. Since lawsuits are usually brought where the parties live, the domiciliary nexus favors application of the *lex fori,* whereas reliance on the *lex patriae* tends to increase foreign law problems. At the same time, the national law principle's success spelled the doom of Savigny's optimistic belief in the eventual possibility of a world-wide uniform body of conflicts rules. Mancini managed to drive a wedge between common law nations, which have steadfastly adhered to the domiciliary principle, and those civil law countries that opted for the *lex patriae*. The resulting rift forever laid to rest the hope that multilateralism could achieve its goal of decisional harmony.

7. Some Observations and Questions

It seems appropriate to conclude this brief historical survey with Mancini, because his contributions largely complete the inventory of conflicts ideas. Little has been added since, except for the elaboration of what civilians usually call the "General Part" of the conflict of laws, a catch-all category that contains a number of conceptual constructs scholars have contrived to cope with the congenital defects that afflict the multilateralist approach. The twentieth century also produced a novel doctrine that attempts to answer the central question why local courts apply foreign law. Like the vested rights doctrine, this so-called "reception" or "local law" theory, which was invented independently by Italian and American authors, deals with the problem by denying its existence. Judges, so the theory goes, neither apply foreign law nor do they enforce rights that have vested abroad; rather they resort to a peculiar kind of *lex fori* created *ad hoc* in the image of the foreign rule. This fatuous explanation, although it appealed to such eminent judges as Learned Hand and Roger Traynor, inspires no more hope for continuing progress in our times than the mental gymnastics exacted by the "General Part."

There have, of course, been recent upheavals in conflicts theory and practice, both in the United States and elsewhere. But while the American "conflicts revolution" and similar trends in Europe have attracted considerable attention, their intrinsic novelty may well be questioned. If one cuts through the modernistic jargon with which much of the recent literature and judicial opinions is larded, one encounters old familiar trains of thought. A glance at some of the opinions the countless American conflicts cases decided since *Babcock v. Jackson*[321] reveals that some American judges still look for the seat of legal relationships, whereas others wonder, as the statutists did, whether forum rules apply to residents traveling abroad and to local activities of nonresidents. Still others share Aldricus' predilection for the better rule of law. Like medieval Italian scholars, American courts tend to run together these various approaches in blissful ignorance of the fact that they contradict one another. Such unabashed eclecticism may be astonishing, but new it is not. More than 150 years ago Judge Porter of the Louisiana Supreme Court, after reviewing the opinions of jurists scattered widely over space and time, reached the resigned conclusion that our discipline is

> a subject, the most intricate and perplexed of any that has occupied the attention of lawyers and courts: one on which scarcely any two writers are found to entirely agree, and on which, it is rare to find one consistent with himself throughout. We know of no matter in jurisprudence so unsettled or none that should more teach men distrust for their own opinions, and charity for those of others.

Since then, matters have not improved. In fact, they have probably worsened. The ever-increasing production of scholarly writing and judicial decisions heaps additional intricacies

---

[321]   12 N.Y.2d 473, 191 N.E.2d 279, 240 N.Y.S.2d 743 (1963).* * *

and perplexities upon the subject. But while the history of conflicts law has been long and rich in detail, legal imagination—even the imagination of conflicts scholars—is limited. With the benefit of hindsight it is possible to venture a few general observations and questions suggested by past experience which, in turn, may help in assessing the merits of current conflicts lore.

First, it is noteworthy that there are hardly any traces of a conflicts system to be found in antiquity, despite the level of civilization and commercial sophistication Greece and Rome had attained. Is it fair to conclude that advanced legal systems can do without choice-of-law rules?

Second, conflicts law seems to flourish best in a peculiar legal setting. Bartolus, Dumoulin, d'Argentre, Huber, Story, Wachter and Savigny lived in different countries, different centuries and different intellectual climates. Yet they all inhabited a similar juridical environment, where law-making power was dispersed and a shared legal tradition, rather than the command of a central authority, made law cohesive. Why are such surroundings particularly conducive to the development of our discipline?

Third, there is an astonishing lack of consensus on a fundamental question, namely why courts, sworn to uphold the forum's laws and constitution, should ever apply foreign law. The Dutch jurists, who first grasped the importance of this inquiry, thought that they had found the answer in the dubious notion of comity. Savigny advanced a pragmatic reason, namely the need achieve uniform results in conflicts cases. Others have proffered conceptualistic explanations, such as the vested rights and local law doctrine. Can any of these responses satisfactorily explain the forum's abdication of legislative power? Are choice-of-law rules a consequence of noble altruism, are they compelled by international law, or can they be justified by purely pragmatic considerations?

Fourth, even if legal theories cannot satisfactorily explain the conflicts enigma, the practical goal of decisional harmony Savigny espoused might warrant the displacement of forum law in appropriate instances. But assuming that the prevention of forum shopping is the true *raison d'etre* of the conflict of laws, can choice-of-law rules in fact guarantee uniform results in multistate cases?

Fifth, if one assumes that decisional harmony can be attained, is that objective important enough to burden trial courts with the onerous task of ascertaining and applying foreign law? Who can vouchsafe that they will correctly apply alien precepts? Given the expense and margin of error inherent in trying suits under rules with which the judge is unfamiliar, is the game worth the candle?

Sixth, consistency and uniformity are surely not the only values in the law. The responses to multistate problems in antiquity were informed by the desire to do substantial justice, and that consideration has never been wholly absent from the conflict of laws. If our discipline, like any other, must pay attention to results, how can that constraint be reconciled with the ideal of decisional harmony?

Finally, what method or approach is best suited to accomplish whatever ends conflicts law should serve? Are thought processes that were conceived in the Middle Ages of any utility in this day and age? Or have all past efforts to reach rational solutions in multistate cases been in vain? As Judge Porter observed in *Saul v. His Creditors,* if "So many . . . men, of great talents and learning, are . . . found to fail in fixing certain principles, we are forced to conclude that they have failed, not from want of ability, but because the matter was not susceptible of being settled on certain principles."[325]

Fortunately, we can at least identify the approaches that have been tried so far, and it is pos-

---

[325]   *Saul,* 5 Mart. (n.s.) 569, 596 (La. 1827).

sible to assess their strengths and weaknesses. The great diversity of theories that muddle our discipline presents a deceptive picture of the range of legal imagination. Looking more closely at the historical record, we find that there are only three basic choice-of-law methods:

(1) The creation of rules of decision that directly govern multistate transactions (the *substantive law approach*);
(2) The determination of the personal and territorial reach of the potentially applicable local rules of decision (the *unilateralist approach*);
(3) The interposition of choice-of-law rules between multistate transactions and legal systems (the *multilateralist approach*).

These three approaches have coexisted since the Middle Ages. But while the "pluralism of methods" is not a new phenomenon, it has assumed renewed importance in our day. In the United States as well as in Europe there are trends away from rigid multilateral choice-of-law rules and towards a revival of unilateralism. At the same time, the idea of resolving multistate problems in a supranational fashion has again become popular, as shown by the current debate about a new *lex mercatoria*. Thus, the question of methodology has moved to the forefront of discussion, a conclusion confirmed by recent Hague lectures of several distinguished scholars.* * *

* * * * *

Comments

1. Professor Juenger is careful to keep his own views on conflict of laws from obscuring his historical account. Like any good historian, he lets the facts speak for themselves. We are left to wonder, then, how conflicts movements as intractably opposed as multilateralism and unilateralism could both be so vital and regenerative in European legal history. A similar question arises later when we consider in Chapter Six the multilateralism-unilateralism debate that continues to rage in this country.

2. Numerous materials and historical studies are cited in Professor Juenger's book. Additional English-language accounts of the development of choice of law (private international law) in Europe include Juenger 1983;[1] Juenger 1985a; North & Fawcett 1992: pp. 15-21, 23-26; Scoles & Hay 1992: pp. 5-11; Yntema 1953; Yntema 1966.

3. Those interested in contemporary European conflicts law will find comprehensive treatment of the subject in Reimann 1995. Additional sources include Guedj 1991; Hanotiau 1982; Jayme 1989; Juenger 1982; Vitta 1982. Writing on conflicts law in other parts of the world is surveyed in Chapter Eleven, Part F (2).

---

[1]   Full citations appear in the bibliography, Chapter Twelve.

CHAPTER THREE

Lex Loci Delicti—The Dominance and Partial Decline of Multilateralism in American Conflicts Law

Part A of this Chapter notes the development and dominance of multilateralism in American conflicts law—that is to say, advancement of a body of choice-of-law rules designed to be administered uniformly throughout a community of jurisdictions. Through the apparatus of *lex loci delicti*, the object was to secure the same choice-of-law result for a particular kind of case, wherever that case may be tried. This is also called the territorial, or jurisdiction-selecting, approach. Part A surveys the high points of this movement: the writing of Joseph Story and Joseph Beale and the adoption of the American Law Institute's original RESTATEMENT OF THE LAW OF CONFLICTS.

We begin with a selection from the work of Joseph Story, the first great American conflicts scholar. Here Story argues that neutral and uniform conflicts rules are necessary among and within nations to avert grave disruption in commerce and human affairs. Story acknowledges that a domestic tribunal can never by bound by a foreign sovereign to apply the foreign sovereign's law. Yet Story maintains that, when the uniform conflicts rule points away from local law and toward the law of another jurisdiction, the local tribunal should follow the rule as a matter of comity. In the next selection Professor Kurt Nadelmann assesses Story's work and explains his great influence.

We then move to an excerpt by Joseph Beale. Like Story, Beale maintains that, while a tribunal cannot be coerced to apply nonforum law, it should do so under a *lex loci delicti* approach. That is, it should use jurisdiction-selecting rules derived from the geographical location of an event common to a particular type of case (i.e., the law of the place of contracting governs issues of contract validity). But Beale bases his argument on a vested-rights conception of governing law, rather than on Story's notion of comity. Beale's view became enshrined in the American Law Institute's original RESTATEMENT OF THE LAW OF CONFLICTS. In his selection, Dean Goodrich (a conflicts scholar and ALI leader) explains how and why the original conflicts RESTATEMENT came about. Part A then concludes with several sections from the original RESTATEMENT, revealing a dichotomy in conflicts law that Story and Beale were never able entirely to resolve: forum neutrality ostensibly imposed by *lex loci delicti* on one hand, and the ultimate authority of the forum to apply its own law on the other.

Conflicts scholars increasingly questioned both the theoretical underpinnings of the *lex loci* approach and the reliability of its operation. Part B of this Chapter samples the writing of a number of these critics. In the first entry, Professor Elliott Cheatham challenges the value of Story's concept of comity. In the next, Professor Hessell Yntema assails Beale's vested rights theory. Professor Walter Wheeler Cook then suggests that the conception of American conflicts law as uniform, mechanical, and certain in application ignores what American courts do in fact. Finally, in one of the most influential conflicts articles, Professor David Cavers notes widespread confusion and doctrinal instability under the *lex loci* approach and reflects on possibilities for conflicts reform.

A. Story, Beale, and the Original RESTATEMENT

Joseph Story, COMMENTARIES ON THE CONFLICT OF LAWS 5-8, 8-9, 193-194, 201-202, 203-204, 222, 233, 234-235 (Boston: Hilliard, Gray & Co. 1834)

* * * * *

§ 4. [I]n the present times, without some general rules of right and obligation, recognised by civilized nations to govern their intercourse with each other, the most serious mischiefs and most injurious conflicts would arise. Commerce is now so absolutely universal among all countries; the inhabitants of all have such a free intercourse with each other; contracts, marriages, nuptial settlements, wills and successions, are so common among persons, whose domicils are in different countries, having different and even opposite laws on the same subjects; that without some common principles adopted by all nations in this regard there would be an utter confusion of all rights and remedies; and intolerable grievances would grow up to weaken all the domestic relations, as well as to destroy the sanctity of contracts and the security of property.

§ 5. A few simple cases will sufficiently illustrate the importance of some international principles in matters of mere private right and duty. Suppose a contract, valid by the laws of the country, where it is made, is sought to be enforced in another country, where such a contract is positively prohibited by its laws; or *vice versa*, suppose a contract, invalid by the laws of the country, where it is made, but valid by that of the country, where it is sought to be enforced; it is plain, that unless some uniform rules are adopted to govern such cases, (which are not uncommon), the grossest inequalities will arise in the administration of justice between the subjects of the different countries in regard to such contracts. Again; by the laws of some countries marriage cannot be contracted until the parties arrive at twenty-one years of age; in other countries not until they arrive at the age of twenty-five years. Suppose a marriage to be contracted between two persons in the same country, both of whom are over twenty one years but less than twenty-five, and one of them is a subject of the latter country. Is such a marriage valid, or not? If valid in the country, where it is celebrated, is it valid also in the other country? Or the question may be propounded in a still more general form, Is a marriage, valid between the parties in the place, where it is solemnized, equally valid in all other countries? Or is it obligatory only as a local regulation, and to be treated every where else as a mere nullity?

§ 6. Questions of this sort must be of frequent occurrence, not only in different countries wholly independent of each other; but also in provinces of the same empire, governed by different laws, as was the case in France before the Revolution; and also in countries acknowledging a common sovereign, but yet organized as distinct communities, as is still the case in regard to the communities composing the British Empire, the Germanic Confederacy, the States of Holland, and the Domains of Austria and Russia. Innumerable suits must be litigated in the judicial forums of these countries and provinces, in which the decision must depend upon the point, whether the nature of a contract should be determined by the law of the place, where it is litigated; or by the law of the domicil of one or both of the parties; or by the law of the place, where the contract was made; whether the capacity to make a testament should be regulated by the law of the testator's domicil, or that of the location of his property; whether the form of his testament should be prescribed by the law of his domicil, or of that of the location of his property, or of that of the place, where the testament is made; and in like manner, whether the law of the domicil, or what other law should govern in cases of succession of intestate estates.

§ 7. It is plain, that the laws of one country can have no intrinsic force, *proprio vigore*, except within the territorial limits and jurisdiction of that country. They can bind only its own subjects, and others, who are within its jurisdictional limits; and the latter only while they remain there. No other nation, or its subjects, are bound to yield the slightest obedience to those laws. Whatever extra-territorial force they are to have, is the result, not of any original power to extend them abroad, but of that respect, which from motives of public policy other nations are disposed to yield to them, giving them effect, as the phrase is, *sub mutuae vicissitudinis obtentu*, with a wise and liberal regard to common convenience and mutual necessities.

* * *

§ 8. This is the natural principle flowing form the equality and independence of nations. It is an essential attribute of every sovereignty, that it has no admitted superior, and that it gives the supreme law within its own domains on all subjects appertaining to its sovereignty. What it yields, it is its own choice to yield; and it cannot be commanded by another to yield it as matter of right. And accordingly it is laid down by all publicists and jurists, as an incontestable rule of public law, that one may with impunity disregard the law pronounced by a magistrate beyond his territory. *Extra territorium jus dicenti impune non paretur*, is the doctrine of the Digest; and it is equally as true in relation to nations, as the Roman law held it to be in relation to magistrates. Vattel has deduced a similar conclusion from the general independence and equality of nations, very properly holding, that relative strength or weakness cannot produce any difference in regard to public rights and duties, and that whatever is lawful for one nation is equally lawful for another; and whatever is unjustifiable in one is equally so in another. And he affirms in the most positive manner (what indeed cannot well be denied) that sovereignty, united with domain, establishes the exclusive jurisdiction of a nation within its territories, as to controversies, crimes, and rights arising therein.

§ 9. The jurisprudence, then, arising from the conflict of the laws of different nations, in their actual application to modern commerce and intercourse, is a most interesting and important branch of public law. To no part of the world is it of more interest and importance than to the United States, since the union of a national government with that of twenty-four distinct, and in some respects independent states, necessarily creates very complicated relations and rights between the citizens of those states, which call for the constant administration of extramunicipal principles. This branch of public law may be fitly denominated private international law, since it is chiefly seen and felt in its application to the common business of private persons, and rarely rises to the dignity of national negotiations, or national controversies.

* * * * *

§ 232. It is easy to see, that, in the common intercourse of different countries, many circumstances may be required to be taken into consideration, before it can be clearly ascertained, what is the true rule, by which the validity, obligation, and interpretation of contracts are to be governed. To make a contract valid, it is a universal principle, admitted by the whole world, that it should be made by parties capable to contract; that it should be voluntary; upon a sufficient consideration; lawful in its nature; and in its terms reasonably certain. But upon some of these points there is a diversity in the positive and customary laws of different nations. Persons, capable in one country, are incapable by the laws of another; considerations, good in one, are insufficient or invalid in another; the public policy of one permits or favours certain agreements, which are prohibited in another; the forms, prescribed by the laws of one, to ensure validity and obligation, are unknown in another; and the rights, acknowledged by one, are not commensurate with those belonging to another. A person sometimes contracts in one country, and is domiciled in another, and is to pay in a third; and sometimes the property, which is the subject of the contract, is situate in a fourth; and each of these countries may have different, and even opposite laws. What then is to be done in this conflict of laws? What law is to regulate the contract, either to determine the rights, the actions, and the defences growing out of it; or the consequences flowing from it; or to interpret its terms, and ascertain its stipulations?

* * * * *

§ 242. (1) Generally speaking, the validity of a contract is to be decided by the law of the place, where it is made. If valid there, it is by the general law of nations, *jure gentium*, held valid every where, by tacit or implied consent. The rule is founded, not merely in the convenience, but in the necessities of nations; for otherwise, it would be impracticable for them to carry on an extensive intercourse and commerce with each other. The whole system of agencies, purchases and sales, credits, and negotiable instruments, rests on this foundation. * * *

§ 243. (2) The same rule applies, *vice versa*, to the invalidity of contracts; if void, or illegal by the law of the place of the contract, they are generally held void and illegal every where.

§ 244. (3) But there is an exception to the rule as to the universal validity of contracts, which is, that no nation is bound to recognise or enforce any contracts, which are injurious to their own interests, or to those of their own subjects. This exception results from the consideration, that the authority of the acts and contracts done in other states, as well as the laws, by which they are regulated, are not, *proprio vigore*, of any efficacy beyond the territories of that state; and whatever is attributed to them elsewhere, is from comity, and not of strict right. And every independent community will, and ought to judge for itself, how far that comity ought to extend. The reasonable limitation is, that it shall not suffer prejudice by its comity. Mr. Justice Best has with great force said, that in cases turning upon the comity of nations (*comitas inter communitates*), it is a maxim, that the comity cannot prevail in cases, where it violates the law of our own country, the law of nature, or the law of God. Contracts, therefore, which are in evasion or fraud of the laws of a country, or the rights or duties of its subjects, contracts against good morals, or religion, or public rights, and contracts opposed to the national policy or institutions, are deemed nullities in every country, affected by such considerations; although they may be valid by the laws of the place, where they are made.

* * * * *

§ 266. Secondly, the obligation of the contract, which, though often confounded with, is distinguishable from, its nature. The obligation of a contract is the duty to perform it, whatever may be its nature. It may be moral, or legal, or both. But when we speak of obligation generally, we mean legal obligation, that is the right to performance, which the law confers on one party, and the corresponding duty of performance, to which it binds the other.

* * * * *

§ 280. The rules already considered suppose, that the performance of the contract is to be in the place, where it is made, either expressly or by tacit implication. But where the contract is either expressly or tacitly to be performed in any other place, there the general rule is, in conformity to the presumed intention of the parties, that the contract, as to its validity, nature, obligation, and interpretation, is to be governed by the law of the place of performance.

* * * * *

§ 282. But although the general rule is so well established, the application of it in many cases is not unattended with difficulties; for it is often a matter of serious question, in cases of a mixed nature, which rule ought to prevail, the law of the place, where the contract is made, or that of the place, where it is to be performed. In general, it may be said, that, if no place of performance is stated, or the contract may indifferently be performed any where, it ought to be referred to the *lex loci contractus*. But there are many cases, where this rule will not be a sufficient guide; and as the subject is important in its practical bearing, it may be well to illustrate it by some cases.

* * * * *

Kurt H. Nadelmann, *Joseph Story's Contribution to American Conflicts Law: A Comment*, 5 AM. J. LEGAL HIST. 230, 234-238, 243-244, 245-246, 252-253 (1961)*

* * * * *

* * * [W]hat is Story's contribution to the American law of conflict of laws? Has Story been the originator of the principal American conflicts rules? Or of some of them? And if so, in his capacity as a judge, or as author of the *Commentaries*?

Some remarks on the status of conflicts law in the United States before Story's appointment to the Bench will help clarify the situation. In the first place, it is not proper to say that, in the early years of the Republic, there was little conflict of laws and, therefore, practically no conflicts law to be found here. The legislatures of the colonies had passed a vast amount of legislation. The result was diversity of law in England and in the Colonies, and again among the Colonies themselves. Conflicts existed in many areas of the law. And there were of course the conflicts of jurisdiction also. The inclusion in the Articles of Confederation of provisions designated to regulate jurisdictional conflicts had its good reasons. The principal conflicts of laws were in specific fields, as they are for each period. One was the differences in the rate of interest. In his attack, in the Virginia Convention on the Adoption of the Federal Constitution, on the planned establishment of federal courts, Patrick Henry asked what law the federal courts would apply in conflicts cases. John Marshall gave the answer—that it would be the laws of the state where the contract was made, that this was an established principle in the jurisprudence of Virginia. And Marshall used, as illustration, a case involving the different interest rates in Virginia and Maryland.

Likewise erroneous is the idea that case law on conflicts was almost nonexistent. Proof of the true status of affairs can be made with the help of Story himself. The Harvard Law Library has a Story manuscript bound in three thick folio volumes, entitled, "Digest of Law," an attempt by Story to present the law in the form of a Digest. Story worked on it while practising law. The case law up to 1808 or 1809 is covered. A digest of the conflicts law appears in the second volume under the heading "*lex loci*" on six pages written in Story's thin handwrit-

---

*   Reprinted with permission.

ing. * * * The chapter has thirteen subheadings: personal rights, real estate, personal property, contracts, actions, bars and discharges, wills, intestate property, marriage and divorce, crimes and punishment, judgments, municipal prohibitions, detached matters. The total number of references made to writers and decisions is 108. Among the writers cited are Huber, Voet, Vattel, Kames, and Erskine. Forty different decisions are referred to, 14 English and 26 American. Of the latter, 10 are from New York, 8 from Pennsylvania, 3 from Massachusetts, 1 from Connecticut, and 2 each from the United States Supreme Court and the Circuit Courts. While the *Digest* is no finished product, it helps give a view of the status of conflicts law as of about the time when Story received his appointment to the Supreme Court (1811).

Another, more convenient, checking on the status of the law on conflicts of laws is possible for the year 1825. In that year, Esek Cowen, reporter of the Supreme Court of the state of New York, brought out a digest, and a very competent one, of what he called "*lex loci* and *lex fori*" in the form of a note to a conflicts decision in his *Reports*. The digest, in the fourth volume of Cowen's *Reports*, runs over twenty-two pages in small print. The material is grouped under twelve headings: the *lex loci contractus*, of the *lex domicilii*, of proceedings in foreign courts of justice, of foreign criminal laws, manner of proving state statutes, manner of proving foreign judgments, decrees and so on, of the *lex loci rei sitae*, of the *lex fori*, law of crimes, of the power of one state over the fugitives from justice of another. The great majority of the cases cited in support of the rules of law stated are from American jurisdictions. A useful compilation, Story referred to it many times in his *Commentaries on the Conflict of Laws*.

Of another character, but no less interesting, is what may be called a "restatement," made shortly thereafter by Henry Wheaton for the benefit of English lawyers. While in London in 1827 (he was on his way to Denmark as newly appointed United States Minister), Wheaton was interviewed by Jabez Henry on the status of American law. Henry asked 40 specific questions, the majority about rules of conflicts, and questions and answers appeared in an English law journal in 1828. This interesting piece has been reprinted in the January 1958 issue of the *New York Law Forum*.

But the best thing is to turn to the case material used by Story himself in his *Commentaries*. This gives the status of the case law as of 1833. Also, it facilitates checking on possible contributions, until 1833, by Story the judge, sitting on the Supreme Court of the United States or riding the Circuit.

On the basis of the Table of Cases, slightly more than 500 decisions were used by Story in the first edition of the *Commentaries*. A breakdown of these cases according to jurisdictions produces the following figures: 216 English, 8 Scottish, and 282 American decisions. The numbers remove the basis for attempts at minimizing the existence of American case law. Of the 282 American cases, 67 each are from New York and Massachusetts, 28 from Louisiana, 16 from Pennsylvania, 12 from Connecticut, 10 from Maryland, 5 from New Hampshire, 3 each from Maine, Virginia, and South Carolina, 2 from Vermont, and 1 each from North Carolina and Alabama; United States Supreme Court decisions referred to are of the number of 45 and United States Circuit Court decisions 19. Of the Supreme Court decisions, 14 are from the time before Story was on the Court and 31 in which he participated. In 5 of the 31, Story wrote the opinion of the Court and in one other he delivered a dissent. For none of the five decisions would it be possible to say that Story, more than any other member, was responsible for the decision; nor could this be said of any of the cases in which other members wrote the opinion. And it can hardly be said that any of the five decisions in which Story wrote the opinion created new conflicts law.

* * * * *

* * * To what an extent have the *Commentaries* suggested rules not yet established by English or American adjudications?

Before attempting any answer, we shall recall the characteristics of this unique work—one of the few international classics on conflicts. Before Story's *Commentaries*, no textbook existed in the English language on conflict of laws. There were only: a chapter on some of the problems, which Kames, the Scottish jurist, had added to the second, 1767, edition of his *Principles of Equity*; the digests of decisions, notably those by Cowen and Laussat, that lack any attempt at systematic presentation; and additions on conflicts aspects made by Kent to some chapters in the second, 1832, edition of his *Commentaries on American Law*. The arrangement of the materials thus was a problem, and Story lists it in the preface to the *Commentaries* as the greatest problem faced by him. Foreign precedents were of little help for they followed the civilian departmentation of the law.

The other serious problem, also noted in the preface, was making proper choice of foreign materials for use in the treatise. The quantity of available foreign writings on conflicts was overwhelming. Story had no doubt that "essential assistance can be derived from foreign jurisprudence to illustrate the questions brought into contestation in the courts." He could draw on his own court experience. Besides he had used the comparative method already in his *Commentaries on Bailment*, published two years before, in which Story took full advantage of the civil law materials used by Sir William Jones in the latter's *Essay on Bailments*.

* * * * *

One claim which Story did not make for his *Commentaries on the Conflict of Laws*, and which he could not have made, is that of asking credit for the collection of the civilian sources used in the work. Two texts had appeared in the English language, one in London in 1823 and the other in New Orleans in 1828, the treatise by Jabez Henry on *Foreign Law* and Livermore's *Dissertations on the Questions which Arise from the Contrariety of the Positive Laws of Different States and Nations*, in which these authorities are quoted or referred to. Indeed, Henry's text is nothing but a summary of the *Traite de la Personnalite et de la Realite des Loix, Coutumes, et Status* by Boullenois. Thus Story had the references to the sources; and, no less important, he had access to the sources themselves. The fabulous Livermore Collection of writings of Civilians had gone to Harvard in 1833.

Story's outstanding, and lasting, contribution through the *Commentaries* to conflicts law derives from the expert use of both adjudications in American, English, and Scottish courts and views expressed by foreign authors for the purposes of a systematic presentation of the conflicts problems as they arise in the various branches of the law. As said by a leading authority on the history of the law of conflict of laws:[88]

> "With the appearance of the Commentaries on the Conflict of Laws by the American, Story, there begins almost a new era in the scholarly treatment of private international law, not only in America and England, but also on the Continent, a complete break with the previous method of treatment, still somehow suffering from the theory of the statutes; work which in its com-

---

[88]   GUTZWILLER, *Der Einfluss Savignys auf die Entwicklung des Internationalprivatrechts* 110 (Freiburg (Switzerland) 1923). Cf. GUTZWILLER, "Le Developpement Historique du Droit International Prive," 29 *Recueil des Cours de l'Academie de La Haye* 287, 338 (1929).

position shows a transition from an earlier to a new school; on the whole probably still a permeation with the old viewpoints, conceptions and maxims, but only as a shell, the core being formed of practical domestic considerations, to a large part already based on court decisions, and arranged according to the most important questions of law."

* * * * *

Today, Story's *Commentaries on the Conflict of Laws, Foreign and Domestic*, show their age. Other problems than those considered by the author have come into the foreground. Interestingly, torts is not dealt with at all in the work—a fact that has not stopped the writer of the opinion in *The Halley* from quoting Story in support of the unilluminating decision rendered by the Privy Council in that case. The treatment of the constitutional provisions affecting conflicts problems in a separate work, the *Commentaries on the Constitution*, also had to develop into a handicap, especially after the broadening of the "constitutional" area in conflicts with the adoption of the Fourteenth Amendment. Thus it can be understood that reediting the *Commentaries on the Conflict of Laws* was abandoned after publication of the 8th edition in 1883.

Less justified would seem to be the very limited use made currently of the work in legal education. The treatise has remained an invaluable instrument of instruction, demonstrating as it does the advantages which can be derived from the study of the labors of others. Story's work "was not merely the first treatise on conflicts law worthy of the name to appear in English but also a pioneer comparative survey of both the civilian doctrines and the English and American precedents, projected with a scholarly understanding of the mass of detail that has not since been surpassed, and but rarely equalled in England, the United States, or indeed elsewhere."[114] Students of the work are likely to see the shortcomings of any attempt at attacking the basic problems of conflicts law without knowledge of what has been tried out before. Having seen the intellectual struggle, over the centuries, of the best with what are unavoidably difficult, and sometimes insoluble, problems, they will develop a healthy scepticism towards new schemes—normally old ones in a new cloth—supposedly capable of solving the difficulties, but doing it, if at all, only at the expense of justice to the parties in the litigation or the respect for the comity among nations, or both.

Joseph H. Beale, *History and Doctrines of the Conflict of Laws, in* 3 A TREATISE ON THE CONFLICT OF LAWS, 1967-1969 app. (New York: Baker, Voorhis & Co. 1935)*

* * * * *

§ 73. **The Doctrine of Vested Rights.**—Instead of the Dutch theory of comity, the common law has worked out indigenously a theory of vested rights, which serves the same purpose, that is, the desire to reach a just result, and is not subject to the objections which can be urged against the doctrine of comity.

---

[114] YNTEMA, "The Historic Bases of Private International Law," 2 Am. J. Comp. L. 297, 307, reprinted in *Selected Readings on Conflict of Laws* 30, 38 (Kulp ed. 1956).

*   Reprinted with permission of Lawyers Cooperative Publishing, a division of Thomson Information Services, Inc.

As early as the time of Story the courts were already saying that an act or obligation valid by the laws of the place where made was valid everywhere; and that a foreign judgment by a court of competent jurisdiction was conclusive of the right it decided. The fullest statement of this new doctrine was by Sir William Scott in Dalrymple *v.* Dalrymple: "The cause being entertained in an English court it must be adjudicated according to the principles of English law applicable to such a case. But the only principle applicable to such a case by the law of England is that the validity of Miss Gordon's marriage rights must be tried by reference to the law of the country where, if they exist at all, they had their origin." Story accepted and developed this theory, which from his time has been the accepted theory in the English and American courts.

This doctrine may be stated and explained as follows. Although the law to be applied to the solution of the Conflict of Laws is the territorial law, this does not mean the law by which such rights as those brought in question would be created within the territory. As Westlake says, "The will which imposes a national law within territorial limits does not necessarily decree the application of that law to all the cases there arising, when great inconvenience would result from so doing." The national law which is applied to the solution of conflicts is that portion of the national law which deals with the solution of conflicts. If by the national law the validity of a contract depends upon the law of the place where the contract was made, then that law is applied for determining the validity of a contract made abroad, not because the foreign law has any force in the nation, nor because of any constraint exercised by an international principle, but because the national law determines the question of the validity of a contract by the *lex loci contractus*. If it were really a case of conflicting laws, and the foreign law prevailed in the case in question, the decision would be handed over bodily to the foreign law. By the national doctrine, the national law provides for a decision according to certain provisions of the foreign law; in the case considered, according to the foreign contract law. The provisions of this law having been proved as a fact, the question is solved by the national law, the foreign factor in the solution — *i.e.*, the foreign contract law — being present as mere fact, one of the facts upon which the decision is to be based.

To explain the territorial theory in other terms, all that has happened outside the territory, including the foreign laws which have in some way or other become involved in the problem, is regarded merely as fact to be considered by the national law in arriving at its decision, and to be given such weight in determining the decision as the national law may choose to give it. The author summarized this theory in 1902 as follows:[2]

> "The topic called 'Conflict of Laws' deals with the recognition and enforcement of foreign created rights. In the legal sense, all rights must be created by some law. A right is artificial, not a mere natural fact; no legal right exists by nature. A right is a political, not a social thing; no legal right can be created by the mere will of parties. Law being a general rule to govern future transactions, its method of creating rights is to provide that upon the happening of a certain event a right shall accrue. The law annexes to the event a certain consequence, namely, the creation of a legal right. The creation of a right is therefore conditioned upon the happening of an event. Events which the law acts upon may be of two sorts; acts of human beings, and so-called "acts of God," that is, events in which no human being has a share. Rights generally follow acts of men; though sometimes a right is created as

---

2   Beale, Summary of the Conflict of Laws (in Cases, Vol. iii), §§ 1-5.

a result solely of an act of God (as lapse of time: accretion). When a right has been created by law, this right itself becomes a fact; and its existence may be a factor in an event which the same or some other law makes the condition of a new right. In other words, a right may be changed by the law that created it, or by any other law having power over it. If no law having power to do so has changed a right, the existing right should everywhere be recognized; since to do so is merely to recognize the existence of a fact."

* * * * *

Herbert F. Goodrich, YIELDING PLACE TO NEW: REST VERSUS MOTION IN THE CONFLICT OF LAWS, 9-11, 14-15, 23-25, 28-30 (The Association of the Bar of the City of New York 1950)*

* * * * *

Among other subjects of the common law first chosen for Restatement * * * was conflict of laws. Those who made this decision well knew that the work to be done in accordance with it would be difficult. They knew, too, that in the course of the undertaking the Institute would be involved in violent controversy and that the conclusions reached could not possibly be satisfactory to everyone.

There were many reasons for this. The name conflict of laws itself was unfortunate because it implied competition or collision among the rules to settle a given piece of litigation. The name alternatively applied in some of the English and many continental treatises was private international law. This, too, was misleading. It carried an implication of afternoon tea and diplomatic receptions and results reached by adjustment and negotiation rather than by rule of law. There was little American literature. Story, Wharton and Minor had written texts. Story's was the continuation through new editions of his Harvard Law School lectures of nearly a hundred years before. There was no such amount of writing, in texts or legal magazines, as had helped so much in the development of ideas in other subjects of the law. Conflict of laws had not been long established as a subject-matter for law school study. It was only at the turn of the century that Professor Joseph Beale of Harvard had compiled his collection of materials and through the success of his course at that law school pretty generally impressed its importance upon those responsible for the curriculum in other institutions. The law book people with whom the Institute was associated in publishing the Restatement shook their heads dolefully at the mention of a volume in the conflict of laws. They predicted that any book bearing that title would be a financial failure because of the unpopularity of the subject. Only when marketed as part of a set of books, they said, would the Restatement volume in conflict of laws reach the shelves of lawyers and law libraries.

In spite of all the difficulties in the way of restatement, the decision to undertake it was right. Here was a body of law which in spite of its name, was not limited to the merchant or banker who did business overseas. Here was, instead, subject-matter which touched every mer-

---

*   Reprinted with permission.

chant who bought goods from a wholesale house in another state; every family who took a vacation trip to visit relatives in another part of the country; every property owner who left upon his death so much as a single cow in another state than his own. This was a developing body of law, a body of law distinct from the regulation of interstate commerce matters by the Congress, a body of law which dealt with every American whose affairs crossed state lines. Its importance was increasing with the opening of every new strip of concrete highway which led from one state to another. Courts and the lawyers who argued before them were presenting and deciding cases and building up precedents without adequate help in the problems involved, often indeed without consciousness that two-state problems presented anything of peculiar significance. It was important that this growing and developing branch of interstate law should be examined and clarified. The start on a restatement of conflict of laws was made in 1923.

It was during the years when this work was going on that Judge Cardozo gave the Carpentier lectures at Columbia. They were brought out in 1928 by the Columbia University Press under the title of "The Paradoxes of Legal Science." In the third lecture he talked of the "equilibration of interests." He pointed out that there are times and places when rest is to be preferred to motion in the law. There is a suggestion that he thought that the field of conflict of laws was one of those places. He speaks of it as "one of the most baffling subjects of legal science." "The walls of the compartments must be firm," he says, "the lines of demarcation plain, or there will be overlappings and encroachments with incongruities and clashes. In such circumstances, the finality of the rule is in itself a jural end." He finds "logic to have been more remorseless here, more blind to final causes, than it has been in other fields." "Very likely it has been too remorseless," he concludes.

The suggestion that conflict of laws is a field in which certainty is almost the only criterion on which to judge whether a given rule is good law, and where rest is preferable to motion, may have come from Judge Cardozo's experience with the group engaged upon the Conflict of Laws Restatement. He attended many of it sessions, especially when they were held in New York. He was greatly interested and always helpful. The Reporter for the subject was Professor Joseph H. Beale. He was a man of strong mind and definite convictions. He had no doubt whatever as to the reasons why his convictions were right. For the most part, these reasons seemed to him inherent in the nature of a moral universe. And he was for many years the foremost of those teaching and writing conflict of laws in this country. Naturally, his strong personality and tenaciously held views set the tone of group discussions, though they did not by any means always determine the conclusions. From the expression of those views it is not in the least surprising that Judge Cardozo gained the impression suggested in the quotation from his lecture.

* * * * *

The Restatement of Conflict of Laws was not intended to stop the growth in its particular field any more than it was elsewhere. The Restatement was never intended as the last word in the law on any subject. It stated the law as of the date of its promulgation. The Institute hoped that it stated the rules in terms which would be in accord with the then developing law; in other words, with a sympathetic eye to the trend of the time. But nobody thought of it as the last word, nor has it proved to be. Courts have used the Restatement of Conflict of Laws 2010 times. But when the Restatement as a whole was checked through a little while ago to see what developments since its issue required revision of text, there were found more changes in conflict of laws than in any other subject.

* * * * *

We turn next to the field of two-state tort law. Here there has been comparatively little dispute about the rule of reference. Courts having before them cases involving facts claimed to constitute a tort refer the matter, by the orthodox rule, to the law of the place of wrong. And the place of wrong is, we find, the place where the last event occurs which is relied upon to create the cause of action.

There has been little complaint about the rule. The suggestion has been made that of the various possibilities of reference that one should be chosen which would give the plaintiff recovery. Why the choice of law rule should favor plaintiff rather than defendant is not clear. There has been some confusion with regard to whether the items to be included in the measure of damages are subject to the foreign law reference or should be decided by local rules. That has pretty well disappeared; the consensus is that elements of damages are matters of "right" and are included in the reference to the appropriate foreign law.

Out of the tort cases there has arisen considerable argument on theory back of the rules. Both Holmes and Cardozo talked what has been called the "obligatio" or "vested rights" theory. The concept is that the place of tort gives plaintiff his right; the forum enforces it. This notion has been vigorously attacked. But the same results can be reached whether one accepts the obligatio theory or not, it is believed, without aligning one's self upon one side or the other of the legal theology argument. Simply stated, the rule of reference to the foreign law is applied in nearly all the cases because of its essential fairness and convenience.

In the torts field, too, we find much talk and some decisions with regard to supposed local public policy and its effect upon the ordinary rules of reference for the two-state cases. On this point there has been considerable literature and the straw has been pretty well threshed out. Judge Cardozo announced the guiding principle when he said in *Loucks v. Standard Oil Co.*, 224 N.Y. 99, 111, 120 N.E. 198, 201 (1918), "We are not so provincial as to say that every solution of a problem is wrong because we deal with it otherwise at home." His own court lost sight of that principle in cases which came up after he had left the state bench, and similar deviations will probably continue to occur when accepted rules of reference reveal a situation in foreign tort law too violently opposed to the local courts' notions on the subject.

Perhaps the persistence of the talk about local public policy comes from the failure to observe a difference which is obvious, once it is expressed. If an American court is asked to apply a rule of some foreign state where the standards of values are fundamentally opposed to our own, it might well be that such a reference, as Cardozo said, would violate what we regard as some "fundamental principle of justice." But as Judge Beach pointed out a number of years ago, that is not the situation among our states and it is in most instances "an intolerable affectation of superior virtue" for one of our states so to look upon the rules of law of another.

* * * * *

Let us conclude the examination of instances of growing in conflict of laws by looking at the field of contracts. Here the case authorities have been more confused than in any other part of the general subject. There are numberless judicial opinions saying, in decision and dicta, that whether the parties' promises have made a contract and, if so, what are its terms, are questions to be determined by reference to the law of the place of making. But there is authority in plenty announcing the rule with equal positiveness that the law of the place of performance governs. There is likewise case law for the proposition that the answer to the question depends upon the presumed intention of the parties. The law review and text book writers have expressed views as varied as those of the courts.

The Restatement announced the rule that the place of contracting governs the validity of the agreement and the scope of the obligation. Professor Beale believed that to be the only rule possible in a rational legal world. The point was one which he had covered at length in a series of papers which had previously appeared. While the existence of conflicting authorities was recognized, the true rule to him seemed very clear.

Beale's Advisers and subsequently the Institute accepted the statement of the rule, though not necessarily accepting the premises upon which the Reporter had reached his conclusions. Quite obviously a restatement of the law could not be in harmony with all the decisions. The rule stated is clear, easy to understand, easy to apply. In most cases it provides a high degree of predictability, a desirable attribute in commercial matters. That it may be arbitrary in some instances, especially those thought up as hypothetical cases for classroom discussion is admitted. A Chicago offer to a New York offeree and the mailing of the acceptance from the offeree's New Jersey country club is a typical instance. The New Jersey contact with such a transaction is of course purely fortuitous. But courts have cited the contract sections approximately 250 times since the Restatement appeared and little complaint about them has found its way into the opinions.

The Restatement referred matters of performance to the law of the place of performance. This provoked little or no discussion, though it must be admitted that the rule has a deceptive simplicity of statement. What is a matter of original obligation and what is a matter having to do with performance? Suppose, for instance, a moratorium on payment of debts because of the outbreak of war in the place of payment. This is a matter of performance, no doubt, and the law of the place of payment will be looked to in determining whether the debtor is excused. But what of a failure to perform due to supervening impossibility? Is the excuse, if any, to be considered as an implied term of the contract and governed by the law of the place of contracting? Or is it a matter of performance governed by the law of the place of performance? The Restatement recognizes that there is a borderland where the boundaries between obligation and performance are not clear and assigning a question to one division or the other may be a matter of judgment in a particular case.

* * * * *

American Law Institute, Restatment of the Law of Conflict of Laws, Secs. 1, 245, 303, 332, 358, 378, 612 (St. Paul 1934)*

* * *

§ 1.   Subject Matter of Conflict of Laws.

(1) No state can make a law which by its own force is operative in another state; the only law in force in the sovereign state is its own law, but by the law of each state rights or other interests in that state may, in certain cases, depend upon the law in force in some other state or states.

(2) That part of the law of each state which determines whether in dealing with a legal situation the law of some other state will be recognized, be given effect or be applied is called the Conflict of Laws.

* * * * *

§ 245. INHERITANCE OF LAND.

The law of the state where the land is determines its devolution upon the death of the owner intestate.

* * * * *

§ 303. DISTRIBUTION OF ESTATE OF INTESTATE.

The movables of one who died intestate which remain in the state after the estate is fully administered are distributed to the persons who are entitled to take by the law of the state of his domicil at the time of his death.

* * * * *

§ 332. LAW GOVERNING VALIDITY OF CONTRACT.

The law of the place of contracting determines the validity and effect of a promise with respect to

(a) capacity to make the contract;
(b) the necessary form, if any, in which the promise must be made;
(c) the mutual assent or consideration, if any, required to make a promise binding;
(d) any other requirements for making a promise binding;
(e) fraud, illegality, or any other circumstances which make a promise void or voidable;
(f) except as stated in § 358, the nature and extent of the duty for the performance of which a party becomes bound;
(g) the time when and the place where the promise is by its terms to be performed;
(h) the absolute or conditional character of the promise.

* * * * *

§ 358. LAW GOVERNING PERFORMANCE.

The duty for the performance of which a party to a contract is bound will be discharged by compliance with the law of the place of performance of the promise with respect to:

(a) the manner of performance;
(b) the time and locality of performance;
(c) the person or persons by whom or to whom performance shall be made or rendered;
(d) the sufficiency of performance;
(e) excuse for non-performance.

* * * * *

§ 378. LAW GOVERNING PLAINTIFF'S INJURY.

The law of the place of wrong determines whether a person has sustained a legal injury.

* * * * *

§ 612. ACTION CONTRARY TO PUBLIC POLICY.

No action can be maintained upon a cause of action created in another state the enforcement of which is contrary to the strong public policy of the forum.

* * * * *

Comments

1. For additional writing on Story, *see* Ehrenzweig 1954: pp. 135-143;[1] Juenger (1993): pp. 29-31; Lorenzen (1934); Watson (1992).

2. Perhaps the reason why Story sought to discourage local bias in the name of comity was that the local tribunal might thus inspire or reinforce similar gestures of comity in other jurisdictions, leading to the ultimate advantage to all nations of uniformity and continuity in choice of law. In the next Part, however, Professor Elliott Cheatham chides Story for failing to clearly develop this or any other practical argument for his emphasis on comity.

3. As Nandelmann observes, numerous American conflicts cases had been decided before Story published his treatise. American commentators prior to Story had wrestled with the subject. The most notable was Samuel Livermore, whose *Dissertations on the Questions Which Arise From the Contrariety of the Positive Laws of the Different States and Nations* was published in 1828. Like Story, Livermore drew heavily on the work of continental authors (surveyed in Chapter Two). However, while Story was greatly influenced by the Dutch multilaterist Huber, Livermore adopted the unilateralist view of the European statutists. While Story's treatise was a great success, Livermore's book had little influence. An interesting portrait of Livermore appears in Juenger 1993: pp. 28-29.

4. Beale's vested rights doctrine had a forceful advocate in Justice Oliver Wendell Holmes. Holmes expressed the doctrine in *Slater v. Mexican National Railroad Co.*, 194 U.S. 120, 126 (1904): "The theory of the foreign suit is that, although the act complained of was subject to no law having force in the forum, it gave rise to an obligation, an *obligato,* which like other obligations, follows the person, and may be enforced wherever the person may be found." For an article-length study of Holmes' approach to choice of law, *see* Reiblich 1938. Additional critiques of Holmes' position appear in Harper 1947: p. 1158; Juenger 1992: p. 93; von Mehren & Trautman 1965: p. 180.

5. It seems evident from Beale's writing and the observation of Holmes quoted above, that the vested rights doctrine rests in significant part on a theory of substantive justice. That is, reference to foreign law (as, for example, the place of contracting or the place of injury) becomes necessary to a proper definition of rights or duties in the case. A contemporary reworking of the vested rights doctrine appears in the excerpt by Professor Perry Dane in Chapter Nine, Part C.

6. Beale's concerns about conflicts law reflected a larger concern for uniformity and stability in American law that led to organization of the American Law Institute in 1923 (Franklin 1934; Goodrich 1951; Wickersham 1927; Wechsler 1969). A prodigious scholar and guiding force in the development of conflict of laws as a law school subject, Beale was the obvious choice as Reporter for the ALI's conflicts restatement. Beale was also hard-headed and overbearing, called by one observer

---

[1]   Full citations appear in the bibliography, Chapter Twelve.

the apostle of dogmatism" (Morris 1973: p. 323). As Dean Goodrich's account suggests, he usually got his way, and RESTATEMENT OF THE LAW OF CONFLICTS is Bealean throughout. Biographical material on Beale and his contributions to conflict of laws includes Chafee 1943; Griswold 1943; Frankfurter 1943; Juenger 1992: pp. 90-92; Williston 1943.

7. Most of the sections in our excerpt from the original RESTATEMENT are hard and fast rules typical of its *lex loci delicti* approach. Thus, Section 332 commits resolution of numerous contract validity issues to the "law of the place of contracting," and Section 378 commits questions of tort liability to the "place of the wrong." In themselves, these sections seem like unqualified commands. Yet judges administering the original RESTATEMENT actually had a fair amount of elbow room. Section 1 makes clear that a court cannot be bound by foreign law, and Section 612 acknowledges that a court may reject foreign law whenever "enforcement * * * is contrary to the strong public policy of the forum." A commentator described the situation as follows:

> [T]he traditional system as exemplified by the first conflicts Restatement is a system of fixed, a priori choice-of-law rules that did *not* contain any built-in escape clauses. * * * However, the fact that the traditional rules did not contain built-in escape clauses does not mean that the traditional *system* lacked escape mechanisms altogether. For example, the Restatement did sanction the *ordre public* exception [Section 612]. Although this exception was meant to be applied very sparingly, it was nevertheless an exception to which *all* the Restatement rules were subject.

Symeonides 1994b: p. 820 (emphasis in original).

8. The extent to which local autonomy could frustrate the *lex loci delicti* approach becomes clear when we learn that the public policy exception embodied in Section 612 (and examined further in Corr 1985b; Harper 1947: p. 1175; McLaughlin 1991a: pp. 983-988; Nussbaum 1940; Paulsen & Sovern 1956) was but one of a series of "escape devices" available to judges administering the original RESTATEMENT. Surveys appear in Bourne 1993: pp. 78-104; McLaughlin 1991a: pp. 981-998; Symeonides 1994b: pp. 820-821. Three of the additional escape devices were as follows. First, courts characterized issues as procedural rather than substantive, and then invoked the rule that procedural matters were invariably governed by forum law (also discussed in Cook 1933; Richman & Reynolds 1993: pp. 153-155; Risinger 1982). Second, courts would characterize an issue under one branch of substantive law rather than another (explained generally in Ehrenzweig 1961; Lorenzen 1947: pp. 115-135; Morse 1949; Robertson 1940) to reach a *lex loci delicti* rule pointing to local rather than foreign law: *renvoi* (explained generally in Griswold 1939; Kramer 1991d; Lorenzen 1918). Third, courts would utilize foreign (as opposed to local) conflicts law, when the RESTATEMENT pointed away from local law.

9. The works cited above make clear that these four devices (public policy, procedural characterization, characterization between substantive areas, and *renvoi*) had appropriate boundaries of application, but that it was difficult in theory and practice to locate them. It was therefore impossible under the original RESTATEMENT to contain the extent to which the four devices diverted the *lex loci delicti* choice of foreign law. At the same time, whether use of these and other escape devices seriously incapacitated the original RESTATEMENT is a matter of debate. For it is clear that courts in numerous cases took the RESTATEMENT's *lex loci* directives at face value and applied foreign over local law.

10. The entire situation may have left the RESTATEMENT's proponents uneasy, but they appeared willing to live with it. The RESTATEMENT's growing number of critics, however, saw matters quite differently. To them, the RESTATEMENT was on the horns of a dilemma: When courts subverted *lex loci* through forum-favoring escape devices, the RESTATEMENT was an instrumental failure and a sham. When courts were true to the directives of the RESTATEMENT and the precepts of the vested rights theory, they promoted confusion and injustice through formalistic, analytically bankrupt decisions. We sample these arguments in the next Part of this Chapter.

B. Classical Theory Under Attack

Elliott E. Cheatham, *American Theories of Conflict of Laws: Their Role and Utility*, 58 HARV. L. REV. 361, 374, 375-376 (1945)*

* * * * *

* * * [C]omity is a word of various applications.

The term is used in public international law to apply to the relation of nation to nation; in conflict of laws, to the action of the courts of one nation or state when asked to use a law or enforce the judgment of a court of another nation or state;[34] in non-conflicts matters, to the use of precedents coming from a tribunal without compelling authority, as, from a court of another nation or from a co-ordinate court in the same nation. In all of these situations, the term may be employed in its ordinary sense of courtesy; or with the wider meaning of expediency; or in the more specialized sense of reciprocity. Throughout there is the common implication that the relation or the action in question is governed by considerations other than compulsion or legal duty.

* * * Story was concerned with emphasizing a negative aspect of the situation, the freedom of the state from compulsion. Especially he wished to establish that when foreign law is employed this is not because the foreign law operates of its own force in the forum, or because there is an international obligation on the forum to use the foreign law, but because the forum with full liberty of action allows the foreign law to operate for the purposes of the case or, in short, by comity. Since in Story's meaning the term indicates only freedom from compulsion, it does not show the affirmative reasons for the use of foreign law and these reasons must be found elsewhere. Taken only in this sense of freedom of a state from compulsion in the nature of law or in international obligation, the term comity would be apt to express a view with which common-law writers and judges agree.

If taken in other applications or other meanings, as has often been done by critics, however, it is certainly unfortunate. Three of these may be mentioned:

1.   It has sometimes been thought that comity is identical with reciprocity or courtesy as showing the reason for the employment of foreign law, and it was this sense that came under the criticism of the strong dissent in *Hilton v. Guyot*. It may be agreed that neither reciprocity nor courtesy is by itself a sufficient explanation of the use of foreign law, but this does not suffice to condemn Story's use of comity in its negative aspect, for in so far as he indicated the

---

[34]   "No law has any effect, of its own force, beyond the limits of the sovereignty from which its authority is derived. The extent to which the law of one nation, as put in force within its territory, whether by executive order, by legislative act, or by judicial decree, shall be allowed to operate within the dominion of another nation, depends upon what our greatest jurists have been content to call 'the comity of nations.' Although the phrase has been often criticized, no satisfactory substitute has been suggested.

"'Comity,' in the legal sense, is neither a matter of absolute obligation, on the one hand, nor of mere courtesy and good will, upon the other. But it is the recognition which one nation allows within its territory to the legislative, executive or judicial acts of another nation, having due regard both to international duty and convenience, and to the rights of its own citizens or of other persons who are under the protection of its laws." Mr. Justice Gray in Hilton v. Guyot, 159 U.S. 113, 163-64 (1895).

affirmative reasons for state action it was in terms much more broadly conceived.

2.   In intranational conflicts there may be a constitutional requirement under the full faith and credit clause to use the law of another state and even in international conflicts there seems to be at times a somewhat similar compulsion on a state under the due process clause. In situations of this sort the freedom of action which Story wishes to convey by the word "comity" does not exist, and the term itself is inappropriate.

If leaving the question, why a *state* employs foreign law, we come to the question, why a *court* or a *judge* employs foreign law, we are in an area where the concept and term comity are misleading. A court is not free to follow the personal desires of the judge, and is under the usual obligation to adhere to statute and precedent. So if "comity" be employed to denote the reasons for action of a court, it can only be in the sense that comity means the rules of conflict of laws of the state.

Story's view of the freedom from international compulsion is valid, but since in the common law there is no sense of such a compulsion to use foreign law and since the term is capable of easy misunderstanding, it had better go out of usage.

* * * * *

Hessell E. Yntema, *The Hornbook Method and the Conflict of Laws*, 37 YALE L.J. 468, 476-477, 478-480 (1928)*

* * * * *

* * * One of the primary difficulties with the vested rights theory is the figurative and undifferentiated character of its terminology. To say that laws "exist" within defined geographical limits; that by these laws rights are "created" and so "exist" until they are destroyed by operation of law; that, furthermore, there are "principles" which invest these rights with the powers of migrating from state to state; and that by virtue of these principles rights so vested are recognized and enforced in foreign courts—is to express in crass symbols the most complex syntheses of phenomena. Even so, the metaphorical expression that principles or rights exist is oftentimes a useful mode of speech and not in itself objectionable, so long as we are aware that we have merely given a label to a complicated experience, real or supposed. We must needs talk and probably also think in symbols of sign and sound. The difficulty is rather that the symbols of the vested rights theory neither correspond to the social and economic factors with which courts deal nor even accurately suggest the things which are done in courts. Hence flows the chief vice of this and similar too abstract conceptualistic theories of law, that, because the symbols used are too few and too remote from reality to represent it, they force those whose thoughts are limited to these symbols finally to regard them as reality and to believe that by employing them in the processes of formal logic, "correct" results may be obtained. A simple illustration will suggest the point. The hypothesis, two plus two equals four, is true as an abstract proposition if we accept certain premises; but it is by no means a universally useful method of stating experience, as the addition of two parts of hydrogen to two of oxygen will demonstrate. If the realm of law were like mathematics, compounded of hypotheses or of the stuff which dreams are made of, no one could object to peopling the legal world with principles, rights or other juristic constructions. But law is not logic, however use-

*   Reprinted by permission of The Yale Law Journal Company and Fred B. Rothman & Company from The Yale Law Journal, Vol. 37, pages 468-483.

fully logic may be made to serve the ends of law. And any system of thought so fragmentary as to base the actual statement or reform of law on purely logical deductions from combinations of abstract symbols without careful analysis of the practical purposes of legal traditions and institutions considered with reference to the concrete case is not merely obscurant but socially dangerous. Only by constantly checking the hypotheses resulting from logical manipulations against observation and experience can we hope to approximate practical truth or justice in the administration of law.

As it is stated, the vested rights theory is either an elliptical tautology which leads us nowhere or otherwise it is disingenuous. In either case, it can scarcely be considered either an appropriate vehicle for describing legal practice or an effective means for directing the decision of a court. If we are told that rights which become vested under the proper law are usually enforced in foreign jurisdictions, the natural inquiry arises as to the process by which this investment occurs. Apparently, we are to believe that the investment takes place under the influence of certain common law principles to the extent that these principles are uniformly adopted in the various jurisdictions as to which there is inquiry. The obvious inference is that rights are vested when and because they are vested, which completes this circle.

* * * * *

If *** we interpret the theory of vested rights to mean that "rights once vested under the proper law" should be enforced in the foreign court, our theory is disingenuous, or perhaps ingenuous, since we are assuming the very point at issue, *i.e.,* whether particular claims should be so enforced. It is doubtless true that in many situations the result is the one to be desired, but it is not satisfying from a practical or even a logical point of view to start out by assuming the conclusion. A mode of analysis is required which will state and estimate the equities and conveniences and so reach its conclusions. To do so efficiently, we shall need not only a more precise and flexible terminology but also both careful study of individual cases from the point of view of social and judicial engineering and information as to the fact-situations and the foreign legal practices with which we are dealing.

The point of view which we are stating will inevitably meet the criticism that, in attempting to secure justice in the individual case, we have discarded the possibility of uniformity and certainty in the administration of cases involving the foreign element. The argument is, in sum, that the so-called "uniform enforcement of vested rights" can only be approximated by assuming the general principle that there is to be uniformity. There are various difficulties with this argument of policy as to how doctrines of the conflict of laws should be formulated. As a preliminary point, we may remind ourselves that it can by no means be assumed that uniformity and certainty are the sole ends to be attained. There may be, and we cannot ascertain until inquiry, situations in which the foreign law may be so obsolete or so inimical to the social interests of the forum that to apply the doctrine would defy justice. Here, as elsewhere in the law, *summum ius summa iniuria.* In fact it may be discovered that a discretionary power of rejecting the foreign law in such cases may in the long run conduce to the sound and uniform development of legal doctrine in this country. Such doctrines as that of a "federal common law" have an importance which we have not as yet attempted to ascertain. Again, a general principle of uniformity, as we have attempted to suggest above, can never correspond to the realities of judicial administration. This is so, far more largely than we dare admit, even within a single system of courts. The probabilities of variation are multiplied when the courts of one system attempt to follow the practices of another, as to which they must remain relatively ignorant so long as we are to rely merely upon vague general principles to inform them. And, in any case, there will always be a large area of questions in which, because of the necessities of an economical administration of justice, courts will necessarily follow their local practice. In this situation, it will probably be safer, if we must suggest a general principle, to insist upon a just decision than upon one which may as well as not be erroneously believed to be uniform.

The argument that uniformity can be secured only by disingenuity in the statement of general principles, is one by which we are not to be moved for an even more potent reason,—it is simply not so. The ideal of a government of laws and not of men is a dream which will have to wait for the time when law becomes calculus to be realized. Still less can it be said that the administration of justice is controlled by general principles. The history of codes and of legislation, or even of language, should have taught us long since that rules and principles are empty symbols which take on significance only to the extent that they are informed with the social and professional traditions of a particular time and place. Those who disbelieve may regard the manner in which the greatest of our codes has been interpreted, the Constitution of the United States. It is not the symbols but the habits of thought that control interpretation and decision. In dealing with situations involving a foreign element, the habits of thought which we encounter in judges and lawyers are not normally concentrated primarily upon the foreign element. Whether the problem be one of the recognition of a foreign judgment or of the effect to be given a complicated letter of credit transaction, the pattern is furnished by the traditions of the forum and the experience of the concrete fact situation. This is properly so, if an efficient result is to be attained, since the foreign element, the circumstance that events transpired in another jurisdiction, is only one, and often an incidental, aspect of the case. Furthermore, of the many things which have been said as to the mystery of the judicial process, the most salient is that decision is reached after an emotive experience in which principles and logic play a secondary part. The function of juristic logic and the principles which it employs seems to be like that of language, to describe the event which has already transpired. These considerations must reveal to us the impotence of general principles to control decision. Vague because of their generality, they mean nothing save what they suggest in the organized experience of the one who thinks them, and, because of their vagueness, they only remotely compel the organization of that experience. The important problem in the conflict of laws is not the formulation of the rule but the ascertainment of the cases to which, and the extent to which, it applies. And this, even if we are seeking solely uniformity in the administration of justice, will lead us again to the circumstances of the concrete case, and to the careful study of foreign practices. The reason why the general principle cannot control is because it does not inform.

* * * * *

Walter W. Cook, *The Logical and Legal Bases of the Conflict of Law*, 33 YALE L.J. 457, 484-488 (1924)*

* * * * *

* * * [W]hile, so long as we have the territorial organization of modern political society, the law of a given state or country can be *enforced* only within its territorial limits, this does not mean that the law of that state or country cannot, except in certain exceptional cases, affect the legal relations of persons outside its limits. As we have seen, "law" is not a material phenomenon, which spreads out like a light wave until it reaches the territorial boundary and then stops. Whatever be the legal limitations upon the power of a state or country to affect the legal

---

    *   Reprinted with permission of The Yale Law Journal Company and Fred B. Rothman & Company from The Yale Law Journal, Vol. 33, pages 457-488.

relations of persons anywhere in the world, they must be found in positive law of some kind—by the same international law or constitutional law, and do not inhere in the constitution of the legal universe. Whether international law imposes limitations and if so, what they are, can be determined only by observation. Personally, I can find no consensus of opinion among civilized countries upon the matter under consideration; in fact, the utmost diversity of opinion seems to exist. I must, however, leave it to others more competent to speak to say whether my observations are in accord with the facts. Constitutional limitations exist, in the case of American states—the due process clause and the full faith and credit clause. Beyond these, I discover no limitations.

The fundamental point of the foregoing discussion may perhaps be expressed as follows: by far the larger number of the rules for the solution of cases involving the conflict of laws do not relate to the "power" or "jurisdiction" of the particular court or state to decide the case before it in a certain way. Cases involving power arise only where some limitation is imposed by some system of positive law—such as the federal constitution. Other limitations on power do not exist.

I shall probably be met with the statement that the view presented in the foregoing discussion is directly contrary to all that the courts have *said*, as distinguished from what they have *done*. To some extent this is true, although it is believed that that extent is not quite so great as imagined. To begin with, apparently few courts have directly said that they were enforcing a foreign-created right. Such expressions are found chiefly in texts. The language of the courts is usually that they are applying the foreign "law" to the case in hand. As I have pointed out, this expression is ambiguous and can be given an interpretation which will describe what the courts actually have done. That the courts have not *consciously* given it the other meaning (equivalent to saying that they are enforcing foreign-created rights) is clear from the fact that they do not in the typical cases go on to find what the foreign law applicable to the very controversy before them really is, but content themselves with ascertaining the foreign domestic rule. The truth is, most of the judges have never had time or taken the trouble to analyze very clearly just what they do mean. In view of the fact that the legal training of most of them did not include a study of these problems, and of the further fact that only a limited time can be devoted by a busy judge to the study of a single case, this is only natural. In the second place, even if the formulation here presented is novel, in the sense of departing from the language of the opinions, if it is true that the courts have actually done certain things, and that the usual way of describing these things is inaccurate and misleading, does it follow that we ought to continue to misdescribe the actual decisions because such has been the loose practice in the past? Surely progress in the science of the law consists in continually reformulating our generalizations so as to make them bring out more clearly just what the past phenomena described really are and just what we predict will happen in the future.

But, I may be asked, if the answer to conflict of laws cases cannot be deduced from certain pre-existing principles relating to "jurisdiction," how are they to be decided? The only answer that can be given, by the same methods actually used in deciding cases involving purely domestic torts, contracts, property, etc. The problem involved is that of legal thinking in general. It requires for its adequate discussion an inquiry into the technique of human reasoning in general and that of reasoning in the field of law in particular. It must be admitted that the "outrageous bit of nonsense" that men think in syllogisms, that they solve the problems of life by deductive reasoning, has apparently ruled in law as well as in morals and theology. Actually, however, in law as in the natural sciences, practice has preceded theory, at least to a considerable extent, and conclusions have not actually been reached deductively. The reason for this is shown by recent investigations into human thinking. These investigations have convinced the leading students of logic that formal logic, the deductive syllogism, is always purely hypothetical reasoning and never of itself assures us of the factual truth of the conclusions reached. Its content seems to be identical with pure mathematics, which, Bertrand Russell tells us, is "the science in which we never know what we are talking about nor whether what we are saying is true."[80] The actual process involved in settling a situation of doubt—a new case, if we are dealing with law—involves a comparison of the data of the new situation with the facts of a large number of prior situations which have been subsumed under a "rule" or "principle" within the terms of which it is thought the new situation may be brought. This comparison, if carried on intelligently, necessarily involves a consideration of the policy involved in the prior decisions and of the effects which those decisions have produced. If the points in which the new situation resemble the older situations already dealt with are thought to be the qualities the existence of which were decisive in leading to the decisions in the prior cases, the new case will be put under the old rule or principle. In doing this, the rule or principle as it existed has not been applied; it has been extended to take in the new situation. In other words, however great the appearance of purely deductive reasoning may be, the real decision where a case presents novel elements consists in a re-defining of the middle term *construction* or *creation of premises* for the case in hand, which premises did not pre-exist. The statement of the premises of the deductive syllogism is therefore a statement of the conclusion which has been reached on other grounds, and not of the real reason for the decision. When once the premises have been thus constructed, the conclusion inevitably follows.

This view does not lead to the discarding of all principles and rules, but quite the contrary. It demands them as tools with which to work; as tools without which we cannot work effectively. It does, however, make sure that they are used as tools and are not perverted to an apparently mechanical use. It points out that the use never can be really mechanical; that the danger in continuing to deceive ourselves into believing that we are merely "applying" the old rule or principle to "a new case" by purely deductive reasoning lies in the fact that as the real thought-process is thus obscured, we fail to realize that our choice is really being guided by considerations of social and economic policy or ethics, and so fail to take into consideration all the relevant facts of life required for a wise decision. * * *

In the field of the conflict of laws, it is unfortunately true that past judicial phenomena are so confused that the formulation of tools with which to work is vastly more difficult than in most fields of the law. This is due largely to the fact that when American courts first began to be confronted with cases involving the problem, there were so few phenomena in the way of decisions to describe that there could hardly be said to be well recognized principles and rules established by prior English decisions. Without adequate guides to go by, and confronted by the chaotic and conflicting views of continental writers as gathered together in Story's treatise, the courts of last resort in our states found themselves on a largely unchartered sea. For this reason a writer attempting to set forth the "American law" upon the conflict of laws is necessarily compelled more often than in any other field to choose between conflicting rules. In making a choice between such rules, it is obvious that here as elsewhere the basis must be a pragmatic one—of the effect of a decision one way or the other in giving a practical working rule. In this connection it may be suggested that in many cases it makes little difference which rule is adopted, so long as it is reasonably simple and definite and after its adoption is not departed from in cases clearly falling within it.

---

[80]   Quoted in A. S. Eddington, *Space, Time, and Gravitation* (1920) 14.

David F. Cavers, *A Critique of the Choice of Law Problem*, 47 HARV. L. REV. 173, 176-178, 182-187, 192-193, 197-200 (1933)*

* * * * *

A change in methodology invites a re-inspection of the problem to be attacked, for the formulation of a problem is likely to be as much the product of an approach as the approach is the product of the problem. A positive methodology applied to a problem which for it, at least, is false will not yield a fair return; and the situation disclosed by the state of authority in cases involving a choice of laws is symptomatic of a false problem.

Where a problem which courts have set themselves is false, one of two results is inevitable. The courts may adhere consistently to a broad principle beneath the shelter of which a variety of results will be concealed, or they may take refuge in a diversity of doctrines. Whether in either event the decisions themselves may be subsumed under some inarticulate premises is another matter. Complete optimism on this count would point the superfluity of much legal study. Since the courts will usually escape the check of criticism directed to these premises, one is justified, perhaps, in suspecting the worst. We have been too ready, I suggest, to trade the dogma of the automatic and inflexible rule for the myth of the rule freely and deliberately manipulated by the courts.

In American conflicts cases, the alternative of diversity in doctrines has probably been resorted to the more frequently. This is in part due to the coincidence of the development of the federal union with the rapid expansion of international and interstate trade. These events brought to the courts an influx of conflicts cases for which adequate authority did not exist. Story's treatise, designed to meet this need, brought to their attention the works of Continental jurists, adepts of the theoretical method, from whose writings Story had selected those views most consonant with his own. But no embargo could be laid on future imports, and when, subsequently, the hard pragmatism of common law jurisprudence could not be reconciled to the result dictated by one of Story's principles, another doctrine was ready to the judge's hand. Rules proliferated, each fashionably tagged with its appropriate Latin phrase. *Lex loci contractus, lex loci solutionis, lex rei sitae, locus regit actum, mobilia sequuntur personam,*—each phrase bears testimony to our common law judges' dalliance with civilian doctrine.

All this is an old story. More significant is the fact that the conditions of whose origin it offers some explanation have persisted to the present time. Lines of decision have hardened here and there, but the article on a conflict of laws topic which does not deplore a current "confusion of authority" is still a rarity. And to account for its origin does not explain its continuance. That same pragmatism of the common law has effected many times before this the absorption of those elements of an alien theory which were congenial to it while it rejected the rest. Why has a century not worked this result in the conflict of laws? The explanation, it is submitted, lies in the nature of the problem which a choice of law case is thought to pose.

When a case arises in which a foreign law is offered in evidence or in which the applicability of the law of the forum is denied, a court faithful to the conventional approach will turn in search of a conflicts of laws rule to determine the *jurisdiction* whose law should govern the question at issue. The conflicts rule indicates in which jurisdiction the appropriate law may be found. Assuming the law offered to be from that jurisdiction, the court will then proceed with the case, employing that law as a rule of decision. Not until its admission for that purpose does the content of that law become material. Both the territorial and the "vested rights" theories

---

sanctioned its disregard. So long as deduction from territorial postulates could indicate only one jurisdiction as a source of law in a given case, the content of that law would be logically irrelevant. Again, so long as the court was in search of a "foreign-created right", it would seek an appropriate jurisdiction, not an appropriate substantive rule, for metaphorical consistency demands that the creation or non-creation of rights be attributed only to states and not to their legal rules. That rules for the determination of the appropriate jurisdiction would ignore the content of its law may not be inevitable as a matter of logic; actually it has seemed inescapable.

With the reaction against the restrictions of theory, there has come a recognition that considerations of justice and social expediency should be, and in many cases have been, the dominant determinants of problems in this field. Yet these considerations are still harnessed to the old task of devising (or justifying) rules for selecting the appropriate jurisdiction whose law should govern a given case. Like the forms of action, in Maitland's telling phrase, the territorial and vested rights theories rule us from their graves, and this dominion is maintained by the problem which they have set and with which we have not broken.

* * * * *

There have been a few avenues of escape from this entanglement which from time to time have been tried by the courts. Among these are the following:

1.   The conflict of laws rule may itself be couched in terms of a result regarded as proper in litigation of a given sort. The most familiar example is the rule generally adopted to govern the choice of a usury law. The decline of the defense of usury in judicial esteem has led many courts to uphold any contract alleged to be usurious when it would be valid by the law of any jurisdiction to which the transaction was materially related. It has been suggested by Professor Lorenzen that this rule be extended wherever the "intrinsic validity" of a contract is in question. This view represents a drastic simplification of the problem and places a low appraisal on the significance of the variations in domestic laws relating to contracts. Perhaps such an estimate is justifiable. In any event, this means of escaping the artificiality of conflicts rules will not be available generally and is itself subject to the qualification implicit in the recognition accorded by its sponsor to the doctrine immediately following.

2.   The conflict of laws rule may be disregarded when the foreign law it selects dictates a result repugnant to the public policy of the forum. In this situation we have a frank discarding of the blindfold. There is, however, no disavowal of the choice-of-law rule which is preserved for use when the results it produces do not run counter to local standards of justice and policy. The invocation of the doctrine has been deprecated quite generally. In certain instances, its employment may be controlled by the Supreme Court. Its very facility is its most unfortunate trait. In its somewhat cavalier dismissal of a foreign law, it dispenses with the necessity for close analysis, for an affirmative appraisal of the situation upon which judgment must be passed. On the Continent efforts have been made to systematize the doctrine of public policy, but the variety of circumstances which may evoke its use is such that generality in the principle evolved has been inescapable. This opens the door to a practice, familiar enough throughout our law, of shifting the focus of inquiry from the narrow issue of policy raised by the case at bar to the broad issue of determining with respect thereto the limits of the principle. Its generality compels resort to other and different cases for aid in its definition.

3.   The conflict of laws rule may refer the court to the intention of the parties as a guide to the selection of the appropriate law. Where this intention has been expressed, as is not infrequent in contracts when at least one party is regularly engaged in interstate business or in wills and trust settlements of importance, the parties themselves will probably have appraised the consequences of an application of the law intended to the controversy in question. If the court is willing unquestioningly to accept their intention as its guide, the blindfold, if preserved, is without consequence. Where, however, the court considers that expressed intent as only one of the factors to be weighed in the selection of an appropriate law, or where the absence of any such expression obliges the court to speculate as to an intention which may never have been conceived, then it should become necessary to take into careful account the results which the competing laws would work in the case at bar. To the extent that the intention rule compels this consideration of the domestic laws, it avoids the anomaly of the blindfold test. To me, this seems a factor in its favor of greater consequence than a preservation of "autonomy of the will," where at least that will becomes well-defined only after conferences with counsel. But the rule trades one false problem for another where intention has not been expressed and is not palpably inferable from the circumstances. A conjectural intent, especially where this is directed to a generality such as "the law of the contract" and not to the consequences of the controversy in litigation, may result in the selection of a different law from that which a considered appraisal of all the factors would have indicated.

4.   The conflict of laws rule may make the choice of jurisdiction depend on the "nature" of the domestic law whose application is in question. A significant instance of such a rule is the familiar doctrine that the forum's rules of procedure will always be employed. If a foreign rule of law is found, when offered, to be procedural in character, it is rejected for the analogous rule of the forum. Recently, Professor Cook has convincingly revealed the inutility of an approach which seeks to derive a solution to this question from pre-existing concepts of "procedure" and "substantive law". But the courts in these cases must at least examine the competing rules of law as a means of determining the appropriate law to be applied. Professor Cook's insistence that this examination include a consideration of the results worked by such rules in the cases would make possible, if heeded, a thoroughly realistic handling of the problem.

These devices are either limited in scope or, although useful at times, more likely to preserve the situation from which on occasion they afford a means of escape than to lead to its ultimate elimination. If the conflict of laws is to keep pace with the development in other fields of the law, courts and commentators alike must abandon the quest for rules which will work justice equally in two contradictory situations. So long as that is the goal of their inquiry, it may be doubted how significant is the choice between the theoretical and the positive methods. Whatever rules may be worked out will in some cases reach results which seem eminently desirable and just as surely will compel courts in others to call upon hitherto undeclared policies of the state or unsuspected intentions of the parties to extricate them from the necessity of pronouncing intolerable judgments.

* * * * *

This effort to portray an approach to problems of conflicting laws which would free the courts from the blindfold of a theory which has compelled them to grope for solutions to problems for which perspicacity is peculiarly essential has been argumentative and decisive. At the risk of distorting an idea not susceptible of blackletter statement, I shall hazard this summary:

When a court is faced with a question whether to reject, as inapplicable, the law of the forum and to admit in evidence, as determinative of an issue in a case before it, a rule of law of a foreign jurisdiction, it should

(1) scrutinize the event or transaction giving rise to the issue before it;

(2) compare carefully the proffered rule of law and the result which its application might work in the case at bar with the rule of the forum (or other competing jurisdiction) and its effect therein;

(3) appraise these results in the light of those facts in the event or transaction which, from the standpoint of justice between the litigating individuals or of those broader considerations of social policy which conflicting laws may evoke, link that event or transaction to one law or the other; recognizing

a)   in the use of precedent, that those cases which are distinguishable only in the patterns of domestic laws they present, may for that very reason suggest materially different considerations than the case at bar, and

b)   in the evaluation of contacts, that the contact achieves significance in proportion to the significance of the action or circumstance constituting it when related to the controversy and the solutions thereto which the competing laws propound.

The end-product of this process of analysis and evaluation would, of course, be the application to the case at bar of a rule of law, derived either from the municipal law of the forum or that of some foreign state if proof of the latter law were duly made. The choice of that law would not be the result of the automatic operation of a rule or principle of selection but of a search for a just decision in the principal case.

* * * * *

Certain of the objections which may be anticipated are sufficiently formidable as to be deserving of more extended treatment * * *. It seems to me that these objections, though they may be advanced separately, are based on a central assumption and may be knitted into a single argument. The assumption and argument may, perhaps, fairly be set forth as follows:

The suggested approach would preclude the attainment of either certainty or uniformity in the conflict of laws because under it the decision of a case involving a choice of law would depend on the content of the conflicting laws and the relative desirability of their application in the light of the facts of the controversy in litigation. A decision now depends on the essentially mechanical application of a rule for the selection of an appropriate jurisdiction, irrespective of the substance of its relevant rule of law. Certainty, in the sense of predictability, is peculiarly important in this field because of the growing importance of interstate and international commercial and social relations. However certain the domestic laws of two states in a given field may be, the issue of controversies arising out of transactions in that field is unpredictable if those laws differ and if the relevant conflict of laws rules are not predictable. In many instances, therefore, the consequences of the application of either law are not as important as the predictability of its application. Uniformity in rule is equally important. Where conflicts rules are not uniform, certainty is measurably diminished since the selection of the forum then enters as a factor which may not be predictable. Moreover it is unjust that the selection of a forum should determine the result of litigation since that empowers the party having control over that choice to select the forum that is most favorable to him. Finally certainty and uniformity are necessary as a curb on local bias which leads to the application of the *lex fori*, or a law similar thereto, in preference to a different law whose claims for consideration, objectively appraised, are superior.

Of course, the basic assumption may be challenged. We have neither certainty nor uniformity despite the formulation of rules and principles of the conflict of laws without regard for the substance of the law whose application they dictate. Moreover, that the formal certainty and uniformity which the wide acceptance of a general formula imparts is deceptive is an observation whose corroboration in the law is becoming so comprehensive that all broad rules are now suspect. On the other hand it must be conceded that the suggested approach would give an impetus to the individualization of cases. This would lead for a time to disagreement both as to the extent to which such a tendency might properly be carried and to the propriety of the results reached in specific instances. But the factors of judgment would be exposed to, not concealed from, the tempering process of criticism. Eventually there would be a tendency toward stability in those fields at least where the factual pattern was relatively stable. The basic assumption is, therefore, by no means axiomatic. There is, however, some risk of augmenting for a time at least the current complaints in this field. But may not these complaints be exaggerated?

One distrusts an argument which proceeds from the persistence of a lack of certainty in a field of law to the exigency of the need for it. Granting, with a reservation, the accelerating increase in interstate and international transactions, nevertheless, the phenomenon is scarcely novel. If the consequences of uncertainty and want of uniformity in the conflict of laws were as intolerable as is often suggested, one would surmise that the problem would have been attacked more vigorously heretofore. One would suppose, for instance, that the first objective of the Commissioners of Uniform State Laws would have been comprehensive legislation enacting statutory rules of the conflict of laws to protect our citizenry during the period that their uniform legislation was being formulated and obtaining acceptance. That this aspect of the problem has been virtually disregarded suggests that while the conduct of business and certain social activities may be embarrassed by a want of uniformity in the laws of the forty-eight states, that embarrassment springs primarily from the cost and difficulty of ascertaining accurately the content of those laws and not from the admitted difficulty of predicting their territorial application.

The willingness, not infrequently encountered in writings on conflict of laws topics, to concede that certainty in rule is of more significance than the rule's content, is more revelatory as an evaluation of conflicts rules than it is significant as a judgment upon the need for certainty in this field. One conflicts rule may point to one jurisdiction as the source of the appropriate law; a second and competing conflicts rule, to another jurisdiction. What consequence the adoption of either rule will have in a given case will depend not on the rule but on the domestic law of the jurisdiction thereby selected. Until a specific case is considered in which the rules work different results, any estimate of their operation must in a large measure be conjectural. Naturally, in such a situation, the importance of certainty will loom disproportionately large. When, instead, the social value of a painstaking balancing of competing considerations to reach just results in specific cases, which the proposed approach would compel, is weighed against the social value of rules to determine such results mechanically, if predictably, the case for certainty becomes dubious. Even though it were conceded that the decisions in many of these cases would not have significant repercussions upon social and economic behavior, the question would remain open. In how many other branches of the law is such a standard set? This indifference to the disposition of individual cases is atypical in the profession and is strongly suggestive of a defense mechanism born of repeat failures to achieve the certainty and uniformity desired.

* * * * *

Comments

1. Professors Cheatham, Yntema, Cook and Cavers produced a great deal of influential writing early on in the choice-of-law revolution. Representative lists appear in the bibliography, Chapter Twelve. Professor Ernest Lorenzen was another important critic (e.g., 1924, 1947[1]). *See*, in addition, Harper 1947.

2. Beale attempted to marginalize the work of his critics, writing:

> In this country a new doctrine, that of the self-styled realists, has been put forward. It may be studied in current articles of W. W. Cook, Lorenzen, and Cavers. It is a very interesting doctrine, but one with which lawyers in practice have little concern; for it is admitted that courts do not accede to it (1935: p. 1879).

3. Criticism of Beale's vested rights approach was realist in spirit. Several of his critics were strongly aligned with the realist movement in jurisprudence (Kalman 1986: pp. 21, 23—locating Cook, Yntema and Lorenzen in the realist camp). Realists did not confine their criticism to conflict of laws. Rather, they attacked formalistic reasoning in the law whenever they found it.

> Most, if not all, varieties of formalistic reasoning can be represented as degenerate species of one or more of the basic attributes of formal reasoning. * * * [A]uthoritative formality degenerates into formalistic reasoning when, for example, a judge ignores gaps in the law, or refuses to acknowledge the nascent and fragmentary character of a piece of pre-existing valid law, and so over-extends that law as if it truly generated * * * reasons governing the issue at hand.

Atiyah & Summers 1987: p. 28.

4. Professor Albert Ehrenzweig would eventually forge the approach of Cook and other conflicts realists into a choice-of-law methodology. Ehrenzweig posed "true rules" describing what courts actually did in conflicts decisions and posed a default rule, "*lex fori*" (choice of forum law), when true rules were not discernable. For elaboration and evaluations of Ehrenzweig's views, *see* Cavers 1965b; Currie 1965; Ehrenzweig 1960, 1965a, 1967, 1971, 1974; Leflar 1965; Rheinstein 1965; Richman & Reynolds 1993: pp. 232-233; Scoles & Hay 1992: pp. 20-23.

---

[1]   Full citations appear in the bibliography, Chapter Twelve.

5. To realists, formalistic reasoning prevented useful thought about what legal institutions did or might best do. Cook later summed up in realist terms the conflicts criticism surveyed in Part B of this Chapter.

> What I mean to suggest is that the seemingly simple and extremely broad principles of the Restatement and of writers like Beale and Story, are inadequate because (1) considered merely as descriptions of what courts have done they are inaccurate and misleading; and (2) as guides for courts in dealing with "new" cases they are too simple and far too broad to furnish an adequate basis for reaching socially useful decisions.

Cook 1943: p. 422.

6. Under the first prong of their attack—that the traditional approach was "inaccurate and misleading"—critics maintained that the supposed uniformity offered to justify the traditional approach did not exist. The innate difficulty of the subject might have frustrated the sincerest efforts of courts to achieve uniformity. But prospects for uniformity were further diminished because courts often resorted to disingenuous use of public policy exceptions, characterization of matters as procedural rather than substantive, characterization as between substantive areas, and *renvoi* to resist the *lex loci delicti* application of foreign law (*see* the commentary following Part A of this Chapter).

7. Under the second prong of their attack—that the traditional approach was insensitive to the goal of "socially useful decisions"—the critics of the traditional approach decried the fact that rules of the original RESTATEMENT directed choice among jurisdictions without reference to the nature and effect of the particular laws in conflict. "The court is not idly choosing a law; it is determining a controversy," Cavers wrote. "How can it choose wisely without considering how that choice will affect the controversy?" Cavers 1933: p. 189.

8. Realist critics gained the upper hand in their academic war with conflicts traditionalists. At the same time, it was much easier for these critics to point out the shortcomings of existing law than to come up with a satisfactory replacement. The next Chapter focuses on the first serious attempt to provide that replacement.

CHAPTER FOUR

Conflicts Revolution—The Watershed Case
of *Babcock v. Jackson*

While scholarly criticism of the vested-rights, *lex loci* approach of the original RESTATEMENT gathered momentum during the second quarter of this century, virtually all courts continued to adhere to the old approach. Finally, in 1963, the New York Court of Appeals made a clean break with tradition in *Babcock v. Jackson. Babcock* is probably the most important choice-of-law decision rendered by an American court. It set the tone for the radical transformation of conflicts law that would follow. It remains a classroom favorite. Because *Babcock* is still so influential, and because it provides an excellent vantage point for the conflicts revolution, it is the focus of Chapter Four.

Babcock was a watershed event in the development of conflicts law and theory for three reasons: timing, the stature of the New York Court of Appeals then, and the fact that the decision was immediately heralded by conflicts scholars. The most significant literary event inspired by *Babcock* was a symposium in the Columbia Law Review, which supplies our material. The symposium opened with the *Babcock* opinions, and an excerpt from the majority opinion is our first selection. The symposium then presented reactions to *Babcock* by leading American conflicts scholars. This chapter draws from four of these comments—by Professors David Cavers, Willis Reese, Robert Leflar, and Brainerd Currie.

Symposium, *Comments on* Babcock v. Jackson, *A Recent Development in Conflict of Laws*, 63 COLUM. L. REV. 1212, 1212-1214, 1215-1217, 1219-1222, 1223-1225, 1233-1235, 1247-1249, 1251-1255, 1255-1257 (1963)*

* * *

BABCOCK V. JACKSON, 12 N.Y.2d 473 * * * (1963).

FULD, J. On Friday, September 16, 1960, Miss Georgia Babcock and her friends, Mr. and Mrs. William Jackson, all residents of Rochester, left that city in Mr. Jackson's automobile, Miss Babcock as guest, for a week-end trip to Canada. Some hours later, as Mr. Jackson was driving in the Province of Ontario, he apparently lost control of the car; it went off the highway into an adjacent stone wall, and Miss Babcock was seriously injured. Upon her return to

---

*   This article originally appeared at 63 COLUM. L. REV. 1212 (1963). Reprinted with permission.

this State, she brought the present action against William Jackson, alleging negligence on his part in operating his automobile.

At the time of the accident, there was in force in Ontario a statute providing that "the owner or driver of a motor vehicle, other than a vehicle operated in the business of carrying passengers for compensation, is not liable for any loss or damage resulting from bodily injury to, or the death of any person being carried in * * * the motor vehicle" (Highway Traffic Act of Province of Ontario [Ontario Rev. Stat. (1960), ch. 172], § 105, subd. [2]). Even though no such bar is recognized under this State's substantive law of torts * * * the defendant moved to dismiss the complaint on the ground that the law of the place where the accident occurred governs and that Ontario's guest statute bars recovery. The court at Special Term, agreeing with the defendant, granted the motion and the Appellate Division, over a strong dissent by Justice HALPERN, affirmed the judgment of dismissal without opinion.

The question presented is simply drawn. Shall the law of the place of the tort *invariably* govern the availability of relief for the tort or shall the applicable choice of law rule also reflect a consideration of other factors which are relevant to the purposes served by the enforcement or denial of the remedy?

The traditional choice of law rule, embodied in the original Restatement of Conflict of Laws (§ 384), and until recently unquestioningly followed in this court * * * has been that the substantive rights and liabilities arising out of a tortious occurrence are determinable by the law of the place of the tort. * * * It had its conceptual foundation in the vested rights doctrine, namely, that a right to recover for a foreign tort owes its creation to the law of the jurisdiction where the injury occurred and depends for its existence and extent solely on such law. * * * Although espoused by such great figures as Justice HOLMES (See *Slater* v. *Mexican Nat. R.R. Co.*, 194 U.S. 120) and Professor Beale (2 Conflict of Laws [1935], pp. 1286-1292), the vested rights doctrine has long since been discredited because it fails to take account of underlying policy considerations in evaluating the significance to be ascribed to the circumstance that an act had a foreign situs in determining the rights and liabilities which arise out of that act. "The vice of the vested rights theory", it has been aptly stated, "is that it affects to decide concrete cases upon generalities which do not state the practical considerations involved". (Yntema, The Hornbook Method and the Conflict of Laws, 37 Yale L.J. 458, 482-483.) More particularly, as applied to torts, the theory ignores the interest which jurisdictions other than that where the tort occurred may have in the resolution of particular issues. It is for this very reason that, despite the advantages of certainty, ease of application and predictability which it affords (see Cheatham and Reese, Choice of the Applicable Law, 52 Col. L. Rev. 959, 976), there has in recent years been increasing criticism of the traditional rule by commentators and a judicial trend towards its abandonment or modification.

Significantly, it was dissatisfaction with "the mechanical formulae of the conflicts of law" (*Vanston Committee* v. *Green*, 329 U.S. 156, 162) which led to judicial departure from similarly inflexible choice of law rules in the field of contracts, grounded, like the torts rule, on the vested rights doctrine. According to those traditional rules, matters bearing upon the execution, interpretation and validity of a contract, were determinable by the internal law of the place where the contract was made, while matters connected with their performance were regulated by the internal law of the place where the contract was to be performed. * * * In *Auten* v. *Auten* (308 N.Y. 155), however, this court abandoned such rules and applied what has been termed the "center of gravity" or "grouping of contacts" theory of the conflict of laws. "Under this theory," we declared, in the *Auten* case, "the courts, instead of regarding as conclusive the parties' intention or the place of making or performance, lay emphasis rather upon the law of the place 'which has the most significant contacts with the matter in dispute'" (308 N.Y., at p. 160). The "center of gravity" rule of *Auten* has not only been applied in other cases in this State, as well as in other jurisdictions, but has supplanted the prior rigid and set contract rules in the most current draft of the Restatement of the Conflict of Laws. (See Restatement, Second, Conflict of Laws, § 332b [Tentative Draft No. 6, 1960].)

* * * * *

The "center of gravity" or "grouping of contacts" doctrine adopted by this court in conflicts cases involving contracts impresses us as likewise affording the appropriate approach for accommodating the competing interests in tort cases with multi-State contacts. Justice, fairness and "the best practical result" (*Swift & Co.* v. *Bankers Trust Co.*, 280 N.Y. 135, 141, *supra*) may best be achieved by giving controlling effect to the law of the jurisdiction which, because of its relationship or contact with the occurrence or the parties, has the greatest concern with the specific issue raised in the litigation. The merit of such a rule is that "it gives to the place 'having the most interest in the problem' paramount control over the legal issues arising out of a particular factual context" and thereby allows the forum to apply "the policy of the jurisdiction 'most intimately concerned with the outcome of [the] particular litigation.'" (*Auten* v. *Auten*, 308 N.Y. 155, 161, *supra*.)

Such, indeed, is the approach adopted in the most recent revision of the Conflict of Laws Restatement in the field of torts. According to the principles there set out, "The local law of the state which has the most significant relationship with the occurrence and with the parties determines their rights and liabilities in tort" (Restatement, Second, Conflict of Laws, § 379[1]; also Introductory Note to Topic 1 of Chapter 9, p. 3 [Tentative Draft No. 8, 1963]), and the relative importance of the relationships or contacts of the respective jurisdictions is to be evaluated in the light of "the issues, the character of the tort and the relevant purposes of the tort rules involved" (§ 379[2], [3]).

Comparison of the relative "contacts" and "interests" of New York and Ontario in this litigation, vis-a-vis the issue here presented, makes it clear that the concern of New York is unquestionably the greater and more direct and that the interest of Ontario is at best minimal. The present action involves injuries sustained by a New York guest as the result of the negligence of a New York host in the operation of an automobile, garaged, licensed and undoubtedly insured in New York, in the course of a week-end journey which began and was to end there. In sharp contrast, Ontario's sole relationship with the occurrence is the purely adventitious circumstance that the accident occurred there.

New York's policy of requiring a tort-feasor to compensate his guest for injuries caused by his negligence cannot be doubted—as attested by the fact that the Legislature of this State has repeatedly refused to enact a statute denying or limiting recovery in such cases * * *—and our courts have neither reason nor warrant for departing from that policy simply because the accident, solely affecting New York residents and arising out of the operation of a New York based automobile, happened beyond its borders. Per contra, Ontario has no conceivable interest in denying a remedy to a New York guest against his New York host for injuries suffered in Ontario by reason of conduct which was tortious under Ontario law. The object of Ontario's guest statute, it has been said, is "to prevent the fraudulent assertion of claims by passengers, in collusion with the drivers, against insurance companies" (Survey of Canadian Legislation, 1 U. Toronto L. J. 358, 366) and, quite obviously, the fraudulent claims intended to be prevented by the statute are those asserted against Ontario defendants and their insurance carriers, not New York defendants and their insurance carriers. Whether New York defendants are imposed upon or their insurers defrauded by a New York plaintiff is scarcely a valid legislative concern of Ontario simply because the accident occurred there, any more so than if the accident had happened in some other jurisdiction.

It is hardly necessary to say that Ontario's interest is quite different from what it would have been had the issue related to the manner in which the defendant had been driving his car at the time of the accident. Where the defendant's exercise of due care in the operation of his automobile is in issue, the jurisdiction in which the allegedly wrongful conduct occurred will usually have a predominant, if not exclusive, concern. In such a case, it is appropriate to look to the law of the place of the tort so as to give effect to that jurisdiction's interest in regulating conduct within its borders, and it would be almost unthinkable to seek the applicable rule in the law of some other place.

The issue here, however, is not whether the defendant offended against a rule of the road prescribed by Ontario for motorists generally or whether he violated some standard of conduct imposed by that jurisdiction, but rather whether the plaintiff, because she was a guest in the defendant's automobile, is barred from recovering damages for a wrong concededly committed. As to that issue, it is New York, the place where the parties resided, where their guest-host relationship arose and where the trip began and was to end, rather than Ontario, the place of the fortuitous occurrence of the accident, which has the dominant contacts and the superior claim for application of its law. Although the rightness or wrongness of defendant's conduct may depend upon the law of the particular jurisdiction through which the automobile passes, the rights and liabilities of the parties which stem from their guest-host relationship should remain constant and not vary and shift as the automobile proceeds from place to place. Indeed, such a result, we note, accords with "the interests of the host in procuring liability insurance adequate under the applicable law, and the interests of his insurer in reasonable calculability of the premium." (Ehrenzweig, Guest Statutes in the Conflict of Laws, 69 Yale L. J. 595, 603.)

Although the traditional rule has in the past been applied by this court in giving controlling effect to the guest statute of the foreign jurisdiction in which the accident occurred * * * it is not amiss to point out that the question here posed was neither raised nor considered in those cases and that the question has never been presented in so stark a manner as in the case before us with a statute so unique as Ontario's. Be that as it may, however, reconsideration of the inflexible traditional rule persuades us, as already indicated, that, in failing to take into account essential policy considerations and objectives, its application may lead to unjust and anomalous results.

* * * * *

David F. Cavers

For a generation, legal scholars have been weeding in the tangled garden of conflict of laws doctrine, directing their critical tools chiefly to extirpating notions of territoriality and vested rights that were choking out judicial concern with realities in the choice-of-law process. For a time it seemed that the scholars would accomplish little more than their weeding, that, being weeders, they had no seed to sow. Perhaps, indeed, no more would have resulted if the responsibility had been theirs alone.

We in the academic branch of the profession have a *metier* which permits us to raise questions that we do not choose to answer, but, fortunately, another branch of the profession, the advocates at the bar, have the task of proposing answers, and still another branch, the judges on the bench, have the duty of decision. Many among today's advocates and, increasingly, among today's judges were once students of the academic critics; they can identify the weeds their teachers complained of; what is more, they can plant something in their place. As a consequence, here and there in the weeded garden decisions have been flowering that thirty years ago could never have broken through the stifling growth of *Restatement* doctrine. Perhaps the most important of these is the latest, *Babcock v. Jackson.*

Some may insist that this distinction should go to *Auten v. Auten,*[4] a decision of the same court, with an opinion by Judge Fuld, who wrote for the majority in *Babcock.* But *Auten,* dealing with a choice of contract law, was concerned with an area that territorial and vested rights doctrine had never been able to dominate, and *Auten,* though plain in its rejection of the *Restatement* place-of-contracting formula, failed to exemplify a satisfactory alternative methodology.

Of late it has been in the area of tort law that the most significant progress has been made, progress that has been all the more consequential because the modern American case law that had to be confronted seemed solid in its support of a single mechanical rule: the application of the law of the place of injury. Some of the new, deviant decisions * * * took advantage of the fact that the tortious act and its harmful consequences were in different jurisdictions and, in applying the law where the act took place, stressed the admonitory function of that law. Others * * * exploited the color of procedure in the laws at issue to sustain the application of the forum's law in situations where this could be justified by other policy considerations. Closer to *Babcock* are such cases as *Emery v. Emery*[11] and *Haumschild v. Continental Cas. Co.*[12] in which the law of the parties' domicile was viewed as controlling questions of intrafamily immunities even though the law of place of injury was recognized as determinative of other issues. Perhaps these cases should be seen as exemplifying the use of the characterization device, allocating the immunity issue to family law rather than to torts, as an escape from the place-of-injury rule.

In *Babcock* not only is the court ready to separate the issue of the host-driver's immunity to his guest-passenger's suit from any issue regarding the tortiousness of his conduct, but also it approaches the former question by seeking to identify the policies embodied in the particular laws in conflict, to ascertain the interests of the states in the application of their respective policies in the light of their contacts with the case, and thereby to decide which state has "the superior claim for application of its law." If the logic of this process is respected, it will produce a decision that governs only those cases that present the same law-fact pattern as the law-fact pattern in the case before the court.

In *Emery* and in *Haumschild* the law of the parties' domicile was chosen without regard to whether that law imposed liability or conferred intrafamily immunity. In other words, domicile was the key used to choose a jurisdiction to supply the governing law, without regard to the content of that law, not as a factor relevant to a choice between a rule conferring immunity and one denying it. Although in the readiness of both courts to focus on the particular issue in dispute and in the policy considerations they invoked, these decisions mark an advance over the omnibus application of the law of the place of injury, nevertheless, the resulting choice-of-law rule was not confined to the law-fact pattern presented by the cases but was cast in traditional terms: it is what I have called a "jurisdiction-selecting rule." Should the opinion in *Babcock* be read as also formulating a jurisdiction-selecting rule? *Babcock*'s claim to a distinctive place among the decisions flowering in the newly weeded conflicts garden depends in part upon whether a negative answer may properly be given to that question.

The significance of the point can be illumined by comparing the court's approach in

---

[4]   308 N.Y. 155, 124 N.E.2d 99 (1954).

[11]   45 Cal.2d 421, 289 P.2d 218 (1955) (law of domicile, rather than place of injury, applied to determine immunity of the defendant father and minor brother from suit by minor plaintiffs).

[12]   7 Wis. 2d 130, 95 N.W.2d 814 (1959) (law of spouses' domicile rather than place of injury, applied to determine immunity of defendant spouse from suit by plaintiff spouse).

Babcock to that of the court in *Haumschild*. In that case the Wisconsin court applied the law of the spouses' domicile, Wisconsin, which permitted one spouse to sue the other for personal injury, and rejected the law of the place of injury, California, which did not allow such an action. In reaching its conclusion that the law of the spouses' domicile should govern the immunity question, the Wisconsin court overruled six decisions. Among them was a case in which the law-fact pattern was just the reverse of that in *Haumschild*: the law of the domicile gave immunity; the law of the place of injury allowed the action. Yet the court's opinion betrayed little recognition that the case it was overruling was different from the case the court was deciding.

To provide a New York parallel to that overruled case, suppose, with *Babcock* in the books, a personal injury action were now to be brought in New York, both parties being from Ontario where they had begun a motor trip that had ended in injury to the plaintiff guest in New York. If the opinion in *Babcock* is read as formulating a jurisdiction-selecting rule, this rule would require the New York court to select Ontario as the jurisdiction to provide the law governing the immunity issue even though Ontario's law is the reverse of the New York law applied in *Babcock*.

In *Babcock*, however, the court did not proceed in disregard of the law-fact pattern before it. On the contrary, it examined the claims of Ontario to the application of its guest-passenger statute in view of the fact that it was the place of injury. It found, quite rightly, that "Ontario has no conceivable interest in denying a remedy to a New York guest against his New York host for injuries suffered in Ontario . . ." since the object of Ontario's guest-passenger statute was "'to prevent the fraudulent assertion of claims by passengers, in collusion with the drivers, against insurance companies'." Noting that the New York legislature had preserved the common-law rule despite persistent efforts to induce a change, the court found "neither reason nor warrant for departing from that policy simply because the accident, solely affecting New York residents and arising out of the operation of a New York based automobile, happened beyond its borders."

* * *

* * * New York had imposed a liability on the host-driver as strict as, or stricter than, would be found in Ontario or in any state he traversed; if any other states, like Ontario, had relieved host-drivers of common-law liability, they would have done so to protect the insurers of their own host-drivers, not out-of-state drivers or their insurers. Therefore, their laws should be held inapplicable.

But should [*Babcock*] be viewed as also calling for the constant application of the law governing the host-driver when that law is a guest-passenger statute and the state of injury has retained the common law? If so, then the statutory immunity (or gross negligence) rule of the host-driver's state would potentially prevail as against the common-law liability rule of every state the automobile entered that had not enacted a guest-passenger statute. Yet the careful demonstration in *Babcock* that Ontario, as the place of injury, had no interest in applying its immunity rule has no relevance to the question whether a state of injury retaining common-law liability has an interest in applying its law to a claim arising out of the guest-passenger relationship. That question is nowhere considered in Judge Fuld's opinion. I find it hard to believe that he meant to dispose so lightly of the case where the plaintiff's injury was sustained in New York and the guest-passenger relationship arose in Ontario. As the state of injury, New York does have a relevant policy, conflicting with Ontario's; its claim to application, as against Ontario's, is entitled to careful evaluation.

The policy of New York is to grant compensation to a plaintiff guest-passenger negligently injured by the defendant host-driver, despite the risk that the plaintiff might collude with the defendant to defraud the latter's insurer. If the plaintiff injured on a New York highway has come from Ontario as a guest of the Ontario defendant, one cannot readily assume that he should be denied the protection of the New York law simply because Ontario law is solicitous for the host's insurer.

There are two considerations that might instead lead a New York court to insist on applying New York law, even though the court would have to recognize a substantial basis for the application of Ontario law. First, the civil remedy of damages for the negligent infliction of personal injury is one of the sanctions that New York employs to induce careful driving on its highways, and clearly its concern with the conduct of the users of its highways is an important one. Second, an injury to a visitor on a New York highway may impose a serious financial burden on persons within the state if the injured person can obtain no compensation for his injury. If the Ontario immunity were to protect the Ontario host and his insurer, it would at the same time subject all those furnishing medical care in New York to the risk that the injured person, lacking compensation, would be unable to reimburse them.

The resulting problem is a difficult one—and a very different one from the essentially false conflict that confronted the court in *Babcock*. I shall exercise my academic prerogative and decline to propound an answer to the question I have posed. My main concern is not that one answer or the other should be given when this case arises. What is important is that the court that is called upon to decide the question employ the process used in the *Babcock* (*that questionable sentence apart*) and, having examined the quite different pattern of interests resulting from the reversal of the law-fact pattern, recognize that it is confronted by a new problem, one that *Babcock* does not control.

* * * * *

WILLIS L.M. REESE

Judge Fuld's opinion in *Babcock v. Jackson* should prove a landmark in the law. It comes at a time when the courts are becoming increasingly dissatisfied with some basic choice-of-law rules and are seeking alternative solutions. It explicitly states a new choice-of-law rule for torts and is almost certain to have a profound effect upon future developments in many other areas of choice of law.

Choice-of-law rules are based upon the principle that a court should apply the law of the most appropriate state to govern the matter at hand. The state whose law should govern may be either the state of the forum or some other state; it is the function of choice-of-law rules to designate which. All persons, including Judge Fuld, who support the principle of choice of law would agree with this, but there is widespread uncertainty as to how many choice-of-law rules should be formulated.

An attempt was made during the first half of this century to regulate the entire field of choice of law by a relatively small number of precise rules. It was said that all questions relating to the validity of a contract are governed by the law of the place of contracting, and that all questions relating to a tort are governed by the law of the state where the defendant's act first caused injury to the plaintiff. In retrospect, it seems clear that rules of this sort, at least in the areas of contracts and torts, could not prove successful. There are many different kinds of contracts and torts. The number of issues that can arise in these two areas of the law and the variety of ways that relevant contacts can be grouped among the interested states border on the infinite. Certainly it would be miraculous if all issues involving, for example, the validity of every kind of contract could be satisfactorily decided by application of the law of the place of contracting. On occasion this place will bear little relation to the parties or the contract.

Application of this law could hardly be expected always to provide the best solution to the particular issue involved.

So much was recognized by the New York Court of Appeals in *Auten v. Auten*.[3] There the court held, in an opinion by Judge Fuld, that the parties' rights and duties under a contract should be determined by the law of the state "which has the most significant contacts with the matter in dispute." The opinion did not provide definite guidelines for the decision of future cases, but it tacitly recognized that choice-of-law rules, like other rules of the common law, must be developed on a case by case basis and that rules based on conceptualistic reasoning, rather than on actual experience, would not prove successful. Thus, the opinion took the first essential step towards the development of satisfactory rules of choice of law by freeing the courts from the shackles of the place of contracting rule and by enjoining them to decide each case as it arose by application of the law of the state of "most significant contacts."

The *Auten* opinion, providing no explicit directions for ascertaining the state of "most significant contacts," left some uncertainty about how to determine the state of the governing law. Undoubtedly, only relevant contacts should be considered, but by what criterion should relevance be judged? Much of this uncertainty has now been removed by the clear statement in *Babcock v. Jackson* that the governing law should be that of the state that "has the strongest interest in the resolution of the particular issue presented." The opinion states that there is no reason why all issues arising out of a claim should be decided by the same law, and indicates that only contacts relevant to a particular issue should be considered in determining what law should govern that issue. The opinion makes clearer than has ever been done before that choice-of-law rules in tort and contract, and presumably in other areas as well, should initially be confined to the issue before the court. As experience develops it will then be possible to determine whether a rule adequate for one issue can properly be applied to others. In this way firmly based, albeit narrow, choice-of-law rules can eventually be developed. Opinions that give an explicit answer to the question posed in *Babcock*, namely, what state "has the strongest interest" in the particular issue before the court, will provide sound basis for the future development of satisfactory rules of choice of law. Some further comments about Judge Fuld's opinion in *Babcock v. Jackson* may be in order:

(1) The opinion clearly supports the basic principle of choice of law that the law of the most appropriate state should govern the matter at hand. To be sure, a court must follow the express directions of its legislature, if constitutional, regarding what law to apply. But in the absence of such directions, which are rarely given, it is for the court to determine whether to apply the law of its own state or that of another. As is made clear in the opinion, the court must make this determination in light of its own evaluation of competing state interests. The relative interests of two or more states in having their law applied will inevitably depend upon the precise issue presented, the facts of the case, and the relationship of these facts and the parties to the states involved. The court is the body best equipped to deal with such variables on a case by case basis. The legislature cannot possibly foresee all of the various situations that will arise in such an immense field. A statute dealing with choice of law in more or less general terms would inevitably encompass unforeseen situations to which it was never intended to apply; it would straitjacket the courts and tend to perpetuate error. On the other hand, a judicial opinion can always be distinguished as involving different facts or issues. In so uncertain and fluid a field as choice of law, progress can best be made through constant experimentation on a case by case basis.

(2) As regards choice-of-law rules in torts, the opinion makes a distinct break with the past.

---

[3]   308 N.Y. 155, 124 N.E.2d 99 (1954).

In contrast to contracts, where the rules were always uncertain, for the normal tort case, where conduct and injury occur in the same state, there was near unanimity for the view that the parties' rights and duties should be determined by the law of that state. This rule provided predictability of result and was easy to apply. Moreover, it called for application of the law of a state that would almost invariably have a substantial interest in the occurrence, since conduct and injury are the most important elements of a tort. Yet, as evidenced by *Babcock v. Jackson* and the cases on intrafamily immunity, there will be situations in which a state other than that of conduct and injury has the greatest interest in a particular issue. In such situations, no reasons would support application of the law of the state of conduct and injury except ease of application and predictability of result. Ease of application is hardly a convincing reason for giving a rule wider application than it otherwise would deserve. And although predictability of result is important to the extent that it facilitates the lawyer's task in advising his client and negotiating a settlement, it is not an all-important value in torts since this is an area where persons will rarely, if ever, give advance thought to the legal consequences of their actions. In any event, continued adherence to a bad rule is a high price to pay for predictability. Furthermore, it is doubtful whether a bad rule will provide predictability since the courts will be inclined to engraft exceptions upon it.

The departure made in *Babcock v. Jackson* from an inflexible choice-of-law rule in torts is believed to be well worth the price. By requiring the courts, at least in the areas of torts and contracts, to tailor their rules to the precise issues involved, the opinion lays the proper basis for the eventual development of a considerable number of relatively narrow choice-of-law rules. Only rules of this type can prove successful in practice. Once they have been developed, the advantages of predictability of result can be enjoyed.

(3) The opinion makes clear that the state of conduct and injury will continue to play an important role in choice of law. It states in dictum that, usually at least, the law of this state will govern standards of conduct, a category that in all probability includes the majority of tort issues. However, if the teaching of the opinion is followed, this law will no longer be applied in a mechanical and arbitrary fashion, but only when the state of conduct and injury "has the strongest interest" in the issue presented.

There will be rare situations in which the state of conduct and injury has so tenuous a connection with the tort that its law should be applied to govern only a few, if any, of the issues presented. Injuries suffered on an airplane in the course of a transcontinental trip may present an instance of this sort. There will be other situations, far greater in number, in which the law of the place of conduct and injury should not govern particular issues involving standards of conduct. An example might be a situation in which, on the facts of the *Babcock* case, the accident would not have occurred if the automobile had been equipped with a safety device as required by New York law but not by the law of Ontario. Here the application of New York law to afford relief in a suit between New York domiciliaries would further New York interests and would hardly seem to be inconsistent with the interests of Ontario.

* * *

(4) The opinion makes clear that in torts and contracts determination of the governing law will depend in part upon the content of the relevant local law rules of the interested states. The reason for this is that the governing law in both these fields is the law of the state with "the strongest interest" in the issue presented, and the degree of a state's interest in the application of its law will depend in part upon the content of that law. Thus in the *Babcock* case, the fact that the Ontario guest statute would have denied the plaintiff recovery was important in the court's determination that Ontario had no interest in having this statute applied. Almost cer-

tainly, the statute was intended to protect Ontario insurance companies, and none were involved in the case. A different problem would have been presented if it had been New York law that denied recovery and Ontario law that allowed it. In such a situation, Ontario interests might be furthered by application of its law so that persons who had aided the injured party would not go uncompensated. New York, on the other hand, would also have an interest in having its law applied because the parties were domiciled there and presumably the defendant's liability insurer either was incorporated in New York or else did substantial business there. Thus, this hypothetical case, in contrast to the one actually before the court, would present an actual conflict of interests between New York and Ontario. Even in this case, however, New York interests would be the greater and New York law should be applied, whether suit were brought in New York or in Ontario or in a third state. For although Ontario might have an interest in protecting persons who had aided the injured party, in the absence of evidence that there were such persons and that the injured party would not otherwise be able to pay them, this interest would seem somewhat hypothetical.

The content of relevant local law rules is an important factor in all cases in which choice of the governing law depends in part upon an evaluation of state interests. However, this may not be so when, as noted below, uniformity of result is the principal choice-of-law value.

(5) The opinion does not discuss whether the issue-by-issue approach, which it advocates for torts and, by way of dictum, for contracts, should be followed in other areas of choice of law. Presumably this should not be done when uniformity of result is the principal value to be attained. Here there is need for relatively simple rules that call for the application of a readily identifiable law. Thus, it is widely held that questions of succession to movables, whether by will or by intestacy, are governed by the law of the decedent's domicile at death, and that the law of the assignor's domicile governs the validity of an assignment of movables for the benefit of creditors. It is believed that the *Babcock* opinion should not be read as applying to rules of this sort.

The issue by issue approach of the *Babcock* case would also seem unnecessary when one state has an obviously dominant interest, as the state of the situs with respect to questions involving land or the state of the parties' common domicile with respect to the validity of a marriage. Here the state of dominant interest would be the same for every issue and without further ado its law should be applied.

* * * * *

ROBERT A. LEFLAR

In *Babcock v. Jackson* the Court of Appeals has promulgated a "center of gravity" or "grouping of contacts" rule for choice of law in torts cases. As often happens when a new rule is announced, the facts of the case were as apt for its application as those of any case likely to come before a court in a long time. The new rule fits these facts perfectly but, as more complex cases arise, a great deal of ingenuity will be required to adapt it to them. Undoubtedly the results will vary with the court and with the facts.

Suppose, for example, that *Babcock v. Jackson* were being tried in Ontario, and the Ontario court were applying this same new choice-of-law rule. It is at least possible that the Ontario court would conclude that the danger of insurance companies' being collusively cheated in Ontario actions arising out of Ontario accidents would give that forum the most significant contacts with the host-guest problem. It is pretty clear that the new rule affords no assurance that on a given set of facts the result will be the same regardless of where the case is tried, even though the facts be simple. One suspects that for one reason or another the forum court will usually find that the most significant contacts are within its own borders, as the New

York court quite understandably did in *Babcock v. Jackson*. This suggests that the real reasons for such a decision will include forum preference, to which Professor Currie attaches prime importance. On the other hand, *Auten v. Auten*,[1] the slightly older brother of *Babcock v. Jackson*, teaches us that New York, at least, will not always find the center of gravity to be in its own backyard.

A great variety of fact situations, with corresponding differences in possibly relevant rules of substantive law, suggest themselves. Suppose that the defendant was domiciled in New York and his car was normally kept there, but the guest came from Ontario. Or suppose that the guest came from a third state or that the lawsuit was brought in a third state. Suppose that the weekend trip started from the third state or was directed primarily to some resort spot in a fourth state. Or suppose that it was not a guest-statute problem, but a family-immunity problem; or a problem involving contributory and comparative negligence with parties domiciled and cars garaged in different states; or a contribution-between-joint-tortfeasors problem with comparable fact variations. Suppose that an injured party had executed a release to one of two joint tortfeasors, or that the question was one of vicarious liability, or of strict liability, or one involving divergent interpretations of the concept of proximate causation, scope of duty and appreciable risk, or of *res ipsa loquitur*.

Common-law judges regularly solve one problem at a time and count themselves lucky if they get the easy one first. As the others come trooping along, the rule that solved the first is likely to be used in the solution of the next, and will probably be modified and improved in the process. After a score of years, or a century, the rule as ultimately stated may resemble but slightly its first formulation. It is unlikely that Judge Fuld will for long recognize in future cases the rule he announced in *Babcock*.

In later years it will be easy to merge the ideas of "significant relationship" and "governmental interests." The supposititious Ontario case stated in the second paragraph of this comment serves to illustrate how this may occur. On the basis of the *Babcock* case, it may be assumed that "grouping of contacts" does not mean mere counting of contacts, that qualitative rather than quantitative evaluation determines "the most significant relationship." Qualitative evaluation is inevitably in terms of policies and interests, the policies and interests that appear important to the evaluator. Often the ones that appear important to a local evaluator (and all evaluators are local unless they sit on the Supreme Court of the United States or some similarly exalted tribunal) are the ones that have a domestic significance, that reflect homegrown attitudes and concerns.

Not all policies that influence courts are local policies, however. The validation of contracts and trusts that are entered into by parties in good faith or the invalidation of some that are deemed oppressive, for example, grow out of policies that transcend strictly local interests. A preference for the law that will compensate tort plaintiffs lurks in the background of some decisions and is another manifestation of a policy not restricted to local interests. The idea that the chosen law should be that which will achieve justice in the individual case is yet another.

Policy-weighing or interest-weighing approaches to choice of law are not actually contrary to New York's "most significant relationship" test. Qualitatively evaluated, significance of a relationship can comprehend almost any policy considerations. The weighing of contacts of which *Auten* and *Babcock* speak could easily turn into a weighing of governmental interests and social policies that grow out of or are discoverable from the contacts. This could happen without much change in either language or sense, and it probably will happen.

---

[1]   308 N.Y. 155, 124 N.E.2d 99 (1954).

* * * * *

BRAINERD CURRIE

The decision of the Court of Appeals in *Babcock v. Jackson* is as heartening as it is historic. It is historic, if for no other reason, simply because it extirpates the rule that substantive matters of tort liability are invariably to be governed by the law of the place of the tort. It is heartening because as a replacement for the discredited rule it provides something very much better than the rather-to-be-expected "center of gravity" or "grouping of contacts" theory.

The trouble with that theory is that the quest for "most significant contacts" that it enjoined was not implemented by any standard according to which significance could be determined. "One 'contact' seems to be about as good as another for almost any purpose. The 'contacts' are totted up and a highly subjective fiat is issued to the effect that one group of contacts or the other is the more significant. The reasons for the conclusion are too elusive for objective evaluation." Judge Van Voorhis could justly say in dissent that "the expressions 'center of gravity,' 'grouping of contacts,' and 'significant contacts' are catchwords which . . . are inadequate to define a principle of law . . . ." But the majority opinion in *Babcock v. Jackson* is very different from earlier opinions treating of the center of gravity.

If the ideal world is one in which a law professor can have his way with the courts, the majority opinion is not ideal. If I could have my way, the courts would abandon "center of gravity" and other such vague and metaphorical phrases. I cannot complain overmuch, however, when the court, while speaking the language of metaphor, explicitly decided the case in the most reasonable and objective way that seems possible: by reference to the policies and interests of the respective states, by construction and interpretation of the respective laws. The center of gravity has come of age.

First of all, the court recognized that the substantive law of a state is not an indivisible corpus. In the calculus of interests a traffic regulation may stand on a different footing from a guest statute. Concentrating, accordingly, on the only provision of foreign law that was in issue—the Ontario guest statute—the court inquired into the governmental policy expressed in that law. "The object of Ontario's guest statute . . . is 'to prevent the fraudulent assertion of claims by passengers, in collusion with the drivers, against insurance companies'. . . ." In what circumstances would it be reasonable for Ontario to claim an interest in the application of that policy? "Ontario has no conceivable interest in denying a remedy to a New York guest against his New York host for injuries suffered in Ontario by reason of conduct which was tortious under Ontario law. . . . [Q]uite obviously, the fraudulent claims intended to be prevented by the statute are those asserted against Ontario defendants and their insurance carriers, not New York defendants and their insurance carriers." Similarly, the court inquired into the policy embodied in New York's law on the same subject and into the circumstances making it reasonable for New York to claim an interest in the application of its policy: "New York's policy of requiring a tort-feasor to compensate his guest for injuries cause by his negligence cannot be doubted . . . and our courts have neither reason nor warrant for departing from that policy simply because the accident, solely affecting New York residents and arising out of the operation of a New York based automobile, happened beyond its borders."

It might have been as simple as that; but, of course, there is more than governmental-interest analysis in the decision. Indeed, the majority opinion contains items of comfort for almost every critic of the traditional system. On the surface, the modern philosophy of conflict of laws gaining the greatest encouragement from the decision appears to be that expressed in the *Restatement (Second)*. Paradoxically, I believe that the decision, rightly understood, spells the doom of all attempts, such as that of the *Restatement*, to solve the problems of conflict of laws by a compendium of choice-of-law rules and in particular of the *Restatement (Second)*'s attempt to solve them by reference to the "law of the state which has the most significant relationship with the occurrence and with the parties."

In a nutshell my argument is: The question whether a particular "contact" is significant is meaningless unless significance is judged in terms of the policies and interests of the states involved. Once this is clear (and *Babcock* makes it clear) we are left simply with the tools of construction and interpretation. When, with the aid of those tools, we find there is no conflict of interests, as in *Babcock*, the proper result is clear: the law of the only interested state is applied. When, by the same process, we find that the interests of two or more states are in conflict, a court has no means of determining which state has "the most significant relationship."

* * * * *

Comments

1. All four of our commentators lauded the result *Babcock* and the modern turn in the thinking of the New York Court of Appeals. In his excerpt, Professor Cavers' sets *Babcock* apart from earlier, more modest attempts to break away from *lex loci* and muses on results suggested by the court's new approach for later, more difficult cases. In the succeeding excerpts, Professors Reese, Leflar and Currie each find in *Babcock* affirmation of their particular views on conflicts reform.

2. Professor Reese applauds in *Babcock* a decisional framework that he will also advocate in the RESTATEMENT (SECOND) OF CONFLICTS (examined in Chapter Eight, Part A). Next, Professor Leflar praises *Babcock* for an eclectic blend of conflicts policies that he will soon refine into his "Choice-Influencing Considerations" approach (examined in Chapter Eight, Part B). Finally, Professor Currie praises an emphasis in *Babcock* on interest analysis—Currie's own approach (examined in Chapter Five).

3. *Babcock* remained a favorite subject for conflicts commentators. *See, e.g.*, Korn 1983: pp. 827-842;[1] Richman 1982: pp. 318-320; Scoles & Hay 1992: pp. 612-613; von Mehren & Trautman 1965: pp. 144-145; Weintraub 1986: pp. 316-317. In 1993, the case again occasioned a symposium. *Celebrating the 30th Anniversary of* Babcock v. Jackson, 54 ALBANY L. REV., 693 (contributions by David D. Siegel, Russell J. Weintraub, Friedrich K. Juenger, Harold G. Maier, Michael E. Solimine, Luther L. McDougal III, Louise Weinberg, Patrick J. Borchers, Gary J. Simson, and Harold L. Korn).

---

[1]   Full citations appear in the bibliography, Chapter Twelve.

CHAPTER FIVE

Interest Analysis—The Emergence of Unilateralism in Modern American Conflicts Law

Other jurisdictions followed the lead of the New York Court of Appeals in *Babcock,* rejecting the *lex loci delicti* approach of the original RESTATEMENT. The task of reforming conflicts law was twofold. Courts had to solve the great problems caused by *lex loci* (indifference to the content of laws vying for acceptance, and to concerns of fairness and justice in the individual case) without creating new problems of theory or application in the process. Interest analysis is the most significant—and controversial—attempt to meet this challenge.

While *lex loci delicti* is a species of multilateralism, interest analysis represents unilateralism. That is to say, interest analysts measure a law's applicability not by jurisdiction-selecting rules but by asking whether the case at hand is one the law is designed to govern. If so, the sovereign creating that law may be said to be "interested" in having it applied. This is an inquiry about the spatial reach of substantive law—will the policies accounting for the existence of that law be sacrificed if it yields to conflicting law? The contact, or geographical feature, of a case most often generating interest is the domicile of the parties. Thus, interest analysis is sometimes called a personal law approach (*lex loci* is, correspondingly, a territorial approach).

This Chapter begins with an introduction to interest analysis by its chief creator and proponent, Brainerd Currie. Currie argues the necessity for interest analysis in conflicts reform and gives the structure of his approach. Professor William Richman then diagrams a series of notable decisions, illustrating three situations encountered in interest analysis: false conflicts (only one sovereign interested), true conflicts (both sovereigns interested), and unprovided-for cases (neither sovereign interested).

Brainerd Currie, *Notes on Methods and Objectives in the Conflict of Laws*, 1959 DUKE L.J. 171, 172-178, 179-180, 181*

* * * * *

* * * Conflict of laws, as we practice it, is concerned with references to foreign law for quite different purposes. Our failure to distinguish between them is to a considerable degree responsible for our troubles. The distinction needs to be clarified and better stated, so that it can

---

*   Reprinted with permission.

be more easily applied; and we need to know more about the class of cases in which foreign law is referred to for some purpose other than that of finding the rule of decision. For the present, however, I divide all conflicts cases into (1) those in which the purpose of the reference to foreign law is to find the rule of decision, and (2) those in which the reference has some other purpose. *The following discussion is strictly confined to the first class.*

The central problem of conflict of laws may be defined, then, as that of determining the appropriate rule of decision when the interests of two or more states are in conflict—in other words, of determining which interest shall yield. The problem would not exist if this were one world, with an all-powerful central government. It would not exist (though other problems of "conflict of laws" would) if the independent sovereignties in the real world had identical laws. So long, however, as we have a diversity of laws, we shall have conflicts of interest among states. Hence, unless something is done, the administration of private law where more than one state is concerned will be affected with disuniformity and uncertainty. To avoid this result by all reasonable means is certainly a laudable objective; but how? Not by establishing a single government; even if such a thing were remotely thinkable as a practical possibility, we attribute positive values to the principle of self-determination for localities and groups. The attainment of uniformity of laws among diverse states is, to put it mildly, a long-range undertaking. Federations could be established wherein the central government, while not disturbing the autonomy of the states in their internal policies, would determine which of several interests must yield in case of conflict. Treaties might be useful in the accomplishment of the same purpose, but this approach to solution has certain inherent difficulties. For various reasons, the political measures which would seem to be the only possible means of avoiding or adequately solving such problems have not done the job.

We do not, however, despair. We turn, instead, to the resources of jurisprudence, placing our faith primarily in the judges rather than the lawmakers. The judicial function is not narrowly confined; we indulge the hope that it may even be equal to the ambitious task of bringing uniformity and certainty into a world whose conflicts political action has failed to resolve. At first, of course, the judges will not be so bold (or so frank) as to avow that they are assuming the high political function of passing upon the relative merits of the conflicting policies, or interests, of sovereign states. They will address themselves to metaphysical questions concerning the nature of law and its abstract operation in space—matters remote from mundane policies and conflicts of interest—and will evolve a set of rules for determining which state's law must, in the nature of things, control. If all states can be persuaded to adhere to these rules, the seemingly impossible will have been accomplished: there will be uniformity and certainty in the administration of private law from state to state. The fact that this goal will be achieved at the price of sacrificing state interests is not emphasized; rather, it is obscured by the metaphysical apparatus of the method.

The rules so evolved have not worked and cannot be made to work. In our times, we have suffered particularly from the jurisprudential theory which has been compounded in order to explain and justify the assumption by the courts of so extraordinary a function. The territitorialist conception has been directly responsible for indefensible results and, what is perhaps worse, has therefore driven some of our ablest scholars to consume their energies in purely defensive action against it. But the root of the trouble goes deeper. In attempting to use the rules we encounter difficulties which do not stem from the fact that the particular rules are bad, nor from the fact that a particular theoretical explanation is unsound, but rather from the fact that we have such rules at all.

First, such rules create problems which did not exist before. * * *

Second, the false problems created by the rules may be solved in a quite irrational way— e.g., by defeating the interest of one state without advancing the interest of another. In at least some instances, this result could be avoided by contriving a different rule; but the substitute rule may be objectionable on other grounds. * * *

Third, despite the camouflage of discourse, the rules do operate to nullify state interests. The fact that this is often done capriciously, without reference to the merits of the respective policies and even without recognition of their existence, is only incidental. Trouble enough comes from the mere fact that interests are defeated. The courts simply will not remain always oblivious to the true operation of a system which, though speaking the language of metaphysics, strikes down the legitimate application of the policy of a state, especially when that state is the forum. Consequently, the system becomes complicated. It is loaded with escape devices: the concept of "local public policy" as a basis for not applying the "applicable" law; the concept of "fraud on the law"; the device of novel or disingenuous characterization; the device of manipulating the connecting factor; and, not least, the provision of sets of rules which are interchangeable at will. The tensions which are induced by imposing such a system on a setting of conflict introduce a very serious element of uncertainty and unpredictability even if there is fairly general agreement on the rules themselves. A sensitive and ingenious court can detect an absurd result and avoid it; I am inclined to think that this has been done more often than not and that therein lies a major reason why the system has managed to survive. At the same time, we constantly run the risk that the court may lack sensitivity and ingenuity; we are handicapped in even presenting the issue in its true light; and instances of mechanical application of the rules to produce indefensible results are by no means rare. Whichever of these phenomena is the more common, it is a poor defense of the system to say that the unacceptable results which it will inevitably produce can be averted by disingenuousness if the courts are sufficiently alert.

Fourth, where several states have different policies, and also legitimate interests in the application of their policies, a court is in no position to "weigh" the competing interests, or evaluate their relative merits, and choose between them accordingly. This is especially evident when we consider two coordinate states, with such decisions being made by the courts of one or the other. A court need never hold the interest of the foreign state inferior; it can simply apply its own law as such. But when the court, in a true conflict situation, holds the foreign law applicable, it is assuming a great deal: it is holding the policy, or interest, of its own state inferior and preferring the policy or interest of the foreign state. Nor are we much better off if we vest this extraordinary power in a superior judicial establishment, such as our federal courts in the exercise of their diversity jurisdiction, or the Supreme Court in the exercise of its power to review state court decisions. True, such a superimposed tribunal escapes the embarrassment of having to nullify the interests of its own sovereign; but the difficulty remains that the task is not one to be performed by a court. I know that courts make law, and that in the process they "weigh conflicting interests" and draw upon all sorts of "norms" to inform and justify their action. I do not know where to draw the line between the judicial legislation which is "molecular," or permissible, and that which is "molar," or impermissible. But assessment of the respective values of the competing legitimate interests of two sovereign states, in order to determine which is to prevail, is a political function of a very high order. This is a function which should not be committed to courts in a democracy. It is a function which the courts cannot perform effectively, for they lack the necessary resources. Not even a very ponderous Brandeis brief could marshall the relevant considerations in choosing, for example, between the interest of the state of employment and that of the state of injury in matters concerning workmen's compensation. This is a job for a legislative committee, and determining the policy to be formulated on the basis of the information assembled is a job for a competent legislative body. We, of course, have such a competent legislative body in Congress; but it has not seen fit to exercise its powers under the full-faith-and-credit clause in such a way as to contribute to the resolution of true conflicts of interest.

* * *

We would be better off without choice-of-law rules. We would be better off if Congress were to give some attention to problems of private law, and were to legislate concerning the choice between conflicting state interests in some of the specific areas in which the need for solutions is serious. In the meantime, we would be better off if we would admit the teachings of sociological jurisprudence into the conceptualistic precincts of conflict of laws. This would imply a basic method along the following lines:

1. Normally, even in cases involving foreign elements, the court should be expected, as a matter of course, to apply the rule of decision found in the law of the forum.

2. When it is suggested that the law of a foreign state should furnish the rule of decision, the court should, first of all, determine the governmental policy expressed in the law of the forum. It should then inquire whether the relation of the forum to the case is such as to provide a legitimate basis for the assertion of an interest in the application of that policy. This process is essentially the familiar one of construction or interpretation. Just as we determine by that process how a statute applies in time, and how it applies to marginal domestic situations, so we may determine how it should be applied to cases involving foreign elements in order to effectuate the legislative purpose.

3. If necessary, the court should similarly determine the policy expressed by the foreign law, and whether the foreign state has an interest in the application of its policy.

4. If the court finds that the forum state has no interest in the application of its policy, but that the foreign state has, it should apply the foreign law.

5. If the court finds that the forum state has an interest in the application of its policy, it should apply the law of the forum, even though the foreign state also has an interest in the application of its contrary policy, and, a fortiori, it should apply the law of the forum if the foreign state has no such interest.

* * * * *

The suggested analysis does not imply the ruthless pursuit of self-interest by the states.

In the first place, the states of the Union are significantly restrained in the pursuit of their respective interests by the privileges-and-immunities clause of article four[30] and by the equal protection clause.[31] Incidentally, employment of this method would give a new importance to those clauses as they affect conflict-of-laws problems. Ironically, and precisely because of their fault of operating mechanically and impersonally, without regard to the real problem of conflicting interests, choice-of-law rules have the virtue that they rarely discriminate in such a way as to raise problems as to the constitutional restraints upon discrimination.

In the second place, there is no need to exclude the possibility of rational altruism: for example, when a state has determined upon the policy of placing upon local industry all the social costs of the enterprise, it may well decide to adhere to this policy regardless of where the harm occurs and who the victim is.

---

[30]   U.S. Const. art. IV, § 2, cl. I.

[31]   *Id.*, Amend. XIV, § I.

In the third place, there is room for restraint and enlightenment in the determination of what state policy is and where state interests lie.

* * * * *

I have been told that I give insufficient recognition to governmental policies other than those which are expressed in specific statutes and rules: the policy of promoting a general legal order, that of fostering amicable relations with other states, that of vindicating reasonable expectations, and so on. If this is so, it is not, I hope, because of a provincial lack of appreciation of the worth of those ideals, but because of a felt necessity to emphasize the obstacles which the present system interposes to any intelligent approach to the problem. Let us first clear away the apparatus which creates false problems and obscures the nature of the real ones. Only then can we effectively set about ameliorating the ills which arise from a diversity of laws by bringing to bear all the resources of jurisprudence, politics, and humanism—each in its appropriate way.

William M. Richman, *Diagramming Conflicts: A Graphic Understanding of Interest Analysis*, 43 Ohio St. L.J. 317, 317-324, 325-326 (1982)*

A revolution in choice-of-law theory has occurred over the last forty or fifty years. At the urging of conflicts scholars, many courts have abandoned the hard and fast rules of the *First Restatement* in favor of content- and policy-oriented choice-of-law theories. The transition, however, has not been smooth. The uncertainty generated by the change, and the difficulty in applying the new systems, have evoked in some courts and in many law students nostalgia for the certainty supposedly available under the *First Restatement*. Brainerd Currie's system for choice of law—governmental interest analysis—epitomizes the difficulty. While the system has an elegance and power that has won it many converts, it is sufficiently sophisticated to generate confusion among courts and sufficiently difficult to produce resistance from law students.

In other areas of the law in which doctrine has proved difficult, scholars have simplified the task of the judge and the student by producing diagrams or charts that visually demonstrate the problem. This Article offers such diagrams for governmental interest analysis. By showing graphically the link between a state's social policy and its factual connection to the dispute, the diagrams illustrate the germ of Currie's insight and thus render interest analysis much more accessible.

II. DIAGRAMMING A CONFLICTS CASE

A. *False Conflicts*

Without regard to choice-of-law strategy, any conflicts case can be diagrammed simply according to its facts. By placing the relevant contacts in the appropriate states, the diagram depicts the problem for decision. Consider *Babcock v. Jackson*.[8] In that case plaintiff and defendant—both citizens of New York—took a weekend trip in the province of Ontario. Defendant lost control of the car and in the resulting collision, plaintiff was injured. She sued defendant

---

*   Reprinted with permission.

8   12 N.Y.2d 473, 191 N.E.2d 279, 240 N.Y.S.2d 743 (1963).

in New York. At the time Ontario had a guest statute that would have prohibited plaintiff's recovery; New York had no such statute.

The facts and the conflicting tort rules can be diagrammed as follows:

Diagram 1

	New York	Ontario
Contacts	Forum Plaintiff's domicile Defendant's domicile domicile Car garaged and insured Trip began	Accident Injury
Law	No guest statute	Guest statute

Under traditional choice-of-law theory this diagram is sufficient, and the only relevant contact is the injury in Ontario.

Currie's system, however, requires us to look beyond the place of injury and to consider the policies behind the conflicting tort rules. The policy behind the New York rule is the traditional one requiring a tortfeasor to compensate his victim for all injuries actually and proximately caused by his fault. The policy supporting Ontario's statute is "to prevent the fraudulent assertion of claims by passengers, in collusion with the drivers against insurance companies." In Currie's terminology the case is a false conflict—only one state's policy is advanced by application of its law. Ontario's interest in avoiding insurance fraud will not be advanced by the application of its guest statute, since defendant's automobile was garaged and insured in New York. In contrast, New York's interest in compensating victims of automobile negligence will be advanced by applying New York law, since plaintiff is a New Yorker.

With these added considerations, Diagram 1 is now insufficient. What is required is a graphic way of presenting the relevant contacts, the differing tort rules and their supporting policies, and *most importantly, the relationship between the policies and the contacts*. Consider Diagram 2.

Diagram 2

	New York	Ontario
Contacts	Forum Plaintiff's domicile Defendant's domicile Car garaged and insured Trip began	Accident Injury
Law	No guest statute	Guest statute
Policy	Compensate auto accident victims	Avoid insurance fraud

The arrows graphically depict Currie's insight. The arrow from New York's policy (compensate auto accident victims) points toward a New York contact: the New York plaintiff. The arrow from Ontario's policy, however, does not point toward an Ontario contact. Rather, it crosses the center line, indicating that Ontario policy has no Ontario referent, and thus, that Ontario's interests will not be advanced by the application of its laws. Since the arrows from both relevant policies point to contacts in New York, the case is a false conflict.[13]

B. *True Conflicts*

A true conflict is a case in which each state's policy would be advanced by the application of its law. In such a case each state has a contact that is relevant to the policy behind its rule.

An example of a true conflict is *Lilienthal v. Kaufman*.[15] Defendant had been declared a spendthrift by an Oregon court and had been placed under a guardianship. He nevertheless contracted with plaintiff, a Californian, in San Francisco to borrow money to finance a joint venture. The guardian declared the obligation void, and plaintiff sued in Oregon. Under Oregon law the obligation was voidable. Under California law, which has no spendthrift statute, the oblig-

---

[13]   Another example of a false conflict is Hurtado v. Superior Court, 11 Cal. 3d 574, 522 P.2d 666, 114 Cal. Rptr. 106 (1974), a wrongful death action. Plaintiff and plaintiff's decedent were domiciliaries of Mexico; defendant of California. The accident took place in California. Mexico had a limit of $1,946.73 on wrongful death recoveries, while in California recovery for wrongful death was unlimited. The court determined that the policy underlying Mexico's damage limitation was to avoid impoverishing tortfeasors and that California's reason for having no such limitation was to deter tortious conduct. The contact relevant to Mexico's policy—the defendant—was in California, as was the contact relevant to California's policy—the accident. The case, a false conflict, diagrams as follows:

Diagram A

	Mexico	California
Contacts	Plaintiff's domicile	Accident
	Domicile of plaintiff's decedent	Defendant's domicile
		Accident (negligence)
Law	Damage limit for wrongful death	Unlimited damages for wrongful death
Policy	Protect defendants	Deter negligent driving

The diagram shows the false conflict. Since Mexico's policy arrow crosses the center line and points to a contact in California, Mexico's interest would not be advanced by the application of its law. California's interest, in contrast, would be advanced since its policy arrow points toward a California contact. Both arrows point toward California—a graphic indication that only California's interests are at stake and the case is a false conflict.

[15]   239 Or. 1, 395 P.2d 543 (1964).

ation was valid. The Oregon court indicated that the policy behind the Oregon spendthrift statute was to protect the family of the spendthrift and the state treasury, lest the spendthrift or his family require public assistance. The court suggested that California's interest was in having its citizen paid and in ensuring the security of contracts made in California. The case is a true conflict[21] and can be diagrammed like this:

Diagram 3

	California	Oregon
	Plaintiff's domicile	Forum
		Defendant's domicile
Contacts	→ Contract made & to be performed	
		Defendant's guardian
		Defendant's ◄ family
Law	No spendthrift statute	Spendthrift statute
Policy	── Ensure security of contracts	Protect family of ── spendthrift and public fisc

The diagram helps to show the true conflict. California's policy arrow points toward a California contact, thus indicating that the application of California law would advance its policy interests. Similarly, Oregon's policy refers to an Oregon contact; that state's interests would also be advanced by the application of its law. The court, following Currie's program for resolving true conflicts, applied the law of Oregon.

---

[21]   Another true conflict is Bernhard v. Harrah's Club, 16 Cal. 3d 318, 546 P.2d 719, 128 Cal. Rptr. 215 (1976). Plaintiff, a citizen of California, was injured when his motorcycle collided in California with a car driven by a Californian. The driver and passenger of the car were intoxicated after a visit to defendant's drinking and gambling club in Nevada. California imposed civil liability on tavern keepers for injuries caused by patrons served alcohol when they are past the point of obvious intoxication; Nevada did not. California's interest was the protection of California citizens upon its highways from drunk drivers. Nevada's interest was the protection of its gambling and tavern industry. Each of these policies has a relevant contact in the appropriate state, as the diagram shows:

Diagram B

	California	Nevada
	Forum	Defendant tavern ◄
Contacts	Plaintiff's domicile	Drinking and tortious offering
	Car driver's domicile	
	→ Collision	
Law	Tavern keeper liability	No tavern keeper liability
Policy	── Protect citizens on highways	Protect gambling ── and tavern industry

C. *The "Unprovided-for Case"*

An "unprovided-for case" is a case in which neither state has an interest. In other words, because of the relevant state policies and the location of the contacts, neither state's policy interests would be advanced by the application of its law.

In *Erwin v. Thomas*[24] plaintiff's husband, a Washington domiciliary, was injured in Oregon as a result of an Oregon defendant's negligence. Plaintiff sued defendant in Oregon for loss of consortium. The law of Oregon permitted a wife to recover damages from a tortfeasor for loss of consortium, while the law of Washington did not. The court made passing reference to the most significant relationship test, but relied principally upon interest analysis. It found that the policy behind the Oregon law was solicitude for the rights of married women. Washington's policy, said the Oregon court, was to protect defendants. The case is displayed below:

Diagram 4

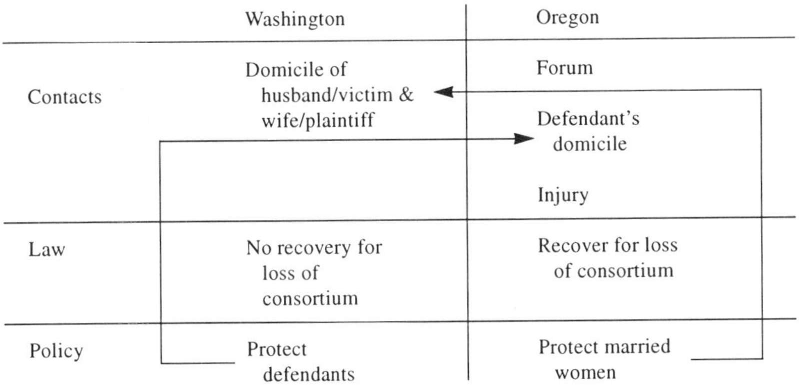

	Washington	Oregon
Contacts	Domicile of husband/victim & wife/plaintiff	Forum
		Defendant's domicile
		Injury
Law	No recovery for loss of consortium	Recover for loss of consortium
Policy	Protect defendants	Protect married women

As Diagram 4 shows, Washington's policy of protecting defendants is not actuated because defendant is domiciled in Oregon, not Washington. Similarly, Oregon's policy interest would not be advanced by the application of its law since plaintiff/wife (the object of Oregon's policy concern) is a Washingtonian. The case, then, is an unprovided-for case: as the arrows

---

[24]   264 Or. 454, 506 P.2d 494 (1973).

demonstrate, neither state's policy refers to an in-state contact. Accordingly, neither state's interest would be advanced by the application of its law.[29]

* * * * *

There are three basic benefits to the diagram technique. The first and most obvious is that it permits classification of a case simply by its shape.

* * * * *

---

[29]   The Oregon Supreme Court adopted Currie's strategy for dealing with the unprovided-for case and applied the law of the forum. See Currie, Survival of Actions: Adjudication Versus Automation in the Conflict of Laws, 10 Stan. L. Rev. 205 (1958). "It is apparent, therefore, that neither state has a vital interest in the outcome of this litigation and there can be no conceivable material conflict if an Oregon court does what comes naturally and applies Oregon law," 264 Or. 454, 459-60, 506 P.2d 494, 496-97 (1973).

Another, more famous example of an unprovided-for case is Neumeier v. Kuehner, 31 N.Y.2d 121, 286 N.E.2d 454, 335 N.Y.S.2d 64 (1972). Neumeier is one in a long line of New York guest statute cases. [Babcock v. Jackson, 12 N.Y.2d 73, 191 N.E.2d 279, 240 N.Y.S.2d 743 (1963); Dym v. Gordon, 16 N.Y.2d 120, 209 N.E.2d 792, 262 N.Y.S.2d 463 (1965); Tooker v. Lopez, 24 N.Y.2d 569, 249 N.E.2d 394, 301 N.Y.S.2d 519 (1969).] Defendant's intestate, a New York domiciliary, drove his car (insured and garaged in New York) to Ontario. There he picked up plaintiff's decedent, an Ontario domiciliary. Both were killed instantly when their car was struck by a train in Ontario. Ontario had a guest statute that prohibited recovery by a guest against a host absent gross negligence; New York had no such statute. The policy behind New York's common-law rule was the compensation of collision victims. The court stated that the policy behind the Ontario statute was a desire to protect defendants from suits by ungrateful guests. The case is depicted below in Diagram C.

Diagram C

	New York	Ontario
	Forum	Plaintiff's (guest's) domicile
Contacts	Defendant's (host's) domicile	Accident
	Car garaged & insured	Injury
Law	No guest statute	Guest statute
Policy	Compensate auto accident victims	Protect hosts from ungrateful guests

This is an unprovided-for case because both arrows cross the center line. The Ontario policy (protect hosts from ungrateful guests) refers to a New York contact, and the New York policy (compensate auto accident victims) refers to an Ontario contact. Thus, Neumeier is a case in which neither state's interest would be advanced by application of its law.

The case was decided in favor of the New York defendant based upon three rules formulated by Judge Fuld to govern guest-host cases. Neumeier generated substantial controversy. Much of it is contained in Neumeier v. Kuehner: A Conflicts Conflict, 1 Hofstra L. Rev. 93 (1973) (comments on the case by Professors Baade, King, Sedler, Shapira, and Twerski).

The key to understanding the * * * diagrams is to note the significance of the arrow's crossing the center line. The arrow, after all, is a policy-contact connector; it shows the relationship between a policy and a contact. When the arrow stays on one side of the center line, it shows that the state's policy refers to an in-state contact and thus that the state's interest will be advanced by application of its law. On the other hand, when the arrow crosses the center line it shows that the state's policy refers to an out-of-state contact and thus that the state's interest will not be advanced by the application of its law.

A false conflict, then, is one * * * in which one arrow crosses the line and one does not; only one state's policy will be advanced by applying its law. In a true conflict * * * neither arrow crosses the center line; each state's policy will be advanced by application of its law. In an unprovided-for case * * * both arrows cross the line, thus indicating that neither state's policy will be advanced by application of its law.

The second advantage of the diagrams is that they forcefully highlight Currie's major insight. Currie was not the first to suggest that policy is important in choice-of-law cases; even under the *First Restatement* courts refused to apply foreign law upon the ground that it violated the forum's public policy. Nor was Currie the first to suggest that contacts are important in choice of law. The *First Restatement* emphasized contacts, albeit only one at a time. The center-of-gravity theory required consideration of all the contacts between a dispute and the several states whose law might govern. Currie's contribution was to point out that what is crucial to the choice-of-law decision is the relationship between a state's contacts with a dispute and the policy behind its law; this is the relationship that is graphically represented in the diagrams.

* * * * *

Comments

1. Much of Currie's conflicts work may be found in a collection of his essays (1963a).[1] A comprehensive and sympathetic discussion of Currie's contributions appears in Kay 1989. Currie's ideas are discussed at length in two symposium *Choice of Law*, 48 Mercer L. Rev. (no. 2 1997) (forthcoming—contributors include Patrick Borchers, David Currie, Friedrich K. Juenger, Herma Hill Kay, Marjorie F. Knowles, Bruce Posnak, John Rees, Jack Sammons, Gene R. Shreve, Joseph W. Singer, Symeon Symeonides, Russell J. Weintraub); *Interest Analysis in Conflict of Laws: An Inquiry into Fundamentals with a Side Glance at Products Liability*, 46 Ohio St. L.J. 457 (1985) (contributions by P. John Kozyris, Lea Brilmayer, Robert Sedler, Russell J. Weintraub, Friedrich K. Juenger, Dimitrios Evrigenis, Donald H. Berman, George A. Zaphirou, Gene R. Shreve, William V. Luneburg, and Symeon Symeonides).

2. Currie deserves the lion's share of the credit for developing interest analysis. Berman 1985; Ely 1981: p. 174; Shreve 1985. Yet several authors, working prior to Currie or when he wrote, captured something of Currie's approach. The very first conflicts scholarship in this country was of a unilateralist bent, in the European statutist tradition. Livermore 1828. Closer to Currie's own time, commentators questioned in various ways the indifference of the Bealean approach to the purposes of laws in con-

---

[1]   Full citations appear in the bibliography, Chapter Twelve.

flict. *See, e.g.,* Cavers 1933: pp. 192-193, 197-200; Cheatham 1945: pp. 380-81; Harper 1947: p. 1161; Lorenzen 1924: pp. 750-751.

3. Currie saw nothing evil in uniformity as such. "[I]n general, like motherhood, everyone favors uniformity of result." Von Mehren & Trautman 1965: pp. 299-300. But Currie did attack what he judged to be the mindless pursuit of uniformity. He made a tongue-in-cheek proposal to replace part of the existing territorial approach with the rule "that the governing law shall be that of the state first in alphabetical order." Currie noted that his proposal would be a modest improvement, "since the existing rules for choice of law are just as arbitrary, and much more complex." 1963a: p. 609.

4. In our selection, Currie appears to acknowledge a risk of at least some forum favoritism from his approach but suggests that the United States Supreme Court can police matters under the privileges-and-immunities and equal-protection clauses. The Supreme Court has in fact largely remained on the sidelines. Proposals for regulation of choice of law under various parts of the Constitution are surveyed in Chapter Ten.

5. For all his influence, Currie was not a consensus builder. Currie's excerpt in this Chapter reveals a number of his controversial positions: his relative indifference to party expectations in choice of law, his refusal to compare intensities of interests in true-conflict cases, his refusal to permit conflicts judges to be influenced by their substantive preferences, and his insistence that the interested forum always apply its own law. Currie's views induced attack by opponents of interest analysis across a wide front, and they prompted most other interest analysts to distance themselves from Currie in one way or another.

6. Later, Currie did moderate his approach in one respect. He shifted to a more cautious determination of state interests, especially of the interest of the forum state.

> [T]o assert a conflict between the interests of the forum and the foreign state is a serious matter; the mere fact that a suggested broad conception of a local interest will create conflict with that of a foreign state is a sound reason why the conception should be re-examined, with a view to a more moderate and restrained interpretation both of policy and of the circumstances in which it must be applied to effectuate the forum's legitimate purpose.

Currie 1963b: p. 757. However, Currie never retreated from his position that the truly interested forum should apply its own law. Cavers 1970: pp. 146-149; Shreve 1985: p. 541.

7. The most successful of Currie's three models was the "false conflict." It provided an excellent argument against the territorial approach of the original RESTATE-MENT by demonstrating how the latter forced the choice of disinterested over interested law. Professor Richman uses the example of *Babcock v. Jackson* (also the subject of Chapter 4) to demonstrate how courts were particularly receptive to the false-conflict idea when the *lex loci delicti* rules of the original RESTATEMENT would have forced them to sacrifice important policies secured by local law. Currie's critics (represented in Chapter Six A) often questioned the value of his false-conflicts analysis. Their most trenchant attacks, however, were directed at his other two models: the "true conflict" and the "unprovided-for case."

8. Currie did not answer clearly all of the questions he raised. One critic observed:

> [I]t is sometimes not even clear which aspects are the defining characteristics of governmental interest analysis. One might accept his methodological premises, but reject or remain agnostic about his illustrative examples. * * * Or one might do the opposite, accepting the examples but not the method. * * * Or one might agree with the critique of Beale but reject the entire alternative program.

Brilmayer 1995c: p. 49. Continuing in this vein, she asked:

> Which is the "real" governmental interest analysis? It would be unprofitable to speculate about which current positions are truly more faithful to the original theorist's intentions because Currie's writings were numerous, varied, and, on occasion, ambiguous. This should not be too surprising given that his major articles were written over the course of a few short years, and that he did not live long enough to systematize his ideas or respond to critics, who are writing twenty or thirty years after his death.

Id. Therefore, Professor Brilmayer suggested, Currie and his governmental interest analysis remain a difficult target for critics.

> It is treacherous work to try to criticize interest analysis as a whole because it has such different aspects. A critic who chooses to criticize aspects of the theory that some other scholar has found uncharacteristic or inessential is vulnerable to accusations of having created straw men. There is probably no authoritative version * * * to criticize.

Id.

CHAPTER SIX

Interest Analysis on Trial

This Chapter depicts the debate over interest analysis that has simmered since Brainerd Currie set forth his approach.

Part A surveys some of the leading criticisms of interest analysis. We see that the most spirited resistance to interest analysis has not come from defenders of the old *lex loci delicti* tradition. It comes instead from commentators who maintain that, while *lex loci* was problematic and reform might have been called for, interest analysis is the wrong path.

Part A begins with Professor Harold Maier's reflections on difficulties inherent in the term, "governmental interests." Professors John Kozyris, Friedrich Juenger and Lea Brilmayer then press their attacks. While the three critics offer different perspectives, they contribute to a common case against interest analysis. Questions raised by their arguments include whether it is possible consistently to determine the intended reach of substantive rules, whether interest analysis has the structure and stability necessary in a choice-of-law approach, and whether interest analysis is not an open door to local favoritism and forum shopping in choice of law. In a selection concluding Part A, Professor Aaron Twerski notes what he regards to be the particular frailties of interest analysis in the "unprovided-for case."

Those reading only Part A of this Chapter might be led by the force, clarity and elegance of arguments encountered there to wonder why interest analysis ever achieved importance in American conflicts law. They might be surprised to learn that about as many conflicts scholars support interest analysis as oppose it. The supporters, represented by Professors Russell Weintraub, Robert Sedler, David Seidelson, Louise Weinberg, and Bruce Posnak, take their turn in Part B of this Chapter. The selections by these commentators are like those of the critics in Part A, in that they utilize a variety of perspectives yet contribute to a common case. Their common case in defense of interest analysis is in large part rebuttal—arguments that the strengths of interest analysis have been underestimated, and that the frailties of the approach in theory and in application have been exaggerated. But their case also includes a challenge—since few wish to return to *lex loci delicti*, what alternative approach is demonstrably better than interest analysis?

A. Critics

Harold G. Maier, *Finding the Trees in Spite of the Metaphorist: The Problem of State Interests in Choice of Law*, 56 Albany L. Rev. 753, 754-755 (1993)*

* * * * *

I am principally concerned with two metaphors fundamental to academic and judicial scholarship in modern choice of law. One is the term "conflict of laws" itself. The other is the term "governmental interests." Like most metaphors, these phrases inform by connotation, calling up images of stereotypical relationships. Often these metaphors obscure, rather than enlighten, choice-of-law analysis.

The metaphor "conflict of laws" suggests struggle among sovereigns who, like medieval rulers, engage in battle to assert the primacy of their local policies. The term emphasizes competition, not coordination and cooperation. Under this view, the forum decisionmaker presides over a zero sum game with respect to the states whose laws are involved in the choice; one wins, the others lose.

The term "governmental interests" is equally metaphorical and in many respects mischievous. Under this metaphor, the courts are directed to use the norms of the state with the greatest governmental interest in the outcome of a particular issue as guides to decision. This metaphor anthropomorphizes the state, inferentially characterizing it as a sentient entity with self-generated feelings, thoughts, and concerns. Governmental interest literature is filled with statements like "State X wants" or "State Y rejects" or "State Z believes," none of which are particularly helpful in determining what the writer means by governmental interests or where those interests lie.

* * *

A choice-of-law case never actually involves a confrontation among the wills or policies of competing sovereigns. Once the forum court is seized of the case, solely forum authority determines that case's outcome. The sovereigns whose laws may be applicable and, therefore, whose interests may be at stake are not usually represented before the court, except indirectly by advocates for private clients who seek to rely on foreign rules and whose arguments may not necessarily reflect the views of the state whose policies they urge upon the court. No evidence exists that state governmental authorities monitor the manner in which sister state courts decide choice-of-law cases or that any political response is engendered if a foreign forum incorrectly borrows or fails to borrow a state's local law. Short of constitutional limitations, the forum is free to do its best to achieve justice in the case before it by giving effect to policies appropriate to the situation.

* * * * *

---

*   Reprinted with permission.

P. John Kozyris, *Postscript: Interest Analysis Facing Its Critics—And, Incidentally, What Should Be Done About Choice of Law for Products Liability?,* **46 OHIO ST. L.J. 569, 572-578, 580-581 (1985)***

* * * * *

* * * Whether states have significant interests in the outcome of private law litigation is itself a questionable proposition, but the problem is even more fundamental. What is the reason that, in conflicts, we should be urging the states to pursue their interests? Are not they doing it on their own anyway? * * *

Perhaps the emphasis on interest serves the function of negating other imperatives such as the traditional ones of vested rights and comity. But what about positive content? If each state is left free to determine what its interests are and where they lie, is not the logical consequence of interest analysis its own self-destruction as a choice of law theory since the issue then will become only a matter of the will and power of each state? Interest analysis, however, in fact goes beyond a mere description of state preferences. Its conflicts values revolve around the home connection and the forum preference, and its methodology of assessing state interests on a case-by-case, issue-by-issue basis is often nothing but a cover for the relentless pursuit of these two values.

Currie's writings, and on this there is no disagreement among his successors, reveal a pervasive belief that states are and should be more interested in their people (citizens, domiciliaries, residents) than in events or actions within their territory. The personalism-versus-territorialism debate is as old as they come. Story himself, the American grandfather of conflicts, recognized the importance of the personality factor; the question being not one of relevance, but of proper balance and proportion. The primacy of the home connection as against the events or property locale, as advocated by interest analysis, is anything but self-evident. That states are interested in or have decided to legislate with regard to persons rather than events or property remains a bold but naked assertion which is supported neither by historical data nor by compelling logic. In fact, at least in the past, legislatures have been territorially oriented, and this trend has not been reversed in recent times despite the assaults of interest analysis. This was evident in the choice of law provisions of the new statutes for no-fault automobile reparations. Furthermore, reliance on the personality factor can produce intractable problems. In a territorial system, the significant events of a multistate transaction can be localized in one state often enough so that the parties have a common connection there. To be sure, what is significant may be controversial, like the resulting harm or conduct in torts, or the making or its performance in contracts. However, the case against the territorial system on this point has been vastly overstated because in the normal situation an acceptable, if imperfect, localization can be made. Also, in a personal system, when all the parties are from the same state, the common connection is strong and the choice is often easy. Yet when they come from different states, we face an impasse. The parties share no connecting factor and, given that the interests of states in their own people are presumably of equal weight, the application of one of the two laws would sacrifice an equally authoritative law.

---

*   Reprinted with permission.

Some interest analysts use different terminology urging us to go then to the law of the place of social impact. If the impact approach were to be taken seriously rather than as a euphemism for the plaintiff's home state, we would be faced again with an equally insoluble problem, because, however it is sliced, what is given to the plaintiff must be taken from the defendant. When the loss is shifted to the defendant, there must be a commensurate negative impact in his home state, and thus there is encountered the original impasse of whose home state is more equal than the other's. In addition, seeking to localize impact and consequences uses the processes of the traditional conflicts methods while it lacks the relative certainty and ease of application of such methods.

Incidentally, another way to come out in favor of the plaintiff, quite unorthodox by Currie's standards, is to introduce the principle of compensation: breaking the split-domicile tie in favor of spreading, rather than concentrating, losses. In this realm of substantive policies which determines conflicts choices (compensation in torts, validation in agreements), we have at least articulated the real basis of the choice.

The additional fact that interest analysis uses the home connection not neutrally, blindly, or bilaterally, and that it does not apply the *lex domicilii* of the tort victim regardless of its content or whether the victim is a domiciliary of the forum, makes matters even worse. If this reduces to the notion that states are interested in applying their protective laws only in favor of their own people and their burdensome laws only against nonresidents, the resulting blatant discrimination not only is unwise, but would violate constitutional standards, especially the privileges and immunities clause. Currie's position on this issue is Delphic if not apocryphal, and it is gratifying that at least some interest analysts expressly disclaim any intent to prejudice the nonresidents. However, even under the best of circumstances and with the best of intentions, the emphasis on both the *lex domicilii* and the *lex fori* in the context of plaintiff's wide choice of fora all too often will bring about such a result and we cannot close our eyes to it.

Equally objectionable is the intimation that states should so calibrate their choice of law that they derive selfish, usually pecuniary, extraneous benefits from it by lightening their welfare burden. Conflicts is not a branch of taxation. This is not to say that a state may not adopt a victim compensation system which reduces welfare expenses in general, or that it may not apply such a system to all situations having an appropriate connection to it. However, such a connection is a precondition that must be met. If the domicile of the parties is the connection used, then due (equal?) deference must be given to the compensation schemes of the states of the domicile of all the affected parties.

The other fundamental normative preference of interest analysis embraces the *lex fori* in all true conflicts. While favoring local law has some basic primitive appeal ("my courts apply my law") and produces certainty, its wisdom has been debated for ages. The litmus test of the even-handedness of any conflicts approach is precisely its position on the question of whether comity and mutual self-limitation, or go-it-alone and beggar-thy-neighbor, should predominate.

In discussing this aspect of interest analysis, I will assume, although it is not entirely clear, that it concedes that a state has no special interest in maximizing the application of its private law just because it is its own. On the other hand, because of the practical reasons of convenience and familiarity, and because local law is the starting point to be applied unless displaced, even in the most forum-neutral conflicts system, it is accepted that in borderline cases the doubts ought to be resolved in favor of the *lex fori*. Interest analysis, however, goes far beyond using the *lex fori* as a residual tie-breaker. Currie's main thesis was that whenever the forum has any measurable interest in the matter, its law should inexorably apply regardless of the importance of the contacts with and the interests and concerns of any other state. The rejection of any balancing and mutuality purportedly derives from Currie's restricted view of the judicial function. According to Currie, it is not for the courts to choose comity over their own law. One could also detect his negativism toward a cooperative effort in conflicts at all levels.

From the perspective of results, given the self-serving fluidity with which litigants and courts can conjure up some local concern, Currie makes the *lex fori* the supreme law of conflicts. This position is quite extreme. Even as dedicated a *lex fori* champion as Professor Albert Ehrenzweig is more restrained than Currie, by aiming at clarity and certainty rather than celebrating provincialism. He combines the *lex fori* with a few forum-neutral hard and fast true rules of conflicts. In addition, he further mitigates the reach of the *lex fori* by relying on tighter jurisdictional rules ("proper law in a proper forum") to eliminate cases having no significant connection with the forum.[36]

It should also be noted that, since it is the plaintiff who ordinarily chooses the forum, *lex fori* easily reduces to *lex actoris*, or in other words, the law of plaintiff's choosing. What happens then to Currie's opposition to substantive objectives such as validation or compensation? In any event, I remain mystified as to why plaintiffs as such should be given a conflicts bonus which can be so readily abused in our world of easy judicial jurisdiction. Would interest analysis remain faithful to the *lex fori* if defendants were allowed to bring declaratory actions of nonliability?

Interest analysis is severely split on the pro-forum bias. The majority of its modern adherents, as well as its judicial practitioners, reject the automatic prevalence of the *lex fori* in true conflicts, preferring to engage in some balancing, weighing, or comparative-impairment evaluation of the interests of all concerned states.

This Postscript is not the place to further debate the *lex fori*. It suffices to say that interest analysis has done a disservice to federalism and internationalism by relentlessly pushing a viewpoint which inevitably leads to conflicts chauvinism or, more accurately, tribalism in view of the emphasis on the nation being a group of people. Any approach which is based on maximum use of power for one's own selfish interest is not only antithetical to the very raison d' etre of conflicts which is to seek the law most suitable to a multistate controversy, but also is bound to become self-defeating by inviting retaliation and by reducing the benefits of affirmative cooperation. The glorification of the *lex fori* is particularly deplorable when considered in the context of our long history of legislative and judicial benevolent acquiescence in, if not outright adoption of, a forum-neutral system of conflicts. If the Restatement of Foreign Relations Law of the United States can afford to limit the reach of the United States' regulatory law in the international sphere to reflect reasonableness and respect for the authority of other nations, should not the reach of state private law within our federal system be so limited?

Finally, I would like to say a few words about the ad hoc methodology developed by Currie and cultivated by his successors. This methodology does away with conflicts rules and requires a case and a custom-made answer to every choice of law question. While its beginnings may be traceable to the antiformalism of realist jurisprudence, reflecting the rule-skepticism of its most prominent intellectural forebear, Professor Walter Wheeler Cook,[42] this methodology has developed into a different kind of an animal. Its focus is not really on how conflicts rules work in practice, or on their actual social impact, but on its own countersystem of abstract normative preferences. Consequently, its modernism is mostly rhetorical.

---

[36]   A. Ehrenzweig, Conflict of Laws 350 (1962). * * *

[42]   Cook, *The Logical and Legal Bases of the Conflict of Laws*, 33 Yale L.J. 457 (1924).* * *

The ad hoc aspect of interest analysis reflects a philosophical position which rejects strict and specific rules (judicial compulsion) in favor of equitable broad standards (judicial discretion), and which eschews abstract commands interpreted deductively (code method) in preference for case-by-case holdings extended inductively (common law method). However, nowhere in interest analysis is there a recognition of the fact that this position is controversial and debatable. Nor is there any attempt to defend it or explain why it is particularly suited for conflicts. This is just another of the axioms that one must add to the interest analysis baggage.

Even a casual perusal of conflicts developments in recent years will show clearly that the cost of the special brand of casuistic "khadi-justiz" (ad hoc decisions deduced from mystical references to interests) called interest analysis has been quite prohibitive. Conflicts has become a tale of a thousand-and-one-cases. When a new case comes down, interest analysts rush to co-opt it, not by arguing that it is the best or the most acceptable, but by rejoicing in that it is supportable and not totally wrong.

Collapsing the conflicts inquiry into the quest for substantive justice, thus confusing questions of power and authority with those of substantive results, and pursuing the holy grail through a self-centered policy analysis compounds the mess. Efforts to make some order out of all this have produced an incredibly voluminous and complex literature. Any attempt to synthesize this literature must live in the shadow of Currie's antirule homilies. Judges, who at first were flattered and enticed by the invitation to freewheeling decision making, are becoming increasingly disoriented in the process of trying to button down policies, contacts, interests, and all that is in between.

These methodological complications are more serious in a field such as conflicts where the crucial issue involving allocation of power (jurisdiction) is preliminary to the resolution of the substantive controversy. The need for clarity and certainty is the greatest in this preliminary stage, and any system calling for open-ended and endless soul-searching on a case-by-case basis carries a high burden of persuasion. With centuries of experience and doctrinal elaboration behind us, we hardly need more lab testing and narrow findings. Rather, we need to make up our minds and make some sense out of the chaos. This is not to say that conflicts rules may not be improved by reducing the generality of their scope, where indicated, or by opening up the realm of relevant contacts and upgrading the status of the personal contacts where appropriate. However, going over to a world of judicial particularistic intuitionism, as called for by the conflicts antirulists, is quite another matter. In my jurisprudential universe, fixed but revisable rules which lead to good results in the overwhelming majority of the cases, and which are supplemented by some general corrective principles to mitigate injustice in the remaining cases, are superior to, and incredibly more efficient than, a system in which each case is decided as if it were unique and of first impression. This is even more applicable to conflicts.

In short, Currie, surely a master craftsman, endowed with high reason and broad vision, may have been right in many of his insights: that conflicts is a game of power and authority; that people sometimes matter more than events; and that considerations such as better law and party expectations as to the applicable law are inappropriate. Furthermore, Currie's system, with its emphasis on the primacy of the *lex fori* to govern in all true conflicts, had a certain internal consistency and practicality which is seriously compromised in the more balancing-oriented versions of his theories. However, while the judgment of history is still ahead of us, looking at the total picture in terms of practical solutions, my current scoresheet shows a few hits (reconsideration of fundamental premises and system, restoration of personal connections) and many misses (fostering parochial and selfish approaches, overstating the existence of governmental interests in the private law sphere, catering to domiciliary plaintiffs, employing a talismanic and cumbersome methodology).

* * * * *

Friedrich K. Juenger, *Conflict of Laws: A Critique of Interest Analysis*, 32 AM. J. COMP. L. 1, 10-12, 33-44 (1984)*

* * * * *

The Principle Features of Currie's Approach

1. The Primacy of Forum Law

While traditional conflicts thinking assumed the equality of local and foreign law, Currie regarded the two as qualitatively different. He believed that the *lex fori* always had a claim to application because "normally, even in cases involving foreign elements, the court should be expected, as a matter of course, to apply the rule of decision found in the law of the forum." Accordingly, local law can be applied even if there is no forum interest to vindicate. A court is required to analyze foreign policies and interests only if the parties raise the foreign law issue. But even then analysis begins at home and is likely to end where it began, because if the forum has no "legitimate interest" it probably cannot take jurisdiction in the first place.

2. Fragmentation

Since Currie's approach is geared to ascertaining the reach of substantive rules, it requires a separate analysis for each rule potentially applicable to a given set of facts. Interest analysis therefore splinters a legal transaction, such as a tort or a contract, into discrete issues. For instance, if the crash in France of a Turkish airliner manufactured in California poses twenty legal issues, each of them may be controlled by a rule of decision from a different legal system. Thus the liability of the pilot could depend on French law, vicarious liability of the airline on Turkish law, the liability of the manufacturer on the law of California and the status of relatives as wrongful death beneficiaries on the law of their (or the dead passengers') home states.

Obviously, such fragmentation entails greater complexities than the First Restatement's jurisdiction-selecting rules, which submit the entire controversy (except for issues considered to be procedural) to the *lex loci delicti*. It follows that the difficulties already implicit in the calculus of policies and interests are exacerbated whenever a case poses more than one issue. Also, if courts are permitted to splice together rules from different legal systems, such *depecage* can yield composite results at odds with those that would follow from applying the local law of any of the interested states.

3. The Personal Law Principle

Any method that purports to ascertain the spatial reach of rules by means of construction and interpretation requires interpretive guidelines. A rule of law may be construed either to apply to people, things and transactions within a state, or to apply to the state's subjects, wherever they may happen to be. Which rules are territorial and which follow the person has been the subject of protracted discussion ever since the Middle Ages. The First Restatement, although it recognized that a state may have "legislative jurisdiction" over its domiciliaries,

---

*   Reprinted with permission.

clearly favored territorial connecting factors. In marked contrast, Currie considered it axiomatic that the personal law principle should be preferred. Even when he did concede relevance to territorial contacts, he attempted to rationalize this conclusion in personal law terms by hypothesizing a governmental concern with local parties who may be indirectly affected by a transaction.

By favoring a personal nexus Currie was able to supply a constructional preference to help to decide the intended reach of legal rules. But that preference poses an obvious difficulty whenever the parties to a transaction are from different states. In a tort action, for instance, whose personal law should the court apply, that of the victim or that of the tortfeasor? Moreover, to the extent that Currie's scheme concedes significance to territorial contacts, it invites a conflict between the laws of the parties' home states and that of the place of the transaction. For example, if the accident state has an interest in compensating victims, should its compensation rules prevail over those of the victim's and the tortfeasor's common home state? According to Currie, the primacy of forum law supplies a simple solution to this seemingly intractable problem: such "true conflicts" are resolved by letting forum law prevail.

But what if application of the *lex fori* does not promote any forum policy? According to Currie it is possible that neither the forum nor any other state has any concern about the outcome of a lawsuit. This strange conclusion follows from the premise that law exists to promote the welfare of a sovereign's subjects. For example, a nonresident victim injured in a state whose laws bar recovery brings an action in the tortfeasor's home state, whose law would grant relief. In that situation neither state has an interest in implementing its protective policy to favor a nonresident, with whose welfare the state is not concerned, at the expense of a resident. Currie called this an "unprovided-for" case. But how can an analysis designed to effectuate state interests resolve cases in which "neither state cares what happens"? Once again Currie had to rely on the rough and ready expedient of applying the *lex fori*.

* * * * *

A Synopsis of Defects

1. The Futility of Ascertaining Policies

Currie purported to ascertain the scope of substantive rules from their underlying policies. This assumes that it is possible to ascribe a specific purpose to each rule of law. However, a rule may be the product of legislative compromise among competing policies or, as Currie recognized, it may lack a discernible policy. Moreover, identical provisions may have been enacted by different legislatures for different reasons. Thus, rules imposing tort liability can be rationalized as serving either a compensatory or a deterrent purpose. Should it matter which of the two was uppermost in the legislative or judicial mind when the rule was adopted? Or should all plausible policies be imputed, including those no one ever considered until an interest analyst supplied them after the fact?

Also, can one really assume that all policies are created equal? This clearly must be the view of those who, like Currie, consider it improper to weigh competing policies. Yet, implicit in a legal system that provides for judicial review and federal preemption is the assumption of a hierarchy of norms. The policies lurking behind guest statutes obviusly cannot command the same reverence as those enshrined in the Bill of Rights. Similarly, the policies of the Sherman Act are more potent than those of contract law. Rules adopted in a conscious effort to reform the law, perhaps to remedy what may be held unconstitutional in the future, seem entitled to greater respect than those "drags on the coattails of civilization" that have somehow managed to escape judicial or legislative scrutiny. Currie's brand of interest analysis makes no allowance for such differences. He firmly believed that even such quaint relics of a bygone era as married women's disabilities and non-survival rules represent government policies, however indefensible, which the courts must effectuate. In fact, the topics selected by some analysts to demonstrate the operation of their method suggest that the less defensible a policy, the greater its appeal. While "choice-of-law experts continue to engage in transcendental meditation over guest statutes," they neglect more timely issues, such as the conflicts problems posed by no-fault plans.* * *

Judicial decisions suggest that the analysts' faith in the courts' ability to isolate the policies behind substantive rules is misguided. Since 1963, when it handed down *Babcock v. Jackson*, the New York Court of Appeals had been "deeply engaged in probing the psychological motivation of legislatures of other States."[219] The judges spent almost ten years trying to identify the possible purposes guest statutes might serve. By the time the court decided *Neumeier v. Kuehner*, the case that marked the demise of interest analysis in New York, it was still not entirely clear which purposes really mattered.

How, in any event, should judges go about ascertaining foreign policies? Commenting on attempts to divine the reasons behind the Ontario guest statute featured so prominently in New York jurisprudence, a * * * trial judge asked, rhetorically,

> is one to subpoena the Prime Minister of Canada, or a knowledgeable Ontario Legislator into a New York Court to give evidence on the issue? And, is it realistic to believe that anyone will admit, under oath, that just plain old political patronage may have been one, or the sole motivation that led to the involved legislative enactment?[220]

A California case demonstrates the dubious nature of judicial attempts to second-guess foreign lawmakers. In *Hurtado v. Superior Court* the California Supreme Court wrestled with an article in the Civil Code of Zacatecas that imposes a low ceiling on recovery for death and personal injury. Lacking the benefit of a foreign law expert the justices relied on their intuitions, guided by the discussion of American wrongful death acts in a book by Professor Cavers, who would be the first to disclaim any familiarity with Mexican tort law and policies.

2. The Vain Search for Interests

Equally implausible is the assumption of interest analysis that one can deduce the reach of rules from their underlying policies. As Rabel put it,

> answers to the regular questions of conflicts law are rarely contained in municipal statutes. Private law rules ordinarily do not direct which persons or movables they include. It is as mistaken to apply such rules blindly to

---

[219]   Neumeier v. Kuehner, 31 N.Y.2d 121, 130, 286 N.E.2d 454, 459, 335 N.Y.S.2d 64, 72 (1972) (Breitel, J., concurring).

[220]   Himes v. Stalker, 99 Misc. 610, 617, 416 N.Y.S.2d 986, 990 (Sup. Ct. 1979).

events all over the world as to presume them limited to merely domestic situations. They are simply neutral; the answer is not in them.[225]

Since policies do not come equipped with labels proclaiming their spatial dimension, interest analysts, like traditionalists, need a localizing mechanism that connects a person, thing or event with a particular legal system. The analysts do not openly avow their reliance on this familiar conflicts technique; they pretend to derive their conclusions directly from an analysis of social concerns. In fact, however, they merely do what conflicts scholars have done for centuries, i.e., they assume that rules of decision are either territorial or follow the person.

Thus, interest analysis is ultimately just as "crudely geographical" as Beale's system. But whereas Beale was quite explicit about when to use one connecting factor or the other, the analysts disagree widely on the significance and legitimacy of the contacts they employ when purporting to construe and interpret. Currie revived the personal law principle on the assumption that laws are passed primarily for the benefit of local residents. He therefore favored the domiciliary nexus, yet he also attributed some continuing relevance to the territorial principle that had once reigned supreme. This left his disciples with two connecting factors but little guidance on when to use which. Their uncertainty and disagreements provide judges with ample arguments to support the application of local law, which they know best, whenever the forum has some personal or territorial link with a transaction. In other words, as in workers' compensation cases, courts are free to apply forum law in almost any case.

This result does not, in any real sense, follow from an analysis of state interests. In fact, there is little to support the analysts' belief in the reality of such interests. To Currie it was an article of faith that governments have an interest in rules of private law, and he viewed the vindication of such interests as an important attribute of sovereignty. However, as we have seen, judges as well as scholars have questioned their existence. True, many judicial opinions, including those of the United States Supreme Court, refer to state interests. But mere reiteration, even by the highest tribunal, cannot fill an empty word with meaning. After all, rights never really did vest, nor did obligations stalk hapless debtors, no matter how often the courts resorted to these figures of speech. Even devout followers of Currie concede that there is nothing reprehensible about the sacrifice of forum interests, although Currie might have thought that such a dereliction of judicial duties borders on an impeachable offense.

No one has ever bothered to adduce empirical evidence for the existence of interests Currie hypothesized; like vesting rights they must be accepted on faith. But skepsis rather than faith is called for in the conflict of laws, a discipline that has so often fallen prey to glib wordplay. If states are indeed deeply concerned about the outcome of private lawsuits, how can they permit private parties to escape from local policies and to defy state interests by simply stipulating the law that governs their bargains and the forum, judicial or arbitral, that decides their disputes? Of course, it might be argued that contracts are sui generis. But even in the law of torts, the litigants can thwart whatever governmental interests there may be in local rules. Long-arm jurisdiction affords ample opportunities to evade local policies through forum shopping and to utilize the very forum preference which is the hallmark of interest analysis as a means of subverting governmental interests.

---

[225]   1 Rabel, *The Conflicts of Laws* 103 (2d ed. 1958).

3. Legal Jingoism

Currie's fixation on local interests and policies made him debunk the conflicts objectives of uniformity and predictability, as well as the system values of federalism and international cooperation. According to him,

> [a] choice-of-law rule does express a policy, but it is not of the same order as the social and economic policies which are normally developed by a state in the pursuit of its governmental interests and the interests of its people. . . . This is but a mild, tentative, and self-denying policy.[233]

That passage, unsupported by authority, contradicts a record compiled over centuries by courts, scholars and legislatures. It also flies in the face of worldwide agreement on the need for conflicts law and express Congressional policy. Finally, it clashes with the rationale of two landmark decisions in which the Supreme Court emphasized the need for worldwide comity, even at the expense of local policies. As the Justices pointed out, multistate transactions involve policies and considerations quite different from those that control purely domestic disputes.

Some interest analysts, concerned about the "balkanization" of multistate transactions, reject Currie's forum-centered resolution of true conflicts. Yet their attempts to take into account competing ideas of comity and federalism not only complicate the interest calculus, they undermine the very foundations of the methodology they espouse. Interest analysis is, after all, an attempt to derive solutions to conflicts problems from the notion of sovereignty. Thus, all proposals to improve on Currie's singleminded forum bias by blending his teachings with traditional conflicts values inevitably contradict the very essence of his approach.

Currie assumed a "Hobbesian state of nature," an assumption that can only produce an anti-conflicts law. It is of course precisely the lawmaking monopoly of states and nations which creates the problem that the law of conflicts is called upon to resolve. No conflicts theory can accomplish the task if it fails to recognize considerations other than those of sovereignty. Fortunately, however, ethnocentricity is not the official policy of modern states. Even countries that defer to the *raison d'etat* with much greater vigor than we do still espouse traditional conflicts ideals. The emphasis of influential Eastern European conflicts commentators on "peaceful coexistence," "equality" and "mutual benefit" at least sounds better than the following passage from an American appellate opinion:

> We are a Court of the United States, an instrumentality created to effectuate the laws and policies of the United States. We conclude that in this case we have no warrant, legal or moral, to frustrate well established American policies by an application of the local policies of a foreign government.[243]

The author of this tribute to the beggar-thy-neighbor principle served on a Circuit that had been admonished by the Supreme Court only three years earlier not to "insist on a parochial concept that all disputes must be resolved under our laws and in our courts."[244] But for the pow-

---

[233]   Currie, [*Selected Essays on the Conflict of Laws* [52-53 (1963)].

[243]   Challoner v. Day and Zimmermann, Inc., 512 F.2d 77, 82 (5th Cir.), vacated and remanded, 423 U.S. 3 (1975).

[244]   The Bremen v. Zapata Off-Shore Co., 407 U.S. 1, 9 (1972).

erful lure of a mischievous doctrine he might have known that an opinion couched in such jingoistic prose would court reversal.

4. The Intractable Personal Law Principle

Since Currie accorded primary importance to the connection between a person and a state, his entire method amounts to little more than a complicated way of saying that the law of the domicile governs. However, exclusive or even primary reliance on a personal nexus poses puzzling problems. First of all, until now the analysts have been unable even to describe with some precision the kind of relationship between a person and a state that is necessary and sufficient to activate governmental interests. Apparently they proceed on the questionable premise that only one state can have a "homelike" interest. One of them has cogently exposed the shortcomings of the domiciliary concept, but he is far less specific about a possible substitute. While domicile may be too technical, "settled residence" is a "clumsy term without precise meaning." Even "home state," an amorphous phrase "used in a deliberate attempt to avoid the complexities of greater precision," hardly fits the situation of jet-setters and migrant laborers. The vaguer the terminology, however, the more complicated the analysis, because with any softening of the definition the number of potentially interested states increases.

Another question the analysts have overlooked is why a person's physical nexus to the state of residence should be more important than the legal and emotional ties to the nation to which that individual owes allegiance. At least in the case of aliens who come from countries that express an interest in their citizens by choosing nationality rather than domicile as the connecting factor, should citizenship be considered irrelevant? Or is a driver's license better evidence of belonging than a passport? Conversely, how can a person's home state be considered "interested" if it indicates its sublime disinterest by refusing to apply its law to foreign events that involve its residents?

Even if all of these difficulties could be surmounted somehow, the personal law principle would still pose intractable problems in two fairly common situations. First, a party may have changed his or her residence after the events that give rise to a lawsuit.* * *

Second, the personal law principle is unsatisfactory whenever the parties to a lawsuit hail from different states. Describing the system of personal laws that prevailed in the early Middle Ages, a medieval author spoke of "five men, each under a different law, . . . walking or sitting together." As the stark facts of *In re Paris Air Crash of March 3, 1974* indicate, modern transportation throws together yet larger crowds from diverse states and nations.* * * Currie proposed to decide the resultant "true conflicts" by recourse to the *lex fori.* * * * But even that jingoistic remedy is no panacea. It does not tell us how to resolve such conflicts in a disinterested forum, and how to deal with the hobgoblin of the "unprovided-for case" in which no state has an interest. The literature on these imaginary problems is bulky; the answers proffered implausible and of little help to busy courts. The analysts' responses are certainly no less bewildering than the traditionalists' endless battles over such problems as *renvoi,* characterization and the incidental question. Currie's major insight was that the territorially-oriented rules he attacked created "problems that did not exist before." It is strange that he never noticed that his personal law principle had precisely the same propensity.

Finally, the home-state preference raises fundamental fairness questions. As Currie realized, to reserve the benefits of local law to local residents may violate the equal protection as well as the privileges and immunities clauses. Several reported cases reveal the problematic nature of the home-state preference, and a recent article by Ely argues that the personal law principle is constitutionally infirm.[262] But even apart from such scruples, it seems unsatisfactory to let justice depend on who sues whom where. Nor can the homestate preference be justified by Currie's "Handmaiden Axiom" that views courts as mere mouthpieces of the legislative will. Even if the judges' role in conflicts cases were in fact that humble, it has been shown convincingly that state legislatures tend not to exclude strangers from the benefits of domestic reforms. Accordingly, there is no reason whatsoever for courts to construe legislation in such a narrow-minded fashion.

5. The *Depecage* Puzzle

Currie's methodology, complex as it is to start with, is further complicated by the requirement of a separate choice-of-law analysis for each issue presented in a multistate case. Such issue-splitting opens up the possibility of *depecage*; i.e., that substantive rules derived from more than one jurisdiction control different aspects of the same transaction. A court may have to piece together an artificial combination of rules from disparate sources, and the resulting construct does not necessarily bear any resemblance to the internal laws of any of the states involved.

Obviously, this possibility should disturb positivists like Currie * * * . The analysts' reaction is understandable: those committed to a method that emphasizes the interests of governments feel uncomfortable about reaching results that none of the "concerned" sovereigns would condone. Yet *depecage* is the price that any issue-oriented approach inevitably exacts. The analysts' discomfort simply reveals an inconsistency in their method: focusing on the policies behind specific rules forces them to disregard whatever interest a state may have in the integrity of its legal system as a whole.

6. Rules After All?

According to the California Supreme Court, the "true function of interest analysis can probably be appreciated only casuistically in its application to an endless variety of choice of law problems."[267] Such judicial candor is refreshing. However, the open avowal of free-form justice is hardly compatible with the role of courts of last resort in a system based on precedent. Neither litigants nor the administration of justice stand to gain if state supreme courts adopt Ambrose Bierce's definition of an appeal, i.e., putting "the dice into the box for another throw." This may explain why some analysts have become sensitive to the charge that their methodology calls for unprincipled decision making. According to one of them stare decisis will ultimately produce rules of choice-of-law, and in tort cases such rules may already have emerged. Another analyst has tried to formulate black letter rules that would resolve conflicts, true and false, as well as the unprovided-for case. Although ventures of this kind contradict Currie's premise that we would be better off without choice-of-law rules, it may indeed be possible to distill the essence from the mass of decided cases that have purported to analyze interests.

---

[262] Ely, [*Choice of Law and the State's Interest in Protecting Its Own*, 23 WM. & MARY L. REV. 173 (1981)].

[267] Bernhard v. Harrah's Club, 16 Cal.3d 313, 321, 546 P.2d 719, 724, 128 Cal.Rptr. 215, 220, cert. denied, 429 U.S. 859 (1976).

While the new learning's vague and abstruse terminology makes it difficult even to read the cases, if one follows Walter Wheeler Cook's advice and pays attention to what courts have done, rather than what they have said they were doing,[272] a clear pattern emerges. The first thing that becomes apparent is that the bulk of recent conflicts decisions deals with tort issues. There are contract cases, but their practical importance is limited. Skilled draftsmen are usually able to avoid subjecting their agreements to the hazards of the conflicts quagmire by appropriate choice-of-law clauses, which can be buttressed with arbitration or forum-selection provisions. Fortunately, the principle of party autonomy has survived the conflicts revolution, for business might well grind to a halt if counsel had to scrutinize each possible issue posed by every agreement they draft to determine the interests and policies of all potentially concerned states. Accordingly, contracts choice-of-law issues will primarily arise in a non-commercial setting or in the case of consumer contracts. Similarly, Art. 9 of the Uniform Commercial Code rescues security interests from the vagaries of interest analysis, and the situs rule still reigns supreme over real property. Party autonomy and the rule of validation prevail in the field of wills and trusts, and marriages as well are customarily upheld, local idiosyncracies notwithstanding. Traditional rules, supplemented by legislation, seem to offer workable solutions for marital property disputes in spite of the fact that the substantive rules vary widely and are in a state of flux. Accordingly, the practical effect of the new learning is largely limited to the area of torts.

The actual results that courts have reached in tort cases can easily be grasped, however convoluted the path judges took to reach them. In almost every case in which courts have resorted to interest analysis they ended up applying forum law. This is hardly surprising, considering that analysts urge judges to apply their own law whenever the forum has some interest, and that judges tend to be more comfortable with their own than with foreign law. Since the forum must have some contacts with the defendant to take the case, and interests are easily conjured up, the state of litigation will rarely be "disinterested." Why then should it be necessary even to consider the multifarious policies of other states and nations? The elaborate conceptual scheme of interest analysis could easily be replaced by a simple rule of non-choice. There is nothing novel or unusual about the *lex fori* principle; it already prevails in the related field of workers' compensation and it may have been the rule in early American tort choice of law. * * * Resurrection of that principle would accurately reflect the holdings of most current tort choice-of-law decisions, and it is simple enough to please busy courts and counsel. It should also satisfy the yen for predictability: as long as the injured party is represented by an artful forum shopper, plaintiff is bound to win. At the same time, that principle should appeal to those analysts who, like Currie, dismiss the relevance of multistate policies out of hand.

It might even be possible to improve on the principle of nonchoice by adding the spice of variety to an otherwise dull rule. The proudest boast of interest analysis is its ability to resolve false conflicts, which in practice means application of the parties' common home state law. Accordingly, a common-domicile rule should be acceptable. To add yet greater diversity, one might think of a re-exception to this qualification of the *lex fori* principle, in the event that the forum is the accident state and provides the victim with a greater measure of protection. Whatever one's preference, it seems possible to reduce the results of the interest analysis to rules. These may not fit the results reached in each and every case that purported to apply the interest approach, but it surely seems justified to disregard occasional deviations (which, after all, may simply be the result of faulty analysis) in favor of some clearcut propositions that

---

[272]   Cook, "The Logical and Legal Bases of the Conflict of Laws," 33 Yale L.J. 457, 460 (1924).

would render cumbersome analysis dispensable. Of course, once there are rules, analysis becomes unnecessary, the analysts are deprived of their stock in trade, the fun and games are over. In fact, if one compares the proposed rules with the immense intellectual effort expended, in thousands of pages, on laying the necessary foundations for such modest propositions, one wonders whether all this revolutionary turmoil was really necessary. The mountains labored mightily only to give birth to a mouse.

Lea Brilmayer, *Interest Analysis and the Myth of Legislative Intent*, 78 MICH. L. REV. 392, 392-393, 397-400, 402-404, 408-411 (1980)*

Modern conflict-of-laws scholarship is the victim of a well-intentioned misrepresentation. Proponents of "governmental interest analysis" have marketed their theory as a species of legislative interpretation, indeed as the definitive approach to construing legislative intent. But while promoted by Brainerd Currie as an antidote to the pernicious metaphysical assumptions that afflicted Beale and the *First Restatement*, interest analysis is in fact nothing of the kind. Interest analysis merely substitutes one set of metaphysical premises for another, leaving the body of conflicts law with a remedy every bit as distressing as the disease it was designed to cure.

Thus far, the interest analysts have been allowed to argue, in effect, "Our method may seem shortsighted and parochial, but it is not the courts' business to second-guess a state legislature." The avowed goal is precise, case-by-case implementation of state statutory policies—loyalty to state policy concerns rather than to "first principles" such as uniformity or predictability. By neglecting to challenge the interest analysts' claims of fidelity to legislative intent, traditionally minded conflicts theorists have by implication left themselves espousing the proposition that a court should decline to honor valid legislative wishes. That posture is unnecessarily vulnerable, conceding the interest analysts far too much. This Article attempts to strip away the defense of mock judicial deference and to criticize governmental interests analysis on its own merits.

* * * * *

Because statutes embodying only regulatory policies are so obviously territorial, their conflict of laws implications are rarely litigated. Regulatory policies, however, are important in conflicts litigation because they are often joined with compensatory or protective policies in a single statute. Regulatory policies are triggered by territorial connecting factors, and protective or compensatory policies by domiciliary ones. The difficult issue, therefore, is what to do when a fact situation triggers one of the interests behind a statute but not the other. What, in other words, should be done when conduct within the state injures a nonresident or when a resident is hurt by conduct outside the state? Apparently, the interest analysts would answer that either the compensatory or the conduct-regulating interest is a sufficient reason to apply forum law. Thus, if the plaintiff is a resident or the tortious conduct occurred within the state, the state has an interest in having its statute applied. This is apparently the reason Currie would have allowed a New Yorker to benefit from New York negligence law even though the accident occurred out of the state: the New York compensatory interest was sufficient. Various cases purporting to apply interest analysis are consistent with this view, and it has been explicitly urged by at least one commentator.

---

*   Reprinted with permission.

Implicit in this calculus of interests are three discernible biases: pro-resident, pro-forum-law, and pro-recovery. The pro-resident bias results from the assumption that protective and compensatory policies of the forum can be invoked only by forum residents. Residents thus have the best of both worlds: they can claim the benefits of these policies in multistate cases without incurring the corresponding costs. The pro-recovery and pro-forum-law biases stem from the assumption that when a statute embodies several policies, any one of them may trigger the finding of an "interest." Thus, a forum statute that embodies regulatory and compensatory policies gives rise to a governmental interest if the plaintiff is a resident of the forum or if the offensive conduct occurred there. This splintering of policies increases the likelihood that the state will have an interest and predisposes the method toward forum law. Furthermore, it creates a bias toward recovery because pro-recovery statutes are the most likely to serve several different policies, namely compensatory and regulatory ones. The plaintiff's power to choose the forum contributes further to the pro-recovery bias; interest analysis permits different courts to reach different results by honoring their respective states' interests, and the plaintiff naturally selects the most favorable forum.

These biases do not bother the interest analysts too much, for the abiding purpose of their theory is case-by-case implementation of state policies. For members of the Currie school, deference to the laws of other jurisdictions and even-handed treatment of nonresidents do not warrant disregard of state substantive goals. Since they think "interests" are the perfect embodiment of legislative intent, the sacrifice of mundane system-coordinating concerns does not distress them. And if their premise is truly sound, their conclusion may be compelling; if interest analysis really holds the key to legislative intent, the sacrifice is not only worthwhile but arguably necessary.

Why do the interest analysts claim that their theory satisfies legislative desires? Saying it's so doesn't make it so. Most traditionally minded theorists would agree that any explicit legislative instructions should be followed; but the problem is what to do when the face of the statute is silent. What sort of evidence would interest analysts use to justify their inferences?

Currie did not envision extensive reliance upon legislative history. Many states do not even publish legislative histories, and those that do rarely document the legislators' views on territorial reach. Currie reached his solutions by generalizing about classes of statutes (married women's contract laws; for instance), apparently assuming that unless otherwise indicated in the statute the policies behind all such statutes could be treated as identical. This assumption alone should make us suspicious about whether Currie was deducing true legislative intent, which one might expect to vary from state to state. It suggests that Currie's principles of inference were rather a product of his own normative beliefs about how far certain policies *ought* to reach.

* * * * *

Interest analysis must therefore be some species of constructive intent: a calculus of *a priori* principles that a court may fall back on when the legislature gives no guidance. Only if this conclusion is correct do interest analysts have a normative base from which to criticize conflicts statutes—for one's approach to constructive intent would probably be to choose what one finds to be the most coherent and convincing theory. This interpretation forces the interest analysts to concede that they reason from *a priori* assumptions, but at least it explains how they are able to draw inferences from a seemingly silent statute, like rabbits from a hat.

* * *

Opponents of interest analysis have frequently objected that the theory allows unpredictable results: that persons who act in reliance on one state's laws may be unfairly surprised by application of another's. One cause of this unpredictability is the assumption that when a statute evidences both a regulatory policy and a compensatory or protective policy, either would suffice to justify application of forum law. Thus, a statute that embodies a strong regulatory policy together with a compensatory policy may be applied on the ground that the plaintiff is a forum resident, a fact that the defendant might well have been unable to ascertain at the time of conduct. This is problematic, since in enacting a regulatory statute a legislature manifests a belief that most people will change their behavior in contemplation of the law. It seems unjust to apply such a law to persons who could have had no notice of the applicable standards, since the legislature could not have expected them to change their conduct to conform. The resulting unfairness can be demonstrated by two hypothetical situations.

Dram-shop acts are statutes that prohibit the sale of liquor to inebriates; some states have interpreted them also to authorize recovery of civil damages from the tavern owner if the inebriate negligently injures someone later. It seems clear under interest analysis that dram shop acts, so interpreted, embody both regulatory and compensatory policies. The compensatory policy seems implicit in the reasoning courts have used to justify imputing civil liability. The regulatory policy is evident both because the statutes make sale of liquor to inebriates illegal and because presumably anyone, resident or nonresident, could sue a tavern owner who made such a sale within the state.

If either of the two policies is a sufficient basis for applying a dram-shop act, then civil liability is appropriate whenever the sale occurs within the state or a state resident is injured. Interest analysis would thus seem to imply that if while on vacation in a state with no dram-shop act, a forum resident is hit by an auto careening out of a local bar's parking lot, then he may return home, sue, and recover from the tavern owner. There may be interest analysts who would not flinch at this result, since the forum has an "interest" in seeing its plaintiff compensated. These theorists would not mind that the tavern owner was surprised by application of forum law, since state courts are not in the business to take pity on dismayed nonresidents, but rather to do as their legislature bids. The legislative command, presumably, is "Thou shalt compensate forum residents."

A second hypothetical, however, indicates that residents, too, may be trapped by the interest analysts' logic. Assume that the forum legislature has learned that installing a special safety guard would reduce the number of accidents caused by power lawn mowers. It orders manufacturers to install the guard on all new mowers and provides that noncompliance shall be negligence per se. A resident manufacturer diligently complies when manufacturing lawn mowers to be sold within the state. The safety guard is expensive, however, and he decides not to put himself at a competitive disadvantage by installing them on mowers he manufactures for sale and use in other states. "After all," he reasons, "my state legislature would have no desire to regulate my sales in other jurisdictions. That's interstate commerce." Will the forum nevertheless apply the negligence per se provision if the person injured in an out-of-state accident turns out, coincidentally, to be a resident? It is unlikely that an interest analyst scholar or a court would go so far. But if not, why not?

* * * * *

A second objection to the interest analysts' methodology is its parochialism, for interest analysis assumes that protective and compensatory policies are intended to benefit residents alone. The consequences of such an assumption are scarcely even-handed. For example, suppose the forum has an automobile guest statute—one requiring a passenger to demonstrate reckless or willful misconduct in order to recover from a host driver. Interest analysis holds that in a negligence action brought by a passenger who is a resident of the forum, a nonresident driver cannot claim the benefit of forum law and require a showing of reckless or willful misconduct. If, however, the nonresident had been the passenger and the resident had been driving, the forum would have an "interest" in applying its guest statute. The out-of-stater must pay if he is the driver but cannot collect if he is the passenger.

Limiting the reach of protective and compensatory statutes to precisely those cases where they benefit residents can lead to other obnoxious results. Suppose, for example, that state A has a statute of frauds provision: according to interest analysis, it was designed to protect the residents of A. Anderson, a merchant from state A, contracts with Becker from state B; the contract does not satisfy A's statute of frauds, but under the law of B it would be binding. Suppose Anderson wants to know if the contract is valid in state A. An interest analyst could not give a straight answer. The contract could be either valid or invalid since A's "interest" in having its statute of frauds applied depends upon which party is seeking to enforce the contract. If Anderson is suing Becker, then A has no interest in supplying a protective defense. If, on the other hand, Becker sues Anderson, state A will have an interest in asserting its statute of frauds on his behalf. State A has, in effect, given its residents the power to bind parties from out of state to a contract without being bound themselves.

In other situations, faithful adherence to interest analysis would require a court to browse through the laws of the states involved in the controversy to pick the one that best served the resident party. Assume that Anderson is injured by a toy designed and manufactured by Billings in state B. Anderson thinks Billings was negligent in designing the product. An A statute provides tort compensation for damages from negligent manufacture, which has been interpreted to include defective design. Does A have an interest in having its law applied? As in the previous example, the answer must be "it depends." If B law excludes recovery for defects in design, then A has an interest in securing compensation for Anderson under its own law, for A's law appears to have a compensatory purpose that makes it applicable to help Anderson. But if B is a strict liability state with no exclusion for design defects, A's interest would vanish since it is no longer to Anderson's advantage that A law apply. In comparison to strict liability, a negligence system appears designed to protect manufacturers, and in this case the manufacturer is from out of state. "Interest" under the Currie approach amounts to an "interest" in getting the best deal possible for the resident party by choosing the most favorable law.

The difficulty with Currie's approach is not its reference to domiciliary factors. If a state declared that its products liability law applied to all injured residents, the problem outlined above would be avoided. Either there would be an interest or there would not, and it would not depend upon comparison with other states' laws. But such a statute would not always benefit forum residents. It would benefit them in some cases and harm them in others. Thus, such a rational statute is irreconcilable with the superficially plausible syllogism that seems to underlie Currie's approach: if a statute is designed to benefit forum residents, it should be applied only when a resident will benefit.

Why should a court accept the suggestion that protective and compensatory policies should be applied only when a forum resident will benefit? The blatant parochialism evidenced by these examples surely imposes costs. It jeopardizes a principle essential to smooth functioning of federal systems: treating nonresidents as fairly as residents. It also raises difficult problems of whether an individual ought to be able to get a change of law by deliberately aquiring a new domicile after the transaction in question occurs. Moreover, these costs might easily be avoided through a more comprehensive investigation of legislative intent, one that projects into the legislative mind some sensitivity to system-coordinating values. * * *

* * * * *

Aaron D. Twerski, Neumeier v. Kuehner: *Where are the Emperor's Clothes?*, 1 Hofstra L. Rev. 104, 106-108 (1973)*

*Neumeier[v. Kuehner]*** presented the New York Court of Appeals for the first time with a choice-of-law case in which, under traditional analysis, neither of the contact states had a legitimate governmental interest. How did this strange result come to pass? It was very simple indeed. In *Neumeier* the defendant was a New York resident who travelled from Buffalo, New York to Ontario, Canada. In Fort Erie, Ontario, he picked up his guest, Neumeier, an Ontario resident. Their trip was to take them to Long Beach, also in Ontario, and back again to Neumeier's home in Fort Erie. On the way to Long Beach, at a railroad crossing, the defendant Kuehner's car was struck by a train. Both the host and his guest passenger were killed in the collision.

This simple fact pattern, superimposed on the legal positions of New York and Ontario as to host-guest liability, was destined to produce an anomalous situation. New York, as we all know, has no host-guest statute. Ontario, on the other hand, requires a guest to prove gross negligence against his host in order to recover. Under interest analysis in order to determine whether there is a true policy conflict one must examine the policies supporting the supposedly conflicting rules. Traditional analysis would lead a court to conclude that New York's policy favoring compensation is not relevant since New York is primarily concerned with the welfare of its domiciliaries. Since the plaintiff is an Ontario domiciliary New York really has no stake or interest as to whether the plaintiff recovers. Conversely, the Ontario host-guest statute has no necessary claim to application. Numerous rationales have been offered for host-guest statutes. Whether the reason be that they were designed to protect insurance companies from host-guest collusion or to protect hosts from ungrateful guests it is clear that Ontario has no strong reason to opt for the operation of the host-guest statute in this instance. The defendant is a New Yorker and if the policies of Ontario's host-guest statute are to protect Ontario domiciliaries or insurance companies doing business in Ontario, then Ontario could care little if compensation were offered off the back of a New York defendant. The late Professor Brainerd Currie, when faced with this kind of dilemma, was quite direct as to its implication. He said: "This is the 'unprovided for case' in a very special sense. Neither state cares what happens."[9] Realizing that this statement was somewhat shocking, Currie went on to defend this position:[10]

> It may be that the laws of neither state, nor of both states together, purport to dispose of the entire universe of possible cases. Identical laws do not necessarily mean identical policies, and different laws do not necessarily mean conflicting policies, when it is remembered that the scope of policy is limited by the legitimate interests of the respective states.

---

*   Reprinted with the permission of the Hofstra Law Review.

**   [31 N.Y.2d 121, 286 N.E.2d 454, 335 N.Y.S.2d 64 (1972).]

[9]   B[RAINED] CURRIE, SURVIVAL OF ACTIONS: ADJUDICATION VERSUS AUTOMATION IN THE CONFLICT OF LAWS, *in* SELECTED ESSAYS ON THE CONFLICT OF LAWS 152 (1963).* * *

[10]   B. CURRIE, *supra* note 9, at 153.

The net result of all this is that the methodology of interest analysis tells the court that it has before it a simple interstate auto accident case for which neither state has any relevant policy. When Currie said that "traditionalists may stand aghast at this anomaly"[11] he understated the reaction considerably. Is it really possible for rational people to conclude that neither New York nor Ontario has any concern with the outcome of this commonplace accident phenomenon? It defies belief. Only the almost mesmerizing effect of the brilliant Currie writing prevented this statement from being subjected to the strongest ridicule.

Why is it that interest analysis met its Waterloo with the advent of the unprovided for case? The answer as this author sees it is rather elementary. In evaluating interests Currie and his academic followers placed tremendous emphasis on the *interest of the domicile state of the parties in granting or denying recovery*. For example, whenever plaintiff hailed from a state granting recovery and defendant was domiciled in a state denying recovery the interest analysts claimed that there was an irreconcilable conflict. After all doesn't the domicile state of one party want him to recover and the domicile state of the other party seek to deny recovery? There was rarely any attempt to view the policies behind these rules in broader perspective. They either protected a domiciliary interest or did not. It was as simple as all that.

In an unprovided for case like *Neumeier* we face a situation where there are no domiciliary interests to protect on the part of the contact states. New York has no domiciliary interests to protect by its pro-compensation rule since the plaintiff is not a New Yorker. Ontario has no domiciliary interests to protect by its anti-compensation rule because the defendant is not an Ontario domiciliary. Thus, the entire structure of interest analysis crumbled. Having defined the interests as domiciliary oriented when you run out of domiciliaries to protect you run out of interests. The emperor indeed stands naked for all to see.

* * * * *

Comments

1.   The belief shared by the contributors in Part A of this Chapter, that it is often impossible to determine the intended reach of substantive rules, has additional adherents. One of the most forceful was the late Professor Maurice Rosenberg, who wrote:

> Searching for governmental interests presupposes that the purposes behind substantive rules are so clear, so singular, so unequivocal that we can hope to discover them with some certainty and some consensus. This is at odds with reality. Even the simple rules that raise rights and duties with regard to personal injuries are a composite of thrusts and counter-thrusts of many kinds. For instance, there are many substantive rules favoring recovery for negligent injuries; but contributory negligence, assumption of risk, workmen's compensation exclusions and other rules are opposed to recovery. To try to bring all the huffing and puffing together into a policy that runs clearly in one direction and that has a measurable intensity that permits comparing it with some contrary policy is, in my judgment, pure fantasy.

Rosenberg 1967a: p. 464.

---

[11]   *Id*. at 152.

2. Another distinguished commentator decried what he saw to be the "irresistible urge" of many interest analysts "to impute to virtually every legal norm some underlying concrete social or political purpose." He further observed:

> The intellectual premise of such a process may become rather shaky as one encounters legal rules whose supporting policy goals are obscure, cumulative, or even contradictory. In the absence of reliable information as to the intended policy function of the legal norm in question, the process may readily degenerate into a speculative postulation, or even fabrication, of putative underlying policies, solely on the ground of their assumed plausibility.

Shapira 1977: p. 262. Other commentators have suggested the process of determining government interest by ascertaining the purpose of a substantive rule becomes even more uncertain when the rule is from a foreign country rather than a sister state. Kahn-Freund 1968: pp. 60-61; Zweigert 1973: pp. 288-289.

3. The geographical facts most often important in interest analysis are the litigants' places of domicile. In torts cases, plaintiff's domicile in a pro-recovery state or defendant's domicile in an anti-recovery state will often make those states "interested" places. Professors Kozyris, Juenger and Brilmayer maintained in Part A that interest analysis inevitably leads judges to parochialism. That is, the party domiciled in the forum who is advantaged by local law (usually plaintiff) receives preferential treatment. The resulting choice-of-law imbalance is pernicious, say these critics, because it wrongs parties urging the application of non-forum law, discredits the judicial process, and encourages forum shopping. Similar arguments have been made by other commentators. *See, e.g.,* Corr 1983; Ely 1981; Laycock 1992.

4. In Part B, Professors Seidelson and Weintraub will dispute the notion that interest analysis invariably favors the interested forum in true conflicts. With other commentators, they maintain that interest analysis can support a forum-neutral, balancing approach to choice of law. Professors Kozyris and Juenger raised and rejected this possibility in Part A. Their view is shared by Bliesener 1994: pp. 704-705; Brilmayer 1995a: p. 477; Ely 1981: p. 175. Other writers have made related points. Borchers 1992a: p. 382 ("lifelong observers of American choice-of-law decisions may be able to detect that most recent cases can be explained by a desire to apply prorecovery forum rules * * * "); Solimine 1989: p. 56 (suggesting the tendency under modern conflicts decisions that "a forum state resolves a true conflict by using its own law, which inevitably favors the forum-shopping plaintiff.").

5. A different kind of criticism of interest analysis may be found in the writing of Judge Richard Posner. Judge Posner writes that reforms in conflict of laws based on interest analysis "appear to have miscarried." Posner 1987: p. 769. The author indicates that the current concept of "interests" in choice of law is at odds with the his law-and-economics approach to the subject. Posner 1985: pp. 304-307; Posner 1992: pp. 587-588.

B. Defenders

Russell J. Weintraub, *A Defense of Interest Analysis in the Conflict of Laws and the Use of that Analysis in Products Liability*, 46 OHIO ST. L.J. 493, 493-503 (1985)*

I return to the field in defense of interest analysis. It is ironic that I should be regarded as a champion of that cause. Brainerd Currie's most charitable characterization of my work would doubtless be heresy. I have spent a good deal of time attempting to articulate forum-neutral solutions to two problems—the true conflict and the unprovided-for case—that he would resolve by application of forum law. Furthermore, identification of the policies underlying domestic laws is not the Alpha and Omega of conflicts analysis. Giving effect to transjurisdictional policies, including the purposes of choice of law, is equally important. Currie and I agree only on the following points: the policies represented by domestic rules can be useful guides in resolving choice-of-law problems; and the conflict of laws should join the mainstream of legal reasoning. It is these propositions that this article will defend; the exposition of Currie's viewpoints will be left to his own superbly crafted articles. This article will first respond to the most common criticisms of basing conflicts decisions on policies underlying domestic rules. * * *

* * * * *

A. *Difficulty of Determining What Policies Underlie a Rule*

Many critics of interest analysis contend that it is difficult or impossible to determine the policies underlying a particular domestic rule. The rule may result from the compromise of competing purposes or may embody no discernible policy at all. Moreover, states do not have interests in litigation between private parties.

The objection that it is difficult to determine the purposes of a rule is the most surprising criticism. There is nothing new or remarkable about the proposition that legal rules have purposes which can be identified. Even in purely local cases, an intelligent decision to apply a rule in a marginal situation (one that does not clearly fall within or without the scope of a rule) depends upon knowing the reasons for the rule. These reasons are not always easy to identify, and sometimes there will be disagreement over them. However, before a rule is applied, the purposes of the rule should be discerned.

When choice-of-law analysis focuses on the reasons underlying putatively conflicting domestic rules, it simply mirrors the form of intelligent analysis employed in all fields of law. Cardozo observed that, under the territorial rules of his day, the conflict of laws was "one of the most baffling subjects of legal science" in which "fundamental conceptions have been developed to their uttermost conclusions by the organon of logic." He indicated his discomfort with the state of conflicts thinking: "[W]hen I view the [conflict of laws] as a whole, I find logic to have been more remorseless here, more blind to final causes, than it has been in other fields. Very likely it has been too remorseless." Cardozo's use of the phrase "too remorseless" indi-

---

*   Reprinted with permission.

cates that he believed conflicts analysis had departed from the flexible policy-oriented approach that wise judges used in other areas. * * *

* * *

The argument is sometimes made that even if determining the purposes underlying domestic rules is feasible in interstate conflicts, it is not practicable in international conflicts because the judge of one country is not likely to understand the purposes of the laws of a nation with an entirely different legal system. The difficulty of finding the policies represented by foreign rules is overstated. Familiarity with other legal systems grows apace. Furthermore, judges have the assistance of counsel who have the time and incentive to make the necessary inquiries and to obtain expert assistance. The greatest flaw in the argument distinguishing international cases from interstate conflicts is that the argument is not for territorial choice of law, but for forum law. The court should not apply foreign law if it does not understand the purposes of that law. Wooden application of misunderstood foreign law is far more likely to result in injustice than the application of forum law.

As for objection to the term "state interests," it refers to the purposes underlying a law of that state. It is probably a needlessly confusing term. I prefer "functional analysis" to "interest analysis."

B. *The Territorial Reach of Policies Is Not Self-Evident*

Another criticism of interest analysis is that even if the purposes of a rule can be discovered, the rule's geographical reach is not apparent. There still must be a territorial connecting factor. The fault with this criticism is that the purposes underlying a rule reveal the social consequences that the rule is designed either to foster or to avoid. Lawyers and judges can determine whether, in the light of a state's contacts with the parties or with the transaction, those consequences will be experienced there if its law is not applied.

If one woke up in the morning with a blank mind, set out to discover the world, and turned to the conflict of laws, he or she would probably create a territorial system; any other method is counter-intuitive. It is easy to conclude that each jurisdiction's law *ought* to apply only to events within it. When pressed for an explanation of the system, one would say, "If a state or nation cannot determine the rules that apply to events that take place within its borders, social consequences would occur there that the state or nation had designed its law to prevent." Once that is said, however, the whole system would crumble. A little reflection would reveal that application of situs law would sometimes cause social consequences elsewhere, while failure to apply lex loci would have no local effects. There are few "nevers" in any rational system of jurisprudence, but there is one candidate: if personal injury is caused by unintentional conduct and the place of injury has no other contacts with the parties, applying the law of the place of injury never will advance the purpose of its rule that denies or limits recovery.

C. *Uncertainty of Result*

Another argument against interest analysis is that a functional analysis, resting on the shifting sands of policy, can lead to chaos. Territorially oriented choice-of-law rules, on the other hand, have the virtue of certainty. A famous series of New York decisions dealing with the application of the "guest" statutes of other jurisdictions, which limit a guest passenger's right to recover against a host driver, illustrates the confusion that can occur when functional analysis is misunderstood. In desperation, the New York Court of Appeals adopted three rules that would thereafter apply to guest statute cases. Rule three, the catchall provision, is a thinly disguised version of the old place-of-wrong rule. If this can occur in New York, which led the judicial revolt against territorial choice-of-law rules, it can, and probably will, happen anywhere.

The New York experience is not a necessary concomitant of adopting a functional conflicts analysis. It is the inevitable result of both misunderstanding and misapplying policy analysis. In the strangest of the New York line of cases, *Dym v. Gordon*,[17] the court applied a Colorado guest statute to deny recovery to a New York guest suing a New York host although New York law would have made the host liable for negligence. In order to work this magic, the New York Court of Appeals had to violate the central teaching of functional analysis. It invented a purpose underlying the Colorado statute that had never before been stated—the preservation of the host's liability insurance proceeds for compensation of occupants of automobiles with which the host collides.

There are certain desirable attributes of any legal system. The characteristics most pertinent to the present discussion are predictability of results, just results, and accessibility. These three characteristics are related, and there is likely to be tension between them. Predictability is necessary to plan transactions and, when disputes arise, to facilitate settlement. Predictability also reduces the cost and complexity of litigation. Justice is important because it is unlikely that any legal rule, no matter how easy to apply, will long survive if it produces results that are perceived to be unjust. The results will be unjust if they are poor responses to the social problem to which the rule is addressed. Accessibility is necessary if the legal system is not to serve only the wealthy and the privileged. Tension is likely to arise between the need for just results on one hand and predictability and accessibility on the other. The more we try to mold each decision to fit the particular circumstances of a case, the less predictable and more costly the administration of justice is likely to become.

The solution to this problem lies in functional rules that are satisfactory responses to underlying social problems and that also yield reasonable predictability when administered by the members of a learned profession. It may well be that there is no other solution. In a system based on case law and precedent, the only reliable rule may be one that summarizes a series of just and reasonable decisions.

The rigid and simple territorial choice-of-law rules seemed child's play to apply. If, for example, the tort rule was place-of-wrong, the court could stick a pin in the map where the plaintiff was injured, find the tort law of that place, and apply it. But intelligent lawyers and judges who unhappy with the result thus obtained found ways around the mechanical rule. Characterization tricks could be played. What was alleged to be a "tort" problem could have its label switched to "procedural" so that the law of the forum rather than of the place of injury applied. This was formerly fairly common in the United States with an issue as important as the measure of damages for tortious injury and is still found in English decisions. Lawyers and judges also circumvented the rule by putting a different substantive label on the problem so that a new territorial rule would emerge and point to a place other than where injury occurred. "Tort" could change in this way, for example, to "contract," or "family law," or "administration of estates." As a last resort, the "public policy" doctrine could preclude application of the law selected by the forum's choice-of-law rule.

<hr />

[17]   16 N.Y.2d 120, 209 N.E.2d 792, 262 N.Y.S.2d 463 (1965).

The reason for recharacterization is that important policies underlying a law not selected by the territorial rule will be impaired and policies of the law selected are either not relevant or should yield. If, as is typical of the label-switching opinions, this reason is not stated, the recharacterization appears arbitrary and the results are unpredictable—far less predictable than they would be under a rule that originally directed attention to maximum accommodation of policies underlying the domestic laws of contact states. A functional approach moves public policy to the foreground to shape the original selection of governing law instead of serving as a last-minute escape from that choice.

There is no reason why functional choice-of-law rules that take account of the purposes of conflicting domestic laws and that also produce reasonably predictable results cannot be stated. Once the different policies of two or more jurisdictions are implicated, the conflict between them should be resolved by result-oriented presumptions. Examples are, for torts, a presumption that the law favorable to the plaintiff should be applied and, for contracts, a presumption that the law that validates the contract should be applied. These presumptions are not pulled out of the air. They reflect widely shared trends in the development of the substantive area involved and in transjurisdictional policies. Moreover, the presumptions as to results are rebuttable. The factors that might rebut them are drawn from the same transjurisdictional trends and policies that formed the basis for the original presumption. Examples are denial of tort recovery for injury to an employee and refusal to validate contracts of adhesion. The rule I propose to govern choice of law for contract validity is: *A contract is valid if valid under the law of the settled place of business or residence of the party wishing to enforce the contract unless the settled place of business or residence of the other party has an invalidating rule designed to protect against contracts of adhesion.* This rule is one that can be administered by judges and lawyers in a way that will yield an acceptable degree of predictability of results and will respond satisfactorily to almost all transjurisdictional contract cases. There are, to be sure, other factors that will affect the proper response to a conflict concerning the validity of a contract. There may be strong rules invalidating contracts that are illegal or immoral even though they are not contracts of adhesion. But the rule I suggest will work well in almost all cases and, when it does not, other relevant factors can be stated as exceptions to this broad validating rule.

D. *Forum Preference for Its Own Law*

It has been charged that functional analysis, particularly the aspect of it that focuses on the policies underlying domestic rules, is a circumlocution for applying the law of the forum. As a practical matter, a court using this method will find a sufficient forum interest to make forum law relevant and then will resolve any clash between forum and foreign policies by finding that forum law is "better."

There is evidence to support this charge. Probably the most notorious example is *Lilienthal v. Kaufman*.[31] This 1964 Oregon Supreme Court opinion refused to enforce the commercial indebtedness of an Oregon resident when suit was brought by a California creditor. Under a unique Oregon procedure, the debtor had been declared a spendthrift. A guardian was appointed, and the guardian exercised his power to avoid the obligation. The Oregon debtor had traveled to California to borrow the money to finance a business venture, and the California

---

[31]   239 Or. 1, 395 P.2d 543 (1964).

creditor was unaware of the debtor's "spendthrift" status. The court resolved the clash between Oregon and California policies by explicitly adopting a forum-preference rule saying "[w]e are of the opinion that in such a case the public policy of Oregon should prevail and the law of Oregon should be applied . . . ." The result has been widely condemned and is probably wrong because the invalidating Oregon rule was aberrational, the California creditor was unfairly surprised, and the preferred transjurisdictional solution would have been to validate this commercial agreement.

But *Lilienthal* is not an example of a decision in which forum law was declared "better." The court was applying Currie's mandate that in the event of a true clash between forum and foreign objectives, forum law should prevail. The court quickly abandoned this notion in a tort case decided three years later. The court probably leaned too far in the opposite direction by denying an Oregon wife damages for injuries to her husband in the course of his employment in Washington. Oregon law gave her the right to recover, but Washington law did not. There would have been no unfair surprise to the Washington employer in holding it liable under the law of the state where the employee resided and where the employer was licensed to do business. The court stated that "state chauvinism and interstate retaliation are dangers to be avoided."

Conklin v. Horner[36] is a classic example of interest fabrication coupled with preference for "better" forum law. That case involved an Illinois host and guest and a crash in Wisconsin. Illinois had a guest statute which would have barred the action by the passenger, but Wisconsin law permitted recovery. The Wisconsin Supreme Court found three Wisconsin policies that would be advanced by permitting recovery: compensation of the injured guest, avoidance of loss to Wisconsin taxpayers or medical creditors, and deterrence of negligent driving in Wisconsin. The compensation policy is simply another way of saying that Wisconsin law should be manna for the injured of the world even though the social consequences of failure to compensate are likely to be experienced in Illinois, which had contrary policies. This is the antithesis of interest analysis. Preventing the cost of medical treatment from falling on Wisconsin taxpayers or doctors is a legitimate concern, but first there should be some showing that, on the facts of *Conklin*, these evils were likely to occur. The contention that the increased chances of civil recovery will make Illinois hosts drive more carefully in Wisconsin is untenable.

Even though *Conklin* was criticized as a distortion of interest analysis, the court did not alter its opinion. In *Hunker v. Royal Indemnity Company*,[39] criticisms of *Conklin* were dismissed as "naive." *Hunker* itself, however, showed that the Wisconsin court would not invariably prefer its own law. In *Hunker*, two Ohio residents were driving in Wisconsin in the course of their employment. After a crash in Wisconsin, the passenger brought a direct action against his fellow employee's liability insurer. Under Ohio law, worker's compensation was the sole remedy, but under Wisconsin law, tort recovery was available. Despite its finding that Ohio and Wisconsin were "both interested jurisdictions," the court applied Ohio law and barred suit. *Conklin* was distinguished as follows:

> The bar of co-employees' actions does not represent merely past thinking. The trend, to the extent that it is discernible, appears to be toward barring these actions rather than permitting them. We cannot conclude, as we did in . . . *Conklin*, that Wisconsin's rule of liability unmistakably represents the better law.[42]

---

[36]   38 Wis. 2d 468, 157 N.W.2d 579 (1968).

[39]   57 Wis. 2d 588, 204 N.W.2d 897 (1973).

[42]   *Id.* at 610, 204 N.W.2d at 908.

Thus, forum preference is not the rule, even in the home of *Conklin v. Horner.*

Another case in which the court used interest analysis and resolved a clash of state policies in favor of the law of a sister state is *Offshore Rental Company v. Continental Oil Company.*[43] A California employer sued a Louisiana company for injury in Louisiana to a key employee. A California statute arguably provided a cause of action for resulting losses to the employer, but no recovery was available under Louisiana law. The California Supreme Court resolved the "true conflict" between California and Louisiana policies in favor of the "stronger, more current interest of Louisiana."

A similar result was reached by the Minnesota Supreme Court in *Bigelow v. Halloran.*[46] The plaintiff lived in Iowa at the time she was shot by her Minnesota boyfriend, who then turned the gun on himself and committed suicide. After she moved to Minnesota, the plaintiff brought suit against her assailant's estate. Under Minnesota law, the action for an intentional tort was terminated by defendant's death, but the claim survived under Iowa law. The court found that "the governmental interests test prove[d] to be inconclusive" because both Iowa and Minnesota policies were implicated. However, the court resolved the conflict in favor of Iowa law as the "better rule" because it was more in accord with trends in the law of survival of actions.

Cipolla v. Shaposka[49] also belies the inevitability of forum preference. Two young men, one from Delaware and one from Pennsylvania, attended school in Delaware. At the end of the school day, the Delaware resident was driving his friend home to Pennsylvania. The car crashed in Delaware. Under Delaware law, the host driver was not liable for his ordinary negligence, but he was liable under Pennsylvania law. A majority of the Pennsylvania Supreme Court resolved the "true conflict" in favor of Delaware law on the ground that the Delaware defendant "should not be put in jeopardy of liability exceeding that created by [his] state's laws just because a visitor from a state offering higher protection decides to visit there." The opposite result should have been reached. The host intended to drive into Pennsylvania. Thus, Pennsylvania had a reasonable nexus with defendant's course of conduct, and, although it was less clear at the time of the case in 1970 than it is today, the Delaware guest statute should have yielded to the Pennsylvania rule which better tracked current liability developments. But whether or not one agrees with the result, *Cipolla* is further evidence that interest analysis is not another way of saying "forum law applies and our resident wins."

The clearest example of a court inventing a nonexistent interest is *Dym v. Gordon*, the guest-statute case in which the New York Court of Appeals, rather than manipulating the analysis to apply forum law, managed to apply Colorado law to deprive one New Yorker of recovery against another.

When one turns to transjurisdictional commercial contracts, the cases are legion in which a forum has upheld an agreement under foreign law against a local defendant. This is so common a result in usury cases that, according to the Second Restatement, validation is the rule. The Restatement would have better reflected the results reached in adjudication if it had taken validation as its basic rule for all contract issues.

---

[43]   22 Cal. 3d 157, 583 P.2d 721, 148 Cal. Rptr. 867 (1978).

[46]   313 N.W.2d 10 (Minn. 1981).

[49]   439 Pa. 563, 267 A.2d 854 (1970).

E. *Interest Analysis Focuses on Domicile at a Time of Great Population Mobility*

It has also been charged that policy analysis is really a complex way of saying that each jurisdiction is interested in making the benefits of its law available to its own citizens but not to others. This not only raises grave questions of unfair discrimination, but also focuses on domicile at a time of unprecedented population mobility.

It is true that insofar as social consequences of applying law are likely to be experienced where the parties live, interest analysis does focus on residence. But there are other contacts that are relevant to policies underlying local law. For example, the place where the defendant acts may have a rule designed to deter his conduct. If so, the purpose of that rule will be advanced by applying it even though none of the parties resides there. It is necessary, however, to be realistic about whether a rule permitting recovery of civil damages will shape conduct. It is unlikely that such a rule will deter negligent driving. If the driver is not made careful by the risk to his life and the lives of his loved ones, or by the threat of criminal punishment, it is unrealistic to think that when he crosses the state line he will say to himself, "I'd better slow down; this state permits guests to recover against their hosts."

Mobility is not as great a problem when dealing with companies as opposed to individuals, and even with individuals there are ways to avoid unfair discrimination against foreigners and to take account of mobility.

First, the benefits of local law should be made available to a nonresident when this will not offend any policy of his state and will accord with the forum's view of appropriate social responsibility. For example, a host driver should be liable to his guest if liable under the law of the host's residence, even if there is no liability under the law of the guest's residence or the place of injury. This will make residents of the host's state responsible loss distributors, and courts in that state should not be so callous as to wish to implement this policy only when their own residents are injured. Certainly the guest's residence will not object to his recovery. And if the guest later moves to the host's state, application of its law has cast bread upon the waters.

Second, mobility should be taken account of directly. In each case, the question of how likely it is that social consequences will be experienced in a state other than the one in which the parties resided at the time of the occurrence should be addressed. Moves that have occurred between the event and decision of the case should be considered, subject to the caveat that doing so should not encourage house shopping, deter a move otherwise in a party's best interest, or be unfair to the other party.

F. *Depecage*

"Depecage" refers to the application of the laws of different states to separate issues in the same case. The problem existed under territorial choice-of-law rules. Many outcome determinative rules were dysfunctionally characterized as "procedural." This was a shorthand way of saying that the law of the forum applied, although the law of another state applied to "substantive" issues. Even with regard to admittedly substantive issues, territorial rules could point in different directions. In products liability cases, for example, the law of the place of injury applied to tort counts and the law of the place where the sales contract was made applied to warranty counts.

In some respects interest analysis will lessen the likelihood of depecage. When adjudicating products liability cases, courts will not automatically be pointed in different directions just because physical injury occurred outside the state of sale. It is true, however, that, on balance, policy analysis may increase the incidence of depecage. Every law in putative conflict requires separate analysis concerning its underlying purposes and the territorial reach of those policies.

In this as in all other matters, there is no substitute for perspicacity and common sense. If depecage produces a result different from the one that would be reached under the law of any jurisdiction, this may be either a superior accommodation of state policies or a horrible and unfair distortion of those policies. In a products liability suit, for example, it may be that the victim is entitled to the generous compensation policies of his domicile if that state has sufficient contacts with the defendant or the defendant's course of conduct to make application of its law fair. It is less justifiable to apply the punitive damages rules of the victim's home state if they permit recovery when none would be permitted in any state where the defendant acted. In a case like *Kilberg v. Northeast Airlines*,[64] however, it is not sensible to apply the degree-of-culpability measure of wrongful death recovery in force at the place of the crash but remove the statutory limit on that recovery. This is likely to produce a higher recovery than would be available under the law of any contact state, advance the policies of none of these states, and therefore be unfair to the defendant.

* * * * *

Robert A. Sedler, *Reflections on Conflict-of-Laws Methodology*, 32 HASTINGS L.J. 1628, 1628-1635 (1981)*

A Tenable Approach for Deciding Choice-of-Law Issues

I have long held the view that the interest analysis regimen, as developed by the late Brainerd Currie, is the preferred approach to resolving conflict of laws because it will provide functionally sound solutions to the choice-of-law issues that arise in actual cases. I also maintain that, in practice, the courts that have abandoned the traditional approach generally employ interest analysis to resolve choice-of-law issues regardless of which "modern" approach to choice of law they are purportedly following. Moreover, in the case of what Professor Currie terms the "true" conflict—the situation in which both the forum and the other involved state each has a real interest in applying its own law in order to implement the policy reflected in that law—the forum, again regardless of its purported method for dealing with the true conflict, will generally apply its own law.

The validity of any approach of law must be tested against the results that it produces in actual litigation. Academic commentators generally agree that the results reached by the courts when dealing with choice-of-law issues are for the most part functionally sound and fair. The disagreement is over which approach the courts should adopt, and the criticism tends to focus much more on the rationale of the courts' decisions than on the decisions themselves. If it is conceded that the courts generally do reach functionally sound results, and if in practice the courts generally are employing interest analysis regardless of their formal pronouncements, then the validity of interest analysis as an approach to choice of law, I would submit, has been empirically demonstrated.

---

[64]   9 N.Y.2d 34, 172 N.E. .2d 526, 211 N.Y.S.2d 133 (1961).

I have always believed that academic commentators tend to take an unduly complex view of the choice-of-law process, and this view sometimes carries over to the courts when they try to provide a rationale for their choice-of-law decisions. Interest analysis has the effect of *simplifying* the choice-of-law process by focusing on the policies reflected in a state's rules of substantive law. This is the same focus a court must have when dealing with the application of a rule of substantive law in a domestic case.

The simplifying effect of interest analysis may explain the courts' practical preference for its approach. Courts tend to see a conflicts case as essentially a domestic case with a foreign element added, and a state's interest in applying its law in order to implement the policy reflected in that law seems to the courts to be a rational approach to deciding whether that state's law should be applied. Thus, when the application of the forum's law in the particular case will not advance the policy reflected in that law, and the application of the law of the other involved state will advance the policy reflected in that state's law, it seems logical to the court to apply the law of the only interested state. Similarly, when the reasons that call for the application of the forum's law in a domestic case are equally present in a conflicts case, it seems logical to the forum court to apply its own law. The courts do not view their function in a conflicts case to be that of "policing the interstate and international order" and are not disposed to subordinate the policy underlying their own law in favor of supposed "multistate policies."

It is my contention, therefore, that interest analysis is a tenable approach for deciding choice-of-law issues because it works. It simplifies the choice-of-law process by carrying over the considerations applicable to the resolution of domestic cases to the resolution of conflicts cases. In practice, it is not difficult to apply, and it produces functionally sound and fair results. While most academic commentators disagree with the view that in the case of the true conflict the forum should apply its own law in order to implement the policies reflected in that law, it nevertheless cannot be demonstrated that the application of the forum's law in the true conflict produces results that are functionally unsound or fundamentally unfair to the parties.

So long as interest analysis and the application of the forum's own law in the case of the true conflict generally produce functionally sound and fair results, Professor Currie's version of interest analysis must indeed be considered the most tenable approach for deciding choice-of-law issues.

The Matter of Identifying Underlying Policies and Interests

I disagree emphatically with the contention that the courts are not equipped to determine the policies underlying a state's law and the interest of a state in having its law applied in order to implement those policies in a particular case. When the court is following an interest analysis, particularly as I have reformulated it for use in the day-to-day process of deciding actual cases, the policy with which it is primarily concerned is the policy embodied in its own law. This is because the court will apply its own law to implement that policy whenever it has a real interest in doing so. The court must determine the policy underlying a law when applying it in a domestic case, and the process is no different when the court is deciding upon the law's application to a situation containing a foreign element.

The alleged difficulty in determining the policies underlying a law often results from confusing legislative purpose with legislative motivation. The distinction between the two is well understood by constitutional commentators; generally, legislative motivation is irrelevant in constitutional analysis, while legislative purpose is central to the determination of a law's constitutionality. If that distinction were equally well understood by conflicts commentators, they would recognize that there is no great difficulty in determining the policies underlying rules of substantive law.

Legislative purpose refers to the objectives that a law is designed to accomplish, while legislative motivation may be defined as the factors stimulating the enactment of a law. Motivation may vary between legislators, and there may be mixed motives for enacting a particular law. Thus, a collective motivation cannot be ascribed to the legislature, but a collective purpose can be so ascribed. This is done by considering what objectives the law was designed to accomplish. These objectives can be determined from the provisions of the law itself, viewed both functionally and in relation to other laws of the state dealing with the same subject. Once the focus is on legislative purpose rather than on legislative motivation, determining the policies underlying a rule of substantive law is not difficult.

Another reason for the alleged difficulty in determining the policies underlying a rule of substantive law is the purported necessity of identifying a single or primary policy that is embodied in the law. For the purposes of interest analysis, a rule of substantive law should be presumed to reflect all legitimate policies that it could possibly serve. When multiple policies are presumed, they will usually support the same conclusion as to which is the interested state.

Thus, if the objectives that the law is designed to accomplish are examined and if multiple policies are assumed, there will be no real difficulty in determining the policies underlying that law. In addition, identifying the policies reflected in one state's rule of substantive law is also likely to serve to identify the policies of the state having the opposite rule. Once those policies are determined, there is little difficulty in determining the interests of the forum and of the other state in having their laws applied in order to implement those underlying policies.

Let us consider a few examples of the matter of identifying underlying policies and interests. Consider first the guest statute. Because a guest statute makes it more difficult for a guest-passenger to recover against a host-driver by requiring a showing of something more than ordinary negligence, it advances the following objectives: (1) to give the host some protection from suits by ungrateful guests; (2) to protect insurers from collusion between guest-passengers and host-drivers; and (3) to reduce the insurer's liability for passenger claims. The state interested in applying a guest statute to implement any or all of these policies is the defendant's home state, which is also the state in which the vehicle is insured, and the state in which the consequences of imposing liability, including the charging of the accident for the purpose of the insurer's loss, will be felt. The state that does not have a guest statute has a policy of allowing all accident victims to recover for ordinary negligence, including guest-passengers injured by the negligence of a host-driver. When the accident victim resides in a state that has not adopted a guest statute, that state has a strong interest in applying its law allowing guest-passengers to recover against host-drivers for ordinary negligence, because the consequences of the accident will be felt in the victim's home state.

Next, consider the example of a conflict between a rule of comparative negligence and a rule of contributory negligence. The policy underlying a rule of comparative negligence is to protect accident victims by permitting recovery, but reduced in some proportion to the victim's own negligence. A rule of contributory negligence, by contrast, furthers a policy of protecting defendants in circumstances in which the negligence of the plaintiff contributed to the accident in any way. As in the guest statute situation, if the plaintiff's home state has a rule of comparative negligence, it has a real interest in applying that rule, while if the defendant's home state has a rule of contributory negligence, it has a similar interest in applying its rule.

Finally, consider the dram shop act situation. The policies underlying a dram shop act are to raise standards of conduct by imposing liability for harm caused to third parties by intoxicated patrons and to provide a financially responsible party in the case of alcohol-related accidents. A state that has not adopted a dram shop act has a policy of protecting dispensers of alcoholic beverages from this kind of liability. The state in which a dispenser of alcoholic beverages carries on its activity has a real interest in applying its dram shop act in order to implement the admonitory policy reflected in that law. The state without a dram shop act has a similar interest in applying its law in order to protect the defendant from the imposition of such liability. When serving alcoholic beverages in a state without a dram shop act forseeably can and in fact does cause harm to a resident of an adjacent state that has enacted a dram shop act, the latter state has a real interest in applying its law in order to implement both its admonitory and compensatory objectives.

The courts generally have had no difficulty in identifying the policies and interests of the involved states. This experience is the best answer to the contention that the courts are not equipped to determine policies underlying a state's law and the interest of a state in having its law applied in order to implement those policies in a particular case.

* * * * *

David E. Seidelson, *Resolving Choice-of-Law Problems Through Interest Analysis in Person Injury Actions: A Suggested Order of Priority Among Competing State Interests and Among Available Techniques for Weighing Those Interests*, 30 Duq. L. Rev. 869, 869-879 (1992)*

To a court committed to resolving choice-of-law problems by the application of interest analysis, either exclusively or in conjunction with other approaches, fashioning an order of priority may be an extremely important element in the process of deciding which state's local law to apply. Such an order of priority can come into play in two different ways. First, if the court is confronted with a true conflict, that is, a case in which each of two states has a significant interest in the application of its own local law, the court must decide which state's interest in the application of its law is the more significant. That necessarily compels the court to determine which of two competing underlying reasons is the more significant. For example, if the reason underlying State A's law is conduct regulation and the reason underlying State B's law is the protection of economic integrity, the court will be required to determine which of those underlying reasons represents the more significant interest. Thus, establishing an order of priority as between a state's interest in conduct regulation and a state's interest in protecting economic integrity may be of enormous assistance in deciding which state's interest in the application of its law is the more significant. Second, in attempting to determine which state's interest in the application of its law is the more significant, the court, through interest analysis, may have available several different techniques. For example, the court could engage in a form of comparative impairment or the court could inquire as to which state's law manifests the more sharply focused concern. Determining which of those techniques should have priority over the other may influence the manner in which the court resolves the choice-of-law problem. Consequently, establishing an order of priority as among underlying reasons and among available techniques could facilitate the judicial task significantly. It is my intention to attempt to establish an order of priority among those underlying reasons and among those available techniques most likely to arise in choice-of-law problems in personal injury actions.

---

*   Reprinted with permission.

Let's fashion a hypothetical case that will begin to create such an order of priority. Plaintiff brings a product liability action against the defendant based on Section 402A of the Restatement (Second) of Torts, asserting that plaintiff was injured while using defendant's defective and unreasonably dangerous product. The defendant attempts to reduce the amount of damages potentially recoverable by alleging that plaintiff was comparatively negligent in the manner in which he utilized the product. The plaintiff is domiciled in State A; defendant is domiciled in State B. Both states have adopted Section 402A as a part of their common law and both states have pure comparative negligence statutes. State A, however, holds that comparative negligence is not applicable to 402A actions. Under State A's local law, the plaintiff, even if negligent in his use of the product, is entitled to recover full damages from the seller of the defective, unreasonably dangerous product. State B, on the other hand, permits the 402A defendant to utilize comparative negligence to reduce the amount of damages recoverable. The action is brought in State A. In response to defendant's assertion of comparative negligence, predicated on State B's local law, plaintiff moves to strike that partial defense, asserting that State A's local law should be applied. How should the court rule on plaintiff's motion?

If the court utilizes interest analysis, it will attempt to identify the reasons underlying each state's local law. State A precludes the 402A defendant from asserting comparative impairment for two reasons: (1) to deter the sale of defective products by making the seller feel an undiluted sting of liability, and (2) to assure that the injured victim does not become an indigent ward of the state. The first reason, aimed at conduct regulation, would convert into a significant interest on the part of State A in having its law applied if the conduct intended to be regulated or the immediate consequences of that conduct occurred in State A or if the ongoing consequences of that conduct would be felt in State A. Even if the manufacture and sale of the defective product occurred in State B, State A would have an interest in the application of its law if the product injured the plaintiff in State A because the injury would be the immediate consequence of the sale of the defective product. Similarly, even if the injury occurred in State B, State A would have an interest in the application of its law if the ongoing consequences of the conduct would be felt in State A, as they would, given the plaintiff's domicile in that state.

Let's assume that sale and injury occurred in State B but the ongoing consequences will be felt in State A, the plaintiff's domicile. In these circumstances, the conduct-regulating reason underlying State A's law would convert into a significant interest on the part of State A in having its law preclude the defendant from invoking comparative negligence applied to this case. Because the plaintiff is domiciled in State A, the second reason for that state's law also would convert into a significant interest on the part of State A in having its law applied: if plaintiff's damages are diminished through comparative negligence, the injured plaintiff may become an indigent ward of State A. Consequently, both of the reasons underlying State A's law convert into significant interests on the part of State A in having its law applied.

State B's local law permitting the 402A defendant to diminish damages through comparative negligence exists to: (1) protect the economic integrity of State B sellers by assuring a more equitable distribution of the economic loss resulting from the negligent use of defective products, and (2) encourage product users to exercise reasonable care. Because the defendant is a State B seller, it falls precisely within the class intended to be protected by the first reason for that state's law; thus, that reason converts into a significant interest on the part of State B in having its law applied. Since the plaintiff's injury-producing product use occurred in State B, the second reason for that state's law, conduct regulation, also converts into a significant interest on the part of State B in having its law applied: the conduct intended to be regulated and the immediate consequences of that conduct occurred in State B.

Interest analysis indicates that the case presents a true conflict: each state has a significant interest in the application of its own local law. In these circumstances, the court, under *Allstate Insurance Co. v. Hague*,[14] would be constitutionally free to apply the law of either state. Neither result would violate the due process rights of the litigant adversely affected thereby and application of the forum's law would not violate the Full Faith and Credit Clause. The forum, however, committed to utilizing interest analysis, will attempt to determine which state's interest in the application of its own law is the more significant and apply the local law of that state.

This final step of interest analysis in this case is somewhat demanding. Not only does the case present a true conflict, it confronts the court with rather evenly balanced competing interests. State A has a significant interest in the application of its law precluding the use of comparative negligence based on that state's desire to: (1) assure that its domiciled victim does not become an indigent ward of that state, and (2) deter the sale of defective products by having the seller feel an undiluted sting of liability. State B has a significant interest in the application of its law permitting the utilization of comparative negligence based on its desire to: (1) protect the economic integrity of its domiciled seller, and (2) deter negligent product use by having the user suffer a diminished recovery. Each state has an interest in protecting the economic integrity of its domiciled litigant and each state has an interest in conduct regulation. How should the court go about determining which state's interest in the application of its own law is the more significant?

Let's begin by weighing each state's interest in protecting the economic integrity of its domiciled litigant. State A wants to assure that the injured victim does not become an indigent ward and State B wants to assure that the seller does not become bankrupt. Which of these competing economic interests is the more significant? I believe that the court should conclude that State A's interest is the more significant. Why? Given an adverse choice-of-law result, the indigence of the injured victim, deprived of his pre-existing capacity to be entirely self-supporting, seems more likely to eventuate than does the bankruptcy of the seller, which retains its commercial capacity to pass on the cost of the undiminished liability. Consequently, looking only at the competing economic interests, State A seems to have the more significant interest in the application of its local law.

But how about each state's interest in conduct regulation? State A wishes to impose on the seller an undiminished sting of liability for the purpose of deterring the marketing of defective products. State B wishes to reduce the plaintiff's recovery for the purpose of deterring the negligent use of products. Each state has a significant interest in conduct regulation and each state's interest in conduct regulation is aimed at protecting and preserving human life. Merely to assert each state's interest in conduct regulation in those terms, protecting and preserving human life, suggests strongly that such a conduct regulating purpose is of greater moment than each state's admittedly legitimate interest in protecting the economic integrity of its domiciled litigant. Protecting and preserving human life must be assigned greater significance than protecting economic integrity. Consequently, the court's resolution of the choice-of-law problem is likely to turn on the determination of which state's interest in conduct regulation is the more significant. How should the court go about making that determination?

I suppose the court could attempt to determine which state's law, State A's law aimed at protecting and preserving human life by deterring the marketing of defective products or State B's law aimed at protecting and preserving human life by discouraging the negligent use

---

[14]   449 US 302 (1981).

of products, is more likely to accomplish the desired effect. There are, however, a couple of problems with attempting to achieve such a determination. First, such an endeavor seems almost surely destined to turn into a judicial determination of which state's local law is the "better rule of law." I am strongly inclined toward the view that the "better rule of law" factor has no legitimate role to play in ingenuous interest analysis. Its use seems almost invariably to lead to the parochial conclusion that "ours" is the "better" rule of law. Second, absent significant empirical evidence, I'm not sure how a court could determine which state's law was the more effective means of protecting and preserving human life. And, even with such empirical evidence (should it exist), I believe that each state would have the right to make its own determination of what credibility to afford such data or which conflicting studies (should they exist) to credit, and therefore each state would have the right to make its own determination of which of the two approaches was the more effective in accomplishing the desired purpose. Consequently, with or without such empirical data, the court's effort to determine which state's local law constituted the more efficient manner of protecting and preserving human life would almost certainly degenerate into an inappropriate determination of the "better rule of law."

Is there some alternative manner of weighing the competing state interests, each aimed at protecting and preserving human life? I think there is. It's apparent that, if State A's law precluding comparative negligence is applied, State B's interest in deterring negligent product use would be wholly frustrated. On the other hand, if State B's law permitting comparative negligence is applied, State A's interest in deterring the marketing of defective products would not be wholly frustrated. While the ultimate sting of liability imposed on the defendant would be diminished to the extent that the plaintiff's negligent use of the product contributed to his injuries, the net liability imposed on the defendant would serve State A's interest to some extent. Since the application of State A's law would wholly frustrate State B's interest in protecting and preserving human life by regulating the conduct of the product user and the application of State B's law would only partially frustrate State A's interest in protecting and preserving human life by regulating the conduct of the product marketer, I believe the court should conclude that State B has the more significant interest in the application of its conduct regulating law. Of course, the application of State B's law permitting the comparative negligence defense and therefore potentially diminishing the plaintiff's recovery would necessarily enhance the possibility that the injured plaintiff might become an indigent ward of State A. Should that dissuade the State A court from applying State B's local law? I think not. Even though we determined earlier that protecting the plaintiff from indigence was of greater significance than protecting the defendant from bankruptcy, each state's interest in protecting and preserving human life through conduct regulation is manifestly more significant than each state's interest in protecting economic integrity. Therefore, that resolution affording the greater play to the conduct regulating interests is the more appropriate resolution. And, while that resolution may enhance the possibility of the plaintiff's indigence, it does not compel that indigence. The plaintiff will still enjoy some recovery and even that diminished recovery serves as some, albeit limited, assurance against indigence. Consequently, I believe that the court should apply State B's law permitting the comparative negligence defense and, therefore, deny the plaintiff's motion to strike that partial defense.

That resolution and the interest analysis by which it was accomplished suggest several conclusions with regard to an order of priority for competing underlying reasons of conflicting local laws. First, an underlying reason aimed at preventing the indigence of an injured person should be given priority over a competing underlying reason aimed at protecting economic integrity generally, because of the greater likelihood that such indigence will result given an adverse choice-of-law result. Second, an underlying reason directed toward protecting and preserving human life through conduct regulation should be given priority over any interest in protecting economic integrity, simply because of the greater value placed on human life. Third, confronted with competing interests in protecting and preserving human life through conduct regulation, the court should attempt to achieve the result that does not wholly frustrate such interest on the part of either state. By applying this order of priority to those competing interests, the court is likely to achieve that choice-of-law result produced by the application of the local law of the state having the more significant interest in the application of its own law.

Something else emerges from the process we utilized in resolving the above choice-of-law problem. Confronted with each state's interest in protecting the economic integrity of its domiciled litigant, State A seeking to avoid the indigence of the injured person and State B attempting to avoid the bankruptcy of the seller, we determined which of those interests was the more significant by asking this question: Given an adverse choice-of-law result, which state's interest would be more frustrated? This question led us to conclude that, given an adverse result, the indigence of the injured party would be more likely than the bankruptcy of the seller and this conclusion, in turn, led us to the determination that, as between those two competing interests, State A's was the more significant. Confronted with each state's interest in protecting and preserving human life through conduct regulation, State A seeking to deter the marketing of defective products and State B attempting to deter the negligent use of such products, we determined which of those interests was the more significant by asking the same question: Given an adverse choice-of-law result, which state's interest would be more frustrated? This question led us to conclude that, while the application of State A's law would wholly frustrate State B's interest in conduct regulation, the application of State B's law would frustrate State A's interest in conduct regulation only in part. This conclusion, in turn, led us to the determination that, as between those two competing interests, State B's was the more significant. Given the primacy accorded to interests aimed at protecting and preserving human life, we ultimately concluded that State B had the more significant interest in the application of its local law. That critical question—given an adverse choice-of-law result, which state's interest would be more frustrated?—is the cornerstone of comparative impairment. And, as we employed that question, it was at the core of determining which state had the more significant interest in the application of its law. This shouldn't be surprising. The question, after all, is simply another way of asking, which state has the more significant interest in the application of its law to this issue in this case? Thus, comparative impairment, when applied directly and exclusively to the interests in conflict, is an integral part of the process of interest analysis in resolving a true conflict. By rephrasing the basic question from, Which state has the more significant interest in the application of its law?, to, Given an adverse choice-of-law result, which state's interest would be more frustrated?, we simply provided the court with a specific perspective to be utilized in resolving the basic question. And that perspective, extremely helpful in our hypothetical, is likely to be equally helpful in resolving any true conflict. After all, the state whose interest will be more frustrated by an adverse choice-of-law result is likely to be the state having the greater interest in the application of its own local law. Thus, this use of comparative impairment, applied directly and exclusively to the conflicting interests, must assume a high priority among the various techniques available to an interest analysis court confronted with a true conflict. The technique thus limited is at the core of determining which state has the more significant interest in the application of its local law.

* * * * *

Louise Weinberg, *On Departing From Forum Law*, 35 MERCER L. REV. 595, 598-601, 626-627 (1983)*

* * * * *

Despite much confused hand-wringing in the literature, modernist writers are in substantial agreement about the uses of forum preference in choice of law. It is true that a myth has arisen that forum preference is the consequence of judicial parochialism, chauvinism, or sloth. It is thought that when a state applies its own law, at least in nonfalse conflict cases, it acts at the expense of widely shared, multistate, or even national policies. Ever since *International Shoe Co. v. Washington*[11] bestowed upon plaintiffs the option of forum shopping, forum preference also, inevitably, has been perceived as a kind of systemic unfairness to defendants, so that conflicts thinking has become politicized on the point. Those writers tending to align themselves with the defendants' bar do not like forum preference, and those tending to align themselves with the plaintiffs' bar do (although these latter, inwardly persuaded of the myth, tend to avoid saying that they do). The foes of forum preference have thus elected themselves the champions of multistate policy, while the apologists for forum preference are occasionally found trying to explain why multistate policy does not count.

This polarization of thinking is quite unnecessary, and conceals what in actuality is a broad-based, if implicit, consensus. It should be a truism that the two positions reconcile.

Current modernist writers are fully aware that forum preference vindicates widely shared policy concerns in the general run of nonfalse conflict cases. It is understood that the choice of forum confers upon plaintiffs some control over choice of law. A proponent of multistate policy would have to be writing in his or her sleep not to have noticed that what the plaintiff seeks in the general run of cases is precisely the vindication of policies all states share: compensation for injury, deterrence of wrongdoing, and enforcement of agreements. Plaintiffs today have the power to seek effectuation of these multistate policies under forum law. It is thus transparent that forum preference promotes multistate policies.

This conviction underlies the virtually universal advice given by modernist writers on when the forum should depart from its own law. Most agree that a departure is justified precisely in those cases in which multistate policy would not be advanced by forum law. Thus (to touch briefly on the more prominent of the proposals), Professors von Mehren and Trautman suggest that forum law that is "regressing" rather than "emerging" be avoided,[16] and Professor Weintraub suggests a similar disregard of forum law that is "aberrational" or "anachronistic."[17] Professor Leflar suggests that the forum choose "the better law."[18] If the law of the forum is not plaintiff-favoring, Professor Weintraub suggests a straight-forward choice of law that is. In a more neutral-sounding fashion, a departure from undesirable local law may be managed through Professor Baxter's "comparative impairment" analysis[20] or some version of "common

---

*   Reprinted with permission.

[11]   326 U.S. 310 (1945).

[16]   A. VON MEHREN & D. TRAUTMAN, [THE LAW OF MULTISTATE PROBLEMS 377 (1965)].

[17]   R. WEINTRAUB, [COMMENTARY ON THE CONFLICTS OF LAW 346 (2d ed. 1980)].

[18]   R. LEFLAR, [AMERICAN CONFLICTS OF LAW § 107 (2d ed. 1977)]. *See* Freund, *Chief Justice Stone and the Conflict of Laws*, 59 HARV. L. REV. 1210, 1214-15, 1223 (1946).

[20]   Baxter, [*Choice of Law and the Federal System*, 16 STAN. L. REV. 1, 10-11, 19 (1963)].

policy" analysis.[21] All of these proposals rest upon the observation that in a typical conflict of laws, both concerned jurisdictions will share fundamental multistate policies.

On the other hand, when there is disfavored law at the forum, by hypothesis only the forum will be concerned in its application. In other words, all states share plaintiff-encouraging policies of compensation, deterrence, enforcement, and validation; one state's occasional idiosyncratic defense need not be deferred to.

Carried to their logical conclusion, then, current approaches to the resolution of nonfalse conflicts will tend to reduce to variations on the 'better law' formulation of Professor Leflar. The litmus test is multistate policy: a departure from forum law will be justified when there is 'better law' in the nonforum state, law more representative of multistate policy—that is, law more favorable (in the usual case) to the plaintiff. So the forum faced with a nonfalse conflict, and hewing to the modernist position, will apply sister-state law when the plaintiff's claim under forum law is generally disfavored, or when forum law favors the defendant and the defense is not generally favored.

What cannot be extracted from current writing on resolution of intractable cases, however, is an understanding of functional difficulties that in fact attend departures from forum law, and thus any recommendation for courts struggling with such difficulties. In particular, there is a failure to perceive that the forum may have a superior option. But before I come to that option, it will be convenient to introduce some perhaps overly fundamental background.

It seems to me that the modern, rationalized approaches to choice of law pretty much boil down to interest analysis, which in turn boils down to ordinary judicial process. The job of a court confronted with extraterritorial facts is not to give such facts any unique treatment, but instead to deal with them just as it would with any other facts raising legal issues. It is elementary that a court handles such facts by finding reasons for the allegedly applicable rules, and identifying the known relevant policies of the sovereign. Once those are discerned a court's task is considerably narrowed. It remains only to determine whether the new facts make a difference, in light of the discerned policies. That much is obvious. Now, the modern view is that extraterritorial facts should be treated in precisely the same way as other problem facts. That was the essential insight of Brainerd Currie.

We have already seen that the various suggested grounds for departure from forum law require a preliminary finding that nonforum law is more closely attuned to multistate policy— in short, that it is "better." But a court that has found the law of a sister state to be "better" than its own, in so doing has inescapably discerned its own current policy. Once that happens, the cleaner, more direct approach would be to make a change in local law. Even a statutory rule may be interpreted to conform to existing local policy, although this later option may not always be practicable; but setting to one side the stumbling-block of outworn or wrong-headed legislation, identification of "better law" in a sister state will inevitably suggest to the forum the advisability of adopting the sister state's view as its own. In some cases, as we shall see, the forum may have no acceptable alternative to that course.

* * * * *

It appears that in nonfalse conflict cases occasions for departure from forum law are even less numerous than suggested by modernist writers. Certainly, the forum is never warranted in departing from its own law on the spurious ground that comity or federalism require it to defer

---

[21]   *See* Sedler, *Interstate Accidents and the Unprovided For Case: Reflections on* Neumeier v. Kuehner, 1 HOFSTRA L. REV. 125, 143-49 (1973).

to some other law, or on the ground that the place of transaction is the more concerned juris-diction. The forum cannot with assurance depart from its law, even when there is a defense or an aberrational or invalidating claim at the forum, unless revision of local law is not a desir-able or practicable alternative, or unless a departure from local law can be managed without dis-crimination between residents of the forum state in conflicts and domestic cases respectively. The forum cannot depart from its own law on the ground that its law is highly disfavored with-out risking the irrationality of returning to explicitly disfavored law in subsequent cases; when feasible the forum must refine local law. When there is repealed or overruled law at the forum, retroactive application of the newer law, when possible, is preferable to a flight to non-forum law. In sum, the forum ought not to depart from its own law on grounds of multistate pol-icy without considering the magnitude of the irrationalities and inequities that can attend a departure from forum law.

I suspect that we should begin to see increased judicial revision of local law by courts con-fronted with invalidating, aberrational, or anachronistic home law, if conflicts analysis, as it should be, is increasingly and successfully assimilated to ordinary judicial process. I suspect, too, that commentators will become increasingly comfortable with choices of forum law, and more sympathetic to courts making such choices, once the role of forum law in administration of multistate policy, and the functional constraints operating on the forum, are more fully under-stood.

Bruce Posnak, *Choice of Law: Interest Analysis and Its "New Crit-ics,"* 36 AM. J. COMP. L. 681, 684-689 (1988)*

* * * * *

Although criticism going to the heart of Currie's theory was slight during the '60s and '70s, the '80s have brought a deluge. Some of the new critics allege that the foundation for interest analysis is defective, and thus, at least imply, that the whole edifice should be torn down. These new critics, renewing some older criticism, assert that the rationale for interest analysis is that: (1) it carries out the intent of the promulgators of the competing laws; or (2) it fulfills the desires of the competing states in regard to the outcome of the case, or both. As one might expect, the critics then demolish this rationale. They do so by making two points: Lawmakers ordinarily do not anticipate a choice of law problem and therefore can have no intent whether the law should apply in a conflicts case; and, except in rare cases (such as those involving tax-ation and eminent domain), states don't care who wins. Voila! Emperor Currie has no clothes. Unwittingly, these critics created strawmen. Neither carrying out the intent of the lawmaker nor furthering the desires of the states * * * is the *raison d'etre* of Currie's interest analysis. In fact, neither is even relevant to interest analysis. The misperception, however, was an honest and even reasonable one. It was probably due in large part to some unfortunate word choices by Currie and his failure to articulate clearly the rationale for his approach.

Although a few writers have tried to show that rationality in terms of the policies of the competing laws (rather than carrying out the lawmaker's intent or the states' desires) is the goal of and justification for interest analysis, we have not succeeded. * * *

---

*   Reprinted with permission.

Currie referred to his approach as "governmental interest analysis." He also made statements such as: "[T]he basic problem in conflict of laws is to reconcile or resolve the competing interests of different states,"[37] and cases were "unprovided for" because "neither state cares what happens."[38] Phrases like these could lead one to believe that Currie was striving to effectuate the lawmaker's intent or the desires of the states, or both. However, upon closer examination of his work, and especially of his criticism of the *First Restatement*, it becomes clear that he was searching for a choice of law method that would bring about rational results in terms of the policies of the competing laws. As Professor Cavers succinctly put it, the label "governmental interests" is "dispensable," and "the decisive factor in Professor Currie's method is the finding that the application of a law is *reasonable* in light of the circumstances of the case and the policies the law expresses."[40] Only when such a finding is made will a state possess an "interest" in the sense Currie intended. Consequently, neither whether the lawmaker intended for the law to apply to the particular set of facts nor whether the state cares who wins the case is even relevant.

To determine whether a state, forum or foreign, has a specific interest, Currie would have the forum identify the law of that state that is vying for application on the issue in question. Then a determination of the policy of that law should be made just as it would if the policy of that law were at issue in a wholly domestic case. With that policy in mind, the court should determine whether, in light of the facts of the case, it is reasonable to conclude that it would be furthered. The intent of the lawmaker would be relevant, but only to glean the domestic policy of a law, not its interstate reach.

Currie was questing for rationality. It is true, however, that in one sense the *First Restatement* might be considered rational; its purported certainty and simplicity might be thought, or at least hoped, to bring about uniform results regardless of the forum, a reasonable goal. This was not the type of rationality Currie had in mind. If a policy of only one of the competing laws could be advanced, as a matter of rationality Currie would apply it. Currie concluded that the goal of uniformity, especially since it proved illusory, was not sufficient to justify irrational results in terms of the policies of the competing laws.

Currie's emphasis was on the results of individual cases; the *First Restatement* was more concerned with the uniformity of results. Attempting to ensure that all courts apply the same law to a set of facts is laudable, but not as important as arriving at a result that makes sense in light of the policies of the competing laws. The vast majority of laws are but means to an end. They are promulgated, judicially or legislatively, to further some policy or policies. Very few laws are promulgated merely to terminate controversy. If two laws are vying for application and it is clear that the policies of only one would be advanced if applied, or thwarted if not applied, the only reasonable, rational, logical, sensible thing to do is to apply that law. To do otherwise was the type of irrationality that was anathema to Currie, and his governmental interest methodology was designed to eliminate it. As David Currie said, ". . . it [interest analysis] has the virtue of recognizing that laws are adopted in order to accomplish social goals and that they should be applied so as to carry out their purposes . . ."[46] Finally the primary goal of a court

---

[37]   [Brainerd] Currie, *Selected* [*Essays on the Conflict of Laws*, 163 (1963)].

[38]   *Id.* at 152.

[40]   [David] Cavers, *The Choice of Law Process* 102 (1965).

[46]   Currie, "Comments on Reich v. Purcell," 15 UCLA L. Rev. 595, 605 (1968). See also Posnak, ["Choice of Law—Rules v. Analysis: A More Workable Marriage Than the Second Restatement; A Very Well-Curried Leflar Over Reese Approach," 40 Mercer L. Rev. (1989)].

should be to properly resolve the controversy between the parties, not to reach the same result some other court would.

Although it is not clear, Currie might have viewed the prevention of "provincialism in jurisprudence" as a secondary justification for his methodology. Currie maintained that the Full Faith and Credit Clause requires the forum to apply the law of a sister state if the latter possesses the only specific interest. Although he never clearly articulated why this should be so, it was probably to prevent the undue denigration of a sister state's sovereignty so as to make this a more perfect union. If the forum, despite concluding that a sister state possesses the only specific interest, applies its own law, it is, in effect, thumbing its nose at that state and inviting retaliation. Whether Currie used this as an additional rationale for his theory is not very important. What is important is that his methodology prevents such gratuitous slaps.

Whether Currie devised his system in part to avoid the undue denigration of a state's sovereignty is problematic; clearly he did not devise his system so that a case could be decided the way the personification of the putatively competing states desire. Consequently, attacking interest analysis by demonstrating either that the states don't care how most cases come out, or that the lawmakers don't have any intent as to the interstate scope of most laws, is demurrable. These attacks, therefore, do nothing to either weaken the foundations of interest analysis or to remove any of the Emperor's clothes.

Professors Juenger and Brilmayer used up many trees criticizing interest analysis but hardly a twig suggesting alternatives. In fact, even though they have both written extensively in the field, it is not clear how they think courts ought to choose between competing laws. * * * There is some similarity, however, between some of these new critics of interest analysis and the pre-Currie critics of the *First Restatement*. Both criticized an existing apparatus for choosing law without offering viable alternatives. And since the pre-Currie critics of the *First Restatement* probably set the stage for Currie, Cavers and others, there is room for such criticism. Indeed, it is probable that others who will or *have* proposed alternatives to Currie's brand of interest analysis were influenced by these new critics who offered no alternatives themselves. Nevertheless, * * * it behooves such critics to put their necks on the line and explain what they would like in place of what they criticize.

Comments

1. The contributors in Part B of this Chapter did not really deny that interest analysis can be a means for judges to give preferential treatment to local litigants under local law. Rather, they differ with critics of interest analysis (and to an extent with each other) over the importance of, and answers to, a number of questions: Is not at least a small amount of local favoritism inevitable in choice of law, given the federal (rather than unitary) character of government in the United States? How much local favoritism is excessive? How much excessive forum favoritism actually occurs in American choice of law? Would excessive forum favoritism diminish significantly if courts did not employ interest analysis?

2. Under our federal system of government, states (rather than the national government) create most of the substantive law governing civil actions in state or lower federal courts. Moreover, while Congress or the Supreme Court has power under the United States Constitution to reduce some or all of conflicts law to federal law, little of that power has been invoked. The consequences of this situation (explored in

Chapter Ten) are that (1) conflicts choices for American courts are usually intra-national (between local state law and that of another state), and (2) choice is largely self-regulated. Serious concern over the possibility of local bias in choice of law also arises in other countries that, like the United States, employ a federal system of government. *See, e.g.*, Nygh 1995: p. 912[1] (Australia); Swan 1995: p. 931 (Canada). In contrast, the common source of substantive law for countries under a unitary form of government obviates most intra-national conflicts. Conflict of laws is therefore a much less significant category in the unitary countries of Germany, Italy and France. Herzog 1992: pp. 311-325.

3. So long as we maintain a federal system of government, it is probably unrealistic to imagine American choice of law utterly free of local bias. The question therefore becomes, when does local bias exceed tolerable limits? The answer must be made with reference to contemporary choice-of-law values. The author has suggested that local bias is excessive when it produces conflicts decisions that "unfairly damage nonforum litigants, exhibit disrespect to nonforum governments, and undermine principles of order and uniformity in choice of law. * * *" Shreve 1996a: p. 276. The critics surveyed in Part A seemed to suggest that local bias is extensive; however, this has not been an unanimous view. According to the late Professor Willis Reese,

> American choice of law is not as unruly and chaotic as is generally supposed. On the basis of the actual court decisions, it appears that there is a fair measure of predictability and uniformity of results in all areas, except torts, contracts in situations where the contract does not contain a choice-of-law clause, and conveyances of interests in movables as between the parties to the conveyance.

Reese 1982a: p. 146. A similar assessment appears in North 1990: pp. 23-24.

4. The critics in Part A tended to blame interest analysis for forum bias. The author has suggested that this notion might be limited in two respects:

> First, critics often seem to forget that domicile-based interest analysis works both ways. Thus, while it is true that it permits forum citizens to win cases nonresidents would have lost, it is equally true that domicile-based interest analysis permits nonresidents to win cases citizens would have lost. Thus, when a nonresident defendant can summon anti-recovery law from his own state and demonstrate that his state would be interested in having that law applied to protect him, he may win a conflicts case when a defendant residing in the forum (hence stuck with the forum's pro-recovery law) would have lost an otherwise identical case. Second, critics take too little account of state courts' capacity for principled forbearance. There are now numerous decisions where judges regarded the forum as interested in avail-

---

[1]   Ful citations appear in the bibliography, Chapter Twelve.

ing a local litigant of forum law yet applied nonforum law out of respect for concerns of party fairness or the interests of another sovereign.

Shreve 1993: p. 921. Professor Weintraub offers several such case examples in his excerpt. In the same vein, Professor Pielemeier notes that the Minnesota Supreme Court (a major local-bias offender in the past) recently choose sister-state law after noting that the forum was interested in having its conflicting law applied. Pielemeier 1994.

5. Several of the critics in Part A indicated that their task of questioning interest analysis was complicated by the fact that advocates of interest analysis varied in their conceptions of the approach. Interest analysts differ, for example, about whether the approach can or should be used to promote forum neutrality in choice of law. Reasoning from somewhat different premises, two leading interest analysts maintain that true conflicts should be resolved by forum law. Through what might be termed a functionalist or realist approach, Professor Weinberg suggested this position in her excerpt appearing in Part B. This view is confirmed in Weinberg 1991a: p. 81. Through arguments close to Currie's own, Professor Herma Hill also concludes that an interested forum should apply its own law. Kay 1980: pp. 611-613; Kay 1989: pp. 150-152. Opposed to this conclusion, a number of interest analysts maintain that interest analysis effectively guides the choice of either forum or non-forum law in true conflicts, depending upon the case. Professors Wientraub and Seidelson took this position in Part B.

6. The classic exposition of interest analysis as a neutral approach appears in Baxter 1963: pp. 19-22. Professor Baxter's views provided the basis for the so-called comparative impairment approach, used extensively by California courts. The comparative impairment approach has been the subject of numerous articles. *E.g.*, Horowitz 1974; Kanowitz 1978; Kay 1980.

7. There is a lack of consensus on whether or to what extent interest analysis should represent but one ingredient in a larger, eclectic approach to choice of law. The eclecticism debate is featured in Part A of Chapter Nine.

8. With rare exceptions (*e.g.,* Foley 1968), critics of interest analysis tend also to be critical of the formalistic regime of *lex loci delicti* that preceded it. Interest analysts thus set up the challenge found in Professor Posnak's selection: Do the critics really have a different and better alternative of their own to offer? Adding to this counterargument, Professor Weintraub suggested that no third option exists, that options are limited to interest analysis or some form of territorial rules, and that to choose the latter is to return to the discredited past.

> Alas, it is probably too late to turn the choice-of-law clock back. Mechanical conflicts rules, like mechanical rules in any field of law, cause covert resistance. An attempt to return to territorial choice-of-law rules would undoubtedly invite, on a greatly accelerated basis, the avoidance techniques used in the past, such as overuse of the proce-

dural category to apply forum law, substantive labels that we make up as we go along * * * and of course, our old friend waiting there to snatch us from the jaws of death, public policy. Attempts to simplify choice-of-law analysis with rigid territorial rules have not worked before, and will not work again, unless we elect or appoint to our courts people who have room temperature IQs.

Weintraub 1989: p. 133. In a similar vein, this author has questioned the practicability of conflicts law designed to prevent courts from reacting to what they perceive to be strong needs of local policy.

> [F]irm conflicts rules may cut too much against the grain of our legal experience to succeed. Much of the history of American conflicts law in this century can be told in the growing rejection of hard rules in favor of method, and the growing distaste of lawyers, judges, and the public with conflicts law that was mechanical and thus blind to the aims of local law and policy. Much as radical critics might try to distance themselves from the thoroughly discredited approach that modern theory replaced, similarities of disfunction are difficult to ignore. If rules ordered judges to ignore important local policies at stake in conflicts cases, would judges be more submissive than they were fifty years ago when old theory made the same demand?

Shreve 1993: pp. 921-922.

9.   Naturally, critics of interest analysis see more than two possibilities for choice of law. That is, they dispute the contention that conflicts law must either embrace some form of interest analysis or return to the Bealean past of *lex loci* and the original RESTATEMENT. Note, for example, the reform proposals of Professors Brilmayer and Dane appearing in Chapter 9, Part C.

CHAPTER SEVEN

Completing the Picture—American Conflicts Theory Apart From Multilateralism and Unilateralism

Not all contemporary choice-of-law policies figure in the debate over multilateralism (territorialism) versus unilateralism (interest analysis). Two additional policies are the subject of this Chapter.

Part A examines the conflicts policy that chosen law should not disturb the reasonable expectations of a litigant. The opening selection by Professor Max Rheinstein suggests the importance of actual party expectations to conflicts law and locates the value of expectations within a broad Western legal tradition. Next, an excerpt by Professors Elliott Cheatham and Willis Reese stresses the importance of protecting actual and reasonable expectations in choice of law. That policy, they maintain, must be differentiated from more general notions of uniformity, certainty, and predictability. Part A concludes with an opposing view by Professor Aaron D. Twerski, who argues against a bright-line distinction between actual party expectations and predictability of results. Professor Twerski urges the latter is an important conflicts policy in its own right because predictability in choice of law fosters a sense of tranquility.

Part B explores substantivism, the policy that the conflicts judges should whenever possible apply the best available substantive law. We begin with a selection by the most influential substantivist, Professor Robert Leflar. Here, Professor Leflar explains and supports his "Better Rule of Law" criterion for choice of law. He notes the traditional use of substantivism in at least a few settings, urges broader application of that policy, and sets up the strongest case for his better-rule approach: when one of the laws in contention is anachronistic. Next, Professor Joseph Singer advocates a substantive perspective in choice of law more extensive than that suggested by Professor Leflar. Judges and theorists, Professor Singer maintains, have failed to undertake searching examination of contemporary substantive values at stake in conflicts cases. Taking the opposite tack, Professor William Baxter challenges the place of substantivism in choice of law. He argues that it is unseemly for judges to inject their own substantive preferences into their conflicts decisions, that the substantive wisdom of such "super-value judgments" is in fact open to question, and that subsantivism will diminish predictability in choice of law.

Part B continues with a selection by Professor Arthur von Mehren on possibilities for special substantive rules for multistate cases. Professor von Mehren explains the practice, how a court might decide a case by fashioning and applying a substantive rule unlike either of the actual laws in conflict. Professor von Mehren counsels restraint in the use of such special rules, but notes three situations where the concept is worth exploring. Finally, Professor Patrick Borchers offers an expansive definition of substantivism. Using an approach he entitles "conflicts pragmatism," Professor Borchers questions whether it is useful to differentiate between substantive-law and choice-of-law policies.

A. Justified Expectations

Max Rheinstein, *The Place of Wrong: A Study in the Method of Case Law*, 19 Tulane L. Rev. 4, 17-23 (1944)*

* * * * *

* * * Presumably, the law of conflict of laws fulfills some useful function in our social order. What is that function?

Assume that John Jones is a druggist in, let us say, Georgia. He believes in competition and wishes to sell his toothpastes, shaving creams, soaps, tooth-brushes, *et cetera*, at a cheaper rate than the manufacturers want them to be sold to the public. He knows that there are other cut-rate drug stores in the state, and he has not heard that any one of them has ever had legal trouble. After several years of successfully conducting his business, he finally decides to retire and to live with his daughter and son-in-law in Chicago. He moves from Georgia to Illinois, transfers his savings from a Georgia bank to one in Illinois and settles down to what he expects to be a peaceful evening of a busy life. Suddenly, he is hailed before a court in Cook County, Illinois, by another druggist, perhaps a former competitor in Georgia, or by a drug manufacturer, and a suit for several thousands of dollars is brought against him. When he asks upon what basis this claim is sought to be justified, he is referred to the Illinois Retail Price Maintenance Act, which declares price-cutting an actionable act of unfair competition. We can safely expect that the court would decide the case in the defendant's favor. Otherwise, we should feel shocked. A Georgia resident who is exclusively engaged in business in Georgia has no reason to expect that his business practices might ever be subjected to scrutiny under the standards of the law of Illinois, or of any other state or country with which neither he nor his business has ever had contact. We regard him as justified in expecting that the legality of his business activities will be gauged by no law other than that of Georgia, or, perhaps, of such other states or countries with which his business activities had some obvious contacts. If the mere fact of his removal to Illinois were suddenly to subject to Illinois liability activities carried on before his removal to that state, we would share his feeling of outrage and would denounce as unjust, unreasonable and even intolerable a law that would result in such a decision. His justified expectations would have been disappointed and we, the public, would not stand for it.

Or let us assume that John Doe sells a piece of land to Richard Roe. Both parties to the transaction are native residents of Indiana, where the land is situated. The deal is negotiated and consummated through an Indiana lawyer, who has drawn the deed in accordance with Indiana law and practice. Roe, the buyer, has taken possession of the land, but after a short while he discovers that the land is charged with an outstanding tax lien of which he had no previous knowledge. When consulting his lawyer he is informed that he has no remedy against Doe, because Doe had not given in his deed any express warranty of freedom from incumbrances and because, under the law of Indiana, no such warranty will be implied. In the course of the conversation, the lawyer casually observes that the law is different in Missouri, where a warranty of freedom from incumbrances is read into a land deal unless it has been expressly contracted out by the vendor. It would help our purchaser little to hail the vendor before a court of Mis-

---

*   Reprinted with permission.

souri, where Doe perhaps owns some property, or where Doe may some day be traveling. Again, it may be safely predicted that no court in Missouri would hold the vendor liable and that, if it did, its decision would be decried as outrageously wrong. The reason is again that, under the circumstances, Doe, when he sold his land had no reason to assume that Missouri law would ever be applied to his transaction.

Finally, let us assume that H has been a lifelong resident of Illinois. In Illinois he went through a ceremony of marriage in accordance with Illinois law and settled down to live there with his wife, a native of the state. After several years of married life, A deserted him, and H obtained a decree of divorce in a court of Illinois, where desertion constitutes a ground for divorce. Some time later, H, still in Illinois, marries B, another native of the state. After three years of married life with B, he moves with her into South Carolina. What would we say if a district attorney of that state would indict H and B for bigamy, alleging that divorce is unknown to its law and that, therefore, as far as South Carolina is concerned, H is still married to A? Or how would we feel if, under such an argumentation, at H's death a South Carolina court would hold that B was not entitled to a widow's share in H's estate or was not entitled to workman's compensation as his widow? Again, we would feel shocked and appalled and, again, the reason would be the fact that justified expectations had been rudely disappointed.

It is for cases like these that the rules of choice of law have been elaborated. The courts of Illinois are organs of the social and political community of Illinois. As a general rule, they are expected to look to Illinois statutes and Illinois precedents. A law other than that of Illinois is of no concern to them. Yet, in the three cases just stated, we would regard it as unfair if the court would decide them under the law of its own state. The cause of this feeling of unfairness, we have already stated, is the fact that legitimate expectations of the parties would be disregarded, and that there would thus be violated a policy which is basic for the entire legal order, and which underlies numerous of the very fundamental institutions of the law, *viz.* the policy of protecting justified expectations.

One of the most obvious applications of this policy is constituted by the doctrine of estoppel, which simply means that a man who through his conduct has raised in others the expectation that he will follow a certain line of conduct, is not allowed to frustrate expenses which those others have incurred in consequence of the expectation raised.

Another expression of the policy that a legitimate expectation ought not to be disappointed, is found in the constitutional prohibition of *ex post facto* laws; and in the maxim of *nulla poena sine lege*, which has been declared to constitute an indispensable part of the rule of law by the most prominent judicial body of the world.

The same idea that one should not be taken by surprise and suffer detriment for the non-obedience of a law of which he could not have any knowledge, is constituted by the rule that no law is to take effect before it has been properly promulgated.

It is within the same order of ideas that the principle of *stare decisis* is being regarded as fundamental in the common law. One ought to be able to rely on the stability of judicial practice. Commercial practices and legal transactions are being based upon the expectation that courts will not easily reverse themselves. Countless are the judicial expressions of the deeply felt necessity to continue a line of precedents, even though it may appear theoretically unsatisfactory once it has become the basis of conveyancers' and business men's practices and property-owners' reliances.

Contract is one of the most basic and most far-reaching institutions of our whole legal and its underlying social order. A promise has been made by an individual and has been relied upon by another. The state with its overwhelmingly powerful machinery of law-enforcement through sheriffs deputies, the militia and, as a last resort of latent power, the army, compels the reneging promisor to live up to his promise or, at least, to make the promisee whole for the damages he has suffered through the disappointment of his expectations. Truly, no more impressive illustration can be imagined of the fundamental importance of the policy of protecting justified expectations than the deputy sheriff who forcibly breaks a debtor's resistance. This application of the state's power machinery becomes understandable, however, when we consider that the entire economic structure of our age is based upon credit, *i.e.,* upon investors' and other creditors' expectations that their debtors will make proper use of the capital entrusted to them and that they will honor the creditors expectations to receive interest and repayment. Only in passing may it be mentioned that the institutions of the trust and the will are nothing but special applications of the same principle. Such considerations will help us recognize that the protection of expectations is indeed one of the deepest necessities of all human life itself, social and individual. We could not live in a world in which we could not foresee that, in general, our expectations will not be disappointed. The forces of tradition, social etiquette, morality and religion combine in stabilizing social life and in thus rendering it predictable; and all our search for the hidden "laws" of nature is motivated by the yearning for greater predictability of the ways of nature, of the weather, for instance, or of the ways of bacteria or of gravitation.

Except where other higher aspirations interfere, expectations must be relied upon, and one of those expectations is that we ought not to be subjected to punishment, liability or other legal detriment for conduct which we had good reason to believe would not subject us to such troubles. It is in this order of ideas that we find the *raison d' etre* of the condemnation of *ex post facto* laws as well as of that branch of the legal order with which we are concerned here, *viz.* choice of law. This statement should not be misunderstood, however. It is not suggested here that the policy of protecting justified expectations is the only explanation of the fact that domestic courts occasionally apply a foreign law. There are others, for instance the policy to assist other friendly states or nations in the enforcement of social policies, which they regard as important. Still less is it suggested that the policy of protecting justified expectations explains those rules of the conflict of laws which are not choice-of-law rules, *i.e.,* rules indicating whether a given case shall be decided under the domestic or under some foreign law. Rules on jurisdiction of courts, on recognition and enforcement of foreign judgments, or on the legal status of aliens are based on peculiar policies of their own. The only proposition made here is that among the policies motivating a state to refrain in certain cases from the application of its own law in favor of some foreign law, the policy of protecting justified expectations plays a prominent role.

* * * * *

Elliott E. Cheatham and Willis L.M. Reese, *Choice of the Applicable Law*, 52 COLUM. L. REV. 959, 970-972 (1952)*

* * * * *

* * * A person's expectations are likely to be disappointed to the extent that choice of law rules do not lead to uniformity, certainty and predictability of result. But in a deeper sense this policy is one of the basic reasons why we have choice of law rules at all. Suppose that in England, defendant, while driving on the left side of the road, as of course he was required to do, were to injure the plaintiff. Would it not be utterly unfair if, in a suit brought in this country, the court were to apply local law to the occurrence and hold defendant liable for not having dri-

---

*   This article orginally appeared at 52 COLUM. L. REV. 959 (1952). Reprinted with permission.

ven on the right? This illustration, obvious as it is, reveals at least one of the reasons for a system of choice of law. It is required on the grounds of elemental fairness in order not to defeat the justified expectations of the parties.

This policy is naturally strongest when all elements of an occurrence are grouped in a single state. It is not, however, limited to such situations. For example, if parties domiciled in New York should enter into a contract in Illinois which contained a stipulation that Illinois law should govern the extent of their rights and obligations, it would seem, in the absence of some cogent reason to the contrary, that this law should be applied wherever the contract might be sued upon. Similarly, if defamatory matter published in an Omaha newspaper, where it enjoyed a privileged status, were by some strange and fortuitous circumstance transported to China, where it was not so privileged, it would seem unfair to hold defendant liable under Chinese law.

Some cautions, however, are necessary. To begin with, parties to multistate transactions frequently do not give thought beforehand to the question of what law will govern any disputes which may arise between them. Presumably this is normally true of negligence cases where the plaintiff usually does not think about the matter at all, and where the defendant is notoriously prone to act without contemplation of possible consequences. Undoubtedly, the same can be said of many informal contracts entered into between laymen without benefit of legal advice. In situations of this sort, the policy does not help for the simple reason that the parties had no expectations whatsoever with respect to choice of law. Again, cases obviously arise where the parties have conflicting expectations on the subject, and here also the policy can furnish no aid.

It should also be emphasized that the policy looks only to the protection of those expectations which are justified. An American citizen in a foreign Country for example, who seeks to monopolize the foreign commerce of the United States, may believe he is outside the reach of the Sherman Anti-Trust Law. Yet he knows or should know that, at the very least, his actions bring him close to the edge of that law and, at the same time, that he is doing something which not only is wrong in American eyes but also will affect economic conditions in the United States. Under such circumstances, few would be shocked if he were to be found guilty of violating the Act. We must further remember that many legal rules are frankly designed to defeat expectations of persons, who, because of their dominant position, seek to take unfair advantage of others, or conversely who, as in the case of minors, stand in need of special protection. The range of application of such protective laws obviously cannot be determined by looking to the expectations of the parties, and the question must be governed by other considerations.

* * * * *

Aaron D. Twerski, *Enlightened Territorialism and Professor Cavers—The Pennsylvania Method*, 9 DUQ. L. REV. 373, 381-382 (1971)*

* * * * *

When I wake in the morning I expect the sun to shine. In the evening, I expect darkness to fall. Do these expectations have juridical significance? I believe they do. Those positing an interest analysis would argue that their significance arises from the fact that expectations affect

---

*   Reprinted with permission.

conduct. I undertake certain activities with an awareness of the amount of light that will be available to me. I suggest, however, that expectations play a far more potent role in our life style. There is a regularity and rhythm to life in which the familiar—the habitual plays a vital role. At times it affects conduct but even when it does not affect conduct, it affects our sense of tranquillity. A meteor streaking along in the sky thousands of miles from us is of interest because it is a departure from the norm. We can take this departure from the norm with a fair degree of equanimity. If, however, we should go outside on a clear night in which the moon is clearly visible and find no stars it would upset us no end. It would upset us not because we depend on starlight, but because we have the right to believe in the regularity of nature.

Law is no stranger to human activity. If we live in a world of nature—we also live in a world of law. A Delaware driver, on a trip in Delaware expects Delaware law to apply. He may be driving a Pennsylvania guest to his home in Pennsylvania but his expectations prior and subsequent to any accident is that whatever the Delaware law may be it will apply to him. It is immaterial whether it affects his conduct. People have a right to expect a regularity and rhythm from the law. If this is what those who argue for certainty as a conflict of law value are concerned with then they have a point in their favor.

It appears to me that this is not the standard stare decisis type of argument. Change is part and parcel of the common law and the populace has learned to live with it. What is difficult to accept is the notion that "time and space elements" play no role whatsoever in the legal framework of choice-of-law. I think we rather underestimate the embarrassment of the lawyer in the *Cipolla* case [*Cipolla v. Shapska*, 439 Pa. 563 (1970)] who had to explain to the defendant that he was being dragged through a trial because no one was quite sure which law governed his activities. The essence of a normal human existence is the ability to integrate one's experience. We can provide for the throwout and the bizarre but it must be just that—bizarre. To demean "time and space" in the law of conflicts is to deny an important facet of the human experience. Delaware drivers driving in Delaware deserve Delaware law—for better or for worse. When the bizarre becomes the norm—we destroy the norm. The schizophrenic is the human symbol of this distorted point of view. It behooves those who advocate fragmented choice-of-law theory to reconsider normal expectancies as an appropriate function of the law.

* * * * *

Comments

1. As noted in Chapter One, the policy of respect for justified party expectations does not seem to be a component of either a multilateral or a unilateral approach to choice of law. Choice-of-law results guided by concern over party expectations would be too case-variable to meet the uniformity goal of multilateralism (territorialism). Similarly, concern over party expectations would be immaterial to the quest of unilateralism (interest analysis)—to determine the spatial reach of rules vying for application.

2. The theme in Professor Rheinstein's selection, that courts should try whenever possible to protect litigants from unfair surprise in choice of law, is not controversial in itself. Chapter Eight indicates that the idea has found its way into the conflicts law of most American courts today. Professor Rheinstein was not alone in placing the party expectations factor at the center of choice of law. *See, e.g.*, Neuner 1942: pp. 482-486.[1] But few commentators or courts have gone that far. Today, party expectations is likely to appear as but one of a number of conflicts policies combined in an eclectic approach to choice of law. Conflicts eclecticism is examined in Chapter 9, Part A.

3. There has been concern that the expectations policy is susceptible to careless overuse by conflicts courts. Professor Amos Shapira wrote:

> The customary juristic enthusiasm about the "vindication of reason-able expectations" desideratum, which on the face of it is nothing but admirable, often proves unwarranted when scrutinized in pragmatic terms. Many of those committed to the parties' foreseeability goal tend to ignore the crucial fact that, in order to merit legal protection, such expectations ought not only to be justified but first of all actual, existing in fact and capable of realistic identification. The compulsive inclination to infer or impute to individuals implicated in a legal controversy private expectations, even where the latter in point of fact do not exist, or cannot be appropriately evidenced, could obscure legal reasoning. Such a juristic indulgence in the assessment of subjective expectability as to the governance of legal rules may readily provide an ideal ground for frequently fictitious speculations. Time and again judges and writers undertake an extremely speculative analysis of the presumed expectations of parties engaged in some sort of a legal interaction. The assumed hypothesis seems to be that, as a rule, individuals can and do in fact form conscious expectations as to the identity of the normative criteria by which their involvements may be tested. Far from being axiomatic, the tenability of such a hypothesis is highly dubious.

Shapira 1970: p. 81.

4. In their excerpt, Professors Cheatham and Reese concurred with the view of Professor Shapira above that the expectations policy should influence decision only in conflicts cases where the expectation of a litigant as to governing law is both actual and reasonable. In the selection concluding Part A, Professor Twerski appeared to argue against this limitation. Confirming this, he observed later that "my main contention has been that expectations have to be looked at in a perspective broader than that of the parties to the transaction." Twerski 1981: p. 159. Others have also maintained that concern for the expectations of litigants is best understood as but part of a larger policy of predictability in choice of law. Goodrich 1930: p. 167; Westbrook 1975: pp. 449-450.

---

[1]   Full citations appear in the bibliography, Chapter Twelve.

B. Substantivism

Robert A. Leflar, *Choice-Influencing Considerations in Conflicts Law*, 41 N.Y.U. L. REV. 267, 295-304 (1966)*

* * * * *

At one time judges deciding choice-of-law cases would have self-consciously denied that they gave any weight to the quality of the rules of law between which choice was made. A vested rights approach called for a choice between states, not between laws and there was thought to be some tinge of the unethical in the conduct of a judge who, unlike blind Justice, deliberately opened his eyes to see the consequences of his choice. Even today some jurists assert the blind ideal, though none would deny the reality, sometimes partially concealed but readily discoverable, of weight given to the content of rules and the results they produce. Choice of law, as distinguished from choice of jurisdictions, is accepted by the courts more by deed than by word, but it is accepted, within limits. It is easiest to accept when the laws of two involved states are substantially identical, or give the same result in the pending dispute, so that a court can apply the rule or reach the result, perhaps as against the contrary rule of a third state, without having to choose between the first two. But choice between laws as such is a common element in ordinary conflicts cases today. Superiority of one rule of law over another, in terms of socio-economic jurisprudential standards, is far from being the whole basis for choice of law, yet it is without question one of the relevant considerations.

"Justice in the individual case" has always been one of the objectives of law, and it has at times been suggested as the best ultimate that could be aimed at in choice-of-law cases.* * * In a sense, justice in a particular case calls for individualization of decisions, a choice of the better party in the litigation rather than of the better law. Such individualization is not outside the function of law, and judges sometimes properly take pride in it, but it at the same time is a bit frightening to one who, remembering that P's justice may be D's damnation, is anxious to maintain "the rule of law as against the rule of men." A choice made between competing rules of law is more impersonal, less subjective, more in keeping with the traditional law-discovering functions of a common-law court. When the choice is deliberately made in favor of applying what by the forum's standard is the better of the competing rules of law, it is likely that justice between the litigating parties, according to the forum's standards, will be approximated too. The larger consideration seems to serve all the purposes of the narrower one, and to serve them more acceptably.

* * *

More often the better law, for any given set of facts, will be the law which undertakes to uphold a fair transaction entered into by the parties in good faith. * * * The usurious contract cases are the ones most often cited to illustrate this operation of the choice-of-the-better-law process, but the others are almost as familiar. This process, while it normally leads to validation, could equally well lead to invalidation, if the subject matter of the contract were deemed grossly immoral or antisocial by the forum court, or if its form or method of execution, as in

---

*   Reprinted with permission of the New York University Law Review.

the case of some sorts of adhesion contracts, savored of what that court regarded as unfair advantage. In choosing between relevant law that would sustain the transaction and another that would defeat it, the court will almost surely be influenced by its strongly held views on these matters; if it has no strongly held views the policy favoring validation will presumably win out.

It is evident that the search for the better rule of law may lead a court almost automatically to its own lawbooks. The idea that the forum's own law is the best in the world, especially better than fancy new sets of laws based on such nontraditional approaches as research and policy analysis, is unfortunately but understandably still current among some members of our high courts. * * * [I]t is altogether possible, and perhaps more likely than not, that a court may conscientiously conclude, after intelligent comparison, that its local rules of law are wiser, sounder, and better calculated to serve the total ends of justice under law in the controversy before it than are the competing rules of the other state or states that are involved in the case. Such a conscientious conclusion is to be respected. But it does not amount to an automatic prefererence for local law, nor is an automatic preference justifiable. Most courts today do not employ any such automatic preference. What has been called the "result-selective approach" in choice-of-law cases, frequently covered up by a facade of reference to conventional conflicts rules, is too clear in its persistent manifestations, including frequent determination that non-forum law is controlling, to be denied. In every case, however, it can be shown that the choice is directed to the rules of law that produce the result rather than to the result as such.

Judges can appreciate as well as can anyone else the fact that their forum law in some areas is anachronistic, behind the times, a "drag on the coat tails of civilization,"[113] or that the law of some other state has these benighted characteristics. When a court finds itself faced with a choice between such anachronistic laws still hanging on in one state, and realistic practical modern rules in another state, with both states having substantial connection with the relevant facts, it would be surprising if the court's choice did not incline toward the superior law. A court sufficiently aware of the relation between law and societal needs to recognize superiority of one rule over another will seldom be restrained in its choice by the fact that the outmoded rule happens still to prevail in its own state. One way or another it will normally choose the law that makes good sense when applied to the facts.

"One way or another." That suggests manipulation of conflicts rules, the deliberate employment of conflicts concepts as gimmicks to enable courts to reach desired results, as "cover-up" devices designed to conceal the real influences that dominate the judicial process in choice-of-law decision. Such deceits are normally regarded as bad. We praise the great judge who knows how to use precedents narrowly or broadly, build up constructive analogies and explain others away, use fictions wisely and reach results that society approves yet clothe them in the garb of traditional law. That is the method, the technique of our common-law system as good lawyers learn and practice it. It is a method that calls for cleverness but not for deceit. At least we do not like it when there is less than the appearance of intellectual integrity in the process, and we ask that the process be purified as soon as possible. That is definitely our attitude today in viewing manipulative gimmicks in choice of law. We do not in general disagree with results that these deceits have enabled courts to achieve in the past, but we do ask that real reasons and not cover-up devices be given now as explanations of past decisions and guides to future ones.

That choice-of-law concepts are susceptible to manipulation has been openly recognized for a long time. The process of characterization, once seriously regarded as the key to many

---

[113]   Cheatham & Reese, Choice of the Applicable Law, 52 Colum. L. Rev. 959, 980 (1952). * * *

choice-of-law problems, was particularly easy to turn into gimmick functioning because it was based on traditional analytical classifications long honored in Austinian jurisprudence yet never much more exact than a key-numbered descriptive word index. The distinction between substance and procedure has been maneuvered back and forth a hundred ways: personal injury cases usually given a tort characterization are sometimes classified as presenting contract problems, survival cases traditionally deemed to sound in tort have been called matters of estate administration, trespass cases can be classified as involving either tort law or land titles, land sale disputes can be characterized as either title or contract problems, and the same dichotomy is possible as to numerous sorts of transactions concerning chattels.

Nor is characterization the only or even the principal gimmick employed to cover up actual choice-of-law reasons. Definitions of domicile and residence as well as fact findings calculated to suit a given definition of one or the other may shift from court to court. Renvoi has been employed to move a case over to another governing law when this was thought desirable. The multiple rules available in contract cases have been picked over and chosen from so as usually to apply a law that would sustain contracts entered upon in good faith. The flexibility of the "center of gravity" or "predominant contacts" rule proposed by the Restatement (Second) for contract and tort cases constitutes one of the major arguments for approving it. Similar flexibility is present in the "specificity" test for statute of limitations cases. Trusts, especially charitable ones, have regularly been sustained by applying to them first one rule as to governing law and then another. The "presumed intent of the parties" as a choice-of-law guide is usually no more than a judicial selection of the law that will most nearly effectuate the socio-economic purposes of the parties' transaction. Many other illustrations could be given. All of them are of courts actually choosing one set of laws over another, rather than choosing one state and then finding out afterward what its law is.

There is nothing new or strange in this choice of law rather than choice of jurisdictions. Every judge and lawyer knows that our courts have engaged in it from time immemorial, and that it was right for them to do so. Some courts probably have engaged in a choice of parties, but that will scarcely be defended. The urge to do justice in the individual case is amply cared for by a wise choice of the better law to govern the parties' claims. The difficulty is in the cover-up, the pretense that the courts do not make a choice of laws but only a choice of jurisdictions. * * *

The lawyer representing one side or the other in a case starts, at least approximately, with the result he wants to reach, whether the case involves choice of law or something else. That we expect. In nonconflicts cases he first endeavors to characterize his problem, to determine what field it falls in; then, when he finds that the governing rule is unsettled he builds an argument for the rule that for his purposes seems the better one. At the same time he seeks a characterization under which he can with reasonable hope of success argue for the preferred rule. In choice-of-law cases the customary process is much the same, up to a point. The typical lawyer, knowing the result he wants to reach and having characterized his problem sufficiently to know what rules of law he is concerned with, checks the laws of the connected states and ascertains those favorable to him. Then he looks at the mechanical conflicts rules which choose a state rather than a law, and selects anew a characterization or a conflicts theory (gimmick) that will, under the mechanical rules, lead him to the previously chosen law with its desired result. When he comes before the court, he reverses the reasoning process and argues first for his ultimate characterization and conflicts theory, then leads on to the concluding result which was in fact his starting point. Since both sides normally present their choice-of-law reasoning in this final form, it is understandable that courts accept the form, and in their decisions adopt it as presented by one side or the other. But it is also expected that a court will see through what the lawyers have done, follow the order of their unstated as well as of their stated argument, and weigh it also in the judicial balance. The court's desire to achieve justice is just as real as that of the opposing lawyers, the difference being that the court's definition of justice is not controlled by the identity of the lawyers' clients. The court can concern itself with the quality of the opposing laws between which it has to choose, and there is plenty of evidence that courts do concern themselves with this question of quality even though they do not often phrase their opinions in terms of it. The lawyer who omits argument on the inherent superiority of the opposing laws, apart from their territorial origins, is crediting the average court with less understanding and wisdom than it really possesses. Argument presented under the label "strong public policy" may serve the purpose, but it would be more to the point if the cover-up were played down and the discussions were directed specifically, as in non-conflicts cases, to the question of which rule of law deserves preference.

* * * * *

Joseph W. Singer, *Real Conflicts*, 69 B.U. L. REV. 1, 59-64, 75-76 (1989)*

* * * * *

* * * [C]onflicts scholars who advise to apply the better law or the underlying common policy of different states have oversimplified the question of which law is better. They either fail to confront the actual conflicts between the policies of different states, or when they do recognize those conflicts, they fail to give an adequate defense of the law they have identified as better. Conflicts scholars, as well as courts deciding conflicts cases, tend to identify the basic policies of different areas of law in a relatively mechanical and simplistic fashion. Perhaps because modern conflicts analysis itself is so complex, scholars tend to avoid the complexities that underlie the substantive field at issue. Seeking some sense of stability, they choose to simplify the policies underlying substantive law while they confront the difficult questions of multistate policy. Thus, their discussions of substantive policy underlying conflicting state laws are devoid of the sophistication that characterizes analyses of domestic cases involving conflicts about the substantive law of torts, contracts, and property.

Yet, the advocates of the multistate interests in uniformity and the better law are not the only ones who have oversimplified multistate policy. The advocates of comity have similarly oversimplified what is involved in defining the appropriate bounds of overlapping state powers in a federal system. Application of forum law promotes the policy of a separate state and therefore could further multistate interests in comity just as easily as application of the law of some other state. If the application of forum law substantially frustrates the ability of another state to further its local policies, we worry about how conflicts cases of this kind will affect the ability of separate states to pursue separate policies for their own communities. But, if application of either state's law will advance one state's interests while interfering with the norms of the other state, the goal of promoting diversity will not tell us which way to go. Abstract references to the norms of comity or the "needs of the interstate system" are not sufficiently determinate to guide us in choosing which state's law to apply.* * *

---

*   Reprinted with permission.

The advocates of comity have not given sufficient thought to the kind of self-governing polities or separate normative communities they are interested in protecting. We are dealing with situations in which application of either state's law will interfere with the other state's norms in a way that should legitimately concern it. In these kinds of cases, the issue that should seize our attention is the relations among overlapping normative communities. When and for what reasons should we protect the right of someone to rely on the law of the place where she acts to limit her liability or to enforce an arguably unconscionable contract? When is a community entitled to govern itself even though its policies affect outsiders adversely? What kinds of foreign social relationships should the forum reinforce or accept, even though the forum would judge them to be unjust or oppressive?

Consider *Western Airlines v. Sobieski.*[186] Western Airlines, like many corporations, incorporated in Delaware. Yet, it did a substantial amount of business in California: more than thirty percent of its stock was owned by California residents; more than sixty percent of its wages and salaries were paid to employees in California; the majority of its passengers traveled between points in California; and its executive and operations offices were located in California. In contrast, it did no business in Delaware. A group of minority shareholders succeeded in electing two directors by voting their shares cumulatively. The corporation responded by amending its certificate of incorporation to eliminate cumulative voting; the amendment was adopted by a shareholder vote of about 450,000 to 200,000. Delaware, the state of incorporation, permitted Western Airlines to so amend its governing charter; California, the principal place of business, required corporations to provide for cumulative voting and thus prohibited such a maneuver. The Commissioner of Corporations of California exercised his statutory authority to disapprove the decision to eliminate cumulative voting. The trial court overruled the Commissioner, applying the traditional rule that relations among shareholders are governed by the law of the place of incorporation. The District Court of Appeals reversed, holding that the forum had significant interests in applying its law to protect resident minority shareholders and to regulate the governance of a corporation whose business activities were centered in the forum. This result is highly unusual and disapproved by many conflicts and corporations scholars.

Clearly, the forum viewed its own policy as better. The case thus presented a real conflict between California's and Delaware's conceptions of the better law. It also presented a real conflict between the multistate policy of enforcing the better, just law to vindicate the forum's interest in regulating business affairs centered in the forum and the multistate policy of promoting diversity by granting comity to the policies of the state where the corporation chose to incorporate. But, the case also highlights a real conflict about the meaning of comity. Does application of forum law illegitimately interfere with the ability of Delaware to govern relations among shareholders who establish corporations under its incorporation law? Does it illegitimately constrict the freedom of shareholders to decide where they will incorporate? Or, conversely, does application of Delaware law illegitimately interfere with the ability of California to regulate business affairs that have a substantial effect on the California economy? Does application of the law of the place of incorporation effectively delegate to Delaware the power to rule the nation?

These ambiguities in the notion of comity remind us that application of either state's law will interfere with the policies of the other. They also remind us that invocation of "critical territorial contacts" cannot decide this case for us; the territorialists must explain to us whether the critical contacts are with the principal place of business or with the place where incorpo-

---

[186]   191 Cal. App. 2d 399, 12 Cal. Rptr. 719 (1961).

ration papers are filed. To answer this question, they need to explain whether or not a business can evade the regulatory requirements of the place where it does business simply by announcing that it resides in another state. Should shareholders be free to determine which state's law will govern their relations among themselves, thereby obliterating entirely the power of the place where they do business to regulate their governance structure?

Initially, application of Delaware law would appear to further interests in comity. The California forum could engage in restrained interpretation of its regulatory policy by altruistically deferring to Delaware's policy of granting a liberty interest in freedom of contract to shareholders to freely determine their governance structure. Deference to foreign law in this situation by the California court would show an admirable willingness to live in a multistate system by enforcing legal relationships centered in other states that the forum views as oppressive or socially harmful.

But, this initial appearance of comity is deceiving. Fortunately—or unfortunately—deference to the law of the place of incorporation will change the behavior of corporations nationwide. Boards of directors that want to minimize the power of minority shareholders will attempt to change the state of their incorporation to the free haven of Delaware; given management's influence over most directors and stockholders, they may succeed quite often. Delaware seeks to have as many corporations incorporate (and operate) in Delaware as possible, as the fees and taxes generated by incorporation add significant revenues to the state budget. To this end, Delaware lowers or abolishes many forms of regulation that hamper management or interfere with its ability to protect itself from being dislodged. The likely result is that hundreds of corporations will change their state of incorporation to Delaware. Other states, surveying the positive economic effects of Delaware policy and recognizing their own desire for corporate fealty, subsequently lower their standards to rival Delaware's. The competition among states thus starts a pathological race to the bottom. Delaware, with its rock bottom standards, effectively rules the nation. The result, far from an advancement of interests in diversity, is one of national uniformity. And it may be uniformity of an unattractive kind—not uniformity of the better law, but of the worst law. Thus, we must ask the question: When does deference [to] the law of another state actually further interests in preserving separate political communities or social laboratories and when does it promote uniform bad law?

On the other hand, application of the supposedly better forum law does not solve the comity problem either. For example, if a few states adopt plaintiff-compensating policies because their legislatures are controlled by their state trial lawyers' associations, their courts may become havens of multistate products liability lawsuits. As the flurry of tort reform legislation of recent years shows us, many people believe that the sentimental policies of a few judges who cannot see around hapless victims are ruining the economy of the nation. Whether they are right or wrong, we should worry about whether the tort victims' ability to choose to sue in plaintiff-favoring states allows these states to rule the nation under the guise of promoting justice, and results in a different—but no less perverse—race to the bottom.

What kind of political community is it in Delaware to which California should defer? If most of the shareholders and business activities of companies incorporated in Delaware are located in other states, what social relationships *in Delaware* does Delaware law protect? Is it the community of pieces of paper in the offices of the Delaware Secretary of State? Does the Delaware law represent an effort of the people of Delaware to constitute themselves as a normative community? Or does the community of Delaware taxpayers merely want to decrease its taxes? Is this enough to justify California's acquiescence in what it views as inefficient and unjust relationships among the resident owners of businesses whose real activities are centered in California? Should shareholders scattered around the country have the right to declare allegiance to Delaware and thus obtain the benefits of Delaware law at the expense of those who claim the protection of the law of their home state?

Identifying what we mean by comity requires us to consider what kinds of issues relate to the idea of a political or normative community. We must identify the kinds of social relationships that the notion of comity should protect. What kinds of policies must we tolerate in the interest of promoting diverse polities? When does a state constitute a normative community? If real conflicts arise between the abilities of different states to further their conceptions of justice, what forms of accommodation should we seek? These questions raise complexities about the meaning of self-government, democracy, tolerance, and political pluralism. They cannot be answered by appealing to the abstract notions of the "most significant relationship" or "comparative impairment" or "real interests." They require us to define, not abstractly, but in context, what we mean by social justice and freedom in the relations among overlapping normative communities.

* * * * *

William F. Baxter, *Choice of Law and the Federal System*, 16 STAN. L. REV. 1, 4-6 (1963)*

* * * * *

As is consistent with the generally healthy concern for pragmatic consequences that has characterized recent jurisprudential thought, most attempts to identify a normative basis for choice criteria have focused upon the interests of the immediate parties to the transaction and thus upon the same factors that would be dispositive in a similar case wholly internal to a single state. I cannot escape the conclusion that a search so oriented must prove unrewarding. Every choice-of-law case involves several parties, each of whom would prevail if the internal law of one rather than another state were applied. Each party is "right," "worthy," and "deserving" and "ought in all fairness" to prevail under one of the competing bodies of law and in the view of one of the competing groups of lawmakers. Fact situations which differ only in that they are internal to a single state have been assessed by the different groups of lawmakers, and each has reached a different value judgment on the rule best calculated to serve the overall interest of its community. If attention is confined to the circumstances of the immediate parties, the conflict between the internal laws and between the value judgments they are intended to implement cannot be resolved by the judge unless he is prepared to impose still another value judgment upon the controversy. The judge who takes this approach must conclude, for example, that legal systems recognizing past consideration in contract cases embody a juster justice than those that do not or conclude that legal systems imposing absolute liability in tort cases achieve results more desirable than those that apply the standard of negligence. The imposition of such super-value judgments is not, of course, intellectually impossible. Courts have, from time to time, resolved cases on this basis, though they seldom make the basis explicit. Super-value judgments have been urged, somewhat more explicitly, by commentators.

The drawbacks of this approach, however, are easily identified. The judge is required to formulate law in a much more frank and open manner than is generally thought compatible with

---

his non-political status. It lacks the protective apparent neutrality of tradional choice rules which, however flexible they actually are, allow the judge to apply them and then announce the result with a tone that suggests he himself was surprised by the outcome. Necessarily a super-value judgment is disputable: the very occasion for its articulation is the existence of a contrary judgment reached by one of the contending bodies of internal lawmakers. Finally, the objective of primary predictability is not likely to be furthered. The uniformity of outcome on which it depends will exist only if the same super-value judgment is reached in all forums, consistently subordinating the same local value judgment. One of the most probable forums is the state that has adopted, for internal purposes, the value judgment to be subordinated. The judges of that state are unlikely to reach a super-value judgment in conflicts cases contrary to judgments they previously reached in internal cases which the approach does nothing to distinguish.

These difficulties can be avoided if normative criteria can be found which relate to the very aspects of a conflicts case that distinguish it from an analogous internal case. That such criteria can be elaborated in many, if not all, conflicts cases has been demonstrated by several writers who have urged that conflicts cases be resolved on the basis of the governmental interests involved.

* * * * *

Arthur T. von Mehren, *Special Substantive Rules for Multistate Problems: Their Role and Significance in Contemporary Choice of Law Methodology*, 88 HARV. L. REV. 347, 356-359 (1974)*

* * * * *

The development by individual legal orders of substantive rules for multistate problems proceeds basically on the assumption that certain situations or transactions having significant connections with more than one legal order cannot be appropriately regulated by the application of the rules and principles applied to comparable situations or transactions whose significant contacts are with only one legal order. * * * The distinguishing characteristic of the substantive-rule technique is its recognition that, on occasion, serious problems are created by regulating situations with significant multistate elements under rules and principles developed for comparable, fully domestic situations.

The substantive-rule approach thus raises the question whether one should, in handling the choice of law problem, work from the beginning with a fundamental distinction between situations and transactions that can, and those that cannot, appropriately be localized, allocating regulation of the former to a domestic law and developing special multijurisdictional rules for the latter. Such an approach encounters several difficulties. In the first place, the propriety in a particular multistate context of a substantive-rule solution cannot be assessed generally or abstractly, but only after considering the domestic-law rules that regulate comparable domestic problems in the various concerned legal orders. The appropriateness of localizing a given situation or transaction will largely depend upon the problem that has arisen, the kind and intensity of the concern that the various implicated legal orders may have in the resolution of the

---

controversy, and the degree to which the expectations and understandings of the parties were, or should have been, shaped by solutions provided in comparable local situations. Moreover, the principle of equality requires that a legal order not distinguish between the treatment of localized and multistate situations or transactions unless the circumstances are such as clearly to justify departing from the norm represented by domestic-law solutions. There is also an economy of effort and an avoidance of complication in utilizing domestic-law solutions insofar as possible. Furthermore, since as a practical matter the legislature is not, aside from special circumstances, likely to be active in developing special substantive rules for multistate problems, the burden of this approach will fall, for the most part, on the judiciary. Here, especially in civil law systems, the traditional hesitancy to accord lawmaking functions to the courts stands in the way of broadscale resort to a substantive rule approach, as does the general reluctance of all contemporary societies to assign additional tasks of great complexity and difficulty to already overburdened courts. Finally the approach might, unless widely adopted, increase opportunities for forum shopping and would reduce legal security generally if decisional uniformity became more difficult to attain.

Accordingly, courts have resorted to the use of multijurisdictional rules only after they have concluded that a minimally apt solution cannot be obtained by applying the domestic-law rule indicated by the choice of law process. For example, after a French law of 1925 permitted arbitration clauses in domestic commercial contracts, the French courts chose to uphold arbitration clauses in international contracts governed by French law concluded before that date, while continuing to refuse enforcement to such clauses in domestic contracts concluded before the effective date of the statute. This result was not based on the proposition that an entirely separate body of rules and principles should be developed for international commercial contracts, but on the perception that, in view of the special requirements of these international transactions, application of the French domestic rule would produce an unacceptable result. Similarly, where various legal systems, by legislation or by judicial action, establish special procedural rules for litigation involving foreign parties or for cases in which evidence must be obtained from abroad, the intent is not to provide an entirely distinct procedural scheme but is to alter the system utilized for purely domestic transactions only where considerations of aptness imperatively require.

Three general classes of situations are encountered in which multistate substantive rules may recommend themselves. In the first type of situation, the forum considers that two legal orders are sufficiently concerned with a given situation that the rules of both should be given effect, but the domestic rules do not lend themselves to cumulative application. The judgment here that the view of more than one legal order must be given effect may reflect simply the force of circumstance—if a witness whose testimony is required in B is available only in A, the B court can hardly ignore A's views respecting the manner in which testimony is to be taken. The second general class comprises situations which, because of their multistate characteristics, involve considerations which do not have particular significance in comparable domestic settings. For example, a state which considers it inappropriate to submit to arbitration claims against itself arising from domestic transactions may be willing to arbitrate disputes arising from multistate transactions, in view of the foreign plaintiff's fear of prejudice if he is forced to litigate a controversy with the sovereign in the sovereign's courts, as well as the state's reluctance to litigate in the courts of other sovereigns. These two classes of solutions thus forward the policy of aptness by introducing needed refinements not provided by the otherwise applicable domestic rules. A third class of situations is presented only by cases of true conflict, that is to say, situations in which two or more legal orders have legitimate reasons to regulate the dispute that has arisen, but hold mutually inconsistent views respecting the form such regulation should take. Here, a multistate solution may be adopted in order to achieve decisional uniformity or other values of conflicts justice without requiring one state to sacrifice entirely its views respecting aptness. By according roughly equal respect to the views of each legal order, a basis may be created for agreement upon a mutually acceptable governing rule.* * *

* * * * *

Patrick J. Borchers, *Conflicts Pragmatism*, 56 ALBANY L. REV. 883, 895-899 (1993)*

* * * * *

* * * [A]lthough conflicts writers seem reluctant to admit it, they do not have a monopoly on the conflict between "systemic" and "individualized" values. For instance, a court attempting to decide, in a purely local case, whether to create a "discovery" exception to a statute of limitations must consider "systemic" values and "substantive" criteria.[109] Such a court is required to consider the values promoted by not creating such an exception (ease of application and uniformity of result) and those promoted by creating an exception (fairness in the individual case). Few would assert that such a choice can be made in a "value-free" manner. Rather, the beacons of substantive law—the utility of each approach for these and future litigants—light the judge's path.

The question then becomes: Why is it that similar choices can be made in a "value-free" manner in multistate cases? Freed from the notion that "legal rules" are a set of concepts, and looking at law pragmatically (or "realistically") as an activity being carried out by judges and other governmental officials, the answer is that such choices *cannot* be made in a "value-free" manner. Judges are engaged in the same activity or enterprise whether they have before them a local or a multistate case.

Recast in this way, it becomes clear that substance has been there all along in choice of law. The best arguments raised in favor of the *First Restatement*—uniformity of result, ease of application, and avoidance of forum shopping—are substantive law arguments. Specifically, they are arguments based on the uniformity of treatment of litigants and the reduction of the costs of litigation. Not surprisingly, these are exactly the arguments that favor a "hard and fast" statute of limitations. The arguments raised to attack the *First Restatement* are no less substantive. The argument that the place-of-the-injury rule in torts cases produces "absurd" and "unjust" results is a species of the argument that any general rule can produce harsh results that must be mitigated. Not surprisingly, this is exactly the argument that favors a "discovery" exception.

Conflicts pragmatism means bridging the perceived gulf between the values that are thought to inform choice of law and substantive law. It means realizing that the considerations which guide a choice between competing ways of deciding a local case are not absent in a multistate one. It means figuring out, as judges have done since the dawn of the common law, whether the decision is a good or a bad one. It means worrying about whether decisions in mul-

---

*   Reprinted with permission.

[109]   *See, e.g.*, Fernandi v. Strully, 173 A.2d 277 (N.J. 1961).

tistate cases make people's lives better or worse instead of whether they will appease some hypothetical "sovereign".

Let me suggest how this task of bridging the imagined gulf between substantive and conflicts values might begin. Many writers and courts have hypothesized a distinction between "conduct-regulating" and "loss-allocating" rules of law. Conduct-regulating rules—including traffic laws, the validity of contracts, and the priority of liens on real property—are such because they are forward looking. Their dominant purpose is to set out guideposts to allow persons to shape their conduct so as to give rise to predictable legal consequences. A person can know that by driving under the speed limit, signing an agreement, or perfecting a security interest, he or she is avoiding or taking certain risks. Loss-allocating rules are different. These rules—including negligence, strict liability, and defenses to non-intentional torts—are such because they are backward looking. Their dominant purpose is to look back to an unplanned transaction, paradigmatically an accident, to determine who should bear the loss and in what proportion.

Of course, the distinction between loss-allocating and conduct-regulating rules is not always sharp, and the classes may well not exhaust all legal rules. Some rules of negligence, most notably malpractice liability, affect conduct in certain ways, such as encouraging the purchase of insurance. But it is a serviceable distinction, just as the distinction between "substance" and "procedure" is serviceable despite well-documented difficulties of application in marginal circumstances.

The substantive values that underlie these two broad classifications are different. In the case of conduct-regulating rules, certainty and predictability are at a premium. Pragmatic choice of law fosters these values in conduct regulation. This can be accomplished by hard and fast rules that are likely to comport with the subjective expectations of the parties. For example, a pragmatic choice-of-law rule for traffic laws, such as speed limits, would be the place of the conduct. One would think it bizarre to have any other rule. A rule that chose, for instance, the place of registration of the car would lead to peculiarities. A person driving a California-registered car through New York on a rural stretch of four lane highway would be immune from a speeding ticket for travelling 60 m.p.h. (because California law allows speeds of up to 65 m.p.h. on such roads), while a driver in a New York-registered car could be ticketed (because the maximum speed in New York is theoretically 55 m.p.h.). Regulating by the law of the place of the conduct avoids the anomalies and vindicates practical expectations.

A pragmatic choice-of-law rule for the priority of liens on real property would be the situs of the real property. In order for a lienholder to make an accurate appraisal of the value of his security interest, he must know who is ahead of him in line at any foreclosure sale. An uncertain, difficult to apply choice-of-law approach would greatly frustrate such an appraisal. The situs rule has the twin virtues of making the choice-of-law calculation easy and comporting with the intuitive expectations of all concerned.

But just as the values that underlie substantive law do not remain constant across its full spectrum, the values that underlie choice of law also vary. Hard and fast rules work well for conduct-regulating rules because of the purpose of those rules. There is, however, no reason to believe that the same approach will work well for loss-allocating rules. Loss-allocating rules, as we have seen, look back to unplanned events and attempt to assign the loss justly. Predictability matters less because the liability-creating event is unplanned. Of course, the most just manner for the allocation of loss can be, and often is, controversial, and courts frequently struggle visibly with these decisions.

However, if courts are to approach conflicts of loss-allocating rules pragmatically and fulfill the substantive values underlying these rules, they must assess the justice of the competing rules. Any non-pragmatic approach will promote justice only by happenstance. It matters not whether the choice is based on the place of the accident (as the *First Restatement* counseled), the domiciles of the parties (as Currie counseled), a combination of the two (as the *Second Restatement* counseled), the alphabetical ordering of the states, or the flip of a coin. Any approach that fails to consider the justice of the competing methods of apportioning the loss will inevitably apportion the loss unjustly in some cases, and thereby frustrate the substantive values.

Of course, justice in loss allocation is a controversial matter, as the variety in United States tort law attests, and choosing the most just of the competing rules is not always easy. However, courts struggle with these same value judgments in local cases. Often courts will consider their own state's law superior, but experience shows that this is not inevitable. Even though disagreements as to the wisdom of each of varying approaches to loss allocation will persist, and even though some forum bias will exist, the alternative is untenable. The alternative—ignoring the merits of the competing rules—will frustrate substantive policies just as surely as would a rule requiring courts to choose the law in real property disputes by a roll of dice. And if choice, in this context, is to be made pragmatically and the gulf with substantive law bridged, the justice of the competing rules must be the determinant.

* * * * *

Comments

1.   Substantivist conflicts policy, that courts should choose the best available law, is difficult to locate within either the multilateral (territorial) or unilateral (interest analysis) movements in American conflicts law. As noted in Chapter One, multilateralism and unilateralism are both concerned with the appropriate sovereign (law source) rather than the best law. Substantivism also stands apart from the justified expectations policy surveyed in Part A of this Chapter, since the latter expresses little if any interest in the innate quality of the law upon which a party reasonably relies.

2.   Conflicts writing in a substantivist vein is surveyed in Borchers 1993a: pp. 901-904;[1] Weinberg 1991a: pp. 65-67. On the European antecedents for conflicts substantivism, *see* Juenger 1980: pp. 120-121; Juenger 1993: pp. 23-24.

3.   Professor Robert Leflar noted in the selection opening Part B of this Chapter that usury cases provided an early example of conflicts substantivism in this country. Beginning in the nineteenth century, American judges who disliked usury laws held that "the parties are presumed to have chosen the law that will sustain the contract." Goodrich 1938: p. 285. Further discussion of this development appears in Cavers 1933: p. 182; Lorenzen 1921: p. 673.

4.   The idea that conflicts cases should be adjudicated in a way promoting substantive justice is not in itself controversial. Substantive justice is, after all, the aim of all civil litigation. Much controversy has arisen, however, about whether or how the choice-of-law process should be manipulated to secure particular substantive results. The positions for and against substantivism in choice of law are arranged around a

---

[1]   Full citations appear in the bibliography, Chapter Twelve.

series of questions: Do conflicts judges frequently take substantive concerns into account, and will they continue to do so whether or not commentators approve of the practice? Is it proper judicial behavior for judges to express through choice of law their personal substantive preferences? Is substantivist policy capable of producing coherent conflicts doctrine? Can it be effectively coordinated with other policies (*e.g.*, interest analysis, party expectations) in a combined choice-of-law approach? Is substantivism in judicial practice little more than forum favoritism? Professor Leflar (the leading proponent of conflicts substantivism) and Professor William F. Baxter (a vocal critic) delivered opposing answers to these questions in their selections appearing in Part B.

5. A number of commentators have endorsed the idea that choice of law should be influenced to at least some degree by the concerns of substantive justice. They include Juenger 1989a: p. 126; Reese 1986: pp. 6-7; Weintraub 1986: p. 284; Zweigert 1973: pp. 289-290, 294-295. On the other hand, many writers have challenged conflicts substantivism as improper, doctrinally incoherent, or simply beside the point. These critics include Baade 1973: p. 165-166; Cavers 1970: p. 175; Currie 1963a: pp. 104-105; Korn 1983: p. 958; McLaughlin 1991b: pp. 396-398; Morris 1973: p. 324; Scoles & Hay 1992: pp. 29-31; Westbrook 1975: pp. 461-462. There are also critics who, while less hostile to conflicts substantivism, are nonetheless skeptical. One such writer observed:

> it is with sincere regret that we report the nonexistence in the world of conflicts of any substantive super law (national consensus law, better law, modern law) applicable to multistate cases. Before this is challenged, consider these words of consolation. There is indeed a life for this super law, but in another world, on the planet of unification. Perhaps my view of the scope of choice of law is too narrow, but I include within it principally those situations where at least two senses of justice, as crystallized in differing substantive rules of equal standing, are potentially applicable. In many areas of the law, even in the field of torts (products liability, defamation), states and nations have different perceptions on where to draw the line of justice. This is likely to continue for the indefinite future. The struggle, then, is not between good and evil, but between at least two goods or two lesser evils. By what authority and on what kind of reason other than pure subjective preference can a judge select one of these senses of justice over that which prevails in his own state?

Kozyris 1985b: p. 571. A similar view is expressed in Weinberg 1991a: p. 94.

6. Conflicts substantivism takes on a somewhat different meaning when argued from the premise that no purely domestic substantive rule suits the multistate character of the case. Professor Arthur von Mehren, who explored the potential for special substantive rules in his selection in Part B, worked with his colleague, the late Professor Donald Trautman, to develop this idea. *See, e.g.*, von Mehren & Trautman 1965: pp. 376-378. The approach has additional support. Juenger 1982: pp. 120-121;

McDougal 1984: pp. 489-491; McDougal 1996: pp. 2483-2484. But Professor Peter Hay has rejected the concept, arguing: "'Better law' as the source of new multistate solutions * * * ultimately suffers from the same *ad hoc* nature as the 'better law' approach from which it derives." Hay 1991: p. 356.

CHAPTER EIGHT

Prevailing Choice-of-Law Approaches

This Chapter examines the forms of conflicts law most often used by America courts today.

Part A treats the most widely adopted choice-of-law approach: the American Law Institute's RESTATEMENT (SECOND) OF CONFLICTS OF LAWS. Part A begins with a selections from the RESTATEMENT (SECOND) that reveal the methodological design of the work and illustrate its applications. Next, Professor Michael Finch discusses the theory and structure of the Restatement (Second) as well as the climate of controversy surrounding it. Finally, Professor Symeon Symeonides' functional critique divides the directives of the RESTATEMENT (SECOND) into a series of categories—from gentle, policy-guided suggestions to courts to stern rules reminiscent of the original RESTATEMENT.

Part B of this Chapter examines the "choice-influencing considerations" recommended by Professor Robert Leflar, an approach that trails only the RESTATEMENT (SECOND) in popularity. Part B opens with a selection by Professor Leflar where he sets the stage for his approach with prior law and commentary, and then presents, explains and defends his five choice-influencing considerations. Next, in an excerpt from another article, Professor Leflar provides a series of examples of his approach in application. Part B concludes with a description by Professor James R. Pielemeier of the experience of Minnesota state courts with Leflar's choice-influencing considerations.

The Chapter ends with a recent study by Professor Symeonides, the leading observer of trends in American conflicts law. This selection provides an annotated map of the choice-of-law in the United States. Professor Symeonides classifies the conflicts law of each state in the areas of torts and contracts.

A. The RESTATEMENT (SECOND)

American Law Institute, RESTATMENT OF THE LAW (SECOND) CONFLICT OF LAWS, Introduction, §§ 6 (with comment), 145 (with comment), 146, 147, 175, 187 (with comment), 188, 196, 236, 260, 270, 278 (St. Paul 1971)*

INTRODUCTION

* * * As those who followed the tentative drafts (1953 to 1965) and the three installments of the proposed draft (1967 to 1969) will readily confirm, the new work is far more than a current version of the old. In basic analysis and technique, in the position taken on a host of issues, in the elaboration of the commentary and addition of Reporter's Notes, what is presented here is a fresh treatment of the subject.

It is a treatment that takes full account of the enormous change in dominant judicial thought respecting conflicts problems that has taken place in relatively recent years. The essence of that change has been the jettisoning of a multiplicity of rigid rules in favor of standards of greater flexibility, according sensitivity in judgement to important values that were formerly ignored. Such a transformation in the corpus of the law reduces certitude as well as certainty, posing a special problem in the process of restatement. Its solution lies in candid recognition that black-letter formulations often must consist of open-ended standards, gaining further content from reasoned elaboration in the comments and specific instances of application given there or in the notes of the Reporter. That technique is not unique to Conflicts but the situation here has called for its employment quite pervasively throughout these volumes. The result presents a striking contrast to the first Restatement in which dogma was so thoroughly enshrined.

One illustration will suffice to make the point. The earlier Restatement treated choice of law in torts and contracts by articulating a closed set of rules derived from vested-rights analysis. The governing law in torts was determined by the place in which the contract became binding or, when performance was an issue, where the contract was to be performed. Restatement Second supplants these rules by the broad principle that rights and liabilities with respect to a particular issue are determined by the local law of the State which, as to that issue, has "the most significant relationship" to the occurance and the parties. The "factors relevant" to that appraisal, absent a binding stautory mandate, are enumerated generally [in § 6].* * *

To be sure, this mode of treatment leaves the answer to specific problems very much at large. There is, therefore, wherever possible, a secondary statement in black letter setting forth the choice of law the courts will "usually" make in given situations. These formulations are cast as empirical appraisals rather than purported rules to indicate how far the statements may be subject to revaluation in a concrete instance in light of the more general and open-ended norm. The reader is thus alerted to the dynamic element in choice of law adjudication, without losing the degree of guidance past decisions may afford. That guidance is enhanced, moreover, by the further exposition in the comments and Reporter's Notes. The comments, it should be noted, no less than the black letter carry the approval of the Institute. The Notes, however, rest on the authority of the Reporter only, though they too have been before the Advisers and the Institute, whose criticism and suggestions the Reporter has invited and considered.

---

* * * * *

Chapter 1—Introduction

§ 6 CHOICE-OF-LAW PRINCIPLES

(1) A court, subject to constitutional restrictions, will follow a statutory directive of its own state on choice of law.

(2) When there is no such directive, the factors relevant to the choice of the applicable rule of law include

   (a) the needs of the interstate and international systems,

   (b) the relevant policies of the forum,

   (c) the relevant policies of other interested states and the relative interests of those states in the determination of the particular issue,

   (d) the protection of justified expectations,

   (e) the basic policies underlying the particular field of law,

   (f) certainty, predictability and uniformity of result, and

   (g) ease in the determination and application of the law to be applied.

Comment on Subsection (1):

   a. Statutes directed to choice of law. A court, subject to constitutional limitations, must follow the directions of its legislature. The court must apply a local statutory provision directed to choice of law provided that it would be constitutional to do so. An example of a statute directed to choice of law is the Uniform Commercial Code which provides in certain instances for the application of the law chosen by the parties (§ 1-105(1)) and in other instances for the application of the law of a particular state (§§ 2-402, 4-102, 6-102, 8-106, 9-103). Another example is the Model Execution of Wills Act which provides that a written will subscribed by the testator shall be valid as to matters of form if it complies with the local requirements of any one of a number of enumerated states. Statutes that are expressly directed to choice of law, that is to say, statutes which provide for the application of the local law of one state, rather than the local law of another state, are comparatively few in number.

   b. Intended range of application of statute. A court will rarely find that a question of choice of law is explicitly covered by statute. That is to say, a court will rarely be directed by statute to apply the local law of one state, rather than the local law of another state, in the decision of a particular issue. On the other hand, the court will constantly be faced with the question whether the issue before it falls within the intended range of application of a particular statute. The court should give a local statute the range of application intended by the legislature when these intentions can be ascertained and can constitutionally be given effect. If the legislature intended that the statute should be applied to the out-of-state facts involved, the court should so apply it unless constitutional considerations forbid. On the other hand, if the legislature intended that the statute should be applied only to acts taking place within the state, the statute should not be given a wider range of application. Sometimes a statute's intended range of application will be apparent on its face, as when it expressly applies to all citizens of a state including those who are living abroad. When the statute is silent as to its range of application, the intentions of the legislature on the subject can sometimes be ascertained by a process of interpretation and construction. Provided that it is constitutional to do so, the court will apply a local statute in the manner intended by the legislature even when the local law of another state would be applicable under usual choice-of-law principles.

Comment on Subsection (2):

   c. Rationale. Legislatures usually legislate, and courts usually adjudicate, only with the local situation in mind. They rarely give thought to the extent to which the laws they enact, and the common law rules they enunciate, should apply to out-of-state facts. When there are no adequate directives in the statute or in the case law, the court will take account of the factors listed in this Subsection in determining the state whose local law will be applied to determine the issue at hand. It is not suggested that this list of factors is exclusive. Undoubtedly, a court will on occasion give consideration to other factors in deciding a question of choice of law. Also it is not suggested that the factors mentioned are listed in the order of their relative importance. Varying weight will be given to a particular factor, or to a group of factors, in different areas of choice of law. So, for example, the policy in favor of effectuating the relevant policies of the state of dominant interest is given predominant weight in the rule that transfers of interests in land are governed by the law that would be applied by the courts of the situs (see §§ 223-243). On the other hand, the policies in favor of protecting the justified expectations of the parties and of effectuating the basic policy underlying the particular field of law come to the fore in the rule that, subject to certain limitations, the parties can choose the law to govern their contract (see § 187) and in the rules which provide, subject to certain limitations, for the application of a law which will uphold the validity of a trust of movables (see §§ 269-270) or the validity of a contract against the charge of commercial usury (see § 203). Similarly, the policy favoring uniformity of result comes to the fore in the rule that succession to interests in movables is governed by the law that would be applied by the courts of the state where the decedent was domiciled at the time of his death (see §§ 260 and 263).

   At least some of the factors mentioned in this Subsection will point in different directions in all but the simplest case. Hence any rule of choice of law, like any other common law rule, represents an accommodation of conflicting values. Those chapters in the Restatement of this Subject which are concerned with choice of law state the rules which the courts have evolved in accommodation of the factors listed in this Subsection. In certain areas, as in parts of Property (Chapter 9), such rules are sufficiently precise to permit them to be applied in the decision of a case without explicit reference to the factors which underlie them. In other areas, such as in Wrongs (Chapter 7) and Contracts (Chapter 8), the difficulties and complexities involved have as yet prevented

the courts from formulating a precise rule, or series of rules, which provide a satisfactory accommodation of the underlying factors in all of the situations which may
arise. All that can presently be done in these areas is to state a general principle, such
as application of the local law "of the state of most significant relationship", which provides some clue to the correct approach but does not furnish precise answers. In these
areas, the courts must look in each case to the underlying factors themselves in order
to arrive at a decision which will best accommodate them.

Statement of precise rules in many areas of choice of law is made even more difficult by the great variety of situations and of issues, by the fact that many of these situations and issues have not been thoroughly explored by the courts, by the generality
of statement frequently used by the courts in their opinions, and by the new grounds
of decision stated in many of the more recent opinions.

The Comments which follow provide brief discussion of the factors underlying
choice of law which are mentioned in this Subsection.

d. Needs of the interstate and international systems. Probably the most important function of choice-of-law rules is to make the interstate and international systems
work well. Choice-of-law rules, among other things, should seek to further harmonious relations between states and to facilitate commercial intercourse between them.
In formulating rules of choice of law, a state should have regard for the needs and policies of other states and of the community of states. Rules of choice of law formulated
with regard for such needs and policies are likely to commend themselves to other
states and to be adopted by these states. Adoption of the same choice-of-law rules by
many states will further the needs of the interstate and international systems and
likewise the values of certainty, predictability and uniformity of result.

e. Relevant policies of the state of the forum. Two situations should be distinguished. One is where the state of the forum has no interest in the case apart from the
fact that it is the place of the trial of the action. Here the only relevant policies of the
state of the forum will be embodied in its rules relating to trial administration (see
Chapter 6). The second situation is where the state of the forum has an interest in the
case apart from the fact that it is the place of trial. In this latter situation, relevant policies of the state of the forum may be embodied in rules that do not relate to trial administration.

The problem dealt with in this Comment arises in the common situation where a
statute or common law rule of the forum was formulated solely with the intrastate situation in mind or, at least, where there is no evidence to suggest that the statute or rule
was intended to have extraterritorial application. If the legislature or court (in the case
of a common law rule) did have intentions with respect to the range of application of
a statute or common law rule and these intentions can be ascertained, the rule of Subsection (1) is applicable. If not, the court will interpret the statute or rule in the light
of the factors stated in Subsection (2).

Every rule of law, whether embodied in a statute or in a common law rule, was
designed to achieve one or more purposes. A court should have regard for these purposes in determining whether to apply its own rule or the rule of another state in the
decision of a particular issue. If the purposes sought to be achieved by a local statute

or common law rule would be furthered by its application to out-of-state facts, this is a weighty reason why such application should be made. On the other hand, the court is under no compulsion to apply the statute or rule to such out-of-state facts since the originating legislature or court had no ascertainable intentions on the subject. The court must decide for itself whether the purposes sought to be achieved by a local statute or rule should be furthered at the expense of the other choice-of-law factors mentioned in this Subsection.

f. Relevant policies of other interested states. In determining a question of choice of law, the forum should give consideration not only to its own relevant policies (see Comment e) but also to the relevant policies of all other interested states. The forum should seek to reach a result that will achieve the best possible accommodation of these policies. The forum should also appraise the relative interests of the states involved in the determination of the particular issue. In general, it is fitting that the state whose interests are most deeply affected should have its local law applied. Which is the state of dominant interest may depend upon the issue involved. So if a husband injures his wife in a state other than that of their domicil, it may be that the state of conduct and injury has the dominant interest in determining whether the husband's conduct was tortious or whether the wife was guilty of contributory negligence (see § 146). On the other hand, the state of the spouses' domicil is the state of dominant interest when it comes to the question whether the husband should be held immune from tort liability to his wife (see § 169).

The content of the relevant local law rule of a state may be significant in determining whether this state is the state with the dominant interest. So, for example, application of a state's statute or common law rule which would absolve the defendant from liability could hardly be justified on the basis of this state's interest in the welfare of the injured plaintiff.

g. Protection of justified expectations. This is an important value in all fields of the law, including choice of law. Generally speaking, it would be unfair and improper to hold a person liable under the local law of one state when he had justifiably molded his conduct to conform to the requirements of another state. Also, it is in part because of this factor that the parties are free within broad limits to choose the law to govern the validity of their contract (see § 187) and that the courts seek to apply a law that will sustain the validity of a trust of movables (see §§ 269-270).

There are occasions, particularly in the area of negligence, when the parties act without giving thought to the legal consequences of their conduct or to the law that may be applied. In such situations, the parties have no justified expectations to protect, and this factor can play no part in the decision of a choice-of-law question.

h. Basic policies underlying particular field of law. This factor is of particular importance in situations where the policies of the interested states are largely the same but where there are nevertheless minor differences between their relevant local law rules. In such instances, there is good reason for the court to apply the local law of that state which will best achieve the basic policy, or policies, underlying the particular field of law involved. This factor explains in large part why the courts seek to apply a law that will sustain the validity of a contract against the charge of commercial usury (§ 203) or the validity of a trust of movables against the charge that it violates the Rule Against Perpetuities (§§ 269-270).

i. Predictability and uniformity of result. These are important values in all areas of the law. To the extent that they are attained in choice of law, forum shopping will be discouraged. These values can, however, be purchased at too great a price. In a rapidly developing area, such as choice of law, it is often more important that good rules be developed than that predictability and uniformity of result should be assured through continued adherence to existing rules. Predictability and uniformity of result are of particular importance in areas where the parties are likely to give advance thought to the legal consequences of their transactions. It is partly on account of these factors that the parties are permitted within broad limits to choose the law that will determine the validity and effect of their contract (see § 187) and that the law that would be applied by the courts of the state of the situs is applied to determine the validity of transfers of interests in land (see § 223). Uniformity of result is also important when the transfer of an aggregate of movables, situated in two or more states, is involved. Partly for this reason, the law that would be applied by the courts of the state of a decedent's domicil at death is applied to determine the validity of his will in so far as it concerns movables (see § 263) and the distribution of his movables in the event of intestacy (see § 260).

j. Ease in the determination and application of the law to be applied. Ideally, choice-of-law rules should be simple and easy to apply. This policy should not be overemphasized, since it is obviously of greater importance that choice-of-law rules lead to desirable results. The policy does, however, provide a goal for which to strive.

k. Reciprocity. In formulating common law rules of choice of law, the courts are rarely guided by considerations of reciprocity. Private parties, it is felt, should not be made to suffer for the fact that the courts of the state from which they come give insufficient consideration to the interests of the state of the forum. It is also felt that satisfactory development of choice-of-law rules can best be attained if each court gives fair consideration to the interests of other states without regard to the question whether the courts of one or more of these other states would do the same. As to whether reciprocity is a condition to the recognition and enforcement of a judgment of a foreign nation, see § 98, Comment e.

States sometimes incorporate a principle of reciprocity into statutes and treaties. They may do so in order to induce other states to take certain action favorable to their interests or to the interests of their citizens. So, as stated in § 89, Comment b, many States of the United States have enacted statutes which provide that a suit by a sister State for the recovery of taxes will be entertained in the local courts if the courts of the sister State would entertain a similar suit by the State of the forum. Similarly, by way of further example, some States of the United States provide by statute that an alien cannot inherit local assets unless their citizens in turn would be permitted to inherit in the state of the alien's nationality. A principle of reciprocity is also sometimes employed in statutes to permit reciprocating states to obtain by cooperative efforts what a single state could not obtain through the force of its own law. See, e. g., Uniform Reciprocal Enforcement of Support Act; Uniform (Reciprocal) Act to Secure Attendance of Witnesses from Without a State in Criminal Proceedings; Interpleader Compact Law.

* * * * *

Chapter 7—Wrongs

Topic 1—Torts

Title A. The General Principle

§ 145 THE GENERAL PRINCIPLE

(1) **The rights and liabilities of the parties with respect to an issue in tort are determined by the local law of the state which, with respect to that issue, has the most significant relationship to the occurrence and the parties under the principles stated in § 6.**

(2) **Contacts to be taken into account in applying the principles of § 6 to determine the law applicable to an issue include:**

(a) **the place where the injury occurred,**

(b) **the place where the conduct causing the injury occurred,**

(c) **the domicil, residence, nationality, place of incorporation and place of business of the parties, and**

(d) **the place where the relationship, if any, between the parties is centered.**

These contacts are to be evaluated according to their relative importance with respect to the particular issue.

Comment:

a. Scope of section. The rule of this Section states a principle applicable to all torts and to all issues in tort and, as a result, is cast in terms of great generality. This is made necessary by the great variety of torts and of issues in tort and by the present fluidity of the decisions and scholarly writings on choice of law in torts. Title B (§§ 146-155) deals with particular torts as to which it is possible to state rules of greater precision. Undoubtedly, this list will lengthen with increased experience. Title C (§§ 156-174) deals with particular issues in tort. It seems clear that the best way to bring precision into the field is by attempting to state special rules for particular torts and for particular issues in tort.

Comment on Subsection (1):

b. Rationale. The principles stated in § 6 underlie all rules of choice of law and are used in evaluating the significance of a relationship, with respect to the particular issue, to the potentially interested states, the occurrence and the parties. The factors listed in Subsection (2) of the rule of § 6 can be divided into five groups. One group is concerned with the fact that in multistate cases it is essential that the rules of decision promote mutually harmonious and beneficial relationships in the interdependent community, federal or international. The second group focuses upon the purposes, policies, aims and objectives of each of the competing local law rules urged to govern and upon the concern of the potentially interested states in having their rules applied. The factors in this second group are at times referred to as "state interests" or as appertaining to an "interested state." The third group involves the needs of the parties, namely the protection of their justified expectations and certainty and predictability of result. The fourth group is directed to implementation of the basic policies underlying the particular field of law, such as torts or contracts, and the fifth group is concerned with the needs of judicial administration, namely with ease in the determination and application of the law to be applied.

The factors listed in Subsection (2) of the rule of § 6 vary somewhat in importance from field to field. Thus, the protection of the justified expectations of the parties, which is of extreme importance in such fields as contracts, property, wills and trusts, is of lesser importance in the field of torts. This is because persons who cause injury on nonprivileged occasions, particularly when the injury is unintentionally caused, usually act without giving thought to the law that may be applied to determine the legal consequences of this conduct. Such persons have few, if any, justified expectations in the area of choice of law to protect, and as to them the protection of justified expectations can play little or no part in the decision of a choice of law question. Likewise, the values of certainty, predictability and uniformity of result are of lesser importance in torts than in areas where the parties and their lawyers are likely to give thought to the problem of the applicable law in planning their transactions. Finally, a number of policies, such as the deterrence of tortious conduct and the provision of compensation for the injured victim, underlie the tort field. These policies are likely to point in different directions in situations where the important elements of an occurrence are divided among two or more states.

Because of the relative insignificance of the above-mentioned factors in the tort area of choice of law, the remaining factors listed in § 6 assume greater importance. These remaining factors are the needs of the interstate and international systems, the relevant policies of the forum, the relevant policies of other interested states and particularly of the state with the dominant interest in the determination of the particular issue, and ease in the determination and application of the law to be applied.

c. Purpose of tort rule. The purpose sought to be achieved by the relevant tort rules of the interested states, and the relation of these states to the occurrence and the parties, are important factors to be considered in determining the state of most significant relationship. This is because the interest of a state in having its tort rule applied in the determination of a particular issue will depend upon the purpose sought to be achieved by that rule and by the relation of the state to the occurrence and the parties. If the primary purpose of the tort rule involved is to deter or punish misconduct, as may be true of rules permitting the recovery of damages for alienation of affections and criminal conversation, the state where the conduct took place may be the state of dominant interest and thus that of most significant relationship (see § 154, Comment c). On the other hand, when the tort rule is designed primarily to compensate the victim for his injuries, the state where the injury occurred, which is often the state where the plaintiff resides, may have the greater interest in the matter. This factor must not be overemphasized, however. To some extent, at least, every tort rule is designed both to deter other wrongdoers and to compensate the injured person. Undoubtedly, the relative weight of these two objectives varies somewhat from rule to rule, and in the case of a given rule it will frequently be difficult to tell which of these objectives is the more important.

A rule which exempts the actor from liability for harmful conduct is entitled to the same consideration in the choice-of-law process as is a rule which imposes liability. Frequently, however, it will be more difficult to discern the purpose of a rule denying liability than of a rule which imposes it. Take, for example, a statute which abolishes the right of action for alienation of affections. Such a statute may have been designed only to spare the local courts from the burden of having to hear such actions. If so, the statute should only be applied to bar actions brought in the state of its enactment. On the other hand, the statute may have had as its sole, or alternative, purpose the protection of defendants against being harassed by such actions. If so, there would be a basis for applying the statute to bar an action brought outside the state of its enactment if the complained-of conduct had taken place in that state and particularly if, in addition, the defendant had been domiciled there.

Frequently, it will be possible to decide a question of choice of law in tort without paying deliberate attention to the purpose sought to be achieved by the relevant tort rules of the interested states. This will be so whenever by reason of the particular circumstances one state is obviously that of the applicable law.

d. The issue involved. The courts have long recognized that they are not bound to decide all issues under the local law of a single state. Thus, in a simple motor accident case that occurred outside the state of the forum, a court under traditional and prevailing practice applies its own state's rules to issues involving process, pleadings, joinder of parties, and the administration of the trial (see Chapter 6), while deciding other issues—such as whether the defendant's operation of the vehicle was negligent— by reference to the law selected by application of the rules stated in this Chapter. The rule of this Section makes explicit that selective approach to choice of the law governing particular issues.

Each issue is to receive separate consideration if it is one which would be resolved differently under the local law rule of two or more of the potentially interested states.

Experience and analysis have shown that certain issues that recur in tort cases are most significantly related to states with which they have particular connections or contacts. So, for example, a state has an obvious interest in regulating the conduct of persons within its territory and in providing redress for injuries that occurred there. Thus, subject only to rare exceptions, the local law of the state where conduct and injury occurred will be applied to determine whether the actor satisfied minimum standards of acceptable conduct and whether the interest affected by the actor's conduct was entitled to legal protection (see §§ 146-147).

On the other hand, the local law of the state where the parties are domiciled, rather than the local law of the state of conduct and injury, may be applied to determine whether one party is immune from tort liability to the other or may be held liable to the other only for injuries resulting from intentional conduct or from some aggravated form of negligence, or conversely, whether one party owes the other a higher standard of care than would be required in the circumstances of the case by the local law of the state where conduct and injury occurred. An example is the issue of intra-family immunity, which, as stated in § 169, is usually determined by the local law of the state of the spouses' common domicil. Likewise, the circumstances under which a guest passenger has a right of action against the driver of an automobile for injuries suffered as a result of the latter's negligence may be determined by the local law of their common domicil, if at least this is the state from which they departed on their trip and that to which they intended to return, rather than by the local law of the state where the injury occurred.

Again the state where the conduct and injury occurred will not necessarily be the state that is primarily concerned with the issue whether tort claims arising from the injury survive the death of the tortfeasor. So when conduct and injury occur in state X but both the plaintiff and the defendant are domiciled in state Y, it would seem that, ordinarily at least, Y would have the greater interest in the issue of survival and that its law should control (see § 167, Comment c). Similarly, whether a charitable corporation can successfully assert the defense of charitable immunity may be determined by the local law of the state where the plaintiff is domiciled and the defendant incorporated rather than by the local law of the state where conduct and injury occurred (see § 168, Comment b). By way of further example, it would seem that the state where all interested persons are domiciled will, usually at least, have the greatest interest in determining the extent to which each shall share in a tort recovery. So it may be that questions relating to the distribution between spouses of a recovery for an injury to one of the spouses should be determined by the local law of their domicil (cf. § 166, Comment b).

Undoubtedly, future cases will provide the basis for constructing special rules for still other issues of choice of law.

Comment on Subsection (2):

e. Important contacts in determining state of most significant relationship. In applying the principles of § 6 to determine the state of most significant relationship, the forum should give consideration to the relevant policies of all potentially interested states and the relevant interests of those states in the decision of the particular issue. Those states which are most likely to be interested are those which have one or more of the following contacts with the occurrence and the parties. Some of these contacts also figure prominently in the formulation of the applicable rules of choice of law.

The place where injury occurred. In the case of personal injuries or of injuries to tangible things, the place where the injury occurred is a contact that, as to most issues, plays an important role in the selection of the state of the applicable law (see §§ 146-147). This contact likewise plays an important role in the selection of the state of the applicable law in the case of other kinds of torts, provided that the injury occurred in a single, clearly ascertainable, state. This is so for the reason among others that persons who cause injury in a state should not ordinarily escape liabilities imposed by the local law of that state on account of the injury. So in the case of false imprisonment, the local law of the state where the plaintiff was imprisoned will usually be applied. Likewise, when a person in state X writes a letter about the plaintiff which is received by a person in state Y, the local law of Y, the state where the publication occurred, will govern most issues involving the tort, unless the contacts which some other state has with the occurrence and the parties are sufficient to make that other state the state which, with respect to the particular issue, has the most significant relationship to the occurrence and the parties (see § 149).

Situations do arise, however, where the place of injury will not play an important role in the selection of the state of the applicable law. This will be so, for example, when the place of injury can be said to be fortuitous or when for other reasons it bears little relation to the occurrence and the parties with respect to the particular issue (see § 146, Comments d-e). This will also be so when, such as in the case of fraud and misrepresentation (see § 148), there may be little reason in logic or persuasiveness to say that one state rather than another is the place of injury, or when, such as in the case of multistate defamation (see § 150), injury has occurred in two or more states. Situations may also arise where the defendant had little, or no, reason to foresee that his act would result in injury in the particular state. Such lack of foreseeability on the part of the defendant is a factor that will militate against selection of the state of injury as the state of the applicable law. Indeed, application of the local law of the state of injury in such circumstances might on occasion raise jurisdictional questions (see § 9, Comment f).

The place where conduct occurred. When the injury occurred in a single, clearly ascertainable state and when the conduct which caused the injury also occurred there, that state will usually be the state of the applicable law with respect to most issues involving the tort. This is particularly likely to be so with respect to issues involving standards of conduct, since the state of conduct and injury will have a natural concern in the determination of such issues.

Choice of the applicable law becomes more difficult in situations where the defendant's conduct and the resulting injury occurred in different states. When the injury occurred in two or more states, or when the place of injury cannot be ascertained or is fortuitous and, with respect to the particular issue, bears little relation to the occurrence and the parties, the place where the defendant's conduct occurred will usually be given particular weight in determining the state of the applicable law. For example, the place where the conduct occurred is given particular weight in the case of torts involving interference with a marriage relationship (see § 154) or unfair competition (see Comment f), since in the case of such torts there is often no one clearly demonstrable place of injury. Likewise, when the primary purpose of the tort rule involved is to deter or punish misconduct, the place where the conduct occurred has peculiar significance (see Comment c). And the same is true when the conduct was required or privileged by the local law of the state where it took place (see § 163, Comment a).

The place where the defendant's conduct occurred is of less significance in situations where, such as in the case of multistate defamation (see § 150), a potential defendant might choose to conduct his activities in a state whose tort rules are favorable to him.

The domicil, residence, nationality, place of incorporation and place of business of the parties. These are all places of enduring relationship to the parties. Their relative importance varies with the nature of the interest affected. When the interest affected is a personal one such as a person's interest in his reputation, or in his right of privacy or in the affections of his wife, domicil, residence and nationality are of greater importance than if the interest is a business or financial one, such as in the case of unfair competition, interference with contractual relations or trade disparagement. In these latter instances, the place of business is the more important contact. At least with respect to most issues, a corporation's principal place of business is a more important contact than the place of incorporation, and this is particularly true in situations where the corporation does little, or no, business in the latter place.

These contacts are of importance in situations where injury occurs in two or more states. So the place of the plaintiff's domicil, or on occasion his principal place of business, is the single most important contact for determining the state of the applicable law as to most issues in situations involving the multistate publication of matter that injures plaintiff's reputation (see § 150) or causes him financial injury (see § 151) or invades his right of privacy (see § 153).

In the case of other torts, the importance of these contacts depends largely upon the extent to which they are grouped with other contacts. The fact, for example, that one of the parties is domiciled or does business in a given state will usually carry little weight of itself. On the other hand, the fact that the domicil and place of business of all parties are grouped in a single state is an important factor to be considered in determining the state of the applicable law. The state where these contacts are grouped is particularly likely to be the state of the applicable law if either the defendant's conduct or the plaintiff's injury occurred there. This state may also be the state of the applicable law when conduct and injury occurred in a place that is fortuitous and bears little relation to the occurrence and the parties (see § 146, Comments d-e).

The importance of those contacts will frequently depend upon the particular issue involved (see Comment d).

The place where the relationship, if any, between the parties is centered. When there is a relationship between the plaintiff and the defendant and when the injury was caused by an act done in the course of the relationship, the place where the relationship is centered is another contact to be considered. So when the plaintiff is injured while traveling on a train or while riding as a guest passenger in an automobile, the state where his relationship to the railroad or to the driver of the automobile is centered may be the state of the applicable law. This is particularly likely to be the case if other important contacts, such as the place of injury or the place of conduct or the domicil or place of business of the parties, are also located in the state (see, for example, § 146, Comment e and § 147, Comment e). On rare occasions, the place where the relationship is centered may be the most important contact of all with respect to most issues. A possible example is where the plaintiff in state X purchases a train ticket from the defendant to travel from one city in X to another city in X, but is injured while the train is passing for a short distance through state Y. Here X local law, rather than the local law of Y, may be held to govern the rights and liabilities of the parties.

* * * * *

f. The tort involved. The relative importance of the contacts mentioned above varies somewhat with the nature of the tort involved. Thus, the place of injury is of particular importance in the case of personal injuries and of injuries to tangible things (see §§ 146-147). The same is true in the case of false imprisonment and of malicious prosecution and abuse of process (see § 155). On the other hand, the place of injury is less significant in the case of fraudulent misrepresentations (see § 148) and of such unfair competition as consists of false advertising and the misappropriation of trade values. The injury suffered through false advertising is the loss of customers or of trade. Such customers or trade will frequently be lost in two or more states. The effect of the loss, which is pecuniary in its nature, will normally be felt most severely at the plaintiff's headquarters or principal place of business. But this place may have only a slight relationship to the defendant's activities and to the plaintiff's loss of customers or trade. The situation is essentially the same when misappropriation of the plaintiff's trade values is involved, except that the plaintiff may have suffered no pecuniary loss but the defendant rather may have obtained an unfair profit. For all these reasons, the place of injury does not play so important a role for choice-of-law purposes in the case of false advertising and the misappropriation of trade values as in the case of other kinds of torts. Instead, the principal location of the defendant's conduct is the contact that will usually be given the greatest weight in determining the state whose local law determines the rights and liabilities that arise from false advertising and the misappropriation of trade values.

The principal location of the defendant's conduct is also the single most important contact in the case of interference with a marriage relationship (see § 154). In situations involving the multistate publication of matter that injures the plaintiff's reputation (see § 150) or causes him financial injury (see § 151) or invades his right of privacy (see § 153), the place of the plaintiff's domicil, or on occasion his principal place of business, is the single most important contact for determining the state of the applicable law.

g. Recovery on some theory other than tort. A plaintiff who cannot obtain recovery in tort under the law selected by application of the rule of this Section may sometimes obtain application of a more favorable law by relying upon some other basis of liability. Thus, the plaintiff may have the basis for a claim that the defendant is liable to him for his injuries on the ground of breach of contract. If so, the applicable law would be that selected by application of the rules of §§ 187-188. Conversely, a defendant who would be liable under the law selected by application of the rule of this

Section may on occasion be able to escape liability because of some provision in a contract. A relationship of master and servant, carrier and passenger or vendor and vendee may provide a basis for a contention that the case should be characterized as one of contract rather than tort. In some situations, the same result will be reached irrespective of whether the problem is characterized as one of tort or of contract. As to characterization, see § 7.

h. Reference is to "local law" of selected state. The reference is to the "local law" of the state of the applicable law and not to that state's "law," which means the totality of its law including its choice-of-law rules (see § 4). Values of certainty of result and of ease of application dictate that the forum should apply the local law of the selected state and not concern itself with the complications that might arise if that state's choice-of-law rules were applied. There is also no basis for supposing that fairness requires the forum to apply the choice-of-law rules of the selected state. To the extent that they may give thought to the possible consequences before engaging in conduct which may be tortious, persons would probably expect that the local law of the state selected by application of the present rule would be applied.

On the other hand, in judging a state's interest in the application of one of its local law rules, the forum should concern itself with the question whether the courts of that state would have applied this rule in the decision of the case. The fact that these courts would have applied this rule may indicate that an important interest of that state would be served if the rule were applied by the forum. Conversely, the fact that these courts would not have applied this rule may indicate that no important interest of that state would be infringed if the rule were not applied by the forum (see § 8, Comment k). It should be reiterated that in the torts area the forum will not apply the choice-of-law rules of another state. The forum will consult these rules, however, for whatever light these rules may shed upon the extent of the other state's interest in the application of its relevant local law rule.

* * *

i. When rule of two or more states is the same. When certain contacts involving a tort are located in two or more states with identical local law rules on the issue in question, the case will be treated for choice-of-law purposes as if these contacts were grouped in a single state.

* * *

§ 146 PERSONAL INJURIES

In an action for a personal injury, the local law of the state where the injury occurred determines the rights and liabilities of the parties, unless, with respect to the particular issue, some other state has a more significant relationship under the principles stated in § 6 to the occurrence and the parties, in which event the local law of the other state will be applied.

* * * * *

§ 147 INJURIES TO TANGIBLE THINGS

In an action for an injury to land or other tangible thing, the local law of the state where the injury occurred determines the rights and liabilities of the parties unless, with respect to the particular issue, some other state has a more significant relationship under the principles stated in § 6 to the occurrence, the thing and the parties, in which event the local law of the other state will be applied.

* * * * *

Chapter 7—Wrongs

Topic 2—Actions For Death

§ 175 RIGHT OF ACTION FOR DEATH

In an action for wrongful death, the local law of the state where the injury occurred determines the rights and liabilities of the parties unless, with respect to the particular issue, some other state has a more significant relationship under the principles stated in § 6 to the occurrence and the parties, in which event the local law of the other state will be applied.

* * * * *

Chapter 8—Contracts

Topic 1—Validity of Contracts and Rights
Created Thereby

Title A. General Principles

§ 187 LAW OF THE STATE CHOSEN BY THE PARTIES

(1) The law of the state chosen by the parties to govern their contractual rights and duties will be applied if the particular issue is one which the parties could have resolved by an explicit provision in their agreement directed to that issue.

(2) The law of the state chosen by the parties to govern their contractual rights and duties will be applied, even if the particular issue is one which the parties could not have resolved by an explicit provision in their agreement directed to that issue, unless either

(a) **the chosen state has no substantial relationship to the parties or the transaction and there is no other reasonable basis for the parties' choice, or**

(b) **application of the law of the chosen state would be contrary to a fundamental policy of a state which has a materially greater interest than the chosen state in the determination of the particular issue and which, under the rule of § 188, would be the state of the applicable law in the absence of an effective choice of law by the parties.**

(3) **In the absence of a contrary indication of intention, the reference is to the local law of the state of the chosen law.**

Comment:

a. Scope of section. The rule of this Section is applicable only in situations where it is established to the satisfaction of the forum that the parties have chosen the state of the applicable law. When the parties have made such a choice, they will usually refer expressly to the state of the chosen law in their contract, and this is the best way of insuring that their desires will be given effect. But even when the contract does not refer to any state, the forum may nevertheless be able to conclude from its provisions that the parties did wish to have the law of a particular state applied. So the fact that the contract contains legal expressions, or makes reference to legal doctrines, that are peculiar to the local law of a particular state may provide persuasive evidence that the parties wished to have this law applied.

On the other hand, the rule of this Section is inapplicable unless it can be established that the parties have chosen the state of the applicable law. It does not suffice to demonstrate that the parties, if they had thought about the matter, would have wished to have the law of a particular state applied.

* * *

b. Impropriety or mistake. A choice-of-law provision, like any other contractual provision, will not be given effect if the consent of one of the parties to its inclusion in the contract was obtained by improper means, such as by misrepresentation, duress, or undue influence, or by mistake. Whether such consent was in fact obtained by improper means or by mistake will be determined by the forum in accordance with its own legal principles. A factor which the forum may consider is whether the choice-of-law provision is contained in an "adhesion" contract, namely one that is drafted unilaterally by the dominant party and then presented on a "take-it-or-leave-it" basis to the weaker party who has no real opportunity to bargain about its terms. Such contracts are usually prepared in printed form, and frequently at least some of their provisions are in extremely small print. Common examples are tickets of various kinds and insurance policies. Choice-of-law provisions contained in such contracts are usually respected. Nevertheless, the forum will scrutinize such contracts with care and will refuse to apply any choice-of-law provision they may contain if to do so would result in substantial injustice to the adherent.

* * *

Comment on Subsection (1):

c. **Issues the parties could have determined by explicit agreement directed to particular issue.** The rule of this Subsection is a rule providing for incorporation by reference and is not a rule of choice of law. The parties, generally speaking, have power to determine the terms of their contractual engagements. They may spell out these terms in the contract. In the alternative, they may incorporate into the contract by reference extrinsic material which may, among other things, be the provisions of some foreign law. In such instances, the forum will apply the applicable provisions of the law of the designated state in order to effectuate the intentions of the parties. So much has never been doubted. The point deserves emphasis nevertheless because most rules of contract law are designed to fill gaps in a contract which the parties could themselves have filled with express provisions. This is generally true, for example, of rules relating to construction, to conditions precedent and subsequent, to sufficiency of performance and to excuse for nonperformance, including questions of frustration and impossibility. As to all such matters, the forum will apply the provisions of the chosen law.

Whether the parties could have determined a particular issue by explicit agreement directed to that issue is a question to be determined by the local law of the state selected by application of the rule of § 188. Usually, however, this will be a question that would be decided the same way by the relevant local law rules of all the potentially interested states. On such occasions, there is no need for the forum to determine the state of the applicable law.

* * *

Comment on Subsection (2):

d. **Issues the parties could not have determined by explicit agreement directed to particular issue.** The rule of this Subsection applies only when two or more states have an interest in the determination of the particular issue. The rule does not apply when all contacts are located in a single state and when, as a consequence, there is only one interested state. Subject to this qualification, the rule of this Subsection applies when it is sought to have the chosen law determine issues which the parties could not have determined by explicit agreement directed to the particular issue. Examples of such questions are those involving capacity, formalities and substantial validity. A person cannot vest himself with contractual capacity by stating in the contract that he has such capacity. He cannot dispense with formal requirements, such as that of a writing, by agreeing with the other party that the contract shall be binding without them. Nor can he by a similar device avoid issues of substantial validity, such as whether the contract is illegal. Usually, however, the local law of the state chosen by the parties will be applied to regulate matters of this sort. And it will usually be applied even when to do so would require disregard of some local provision of the state which would otherwise be the state of the applicable law.

Permitting the parties in the usual case to choose the applicable law is not, of course, tantamount to giving them complete freedom to contract as they will. Their power to choose the applicable law is subject to the two qualifications set forth in this Subsection (see Comments f-g).

e. Rationale. Prime objectives of contract law are to protect the justified expectations of the parties and to make it possible for them to foretell with accuracy what will be their rights and liabilities under the contract. These objectives may best be attained in multistate transactions by letting the parties choose the law to govern the validity of the contract and the rights created thereby. In this way, certainty and predictability of result are most likely to be secured. Giving parties this power of choice is also consistent with the fact that, in contrast to other areas of the law, persons are free within broad limits to determine the nature of their contractual obligations.

An objection sometimes made in the past was that to give the parties this power of choice would be tantamount to making legislators of them. It was argued that, since it is for the law to determine the validity of a contract, the parties may have no effective voice in the choice of law governing validity unless there has been an actual delegation to them of legislative power. This view is now obsolete and, in any event, falls wide of the mark. The forum in each case selects the applicable law by application of its own choice-of-law rules. There is nothing to prevent the forum from employing a choice-of-law rule which provides that, subject to stated exceptions, the law of the state chosen by the parties shall be applied to determine the validity of a contract and the rights created thereby. The law of the state chosen by the parties is applied, not because the parties themselves are legislators, but simply because this is the result demanded by the choice-of-law rule of the forum.

It may likewise be objected that, if given this power of choice, the parties will be enabled to escape prohibitions prevailing in the state which would otherwise be the state of the applicable law. Nevertheless, the demands of certainty, predictability and convenience dictate that, subject to some limitations, the parties should have power to choose the applicable law.

On occasion, the parties may choose a law that would declare the contract invalid. In such situations, the chosen law will not be applied by reason of the parties' choice. To do so would defeat the expectations of the parties which it is the purpose of the present rule to protect. The parties can be assumed to have intended that the provisions of the contract would be binding upon them (cf. § 188, Comment b). If the parties have chosen a law that would invalidate the contract, it can be assumed that they did so by mistake. If, however, the chosen law is that of the state of the otherwise applicable law under the rule of § 188, this law will be applied even when it invalidates the contract. Such application will be by reason of the rule of § 188, and not by reason of the fact that this was the law chosen by the parties.

* * *

f. Requirement of reasonable basis for parties' choice. The forum will not apply the chosen law to determine issues the parties could not have determined by explicit agreement directed to the particular issue if the parties had no reasonable basis for choosing this law. The forum will not, for example, apply a foreign law which has been chosen by the parties in the spirit of adventure or to provide mental exercise for the judge. Situations of this sort do not arise in practice. Contracts are entered into for serious purposes and rarely, if ever, will the parties choose a law without good reason for doing so.

When the state of the chosen law has some substantial relationship to the parties or the contract, the parties will be held to have had a reasonable basis for their choice. This will be the case, for example, when this state is that where performance by one of the parties is to take place or where one of the parties is domiciled or has his principal place of business. The same will also be the case when this state is the place of contracting except, perhaps, in the unusual situation where this place is wholly fortuitous and bears no real relation either to the contract or to the parties. These situations are mentioned only for purposes of example. There are undoubtedly still other situations where the state of the chosen law will have a sufficiently close relationship to the parties and the contract to make the parties' choice reasonable.

The parties to a multistate contract may have a reasonable basis for choosing a state with which the contract has no substantial relationship. For example, when contracting in countries whose legal systems are strange to them as well as relatively immature, the parties should be able to choose a law on the ground that they know it well and that it is sufficiently developed. For only in this way can they be sure of knowing accurately the extent of their rights and duties under the contract. So parties to a contract for the transportation of goods by sea between two countries with relatively undeveloped legal systems should be permitted to submit their contract to some well-known and highly elaborated commercial law.

g. When application of chosen law would be contrary to fundamental policy of state of otherwise applicable law. Fulfillment of the parties' expectations is not the only value in contract law; regard must also be had for state interests and for state regulation. The chosen law should not be applied without regard for the interests of the state which would be the state of the applicable law with respect to the particular issue involved in the absence of an effective choice by the parties. The forum will not refrain from applying the chosen law merely because this would lead to a different result than would be obtained under the local law of the state of the otherwise applicable law. Application of the chosen law will be refused only (1) to protect a fundamental policy of the state which, under the rule of § 188, would be the state of the otherwise applicable law, provided (2) that this state has a materially greater interest than the state of the chosen law in the determination of the particular issue. The forum will apply its own legal principles in determining whether a given policy is a fundamental one within the meaning of the present rule and whether the other state has a materially greater interest than the state of the chosen law in the determination of the particular issue. The parties' power to choose the applicable law is subject to least restriction in situations where the significant contacts are so widely dispersed that determination of the state of the applicable law without regard to the parties' choice would present real difficulties.

No detailed statement can be made of the situations where a "fundamental" policy of the state of the otherwise applicable law will be found to exist. An important consideration is the extent to which the significant contacts are grouped in this state. For the forum will be more inclined to defer to the policy of a state which is closely related to the contract and the parties than to the policy of a state where few contacts are grouped but which, because of the wide dispersion of contacts among several states, would be the state of the applicable law if effect were to be denied the choice-of-law provision. Another important consideration is the extent to which the significant contacts are grouped in the state of the chosen law. The more closely this state is related to the contract and to the parties, the more likely it is that the choice-of-law provision will be given effect. The more closely the state of the chosen law is related to the contract and the parties, the more fundamental must be the policy of the state of the otherwise applicable law to justify denying effect to the choice-of-law provision.

To be "fundamental," a policy must in any event be a substantial one. Except perhaps in the case of contracts relating to wills, a policy of this sort will rarely be found in a requirement, such as the statute of frauds, that relates to formalities (see Illustration 6). Nor is such policy likely to be represented by a rule tending to become obsolete, such as a rule concerned with the capacity of married women (see Illustration 7), or by general rules of contract law, such as those concerned with the need for consideration (see Illustration 8). On the other hand, a fundamental policy may be embodied in a statute which makes one or more kinds of contracts illegal or which is designed to protect a person against the oppressive use of superior bargaining power. Statutes involving the rights of an individual insured as against an insurance company are an example of this sort (see §§ 192-193). To be "fundamental" within the meaning of the present rule, a policy need not be as strong as would be required to justify the forum in refusing to entertain suit upon a foreign cause of action under the rule of § 90.

* * *

Comment on Subsection (3):

h. **Reference is to "local law" of chosen state.** The reference, in the absence of a contrary indication of intention, is to the "local law" of the chosen state and not to that state's "law," which means the totality of its law including its choice-of-law rules. When they choose the state which is to furnish the law governing the validity of their contract, the parties almost certainly have the "local law," rather than the "law," of that state in mind (compare § 186, Comment b). To apply the "law" of the chosen state would introduce the uncertainties of choice of law into the proceedings and would serve to defeat the basic objectives, namely those of certainty and predictability, which the choice-of-law provision was designed to achieve.

i. **Choice of two laws.** The extent to which the parties may choose to have the local law of two or more states govern matters that do not lie within their contractual capacity is uncertain. For example, it is uncertain whether the parties may effectively provide that their capacity to make the contract shall be governed by the local law of one state and the question of formalities by the local law of another. When the parties are domiciled in different states and each has capacity to enter into the contract under the local law of his domicil, they should, subject to the conditions stated in the rule of this Section, be able effectively to provide in the contract that the capacity of each shall be determined by the local law of his domicil.

* * *

§ 188 LAW GOVERNING IN ABSENCE OF EFFECTIVE CHOICE BY THE PARTIES

(1) **The rights and duties of the parties with respect to an issue in contract are determined by the local law of the state which, with respect to that issue, has the most significant relationship to the transaction and the parties under the principles stated in § 6.**

(2) **In the absence of an effective choice of law by the parties (see § 187), the contacts to be taken into account in applying the principles of § 6 to determine the law applicable to an issue include:**

(a) **the place of contracting,**

(b) **the place of negotiation of the contract,**

(c) **the place of performance,**

(d) **the location of the subject matter of the contract, and**

(e) **the domicil, residence, nationality, place of incorporation and place of business of the parties.**

These contacts are to be evaluated according to their relative importance with respect to the particular issue.

(3) **If the place of negotiating the contract and the place of performance are in the same state, the local law of this state will usually be applied, except as otherwise provided in §§ 189-199 and 203.**

* * * * *

Chapter 8—Contracts

Topic 1—Validity of Contracts and Rights Created Thereby

Title B. Particular Contracts

§ 196 CONTRACTS FOR THE RENDITION OF SERVICES

The validity of a contract for the rendition of services and the rights created thereby are determined, in the absence of an effective choice of law by the parties, by the local law of the state where the contract requires that the services, or a major portion of the services, be rendered, unless, with respect to the particular issue, some other state has a more significant relationship under the principles stated in § 6 to the transaction and the parties, in which the event the local law of the other state will be applied.

* * * * *

Chapter 9—Property

Topic 2—Immovables

Title G. Succession on Death

§ 236 INTESTATE SUCCESSION TO LAND

(1) The devolution of interests in land upon the death of the owner intestate is determined by the law that would be applied by the courts of the situs.

(2) These courts would usually apply their own local law in determining such questions.

* * * * *

Chapter 9—Property

Topic 3—Movables

Title E. Succession on Death

§ 260 INTESTATE SUCCESSION TO MOVABLES

The devolution of interests in movables upon intestacy is determined by the law that would be applied by the courts of the state where the decedent was domiciled at the time of his death.

* * * * *

Chapter 10—Trusts

Topic 1—Movables

§ 270 VALIDITY OF TRUST OF MOVABLES CREATED INTER VIVOS

An inter vivos trust of interests in movables is valid if valid

(a) under the local law of the state designated by the settlor to govern the validity of the trust, provided that this state has a substantial relation to the trust and that the application of its law does not violate a strong public policy of the state with which, as to the matter at issue, the trust has its most significant relationship under the principles stated in § 6, or

(b) if there is no such effective designation, under the local law of the state with which, as to the matter at issue, the trust has its most significant relationship under the principles stated in § 6.

* * * * *

Chapter 10—Trusts

Topic 2—Land

§ 278 VALIDITY OF TRUST OF LAND

The validity of a trust of an interest in land is determined by the law that would be applied by the courts of the situs.

* * * * *

Michael S. Finch, *Choice-of-Law Problems in Florida Courts: A Retrospective on the Restatement (Second)*, 24 STETSON L. REV. 653, 655-71 (1995)*

* * * * *

THE ORIGINS AND STRUCTURE OF THE RESTATEMENT (SECOND)

"[W]e wish that we had done a better job. The only thing that prevented us from doing so was that we could not come anywhere near to agreement on anything else."

> Robert Leflar, Member
> Committee of Advisors
> *Restatement (Second).*[7]

A. The Dynamics of the *Restatement* Process

The most important interpretive clue to the *Restatement (Second)* may be found in the above-quoted excerpt from Professor Robert Leflar, who played a significant role in the development of the *Restatement*. From beginning to end, the *Restatement* was an attempted "reconciliation." It was drafted and redrafted over a period of eighteen years, barely two decades after the promulgation of the first Restatement, whose "vested rights" territorialism had suffered withering attack in the academic community.

---

*   Reprinted with permission.

[7]   Robert A. Leflar, *The Torts Provisions of the Restatement (Second)*, 72 COLUM. L. REV. 267, 278 (1972).

As scholars attempted to free themselves from the conceptual restraints of the first *Restatement*, the conflicts literature enjoyed a renaissance of theorizing. A variety of conflicts jurisprudes—including several members of the American Law Institute (ALI) who would attempt to reconcile their theories in the *Restatement (Second)*—advocated novel goals and methods for the resolution of choice-of-law problems. A bold group of state court jurists, in turn, attempted to implement the new learning in their courts.

Clearly, parts of the first *Restatement* were becoming obsolete by the time work commenced on the new restatement. But there was sharp disagreement over whether the time was ripe for a second "restatement" of conflicts doctrine. How could one restate what had yet to be fully stated by the courts? And how could the ALI condense into a coherent document the high degree of tentativeness and dissensus that was characteristic of evolving conflicts doctrine? In open pleas to the ALI, some conflicts scholars asked that the attempt to restate the law be abandoned for the indefinite future.

The only means of restating such a heterogeneous phenomenon as conflicts law in the 1960s was, as Professor Leflar would describe it, through "an impossible degree of reconciliation." Such is the nature of the *Restatement (Second) of Conflict of Laws*, and any attempt to understand that document must begin with the recognition that it does not "restate" what was happening in any particular court. Rather, the *Restatement (Second)* is more accurately described as a negotiated settlement of conflicting judicial and academic approaches to a subject that was in the throes of change. As the reporter to the *Restatement (Second)* candidly observed, it is an eclectic document that relies on a variety of theories.[17]

This admixture of case law and academic theory was inherently unstable—particularly in comparison to the formalistic, blackletter rules of the first *Restatement*. Indeed, from its inception, the *Restatement (Second)* was self-conscious of its "transitional" nature and specifically anticipated evolution in its provisions.

The provisional nature of the *Restatement* should not obscure, however, the fact that it does have several determinate features: It sets forth a structured, if malleable, methodology, and it builds upon discrete choice-of-law concepts that have relatively specific meanings in the discipline. To appreciate this structure and content, it is essential to understand the evolution in the drafts of the *Restatement (Second)*.

B. The Layering of the *Restatement*

At the outset, the *Restatement (Second)* rejected the "vested rights" territorialism of the first *Restatement*, under which the state of a tortious injury (the "lex loci delicti," or "LLD") was deemed to have exclusive jurisdiction to legislate the consequences of tortious conduct. Banished from the *Restatement (Second)* were tort rules that inexorably called for application of the law of a state where some particular activity had occurred. Early drafts of the *Restatement (Second)* did not repudiate, however, the importance of territorialist connections in resolving choice-of-law problems. Instead, the *Restatement (Second)* expanded the scope of territorialist considerations by including, in addition to the place of injury, the place of tortious conduct, the residence of the parties and other locational facts that connect a tort to a particular state. According to early drafts of the *Restatement (Second)*, consideration of these various factual contacts would enable a court to determine which state had the "most significant relationship"

---

[17]   *See* Willis L. Reese, *The Second Restatement of Conflict of Laws Revisited*, 34 MERCER L. REV. 501, 508 (1983). * * *

to the tort and hence, which state's law should apply. Thus was born the "significant relationship" test which, more than any other phrase, has come to characterize the *Restatement (Second)* approach to conflicts.

It is helpful to consider the historical context in which the phrase "significant relationship" was developed. Early drafts of the *Restatement (Second)* were circulated at a time when the New York courts were experimenting with a multiple-fact approach to resolving conflicts problems. The "center of gravity" test employed by the New York courts—some version of which was later incorporated into the *Restatement (Second)* as the "significant relationship" test—called upon courts to identify all relevant factual contacts with the concerned states and to apply the law of the state having the greatest relationship to the controversy. But the precise meaning of this approach seems to have varied from opinion to opinion. In some cases, the New York courts appeared to emphasize the sheer number of factual contacts connecting a state with a legal dispute—what has been uncharitably referred to as "contact counting"—while in other cases, the courts indicated that factual contacts were important only insofar as they established which state was most "interested" in the legal issue, thus suggesting some form of policy analysis.

The important methodological lesson is that, by focusing on multiple fact contacts in ascertaining the state with the most "significant relationship" to a legal dispute, the earliest draft of the *Restatement (Second)* gave arguable textual support to the disreputable practice of "contact counting." In later drafts of the *Restatement*, there was obvious attempt to correct such misimpressions by emphasizing that contacts were to be assessed based on their *qualitative* relationship to legal policies, rather than by their sheer quantity. Thus, the fact-enumerating section of the tort chapter of the *Restatement (Second)*—presently contained in section 145—specifically provides that the enumerated contacts are "to be taken into account in applying the principles of section 6." Nonetheless, contact counting remains a way of life for a surprisingly large number of courts, including courts in Florida.

The introduction of section 6 into the *Restatement (Second)* constitutes the next critical step in its evolution. Section 6 has been described by the *Restatement's* reporter as the document's "central theme." In section 6, one finds the various policies and choice-of-law values that are said to underlie *all* other sections of the *Restatement*.

Section 6 was added to intermediate drafts of the *Restatement* in part to reflect developments in the case law of certain adventurous jurisdictions, but perhaps in larger part to reflect the contributions of leading conflicts scholars.* * *

It bears re-emphasis that all other sections of the *Restatement* ultimately trace back to section 6. Thus, the factual contacts pertaining to torts as set forth in section 145 are only relevant insofar as they relate to one of the section 6 principles. Most importantly, the "significant relationship" test that constitutes the general principle for resolving tort issues under section 145 is specifically defined by reference to the more detailed principles of section 6. Thus, section 145 affirms that tort issues are to be generally governed by the law of the state "which . . . has the most significant relationship to the occurrence and the parties *under the principles stated in [section] 6.*"

C. The Theory of the "Significant Relationship"

Two important methodological issues arise when determining the state of the most significant relationship under the section 6 principles: first, what specific meanings are intended by these succinct "principles," and second, how are these principles to be compared or weighed to determine which state bears the most significant relationship to a tort issue? These questions will be considered in order.

The proper interpretation of section 6 principles is not a matter of pure conjecture, even though some courts adjudicate as if it were. Both the official comments accompanying section 6 and the secondary writings of the *Restatement*'s reporter, Professor Willis Reese, provide important guides to the interpretation of section 6 principles.

Subsection 6(1) states what hardly needs stating. When legislation mandates a particular resolution of choice-of-law disputes, state courts should follow their legislature's directive. As noted in the *Restatement*'s comments, however, legislatures rarely address conflicts issues by statute, and this is particularly true regarding tort issues. In most tort disputes, accordingly, section 6(1) adds nothing to the analysis.

Subsection 6(2)(a) sets forth a principle that, in the great majority of cases, also has little pertinence to the resolution of conflicts issues. While "interstate" and "international" needs are of obvious concern in the greater development of choice-of-law doctrine, they will seldom have pertinence to the resolution of conflicts issues in a particular tort dispute.* * *

As one moves to subsections 6(2)(b) and (c), one moves into the heart of the section 6 principles. Principles (b) and (c) of subsection 6(2) embody the most influential conflicts theory to emerge since the "vested rights" territorialism of the first *Restatement*: what has been termed "governmental interest analysis." Although the leading exponent of interest analysis, Professor Brainerd Currie, was opposed to the new restatement effort, his writings have had conspicuous impact on the drafting of the *Restatement (Second)*.

* * * * *

Without question, the most significant contribution of governmental interest analysis is its identification of the "false conflict." When a false conflict is presented, the solution is obvious: Apply the law of the only "interested" state. In this manner, one state's legal policies are promoted, without harming the legal policies of other states. It is just such a false-conflict case that has prompted numerous state courts * * * to adopt methodologies like the *Restatement (Second)* which employ interest analysis.

There is considerable dispute about which state's law to apply when the court is presented either with a true conflict or an unprovided-for case. Professor Currie contended that a court should apply its own law ("lex fori") when presented with a true conflict, but most courts have not followed this suggestion. Alternative methods for resolving true conflicts include applying the law of the "most" interested state, applying the "better" law, or applying the law of the state where the injury occurred (the LLD state under territorialist methodology).

As previously stated, it is clear that the *Restatement (Second)* incorporates a substantial element of interest analysis. More particularly, the *Restatement (Second)* affirms the "false-conflict" solution of interest analysis by indicating that, when only one state is truly interested in applying its law to a tort dispute, that state's law should apply. But the *Restatement (Second)* is less clear about the means of resolving true conflicts. As will be discussed subsequently, it is arguable that the *Restatement* calls for the "weighing" of state interests and application of the law of the "most" interested state, but it is also arguable that the *Restatement* calls for use of the territorialist, LLD law in some situations where state interests conflict.

The *Restatement (Second)* also perpetuates several of the ambiguities that have troubled interest-analysis methodology throughout its history. For example, which state is "interested" in parties domiciled in more than one state? The *Restatement* provides no definitive resolution of how to determine which states are "interested" in multi-state businesses that arguably "reside" in many states. * * * [M]uch may turn upon whether a state is interested only in those businesses that are incorporated locally or have their principal place of business within the state, or whether a state's interest extends to any entity transacting some business within the state. Similarly, the *Restatement* expressly declines to resolve the issue of whether a state is interested in persons or businesses that establish domicile *after* the occurrence of a tort, as occurs with some frequency in conflicts litigation.

Whatever their ambiguities, principles 6(2)(b) and (c) incorporate some version of interest analysis as a means of determining which state has the most "significant relationship" to a choice-of-law issue. If, as has happened surprisingly often when courts apply the *Restatement (Second)*, there is no consideration of state interests, the court has omitted a key element of the significant relationship test.

The next of the section 6 principles—the "protection of justified expectations"—is largely intended for use in transactional settings, including the resolution of contractual and property issues. This principle has little application to most tort issues, where there is seldom any expectation concerning the consequences of unintended torts, but may indirectly arise in tort litigation insofar as contractual insurance coverage is pertinent to recovery.

Principle 6(2)(e) calls attention to the "basic policies underlying the particular field of law." It is unclear what relevance, if any, this principle has to tort litigation. Comments to this principle provide illustrations, but none of these pertains to tort issues. Consequently, this principle appears to have had little impact on resolution of tort problems under the *Restatement*.

The final two principles of subsection 6(2) are often discussed together. These principles focus on the need for "certainty, predictability and uniformity of result" and "ease in the determination and application of the law to be applied." Legal professionals who have a passing familiarity with conflicts problems will attest to the importance of these principles. The great bulk of conflicts issues sounding in tort will be resolved through negotiations with personal injury attorneys and insurance company representatives. It is vital to the dispute resolution process that, at a minimum, the participants be able to make a reliable forecast of the basic tort law principles that govern liability. If conflicts doctrine is exceedingly complex or indeterminate, a foundation for settlement will be more difficult to discover.

Whatever the conceptual vacuity of the first *Restatement*, if interpreted literally it usually was predictable, uniform, and easy to apply. This is particularly true concerning tort conflicts given the pervasiveness of the LLD rule and the usual ease with which a court could determine where the plaintiff's injury was inflicted.

Although the *Restatement (Second)* gives prominence to the principles of predictability and simplicity, the comments accompanying the text adopt a surprisingly apologetic tone. Thus, the drafters take pains to note that the "certainty" principles should not be "overemphasized" to the point of interfering with the achievement of "desirable results." At this point, one is reminded that the new restatement is indeed an "impossible reconciliation" among advisors who would simultaneously seek stability and change.

* * *

D. The Vestiges of Territorialism

The *Restatement*'s ambivalent attitude toward the classical conflicts goals of predictability and simplicity illustrates a final characteristic of the *Restatement (Second)* that pervades the work: notwithstanding the centrality of section 6 and its diverse principles, and notwithstanding its open-ended invitation to courts to search for the state of the "most significant relationship," the document sounds a strong and recurring note of territorialism. This is acutely manifest in a final feature of the *Restatement (Second)* that requires discussion—its abundant use of the presumption that the law of the place of injury will govern *unless* some other state has a more significant relationship to the tort problem.

A point about the organization of the *Restatement (Second)* is in order. If one were to open the text of the *Restatement* and turn to the chapter on "Wrongs" (whose lead topic is "Torts"), one would first encounter section 145. That section, as previously discussed, calls for the application of the law of the state with the "most significant relationship" to a tort issue under the principles of section 6 and further enumerates miscellaneous factual contacts that are to be considered in applying the section 6 principles.

The *Restatement*'s treatment of torts does not conclude at this point, however; indeed, one finds that section 145 is followed by *forty* additional sections pertaining to the subject. Some of these sections home in on particular types of torts (e.g., defamation or wrongful death actions), while others focus upon particular tort issues (e.g., contributory fault or charitable immunity). The question arises: Why these additional sections?

In part, these additional sections can be viewed as in-depth elaboration of how the "significant relationship" test should apply to discrete problems. That is, given the complexity and openendedness of sections 145 and 6, the drafters have sometimes provided detailed guidance as to how those sections play out in the context of particular tort issues. The value of these particularized sections cannot be overemphasized. Accompanying these sections are detailed "comments" and "illustrations" that offer practical application of the significant relationship test. In these sections, one may find an elaboration of the policies that underlie some of the more common tort rules, together with discussion of the various states that might be interested in applying their law to a problem. Furthermore, one finds helpful annotations of relevant case law from other jurisdictions.

But these particularized sections do more than merely elaborate on analysis under the "significant relationship" test. Many of them also contain choice-of-law presumptions (or recommendations) that call for application of the traditional LLD law unless some other state has a more significant relationship to the tort issue.* * *

The *Restatement*'s use of the LLD presumption as a starting point for many tort issues constitutes a methodologically important—and controversial—step. Taken literally, this presumption has potential to reinstitute the influence of the territorialist touchstone whose predominance in the past was thought to be the very reason for undertaking a new restatement.

The reporter to the *Restatement (Second)* has made clear that the LLD presumption is neither premised on antiquated "vested rights" jurisprudence nor co-equal with the "significant relationship" test. The LLD presumption is just that—a presumption that is always subject to displacement under the "significant relationship" test. But this presumption serves several important functions.

First, to the extent that the *Restatement* is, at least in part, a "restatement" of what the courts were doing at the time of its promulgation, recognition of the LLD presumption is an accurate description of case-law reality. Second, the LLD presumption is often perceived as a "fair" outcome, insofar as persons intuitively assume that they become subject to a state's laws when they enter its territories and are involved in tortious occurrences. Third—and here the justifications tie in more specifically to the "significant relationship" methodology—the LLD state often *is*, according to the *Restatement*, the state that will have the dominant interest in applying its law to a tortious occurrence. Fourth, application of the LLD presumption, consistent as it is with prevailing conflicts theory in many states and simple as it usually is to apply, will serve two of the principles set forth in section 6, namely, the attainment of a predictable and simple means of resolving tort disputes. In some sense, the section 6 principles stressing predictability and simplicity shore up the argument for following the LLD presumption.

The recognition of a LLD presumption raises a critical question of methodology: Exactly how does a litigant overcome the presumption?

Comment to section 146 (which, again, recognizes an overarching LLD presumption for personal injury actions) states that the determination of whether a state has a more significant relationship to the tort issue than does the LLD state depends "in large part" upon whether that state "has a greater interest in the determination of the particular issue than the state where the injury occurred." The reference to some form of interest analysis seems unmistakable. According to the *Restatement*'s reporter, the LLD presumption is rebutted when the state of injury has *no* interest in the tort issue. Thus, the "false conflict" analysis discussed earlier remains a useful means of resolving tort disputes.

It is less certain how the LLD presumption should be handled when a "true conflict" exists. Discussion accompanying section 6 would indicate that a court should seek to apply the law of the state with a "dominant" interest in a torts issue, but nowhere does the *Restatement (Second)* provide a means of weighing or ranking interests. Furthermore, interest analysis is not the sole criterion of the "significant relationship" test, and when one adds to the analysis the predictability and simplicity principles—with their implicit appeal to straightforward solutions like the LLD presumption—the proper means of resolving "true conflicts" becomes more debatable.

At the same time, certain means of resolving true conflicts probably can be ruled out under the *Restatement (Second)* and so reduce the field of uncertainty somewhat. Nowhere in the *Restatement* is there recognition of the principle that a court should fall back on lex fori (the law of the forum) when it is confronted with a "true conflict." In this respect, the *Restatement (Second)* rejects the solution to "true conflicts" proffered by the leading exponent of interest analysis, Professor Currie. Similarly, the *Restatement (Second)* does not authorize a court to apply "the better law" (which in practice might translate into a lex fori solution given courts' predictable preference for their own state's law), a solution that has been advocated by one of the committee members who worked on the *Restatement*.

E. A Tentative Approach to Methodology under the *Restatement (Second)*

Although the matter is not free of controversy, one might sketch out the methodology of the *Restatement (Second)* as follows. In the resolution of most tort issues, a court will begin with the presumption that the law of the place of injury applies. The court will then consider the section 6 principles—through which the state of the most "significant relationship" is determined—foremost of which are those calling for a determination of which states are "interested" in applying their law. If only one state is "interested" in the tort issue, the court should apply the law of the interested state whether it be the state of injury or some other state. If two or more states are interested, then the court should attempt to ascertain which state has the "dominant" interest in the issue. If the state of dominance can in fact be determined, then that state's law should apply. If no state's interest is clearly dominant, however, this equilibrium should arguably be resolved by reversion to the presumptive rule (which incidentally serves the section 6 principles of predictability and simplicity.)

If a court is confronted with one of the appreciable number of tort issues lacking a presumption, or if the place of injury is not one of the several interested states, the court must by necessity engage in a relatively unguided exercise in interest analysis. At this point, a court that sincerely attempts to hew to the *Restatement (Second)* methodology may find itself hoping that, somewhere in the comments or illustrations accompanying the relevant *Restatement* section, the drafters have already devised a solution.

One has profound sympathy with those courts who must negotiate this relatively complex methodology.* * *

* * * * *

Symeon C. Symeonides, *Exception Clauses in American Conflicts Law*, 42 AM. J. OF COMP. L. 813, 825-830 (1994)*

* * * * *

* * *[T]he Restatement Second is, to date, the dominant methodology within the modern camp, being followed in twenty-two states. It is the epitome of an "approach." Its fundamental premise is that the choice-of-law process should proceed on the basis of open ended guidelines leaving ample discretion to the judge for individualized choice-of-law decisions. It would seem that, in such a system of almost unfettered judicial discretion, there would be little need for escape clauses as such.

A more complete answer to this question, however, can be obtained by dividing the provisions of the Restatement into the following four groups: (a) The first group encompasses those sections of the Restatement in which the drafters provide open ended guidelines that leave the choice of the applicable law entirely to the court. For lack of a better name and for the sake of brevity, this group will be referred to hereafter as the "ad hoc group;" (b) The second group encompasses those sections in which the drafters take the next step of telling the court what the applicable law will "*usually*" be. This group is referred to hereafter as the "usually group;" (c) The third group encompasses sections in which the drafters actually designate the applicable law, but then authorize the judge to disregard such designation in appropriate cases. This group is referred to hereafter as the "unless group;" (d) The fourth group encompasses those very few sections in which the drafters dare designate the applicable law *a priori*, without providing an escape mechanism. This group is referred to hereafter as the "rule group." Strictly speaking, true escape clauses are only those which are provided in the third group.

(a) The Ad Hoc Group

The ad hoc group is grounded on two cornerstones. The first is the famous section 6 of the Restatement, which lists the general factors and policies that should guide the court's choice of the applicable law.[74] The second cornerstone is the "most significant relationship" formula,

---

*   Reprinted with permission.

[74]   Section 6 provides that in the absence of contrary statutory directive in the forum's law, "the factors relevant to the choice of the applicable rule of law include (a) the needs of the interstate and international systems, (b) the relevant policies of the forum, (c) the relevant policies of other interested states and the relative interests of those states in the determination of the particular issue, (d) the protection of justified expectations, (e) the basic policies underlying the particular field of law, (f) certainty, predictability and uniformity of result, and (g) ease in the determination and application of the law to be applied."

encountered throughout the Restatement Second, which provides that the objective of the choice of law process is to apply the law of that state which, with regard to the particular issue, has the most significant relationship with the parties and the dispute.

In a great number of cases, the drafters studiously avoid determining in advance the state of the most significant relationship, leaving that determination entirely to the court. The court is simply instructed to "take into account" an illustrative list of factual contacts and to consider those contacts "in light of the policies of section 6." The list of physical contacts differs from one subject matter to another. In torts, these contacts include the place of the injury, the place of the conduct causing the injury, the domicile, residence, nationality and place of business of the parties and the place where the relationship, if any, between the parties, is centered.[75] In contracts, the factual contacts to be taken into account include the places of contracting, negotiation and performance of the contract, the location of the subject matter and the domicile, residence, nationality, or place of business of the parties.[76]

Neither the physical contacts of the particular sections, nor the policy factors of § 6 are listed in the order of their relative importance. It is even officially acknowledged that the policy factors of § 6 may well point in opposite directions.[77] Something similar is possible with respect to factual contacts. "These contacts are to be evaluated according to their relative importance with respect to the particular issue."[78] Thus, judicial discretion reigns supreme in the choice of law process under these sections without any restriction from the drafters.

(b) The "Usually" Group

In some instances, the drafters of the Restatement Second feel confident enough to proclaim that the state of the "most significant relationship" will "usually" be one particular state. For example, in the area of tort conflicts, the Restatement devotes nineteen sections to specific tort issues. Ten of these conclude with the adage that "[t]he applicable law will usually be the local law of the state where the injury occurred" in the following issues: § 156, tortious character of conduct; § 157, standard of care; § 158, interest entitled to legal protection; § 159, duty owed plaintiff; § 160, legal cause; § 162, specific conditions of liability; § 164, contributory fault; § 165, assumption of risk; § 166, imputed negligence; and § 172, joint torts. One section, § 169 provides that for intrafamily immunity the applicable law "will usually be the local law of the state of the parties' domicil." Only the remaining seven sections (161, 163, 168, 170-71, and 173-174) are left unaided by such a presumption.

In contract conflicts, section 188 provides that, subject to some exceptions, "[i]f the place of negotiating the contract and the place of performance are in the same state, the local law of this state will usually be applied." Similarly, section 198 provides that "[t]he capacity of a party to contract will usually be upheld if he has such capacity under the local law of the state of his domicil," while section 199 provides that contractual "[f]ormalities which meet the require-

---

[75] See § 145.2.

[76] See § 188.2.

[77] "At least some of the factors mentioned in this subsection will point in different directions in all but the simplest case." Comment c to § 6.

[78] § 145.2.

ments of the place where the parties execute the contract will usually be acceptable." Similar language is to be found in many other sections of the Restatement Second.[80]

The word "usually" is inherently vague and equivocal. Although it is somewhat less equivocal than the word "perhaps," which is used in another Restatement,[81] the word "usually" is also inherently nonprescriptive. Rather, it is, at most, descriptive. This is why it is rarely, if ever, encountered in statutes. Of course, the Restatement is not a statute. It is not even supposed to be a pre-statement of what the law ought to be, but rather a re-statement of what the law is. Be that as it may, the inherently vague and loose word "usually" accomplishes the drafter's intent of empowering the court to decide individual cases with maximum freedom. This freedom obviates the need for any other escape mechanisms.

(c) The "Unless" Group

In some instances, the drafters of the Restatement Second feel even more confident and designate specifically the state of the most significant relationship. In many of these cases, however, the drafter's confidence is tempered with an equally express authorization to the court to reach a different conclusion if the circumstances of the individual case so warrant. This authorization is expressed in provisos that usually begin with the word "unless."

For example, in the area of tort conflicts, the Restatement provides ten sections designating the applicable law for ten particular types of torts. In all sections, the designation by the drafters of the state of the most significant relationship and thus of the applicable law, is followed by the following escape clause: "unless, with respect to the particular issue, some other state has a more significant relationship under the principles stated in section 6 to the occurrence and the parties, in which event the local law of the other state will be applied." This clause is one of the most repeated phrases in the entire Restatement.[85] In the area of contract conflicts, the "unless" clause appears in most of the sections devoted to particular contracts.

These "unless" clauses are classic examples of escape clauses of the general, open-ended type. The court is vested with ample discretion, not only in determining whether the clause should be invoked or applied, but also in choosing the applicable law once it is determined that the clause is applicable. This discretion is restrained only by "the principles stated in section 6," which are very broad and flexible. Thus, the threshold for employing these clauses is much lower, and the court's hand much freer, than is the case in comparable clauses found in the Swiss or Austrian conflicts statutes, the EEC Contracts Convention and other European codifications or conventions.

In a few instances, however, the drafters provide more specific guidance to the court. For example in the all-important section 187 which defines the limits of party autonomy, the court's freedom to disregard the law chosen by the parties is delineated with more precision.

---

[80]   See, e.g., §§ 284 (marriage); 287-88 (legitimacy); 290 (adoption); 244 (conveyance of interest in chattel); 250 (voluntary assignment for benefit of creditors); 251 (security interest in chattel); 253 (effect on security interest of a dealing with chattel in state to which it has been removed); 254 (enforcement and redemption of security interests); 255 (exercise of power created by operation of law); 256 (exercise of consensual power).

[81]   See American Law Institute, *Restatement of the Law of Foreign Relations 3rd*, § 404 (1987).

[85]   See § 146 (personal injuries); § 147 (injuries to tangible things); § 148 (fraud and misrepresentation); § 149 (defamation); § 150 (multistate defamation); § 151 (injurious falsehood); § 153 (multistate invasion of privacy); § 154 (interference with marriage relationship); § 155 (malicious prosecution and abuse of process). See also § 175 (right of action for death).

The court may disregard the chosen state law, only if "(a) the chosen state has no substantial relationship to the parties or the transaction and there is no other reasonable basis for the parties' choice, or (b) application of the law of the chosen state would be contrary to a fundamental policy of a state which has a materially greater interest than the chosen state in the determination of the particular issue and which, under the rule of section 188, would be the state of the applicable law in the absence of an effective choice of law by the parties."[91]

The same is true with regard to the most recently revised section of the Restatement, section 142, which deals with statutes of limitations. Subsection 3 of that section provides that "The forum will apply its own statute of limitation permitting the action unless (a) maintenance of the action would serve no significant interest of the forum; and (b) the action would be barred under the statute of limitations of a state having a more significant relationship to the parties and the occurrence." As evidenced by the words "significant interests" in clause (a) and "significant relationship" in clause (b), the court retains ample discretion in deciding whether to deviate from the presumptive rule of applying the law of the forum. However, the fact that both clauses must be satisfied before applying another law suggests that this should not be done lightly. The same is true with regard to subsections (1) and (2) of section 142 which provide that "[i]n the absence of exceptional circumstances which make such result unreasonable: The forum will apply its own statute of limitations barring the action." The fact that the words "exceptional" and "unreasonable" are not given more specific content suggests that a certain degree of judicial discretion was contemplated. However, the accepted meaning of these words, as well as the fact that both must be satisfied before displacing the presumptive rule of applying forum law, suggests that the court's discretion is not un-restrained.

(d) The Rules Group

Finally, in very few sections, the drafters of the Restatement designate the applicable law without providing the judge with an express escape clause attached to that section. This is the case with most sections devoted to property and successions issues.[93] In cases involving land,[94] the applicable law is almost invariably the "law that would be applied by the courts of the situs."[95] This is as close the Restatement Second comes to prescribing black-letter choice

---

[91] Restatement Second § 187. The quoted part of the section applies only for issues that "the parties could not have resolved by an explicit provision in their agreement." The parties' freedom to choose the applicable law is totally unrestricted "if the particular issue is one which the parties could have resolved by an explicit provision in their agreement directed to that issue." Id.

[93] See also the unilateral choice-of-law rules contained in Restatement Second §§ 285 (divorce); 286 (nullity of marriage); and 289 (adoption).

[94] For succession to movables see § 260 which provides that successions to movables is governed by the whole law of the last domicile of the decedent. Also to the same effect are §§ 263 (validity and effect of will of movables); 264 (construction of will of movables); 265 (forced share interest of surviving spouse and election). For sections sanctioning the situs rule for inter vivos transactions in movables, see §§ 245 (effect of conveyance on pre-existing interests in chattel); 246 (acquisition by adverse possession or prescription of interest in chattel); 248 (chattel embodied in a document); 249 (embodiment of right in document); 253 (effect on security interest of a dealing with chattel in state to which it has been removed); 255 (exercise of power created by operation of law).

[95] See Restatement Second, §§ 223 (conveyance of interest in land); 225 (equitable conversion of interests in land); 226 (transfer of interest in land by operation of law); 227 (acquisition by adverse possession or prescription of interest in land); 228 (mortgage on land); 229 (foreclosure of mortgage on land); 230 (lien on land); 231 (exercise of power created by operation of law); 232 (exercise of power of attorney to transfer an interest in land); 236 (intestate succession to land); 239 (validity and effect of will of land); 240 (construction of a will devising land); 241 (common law or statutory interest of surviving spouse); 242 (forced share interest of surviving spouse and election). This phrase is often accompanied by the prediction that these courts will "usually" apply their own law. * * *

of law rules. However, even these rules are subject to escape mechanisms of the generic type, such as the *ordre public* exception and the *renvoi* technique. For example, the above quoted phrase is an explicit authorization for *renvoi*, which contains the potential for applying, in appropriate cases, a law other than that of the situs. Indeed, the Restatement Second adopts a much more favorable position towards renvoi than its predecessor, the first Restatement. Section 8 of the Second Restatement authorizes *renvoi* "When the objective of the particular choice-of-law rule is that the forum reach the same result on the very facts involved as would the courts of another state, the forum will apply the choice-of-law rules of the other state, subject to considerations of practicability and feasibility . . . [or] When the state of the forum has no substantial relationship to the particular issue or the parties and the courts of all interested states would concur in selecting the local law rule applicable to this issue, the forum will usually apply this rule."

* * * * *

Comments

1.   While retaining the original *Restatement*'s outward appearance of providing an extensive regime of rules, the RESTATEMENT (SECOND) differs sharply by emphasizing party fairness and an instrumental sensitivity to the policies behind rules vying for selection. Consequently, "[a] comparison [of the RESTATEMENT and the RESTATEMENT (SECOND)] at almost any point will illustrate the shift away from the rule orientation of the former toward the rather general, often amorphous 'principles' of the latter." Holland 1980: p. 619.[1]

2.   The actual extent of difference between in positions taken by the RESTATEMENT (SECOND) and the original RESTATEMENT varies depending on the conflicts issue. Despite differences in wording, the positions of the two seem on some points about the same. For example, both section 303 of the original RESTATEMENT (reprinted in Part A of Chapter Three) and section 260 of the RESTATEMENT (SECOND) (reprinted in Part A of this Chapter) take the same approach concerning intestate succession to movables, by choosing law of the place where the decedent was domiciled.

3.   Local policies were acknowledged in the public policy exception of the original RESTATEMENT (section 612, reprinted in Part A of Chapter Three). The RESTATEMENT (SECOND) acknowledges them differently, through the choice-of-law factor: "the relevant policies of the forum" (section 6 (2) (b), reprinted in Part A of this Chapter). By including local policies on its list of choice-of-law concerns, the RESTATEMENT (SECOND) eliminates any remaining justification for the public policy exception to choice of law. Symeonides 1994b: p. 824.

4.   Differences between the two restatements can be dramatic. Thus, while the original RESTATEMENT did not recognize the power of parties to choose law by contract (Scoles & Hay 1992: p. 36), the RESTATEMENT (SECOND) gives contracting parties con-

---

[1]   Full citations appear in the bibliography, Chapter Twelve.

siderable authority to choose law (in section 187, reprinted in this Chapter). Discussions of section 187 appear in Part A of this Chapter (in the ALI commentary following section 187 and in the commentary of Professor Symeonides). Additional treatments of this important section appear in Richman & Reynolds 1993: pp. 202-206; Scoles & Hay 1992: pp. 673-675; Trautman 1984: pp. 543-545. *Cf.* Juenger 1993: p. 17 (dating the use of choice-of-law clauses in Europe from the Middle Ages).

5. The RESTATEMENT (SECOND) "is written from the viewpoint of a neutral forum which has no interest of its own to protect and is seeking only to apply the most appropriate law." Reese 1963: p. 692. It is a highly eclectic approach, embracing in various parts of section 6 (2) conflicts policies of multilateralsm (subsection 6 (2) (a)), unilateralism (subsections 6 (2) (c) and (d)) and party expectations (section 6 (2) (d)). However, as Professor Finch suggested in his selection, the RESTATEMENT (SECOND) does not endorse the substantivist policy of choice of the better law. This is a significant difference between the RESTATEMENT (SECOND) and its closest competitor, Professor Leflar's "choice-influencing considerations" (the subject of Part B of this Chapter).

6. In deciding whether to publish a second conflicts restatement, the American Law Institute seems to have been on the horns of a dilemma. It was clear that the original RESTATEMENT was in deep trouble with commentators and a growing number of courts (the subject of Chapter Three B). However, as the Introduction to the RESTATEMENT (SECOND) (reprinted in Part A of this Chapter) and Professor Finch's narrative make clear, the ALI was well aware that the condition of American conflicts law was so troubled and uncertain that it would be impossible for a new work either to report or create a consensus on the subject. The Reporter for the project, Professor Willis Reese, acknowledged that:

> revision of the *Restatement* at this time poses many difficulties. More, perhaps much more, is known about choice of law than when Professor Beale wrote. But this additional knowledge has not brought certainty and definiteness in its wake. Instead it has brought disagreement, a renewed search for fundamental values, and perhaps more uncertainty than ever before.

Reese 1963: pp. 680-681. Despite pleas that the project be abandoned (*see, e.g.* Ehrenzweig 1965b), the RESTATEMENT (SECOND) was completed in 1969 and finally published in 1971. The ALI apparently felt that a controversial new conflicts restatement was easier to live with than a discredited old one.

7. The RESTATEMENT (SECOND) has been well-received by American courts.

> Measured in terms of acceptance by courts * * * the Second Restatement has been a smashing success. It is by far the most widely used approach to choice of law in the state courts, and it has proved equally attractive to federal courts applying federal common law. For better or worse, this is the age of the Second Restatement.

Kramer 1991a: p. 486. Similar assessments appear in Bourne 1993: p. 113; Symeonides 1994b: p. 825. A general survey of choice-of-law approaches now in use in the United States follows in Part C of the is Chapter.

8.   In contrast to the cordial judicial reception given the RESTATEMENT (SECOND), reaction within the academic community has varied greatly. At one end of the spectrum, a number of commentators have applauded it. *See, e.g.,* Bourne 1993: pp. 113-118; Korn 1983: pp. 816-819; McLaughlin 1991b: pp. 75, 108-110; Morris 1973: pp. 326-327; Thatcher 1990: pp. 399-401; Westbrook 1975: p. 463. Others have had mixed impressions about the RESTATEMENT (SECOND). *See, e.g.,* Borchers 1992b: pp. 132-133; Hay 1991: p. 362; Lowenfeld 1972: p. 384; Peterson 1972: p. 264; Shreve 1982: pp. 343-344. At the other end of the spectrum are critics who have been quite critical of the RESTATEMENT (SECOND). *See, e.g.,* Currie 1963c: pp. 1233-1234; Ehrenzweig 1963; Juenger 1969: pp. 212-213; Kramer 1991: pp. 486-487; Singer 1989: p. 77.

9.   Two favorite targets for critics are the "most significant relationship" test recurring throughout the RESTATEMENT (SECOND) (and explained by Professor Finch in Part A of this Chapter) and what critics believe to be a diffuse, over-inclusive general approach. Concerning the latter, one observer complained that the RESTATEMENT (SECOND) "was a hodgepodge of all theories. A court was to compare apples, oranges, umbrellas, and pandas, and to determine which state's law to apply by the relative importance assigned to these factors." Gottesman 1991: p. 8. Another wrote of the RESTATEMENT (SECOND) that, "[t]rying to be all things to all people, it produced mush." Laycock 1992: p. 253.

10. Additional perspectives on the RESTATEMENT (SECOND) appear in a forthcoming symposium devoted to its twenty-fifth anniversary. 56 Md. L. Rev. No. 4 (1997) (Contributions by Patrick J. Borchers, William L. Reynolds, William M. Richman, Symeon C. Symeonides, Louise Wemberg, and Russell J. Weintraub).

B. Leflar's Choice-Influencing Considerations

Robert A. Leflar, *Choice-Influencing Considerations in Conflicts Law*, 41 N.Y.U. L. Rev. 267, 279-295 (1966)*

* * * * *

The Choice-Influencing Considerations

The Cheatham-Reese summary of nine policy factors affecting choice-of-law rules and results, * * * is the basic study from which any analysis of choice-influencing considerations must commence. A mere listing, without the explanation that accompanied them, reveals their significances only partially, but it is still useful as a preliminary to further inquiry. They are, in the order of importance assigned to them by Cheatham and Reese:

    (1) The needs of the interstate and international systems;
    (2) A court should apply its own local law unless there is good reason for not doing so;
    (3) A court should seek to effectuate the purpose of its relevant local law rule in determining a question of choice of law;
    (4) Certainty, predictability, uniformity of result;
    (5) Protection of justified expectations;
    (6) Application of the law of the state of dominant interest;
    (7) Ease in determination of applicable law, convenience of the court;
    (8) The fundamental policy underlying the broad local law field involved;
    (9) Justice in the individual case.[50]

Professor Hessel E. Yntema, covering the same ground, listed seventeen policy considerations that have been said to be relevant in the choice-of-law process * * *.[51]

* * *

Professor David F. Cavers has elaborated the same idea in his recent Cooley Lectures.[54] He has carried the process of evaluating the various policy factors (that Cheatham, Reese, Yntema and others have described) to the extent of formulating for some fact situations a few fairly specific rules, or almost-rules, which he derives from his evaluations. He does not call them rules, however, but "principles of preference," and would have the courts use them not as controls but rather as guides to choice-of-law decision. Whether the Cavers approach is or is not accepted by the courts, it illustrates cogently the possibility of using the policy evaluating process as a means of getting away from broad generalizations and arriving at specific results, or guides to results.

---

*   Reprinted with permission.

[50]   Cheatham & Reese, *Choice of the Applicable Law*, 52 COLUM. L. REV. 959 (1952). * * *
[51]   Yntema, *The Objectives of Private International Law*, 35 CAN. B. REV. 721, 734-35 (1957).* * *
[54]   CAVERS, THE CHOICE-OF-LAW PROCESS 139-203 (1965).

The present writer's approach does not carry him as far as Cavers goes. It is my belief that these choice-of-law policies, which I call choice-influencing considerations, can and should be restated and defined with sufficient particularity that they themselves can be used as a practical (though not a mechanical), test of the rightness of choice-of-law rules and decisions. This involves reducing the considerations to manageable number and identity. Some of the policy factors listed by Cheatham and Reese, by Yntema, and by others will appear in or affect more than one of the ultimate considerations, but there should be a minimum of overlapping among them. There must be frank recognition of some contradiction among them, because all of the opposing values must be included in the restated list of considerations. Testing of rules or decisions under such a set of standards will be a qualitative process of evaluation, and there will be clear room for difference of opinion in it. That is inherent in the nature of conflicts problems; solutions to them should usually not be mechanical, but the relevant considerations should include an indication of when mechanical rules are appropriate.

Testing in these terms will commonly justify choice-of-law rules that apply to categories of cases, so that reexamination of the considerations will not be required for every case that comes along, though oftentimes uniqueness or divergencies of fact or law will make standardized generalizations inappropriate. Such inexactness is not new in conflicts law, and any effort to eliminate it would today be a step backward toward mechanical jurisprudence. The societal function of each area of law in which a conflict arises, as well as the locally conceived functions of the specific rules between which conflict exists, ought to be tied into the choice-of-law process. Identification of choice-influencing considerations will aid in achieving predictability for some types of transactions, but different values will be promoted for other types of transactions. In any event, it seems that an effort to identify and clarify the choice-influencing considerations is worthwhile. The present effort can make no claim to originality nor much to new insight. It merely undertakes to restate the considerations that have, expressly or impliedly, always underlain common-law choice-of-law decisions, as others have from time to time identified them. The result is a list of five, which seem to incorporate all that are in the longer lists:

> A. Predictability of results;
> B. Maintenance of interstate and international order;
> C. Simplification of the judicial task;
> D. Advancement of the forum's governmental interests;
> E. Application of the better rule of law.

No priority among the considerations is intended from the order of listing. Their relative importance varies according to the area of the law involved, and all should be considered regardless of area. A brief summary of the content of each will be attempted.

A. Predictability of Results

Predictability of results includes the ideal that the decision in the litigation on a given set of facts should be the same regardless of where the litigation occurs, so that "forum shopping" will benefit neither party. It also includes the companion ideal that parties to a consensual transaction should be able to know at the time they engage upon it that it will produce, by way of legal consequences, the same set of socio-economic consequences (usually but not necessarily based upon the assumed validity of the transaction) regardless of where disputes occur. They should be able to plan their transaction as one with predictable results. At least this is an ideal for some kinds of transactions.

Protection of the justified expectations of parties to a transaction is achieved to the extent that the results are reasonably predictable in advance. A rule that permits parties to select at the time of their transaction the state whose law is to govern it serves this purpose, but we are concerned with serving the purpose even when parties do not know enough about the laws of the two or more states involved to make an advance choice between them, and even when the parties do not think about choice of law at all. Many courts discover a "presumed intent" of the parties, for such cases, to have as governing the law that would sustain their transaction as otherwise planned. When this is done, the court is making a choice of law itself, protecting justified expectations in terms of substantive results by basing its choice on the content of the law more than on territorial reasons. This is true also of Ehrenzweig's closely related "basic rule of validity," applied in favor of most but not all contracts, trusts, wills, commercial instruments, marriages, legitimations, and other socially favored legal arrangements. Under either approach predictability is furthered by making what Professor Cavers has called a choice between laws as distinguished from a choice between jurisdictions. An overt "choice between laws" gives a forum court the opportunity to weigh its decision in terms both of socio-economic results anticipated by the parties and of whatever governmental interests may be present. Most of the other considerations that are relevant in choice-of-law cases can also be furthered by the same choice-between-laws approach.

The eighth item in the Cheatham-Reese list of choice-of-law policies is "the fundamental policy underlying the broad local law field involved." This has to do not with specific rules of forum law but with the broad policy of the society and its law, and it is recognized that this broad policy may even be opposed to some specific local rules, such as those dealing with usurious contracts, or the Rule Against Perpetuities, or accumulations on charitable trusts. For some types of transactions, the forum state's "fundamental policy underlying the broad local law field involved" may well, for multistate cases, be one favoring predictability of socio-economic consequences by sustaining transactions entered into by parties acting in good faith.

A comprehensive element in the predictability consideration is "security," the first of the two policy heads to which Yntema reduced his analysis. Predictability gives security, and without predictability security is appreciably lessened. Lack of security under the law is generally produced by the same opposing considerations that produce lack of predictability in choice of law. These are well illustrated by two claims to security which constantly compete against each other—security of titles and security of transactions (unauthorized transfers of title). No conflicts rule can completely protect both interests simultaneously, any more than can a single rule of substantive law. When interests represented by the predictability consideration fight to a draw, the balance of interests which leads to a decision will have to be based on other considerations. That will often be the case where contradictory claims to movable chattels, as between an owner and a bona fide taker from a bailee, are at issue. Even more clearly, predictability might not be the major consideration if title claims be pitted against interests of some other character.

B. Maintenance of Interstate and International Order

Most countries have single nation-wide systems of law on most subjects, so that in them the formulation of conflicts law requires only international accommodations. In the United States, accommodations to a unique system of federalism must be added. International accommodations may be quite meager where chauvinistic nationalism prevails, but as chauvinism recedes treaties or other agreements dealing with conflicts matters are likely to develop side by side with domestic conflicts law. As "one world" gradually becomes reality, both of these side-by-side methods of international accommodation will serve to match its growing reality. They will appear in this country both from Washington as federal statutes, treaties, and executive agreements and from the states as common law and statute. Increasing accommodations to our federal system will similarly appear, for the most part in statutes enacted in Washington, but in state law as well, as centralization persistently changes the character of our federalism.

Specific clauses in the federal constitution (full faith and credit, due process, privileges and immunities, equal protection, interstate commerce, and perhaps others) as well as the inherent federal control over foreign and national affairs, all as interpreted by the United States Supreme Court, have imposed outer limits on the states beyond which they must not go in interfering with basic requisites to international and interstate orderliness. The latest area for which these limits have been established concerns escheat to the states of choses in action abandoned by their owners.[66] Previously, either a plural escheat or a first-claiming-state-takes-all theory appeared to prevail, with resultant injustice either to the debtor or to the less diligent state. The new due process rule on escheat assures that the debtor will pay once, and only once, to a state mechanically selected on a basis that is fair to all states. The imposition of such outer limits constitutes a proper function of a court interpreting a constitution. But there are factors affecting relationships between states and nations, in choice-of-law cases, that ought to be taken into account yet which ought not (not yet, at least) to be hardened into constitutional limitations. These are properly considerations in the common-law judicial process.

The concern with claims to sovereignty that enters into international choice of law ought not to be very important where the choice is between laws of the states of the United States. The political concern of the states, apart from mere preference for local law and local persons, is primarily with a need for systematization, for an orderliness that will make our federal system work with reasonable efficiency in the complicated choice-of-law field.

The free and unpenalized movement of people and goods from state to state, and freedom in commercial intercourse, are essential to the success of our federal system, and it is part of the law's task to assure them. Deference to sister state law in situations in which the sister state's substantial concern with the problem gives it a real interest in having its law applied, even though the forum state also has an identifiable interest, will sometimes usefully further this aspect of the law's total task. This will sometimes be a deference to what has been called the "stronger law," meaning the law of the state that is in the best position to insist upon ultimate enforcement of its rule, as is the state of situs when title to a tangible res (movable or immovable) is in question, or possibly the state of the domicile when the existence of a familial status is the issue. The sixth of the Cheatham-Reese list of policies, "favoring application of the law of the state of dominant interest," ties in functionally with this deference to the primarily concerned state. It must be recognized that if nearly all of a transaction's significant contacts are with one state (X), yet the forum state (F) applies its own law to the transaction despite its lesser contacts, resentment in X may induce later retaliation in kind. Avoidance of the interstate friction that can develop from this sort of retaliatory comity is a proper choice-of-law objective.

The regulation of forum shopping, both by permitting it within reasonable limits and by barring it under forum non conveniens rules, has bearing on this consideration since it affects

---

[66]   *See* Texas v. New Jersey, 379 U.S. 674 (1965).

choice of law at least as to so-called procedural matters and, where a court employs forum preference among substantive rules, as to them also. Any deliberate employment of forum preference is suspect, since on its face it leaves interstate and international concerns out of account. The balancing process here, however, is particularly delicate, since discrimination against the interests of other governments can be a subtle thing, and the interests of other governments in private litigation are seldom large enough by themselves to dictate the choice of law that a court should make. The most that can be safely said of them is that they constitute a relevant factor for consideration, and that failure to consider them may produce results that, though within the permissible limits of constitutionality as now defined, are troublesome and unfortunate. A neat and orderly system of choice of law, with states' rights clearly identified and allocated, is in our federalism an unrealizable ideal, yet one that should not be discarded.

C. Simplification of the Judicial Task

An easy cliche is that law does not exist for the convenience of the court that administers it, but for society and its members; therefore, simplification of the judicial task should be a minor consideration in determining what any rule of law should be. The statement is true enough. But overcrowded dockets can become a real problem, and complicated rules of law may encourage the delay in decision that is sometimes a reason why dockets lengthen. Also, complex rules are sometimes difficult to apply, especially to complex facts, and even reasonably competent courts, both trial and appellate, may misapply them. The danger of this is multiplied when juries have to deal with foreign law. The strange handling which some good courts have given to renvoi furnishes a convincing illustration. Simplicity in law is a virtue. Judicial efficiency often depends upon it.

It has been argued that a court should apply its own local law unless there is good reason for not doing so. No one can deny the propriety of this argument so long as the "unless" clause is adequately emphasized. It will usually be easier for the forum court to apply its own law than any other. The court is presumably already familiar with it and is already accustomed to administering it.

That is without question a good reason for a court's applying its own procedural rules, since it would be utterly impracticable for a court in F to import the whole procedural machinery and technique of X even in a case that is otherwise clearly governed by X law. But the reasons of practicality which justify that generalization stop short when the rule in question is an outcome-determinative one that would be no harder for the F court to apply than any other X rule of substantive law. If the procedure concept is broadened to cover such matters as statutes of frauds, measure of damages, and the survival of tort claims, one may suspect that the real reason for the decision is some consideration other than the one that supports a forum court's application of its own procedural rules. The true reason may be outright chauvinistic preference for forum law, or an effort to select what is regarded as the sounder of the two competing rules of law, or an effort to do justice in the individual case, or something else. Whatever the true reason is, it ought to be brought out in the open and either accepted or rejected on its own merits. The procedure-substance dichotomy has real justification, but use of it as a cover-up gimmick affording technical legal support for results justifiable only by other real reasons is wrong.

Preference for forum law is of course not the only approach that can simplify the judicial task in choice-of-law cases. Any simple mechanical rule, such as that the law of the place of contracting governs in contract cases and the law of the place of first harmful impact governs torts, is also easy to apply. That is a virtue, and was some justification for these purported rules.

Their ultimate rejection did not deny this virtue, but was based rather on a recognition that other relevant considerations were more important. Yet simplicity and ease of application remain a significant consideration that is properly taken into account in passing upon the utility of any choice-of-law rule that may be suggested for any area of law.

Minimization of conflicts problems by weeding out "false conflicts," a technique not yet adequately developed, should be one of the most fruitful and expandable methods of simplifying choice of law. The method will not be useful in cases where one state's contacts with a set of facts are few and relatively insignificant as compared with those of another state whose law is different; in that situation a choice of law still has to be made even though the choice may be a comparatively quick one. That is an easy conflicts case, not a false one. But if the laws of both states, relevant to the set of facts, are the same, or would produce the same decision in the lawsuit, then there is no real conflict of laws at all, and the case ought to be decided under the law that is common to both states. Some of the strangest decisions with some of the lengthiest and most convoluted opinions in the books could have been handled simply and easily if the false conflict analysis had been understood and accepted. This of course is a facet of Professor Cavers' extremely helpful emphasis on the conflicts problem as one of "choice of laws" rather than "choice of jurisdictions."

D. Advancement of the Forum's Governmental Interests

Entirely apart from the simplification of judicial tasks that comes from a forum court's application of its own rather than some other state's law, a court has a natural and largely justifiable primary concern with advancement of the governmental interests of its own state. These interests are not always clearly reflected, or even reflected at all, by the state's private law, either legislative or judge-made, but they often are. If they are, it is reasonable that in a choice-of-law situation a court will, and should, endeavor to effectuate these interests and purposes insofar as it can identify them. To the extent that the elusive concept "local public policy" can be correlated with local positive law, it constitutes an affirmative pull on any court to prefer its own law over any foreign law. This is a reasoned basis for forum preference. It differs sharply from that "counsel of despair" which is said to be the last resource of puzzled critics who ignore true choice-of-law considerations, give up the effort to effectuate them, and take instead an easy way out by a selection of forum law which gets by as long as the forum state has the minimum fact contacts required by the federal constitution.

Such an unreasoning fall-back on forum preference as a substitute for choice-of-law thinking is not calculated to advance the governmental interests of the forum or any other state, nor is it what the commentators have been talking about in that context. True governmental interests of a state are not discoverable by blind matching with any old law that may be on the state's books. They can be identified, and in turn implemented, only by thoughtful and intelligent analysis of the legal materials in the light of current socio-economic, cultural, and political attitudes in the community. Ascertainment of a state's governmental interests is no small task, not one to be solved by locating a statutory section or a paragraph in an old judicial opinion. Courts should not lightly undertake the task, but it is a task sometimes within the judicial function.

Too often the search for governmental interests in a particular case, especially for the purpose of sustaining application of forum law, is artificial. It turns into something like the argument of amateur debaters who seek as many "points" as possible to support their side without recognizing that one really relevant consideration can outweigh a dozen "points."

A governmental interest in a choice-of-law case, in its simplest sense, is discoverable by putting together (a) the reasons supporting the rule of law in question (F's or X's law) and (b) the state's (F's or X's) factual contacts with a case, or the issue in a case, to see if they match. Since some reasons, usually a variety of them, can be called up in support of almost any rule of law that is on the books anywhere, it is nearly always possible for a good lawyer to conjure up governmental interest in just about any state that has any connection with a set of facts. It is not at all unusual for one state to discover that it has such interests in a set of facts though another state's courts would say otherwise. A court is usually more discriminatingly hard-boiled in analyzing another state's interests than in analyzing its own. It has been suggested, for example, that in *Babcock v. Jackson* New York was the only state that had a governmental interest in the operation of host-guest laws because all the parties were domiciled in New York and were riding in a New York car on a trip that was to begin and end in New York even though the accident occurred in Ontario. Yet an Ontario court could well say, if the action were before it, that its guest statute was designed to prevent collusive suits directed against insurance companies (not just Ontario insurance companies) in Ontario courts, at least on Ontario facts.

The original policy that underlay the Statute of Frauds was at least arguably stated in its title "An Act for the Prevention of Frauds and Perjuryes," which would tend to locate the interest behind the statute at the place where fraud and perjury might occur—the forum where suit is brought on an oral contract. Yet most courts today tie their search for interest in oral contracts cases to other connecting factors. As to a recent case involving effect of a time-for-suit limitation in an Illinois personal property insurance contract on a Florida action for losses suffered after the insured and his property had moved to Florida, Professor Currie thought that the interest of Illinois was exclusive while Michael Traynor, certainly a perceptive analyst, thought Florida's interest was superior. Probably the difficulty in all these cases is one of definition. The simple definition at the beginning of the preceding paragraph does not cover all that must be taken into account. Governmental interest is too large a notion to be narrowly defined or rigidly confined. It must include all the relevant concerns that the particular government, not only as a sovereign entity but also as a repository of justice, may have in a set of facts or an issue. A different legal entity, even though it has a differing statute or judicial precedent on its books, might have about the same total governmental interest in reference to the facts of a particular case.

Use of the connecting factor of domicile as a base for discovering or denying the existence of governmental interests illustrates this. A state of course has some special interest in its domiciliaries, and there are a number of choice-of-law purposes for which domicile is traditionally relevant or even controlling. In many of these areas, however, factors other than a state's concern with protecting its domiciliaries are involved. Where intestate succession to movables is the issue, or marital property titles in movables, or assignments of such property, it is desirable to have some single law to govern so that unity of results can be assured, and domiciliary law is chosen for the sake of convenience. The motivating considerations are predictability of results and simplification of the judicial task more than governmental concern for domiciliaries. The once powerful concern of the domiciliary state with matters of familial status is weakening. In the United States, increasing mobility of the citizenry is decreasing the importance attached to the socio-political idea of each person's having a preeminent headquarters at some one place. The fact that in this country the states are becoming more alike, less chauvinistic in their eccentricities, contributes to this. Most of the states are becoming accustomed to the fact that a large proportion of the human beings who at any given moment are working or playing within their borders will have ties with other states as well. An effect of this is that the states are less concerned than they once were with protection of the local citizen as distinguished from the "stranger," and more inclined than they once were to promulgate and enforce laws that apply to both equally, well beyond the minimum equalities prescribed by the federal constitution. Visitors as well as residents may be protected by "good" local laws. The domicile of parties in one state or another has less significance today, and may well have far less in another generation, than it once had as a basis for locating true governmental interests.

It has been remarked that a state's governmental interests in a given multistate set of facts may be contrary to the state's own law. An obvious response is that a court should be reluctant to find that this is so. It is said that courts should take their social policy from their legislatures, not make it themselves. That is sound enough where the law from which the policy is to be derived is enacted law, or at least enacted law that is to a fair extent in tune with the times. But suppose, as is most often the case, that the opposing rules of states F and X are judge-made. In that case must the court find that the governmental policies of the states are as surely opposed to each other as their judge-made laws are?

This is a situation in which if either state had a clean slate today, instead of precedent, it might now for good socio-legal reasons adopt the other state's rule as its own. True, there are some states whose mores are actually far apart, as Nevada's and Kansas' probably are on gambling transactions. But that is exceptional. Ordinarily differences in common-law rules between states do not represent deep and genuine differences in social policy. They may result from the accident of court membership (the accidents of politics, or sometimes the deliberate schemings of politics), the accident of timing (the early social era when litigation produced a precedent in F as against the middle or later era when one was produced in X), or the accidents of legal education. As far as social policy in the two states is concerned, despite the differing decisions, it is apt to be about the same. There are likely to be in each state two, or possibly more than two, opposing sets of socio-economic interests, one favoring one rule of law, with the other or others to the contrary. These differing interests are not much more likely to be bounded by state lines today than is the air we breathe. The fact that one set of interests has at some past period prevailed in F is relevant, but only as a precedent for deciding cases clearly governed by F law. This precedential effect does not have anything to do with governmental interests in their choice-of-law sense. The prior decision is not a choice-of-law precedent. And a real search for governmental interest relevant to choice of law may or may not reveal that a result opposite to the local precedent is really preferable.

It does no harm to say that this policy analysis is a continuing search for governmental interests, provided we recognize that what we ought to do in any event is to analyze the problem in terms of all the relevant, choice-of-law considerations, of which the interest behind the forum's internal rule is only one. If we classify the process as a search for and effectuation of the state's governmental interests, we should think of them in terms of the total governmental concerns of a justice-dispensing court in a modern American state. Despite the increasingly common character of the states of the United States, there are still significant differences among them on some but not on most matters. If two states really have opposing governmental interests, then advancement of the forum's interests as against those of the other state must be accepted as a legitimate part (but not all) of the choice-of-law process.

E. Application of the Better Rule of Law*

* * * * *

Robert A. Leflar, *Conflicts Law: More on Choice-Influencing Considerations*, 54 CAL. L. REV. 1584, 1588-1598 (1966)*

* * * * *

There are areas in which analysis in terms of the five major choice-influencing considerations leads almost automatically to the conflicts rules that have already been developed. These considerations almost always demand that land title cases, for example, be governed by situs law. On the other hand in cases involving torts, trusts of personalty, and contracts, choice-of-law rules are traditionally less exact, and application of these considerations to the cases mirrors the inexactness. Analysis in terms of the choice-influencing considerations shows why the old rules are inexact, and at the same time justifies most of the results that have actually been reached under them. Nor is this kind of analysis of specific cases as complicated or difficult a process as might be supposed. It is about as easy as the older and more familiar approaches to conflicts cases. A few recent cases can be used as illustrations.

Case (1). H and W, husband and wife who are Spanish nationals and domiciliaries, owned Spanish cash and securities as community property. Between 1919 and the late 1930's they transferred these to a New York bank in a joint custody account, the account agreement providing for joint ownership with survivorship. Under Spanish law this agreement would be void and the property would retain its community character. Under New York law the agreement would be valid. H died first, then W died. H's estate claimed half the property as community; W's estate claimed all of it by survivorship.[19]

Merely bringing the cash and securities from Spain to New York clearly did not change the community character of the spouses' ownership. The question is the legal effect of the subsequent creation of the joint custody account with the New York bank. That was a New York transaction to which New York law may constitutionally be applied. But should it be?

It has traditionally been said that marital property interests in movables are governed by the law of the spouses' domicile regardless of where the things were acquired or where transactions concerning them may have occurred. That is a good rule for most purposes because it assures unity of spousal ownership of all their personalty and tends to provide a unified system of distribution when one of the spouses dies. If this mechanical rule had been automatically applied here, H's estate would have won the cited case as three of the seven judges of the New York Court of Appeals thought it should. But the majority of the judges held that New York's law should govern and that W's estate should prevail. The following analysis of the facts in the light of the relevant choice-influencing considerations appears to sustain the majority position:

A. Predictability of results at the time the spouses set up their New York custody account was important. They deliberately planned for joint ownership and survivorship in accordance with New York law by a bona fide transaction which they in good faith expected would produce that result. Their expectation was a reasonable one under the circumstances. The predictable result which they anticipated would be defeated if New York law were not applied.

---

* [This material appears at pp.139.]

** Copyright © by California Law Review, Inc. Reprinted from CALIFORNIA LAW REVIEW, Vol. 54, No. 4, October, pp. 1588-1598, by permission.

19 The facts are taken from Wyatt v. Fulrath, * * * 239 N.Y.S.2d 486 (Sup.Ct. 1963), *aff'd* . . . 254 N.Y.S.2d 216 (1964), *modified and aff'd* * * * 264 N.Y.S.2d 233 (1965). * * *

B. To apply New York's law encourages international transactions of this character; to apply Spain's law would discourage them. They are worthy of encouragement. It is scarcely conceivable that Spain would feel that New York, by applying its law, was impugning Spanish claim to sovereignty in any sense. Neither state's concern with the facts is so clearly superior to the other's as to give rise to any danger of international ill feeling if the other's law is applied.

C. Simplification of the New York court's judicial task is almost irrelevant here. It might be a little easier for a New York court to apply its own rather than Spanish law, but here both rules are simple and the judicial complications under either are insignificant.

D. The forum does not have any major governmental interest that demands advancement here. An advocate, if he tries, can always spell out a local interest in any partly local set of facts. Here he could assert a New York interest in sustaining local banking transactions valid by local law, and the interest in the freedom of spouses to deal with their marital property which induced promulgation of the New York rule permitting transactions such as this one. That the spouses are not New York domiciliaries would scarcely reduce the force of this argument. However, although New York interests exist, they are not strong ones.

E. A New York court can be expected to regard its rule permitting marital freedom in property and contract matters as superior to Spain's rule invalidating such agreements. The Spanish rule, after all, is pretty medieval, although judges might differ and hold strong opinions about this. A majority on any American court would probably be certain that New York's is the better law.

The conclusion from this analysis is clear. Considerations A, B and E all direct us to New York's law as the proper governing law, while considerations C and D do not direct us elsewhere. This is a case in which the values that admittedly support the old mechanical reference to the law of the domicile in the ordinary marital property case are outweighed by other values inherent in the facts of the particular case.

Case (2). H was driving his car, with his wife W and their child T as passengers, through Colorado on the way to their home in Pennsylvania. Due to H's negligence the car was wrecked and T was killed. W sues H in Pennsylvania for T's wrongful death. Under Colorado law a wife may maintain such an action against her husband, but under Pennsylvania law she may not.

A straight characterization approach leading to application of traditional rules would have made this either a torts case, governed by the law of the place of the harmful impact (Colorado), or a family law case, governed by the law of the family domicile (Pennsylvania). It is possible that a choice between these two characterizations might be motivated by considerations other than those which inhere in pure logic.

Predictability (A) has absolutely no bearing on this problem, because nothing was planned or done with any reference to the wife-husband action rule of either state. If the question had been whether H drove negligently, predictability would have been all-important because both H and others on the same highway had to know what rules of the road applied at the immediate time and place—a question to which only Colorado law could give a definite answer. But that is not the question in our case. Interstate orderliness (B) is not involved here, since no possibility of impairing claims to sovereign power are presented and interstate automotive movement by citizens will scarcely be affected by a choice of either law. Both state's rules are simple (C), and neither can be more easily applied by the Pennsylvania court than the other. But Pennsylvania does have a genuine governmental interest (D) in the set of facts. The permanent presence of the spouses as domiciliaries identifies Pennsylvania as the state having the prime interest in their marital relationship, to which the rules of law in question directly relate. Relationship with a liability insurer and fear of spousal collusions against the insurer also center at the place which is both the forum for the possibly collusive action and the place where the insurance relationship would normally be entered into. Pennsylvania can easily conclude that its total concern with the case is much greater than Colorado's. Moreover, Pennsylvania's rule prohibiting a wife suing her husband for his unintended injuries to their child is not so anachronistic or otherwise contrary to currently accepted social standards (E) as to induce the court to regard Colorado's as the better law.

Analysis in terms of the choice-influencing considerations, with (D) this time being overwhelmingly important, leads to application of Pennsylvania law. That was the result reached by the Pennsylvania court for substantially the same reason.[26] The court's opinion, after adverting to most of the relevant policy considerations, fell back on a comparison of Pennsylvania's interests with those of Colorado, and held that comparison to be controlling. The inference was that if other choice-influencing considerations had been more significant in relation to the facts, they would have controlled, or would at least have been taken into affirmative account. The opinion very nearly serves as a model for the sort of choice-of-law analysis that this study proposes.

Case (3). In Pennsylvania, T, a citizen of Pennsylvania, bought from defendant New York corporation an airlines ticket for a round-trip from Philadelphia to Puerto Rico. On the return trip the plane carrying T disintegrated in the air above Maryland and there fell to the ground. A New York action for T's wrongful death was brought on behalf of his brothers and sisters, his closest surviving relatives. Pennsylvania law allows recovery by surviving brothers and sisters, but Maryland law permits such recovery only by spouses, parents, children or dependents.

New York as forum is in the position of a disinterested third state. It has no substantial connection with the facts, and application of New York's wrongful death laws would probably be violative of the due process clause in the federal Constitution. The choice is between the laws of Pennsylvania and of Maryland. The traditional place-of-the-wrong rule for torts would make Maryland law controlling. A contracts characterization would also be possible. A "center of gravity" or most significant relationships analysis would presumably lead to application of Pennsylvania's law,[32] regardless of characterization. Analysis in terms of the relevant choice-influencing considerations would necessarily produce a reference to the law of one of these two states. Hence, it could not greatly affect the result, but it can avoid a mechanical or a disguised basis for the choice and give the real reasons for it.

As in case (2), predictability (A) has little or no relevancy here. Since the accident was not planned with reference to any state's law, the choice of forum by one party cannot be seen as an attempt to defeat the other's pre-litigation expectations. Maintenance of interstate order (B) is important in the sense that a disinterested third state as forum especially needs to do a good job of deciding between the competing laws and interests of other states, rather than taking sides unfairly between them, to sustain stability and confidence in our system of federalism. Simplification of the judicial task (C) affords no guidance when the choice is between the laws, both fairly short and plain, of two other states. The forum has no particular governmental interests of its own to be advanced (D) other than its general concern with administering justice well and fairly. In furtherance of this general concern, however, the forum may prefer what it regards as the more enlightened rule of law (E). In this instance, it would be Pennsylvania's since the rule allowing recovery there is a modern one which, incidentally, more nearly corresponds with

---

[26]   McSwain v. McSwain, * * * 215 A.2d 677 (1966) * * *

[32]   That was the result in Long v. Pan Am World Airways, * * * 213 NE 2d 796 * * * ([NY] 1965), from which case (3) is derived. * * *

the civilized rule that prevails in New York. This correspondence could legitimately influence a court. The most relevant considerations here are: (C), which requires the court, for the sake of maintaining good order in a complex federalist system, to weigh carefully the interests of the non-forum states and of the parties with relation to the states in the interstate situation; and, with lesser weight, (E), which may give a preference to what might be regarded as the better law of Pennsylvania. The totality of considerations leads to a choice of the Pennsylvania rule.

Case (4). H is domiciled in Ontario where he regularly keeps his car and has it insured. H invites G, also an Ontario domiciliary, to ride with him on a pleasure trip from Ontario into New York and back. While in New York, H drives negligently and injures G. Under New York law the standard for the host's liability to his guest is ordinary negligence. By Ontario statute a host is not liable to his guest for injuries caused by the host's negligent driving. G sues H in New York.

Under the old place-of-the-tort rule, New York law would govern. A contract characterization is scarcely feasible. The center-of-gravity or dominant-contacts approach, to which New York is committed, apparently would require application of Ontario law, though it should be noted that the New York court before which the case was brought held that even under this approach New York law should control.[35] It may be suspected that some perfectly legitimate choice-influencing considerations not expressly mentioned in the court's opinion helped produce this result. How would they operate if they were brought out into the open?

Predictability (A) again is irrelevant. Auto accidents are seldom planned, and there is no evidence that any aspect of this one was. The host-guest rule does not relate to the manner of driving or the rules of the road. It therefore does not fall within that part of automobile negligence law as to which certainty concerning the governing law is of first importance. Although uncertainty as to what law governed may have encouraged the filing of the suit in New York rather than elsewhere—a fact that has forum-shopping overtones—New York is certainly an appropriate place to try the lawsuit. Neither international order (B) nor ease of judicial administration (C) has much bearing on the case. Automotive intercourse between the United States and Canada, or between New York and Ontario, will not be discouraged by application of one state's rule or the other's, nor will either sovereign be offended. No international discomfiture will ensue. And the forum will have no administrative difficulty in applying either rule.

The New York forum does have some governmental interest (D) in the case, however. Its interest is not the intensely practical one which relates to supervision and safety of the state's highways, since the rule in question, unlike rules of the road and definitions of negligence, does not bear upon vehicle operation as such. A governmental interest connected with any particular rule of law has to do with the operative effect of that rule. In this instance the relevant effect is the bearing of the New York negligence rule on the duty of a host to a guest, and the danger of collusion between host and guest to defraud the host's insurer. New York's interest in applying its own law rather than Ontario's on these issues is based primarily on its status as a justice-administering state. In that status it is strongly concerned with seeing that persons who come into New York courts to litigate facts with substantial New York connection have their cases determined according to rules consistent with New York's concepts of justice, or at least not inconsistent with them. That will be as true for non-domiciliary litigants as for domiciliaries. This interest will not manifest itself clearly if the out-of-state rule does not run contrary to some strong socio-legal policy of the forum, but it will become a major consideration if there is such a strong opposing local policy.

---

[35]   Kell v. Henderson, * * * 263 N.Y.S.2d 647 (Sup. Ct.), *aff'd,* . . . 270 N.Y.S.2d 552 (1965).

That consideration leads to (E), preference for what is regarded as the better rule of law. In this instance New York has such a preference, and it is a vigorous one. New York is one of the states that never succumbed to the insurance lobby's campaign for host-guest statutes, and on the whole regards such enactments with justified distaste. Many of the states that acquired these acts in the 1930's are coming to share New York's attitude. The hitchiker era that produced them is past, and current feeling is that they are both unfair to guests and contrary to the enterprise liability, spread-the-loss concept that prevails in the automobile tort area today. Moreover, the Ontario act, barring as it does all guest recovery even for gross negligence, may well be regarded as the most undesirable of all the enactments. A New York court would probably think that its negligence rule makes better socio-economic-legal sense than Ontario's host-guest statute, and that the functions of law in society would accordingly be better served by applying New York's rule. The combination of considerations (D) and (E), therefore, seems to call for the application of New York law.

Case (5). P, a Delaware corporation, operates a licensed gambling casino in Puerto Rico. G, a New York domiciliary, gambled at P's casino. He there gave P a check on G's New York bank account for 3,000 dollars to pay for chips which he then lost. G stopped payment of the check before it was cashed. Under Puerto Rican law the check constituted a valid contractual obligation; under New York law it was an illegal gaming contract. P sues G in New York for the amount of the check.

If the law of the place of making governed, the contract would be valid under Puerto Rican law. If place of performance governed, the law of New York, the place of payment of the check, would invalidate it. Assuming good faith on both sides in issuance and acceptance of the check and an intention that the law of Puerto Rico should govern, an intention-of-the-parties rule would require reference to Puerto Rican law. The same result would follow if Ehrenzweig's "basic rule of validation" were employed. Under a "center of gravity" or most-significant-relationship approach, it would be difficult to predict whether the Puerto Rican gaming parts of the transaction, or the New York domicile plus the check being drawn on and payable at a New York Bank, would be deemed to give rise to the dominant contacts. Actually, the New York Court of Appeals ignored that question, assumed that Puerto Rico's law governed so that the check was valid, and devoted its opinion to the separate question whether any strong New York public policy barred enforcement of the valid contract. The majority permitted enforcement.[43] Nevertheless the validity question is an interesting one.

Predictability (A) is always important in contracts cases. Parties contracting in good faith presumably desire a valid contract. They want their contract governed by a law that will protect the expectations under which they act. Public policy generally favors sustaining transactions that are not anti-social. Maintenance of good relations between New York and Puerto Rico as states (B) also favors recognition of the Puerto Rican claim. This consideration is more important here than it would be in most cases between states of the United States, or between American states and a foreign nation, because of Puerto Rico's special relationship to this country and her extraordinary efforts, with state-side encouragement, to build up her economy and political status. Simplification of the forum court's judicial task (C) is practically irrelevant since both rules of law are clear and easy to apply to the facts. New York has no strong governmental interest (D) in its anti-gambling rules as applied to policed gambling occurring in and regulated by another responsible jurisdiction, particularly since New York allows other forms of policed gambling (pari-mutuel betting at race tracks and church bingo games) within its own territory. The degree of New York's interest is not appreciably affected by the involvement of

---

[43]   Intercontinential Hotels Corp. (P.R.) v. Golden, * * * 254 N.Y.S.2d 257 (1964). * * *

a New York domiciliary and payment which was to be made out of his New York bank account. These facts are only incidental to the larger issues in the case. Finally, New York probably has no strong feeling about its rule being any better, as law, than Puerto Rico's. Some states (Kansas for example) might have such a feeling, but New York is more placid. The weight of considerations (A) and (B), plus the unimportance of (C), (D) and (E), make the New York decision sustaining the contract a proper one.

Case (6). P, an American citizen domiciled in New York, was in Brazil on business. There he bought a airline ticket for an air flight, wholly in Brazil, on defendant Brazilian airline. P was injured as a result of the pilot's negligence in landing at a Brazilian airport. Under Brazilian law the maximum allowable recovery is 100,000 cruzeiros, now worth about 140 dollars in United States money. New York law sets no top limit on recoveries. P sues in New York, where defendant Brazilian airline is effectively brought into court and defends on the merits.

Measure of damages questions have sometimes been characterized as procedural and hence governed by the law of the forum. A more realistic view, however, acknowledges that the difference between 140 dollars and 14,000 dollars is substantive. Not all substantive issues arising from a particular set of facts need necessarily be governed by the same law, but most courts would agree that forum law as such ought not to control. The choice-influencing considerations ought to be employed with specific reference to the facts of the particular case.

Though predictability (A) as to governing law has no relevance to the unplanned air crash itself, it does have bearing on amounts payable under the airline's liability insurance. Since the airline operated wholly in Brazil, whatever insurance it carried, and its economic planning with reference to amounts of liability, were surely related to Brazil's law. And forum-shopping by plaintiffs would be definitely encouraged if law other than Brazil's could control measure of damages.

International relationships (B) are very important in this case. Brazil's rule apparently represents a deliberate national policy to assist an infant industry, important to the nation's growth, by holding down its operating costs. This comes close to the character of a sovereign concern in a friendly nation, with which any state should be reluctant to interfere.

Simplification of the judicial task (C) is the consideration that normally justifies a forum court in applying its own procedural rules regardless of where the facts arose. Applying Brazilian procedure in a New York trial would be burdensome, inefficient, and impossible. Yet Brazil's rule of damages can be easily applied. The reasons for the substance-procedure dichotomy have no bearing on the damages rule. And as to New York's governmental interest in the case (D), P's domicile in the state is the only connecting factor on which it could be grounded. A state, of course, has some concern with the welfare of its domiciliaries, but that concern in itself is minor when it relates to the measure of damages for extrastate injuries on such facts as these. Domicile as a choice-influencing factor is currently decreasing in importance, except as it affects considerations other than governmental interest. A New York court would without any doubt feel that its damages rule is, as law, decidedly superior to Brazil's (E), but this consideration declines near to zero in importance compared to considerations (A) and (B) on these facts. The forum court probably will not really prefer Brazil's law, but the balance of considerations will nevertheless impel it to apply the disliked law.[48]

* * * * *

---

[48]   Ciprari v. Servicos Aereos Cruzeiro, 245 F. Supp. 819 (S.D.N.Y. 1965), *aff'd*, 359 F.2d 855 (2nd Cir. 1966). * * *

James R. Pielemeier, *Some Hope for Choice of Law in Minnesota*, 18 HAMLINE L. REV. 8, 12-14, 18-19, 24-25, 28-29, 33-35, 42-48 (1994)*

* * * * *

Minnesota began its departure from the territorialist approach with the 1957 case of *Schmidt v. Driscoll Hotel, Inc.*,[29] an action against a Minnesota bar for injuries incurred in a Wisconsin auto accident as a result of the bar's illegal sale of intoxicants in Minnesota. Strict application of territorialist rules would have required application of Wisconsin law, the place of the injury, which would not impose liability on the bar. Emphasizing that the bar's allegedly wrongful conduct took place completely in Minnesota, which was also the residence of all the parties, the Minnesota Supreme Court declined to follow that course, referring to "principles of equity and justice," its interest in regulating conduct within its borders, and its view of legislative intent.

Beginning nine years later in 1966, the court continued to reject application of territorialist principles. In a series of five cases spanning a period of six years, the court refused to apply a family immunity rule and guest statutes of states where accidents occurred. Although its doctrinal approach seemed to shift from case to case, the court apparently was ready to make a clean break from the past.

The court formally made that break in the 1973 case of *Milkovich v. Saari*.[36] *Milkovich* was a suit by an Ontario resident against two other Ontario residents for injuries arising out of an auto accident in Minnesota. Ontario had a guest statute, under which the plaintiff would have to establish gross negligence to recover. Minnesota had no similar law, and the issue was whether the Ontario guest statute should apply. After reviewing the earlier Minnesota decisions that departed from the traditional choice of law rules, the court read them as indicating its "preference" for the approach that has been characterized as the "choice-influencing considerations," or the "better rule" approach. This methodology had its genesis in two law review articles written by Professor Robert A. Leflar.[42]

* * *

In applying these considerations and holding that Ontario law did not apply, the *Milkovich* court heavily discounted the importance of the first three. The first, predictability of results, was deemed unimportant because "basically this test relates to consensual transactions where people should know in advance what law will govern their act. Obviously, no one plans to have an accident, and, except for the remote possibility of forum shopping, this test is of little import in an automobile accident case."

---

*   Reprinted with permission.

[29]   82 N.W.2d 365 (Minn. 1957).

[36]   203 N.W.2d 408 (Minn. 1973).

[42]   Robert A. Leflar, *Choice-Influencing Considerations In Conflicts Law*, 41 N.Y.U. L. REV. 267 (1966)* * *; Robert A. Leflar, *Conflicts Law: More on Choice-Influencing Considerations*, 54 CAL. L. REV. 1584 (1966)* * *.

With respect to the second consideration, maintenance of interstate and international order, the court stated that "no more is called for than that the court apply the law of no state which does not have substantial connection with the total facts and the particular issue being litigated." The court concluded that the requirement of a substantial connection was "amply met by the fact that the accident occurred in Minnesota, as well as by the fact that plaintiff was hospitalized for well over a month in the state."

* * * * *

Application of the Five Choice-Influencing Considerations

1. Predictability of Results

* * * Following the supreme court's lead in *Milkovich*, the Minnesota appellate courts have continued to downplay the importance of the first of the choice-influencing considerations, predictability of results. In the tort and insurance context, the only case that gives predictability significant weight is a decision to give effect to a written choice of law agreement. As a general rule, however, this factor has been, at best, of minimal concern. Relying on the notions that predictability applies primarily to consensual transactions, and that accidents are unplanned, some opinions flatly state that this consideration is not relevant to tort cases.

Predictability did get some lip service in *Blamey v. Brown*, where the issue was whether dram shop liability should be imposed on a Wisconsin bar when it was not available under Wisconsin law. The supreme court noted that the defendant "failed to procure liquor liability insurance since he assumed that only the laws of Wisconsin created his liability." While the court conceded that "if Minnesota law is applied some injustice will result to the defendant since the legal ramifications of his actions were not predictable to him at the time he acted," the court concluded that the other choice-influencing considerations outweighed this concern, and justified application of Minnesota law.[72]

When the issue has involved the validity or construction of liability insurance provisions, predictability has similarly been downplayed. In perhaps its most controversial decision, *Hague v. Allstate Insurance Co.*,[73] the issue was whether Minnesota law permitting "stacking" of uninsured motorist benefits was applicable to a Wisconsin accident involving a Wisconsin decedent insured under a policy issued in Wisconsin. The court conceded that Wisconsin's law prohibiting "stacking" of insurance "may be based in part on a desire to keep insurance premiums low." While noting that a concern with setting standard rates made predictability weigh "slightly in defendant's favor," the court concluded that "the fact that one cannot predict automobile accidents because they are unplanned makes predictability of results less important in automobile liability insurance cases than in other contract cases." On rehearing, the court attempted to bolster this rationale, characterizing motor vehicle insurance contracts as being "in a class by themselves." By knowing that the insured auto will be driven from state to state, "[t]he company, therefore, accepts the risk that the insured may be subject to liability not only in the state where the policy is written, but also in states other than where the policy is written, and that in many instances those states will apply their own law to the situation."

---

[72]   *Blamey*, 270 N.W.2d at 891.
[73]   289 N.W.2d 43 (Minn. 1979), *aff'd*, 449 U.S. 302 (1981).

* * * * *

2. Maintenance of Interstate and International Order

* * *Since *Milkovich* stated that "interstate and international relations are maintained without harm where . . . the forum state has a substantial connection with the facts and issues involved," maintenance of those relations has also been given minimal consideration in the majority of Minnesota appellate opinions.

At the Minnesota Supreme Court level, two opinions are simply to the effect that this factor is not relevant to tort cases. Others merely recite some contacts with the state whose law is determined to be applicable, and quickly deem them sufficient to satisfy the demands of this factor. Although there is some language to the effect that courts should consider "retaliation by one state for mere forum preference of another," and whether the "choice of law will promote forum shopping," the court has given these considerations no significant weight. One case appears to hold that if the contacts are sufficient to permit application of a state's law under the due process clause, they lead to the conclusion that the plaintiff "cannot be regarded as simply forum shopping," and satisfy the maintenance concern. And considering this factor in another case applying Minnesota law, the court displayed an embarrassing misunderstanding of this concern: "[s]ome ruffling of interstate relations might occur if Wisconsin law is applied and consequently maintenance of interstate order might be affected."

* * * * *

3. Simplification of the Judicial Task

In determining the choice of "substantive law," the simplification factor has very rarely been important in Minnesota appellate decisions. Almost all follow the view of *Milkovich* to the effect that Minnesota courts have confidence that they could easily apply the law of another state. In the only supreme court decision in which it was a factor, *In re Discipline of Hoffman*, the court simply stated, "Applying Alaska law to an Alaska claim determined in an Alaska tribunal also simplifies the judicial task. . . ." The only "substantive" decision in which it was deemed important is that of the court of appeals in *Board of Regents v. Royal Insurance Co.*[127] In that case, the issue was whether claims against insurers for indemnification for damages associated with asbestos abatement were governed by Minnesota or New York law. In holding Minnesota law to be applicable, the court relied on the simplification factor, referring to orders of the Minnesota Supreme Court that all asbestos-related claims brought in Minnesota state courts be heard and decided by a single judge. The court stated, "It would be consistent with the supreme court's orders to apply a consistent body of law, i.e. Minnesota law, to all Minnesota asbestos-related claims brought before the judge assigned to hear those claims."

* * * * *

---

[127]   503 N.W.2d 486 (Minn. Ct. App. 1993), *aff'd in part, rev'd in part*, 517 N.W.2d 888 (Minn. 1994) (without discussion of the conflicts issue). * * *

4. Advancement of the Forum's Governmental Interests

* * * Analysis of the forum's governmental interests is perhaps the most problematic area in Minnesota appellate conflicts analysis. The supreme court got off to a poor start on this factor, and its early analysis has haunted decisions ever since.

* * * *Milkovich*, in discussing this factor, declined to rely heavily on some policies that arguably underlie Minnesota law, such as deterrence and assuring payment of local medical costs. Instead, *Milkovich* labelled Minnesota's interests as being that of a "justice-administering state," and avoiding resolutions that are "inconsistent with our own concept of fairness and equity."

This very general discussion of Minnesota's interest was continued in *Schwartz v. Consolidated Freightways Corp. of Delaware*,[151] where the issue was whether to apply Indiana's contributory negligence rule or Minnesota's comparative negligence rule in litigation arising out of an Indiana accident. The court there began its analysis with the incredibly vague statement, still repeated in other cases, that "Advancement of the forum's governmental interests contemplates application both in terms of factual contacts with the forum and in terms of the state's policy considerations relevant to its choice of law." * * *

* * * * *

Later cases, both in the supreme court and the court of appeals, continue the same themes. Although they occasionally refer to policies that arguably underlie the Minnesota rule in question, such as compensation of residents and keeping them off the welfare roles, discussions of Minnesota's governmental interests continue to focus on the "justice-administering state," "fairness and equity," and other undefined interests supposedly arising from a listing of factual contacts.

* * * * *

5. Application of the Better Rule of Law

In discussing his fifth choice-influencing consideration, Professor Leflar argued that application of the better rule of law had been an apparent, but unstated reason for many earlier choice of law decisions. He suggested that the employment of this factor had been masked by "manipulation of conflicts rules, the deliberate employment of conflicts concepts as gimmicks to enable courts to reach desired results, as 'cover-up' devices designed to conceal the real influences that dominate the judicial process in choice-of-law decision."

Commenting further in urging courts to explicitly consider and explain their use of this factor, he stated:

> [W]e do not like it when there is less than the appearance of intellectual integrity in the process, and we ask that the process be purified as soon as possible . . . . We do not in general disagree with results that these deceits have enabled courts to achieve in the past, but we do ask that real reasons and not cover-up devices be given now as explanations of past decisions and guides to future ones.

---

[151]   221 N.W.2d 665 (Minn. 1974).

In applying this consideration, the Minnesota decisions have been neither particularly surprising nor enlightening. After concluding that the first four factors pointed in a particular direction, a number of cases state that the better rule factor need not be considered. Supreme court decisions that have considered it have found one state's laws (usually Minnesota's) to be "better" on a variety of grounds. These have included a conclusion that the rationale of the other state's law was not persuasive, reference to the rationale of an earlier Minnesota decision establishing the rule in question, noting that the chosen rule was the majority rule or in the current trend, or that the disfavored rule was relatively antiquated. Court of appeals decisions have not strayed far from the path set by the supreme court, sometimes relying on its conflicts decisions and sometimes on recent non-conflicts decisions in explaining [why] the chosen law was "better." Some confusion (and potential controversy) exists regarding the degree to which the Court should defer to extant Minnesota legislation in determining the "better rule." Beyond this, however, none of its decisions appears particularly striking on this point.

* * * * *

A Breath of Fresh Air

In March of 1994, the Minnesota Supreme Court issued a conflicts opinion that is markedly different in approach and tone from the cases just discussed. *Jepson v. General Casualty Co. of Wis.*[196] arose out of an Arizona accident resulting in injuries to a Minnesota plaintiff. The plaintiff had purchased a general liability automobile insurance contract through a Minnesota agency with the named insureds being himself, his spouse, and two corporations. Both corporations were North Dakota corporations and the address of one, in North Dakota, was listed in the policy as the address for the named insureds. The policy covered seven vehicles, six of which were registered in North Dakota and one in Indiana. The policy was paid at North Dakota rates by one of the corporations, and testimony indicated that Minnesota rates were substantially higher. Testimony also indicated that had the policy been written at the higher Minnesota rates, the insurance agent might have lost the sale.

After the Arizona accident, which occurred in a real estate agent's car, Jepson settled with the person who caused the accident for the policy limits of that person's liability insurance. Then, after bringing an action in North Dakota against General Casualty for North Dakota personal injury protection benefits, which was settled prior to its being filed with a court, Jepson brought a declaratory judgment action in Minnesota. In this Minnesota action, he sought underinsured motorist benefits under the General Casualty policy, insisting that those benefits be "stacked." Under Minnesota law effective at the time of the accident, stacking was permitted, but under North Dakota law it was not. The trial court found Minnesota law to be applicable, and the court of appeals affirmed. The supreme court, however, in a unanimous opinion written by Justice Alan Page, reversed and held North Dakota law to be applicable.

After concluding with brief discussion that either Minnesota or North Dakota law could constitutionally be applied, the court turned to the choice-influencing considerations. In an apparent somewhat gentle repudiation of the practice of earlier decisions, Justice Page's discussion of the factors began on a note eschewing superficial consideration.

---

[196]   513 N.W.2d 467 (Minn. 1994). * * *

> [The choice influencing] factors were not intended to spawn the evolution of set mechanical rules but instead to prompt courts to carefully and critically consider each new fact situation and explain in a straight-forward manner their choice of law. The lower courts need to wrestle with each situation anew. While prior opinions may be helpful to a court's deliberations, the court's obligation is to be true to the method rather than to seek superficial factual analogies between cases and import wholesale the choice of law analysis contained therein.

The court then turned to predictability of results. In sharp contrast to earlier decisions demeaning its importance in cases involving torts and liability insurance, the court emphasized that because the case involved insurance coverage, this contractual element implicated predictability concerns:

> While where an accident occurs is unimportant, the obligations the insurer has to the insured at that time are important. The heart of the bargain between the insurer and the insured is the coverage the insured purchased. The parties enter into the insurance contract with the expectation that, should a dispute arise, the legal system will endeavor to give each side the benefit of their bargain. To the extent the choice of law in this case contributes to giving the parties the benefit of their bargain, it enhances the predictability of the parties' contractual arrangements.

The court then noted that the evidence reflected a mutual expectation by the parties that they had negotiated a North Dakota contract, with the premiums calculated at North Dakota rates. While stating the parties might have expected Minnesota law to apply had the accident occurred in Minnesota, the court recognized that this expectation would not likely hold when the accident occurred in another state. Concluding with its doubts that other states would apply Minnesota law to a case involving similar facts, and the desirability of courts of different states reaching similar results on choice of law in a given dispute, the court held that "The factor of preserving the parties' justified expectations and enhancing the predictability of what state's law will govern in a contractual dispute points away from the application of Minnesota law."

The court's discussion of the second factor, maintenance of interstate order, was also sharply different from earlier treatments of it. Instead of briefly recounting some factual contacts to justify its choice of law under this factor, the court, for the first time, expressed serious concern for the interests that it reflects:

> In discussing . . . the maintenance of interstate order, we are primarily concerned with whether the application of Minnesota law would manifest disrespect for North Dakota's sovereignty or impede the interstate movement of people and goods. An aspect of this concern is to maintain a coherent legal system in which the courts of different states strive to sustain, rather than subvert, each other's interests in areas where their own interests are less strong. By approaching choice of law questions with these considerations in mind, the opportunities for forum shopping may be kept within reasonable bounds.

The court then noted the parties' arguments about "most significant contacts," but seemed to ignore them in its application of this factor. Instead it noted, in part because of the earlier suit commenced and settled in North Dakota, that the suit in Minnesota appeared to be an act of forum shopping. It continued:

> Minnesota does not have an interest in encouraging forum shopping, particularly where we would be sending a message to those people living on our borders to take advantage of the benefits our neighboring states offer in terms of lower insurance rates, lower vehicle registration fees, and sales taxes, and then, if they are injured, take advantage of Minnesota's greater willingness to compensate tort victims.

The court then concluded that this factor also favored application of North Dakota law, noting:

> North Dakota has the authority to regulate the terms of insurance for vehicles licensed and titled in that state. We interfere with the sovereignty of a sister state when we make our law available for people who seek Minnesota benefits while burdening the North Dakota insurance rate base and regulatory system.

After noting, consistently with earlier cases, that simplification of the judicial task was not a significant factor here, the court turned to the fourth consideration, advancement of the forums' governmental interest. Again, in contrast to earlier cases, absent was any reference to the interest in being a "justice-administering state," or an interest in "fairness and equity." Instead, the court explicitly referred to a policy clearly underlying Minnesota's stacking rule, the policy of compensating tort victims, and noted the parties' arguments on whether this was implicated in light of the plaintiff's post-accident move out of state. Acknowledging the existence of this Minnesota interest, the court then noted other Minnesota interests that were also implicated in the case—the interests of assuring predictability of results and maintenance of interstate order. It concluded that while it might apply Minnesota law if the state's governmental interest was the only concern, its choice in this case was more influenced by these other factors.

Finally, the court turned to the last "better law" consideration. It noted the parties' sparring on whether the court of appeals' decisions * * * reflected the appropriate conclusion on the better rule regarding stacking. Instead of expressing a subjective view on this point, the court demanded a rational explanation, and found the cases and the parties lacking:

> On our reading of the cases and briefs, neither *Stenzel,* nor *Wille,* nor the parties offer a compelling explanation of exactly why stacking or anti-stacking is a better rule. *Stenzel* wrongly asserts that, because the legislature prohibited stacking, we must find it to be the better rule of law. If that were true, forum law would always be the better law and this step in our choice of law analysis would be meaningless. *Wille* simply states that because stacking provides greater compensation, it is a better rule.
>
> . . . .
>
> From our present day vantage point, neither the law Minnesota had then, nor the law we have now, is clearly better. Sometimes different laws are neither better nor worse in an objective way, just different. Because we do not find either stacking or anti-stacking to be a better rule . . . this consideration does not influence our choice of law.

Particularly when contrasted with earlier opinions, the court's opinion in *Jepson* is refreshing. Instead of sloughing off the first three concerns, it considers them seriously and appropriately. Regarding the forum state's interest, one can hope that it will be read as implicitly disavowing the interest in "fairness and equity," and as requiring a focus on the policies underlying the competing laws. In requiring an objective explanation of which law is better, the opinion also creates the potential of ensuring well-reasoned explanations on this point in the future. In short, the opinion goes a long way towards rectifying several of the problems with earlier analyses that have been noted in this article.

One might argue that the crux of the decision rested on two points not present in earlier cases: clear evidence of the disparity of insurance rates among the states, and better evidence than usual of forum shopping. The entire tone of the decision, however, suggests the beginning of a new era of serious and thoughtful consideration of the choice-influencing considerations.

* * * * *

Comments

1. The primary sources for Professor Leflar's choice-influencing considerations are his two articles excerpted in Part B of this Chapter and his treatise, Leflar, McDougal & Felix 1986: pp. 290-303. Leflar's work is discussed at length in *Symposium: Leflar on Conflicts*, 31 S.C. L. Rev. 409 (1980) (contributions by Robert L. Felix, Friedrich K. Juenger, John J. Todd, Maurice Rosenberg, and Professor Leflar).

2. By adopting a better-rule criterion as his fifth choice-influencing consideration, Professor Leflar became the leading substantivist among conflicts commentators. The late Professor James Martin wrote:

> Despite the fact that Leflar does not claim to have originated the idea, it is usually associated with him. Likewise, although it is not clear whether Leflar is an enthusiastic supporter of the idea or merely a moderate supporter and an observer who has pointed out that the phenomenon exists, he is usually identified as its chief proponent.

Martin 1980b: p. 183.

3. Professor Leflar's explanation and defense of his better-rule criterion appeared in the earlier survey of substantivism debate (Chapter Seven, Part B). The better rule became, as Professor Leflar acknowledged, "the most controversial of the considerations." Leflar 1966b: p. 1587. It is also the best known. Yet Leflar did not intend to assign it an importance greater than that of his other four choice-influencing considerations. He wrote:

> No one can sensibly contend that this fifth consideration, favoring application of the better rule of law, outweighs the other four considerations. It is given special emphasis * * * because in years gone by the other considerations, or at least their content, were more often discussed while this fifth one was overlooked or not clearly identified. The fact remains that it is only one

of the five, more important in some types of cases than in others, almost controlling in some but far in the background in others.

Leflar 1966a: p. 304.

4. A second distinctive feature of Professor Leflar's "choice-influencing considerations" approach is its brevity. It seems clear that Leflar, a judicial realist, wanted to streamline choice-of-law method to fit the practical pressures and workloads of American courts. Leflar's approach stands in striking contrast to the extensive rule, method and policy paraphernalia that make up the two hundred and twenty one sections of the RESTATEMENT (SECOND). Leflar's approach only recognizes conflicts policy, and even his statements of policy considerations are quite condensed. To some commentators, such an approach sacrifices too much for the sake of brevity. *See, e.g.,* Reese 1963: p. 680; Singer 1990: p. 732; Westbrook 1975: p. 460.

C. Surveying Judicial Preferences

Symeon C. Symeonides, *Choice of Law in the American Courts in 1995: A Year in Review*, 44 Am. J. of Comp. L. 181, 193-203 (1996)*

* * * * *

III. UPDATING THE METHODOLOGICAL MAP

In the surveys conducted in previous years, this author has used the term "methodological map" in a metaphorical sense to describe the manner in which the states of the United States congregate in the various methodological camps. This time, graphic technology has made it possible to provide actual maps, one for tort conflicts and another for contract conflicts. The two maps reproduced below show the major methodological camps in tort and contract conflicts, respectively, as of December 31, 1995.

MAP 1. TORT CONFLICTS

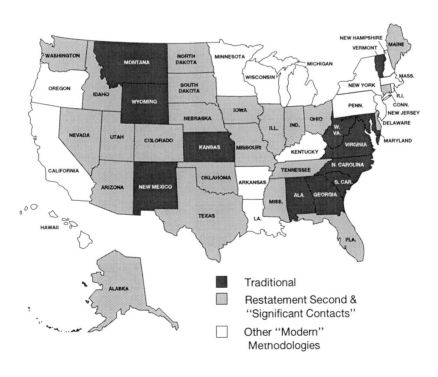

■ Traditional

▨ Restatement Second & "Significant Contacts"

☐ Other "Modern" Methodologies

---

*   Reprinted with permission.

MAP 2. CONTRACT CONFLICTS

■ Traditional

▨ Restatement Second &
"Significant Contacts"

☐ Other "Modern"
Methodologies

In both maps, the traditional states are shown in black, the Restatement Second, or "significant relationship," or "significant contacts" states are shown in grey, and the states that follow "other modern" approaches are shown in white. Included in this latter group are states that follow interest analysis, the *lex-fori* approach, the better-law approach, and other "combined modern" approaches. The fact that a single color is used for states that follow such diverse approaches exemplifies the limitations of graphic technology available to this author. In fact, even the black color which is used to indicate the states belonging to the traditional camp may be somewhat misleading in that it gives the impression that the states belonging to that group are a solid, homogeneous group. They are not. For example, some of those states are firmly committed to the traditional theory and have recently reaffirmed their commitment to it,[83] other states have made small steps in the direction of abandoning it,[84] while other states appear ready to abandon it on the first available opportunity.[85]

Similarly, the fact that the "grey group" lumps together the states following the Restatement Second and the "significant contacts" approach misleadingly blurs the significant differences between these two approaches. Moreover, even if one were to focus solely on the states following the Restatement Second, the use of a single color for all those states gives the misleading impression that those states share the same degree of commitment to the Restatement Second. They do not. Some states use the Restatement Second solely as an escape from a traditional choice-of-law rule that coexists with the Restatement. Some states use the Restatement Second as a camouflage for a "grouping of contacts" approach, while other states use it as a vehicle for restraining interest analysis. Unfortunately, all of these gradations of commitment

---

[83]   To this category belong Alabama, Maryland, and Wyoming, with regard to tort conflicts.

[84]   To this category belong Maryland and South Carolina, with regard to contract conflicts.

[85]   In this category are Kansas and Vermont with regard to tort conflicts, and Tenessee, with regard to contract conflicts.

cannot be shown on these maps without using all the colors in the spectrum. It is still hoped, however, that these maps can be helpful to the reader and that the accompanying tables and textual material can prevent most erroneous impressions.

In these tables, the names of states are accompanied by citations only: (a) if the classification of the particular state is questionable; or (b) if such classification results from a decision rendered in the last three years. In addition, cases decided during 1995 are cited even when they do not affect that state's classification or are otherwise insignificant. * * *

As the two maps indicate, as of December 31, 1995, only twelve states follow the *lex loci delicti* rule and only ten states follow the *lex loci contractus* rule. These states are listed below.

Table 1: Traditional States

TORTS	CONTRACTS
Alabama[87]	Alabama[88]
	Florida[89]
Georgia	Georgia[90]
Kansas[91]	Kansas[92]

---

[87] Alabama's reaffirmation of the *lex loci delicti* rule is fairly recent. See Fitts v. Minnesota Mining & Mfg. Co., 581 So.2d 581 (Ala. 1991); Griffin v. Summit Specialties, Inc., 622 So.2d 1299 (Ala. 1993); Etheredge v. Genie Industries, Inc., 632 So.2d 1324 (Ala. 1994).

[88] In Cherry, Bekaert & Holland v. Brown, 582 So.2d 502 (1991), the Supreme Court of Alabama relied heavily on § 187 of the Restatement Second and quoted liberally and favorably from its comments. Nevertheless, because the court's decision was based primarily on Alabama traditional precedents, see id. at 506, Alabama must remain classified as a traditional state for contract conflicts.

[89] After having abandoned the *lex loci delicti* rule, the Supreme Court of Florida has specifically refused to abandon the *lex loci contractus* rule. See Sturiano v. Brooks, 523 So.2d 1126 (Fla. 1988).

[90] In Amica Mutual Ins. Co. v. Bourgault, 263 Ga. 157, 429 S.E.2d 908 (1993), an insurance contract conflict, the Supreme Court of Georgia relied on § 193 of the Restatement Second. Nevertheless, the court's decision was based primarily on a Georgia statute and relied on the Restatement Second merely as supporting authority. Thus, it is doubtful that this decision signals an impending adoption of the Restatement Second for contract conflicts in general.

[91] The Supreme Court of Kansas has "reserve[d] consideration of the Restatement's 'most significant relationship' test for a later day," but appeared to be sympathetic to it. See St. Paul Surplus Lines Ins. Co. v. International Playtex, Inc., 245 Kan. 258, 777 P.2d 1259 (1989). Nevertheless, three 1995 federal cases decided under Kansas' conflicts law have followed the *lex loci delicti* rule. See Carl v. The City of Overland Park, Kansas, 65 F.3d 866 (l0th Cir. 1995); Stover v. Eagle Products, Inc., 896 F. Supp. 1085 (D. Kan. 1995); Crouch v. Challenger Motor Freight U.S., Inc., 1995 WL 584494 (D. Kan. 1995).

[92] But see Mark Twain Kansas City Bank v. Cates, 248 Kan. 700, 810 P.2d. 1154 (Kan. 1991) (upholding a choice-of-law clause under a non-traditional rationale). According to Jameson v. Pack, 815 F. Supp. 410 (D. Kan. 1993), "Kansas follows '*lex loci contractus*'." Id. at 413. *Accord* Cummings v. LTC, Inc. (D. Kan. 1993); Heatron, Inc. v. Shackelford, 898 F.Supp. 1491 (D. Kan. 1995).

Maryland [93]	Maryland?[94]
Montana	
New Mexico	New Mexico
North Carolina[95]	
	Rhode Island
South Carolina	South Carolina[96]
	Tennessee[97]
Vermont[98]	
Virginia[99]	Virginia[100]

---

[93]   See CHAMBCO v. Urban Masonry Co, [659 A.2d 297 (Md. 1995)]. But see Bishop v. Twiford, 317 Md. 170, 562 A.2d 1238 (Md. 1989) (continuing Maryland's differentiation between tort conflicts, which are governed by the *lex loci delicti,* and worker's compensation conflicts, which are governed by the law of the "jurisdiction that has the greatest interest at stake." Id. at 1241).

[94]   But see [American Motorists Insurance Co. v. Artra Group, Inc., 659 A.2d 1295 (Md. 1995)].

[95]   But see Boudreau v. Baughman, 322 N.C. 331, 368 S.E.2d 849 (1988) (interpreting the phrase "appropriate relation" in the forum's version of U.C.C. art. 1-105 as being equivalent to the phrase "most significant relationship"). See also Terry v. Pullman Trailmobile, 376 S.E.2d 47 at 50 (N.C. App. 1989) (interpreting *Boudreau* as having adopted the Restatement Second); Daussault Falcon Jet Corp. v. Oberflex, Inc., 1995 WL 545331 (M.D.N.C. 1995) (*accord*). But see Jacobs v. Central Transport, Inc., 891 F. Supp. 1088 (E.D.N.C. 1995) (following *lex loci contractus*).

[96]   But see In re Merritt Dredging Co., 839 F.2d 203 (4th Cir. 1988), *cert. denied,* Compliance Marine, Inc. v. Campbell, 487 U.S. 1236, 108 S. Ct. 2904, 101 L. Ed. 2d 936 (1988) (interpreting the phrase "appropriate relation" in South Carolina's version of U.C.C. art. 1-105 as being equivalent to the phrase "most significant relationship" as used in the Restatement Second).

[97]   Having abandoned the *lex loci delicti* rule in 1992, see Hataway v. McKinley, 830 S.W.2d 53 (Tenn. 1992), the Supreme Court of Tennessee has not had occasion to reconsider its adherence to the *lex loci contractus* rule. Lower courts continue to apply the *lex loci contractus* without hesitation. See Lovett v. Wal-Mart Stores, 1993 Tenn. App. Lexis 140 (1993). See also Walker v. Freeman, 1995 WL 749692 (Tenn. App. 1995) (interpreting *Hathaway* as being confined to tort conflicts and refusing to extend it to a banking transaction).

[98]   See Calhoun v. Blakely, 152 Vt. 113, 564 A.2d 590 (1989), *reh'g denied*, 189 Vt. Lexis 282 (Vt. 1989) (adhering to the *lex loci delicti* rule but showing openness in reconsidering it in a "better case"); Vermont Plastics, Inc. v. Brine, Inc., 1993 U.S. Dist. 8631 (D. Vt. 1993), and Nordica USA, Inc. v. Deloitte & Touche, 839 F. Supp. 1082 (D. Vt. 1993) ("predicting" that the Supreme Court of Vermont will adopt the Restatement Second as soon as the opportunity arises); Washington Electric Coop., Inc. v. Massachusetts Municipal Wholesale Electric Co., 894 F. Supp. 777 (D. Vt. 1995) and Donnelly v. McLellan, 889 F. Supp. 136 (D. Vt. 1995) (applying the *lex loci delicti* rule without hesitation).

[99]   See Jones v. R.S. Jones Assoc., Inc., 246 Va. 3, 431 S.E.2d 33 (1993).

[100]   See Buchanan v. Doe, 246 Va. 67, 431 S.E.2d 289 (1993).

West Virginia			
Wyoming[101]			
Total	12	Total	10

The maps also show that 23 jurisdictions follow the Restatement Second or the "significant contacts" approach in tort conflicts, and 29 jurisdictions do likewise in contract conflicts. These jurisdictions are listed in Table 2, infra, which separates pure Restatement Second states from states following a "significant contacts" or "significant relationship" approach.

Table 2. Restatement (Second) and "Significant Contacts" Status

T O R T S		C O N T R A C T S	
Restatement Second	Significant Contacts	Restatement Second	Significant Contacts
Alaska[103]		Alaska[104]	
Arizona		Arizona	
			Arkansas[105]
Colorado		Colorado	
Connecticut		Connecticut[106]	
Delaware		Delaware	
Florida			
Idaho		Idaho	
Illinois		Illinois	

---

[101] See Jack v. Enterprise Rent-A-Car Co. of Los Angeles, [899 P.2d 891 (Wyo. 1995)].

[103] See Ehredt v. De Havilland Aircraft Co. of Canada, 705 P.2d 446 (Alaska 1985)* * *.

[104] See Palmer G. Lewis Co. Inc. v. ARCO Chemicals, [904 P.2d 1221 (Alaska 1995)].

[105] Arkansas' classification in this column is not entirely safe. Standard Leasing Corp. v. Schmidt Aviation, Inc., 264 Ark. 851, 576 S.W.2d 181 (Ark. 1979), and McMillen v. Winona National & Savings Bank, 279 Ark. 16, 648 S.W.2d 460 (Ark. 1983), applied a "significant contacts" approach. See also Vandiver Food Stores, Inc. v. Insurance Co. of North America, 1995 WL 759504 (E.D. Ark. 1995) (applying the Restatement Second to an insurance contract). However, Stacy v. St. Charles Custom Kitchens, Inc., 683 S.W.2d 225 (Ark. 1985), seemed to revert to the *lex loci contractus* rule. A lower court case, Threlkeld v. Worsham, 785 S.W.2d 249 (Ark. App. 1990), applied the "better law" approach to a sale contract.* * *

[106] See Williams v. State Farm Mut. Auto. Ins. Co., 229 Conn. 359, 641 A.2d 783 (1994).

	Indiana[107]		Indiana[108]
Iowa		Iowa	
		Kentucky[109]	
Maine[110]		Maine	
		Michigan[111]	
Mississippi		Mississippi	
Missouri[112]		Missouri[113]	
		Montana[114]	

---

[107]   See Hubbard Mfg. Co., Inc. v. Greeson, 515 N.E.2d 1071 (Ind. 1987) (holding that "when the place of the tort is an insignificant contact," the court will turn to the Restatement Second, but stopping short of embracing the policy-analysis component of the Restatement or of abandoning the *lex loci* rule in general).

[108]   For a 1995 case, see OVRS Acquisitions Corp. v. Community Health Services, Inc., 657 N.E.2d 117 (Ind. App. 1995).

[109]   For a 1995 case blending the Restatement Second with interest analysis and the *lex fori* approach, see Tractor & Farm Supply, Inc. v. Ford New Holland, Inc., 898 F. Supp. 1198 (W.D. Ky. 1995).

[110]   For a 1995 case, see Collins v. Trius, Inc., 663 A.2d 570 (Me. 1995) * * *.

[111]   See [Chrysler Corp. v. Skyline Industrial Services, Inc., 528 N.W.2d 698 (Mich. 1995)].

[112]   For 1995 cases, see Harter v. Ozark-Kenworth, Inc., 904 S.W.2d 317 (Mo. App. 1995); D.L.C. and J.L.C. v. Walsh, 1995 WL 507447 (Mo. App. 1995); Moses v. Union Pacific Railroad v. Mid-South Milling Co., 64 F.3d 413 (8th Cir. 1995).

[113]   For a 1995 case, see CIT Group/Equipment Financing, Inc. v. Integrated Financial Services, Inc., 910 S.W. 722 (Mo. App. 1995).

[114]   See Casarotto v. Lombardi, 268 Mont. 369, 886 P.2d 931 (1994) * * *.

Nebraska		Nebraska[115]	
	Nevada[116]		Nevada[117]
		New Hampshire[118]	
			North Carolina[119]
	North Dakota		
Ohio		Ohio	
Oklahoma		Oklahoma?[120]	
	Puerto Rico		Puerto Rico
South Dakota		South Dakota	
Tennessee			
Texas		Texas	
Utah		Utah[121]	

[115]   See Powell v. American Charter Federal S&L Assn., 245 Neb. 551, 514 N.W.2d 326 (1994) * * *.

[116]   See Hermanson v. Hermanson, 887 P.2d 1241 (Nev. 1994), * * *. For a 1995 case, see Insurance Co. of North America v. Hilton Hotels U.S.A., Inc., 1995 WL 691927 (D. Nev. 1995).

[117]   See *Hermanson*, supra n. 116.

[118]   See Green Mountain Ins. Co. v. George, 634 A.2d 1011 (N.H. 1993); Glowski v. Allstate Ins. Co., 134 N.H. 196, 589 A.2d 593 (1991).

[119]   The classification of North Carolina in this column may be questionable. It is based on Boudreau v. Baughman, 322 N.C. 331, 368 S.E.2d 849 (1988), which interpreted the phrase "appropriate relation" in the forum's version of U.C.C. art. 1-105 as being equivalent to the phrase "most significant relationship."

[120]   The classification of Oklahoma in this column is doubtful. In Bohannan v. Allstate Ins. Co., 820 P.2d 78, 797 (Okla. 1991), the supreme court of that state appeared willing to apply the law of a state other than that of the *locus contractus* upon a showing that the former state "has the most significant relationship with the subject matter and the parties." Id. at 797. However, knowledgeable observers believe that Oklahoma should be listed as a *lex loci contractus* state because an Oklahoma statute, although often disregarded, compels adherence to that approach. * * *

[121]   In Prows v. Pinpoint Retail Systems, Inc., 228 Utah Adv. Rep. 23, 808 P.2d 809 (Utah 1993), * * * the Supreme Court of Utah relied extensively on § 187 of the Restatement Second in deciding not to honor a choice-of-law clause. In general, reliance on § 187 with regard to choice-of-law clauses does not necessarily portend a more general adoption of the Restatement Second for other issues of contract conflicts. Nevertheless, Utah's classification in this column seems rather assured because the court's reliance on the Restatement Second was unhesitant and unqualified.

		Vermont[122]	
Washington		Washington	
		West Virginia[123]	
		Wyoming[124]	
Total	20	4	25	5

Finally, three jurisdictions follow a pure interest analysis, and two other jurisdictions follow the kindred *lex-fori* approach in tort conflicts. No jurisdiction follows these approaches in contract conflicts. Five states follow Professor Leflar's better-law approach in tort conflicts and two of the five do likewise in contract conflicts. Six jurisdictions follow an eclectic approach in tort conflicts and nine do so in contract conflicts. For lack of a better term, the latter approach is called a "combined modern" approach. These states are listed in Table 3, infra.

---

[122]   For a 1995 case, see Green Mountain Power Corp. v. Certain Underwriters At Lloyd's London, 1995 WL 433597 (D. Vt. 1995).

[123]   The Supreme Court of West Virginia has not adopted the Restatement Second for contracts in general but has drawn heavily from it in insurance contract conflicts. See Lee v. Saliga, 179 W.Va. 762, 373 S.E.2d 348 (1988); Nadler v. Liberty Mutual Fire Ins. Co., 424 S.E.2d 256 (W. Va. 1992); Clark v. Rockwell, 435 S.E.2d 664 (W. Va. 1993); Adkins v. Sperry, 437 S.E.2d 284 (W. Va. 1993). In Cannelton Industries, Inc. v. Aetna Cas. & Sur. Co. of America, 460 S.E.2d 1 (W. Va 1994), the court described its precedents as standing for the proposition that "the place the insurance contract was entered into will control with two exceptions. First, it will not apply if there is a 'more significant relationship to the transaction and the parties' in another state or, second, if it results in a conflict of public policy." Id. at 10. For a 1995 case applying the Restatement Second, see Penn Coal Corp. v. William H. McGee & Co., Inc., 903 F. Supp. 980 (S.D. W.Va. 1995).

[124]   Wyoming's classification in this column is doubtful. Cherry Creek Dodge Inc. v. Carter, 733 P.2d 1024 (Wyo. 1987), cited the Restatement Second favorably but relied mostly on the "reasonable relationship" language of the forum's version of the U.C.C. Amoco Rocmount Co. v. The Anschutz Corp., 7 F.3d 909 (10th Cir. 1993), interprets Cherry Creek as having adopted the Restatement Second for contract conflicts.

Table 3. "Other States"

Interest	Analysis	Lex	Fori	Better	Law	Combined	Modern
Torts	Contr.	Torts	Contr.	Torts	Contr.	Torts	Contract
				Ark.			
Cal.[125]							Cal.[126]
D.C.[127]							D.C.[128]
						Hawaii[129]	Hawaii[130]
		Ky.[131]					
						La.[132]	La.[133]
						Mass.[134]	Mass.[135]
		Mich.					

[125]   California, of course, combines interest analysis with comparative impairment in true conflicts cases.

[126]   See Nedloyd Lines, B.V. v. Superior Court, 3 Calif. 4th 459, 834 P.2d 1148 (Cal. 1992) (heavy reliance on the Restatement Second but without abandoning interest analysis).

[127]   For a 1995 case, see District of Columbia v. Coleman, 667 A.2d 811 (D.C. 1995) * * *.

[128]   See District of Columbia Ins. Guaranty Ass'n v. Algernon Blair, Inc., 565 A.2d 564 (D.C. App. 1989) (combining interest analysis with the Restatement Second).

[129]   Hawaii follows a combination of interest analysis, the Restatement Second, and Leflar's choice-influencing considerations. See Lewis v. Lewis, 69 Haw. 497, 748 P.2d 1362 (1988) (contract conflict interpreting Peters v. Peters, 63 Haw. 653, 634 P.2d 586 (1981), a tort conflict, as having adopted a "significant relationship" test with primary emphasis on the state with the "strongest interest.").* * *

[130]   See supra n. 129.

[131]   For a 1995 case, see Phar-Mor, Inc. Securities Litig. v. Ratcliffe, 1995 WL 600240 (W.D. Pa. 1995) (decided under Kentucky conflicts law pursuant to *Van Dusen* and reluctantly applying "the highly parochial choice of law rules of Kentucky." Id. at *2). See also Tractor & Farm Supply, Inc. v. Ford New Holland, Inc., 898 F. Supp. 1198 (W.D. Ky. 1995).

[132]   Louisiana's new comprehensive codification combines elements from many modern American and European approaches into a distinct identity. For discussion of this codification by its drafter, see, *inter alia*, Symeonides, "Private International Law Codification in a Mixed Jurisdiction: The Louisiana Experience," 57 *Rabels Zeitschrift far auslandisches und internationales Privatrecht*, 460 (1993); Symeonides, "Les grands problemes de droit international prive et la nouvelle codification de Louisiane," 81 *Revue critique du droit int'l prive* 223, 233-281 (1992); Symeonides, "Louisiana's New Law of Choice of Law for Tort Conflicts: An Exegesis," 66 *Tul. L Rev.* 677 (1992).

[133]   See supra n. 132.

[134]   Massachusetts follows a combination of interest analysis, "functional analysis," and the Restatement Second. See Bushkin Associates, Inc. v. Raytheon Co., 473 N.E.2d 662 (Mass. 1985). For a 1995 case, see Tidemark Bank for Savings v. Morris, 57 F.3d 1061 (1st Cir. 1995).

[135]   See supra n. 134

				Minn.	Minn.		
				N.H.			
N.J.							N.J.[136]
						N.Y.[137]	N.Y.[138]
							N.D.[139]
						Ore.[140]	Ore.
						Pa.[141]	Pa.
				R.I.			
				Wis.	Wis.		
3	0	2	0	5	2	6	9

* * * * *

---

[136]   See Gilbert Spruance Co. v. Pennsylvania Mfrs. Ass'n Ins. Co., 134 N.J. 96, 629 A.2d 885 (1993) (combining interest analysis with the Restatement Second).

[137]   New York follows interest analysis combined with the *Neumeier* rules in tort conflicts and with a "significant contacts" analysis in contract conflicts, See Cooney v. Osgood Machinery, Inc., 81 N.Y.2d 66, 612 N.E.2d 277 (1993); In re Allstate Ins. Co. v. Stolarz, 81 N.Y.2d 219, 613 N.E.2d 936 (1993), discussed in Symeonides, 1993 Survey at 622-28.

[138]   See supra n. 137.

[139]   North Dakota follows a combination of interest analysis, the Restatement Second, and Leflar's choice-influencing considerations. See American Family Mut. Ins. Co. v. Farmer's Ins. Exchange, 504 N.W.2d 307 (N.D. 1993); Starry v. Central Dakota Printing, Inc., 530 N.W.2d 323 (N.D. 1995).

[140]   Oregon follows a combination of interest analysis and the Restatement Second "coupled with an almost irresistible forum presumption." See [Symeon C. Symeonides, "Choice of Law in the American Courts in 1994: A View from the Trenches." 43 *Am J. Comp. L.* 1, 3 n.6 (1995)] (quoting Professor Nafziger).

[141]   Pennsylvania follows a combination of interest analysis and the Restatement Second, but also draws from Cavers' principles of preference.

Comments

1. For additional surveys of choice of law in American courts, *see* Borchers 1994[1]; Kay 1982; Kramer 1991; Kozyris 1988; Kozyris & Symeonides 1990; Smith 1987; Solimine 1992; Symeonides 1989a; Symeonides 1994; Symeonides 1995.

2. General discussions of the subject of American conflicts law, while not intended to be as comprehensive as the surveys noted above, do note case developments in many jurisdictions. These sources include Brilmayer 1995c; Cavers 1970; Korn 1983; Leflar, McDougal & Felix 1986; Richman & Reynolds 1993; Scoles & Hay 1982; von Mehren 1975; Weintraub 1986.

---

[1] Full citations appear in the bibliography, Chapter Twelve.

CHAPTER NINE

Consensus or Chaos in American Conflicts Law?

This Chapter surveys some of the most difficult and disturbing questions raised in the study of conflict of laws. Modern conflicts law has had a prolonged adolescence. For about fifty years, it has pursued multiple, perhaps competing objectives in theory, and has often seemed uncertain in application. This has prompted innumerable debates over what conflicts law is or should be. Some commentators view the varied, contingent character of choice of law as actually beneficial. Others disagree, believing conflicts law is badly flawed. These critics disagree among themselves about how to reform conflicts law, or whether it is even worth saving. Reform-minded critics offer competing proposals for revamping the subject. More pessimistic critics simply reject conflicts law. They are primarily interested in ways to confine or marginalize the subject.

Part A of this Chapter examines the eclecticism debate—whether the variety of conflicts values and methods can be merged into a single, modern approach, and whether the fluidity of modern conflicts law is beneficial or problematic. Professor Robert Leflar maintains in the opening selection that conflicts law has become relatively settled. He contends that most decisions can be explained under an eclectic list of conflicts policies that most American courts have adopted by consensus. In the next excerpt, Professor James Westbrook endorses eclecticism. Not only do opportunities for picking and choosing from a variety of conflicts approaches enrich conflicts decisions, states Professor Westbrook, but it would be practically impossible today for courts to decide conflicts cases in a non-eclectic way.

Arguing the other side, Professor William Reppy rejects the contention that there is a single eclectic model for choice of law. He also maintains that an eclectic approach leads to bad conflicts law in almost all of its applications. Finally, Professor Joseph Singer argues that, beneath the appearance of consensus among modern choice-of-law approaches, there is actually a great deal of disorder. He concludes that, in application, all of the so-called modern approaches have led to oversimplification and misunderstanding.

Part B of this Chapter treats the rules-versus-approach debate. In the opening selection, Professor Maurice Rosenberg argues for the greater structure provided by rules in conflicts law. Professor Rosenberg contends that rejection of many of the rules in the original RESTATEMENT OF THE LAW OF CONFLICTS should not connote rejection of conflicts rules per se and points to the RESTATEMENT (SECOND) as an example of successful utilization of conflicts rules. Like Professor Rosenberg, Professor Robert Sedler associates rejection of rules in favor of approach with Currie's interest analysis. But, differing with Professor Rosenberg, Professor Sedler favors the use of approach (*viz.*, loosely structured method) over rules in conflicts law. Professor Sedler questions the value of the latter as preset or a priori devices for deciding conflicts cases. Finally, Peter Hay and Robert Ellis seek in their co-authored selection to mediate the differences between the rule and the approach factions. They maintain that the suggestion of a dichotomy between rule and approach in conflicts law has become dated. In reality, argue the authors, it is possible to synthesize many of the best features of rule and of approach thinking into a single model of conflicts law.

Part C collects some of the most ambitious and analytically demanding writing on contemporary conflicts theory. All of the contributors express dissatisfaction with the present condition of American conflicts law. Each proposes a different cure. In the opening selections, Professors Larry Kramer and Gary Simon consider in turn possibilities for recalibrating interest analysis. Then, new opportunities for substantivism in choice of law are explored in successive works by Professors Arthur von Mehren and Joseph Singer. Professor Perry Dane follows with a contemporary reworking of vested-rights theory. Finally, Professor Lea Brilmayer offers a theory of litigant rights and fairness for choice of law, in part utilizing analogies to personal jurisdiction law and theory.

The ferocity of criticism reaches its peak in Part D of this Chapter. In the opening selection, Professor Michael Gottesman maintains that contemporary conflicts law is incoherent, frustrates the expectations of litigants, and is often biased. Pressing the attack further, Professor Stewart Sterk then contends that, stripped of pretense, conflicts law is hopelessly confused and inconsequential. Professor Westbrook takes a much kinder view toward the subject in his excerpt. He argues that what some might mistake for incoherence in conflicts law is in fact a pluralism that makes for good, serviceable decisions. In the concluding selection, Professor von Mehren suggests why we should learn to live with the fact that, to a significant extent, conflicts decisions will always be more complicated and more controversial than domestic cases.

A. The Eclecticism Debate

Robert A. Leflar, *Choice of Law: A Well-Watered Plateau*, 41 LAW & CONTEMP. PROBS. 10, 10-11, 26 (1977)*

American decisional law on choice of law in conflicts cases has arrived at a level of stability, perhaps unsteady and impermanent yet very real, the like of which has not existed in the area for many years. It is a stability to be found in the opinions of appellate courts, not in the law reviews. Academic writing still stirs the ashes of recent controversy and fresh thinkers propose new approaches that might re-revolutionize the law. That is the privilege and the function of active legal minds. But most courts deciding choice-of-law cases have now settled down on a sort of policy plateau which is well above the level of Bealian conceptualism and which, though watered by the life-giving insights of American conflicts scholars among whom David F. Cavers stands out pre-eminently, does not conform in its features to the maps previously publicized by any one of them.

Analysis of opinions handed down within the last year reveals no truly new developments, no changes in the terrain but rather a smoothing over of the plateau's surface. There are still states that repeat the old mechanical rules, but there are fewer of them. Most of the current cases follow a pattern of multiple citation, seldom relying solely upon any single modern choice-of-law theory, but combining two or more of the theories to produce results which, interestingly, can be sustained under any or nearly all of the new non-mechanical approaches to conflicts law.

There are fewer choice-of-law cases reported in the advance sheets nowadays than there were a few years ago, despite the fact that the total number of all reported cases has steadily increased. The current appellate cases either typify another state's breakaway from the old mechanical rules represented generally by the first conflicts *Restatement* or come from states which, having already rejected the old rules, are still fumbling among the newer approaches favored by academic commentators. Some states are engaged in more fumbling than are others. Those that fumble least achieve their stability by lumping most of the recent commentators together, taking their differences less seriously than do the academic theoreticians. Their judicial opinions tend to speak simply of the "new" law of choice of law as distinguished from the "old," and to conclude that results arrived at can be supported by citation to the work of just about any of the conflict-of-laws writers who have proposed new ways to solve the old problems.

The average American appellate court today is handling more cases, including complex cases as well as a mass of less significant ones, than our courts have ever before had to adjudicate. Despite judicial education programs and aid from research assistants, appellate judges have less opportunity for study and broad-based inquiry than did judges in times past. The bulk of published material on all aspects of law, and especially of articles in the legal periodicals, is such that no human being can keep up with all of it, or even read in a week's time all the writing that is relevant to any one of the twenty-five or more cases an appellate judge has to pass on in the course of a typical month.

It is a fair guess that no American judge, trial or appellate, has read anything like all of the useful writing on conflict of laws that a specialized conflicts teacher must be familiar with. Much of this writing has appeared since the judge was in law school. An able and conscientious

---

* Reprinted with permission.

judge can cite Cavers' great book, *The Choice-of-Law Process,* some of Brainerd Currie's and Ehrenzweig's work, and a scattering of other writings, but that is about all. Even the hardest working student in a law school conflicts course could not read all of the "literature" on the subject, if he were taking three or four other law courses at the same time. The most that an average appellate judge working on a choice-of-law case could do would be to study an overall analysis and then read up on approaches that appealed to him. If his court had already handed down cases that broke with old concepts he would try to accommodate his thinking to those cases and would hope they fitted in with later approaches used in other states. He would cite leading cases from other states if they support his conclusion in the case before his court regardless of whether they employ the same theoretical reasoning that his court uses. The common feature of all the cases cited and the one being currently decided would be, quite often, simply the rejection of lex loci delicti, or lex solutionis, or some similar formula. Beyond that, analysis of governmental interests, dominant contacts, most significant relationships, principles of preference, choice-influencing considerations, and (often but not always) preference for the forum's own law would all ordinarily lead to the same conclusion as to who should win the case.* * *

* * * * *

* * *[O]ne trend in American choice-of-law decision appears to be a kind of escape from conflicts law, or at least from the multiplicity of academic theory that clusters about and mystifies conflicts law. No court can in a single case follow all the theories that are currently proposed, but it can agree with their general effect, which is that there are better ways of deciding choice-of-law issues than under the old mechanical rules prescribed by Professor Beale and the first conflicts *Restatement.* Every one of the new proposals calls for decision based upon real reasons relevant to the functions of law in our society, as distinguished from decision based upon formulas merely. Some of the proposals call for less judicial honesty in stating the real reasons for decision than do others, and a theory which leaves room for discreet cover-up of some real reasons has lingering appeal for judges still tied to the notion that all law must consist of rules and formulas. But real reasons generally underlie all of the modern approaches.

It is easy to understand why the courts are running the approaches together. They relate to each other, and each has sustainable merits, yet there are too many of them, and some of them are subtle and call for fine distinctions. Busy judges have no time to study and master all of them, then choose among them. Some afford more flexibility than others. The personalities of proponents influence some courts. Courts are also avoiding conflicts issues when they can reasonably do so. Explanations are easy, but the fact is what is important. The fact is that most American courts today are moving to what they call "the" new law of conflict of laws. It is a conglomerate, and not a bad one.

In terms of location, this body of law is being lifted up by the courts to a well-watered plateau high above the sinkhole it once occupied. No location lasts forever, and there are vistas beyond the plateau, but it is a rest-stop now.

James E. Westbrook, *A Survey and Evaluation of Competing Choice-of-Law Methodologies: The Case for Eclecticism*, 40 Mo. L. Rev. 407, 408-409, 409-411 (1975)*

* * * * *

Although there was widespread rejection of old concepts, one is hard pressed to find anything approaching a consensus on new concepts to take their place. The judge, practitioner, or law student who attempts to survey scholarly thinking in the conflicts field must surely come away from his reading with the impression that the law review articles outnumber the significant cases and that these articles were written by members of countless contending factions, each convinced that it has the only sensible solution to choice-of-law problems.

Although scholars indicate clearly and often rather testily the basis of their disagreements, the courts which have rejected traditional rules often write opinions which mean all things to all people. New York, one of the first states to break away from the traditional approach, has, according to the authors of a leading conflicts casebook, "hopped frenetically from one theory to another like an overheated jumping bean."[7] The typical judicial opinion which rejects traditional learning does not endorse and consistently rely upon a particular methodology. Instead, the tendency is to combine a reference to significant contacts or relationships—the nomenclature of the *Restatement (Second) of Conflict of Laws*—with a discussion of the policy considerations which the court considers relevant. The courts' use of terminology and techniques from competing methodologies—what some commentators have aptly described as eclecticism—has enabled scholars of diverse points of view to unite in their praise of some decisions. While praising specific decisions, scholars often indicate that there is a need to tie a series of cases together by use of a more coherent methodology. Yet there is much to be said in behalf of the tendency to pick and choose from among competing approaches in fashioning a solution to a particular choice-of-law problem. Eclecticism may be a strength rather than a weakness.

* * *

The reaction of scholars to the thrust and counterthrust of the contemporary debate varies according to the point of view of the writer and whether he is defending himself from attack, taking the offensive, or seeking to explain what the tumult is all about. In response to charges that the new functional, state-interest methodologies are unduly complex, it has been asserted that this is simply not true. Implicit in such answers to criticism is the suggestion that the critics do not fully understand the new methodology or that the criticism is motivated by an unwillingness or inability to discard old ways of thinking about choice-of-law problems. Another reaction one finds in the literature is a concession that the present situation is less than satisfactory, coupled with a suggestion that the choice-of-law field is in a transitional phase and that the problems will gradually be brought under control. Some of those who hold this view believe that the difficulties in choice-of-law are caused primarily by the youth and fluidity of the subject. One could also point to the vacuum created by the demise of the first *Restatement* as the

---

*   Copyright © 1975 by the Curators of the University of Missouri. Reprinted with permission.

[7]   R. CRAMTON & D. CURRIE, CONFLICT OF LAWS 258-59 (1968).

primary cause. Still others seem to believe that the transition will be completed and the major problems solved when everyone is finally persuaded to adopt one particular methodology.

An underlying assumption in much of the writing on choice-of-law is that we will gradually perfect our methodologies or our understanding of the subject and eventually arrive at a "fail-safe" system. Yet absent fundamental changes in our federal system, we will achieve only partial solutions, and any consensus we may achieve will be temporary. The promise of an ultimate solution will only raise false expectations. To be blunt about it, choice-of-law problems are and will continue to be unmitigated nuisances for the judge and practitioner. At the same time, these problems are and will continue to be a source of fascination for the scholar because of the very complexity and intractability that make them a source of discomfort for the bench and bar. The most important causes of this state of affairs are not the youth of the subject, the fascination of scholars with complexity, or the refusal by too many judges and lawyers to rid themselves of outmoded patterns of thought. The basic causes are more fundamental than any of these. This is not, however, a counsel of despair. Although the resources of jurisprudence may not be adequate to produce a completely satisfactory methodology, it is possible to decide cases in an informed manner while developing choice-of-law principles which take account of the needs of the various persons, groups, and institutions affected by the choice-of-law process. Moreover, to argue that we will not perfect a "fail-safe" system is not to argue that improvement is impossible. Improvements have been and are being made. But it is essential to remember that the choices that must be made are not between alternatives that are clearly good or bad, or between methodologies that are essentially defective or completely satisfactory. Professors Cheatham, Reese, and Leflar have demonstrated that a number of values are at stake in the choice-of-law process. Some values can be advanced only by sacrificing others. Some problems can be solved only by ignoring others. In the final analysis, the acceptance of a particular methodology usually involves a decision that some values are more important than others and that some problems must be dealt with while others can be tolerated.

* * * * *

William A. Reppy, *Eclecticism in Choice of Law: Hybrid Method or Mishmash?*, 34 MERCER L. REV. 645, 645-646, 650-654, 708 (1982)*

Several conflicts scholars have identified a trend in choice of law opinions toward the use of what has been termed 'eclecticism.' This approach involves use by the court of two or more distinct choice of law methods, or parts of those methods, in deciding a single choice of law issue. For example, one common form of eclecticism is an opinion that announces that the law of state X applies because *both* an interest analysis approach and a center of gravity, or most significant relation, approach point to the law of X.

The distinguished conflicts scholar Robert Leflar seems to applaud this development; certainly he openly accepts it. Professor James Westbrook is thrilled. With this article I join the ranks of those who are critical. Indeed, I find most examples of eclecticism deplorable. The technique usually deprives choice of law of any certainty; it becomes incomprehensible to

---

*   Reprinted with permission.

lawyers and lower court judges who cannot deal with a choice of law problem in ignorance of the choice of law method employed by the forum.

This Article repudiates eclecticism except in instances in which a jurisdiction formulates one single, new choice of law method by piecing together aspects of choice of law methods in use in other states, as, for example, when a court that follows interest analysis borrows center of gravity as a device for breaking true conflicts. In urging the abandonment of eclecticism, this Article certainly does not intend to suggest that a state should turn away from the 'modern' approaches to choice of law and reembrace the lex loci. Instead, a state supreme court that currently tolerates or engages in the type of eclecticism that applies multiple methods, as distinct methods, in the same opinion should adopt forthrightly one of them as *the* method for the state and should reject expressly the others. There is no reason at all that a modern, flexible, justice-seeking method cannot coexist with the important values of certainty and comprehensibility. Renouncing purposeless eclecticism will be an important step towards achieving that goal.

* * * * *

Types of Eclecticism

An analysis of what actually is going on in the numerous 'eclectic' choice of law cases that Professor Leflar and others have found must begin with a demonstration of the falsity of the cornerstone of Leflar's approval of them: that all of the modern methods "are consistent . . . and likely to produce about the same result on a given set of facts."[21] A brief look at three oft-litigated fact patterns reveals that this is not so. First, the situation of a false conflict in favor of 'bad' law, that is, prodefendant, with territorial connection to a state with 'good' law illustrates the error of Professor Leflar's theory. Two examples of this situation are *Kell v. Henderson*[22] and *Milkovich v. Saari.*[23] The plaintiff prevails under the pure better law method, maybe under center of gravity, and, depending on how bad the bad law is, under Wisconsin's brand of interest analysis, which reserves a drag-on-coattails exception to allow application of pure better law. Under all other forms of interest analysis, the defendant prevails.

The second situation that shows the weakness of Leflar's theory is the true-true conflict in which the only connecting factor to the 'good' law is the domiciliary status of the plaintiff. Examples of this situation are the cases of *Rosenthal v. Warren*[25] and *Maguire v. Exeter & Hampton Electric Co.*[26] Plaintiff wins under pure better law; under interest analysis with a forum law break device, if the forum has the good law; and under interest analysis with a better law break device. Defendant wins under center of gravity; restrained better law New Hampshire style; interest analysis with either a lex loci or center of gravity break; interest analysis with a forum break, if the forum has the bad law; and, with respect to some issues, interest analysis with a comparative impairment break.

---

[21] R[OBERT] LEFLAR, AMERICAN CONFLICTS LAW § 109 (3d ed. 1977) * * *. Writing in 1972, however, Leflar realized that the various 'modern' choice of law methodologies did point to different results in many cases. Leflar, *The Torts Provisions of the Restatement (Second)*, 72 COLUM. L. REV. 267, 270 (1972) * * *.

[22] 26 A.D.2d 595, 270 N.Y.S.2d 552 (1966).

[23] 295 Minn. 155, 203 N.W.2d 408 (1973).

[25] 475 F.2d 438 (2d Cir.), *cert. denied*, 414 U.S. 856 (1973) (damages limitation); 374 F. Supp. 522 (S.D.N.Y. 1974) (charitable immunity issue on remand).

[26] 114 N.H. 589, 325 A.2d 778 (1974).

The third example in which modern choice of law methods reach different results is the true-disinterested conflict with the heaviest territorial connections in the plaintiff's home state, which has the bad law. Again, under pure better law, plaintiff wins, as he does if he sues defendant at defendant's home and the method employed is interest analysis with a forum break. No matter where he sues, plaintiff wins under interest analysis with a common policy break device in situations in which that device can be employed. Defendant wins under center of gravity, under New Hampshire's restrained better law method, and under interest analysis with a lex loci or center of gravity break.

The only time all modern methods will reach the same result is in a false conflict in which the bad law is involved only territorially and the territorial connection is fortuitous because the center of gravity is elsewhere. That is, the sole point of agreement is that a fortuitous event occurring in a state with bad law should not be the basis for applying that bad law. Accordingly, an 'eclectic' opinion in which the court employs two or more distinct methods cannot be explained on the theory that there really is only one modern method that can be stated in different ways, as the court has done.

I have tried to imagine why eclectic opinions tend to be written and have come up with the possibilities that follow.

Methodless Ad Hoc Decisionmaking. The judge decides simply on the basis of sympathy factors which party should win and then tells his law clerk: "Write me an opinion for plaintiff employing all choice of law methods that produce a victory for plaintiff." If the clerk determines that twelve methods exist in the various states for dealing with the problem and defendant wins under nine of them, the clerk ignores those nine and writes an opinion showing how plaintiff wins under the three that favor him.

I hope this is not what is happening in any of the eclectic cases. It would be deplorable to have the outcome turn on a value judgment on which *party* was more deserving, even to a conflicts scholar who finds it tenable to base the decision on which *law* is better.

Pure Better Law in Disguise. The judge proceeds in the secrecy of chambers just as a Minnesota judge does openly: deciding what law is better. But the judge is too embarrassed to allow his opinion to reveal that this was the method he employed. Therefore, he gives the law clerk the same instruction as above: "Write an opinion under which plaintiff prevails, and employ all methods that support the result." Among those methods will be the better law method, which of course becomes more palatable when it is described instead as Leflar's five choice-influencing considerations. But the significance of better law will be disguised when the opinion also incorporates all other choice methods that reach the same result. The remaining methods that lead to the opposite result are not mentioned in the opinion.

I suspect that this is indeed what is happening in many of the eclectic opinions. Since the upshot is use of a 'closet' better law methodology, no wonder Leflar is so pleased with eclecticism. He should call on these secret adherents to come out of the closet. It is appalling to hide needlessly from the practicing bar and lower court judges the method actually used.

Confused Lower Court or Federal Court Judge. This confusion must explain a large number of eclectic cases. The federal judge or state intermediate appellate court judge reads the various opinions of the high court of the state and cannot understand what is going on. One case is decided by center of gravity; the next one, without overruling the former, is decided by interest analysis, and so forth. The author of the opinion is not sure whether the state's high court really intends a mishmash or just does not know what it is doing. Therefore, he applies each method he has seen in a recent opinion of the high court. If there is an odd number of such methods, a result always can be reached (for example, 3-2 for defendant). Perhaps ties can be broken in favor of the plaintiff by giving the better law method one and one-half rather than one vote, if better law is one of the methods on the list of those he has found in the state supreme court's opinions.

Kitchen Sink. Although I do not seriously believe that any eclectic court intends to adopt eclecticism itself as a method, this possibility is a conceivable explanation of eclecticism. The judge keeps a master list of all methods he recognizes. These could include all those in use in the United States at the time of the decision, or all of them plus scholarly methods such as Cavers' principles of preference and Ehrenzweig's proper law in a proper forum, which have yet to be adopted at the state level. He then has the law clerk, because he is too busy to do it himself, apply each method to the fact-law pattern and tally one 'vote' for the plaintiff or the defendant based on the result reached under each method. Interest analysis should get as many votes as there are distinct break devices for dealing with the particular case.

If the total number of methods is an even number, a tie is possible, and the kitchen-sink method must have a tie-breaking device. One possibililty: give forum law, if it is constitutionally eligible, one and one-half votes, or give the better law one and one-half votes.

Odd-Numbered Mishmash. This article uses the term 'mishmash' to describe an eclectic method of choice of law that deliberately uses three or five or seven of the other recognized methods. (Any more than that and the jurisdiction will be in the kitchen sink, I suspect.) The court is to apply each method in the mishmash to the fact-law pattern, and each produces one vote for the plaintiff or the defendant. For example, a three-method mishmash might consist of center of gravity, better law, interest analysis with a forum break. The application of this mishmash to *Milkovich v. Saari*,[37] for example, results in one vote for the plaintiff because the common-law rule of liability for ordinary negligence is 'better' than a guest statute, and the defendant gets one vote because the case is a false conflict in favor of Ontario's guest statute. The outcome depends on the location of the center of gravity.

It should be clear that an even-numbered mishmash is impossible, as a method, because there must be some way to break ties, and whatever that device is becomes the odd prong of the mishmash. For example, Wisconsin has declared that it uses both center of gravity and better law in contract cases. But Wisconsin must be able to decide the case in which the territorial factors lie in the jurisdiction with the worst law, with only a domiciliary connection to better law. If the tie is to be broken in favor of the better law, there is no mishmash. Center of gravity can never prevail unless the better law comes from the territorially involved jurisdiction. Thus, the method would be pure better law. If the tie-breaking device is a third method, the mishmash is triple and not double.

Blend of Coffee. This is Professor Rosenberg's analogy to describe the only type of eclecticism that this Article finds acceptable. The blending has occurred in some interest analysis jurisdictions. When the conflict before the court is not false, the forum may turn to better law or center of gravity as a basis for breaking the conflict and applying the law of one of the domiciliary states.

Uninformed Judge. The writer of the opinion, because of the lousy briefs of counsel, does not understand that there is a difference between interest analysis and, for example, the most significant relation method or center of gravity. Sadly, this probably explains a sizeable fraction of the eclectic opinions.

---

[37]   295 Minn. 155, 203 N.W.2d 408 (1973).

* * * * *

Each American jurisdiction should not only choose one method of choice of law—a pure method or a hybrid like New York's—but must also explain it with clarity and particularity to attorneys and lower court judges. For example, although I *think* I know what New York's present choice of law method is, its court of appeals should have taken the opportunity since the 1972 *Neumeier* decision to explain the significance of the large and critical shift in theory that *Neumeier* made. But all it has provided is a cryptic and actually misleading snippet to the effect that lex loci is the "general rule." I have the curiosity of the scholar to learn if my interpretation is correct; but the bench and bar of New York must view the needed assistance as an absolute necessity.

Joseph W. Singer, *A Pragmatic Guide to Conflicts*, 70 B.U. L. REV. 731, 731-739 (1990)*

* * *

* * *At first glance, conflicts law seems quite simple; it can be summarized in a couple of sentences. Modern choice-of-law approaches require courts to analyze the policies underlying conflicting state laws and to consider the justified expectations of the parties. Then, in light of those considerations, the courts are to apply the law of the state that has a real interest in having its law applied. If more than one state has a real interest in the case, the courts should apply the law of the state that has the most significant relationship to the parties and the transaction or occurrence, taking into account the relevant policies and expectations.

Yet when courts and scholars apply this deceptively simple prescription, their analysis seems both complex and disordered. They address a hodgepodge of factors, often with insufficient explanation of how they decided the weight given to each. Nor do the various modern approaches to conflicts law provide determinate answers to concrete cases. Some approaches provide no standard at all. Leflar's better law approach, for example, lists five relevant factors to consider, but identifies no standard for applying them—he does not tell us what to do with the factors, other than to *consider* them. This approach, however, is not unique.

The approaches that do offer standards do not really answer choice-of-law questions; instead, they require decisionmakers to make difficult judgments, just as Leflar does. For example, the Second Restatement requires application of the law of the state that has the most significant relationship with the case; yet, beyond listing factors to consider, it gives little guidance on how to determine significance. Moreover, both courts and scholars substantially disagree as to how to evaluate the relative significance of different factors in particular cases. Similarly, the comparative impairment approach requires application of the law of the state whose policies will be most impaired if its own laws are not applied to the case. In making this judgment, many disagreements can arise on how to judge the strength and scope of substantive policies. Finally, interest analysis requires application of the law of interested states, but interest analysts differ significantly in their interpretations of when states do and do not have real interests in applying their law to a case.

Individual scholars do have consistent and relatively determinate approaches. It is possible to describe in detail both the methods of analysis and the proposed results that would be reached by such accomplished scholars as Louise Weinberg, Robert Sedler, Herma Hill Kay,

---

*   Reprinted with permission.

and Russell Weintraub. No court, however, adopts the approach of a particular scholar *in toto*. Instead, the courts borrow from all the modern approaches, using whatever pieces of the analyses seem useful and compelling in a particular case.

Because the courts borrow from the vast array of modern scholarship, it often seems—quite correctly—that decisionmakers have initial intuitions about the correct result and simply manipulate the factors to justify reaching that result. At other times, the opposite problem ensues: It is not uncommon for judges to conclude that several states have significant contacts with the dispute and that they have no way to determine which contacts are more significant. In such cases judges often throw up their hands and retreat to arbitrary territorial rules like the place of the injury.

The prevalent modern approaches—interest analysis, the most significant relationship test, the comparative impairment test, and the better law approach—organize conflicts analysis by listing factors to consider. Five factors generally appear—in different guises—in the various lists. Interest analysis focuses initially on (1) the *policies* underlying conflicting substantive laws and on the persons or events toward which those policies are directed. It then supplements this factor with consideration of (2) the *justified expectations* of the parties who may have relied on the law of a particular state in planning their conduct or who would be unfairly surprised by the application of another state's law. In addition to these two factors, the Second Restatement's most significant relationship test and the better law approach require consideration of (3) *comity*; (4) *predictability*; and (5) the *better law*. Comity concerns include determining the relative strength of the respective state policies in the context of the case and the legitimacy of applying aberrational or minority policies to extraterritorial cases. Comity concerns also include consideration of the circumstances in which it is appropriate for a state to defer to the ability of another normative and political community to govern a particular case. This may entail either deference of the forum to foreign law or deference of a foreign state to application of forum law. Predictability concerns include enabling citizens to predict the legal consequences of their conduct and thus, to the extent possible, fostering uniform results in conflicts cases.

Although it remains controversial, most courts consider, either explicitly or implicitly, which set of applicable laws is better as a matter of social policy and justice. Additionally, many conflicts scholars have recently argued explicitly for consideration of the better law. For example, many interest analysts propose a rebuttable presumption in favor of plaintiff-favoring forum law on the grounds that (1) when two states have real interests in furthering their social policies, there is generally little reason for the forum to give up what it sees as the better forum law in deference to the worse law of another state; or (2) that plaintiff-favoring policies generally promote better, widely shared norms of recovery in typical torts and contracts cases. In the same vein, the Second Restatement requires analysis of the *basic policies* underlying the particular field of law involved in the case. I have argued that there is no way to determine the basic policy of an entire field of law, like torts or contracts, without making value judgments about which substantive policies should be favored; that is, without identifying the better law.

This list of factors provides a useful reminder of the kinds of considerations generally thought to be relevant to choice-of-law determinations. It fails, however, to present a clear picture of how courts are to apply these factors. Nor does it give sufficient information on how to structure the analysis in either a legal brief or a judicial opinion.

Both the First and Second Restatements of Conflicts failed to provide generally acceptable approaches to analyzing and resolving cases involving choice-of-law questions. The First Restatement failed because it arbitrarily picked particular contacts as determinative. It identified the contact that was *temporally last* among the elements of a cause of action as the most significant contact. For example, in a torts case, the injury generally follows the defendant's conduct and breach of duty, and, in a contracts case, the acceptance follows the offer. But there is no good reason to presume that the last event is more significant than the first. It is true that there is no tort without an injury and no contract without an acceptance, but it is also true that there is no tort without tortious conduct, and there is no contract without a valid offer. For this reason, the rigid application of these jurisdiction-selecting rules often resulted in arbitrary and unjust outcomes. More than one contact is significant in every contested conflicts case, and the significance of particular contacts varies depending on both the circumstances of the case and the policies underlying the conflicting laws.

The arbitrariness and injustice of the First Restatement rules forced judges to invent more and more escape devices, such as recharacterization, *renvoi*, public policy exceptions, and substance/procedure distinctions. Yet these escape devices were as arbitrary as the basic rules; they were both manipulable and unrelated to the underlying policy concerns of the states. The combination of seemingly rigid rules and arbitrary exceptions created a system that was not only unpredictable but irrational. It directed analysis away from the actual underlying concerns, such as policy goals and value choices, implicated in choice-of-law cases. The current resurgence of interest in territorial rules divorced from the policy concerns of the affected states is therefore misguided. Any revival of such a rule system is bound to face the same difficulties as the First Restatement.

The Second Restatement is far superior to the First Restatement because it directs the courts to consider both the substantive and multistate policies implicated in choice-of-law cases. Yet it has its own problems. First, the Second Restatement attempts to combine policy analysis with rules by essentially presenting a long list of presumptions. This goal is a good one and has been accepted by many, if not most, conflicts scholars. The particular presumptions adopted by the Second Restatement, however, are faulty. They are, for the most part, restatements of the rules in the First Restatement. The only difference is that the Second Restatement downgrades the rigid rules to rebuttable presumptions. Yet, the rules in the First Restatement were rejected, not only because they were divorced from policy concerns and overly rigid, but because they often emphasized the wrong contacts. It has thus become necessary for the courts and commentators to attempt to invent new rules more consistent with contemporary notions of the factors that are significant in analyzing conflicts in law. The Second Restatement's presumptions do not achieve their goal of increasing predictability because the courts do not view them as useful and, therefore, do not follow them.

Second, the policy analysis in the Second Restatement is also faulty. It wrongly eschews explicit consideration of the better law. Yet it allows such consideration through the back door, by requiring courts to consider the "basic policies" underlying particular fields of law. Framing the issue in this inappropriate manner wrongly asks courts to distinguish between the basic rules and the exceptions in large areas of law without addressing the underlying wisdom and justice of those rules. This procedure is not only impossible; it makes no sense. The law of torts represents a compromise between requiring actors to compensate the victims of their conduct and encouraging socially useful, but harmful, activity by immunizing actors from liability for the harms they cause. The law of contracts represents a compromise between the policy of consistently enforcing agreements and regulating them to promote individual interests in autonomy and social interests in efficiency and justice. There is no basic policy to identify; the rules in force represent complicated accommodations among competing interests. Identifying a policy as "basic" to a field represents a judgment that it constitutes the preferred fallback position. This necessarily represents a judgment that, all other things being equal, it constitutes the better policy.

The Second Restatement's policy analysis is also defective because it is often one-sided. For example, it argues that allegations of negligence generally concern situations in which "the parties act without giving thought to the legal consequences of their conduct or to the law that may be applied" and that in such circumstances, "the parties have no justified expectations to protect." Although it is true that people do not plan to have accidents, it is also true that defendants, especially businesses, often take into account the applicable tort laws in determining how much to invest in safety or how much insurance to buy. Similarly, the Restatement argues that justified expectations almost always point in the direction of enforcing contractual arrangements. Yet one reason a state may refuse to enforce an agreement is that particular expectations based on the agreement are not justified. This may be because one of the parties has acted in bad faith by unfairly slipping through an unintended loophole in the agreement. Or it may be because the contract was the result of unequal bargaining power, or because it violates important public policies such as promoting competition and alienability of property or preventing discrimination.

Interest analysis and comparative impairment analysis also have defects. Neither approach sufficiently takes account of the difficulties in determining the strength or scope of state policies. I do not mean that it is impossible to make judgments of this sort, only that some scholars fail to confront adequately the competing considerations involved in making these determinations. This problem is exacerbated as these approaches ask the decisionmaker to search for false conflicts. This procedure often induces analysts to understate or ignore the legitimate interests of one of the parties and one of the states involved in the case.

Nor have the Second Restatement or interest analysis always been used wisely by the courts. Many judicial opinions that discuss conflicts issues are both oversimplified and illogical. It is commonplace to find arguments in judicial opinions that mistakenly overlook the legitimate interests of one of the parties and the regulatory concerns of one of the affected states. As a result of this one-sided analysis, judges often wrongly attribute plaintiff-protecting policies to defendant-protecting states. They also often fail to recognize the limits to plaintiff-protecting policies in all states. This failure manifests itself in oversimplified analyses of the substantive policies underlying tort and contract law.

The reasoning in conflicts opinions involving torts is heavily weighted toward plaintiffs. Conflicts scholars hotly dispute whether this is a virtue or an unfortunate bias. It is counted as a virtue by most, but not all, of the conflicts scholars who support the modern policy-oriented approach. In contrast, most of the scholars who tend to support territorial rules, favor giving greater protection to the interests of defendants in conflicts cases. They assume that interest analysis leads in most cases to application of forum law, which usually favors the plaintiff. This is often, but not always, true. For this reason, cases and scholarly commentary applying modern conflicts law do not easily allow lawyers for defendants to develop persuasive arguments for application of the law of defendant-protecting states. Although I believe plaintiffs in torts cases generally should get the benefit of the plaintiff-favoring law of the forum, I believe this choice cannot be adequately justified if the interests of defendants and defendant-protecting states are ignored. Moreover, defendants sometimes *are* entitled to the protection of defendant-protecting laws. The analysis presented here should serve to equip defendants' attorneys to do a better job of developing the most persuasive arguments possible in the context of the plaintiff-favoring modern conflicts system.

A somewhat different situation obtains in conflicts cases involving contracts. With some exceptions, the reasoning in conflicts opinions and scholarly commentary involving contracts heavily favors enforcing contractual arrangements. This means that attorneys representing clients seeking to escape from onerous contractual obligations, or unfair interpretations of ambiguous contractual language, may have difficulty formulating persuasive arguments. I hope to help remedy this problem by clarifying the most widely accepted arguments in favor of choosing the law that regulates the contract.

Judges oversimplify and mischaracterize conflicts cases for several reasons. The most immediate reason is that the prevailing approach to interest analysis encourages oversimplification by requiring analysts to seek out and identify purportedly false conflicts. False conflict analysis is only plausible in most cases that raise interesting conflicts questions if state interests are defined in an overly narrow way or if the states are incorrectly said to share basic underlying policies. The more fundamental reason courts oversimplify conflicts cases is that false conflict analysis appears to relieve the decisionmaker of responsibility for choosing among incompatible values and goals. It therefore creates the illusion of neutrality while seemingly making real conflicts disappear.

* * * * *

Comments

1.   Eclecticism much like that surveyed in Part A appears to be a perennial feature of conflicts law. It is even discernable in the writing of medieval theorists. Juenger 1993: pp. 13-14.[1] Professor Juenger found this phenomenon curious. He wrote of unilateralism and multilateralism that "[t]he coexistence of these two methods in early conflicts literature is remarkable. Unilateralism and multilateralism proceed from different assumptions, focus on different questions, and yield different conclusions." *Id.* at 13.

2.   The selections by the contributors in Part A indicate how lines in the eclecticism debate have been drawn. Professor Leflar is the leading member of the pro-eclecticism camp. Later, he attempted to distill his position.

> [T]he modern decisions, regardless of exact language, are all substantially consistent with each other. Whether the opinion language is that of Restatement (Second) most significant relationship, or of Brainerd Currie's governmental interest analysis, or of Leflar's choice-influencing considerations, or of Cavers' principles of preference, or of Ehrenzweig's more diverse analyses, the real reasons and the result are likely to be about the same. As far as opinion language is concerned, the tendency is, quite properly, to cite all these authors, along with current articles by any other authors who may have discussed the court's specific problem, plus a selection of recent judicial opinions which, regardless of reasoning, have broken away from old-time mechanical choice-of-law rules. Such a collection of authority will almost surely support any sensible non-mechanical choice of law that an intelligent and conscientious court is likely to arrive at.

Leflar 1972b: p. 474. Additional commentators are in general agreement with Pro-

---

[1]   Full citations appear in the bibliography, Chapter Twelve.

fessors Leflar and Westbrook that contemporary decisions usually reflect a consensus view of conflicts law and theory. *See, e.g.,* McLaughlin 1991b: p. 89; Shreve 1993: p. 912.

3. In contrast, other commentators have doubted along with Professors Reppy and Singer either the fact or possible value of conflicts eclecticism. Some, *e.g.,* Rosenbereg 1980: p. 444, doubt the existence of a consensus among American courts. Others doubt that eclecticism could ever bring about good conflicts law. American conflicts law suffered, according to Professor Amos Shapira, from "inflated investment with a variety of policy goals." He added that "[t]he choice of law process, even in its most sophisticated version, just cannot effectively serve too many, often irreconcilable, masters simultaneously." Shapira 1977: p. 249.

B. Rules or Approach?

Maurice Rosenberg, *The Comeback of Choice of Law Rules*, 81 COLUM. L. REV. 946, 958-959 (1981)*

* * * * *

Today no one would defend the system of broad and mechanistic choice-of-law rules that held sway through the first half of this century and that was largely embodied in the first *Restatement of Conflict of Laws*. Currie's attacks on the system and his proposal for a policy-centered approach helped bring about a healthy shift of focus away from the mechanics and toward the objectives of the choice-of-law process. As reporter for the second conflicts *Restatement*, Reese made good use of Currie's insights; particularly, these inclined him to bring greater flexibility into the rules and to make them sensitive to local-law policies of varying types and intensity. But experience is proving that Reese was right to hold fast to his conviction that rules are necessary and feasible and that he was right not to embrace the theory that the interest-analysis approach is the best answer to the choice-of-law problem. That theory rests on a faulty conception of the nature of a conflicts question and does not reflect how the law does or should deal with multi-state cases.

It is true that in conflicts cases, just as in domestic cases, if the legislature has said explicitly that it intends a court to apply a particular rule to a case like the one at bar, the court will follow the expressed intent. However, if the court is unable to discover from the statutory text or history what the legislature desires, single-state and multi-state cases are handled differently. In a domestic case the court reconstructs the absent legislative intention by examining the intensity of the policies or purposes underlying the competing rules. The more intense a policy, the more likely the legislature intended it to apply to a marginal situation. In a multi-state case, however, it is not the intensity of the policies in competition that is the key to decision. Regardless of how strong or weak the policy embodied by the rule is, the decisive question is simply: Did the legislature intend this rule to apply to a situation that has important elements in two or more states? Considerations entirely apart from the intensity of the substantive statutory policy come into play. * * * [T]he big difference is the prominence of the "where" factors in the multi-state cases in contrast to their total absence in the domestic cases.

If a legislature wishes to specify explicitly the territorial reach of a statute by taking account of geographical factors, it often does so, as scores of statutes illustrate. If by design the legislature remains silent on the matter, the effect is to leave it to the courts to determine the statute's reach. When this occurs, a court should decide the statute's reach in accordance with applicable principles of conflict of laws, as Justice Traynor urged in *Bernkrant***. Those principles are based on system-coordinating needs and values, and not alone on the substantive purposes of the competing rules.

---

*   This article orginaaly appeared at 81 COLUM. L. REV. 946 (1981). Reprinted by permission.

**   [Bernkrant v. Fowler, 55 Cal. 2d 588, 360 P. 2d 906 (1961).]

If a legislature has simply failed to consider the possibility that multi-state cases will arise in the course of implementing its legislation, it becomes necessary for the courts to fill the gap, case by case. The interest analysis does not help fill the gap. Probing ever deeper into the substantive policies is most unlikely to illumine the question of the statute's geographical reach in a case with elements dispersed in other states. This seems to be recognized by more and more scholars. The courts should not lag far behind.

Robert A. Sedler, *Rules of Choice of Law Versus Choice-of-Law Rules: Judicial Method in Conflicts Torts Cases*, 44 TENN. L. REV. 975, 977-979 (1977)*

* * * * *

Since I am clearly an adherent of the Currie version of interest analysis, it should not be surprising that I would be highly critical of a rule-oriented approach to choice of law or that I have attacked such an approach elsewhere, both generally and in the context of the *Neumeier*** rules. My criticism, however, goes to *choice-of-law* rules and to a rule-oriented approach to choice of law. There is a crucial distinction, in my view, between choice-of-law rules, such as those proposed by Professor Reese and articulated by the New York Court of Appeals in *Neumeier*, which are formulated a priori and then applied to the facts of particular cases, and rules of choice of law, which evolve from the decisions of the courts in actual cases and result from the normal workings of binding precedent and stare decisis. It is my contention that the courts should resolve conflicts problems on a case-by-case basis with reference to considerations of policy and fairness to the parties, and that in time, through the normal workings of binding precedent and stare decisis, a body of conflicts decisional law will emerge in each state. I call this process "judicial method." The policy-centered conflict of laws and the rules of choice of law that will emerge from judicial method differ sharply from the choice-of-law rules, howsoever narrow and policy-based they may be, that are formulated a priori to cover *categories* of cases and then are applied deductively to all cases coming within each category.

The alternatives, therefore, are not choice-of-law rules versus no rules and "ad hoc" decisions. The alternatives rather are choice-of-law rules developed a priori and applied deductively to particular cases versus rules of choice of law developed through the normal workings of binding precedent and stare decisis in the common-law tradition and applied to like cases with such extensions or modifications as the court deems appropriate. Whatever advantages claimed for choice-of-law rules will be equally realized by rules of choice of law. The rules of choice of law will not have the built-in disadvantages of (1) being developed in the abstract, without regard to the concrete situations and differing policy considerations presented in particular cases, and (2) countenancing unsound results in a particular case by the application of a rule that "works well in the great majority of situations." In short, we do not need choice-of-law rules once we recognize that by applying judicial method to the conflict of laws we will have rules of choice of law.

* * * * *

---

*   Reprinted with permission.

**   [Neumeier v. Kuehner, 31 N.Y.2d 121, 286 N.E.2d 454, 335 N.Y.S.2d 64 (1972).]

Peter Hay and Robert B. Ellis, *Bridging the Gap Between Rules and Approaches in Tort Choice of Law in the United States: A Survey of Current Case Law*, **27** INT'L LAWYER **369, 371-375, 383-384, 386-395 (1993)***

* * * * *

The Rules States: New York and Louisiana

A. NEW YORK AND THE *NEUMEIER* RULES

1. *New York Choice of Law in Tort Before* Neumeier

New York departed from territorially oriented rules for the choice of the applicable law in tort in the well-known decision of *Babcock v. Jackson.*[8] In *Babcock*, the New York court regarded the place of the accident as too fortuitous to justify the application of its law to the question of a New York driver's immunity from liability to his New York host. *Babcock* was factually a simple case, and the rule that it furnished therefore proved inadequate for cases of greater complexity. Ensuing New York decisions attempted to fit different fact patterns into the general "center of gravity" idea, providing lower courts and the bar with little or no guidance. When *Tooker v. Lopez*[10] reached the New York Court of Appeals in 1969, the court was ready to abandon contact counting, analysis of the center of gravity of the host/guest relationship, and the like. The *Tooker* court embraced interest analysis, holding that New York had an interest in affording recovery to a New York domiciliary killed elsewhere as the result of the alleged negligence of another New Yorker. The concurring judges were troubled by the uncertainty that inheres in such an open-ended approach. For instance, what should the applicable law be if the non-New York third party, also injured in the *Tooker* accident, were to sue the driver? The chance to limit the open-endedness came with *Neumeier*.

2. *The* Neumeier *Rules*

The facts of *Neumeier v. Kuehner*[12] were simple. Kuehner, a resident of Buffalo, New York, drove his car to Ontario, Canada, to pick up his friend Neumeier who lived there. They planned a day's trip to another part of Ontario where, apparently, they were to prepare cottages Kuehner owned for the coming rental season. On the way, both were killed when a train hit their car as it crossed railroad tracks in Ontario. Neumeier's wife brought a wrongful death action

---

*   Copyright © 1993 by the American Bar Association. Reprinted by permission.
[8]   191 N.E.2d 279 (N.Y. 1963).
[10]   249 N.E.2d 394 (N.Y. 1969).
[12]   286 N.E.2d 454 (N.Y. 1972).

against Kuehner's estate and the railroad company. At issue was the applicability of the Ontario guest statute, which prevented guests in an automobile from bringing negligence actions against their host drivers. New York did not have such a statute.

The court first distinguished its previous holding in *Tooker v. Lopez*. There, both the guest passenger and host driver were New York domiciliaries, and it was on that basis that New York law controlled. The court noted that *Tooker* had expressly left open the question whether New York law would apply in the present situation stating:

> What significantly and effectively differentiates the present case is the fact that, although the host was a domiciliary of New York, the guest, for whose death recovery is sought, was domiciled in Ontario, the place of accident and the very jurisdiction which had enacted the statute designed to protect the host from liability for ordinary negligence. It is clear that although New York has a deep interest in protecting its own residents, injured in a foreign state, against unfair or anachronistic statutes of that state, it has no legitimate interest in ignoring the public policy of a foreign jurisdiction—such as Ontario—and in protecting the plaintiff guest domiciled and injured there from legislation obviously addressed, at the very least, to a resident riding in a vehicle traveling within its borders.[15]

This passage was the basis for the rules that were announced. Referring to his own concurring opinion in *Tooker*, Chief Judge Fuld, writing for the majority in *Neumeier*, declared that the time had come to "minimize what some have characterized as an ad hoc case-by-case approach by laying down guidelines, as well as we can, for the solution of guest-host conflicts problems."[16] The guidelines took the form of three rules:

> 1. When the guest-passenger and the host-driver are domiciled in the same state, and the car is there registered, the law of that state should control and determine the standard of care which the host owes to his guest.

> 2. When the driver's conduct occurred in the state of his domicile and that state does not cast him in liability for that conduct, he should not be held liable by reason of the fact that liability would be imposed upon him under the tort law of the state of the victim's domicile. Conversely, when the guest was injured in the state of his own domicile and its law permits recovery, the driver who has come into that state should not—in the absence of special circumstances—be permitted to interpose the law of his state as a defense.

> 3. In other situations, when the passenger and the driver are domiciled in different states, the rule is necessarily less categorical. Normally, the applicable rule of decision will be that of the state where the accident occurred but not if it can be shown that displacing that normally applicable rule will advance the relevant substantive law purposes without impairing the smooth working of the multistate system or producing great uncertainty for litigants.[17]

Neumeier itself presented a rule 3 situation. The court applied the law of the place of injury;

---

[15]   *Id.* [at 455].

[16]   *Id.* at 457 (internal quotation omitted).* * *

[17]   [*Id.*] at 457-58.* * *

it did not utilize the proviso of the second sentence because displacing the otherwise applicable law would not advance the substantive law purposes of New York without impairing the smooth workings of the multistate system.

In some ways the *Neumeier* rules resemble both interest analysis and the *Restatement (Second)*. The rules can be seen as a "particularization of *Restatement (Second)* principles . . . establishing priorities of the kind the *Restatement's* drafters were unwilling to do."[19] The rules are also similar to interest analysis—New York's methodological orientation by the time *Tooker* was decided—in that they weigh interests. They do so, however, in advance of the actual case, thus facilitating predictable results while retaining the flexibility that a weighing of interests can give. And while the interests weighed in advance were not specifically delineated in the *Neumeier* opinion, they can be easily ascertained.

The *Neumeier* rules date to the recognition in *Babcock v. Jackson* that mechanical application of the lex loci rule can produce unsatisfactory results. Both parties in *Babcock* shared New York as their domicile. The fact that the accident occurred in another state was "purely adventitious."[22] Thus, out of *Babcock*, *Neumeier* rule 1 was created, calling for the application of the law of the parties' common domicile in order to protect them from the "unfair or anachronistic" laws of another state.[23] But the purpose of *Neumeier* rule 1 goes beyond this. It is designed to protect the expectations of the parties, to the extent that expectations exist in tort. Furthermore, as the court of appeals subsequently recognized in *Boy Scouts of America, Inc. v. Schultz*,[24] application of the law of the parties' common domicile serves to reduce forum shopping, rebuts charges that the forum-locus decides in favor of its own laws or laws favoring recovery, and, perhaps most important, it "brings a modicum of predictability and certainty to an area of law needing both."[25]

Neumeier rule 2 is an offshoot of rule 1. It also protects party expectations by guarding against an unfair result in situations where the place of injury is fortuitous. The first sentence of *Neumeier* rule 2 applies the law of the defendant's domicile when the tort occurred there and that state's law would not hold the defendant liable. This rule has two discernable purposes. It discourages forum shopping by consistently applying the law of the place of the defendant's conduct (when that law is more favorable to the defendant), no matter where the plaintiff's domicile is or where the plaintiff brings suit. The rule also protects party expectations in the sense that it gives defendants the ability to predict the consequence of their actions within their home state and plan their conduct accordingly.

Rule 2, second sentence, also protects party expectations; this time the plaintiff's. In a rule 2, second sentence, fact pattern, application of the plaintiff's protective home state law will further that state's interest. At the same time, the defendant's home state will not have been disfavored, presumably because it does not have an interest in the application of its protective law to actions that occur outside its borders.

Finally, *Neumeier* rule 3 embodies what remains of the traditional lex loci approach; it is the default rule, which applies when party expectations or the protection of domiciliaries from "unfair or anachronistic" laws of a foreign state are not a concern. That facts of *Neumeier* itself

---

[19]   [Peter] Hay, [*Flexibility versus Predictability and Uniformity in Choice of Law*, 226 RECUEIL DES COURS 281, 386 (1991)].

[22]   [Babcock v. Jackson, 191 N.E.2d 279, 284 (N,Y. 1963)].

[23]   *See*, Neumeier v. Kuehner, 286 N.E.2d 454, 456 (N.Y. 1972).

[24]   480 N.E.2d 679 (N.Y. 1985) * * *.

[25]   Hay, *supra* note [19], at 366-367 * * *.

fell into the rule 3 category: A Canadian domiciliary died in an accident in Canada as the result of the alleged negligence of a New York resident. The court applied Canada's guest statute, holding that:

> It is clear that although New York has a deep interest in protecting its own residents, injured in a foreign state, against unfair or anachronistic statutes of that state, it has no legitimate interest in ignoring the public policy of a foreign jurisdiction—such as Ontario—and in protecting the plaintiff guest domiciled and injured there from legislation obviously addressed, at the very least, to a resident riding in a vehicle traveling within its borders.[28]

Neumeier rule 3's proviso gives it flexibility in situations where displacing the lex loci will advance relevant substantive law purposes without impairing the smooth workings of the interstate system. However, in order to maintain the rule's predictability, the rule 3 proviso should be used sparingly; resort to it should serve the purpose of discouraging forum shopping or protecting any existing party expectations.

By identifying the relevant values and interests in advance of an actual case, the *Neumeier* rules (and perhaps most New York decisions whether or not they follow the rules specifically) have created predictable results while avoiding, to a large extent, the inflexible results to which the lex loci may lead. Choice-of-law approaches, such as California's comparative impairment approach, and the *Restatement (Second)*'s "most significant relationship" test, may also contain a priori value judgments. As approaches, rather than rules, however, they are designed as tools for the decisions of individual cases and, absent a body of case law with precedential force, may therefore provide far less predictability of result.

The sections that follow examine post-*Neumeier* choice-of-law decisions in New York and survey the decisional law of selected states in order to explore whether decisions based on approaches display a pattern giving them some of the rules certainty of New York's *Neumeier* rules.

* * * * *

B. Louisiana: A New Rules State

With the recent codification of its conflicts law, Louisiana joined New York as a state following specific rules rather than a generalized approach. Although phrased in terms of California's "comparative impairment" approach, the Louisiana Code's (Code) broad policy objectives remind of the *Restatement (Second)*. They focus on the contacts of the state to the parties and the events in light of policies similar to those listed in section 6 of the *Restatement (Second)*. The Code goes beyond the *Restatement (Second)*, however, by setting forth a priori legislative determinations, in the form of specific rules, of the general policy goals listed in article 15. These rules, with respect to tort, as well as the reasoning behind them, resemble the *Neumeier* rules as modified in *Schultz*.

The Code adopts the *Schultz* distinction between conduct-regulating and loss-allocating rules providing for the application of the lex loci in cases involving issues of conduct regulation when conduct and injury occur in the same state. For cases involving loss-allocating rules, the Louisiana Code adopts *Neumeier* rule 1. Also, as a result of the focus of article 44 on the parties' domiciles and their expectation that they will be subject to their own laws, the Code

---

[28]   Neumeier v. Kuehner, 286 N.E.2d 454, 456 (N.Y. 1972).

will reach results consistent with *Neumeier* rule 2. Louisiana's Code also creates an approach governing situations where conduct and injury occur in different states.

* * * * *

Approach-Oriented States

The *Neumeier* rules were born of a synthesis of case law that sought an alternative to the classic lex loci rule in tort conflicts law. The pre-*Neumeier* case law had adopted an approach to the choice-of-law problem, namely, to determine the center of gravity or some similar focal element of the particular case. As noted earlier, such an approach may leave the resolution of concrete cases very much in the eye of the beholder; *Neumeier* returned to rules precisely to guard against that kind of uncertainty. The difference between the rules of traditional conflicts law and those of the *Neumeier* decision is that the latter proceed on the basis of predetermined interests and values: they do not envision ad hoc determinations, they are "principled rules."

"Interest analysis," in the form proposed by Currie (and not pursued further in this survey), does not weigh interests, either in an a priori fashion or case by case. In the main, it applies the lex fori whenever the case presents a "true conflict." A variation of interest analysis, Currie-style, developed and took hold in California: the "comparative impairment" approach does undertake to weigh "interests," as does the *Restatement (Second)* when it calls for the application of the law of the place of "the most significant relationship" to the issues and to the parties. Both approaches are relatively open-ended, and therefore raise the question whether subsequent judicial practice displays any kind of a pattern with predictive value. The sections that follow explore this question and take the *Neumeier* rules as the benchmark.

A. CALIFORNIA: THE COMPARATIVE IMPAIRMENT APPROACH

One variant of interest analysis undertakes to compare and weigh the competing policy interests of the states involved. The approach adopted several years ago by California seeks to determine the state whose policies would be more impaired than those of another state by not having its law applied. The state that would be disadvantaged in this way, and whose law therefore should be applied, may well be a state other than the forum. California's application of its comparative impairment approach reveals only slight, and perhaps somewhat sporadic, decisional patterns that parallel the *Neumeier* rules.

In *Nicolet, Inc. v. Superior Court*,[94] for example, a California appeals court did not apply the common domicile rule to a bad faith insurance claim brought by an insured Pennsylvanian against a Pennsylvania insurance company. Other California decisions, however, applied the comparative impairment approach in a manner consistent with both the reasoning and results of *Neumeier* rule 2. In *Denham v. Farmers Ins. Co.*[96] the court applied Nevada law, consistent with *Neumeier* rule 2, first sentence, to a bad faith insurance case that arose out of a Nevada accident between California plaintiffs and a Nevada driver insured by the defendant insurance

---

[94]   188 Cal. App. 3d 28, 224 Cal. Rptr. 408 (Ct. App. 1986), *dismissed as moot,* 736 P.2d 319 (Cal. 1987).

[96]   213 Cal. App. 3d 1061, 262 Cal. Rptr. 146 (Ct. App. 1989).

company. A similar conclusion was reached in *Zimmerman v. Allstate Ins. Co.* as well as in other cases.[98] *Neumeier* rule 3 is also represented in several California decisions.

This brief survey of California's experience with the comparative impairment approach suggests, perhaps, an implicit adoption of predetermined values similar to those underlying New York's *Neumeier* rules. Of the cases surveyed, only three would have come out differently under the *Neumeier* rules. No cases explicitly applied principled rules, but several decisions did reach results consistent with the *Neumeier* rules, engaging in *Neumeier*-like reasoning.

* * *

B. *Restatement (Second)* States

For some areas, for example, those related to property, the *Restatement (Second)* retains the traditional rules. For many others, including tort and contract, it introduces an approach for the determination of the applicable law. The court should identify "the place of the most significant relationship" to the issue and the parties and then apply its law. For torts, section 145 lists a number of nonexclusive factors (for example, place of the tort, domicile of the parties, and so forth) that should be considered in making the decision and refers to the pervasive general principles of section 6, on the basis of which these factors should be evaluated.

The general principles are broadly phrased and can accommodate virtually all points of view. Moreover, neither they nor the specific connecting factors assign priorities: They are co-equal. In addition, they are designed to apply to particular issues and not necessarily to the whole case. The first aspect—co-equal factors and considerations—means that no a priori judgments have been made; the courts are encouraged to weigh these considerations on a case-by-case basis. The second aspect, issue splitting (*depecage*), could mean that law-fact patterns will multiply rather than be reduced to a few basic archetypal situations, such as in the *Neumeier* rules. The case law must thus develop decisional patterns that reduce the risk that, while opinions pay lip service to systemic values and policies, the decisional process in fact is so flexible as to be ad hoc and, thus, unprincipled. Case law in several *Restatement (Second)* states appears, to some extent, to adhere to discernible decisional patterns.

Illinois, in *Estate of Barnes*,[111] explicitly adopted the common domicile rule embodied in *Neumeier* rule 1 and other Illinois courts have followed. However, one Illinois court declined to apply the common domiciliary law when it analyzed the case on the basis of the distinction between conduct-regulating and loss-allocating rules.

Colorado has embraced *Neumeier* rule 1's common domicile rule (as well as *Neumeier* rule 2), although few, if any, Colorado courts subsequently followed the specific rules. Florida and Texas, while not adopting it specifically, also appear to follow a common domicile rule. Indeed, of the sixteen *Restatement (Second)* decisions involving common domicile fact patterns surveyed, only one failed to apply the law of the parties' common domicile.

---

[98]   179 Cal. App. 3d 840, 224 Cal. Rptr. 917 (Ct. App. 1986) (Oklahoma law prohibiting third-party bad faith insurance claims applied when Illinois resident was injured in Oklahoma by Oklahoma resident; Oklahoma law protecting Oklahoma insurers from third-party bad faith claims, and their insureds who would be forced to pay for claims through higher premiums, would be more impaired if not applied). * * *

[111]   478 N.E.2d 1046 (Ill. App. Ct. 1985).* * *

Decisions in several *Restatement (Second)* states reveal patterns that may also suggest implicit value choices similar to those underlying *Neumeier* rules 2 and 3. Illinois decisions, for instance, have used "*Neumeier*-like" reasoning in cases involving *Neumeier* rule 2 fact patterns, but many Illinois decisions may not expressly address the policy decisions underlying *Neumeier* rule 2, instead applying the *Restatement (Second)* in a contact counting manner. Florida and Texas decisions have also applied the *Restatment (Second)* with results consistent with *Neumeier* rules 2 and 3. However, again, few cases apply a predetermined set of policy choices similar to those underlying *Neumeier* rules 2 and 3, instead focusing on contact counting.

Conclusions: Bridging the Gap Between Rules and Approaches

If one only looks at numbers, this brief survey reveals a striking similarity between the results reached in particular cases by states applying free-wheeling approaches and the results that would be reached under the *Neumeier* rules. Of the cases surveyed few (approximately twelve) would have come out differently under the *Neumeier* rules; and four of those decisions were New York cases failing to apply *Neumeier*.

However, numbers are only part of the story. The reasoning supporting the decisions reveals the *Neumeier*-like flexibility and predictability that principled analysis can achieve. Most approach states, for example, have followed the common-domicile rule articulated in *Neumeier* rule 1 and adopted in several countries abroad. Louisiana has codified the common-domicile rule, and Illinois and Colorado have explicitly recognized the application of the law of the parties' common domicile through decisional law. In addition, the decisional law of Florida and Texas has almost invariably applied an unarticulated common domicile rule for reasons similar to those underlying *Neumeier* rule 1. Decisions refusing to apply common domiciliary law have done so by giving preference to a "better law" approach that has produced a plaintiff-favoring result.

The most notable common element in approach state decisions that reach results consistent with the *Neumeier* rules is their focus on party expectations. This should not surprise. The *Neumeier* rules focus on party expectations: *Neumeier* rule 1 focuses on the expectations of both parties; rules 2 and 3 focus on the expectation of one party and the concomitant conclusion that it would not be unfair to subject the other party to the law expected by the first. By focusing on the same value goals (for example, party expectations) in recurrent fact patterns, approach states can achieve a level of predictability similar to that of jurisdictions with articulated principled rules and, at the same time, retain some of the flexibility that choice-of-law approaches were meant to provide.

The perception of a gap, of something irreconcilable, between legal systems with rules and those following approaches for the determination of the applicable law is itself dated. Its articulated or intuitive basis is, on the one hand, that rules are rigid, (therefore bad on principle or, at best, of limited utility in a world of differentiated fact patterns and various constellations of interests) and, on the other hand, that approaches will result in, and indeed invite, ad hoc decision making, "Khadi-justice." Both views misstate today's situation, if indeed they were ever entirely correct. "Rules" may of course be rigid. But this is so because they are drawn too sweepingly, not because they are value-neutral. All rules, as do even ad hoc decisions, express value judgments. The lesson of the new European codifications (principally the Rome Convention on choice of law in contract) is that rules can be fashioned more narrowly with more regard to the variety of interests to be addressed. The Louisiana codification, with its roots in the comparative impairment approach, goes in the same direction, as do New York's *Neumeier* rules for tort choice of law.

Similarly, approaches may lead to free-wheeling, ad hoc decision making. Undeniably, they have done so in a large number of cases since U.S. conflicts law began to undergo its revolution. The U.S. approaches gave courts little or no guidance, and the course of decision making became unpredictable.

As rule formulation can become more differentiated, decision making on the basis of approaches can become more principled. A priori identification of values and interests, basic to rule-based systems, whether statutory or decisional, is not part of most U.S. choice-of-law methodologies. Decisional patterns may emerge, however, simply because there is agreement on certain basic propositions. These decisional patterns then can furnish insights and have predictive value. Discerning decisional patterns is not as easy as when value goals are predetermined by rule. But approach-based systems have a degree of certainty, just as rule-based systems have a measure of flexibility.

Comments

1. Professor Willis Reese framed the issue posed in Part B of this Chapter in this way.

> The principal question in choice of law today is whether we should have rules or an approach. By "rule" is meant a phenomenon found in most areas of the law, namely a formula which once applied will lead the court to a conclusion. * * *
> By "approach" is meant a system which does no more than state what factor or factors should be considered in arriving at a conclusion.

Reese 1972: p. 315.[1] Twenty years later, Professor Larry Kramer termed this "a long-standing debate," describing it as follows.

> Rules advocates emphasize the importance of consistency and uniformity and argue that these values are best achieved with a shared system of rules. Advocates of the case-specific analysis counter that judges should be concerned primarily with implementing substantive policies and that this is best done by approaching each case on its own terms.

Kramer 1991c: p. 2137. A survey of authorities from both the rule and the approach camps appears in Cramton, Currie, Kay & Kramer 1993: pp. 234-235.

2. The initial rules-versus-approach debate shadowed to an extent the debate over interest analysis featured in Chapter Six. Recall that interest analysis was a weapon used by legal realists against the rule-bound, formalistic conflicts law promoted in the original RESTATEMENT. Interest analysts therefore tended to be "approach" proponents. That is, they were "inclined to approve of the tendency of modern theory to deny judges sanctuary in territorial or other mechanical rules and to force them instead to grapple with choice-of-law values out in the open." Shreve 1993: p. 913. Professor Sedler's excerpt in Part B is representative.

---

[1]   Full citations appear in the bibliography, Chapter Twelve.

3. For a while, rule proponents were forced to debate from a defensive position—they had to disavow any intention to return to the discredited territorialism (hard-and-fast rules) of the original conflicts RESTATEMENT. Their mission, illustrated by the excerpt by Professor Rosenberg, seemed to be to preserve at least some role for conflicts rules in an era dominated by approach. Another rules supporter of the time was forced to concede: "We have probably reached the stage where most areas of choice of law can be covered by general principles which are subject to imprecise exceptions." But he closed on a stronger note. "We should press on, however, beyond these principles to the formulation of precise rules. A choice of law rule that works well in the great majority of situations should be applied even in a case where it might not reach ideal results. Good rules, like other advantages, have their price." Reese 1972: p. 334.

4. Now, something closer to parity exists between the rule and approach positions. Two trends may explain this. First, the influential *Neumeier v. Kuehener* case, discussed in Part B, sparked at least a partial revival of rules as instruments in American conflicts law. On the continuation of that trend, *see* Sedler 1994a; Silberman 1994; Twerski 1994. Belief in the superiority of approach over rules in choice of law may have suffered a corresponding decline. *See, e.g.*, Kramer 1990: p. 321. Second, the notion of declaring a truce and amalgamating the best features of rules and approach (argued in the excerpt by Hay and Ellis in Part B) appears to be gaining ground. The American Law Institute took this tack in its choice-of-law recommendation for complex litigation, a proposal examined in *American Law Institute Complex Litigation Project: A Symposium*, 54 LA. L. REV. 833 (1994) (contributions by Donald T. Trautman, Symeon C. Symeonides, Edward H. Cooper, Friedrich K. Juenger, Peter J. Kalis, James R. Segerdahl, John T. Waldron, P. John Kozyris, Linda S. Mullenix, James A.R. Nafziger, Robert A. Sedler, David E. Seidelson, Gene R. Shreve, and Herbert P. Wilkins).

C. Conflicts Theory at the Crossroads

Larry Kramer, *Rethinking Choice of Law*, 90 COLUM. L. REV. 277, 290-293, 304-308, 309-319, 323, 324-328, 329-330, 334-335, 336-338, 339, 340-342 (1990)*

* * * * *

A. *The Congruence of Domestic and Multistate Choice of Law Cases*

The first—and most important—point to recognize is that moving from wholly domestic cases to cases with multistate contacts does not change the essential nature of the interpretive problem. A lawsuit with multistate contacts is still just a lawsuit: the plaintiff still alleges that because something happened, he is entitled to a remedy; the court must still determine whether the facts alleged are true, and whether, if these facts are true, some rule of positive law confers a right to recover. Making this determination is still a problem of interpretation. The only difference is that some of the facts are connected to different states, and the court must determine if that affects whether the law or laws at issue confer a right. While this determination may be difficult, it does not alter the nature of the problem confronting the court, which remains to decide what rights are conferred by positive law.

It follows that many features of domestic choice of law analysis are also present in multistate cases. As in the domestic context, not every case presents a choice of law problem. Sometimes the multistate contact is obviously irrelevant to the applicable law* * *. * * *Consequently, unless there is a domestic choice of law problem, this case will not require the court to make a choice between laws.

Moreover, as in the domestic context, it is up to the parties to raise a choice of law issue. Suppose, for example, that a plaintiff from Illinois is involved in an accident in Wisconsin with a defendant from Wisconsin. Plaintiff files a complaint seeking damages under Illinois law. Defendant could probably make a strong argument for Wisconsin law. But defendant may waive this argument, just as defendant may always waive an argument that plaintiff has failed to state a claim.

Third, also as in domestic cases, "choosing" and "applying" are not analytically distinct processes. As explained above, a court "applies" a law by interpreting it to clarify what facts a party relying on that law must establish to obtain relief. If the parties disagree about the applicable law, the court "chooses" from the laws in contention by the same process of interpretation. This is true whether the laws at issue are from the same or from different jurisdictions. In both cases, the court's task is to interpret the laws to determine whether either confers a right to recover on the facts alleged in the particular case.

The thesis of this article is that domestic and multistate cases share a fourth feature: if the parties do raise a choice of law problem in a multistate case, it can be resolved with basically the same two-step process used in domestic choice of law cases. Thus, the court should first examine the laws in issue to determine whether both apply, i.e., whether there is a conflict. If there is a conflict, the court should then employ some second-order rule of interpretation to choose between these laws.

---

*   This article originally appeared at 90 COLUM. L. REV. 277 (1990). Reprinted with permission.

B. *The First Step: Determining Whether There is a Conflict of Laws*

Suppose that plaintiff asserts a claim under the law of one state, and defendant responds that plaintiff's rights are governed by another state's law. How should the court resolve this dispute? To begin with, the court does not have to choose between these laws unless they both apply on the facts alleged. As in a domestic case, then, the first step is to determine whether each law applies to the particular dispute. I will call this determining a law's "prima facie applicability" to distinguish it from the second step of the analysis, in which the court chooses among laws that are applicable in this sense.

This step should sound familiar: Currie advised courts to do something like this to determine whether a case presents a "false conflict." According to Currie, only one state may have an interest, in which case the conflict is false and the proper solution is to apply the law of the only interested state. My understanding—though the matter is not free from doubt—is that when Currie says that a state is "interested" he means that the state's law confers a right in the particular case. Nonetheless, while determining whether a case presents a false conflict may be similar to determining prima facie applicability, I cannot leave this subject merely by citing interest analysis. Neither Currie nor his followers fully explained or justified the assumptions underlying the process by which they identify interests. Moreover, a number of important questions raised by critics of interest analysis remain unanswered: Are a state's interests limited to protecting citizens of the state, or do states have interests that are triggered by where an event occurs? Are there principled means for identifying interests, or is the process an arbitrary one that reflects only the preferences of the interpreter? Is there any justification for limiting state interests to protecting local citizens and domestic concerns, or is this limitation unrealistic and hopelessly parochial? Is there any justification for determining another state's interests other than by that state's choice of law rules? The discussion below addresses these questions while describing how to interpret a state's law where elements of a claim are located in other states.

1. *Prima Facie Applicability.*—Sometimes a law will specify what elements of a claim must be connected to or located in the state for the law to apply. With such laws, the court need not look beyond the face of the statute to determine prima facie applicability. Unfortunately, the great majority of laws are silent with respect to extraterritorial reach, and determining their prima facie applicability is more difficult.

* * * * *

2. *Using the First Step to Resolve Choice of Law Issues: Illustrations.*—As in domestic choice of law cases, determining the prima facie applicability of the laws relied on by the parties may produce three different results: no law may confer a right, only one law may confer a right, or several laws may confer rights. Moreover, again as in the domestic context, in cases of the first two types, and in some cases of the third type, the choice of law dispute is resolved at this first stage of analysis. The parties' rights are clear, for there is no conflict between laws.

a. *No Law Confers a Right.*—*Erwin v. Thomas*[79] is a well-known example of a case in which "no law confers a right." Erwin, a Washington resident, was injured in Washington by Thomas, an Oregon resident. Erwin's wife sued Thomas in Oregon for loss of consortium. Washington followed the common law rule that a wife cannot sue for loss of consortium; Oregon had abrogated this rule by statute.

On these facts, plaintiff had no right to recover under either Washington or Oregon law. While Oregon allows wives to recover for loss of consortium, the Oregon court recognized that

---

[79]   264 Or. 454, 506 P.2d 494 (1973).

"it is stretching the imagination more than a trifle to conceive that the Oregon Legislature was concerned about the rights of all the nonresident married women in the nation whose husbands would be injured outside the state of Oregon."[81] Rather, based on principles of comity and the desire to avoid unnecessary conflicts of law, Oregon can be presumed (absent a clear statement to the contrary) to limit its law to cases in which the contacts in Oregon implicate one of the purposes that led Oregon lawmakers to confer this right in cases having no multistate contacts. Here there are two such purposes: (1) to relieve an innocent victim of the economic consequences of injury by shifting costs to a culpable tortfeasor, and (2) to deter conduct deemed wrongful. Therefore, Oregon gives a right to recover only to wives who are from Oregon and to wives who are married to someone injured in Oregon. Since plaintiff could allege neither of these facts, Oregon confers no cause of action. Plaintiff can only state a claim, then, under the law of either her home state or the state where her husband was injured—both of which happened to be Washington.

Unfortunately for the plaintiff in *Erwin*, Washington adhered to the common law rule that a wife cannot recover for loss of consortium. At common law, a husband could recover for loss of consortium because defendant's negligence deprived him of services his wife owed him by law; a wife had no similar claim because husbands did not owe wives these services. Plaintiff's claim for loss of consortium therefore fails under Washington law because she is not deemed to have suffered an injury.

This analysis suggests that the choice of law dispute is rather easily resolved, for there is no conflict of laws. More importantly, the analysis suggests that plaintiff's claim should be dismissed for failure to state a claim upon which relief can be granted. Because Washington does not recognize her injury, plaintiff seeks to recover under Oregon law; she relies on the fact that defendant is an Oregon resident. But Oregon does not extend a right to recover simply because an injury was caused by someone from Oregon. Therefore, plaintiff has no cause of action—just as she would have no cause of action against a defendant from Washington in a wholly domestic case.

This is not how the Oregon court analyzed the case. Applying Currie's interest analysis, the court reasoned that Washington was interested in protecting defendants and that Oregon was interested in protecting married women. Since the defendant was not from Washington and the plaintiff was not from Oregon, however, the court concluded that "neither state has a vital interest in the outcome of this litigation."[85] Interest analysts call this an "unprovided-for case." Currie argued[87] —and the Oregon court agreed—that if state interests provide no solution the court should apply forum law. In *Erwin*, this meant that plaintiff recovered. Other interest analysts, dissatisfied with the lex fori approach, have offered alternative solutions to unprovided-for cases, suggesting that the court apply the other state's law "even though that law doesn't want to be applied,"[89] or that the court apply the "better law,"[90] or that the court apply the law that

---

[81]   264 Or. at 459, 506 P.2d at 494.

[85]   Id. at 459, 506 P.2d at 496.

[87]   See B. Currie, *On the Displacement of the Law of the Forum, in* [SELECTED ESSAYS ON THE CONFLICT OF LAWS 3, 64-65 (1963)]* * *; B. Currie, [*Survival of Actions: Adjudication Versus Automation in the Conflict of Laws, in* SELECTED ESSAYS], 156-57.

[89]   D. Cavers, [THE CHOICE OF LAW PROCESS 106 (1965)].

[90]   Posnak, [*Choice of Law: A Very Well-Curried Leflar Approach*, 34 MERCER L. REV. 731,] 777-80.

reflects a shared general policy,[91] or that the court re-examine the state interests and create a policy that will be advanced by applying the law of one of the states.[92]

This fuss is unnecessary. Interest analysts have created a problem where none exists by conceptualizing choice of law as a distinct threshold question that must be resolved before the court can render a decision on the merits. Ordinarily, interest analysts believe that an applicable law can and should be chosen on the basis of state interests. But if state interests fail to yield an answer—as in an unprovided-for case—some other way must be found to choose the law under which the merits are to be decided. Hence, the mental gyrations that produce the solutions listed above.

But to say that no state is interested is merely to say that no state gives plaintiff a right to recover; to say that no law applies is merely to say that plaintiff has no cause of action. The court does not first "choose" a law and then "apply" it. The court determines whether any state's law confers a cause of action. In *Erwin*, the answer is no: Oregon does not give plaintiff a cause of action because it does not extend a right to nonresident wives injured outside the state; Washington does not give plaintiff a cause of action because it does not view her as having suffered a cognizable injury. Therefore, unless the Constitution otherwise requires, plaintiff's complaint should be dismissed.

b. *Only One Law Confers a Right.*—In other cases, determining the prima facie applicability of the laws at issue will reveal that only one state's law applies, again resolving the choice of law dispute. Consider, for example, the now-classic case of *Babcock v. Jackson*.[94] Plaintiff, a New York resident, was injured in Ontario when defendant, also a New York resident, lost control of the car in which they were driving and crashed into a wall. Plaintiff brought suit in New York, basing his right to recover on New York law. Defendant answered, pleading an affirmative defense under Ontario's guest statute.

New York's tort law is prima facie applicable. Because tort recovery rules serve both regulatory and protective purposes, New York is presumed to give a right to recover to persons injured in New York and to persons from New York wherever injured. Plaintiff satisfies the latter condition, and therefore he can state a claim under New York law.

Defendant sets up a defense based on Ontario's guest statute. As noted above, guest statutes are designed to reduce insurance rates by preventing guests and hosts from colluding to defraud insurers. Accordingly, Ontario's guest statute applies if defendant's insurance costs are part of the insurance base of Ontario citizens, i.e., if defendant's car is garaged in Ontario. Since defendant's car was garaged in New York, defendant cannot assert a defense under Ontario's guest statute. Consequently, plaintiff should recover under New York law.

Interest analysts call cases like *Babcock* "false conflicts" because only one state has an interest and the laws therefore do not conflict. While I do not necessarily agree with the way interest analysts identify false conflicts, there is undoubtedly a subset of cases in which interpreting the laws at issue reveals that only one law is prima facie applicable. Several commentators have suggested that this subset is limited to cases in which the parties share a common residence. But this misunderstands the analysis. Different laws are applicable on the basis of different contacts with a state, depending on the purpose of the particular law. Consequently, there are various situations in which the facts and laws may be such that only one state's law applies. *Babcock* presents a choice between a New York law that is applicable

---

[91]   Sedler, [*The Governmental Interest Approach to Choice of Law: An Analysis and a Reformulation*, 25 UCLA L. Rev. 181, 233-36 (1977)].

[92]   R. Weintraub, [Commentary on the Conflict of Laws § 6.23 (3d ed. 1986)].

[94]   12 N.Y.2d 473, 191 N.E.2d 279, 240 N.Y.S.2d 743 (1963).

because plaintiff is a New York resident, and an Ontario law that is inapplicable because the critical consequence is felt in New York. The fact that both parties were New York residents is incidental to the analysis, though it may seem important because the consequence that triggers a guest statute (an affect on insurance rates) is closely associated with residency. But this will not always be the case. There may be other situations in which the parties do not share a common domicile but the facts and laws are still such that only one state's domestic interests are affected.

* * * * *

c. *Both Laws Confer Rights.*—Finally, in some cases more than one law is prima facie applicable. This occurs whenever the multistate contacts are arranged in a way that affects more than one state's domestic policy. Of course, the fact that two laws apply to the same facts is not always problematic. Overlapping laws may comfortably co-exist if applying either law is not inconsistent with and does not undermine the other. This is often the case in wholly domestic situations, and it is true in some multistate cases as well. Consider, for example, *Hurtado v. Superior Court*,[103] which most interest analysts mistakenly treat as an unprovided-for case. A resident of Mexico was killed in California by a California tortfeasor. His surviving widow and children, also residents of Mexico, filed a wrongful death action in California. Both Mexico and California provided a cause of action for wrongful death, but Mexico limited the damages that could be recovered.

On these facts, plaintiff can state a claim under the law of either California or Mexico, for giving plaintiff a right to recover furthers both the regulatory purpose of California tort law (in deterring wrongful conduct in California) and the protective purpose of Mexican tort law (in providing compensation for tort victims who live in Mexico). Of course, it is unlikely that plaintiff would elect to sue under Mexican law, since Mexico authorizes the court to award only limited damages. But if plaintiff made this choice, it would not be inconsistent with or undermine California law. California *allows* but does not *require* plaintiffs to sue for unrestricted damages. In a wholly domestic California case, the plaintiff could settle for less than full recovery if he believed that to be in his interest. Hence, if plaintiff chooses to seek only the limited damages provided under Mexican law, this would not violate California law.

Suppose, however, that plaintiff adopts the more likely course and elects to sue under the law of California. Can defendant successfully argue that plaintiff *must* proceed under Mexican law? We presume that Mexico gives plaintiff a cause of action because it has an interest in seeing that plaintiffs from Mexico are adequately compensated: if an injured person lives in Mexico, the consequences (economic and otherwise) of an injury will be felt primarily in Mexico. But allowing plaintiffs to recover under the more generous law of some other state is not inconsistent with this purpose and therefore does not undermine Mexican law.

Why, then, does Mexico limit the amount of damages a plaintiff can recover? Damages limitations on wrongful death serve a protective purpose: concerned that sympathy will move factfinders to inflate the intangible losses associated with death, the legislature fixes a maximum amount that can be awarded. However, * * * we presume that Mexico limits this protection to defendants from Mexico, leaving other states free to determine the liability of non-Mexican defendants. Allowing plaintiff to recover damages from a California defendant under California's more generous law is therefore not inconsistent with and does not undermine Mexican law. Accordingly, plaintiff is free to pursue a remedy under the law of either California or Mexico.

---

[103] 11 Cal. 3d 574, 522 P.2d 666, 114 Cal. Rptr. 106 (1974).

Hurtado is a case in which the laws of different states provide alternative remedies. Most of the time, however, if different laws from more than one state are prima facie applicable, the domestic policies of the states will be incompatible, and applying the law of one state will undermine the law of the other. In such cases, it no longer makes sense to assume that plaintiff is free to choose the remedy. Suppose, for example, that the defendant in *Hurtado* was from Mexico. California would give plaintiff a right to recover unrestricted damages, since the accident occurred in California; Mexico would limit plaintiff's damages. Allowing plaintiff to recover unrestricted damages under California law would undermine Mexico's law, which protects Mexican defendants from excessive damages in wrongful death actions. But denying plaintiff the opportunity to seek full damages by applying Mexico's law would undermine California's regulatory policy respecting deterrence of conduct in California.

In cases like this, the choice of law dispute is not resolved by the first step. The problem remains and requires further analysis.

C. *The Second Step: Resolving "True Conflicts"*

It will be helpful in understanding the second step of the analysis briefly to summarize what the first step accomplishes. A choice of law problem is presented whenever parties disagree about what law governs their dispute. However, the mere fact that the parties disagree about the applicable law does not mean that there is a conflict of laws. On the contrary, the court's first task in addressing a choice of law problem is to determine whether there is such a conflict; special principles of conflict resolution are needed only if more than one law applies to the same facts. Since we know that laws are not intended to regulate universally, the possible cases must be divided into two groups: (1) those that are connected to a state in such a way that the state wants to regulate them, and (2) those that are not so connected. A multistate conflict of laws exists only when contacts are distributed such that more than one state wants to regulate the case.

It is obviously critical, then, to define the line between cases in the first group and cases in the second. This is difficult because lawmakers seldom say anything about extraterritorial applications. The first step of the analysis seeks to overcome this difficulty: it describes a method of interpretation to fill these gaps and identify which contact or contacts must be located in a state for that state's law to apply. This reveals which cases present conflicts, and, at the same time, clarifies the applicable law in cases that do not. Further analysis is still required in the cases identified as true conflicts: since more than one state's law applies, the court must employ some second-order principle to determine whose law should give way. This is the second step of the analysis.

1. *The Inadequacy of Forum Law.*—Suppose, then, that a court in State *A* finds itself faced with a true conflict between State *A* law and State *B* law: how can this conflict be resolved? At first blush, the obvious solution for a State *A* court might seem to be to apply State *A* law. The case is, by hypothesis, connected to State *A* in a way that affects a domestic policy embodied in State *A* law, and failure to apply State *A* law will impair that policy. This is, to be sure, also true for State *B*. But the primary concern of a State *A* court is and must be State *A* law. State *A* courts are, after all, agents of State *A*'s citizenry and lawmakers, and their paramount responsibility should be the implementation of State *A* law. It is one thing to make room for the laws of other states in cases that do not implicate State *A* law. But when State *A* law is at stake, State *A* lawmakers can be presumed to want it applied. Ideally, State *A* lawmakers probably want State *A* law applied regardless of the forum. But if that is too much to expect given State

B's interest, State *A* lawmakers should at least be able to count on having State *A* law applied in a State *A* forum.

This argument for resolving true conflicts by applying forum law assumes that if a court interprets State *A* law to apply only when a particular contact is located in State *A*, it should also interpret that law always to apply when that contact is located in the state. State *A* could do this if it wanted. But we are dealing with laws that say nothing about extraterritorial applications. I have argued that courts should interpret these laws to apply only in cases that are connected to the state in a way that implicates the domestic policy justifying the law in wholly domestic cases. But it does not follow that courts should necessarily interpret these laws always to apply in such cases. On the contrary, there are at least three good reasons not to interpret State *A* law this way unless State *A* lawmakers have said so explicitly.

First, apart from the specific policies reflected in particular laws, states share what are usually called "multistate policies" that may point toward the application of another state's law: policies like comity toward other states, facilitating multistate activity and providing a legal regime whose enforcement is uniform and predictable. Presuming that forum law is intended to apply in every case that implicates the specific policy underlying that law ignores these multistate policies. Yet there are certainly cases in which the state's interest in effectuating multistate policies should override the domestic policies underlying a particular law.

Second, resolving true conflicts by applying the law of the forum encourages forum shopping. A few scholars have suggested that the evils of forum shopping are exaggerated, but most commentators agree that rules facilitating this strategic behavior are undesirable. Put to one side the argument that allowing plaintiffs to choose the forum is "unfair" to defendants— an argument more complicated and less obvious than is generally recognized. Forum shopping still encourages the selection of forums that may be uneconomical for one or both parties. And the incentive to find a forum with favorable law leads plaintiffs to sue in courts whose power over the defendant is doubtful, thereby engendering unnecessary jurisdictional disputes. Thus, even if the costs of forum shopping are smaller than is commonly supposed, there are still costs to be avoided if possible.

Third, always applying forum law is not necessarily in State *A*'s best interests even if those interests are defined narrowly in terms of the domestic policies underlying particular laws (i.e., even if multistate policies are ignored). If every state adopts the "law of the forum" solution, State *A*'s policies will be advanced only in true conflicts that are litigated in State *A* courts. But there is no guarantee that this will include even half the cases. For instance, many cases that implicate prodefendant State *A* laws will not be brought in State *A*, since plaintiffs may shop for a more favorable forum. And the availability of declaratory relief—which allows potential defendants to seize the initiative in filing suit—makes uncertain even the likelihood that cases involving proplaintiff State *A* laws will be brought in State *A*. Moreover, State *A* probably cares more about some true conflicts than others, and there is no assurance that the cases in which State *A* most wants its law applied will be brought in State *A*. From a selfish and parochial point of view, then, it may still be in State *A*'s interests to apply other states' laws in some true conflicts in State *A* courts, thereby inviting reciprocal action that advances State *A* policies in cases brought elsewhere.

Accordingly, unless a law clearly specifies that it applies without regard for any other state's law, it makes sense to assume that some true conflicts should be resolved by applying another state's law. The question is: which ones?

2. *The Idea of a Constructive Multistate Compact and Baxter's Principle of Comparative Impairment.*—Professor Baxter offered a helpful way to think about this question in his

insightful 1963 article, *Choice of Law and the Federal System*.[121] Baxter asks what would happen if lawmakers from two states were to negotiate a multistate agreement on the respective application of their laws in conflict cases. Although Baxter does not explain why this inquiry is appropriate, the question follows from the analysis above. All three arguments for rejecting a forum law solution suggest the need for states to compromise with one another in order to maximize the extent to which they can successfully implement their domestic and multistate policies. In an ideal world, then, states would negotiate multistate choice of law compacts with solutions to true conflicts. These agreements would be part of the states' positive law, and the problem of resolving conflicts of law would disappear.

Such agreements represent a multistate analogue to the idea that a single state's laws are part of a system of laws that are intended to fit together. Just as this system provides a basis for resolving domestic conflicts of law by establishing principles for making choices, so a multistate agreement would provide principles for choosing between the competing laws of different states.

Unfortunately, states have not made such agreements. As with the question of what contacts make a law prima facie applicable, state lawmakers usually say nothing about how to resolve conflicts of laws. Thus, courts must fill this gap as well. Baxter's hypothetical interstate negotiation is simply an application of the same conventional method of interpretation used to resolve domestic conflicts of law and to determine prima facie applicability. Lacking specific guidance from state lawmakers, "the judge must decide what attribution of meaning . . . will yield the most reasonable result in the case at hand."[124] Since the ideal solution would be a negotiated compromise, the court should ask what lawmakers would likely do if they negotiated a multistate agreement—in effect creating a constructive multistate compact. Then, if the courts' interpretations are wrong, the legislature can overrule them.

But what should this constructive multistate agreement look like? Baxter argues persuasively that no state would agree to subordinate its law on the ground that the state's law reflects value judgments that are less worthy or important than those of another state. But that need not end the negotiations. For even conceding that states would not agree that any one state's law is "better," negotiators would presumably recognize that there is a range of cases affecting their policies in different ways and to different degrees. Each state, moreover, would especially want its law applied in the cases that most affect the state's policy. Thus, as the negotiations proceed, each state "would cautiously give up what it wanted less to obtain what it wanted more, . . . and the final agreement would approximate maximum utility to each."[126]

According to Baxter, courts can replicate the likely outcome of such multistate negotiations with a principle of "comparative impairment": "to subordinate, in the particular case, the external objective of the state whose internal objective will be least impaired in general scope and impact by subordination in cases like the one at hand."[127] A state's "internal objective" is the policy that led the state to enact a law for domestic cases; a state's "external objective" is its desire to extend that law to multistate cases that implicate the state's internal objective. In other words, Baxter concludes that courts should resolve true conflicts by applying the law of the state whose domestic policy would be more impaired if that state's law were not applied. This

---

[121]   Baxter, [*Choice of Law and the Federal System*, 16 STAN. L. REV. 1, 9-10 (1963)].

[124]   R. Posner, [THE FEDERAL COURTS: CRISIS AND REFORM 286 (1985)] at 287* * *.

[126]   [Baxter, *Choice of Law and the Federal System*, 16 STAN. L. REV. 1, 7-8 (1963)].

[127]   *Id*. at 18.

approach, Baxter argues, maximizes the likelihood that each state's law will be applied in the cases that are most important to it.

While the principle of "comparative impairment" is conceptually appealing, it is not a practical solution for most multistate cases. This can be demonstrated with Baxter's own illustrations of the method. Precisely because these are illustrations, one expects them to be easy and clear; that they are not suggests the limits of comparative impairment analysis as a workable means of resolving true conflicts.

Baxter's first example involves a highway accident in which one State Y resident injures another State Y resident while driving on State X highways in violation of the X speed limit. Speeding is per se negligent under the law of State X, but not State Y. On these facts, State X has a regulatory interest in deterring unsafe driving on State X highways; State Y has a protective interest in not shifting costs between State Y residents in circumstances it deems inappropriate (Baxter calls this a "loss-distribution" interest). Hence, the case presents a true conflict. Applying comparative impairment analysis, Baxter concludes that State Y's law should apply:

> [T]he X regulatory interest will not be impaired significantly if it is subordinated in the comparatively rare instances involving two nonresidents, who are residents of a state or states that reject the per se subrule. Conduct on X highways will not be affected by knowledge of Y residents that the X per se rule will not be applied to them if the person they injure happens to be a co-citizen.[131]

This is undoubtedly correct: because accidents in State X between State Y residents are rare, applying State Y law in such cases will only marginally impair State X's deterrent policy. But then is it not also true that if State X law is applied the impairment of State Y's loss-distribution policy will be minimal for the same reason? What is the basis for Baxter's confident assertion that the (incremental) impairment of State Y's loss-distribution policy is greater than the (incremental) impairment of State X's deterrence policy? Note that the problem is not merely that the degree of impairment of the two laws is close. The problem is that Baxter is comparing apples and oranges—a regulatory policy of deterrence is qualitatively different from a distributive policy for allocating losses. There is no metric for making a comparison.

In addition, comparative impairment analysis cannot account for differences in the intensity of state interests. Consider Baxter's discussion of a case in which a State Y driver injures a State X resident in State X. According to Baxter, State X's per se negligence rule should apply because "X has an interest in implementing its regulatory provision, and its interest in the application of its loss-distribution rule (which arises because an X resident was injured) offsets Y's corresponding loss-distribution interest."[133] This is true if both states are equally committed to their loss-distribution policies. But what if State Y is more deeply committed to its loss-distribution policy than State X? How does Baxter know that State Y lawmakers do not care more about the impairment of State Y's loss-distribution policy than State X lawmakers care about the combined impairment of State X's loss-distribution and deterrent policies? These questions are especially nettlesome if—as is usually the case—the extent to which either state's policy will be impaired is small.

Baxter dismisses the suggestion that comparative impairment analysis is too difficult to use, protesting that as with any legal rule we must expect hard cases. But all of Baxter's examples can be similarly criticized, and these are supposed to be the easy cases. The judgments

---

[131] *Id.* at 13.

[133] *Id.*

required to determine comparative impairment are simply too subjective and too complex for judges to make in practice. For further proof, one need only examine actual cases decided under comparative impairment analysis.[135]

I do not mean to suggest that the principle of comparative impairment is useless. On the contrary, I suggest a limited but important role for comparative impairment analysis * * *. My point is rather that we cannot rely on comparative impairment to resolve all or even most true conflicts. Moreover, I seriously doubt that lawmakers negotiating an actual multistate agreement would approach the problem this way. Elaborating the range of possible cases and bargaining about which state cares more about which cases would be too difficult and time-consuming.

This conclusion does not affect my earlier conclusions that the ideal way to resolve true conflicts would be by multistate compact, and that courts should analyze the problem in terms of a constructive multistate agreement. The discussion above suggests only that the contours of this constructive agreement cannot be determined by comparative impairment analysis.

3. *Developing Multistate Canons of Construction.*—In domestic cases, courts employ techniques like comparative impairment to solve some cases, but once these methods are exhausted, the courts turn to simpler canons of construction developed specifically to guide choice of law decisions. These canons embody judicial assumptions about how the state's system of laws should be organized. They operate as default rules, directing the court's decision about which law to apply absent a clear statement of actual intent.

The same strategy is appropriate in the multistate context. Lacking specific guidance from state lawmakers about how to integrate forum law with the conflicting laws of other states, courts should articulate presumptive rules of construction that serve this purpose. Like the canons used to resolve domestic conflicts, these principles of construction would operate as default rules—guiding the court's decision about whose law to apply absent specific directions to the contrary from state lawmakers. A set of such canons would give content to the metaphor of a constructive multistate agreement.

Of course, the content of multistate canons will differ from the canons used in the domestic context. The canons developed for domestic cases reflect assumptions unique to organizing laws within a single sovereignty. Thus, these canons are either justified by the fact that the conflicting laws come from a single lawmaker, or they are grounded in a normative preference for the authority of one lawmaker over another. Such thinking is inappropriate in a multistate setting, where a fundamental assumption is that competing laws are enacted by separate, but co-equal sovereigns. Multistate canons must reflect the kind of compromises co-equal sovereigns would be likely to make. At the very least, such canons should leave states better off than if they always applied forum law with respect to the three considerations discussed above: (1) the advancement of multistate policies, (2) the reduction of forum shopping, and (3) greater assurance that each state's law is applied in the cases the state cares about most.

Some Proposed Canons of Construction for True Conflicts

* * * * *

A. *A Comparative Impairment Canon: If there is a conflict between two states' laws, and failure to apply one of the laws would render it practically ineffective, that law should be applied*

---

[135]   See, e.g., Offshore Rental Co. v. Continental Oil Co., 22 Cal. 3d 157, 583 P.2d 721, 148 Cal. Rptr. 867 (1978); Bernhard v. Harrah's Club, 16 Cal. 3d 313, 546 P.2d 719, 128 Cal. Rptr. 215, cert. denied, 429 U.S. 859 (1976). * * *

I suggested above that Baxter's comparative impairment analysis is too subjective and too complex to use as a general principle for resolving true conflicts. There are, however, a few cases in which the impairment is such that courts can safely conclude that both states would agree whose law applies. * * *

* * * * *

* * * When one state's law may be rendered unenforceable if it is not applied, it is fair to assume with Baxter that both states would agree to apply that law (since both states are likely to have some laws that fit this description).

It makes sense, moreover, to apply this canon first, resolving cases covered by it before turning to other canons. Most true conflicts pose only a minor threat to either state's domestic policy, since failure to apply a law in multistate cases seldom affects the law's efficacy in the domestic cases that constitute most of its applications. But the stakes are higher where non-application in multistate cases will also frustrate the state's policy in domestic cases—as was true of Oregon's spendthrift law in *Lilienthal*. Since this may describe some laws in every state, it is in every state's interest to resolve such conflicts by preventing any state's law from being rendered entirely ineffective.

B. *A Substance/Procedure Canon: In a conflict between a substantive policy and a procedural policy, the law reflecting the substantive policy should prevail unless the forum's procedural interest is so strong that the forum should dismiss on grounds of forum non conveniens*

The First Restatement provides that "[a]ll matters of procedure are governed by the law of the forum."[159] This rule is justified on grounds of necessity: to achieve "theoretically complete uniformity of right and duty" the forum should adopt the procedures of the state whose substantive law is to determine the outcome, but the difficulty of learning foreign procedural rules makes this impractical. The First Restatement therefore draws a bright line between laws that define a "right" (which are "substantive" for choice of law purposes), and laws that define a "remedy" (which are "procedural"). Under this rubric, such matters as trial by jury, burden of proof, statutes of limitations and damages limitations are treated as questions of procedure.

Commentators have long recognized that the First Restatement's treatment of substance and procedure is inadequate. Today, most choice of law scholars agree that there is more to classifying a rule as "substantive" or "procedural" than simply determining whether the rule formally regulates the process of obtaining a remedy. Rather, as with other choice of law issues, the classification of a state's procedural rules depends on their purpose.

Generally speaking, rules of procedure are designed to organize the litigation process. The "procedural" label refers to the fact that the purpose of these rules is to facilitate efficient and accurate adjudication. Such rules are regulatory—the conduct regulated being the conduct of litigation—and they are triggered whenever litigation is conducted in the state's courts.

Some rules, however, regulate the trial process in order to affect primary conduct or for some purpose other than to facilitate efficient or accurate adjudication. Evidentiary privileges are a familiar example of this kind of rule, as is the rule of evidence excluding proof of subsequent remedial measures. The applicability of these rules depends on whether the lawsuit affects the conduct or parties that the rule targets, and they do not become applicable simply because a lawsuit is being litigated in the state's courts. These rules are "substantive" rather than "procedural."[164]

---

[159] Restatement of Conflict of Laws § 585 (1934).

[164] See 2 J. Weinstein & M. Berger, Weinstein's Evidence ¶ 407[2], at 407-14- -15 (1989) (subsequent remedial measures); id. ¶ 501[2] (privileges).

Some rules, finally, are both substantive and procedural in that they have both substantive and procedural purposes. Consider, for example, statutes of limitations. On the one hand, a statute of limitations serves a "substantive" purpose by giving potential defendants a definite time after which they need not worry about liability; this provides psychological comfort and allows the defendant to free assets he or she might otherwise hold in reserve.

On the other hand, a statute of limitations also serves a "procedural" purpose by ensuring that cases are not decided on the basis of stale evidence and by allocating limited judicial resources to more recent cases. Examples of other rules that are both substantive and procedural include burdens of production and persuasion, Dead Man's rules and statutes of fraud.

* * *

Conflicts between the forum's procedural policies and another state's substantive policies are especially likely with respect to rules that serve both substantive and procedural purposes. * * *

The traditional solution calls for these cases to be resolved by applying forum law. Surprisingly, most contemporary scholars would still do the same. The modern learning defines "substance" and "procedure" differently than the First Restatement. As a result, certain rules —like privileges—that were once treated as procedural are now regarded as substantive. But most scholars still feel that if the forum has a legitimate procedural interest, forum law should be applied. This preference for forum procedural interests contrasts sharply with the treatment of substance procedure conflicts in the analogous context of diversity cases. Under the *Erie* doctrine, the Supreme Court has recognized that federal procedural rules can trump conflicting state rules, but it has consistently applied the state rule when that rule served a substantive purpose— subordinating legitimate federal procedural policies to state substantive policies.

The proposed canon adopts the balance struck in the *Erie* context. This conclusion rests on the assumption that states generally prefer substantive to procedural policies. After all, the ultimate purpose of procedural law is to implement substantive law accurately and efficiently. Moreover, when conflicts arise in domestic cases between substantive and procedural laws, the usual solution is to favor the substantive rule.

* * * * *

C. *A Canon for Contract Cases: In contract cases, true conflicts should be resolved by applying the law chosen by the parties, or, if no express choice is made, by applying whichever law validates the contract*

As the discussion below indicates, I advance this canon somewhat tentatively. Let me begin by making clear its intended scope. First, I am not proposing that parties should always be free to choose the law that governs their contract. That would be tantamount to repealing the law of contract by enabling parties to opt out of any limitation not imposed by every state or nation in the world. But states are entitled (within constitutional limits) to deprive parties of the freedom to make choices the state's lawmakers deem undesirable, and such laws are routinely enforced in ordinary domestic litigation. What is true for wholly domestic cases, moreover, is also true for multistate cases in which only one state's law is prima facie applicable. A state has no reason to defer to the parties' choice if its law is not in conflict with the law of another state. Where there is such a conflict, however, the state must find a way to choose between the potentially applicable laws. One way to make this choice is to delegate it to the parties.

The parties should thus be allowed to choose only when there is potential for a true conflict. And even in those cases, the parties should not be allowed to choose any law they like.

If a state forgoes applying its law in true conflicts, it is only to accommodate the applicable law of another state. Even if the state decides to resolve true conflicts by delegating the power to choose to the parties, it has no reason to make the parties' choice broader than the conflicting laws.

But why should a state delegate to the parties even this limited power to resolve true conflicts? First, assuming that parties usually choose the law that gives them the most freedom, this canon favors less restrictive laws in true conflict cases. This is preferable to simply applying forum law because, while all states have laws restricting or limiting parties' power to make contracts, these laws are exceptions to a general, pervasive policy favoring freedom of contract. Under this canon, then, each state is "compensated" for subordinating its restrictive policies by the advancement of its more fundamental policy of freedom of contract when that policy conflicts with the restrictive laws of other states.

In addition—perhaps I should say more importantly—allowing the parties to choose advances a shared multistate interest in fostering certainty and predictability. While this policy is generally beneficial, it is particularly important in the area of contracts. Providing an efficient and profitable commercial environment depends on the parties' ability accurately to foretell their rights and liabilities under a contract. Hence, a predictable solution to true conflicts is essential. What better way to facilitate this goal than to let the parties choose for themselves?

In truth, neither of these arguments is completely convincing, which is why I propose this canon only tentatively. * * *

* * * * *

D. *A Canon for Laws that are Obsolete: Where one of two conflicting laws is obsolete (i.e., inconsistent with prevailing legal and social norms in the state that enacted it), the other law should be applied.*

In his celebrated book, *A Common Law for the Age of Statutes*, Dean Calabresi advances the thesis that courts should be able to "overrule" statutes that are obsolete without having to declare them unconstitutional. Over time, Calabresi notes, statutes that were functional when enacted may become dysfunctional without being officially laid to rest by legislative repeal. Instead, these laws remain on the books to be rediscovered from time to time. When they are invoked, observers agree that these outdated statutes are silly, if not manifestly unjust, yet no action is taken to repeal them. There are a number of ways to explain this: legislators seldom monitor their laws effectively and may be unaware of these infrequent decisions; even if they are aware, legislators are generally too occupied with new business to devote time to old problems that are not pressing; legislators rarely disturb the status quo without pressure from some interested group, and the effects of obsolete laws are usually too diffuse or too sporadic to generate organized lobbying efforts. Whatever the explanation, these obsolete laws remain formally viable even though they no longer have majoritarian support and cannot realistically be said to reflect commitment to any actual policy. They are leftovers—vestiges to be removed when lawmakers find the time, the inclination and the immediate need to deal with them.

Just when a law becomes obsolete is not always obvious. Dean Calabresi argues that at some point legislative and judicial innovations will have altered the legal landscape enough that it will be apparent that a law no longer "fits" the "legal topography."[197] The signs to watch for include whether the law reflects judgments appropriate to an earlier time but inconsistent with prevailing social norms; whether the law is based on a theory of liability or obligation that has

---

[197]   [G. CALABRESI, A COMMON LAW FOR THE AGE OF STATUTES 21 (1982)].

been repudiated in subsequent laws dealing with related issues; and whether the law, which was once similar to laws in other states, is now inconsistent with more recent enactments in those states. In any event, even giving most laws the benefit of the doubt to minimize error, some are obviously anachronistic and obsolete.

Examples of obsolete laws are found in many well-known choice of law cases. *Grant v. McAuliffe*,[200] for example, involved an Arizona rule that tort actions abate if not brought before the death of the tortfeasor. This rule rested on an outmoded theory that civil liability is punitive, whereas the rest of Arizona's tort law had long since been modified to reflect modern notions of compensation and deterrence. Other illustrations include the Massachusetts law at issue in *Milliken v. Pratt*,[202] which prohibited married women from making contracts to guarantee a third person's debts (and was already obsolete in 1878); and the Washington law at issue in *Erwin v. Thomas*,[204] which prohibited wives but not husbands from recovering for loss of consortium.

* * * * *

E. *A Canon for Actual Reliance Interests: Where two laws conflict, but the parties actually and reasonably relied on one of them, that law should be applied*

Courts sometimes decide cases by determining the "reasonable expectations" of the parties, and it is tempting to use this construct as a basis for developing additional canons. The problem is that the existence of "reasonable expectations" is not an objective question. Statements about the parties' reasonable expectations mask normative judgments reflecting what a court believes the parties ought to expect. Consequently, one must defend the judgments underlying such canons.

Of course, some judgments about what parties ought to expect are so widely shared as to be uncontroversial. These judgments (intuitions may be more accurate) are usually incorporated into the due process clause of the fifth or fourteenth amendments to the Constitution. In choice of law, for example, a state's law cannot be applied unless there is some connection between the state and the dispute.[210] A defendant from Illinois involved in an accident in Wisconsin can "reasonably" expect that the law of Timbuktu will not be applied. Unfortunately, we cannot say much more than that. For example, the defendant could, as a matter of due process, reasonably expect either Illinois or Wisconsin law to be applied.

Because most laws are prima facie applicable only if there is a significant connection to the state, few true conflicts can be decided based on the reasonable expectations protected by the due process clause. But it is difficult to go farther and justify choosing one state's law as the law parties must "reasonably" expect. As a result, arguments to resolve conflicts according to the parties' reasonable expectations tend to be conclusory and circular. Consider, for example, Professor Cavers' "principles of preference." Cavers favors the place of injury in many tort cases because he believes that this connecting factor embodies what most people reasonably expect. Moreover, the presumption is prescriptive since Cavers would insist on this result even if the parties' actual expectations were different. But Cavers cannot justify his belief beyond observing that it is widely shared, and it is widely shared mostly because it has been

---

[200]   41 Cal. 2d 859, 264 P.2d 944 (1953).

[202]   125 Mass. 374 (1878).

[204]   264 Or. 454, 506 P.2d 494 (1973).

[210]   *See* Allstate Ins. Co. v. Hague, 449 U.S. 302, 308 (1981).

observed in the past. There is nothing natural or prelegal about this expectation. In an earlier era, when the applicable law turned on nationality, people undoubtedly had different expectations.

Now suppose instead that among the various laws that could be applied, we know that the parties actually did rely on a particular one. Is that fact entitled to recognition in the choice of law analysis? The law often gives weight to actual reliance. This corresponds to a generally accepted principle of fairness: where the choice among legitimate options is ambiguous, a party is presumptively entitled to the benefit of the option on which he actually relied. To be sure, this consideration is often outweighed by the state's desire to advance a different policy deemed more important. But actual reliance is a factor to take into account, and where other factors are in equipoise it may provide a basis for decision.

The argument for making a canon out of this principle should be familiar by now: all states probably agree that actual and reasonable reliance on one of several options deserves consideration. In wholly domestic cases, this consideration might be subordinated to one of the state's substantive policies. In a multistate conflict situation, however, this other policy is matched by the policy of the state upon whose law the parties relied. Since the court cannot choose between these laws, the case is—for all practical purposes—in equipoise. We can therefore break the tie by choosing the law on which the parties actually relied. The state whose law is not applied forgoes an opportunity to advance the policy underlying its law, but enhances the likelihood that its law will be applied in other cases if the parties rely on it. In addition, both states advance the shared policy of fairness.

* * * * *

The Role of Reciprocity

* * * * *

But are such canons likely to succeed? This depends first on whether the canons accurately reflect policy preferences, which depends in turn on arguments like those [above]. But even if the canons are successful in this regard, in deciding whether to adopt them, a state must consider the extent to which the canons depend on reciprocity from other states. Should State A adopt canons that subordinate State A law in some true conflicts if other states do not follow suit? The canons will advance multistate policies and reduce forum shopping to some extent even if other states do not reciprocate. Although these gains would obviously be greater if other states applied the canons, the benefits might still be large enough to justify the sacrifice of forum policies called for by the canons.

In fact, I doubt that adopting the canons leaves State A better off than applying forum law if other states do not reciprocate. Without reciprocity, any gains in multistate policies and reduced forum shopping are likely to be too small to compensate for the sacrifice of State A's domestic policies. In that case, State A may not want to adopt the canons unless State B does too, so that State A's sacrifice is offset by the application of State A law in some true conflicts brought in State B.

State A must therefore consider whether it can expect reciprocity from other states before adopting the canons. At first blush, the situation does not look promising. State B is arguably better off not adopting the canons if State A adopts them, since State B law will then be applied in all true conflicts brought in State B plus some true conflicts brought in State A. Therefore, once State B learns that State A has adopted the canons, is it not in State B's interest to adhere to a lex fori approach more strongly than ever? But if State B will not reciprocate, why should State A adopt the canons in the first place? Better to follow Currie's original advice by applying forum law in all true conflicts and leaving it to other lawmakers to negotiate an alternative.

States A and B thus seem to be caught in a choice of law version of the prisoner's dilemma.[224] Each state must choose a strategy. The states could appoint representatives to negotiate a cooperative choice of law solution, but they have not done so. Instead, the states have left the choice of strategies to judges. Since the judges cannot negotiate, they must choose independently. There are several possible outcomes. First, State A and State B could both always apply forum law. This strategy produces some benefit to each state in that it assures the application of each state's law in cases brought in the state. But it is less than perfect because it sacrifices multistate policies altogether, because it encourages forum shopping and because each state's law is only applied in cases litigated in that state's courts.

Alternatively, both states could cooperate by applying canons like those proposed in Part IV. As I argued there, this will leave both states better off by reducing forum shopping and by advancing both multistate and domestic policies. The risk is that judges from State A will choose the canons while judges from State B will adhere to applying forum law. This leaves State B better off than if both states apply forum law: State B's domestic policy is now advanced in all cases brought in State B and in some cases brought in State A. But it also leaves State A worse off than if both states always apply forum law: whatever minimal gains State A realizes in reduced forum shopping and the advancement of multistate policies do not compensate for the sacrifice of State A domestic policies.

Hence, the best mutual decision is for both states to apply the canons. But if either state takes this step without cooperation from the other, that state is worse off than if it just applies

---

[224]   In this familiar hypothetical, X and Y are arrested on suspicion of having committed a serious offense. Without a confession, the District Attorney has only enough evidence to obtain a conviction on a lesser included offense. The DA therefore puts X and Y in separate cells and offers each a deal whereby if one confesses and the other does not, the confessor will get three months imprisonment while the silent partner gets five years; if both confess, they will both get two years; and if neither confesses, they will both get six months.

If X and Y could coordinate their responses to the DA, they would probably agree that neither of them should confess. To be sure, each one might want to hold out for the option in which he confesses and his compatriot does not, since this gives the confessing prisoner the shortest possible sentence. This might even happen if there was a great disparity in bargaining power or if a side-deal could be arranged. (For example, if X can have Y killed, X can give Y a choice between death and five years.) But absent such circumstances, and if there is any willingness to cooperate, the obvious solution is for neither X nor Y to confess.

Game theory nonetheless posits that if X and Y do not consult, they will both confess and go to jail for two years. Consider the situation from X's perspective: If Y confesses and X remains silent, X goes to jail for five years; by confessing, X can lower this sentence to two years. If Y does not confess and X remains silent, X goes to jail for only six months; but if X takes advantage of Y's silence and confesses, X can reduce this sentence to three months. X is thus better off confessing no matter what Y does. Moreover, because the situation is symmetrical, Y faces the same array of possible outcomes. Therefore, both X and Y will confess.

Interestingly, because X and Y acted rationally, both are worse off: if both had cooperated by remaining silent, they would have gotten only six months. But without the opportunity to negotiate, neither can afford to take this risk. Because each is choosing only his own strategy, he must confess or run the risk that the other player will (in which case he goes to jail for five years). This risk makes defection rational under the circumstances. See M. Bacharach, Economics and the Theory of Games 61-64 (1976); R. Luce & H. Raiffa, Games and Decisions: Introduction and Critical Survey 94-97 (1957).

its own law. Thus, if both states act rationally, the analysis above suggests that they will both choose to apply forum law.

In fact, the situation is less bleak than this explanation suggests. The prediction above applies to a game that is played only once. But game theory further posits that if A and B are forced into this situation repeatedly, they will find the cooperative solution and adhere to it. The intuition underlying this prediction is easily explained. If A and B must "play" the prisoner's dilemma repeatedly, the costs of not cooperating on many plays become greater than the costs of being the only player to cooperate on a single play. At some point then, one or both participants will likely take a chance by cooperating. While the risk-taker may suffer on that one play, the cost is worth incurring to signal a willingness to cooperate. Within a few plays, both participants should discover the benefits of cooperation.

* * * * *

Gary J. Simson, *Plotting the Next "Revolution" in Choice of Law: A Proposed Approach*, 24 CORNELL INT'L L.J. 279, 279, 280, 282-284, 287, 288-289, 289-890, 291-294 (1991)*

In this essay I invite readers to consider the attractiveness of the following approach for resolving choice-of-law problems:

1. Ascertain whether any state has a greater *interest in determining the outcome of the case* at hand than the forum state.
2. If so, make the choice(s) of law that a court sitting in the foreign state and applying that state's conflicts law would make.
3. If not, apply forum law with regard to each issue in the case unless:

   a. The foreign elements in the case bring into play a policy that would not be materially implicated if the case were confined in its elements to the forum state;
   b. Such policy militates strongly in favor of a choice of nonforum law; *and*
   c. The policy preference expressed in the forum state's internal law is not so strong as to belie the possibility that the forum state's lawmakers could intend it to yield to another policy in a multistate case.

I outline below reasons for adopting an approach along these lines and expand upon its possible ingredients.* * *

I. The Initial Choice of Jurisdiction

In essence, my proposed approach calls upon a court to make a choice of jurisdiction (identify the state that should have authority to determine the outcome of the case before the court)

---

and then a choice of law (decide the case as the selected jurisdiction would decide it by applying the selected jurisdiction's conflicts law from the perspective of a court sitting in that jurisdiction). Under the approach, the forum state is the selected jurisdiction unless another state has a greater interest in determining the outcome of the case at hand.

A. The Policy Objective and Means-End Strategy

I propose this initial choice of jurisdiction as a means for courts to serve an important policy: maximizing long-term enforcement of the forum state's interests in determining the outcomes of cases with some connection to the forum state. In characterizing this policy as an important one, I do not assume that states ordinarily have interests in the outcome of a conflicts case similar in magnitude to their interests in the outcome of litigation in which the states themselves, rather than private litigants, are the parties. I do assume, however, that at least in the aggregate a state has a material stake in the way in which conflicts cases with some connection to the state are decided.

The proposed approach seeks to implement this interest-maximizing policy by a strategy of identifying the forum state as the selected jurisdiction unless another state has a greater interest. As is probably apparent, this strategy is based on notions of reciprocity. It reflects an assessment of whether, in light of the relative magnitude of state interests, the enforcement of forum state interests is maximized in the long run by (a) enforcing the nonforum interest and thereby inviting reciprocal treatment in cases heard in other states' courts or (b) enforcing the forum interest and thereby forgoing the possible benefits of reciprocity.

* * *

B. Outcome-Determining Interests

In outlining my approach in the introduction, I used italics in the phrase "interest in determining the outcome of the case" to signal the reader that I would not be discussing interests in the usual Currie sense of interests in applying the policies underlying the states' internal laws. After spelling out below more fully the type of interests I have in mind, I contrast them more clearly to Currie-style interests.

Basically, I suggest that a state should be found to have an interest in determining the outcome of a case if and only if the outcome will affect the welfare of people who make their home in the state. As a corollary, I suggest that the magnitude of a state interest of this sort depends upon the magnitude of the effect of the outcome on these people's welfare.

These outcome-determining interests share with Currie-style interests the assumption that a state's interests should in some way be measured in terms of impact on local residents. Under the Currie approach, a policy underlying a state law gives rise to an interest only if application of the policy in some way benefits the residents of the law-making state. In my view—and apparently Currie's as well—an understanding of state interests that attaches special significance to impact on local residents is appropriate in light of the fact that the people who settle in a state are those most likely to benefit or burden its operations.

The outcome-determining interests featured in my approach differ from Currie-style interests, however, in two fundamental ways. First and most obviously, their focus is markedly different. They look at possible outcomes of litigation, while Currie interests look at policies underlying states' internal laws. Moreover, they take into account impact on local residents regardless of its beneficial or disadvantageous nature, while Currie interests take into account only beneficial effects. As may be immediately apparent and as Part II should in any event make clear, the outcome-determining interests in my approach implicitly embrace, by virtue of these differences in focus, a much broader range of state interests than those recognized by the Currie approach. They tacitly acknowledge that states may have interests in applying not only their own internal laws but also—for purposes of furthering such choice-of-law policies as protecting justified expectations or serving the needs of the interstate and international systems—other states' internal laws. Moreover, they tacitly recognize that states may have interests in applying their own internal laws not only to advantage local residents but also—for reasons of basic fairness and morality—to disadvantage them.

The second basic respect in which the outcome-determining interests that I have described differ from Currie interests is that the former are "objective" in the sense of being independent of any wishes, desires, or thought processes on the part of the state. * * * The outcome-determining interests that I describe are ascertained by the court without any such subjective inquiry. The court may not always find it easy to ascertain the effect of the outcome on the residents of the different states with some connection to the facts of the case. I suggest, however, that this inquiry is substantially more manageable and concrete than one, like Currie's, that significantly turns on articulating what state lawmakers had in mind.

* * * * *

II. The Subsequent Choice of Law

* * *

A. When the Forum State is Not the Selected Jurisdiction

Under the proposed approach, if a court concludes that a foreign state has a greater interest in determining outcome than the forum state, it makes the initial choice of jurisdiction in favor of the foreign state and defers to that state's outcome-determining interest as a means of maximizing long-term enforcement of forum interests. The court decides the case as the foreign state would decide it in the hope that its deference to a superior foreign interest will be repaid in kind in cases brought in the foreign state's courts. To decide the case as the foreign state would decide it the court applies the foreign state's conflicts law as if it were sitting in that state.* * *

* * *

Although the policy underlying the proposed choice of jurisdiction broadly dictates deference to the conflicts law of a selected foreign jurisdiction, it allows for nondeference in two types of situations. Most obviously, a court cannot be expected to defer to foreign conflicts law that fails to observe constitutional limitations. In addition, a court need not defer to the foreign conflicts law in resolving a particular issue if the court's resolution of the issue by a law other than the one indicated by the foreign conflicts law presents no material likelihood of affecting the outcome of the case. The latter exception essentially recognizes that deference to another state's outcome-determining interest leaves some room for forum "procedures." In keeping with the policy underlying the proposed choice of jurisdiction, however, the exception limits "procedural" departures from foreign conflicts law to ones that pose no apparent threat of undermining the paramount foreign interest in determining outcome.

* * *

B. When the Forum State Is the Selected Jurisdiction

Under the proposed approach, if a court identifies the forum state as the selected jurisdiction, it should exercise the forum interest in determining the outcome of the case by applying forum law as to each issue in the case unless each of three conditions is satisfied: (1) the foreign elements in the case bring into play a policy that would not be materially implicated if the case were confined in its elements to the forum state; (2) such policy militates strongly in favor of a choice of nonforum law; and (3) the policy preference expressed in the forum state's internal law is not so strong as to belie the possibility that the forum state's lawmakers could intend it to yield to another policy in a multistate case. The basic rationale behind this recommendation is two-fold. First, forum law represents the forum state's considered judgment as to the fairest or most socially beneficial way of resolving cases confined in their elements to the forum state. Second, unless it is reasonably clear that the substitution of one or more out-of-state elements for intrastate ones brings into play a factor that significantly alters the policy balance struck for the intrastate case, respect for that policy balance requires that the court assume that the fairest or most socially beneficial way of resolving the multistate case at hand is by applying forum law.

1. The Forum Law Presumption and State Interests

The presumption in favor of forum law central to this recommendation often may lead a court to vindicate a forum state interest in determining outcome in a way that the Currie school may find anomalous. Assume, for example, that in Y's suit against the tavern, the state B court identifies state B as the selected jurisdiction and goes on to apply the state B dram-shop act on the view that the conditions for nonapplication of forum law are not satisfied. In essence, the court vindicates the forum state's interest in determining outcome—an interest predicated on the forum state's concern for the welfare of one of its residents, the tavern—by applying a law that disadvantages its resident. To Currie-style interest analysts this may appear the height of illogic. A state vindicates its interests, they may protest, by benefiting its residents, not by disadvantaging them.

I suggest that any flaw in logic that this illustration brings to the fore lies in the Currie conception of state interests. There is nothing incongruous about the notion that state B is expressing its interest in the tavern's welfare by applying its law to deny the tavern the protection from liability that the tavern desires. State B's interest in the tavern's welfare is vindicated by applying a law that state B believes deals fairly with defendants who act as the tavern did in the case at hand. In short, a state's interest in its residents' welfare is served when they are treated fairly, not necessarily when they get what they want. * * *

2. Reasons for Departing from Forum Law

In deciding whether the three specified conditions for nonapplication of forum law are met, a court probably should be especially mindful of two policies: protecting justified expectations, and serving the needs of the interstate and international systems. Although other policies may legitimate a departure from forum law, these two seem by a sizable margin those most likely to do so. It is beyond the scope of this essay to attempt to specify criteria for deciding when these policies militate strongly in favor of choosing nonforum law. To provide some guidance, however, as to the kinds of circumstances in which nonapplication of forum law would be appropriate under my proposal, I discuss below the soundness of choices of nonforum law in two well-known cases that implicate these policies. To place my discussions of the cases in proper perspective, I underline that I selected them for purposes of illustration because of their facts, laws, and results, not because of the opinions that the courts wrote in deciding them. Although I refer in places to the courts' opinions in the cases, my concern here is not with the adequacy of the courts' express reasoning, which I do not relate in any detail. Instead, it is with the validity under my proposal of the results they reached.

a. Protecting Justified Expectations

The policy of protecting justified expectations has long been regarded as a policy basic to a fair legal order. Though not peculiar to multistate cases, it may come into play with special force in multistate contexts. *Intercontinental Hotels Corp. v. Golden*,[27] a 1964 decision of the New York Court of Appeals, offers a fact situation in which it does.

Golden, a New York resident, lost $12,000 while gambling on credit in a government-licensed casino in Puerto Rico owned and operated by Intercontinental Hotels Corporation. Under the law of Puerto Rico, the gambling debt was validly contracted and enforceable. Under New York law, it was illegal to operate a gambling casino and any contract made with the operator of such an establishment was void. Intercontinental sued Golden in New York to recover on the gambling contract. On appeal from a judgment dismissing the complaint, the New York high court held that Puerto Rican law governed.

Under the circumstances of the case, the policy of protecting justified expectations provided cogent support for the court's ruling. On the one hand, the policy appeared to militate strongly in favor of choosing Puerto Rican law. Since the contract was entered into in Puerto Rico and covered only gambling that would take place in Puerto Rico, both parties very probably and quite reasonably expected at the time of their agreement that it would be governed by Puerto Rican law. Furthermore, in extending $12,000 in credit to Golden, the plaintiff plainly relied to its detriment on the expectation that Puerto Rican law applied and that the contract was therefore valid and enforceable. Finally, not only was the plaintiff obviously aware that the agreement was valid and enforceable under Puerto Rican law; it is virtually inconceivable that this New York defendant, temporarily in Puerto Rico at least in part to take advantage of its government-licensed gambling facilities, was not aware of this fact as well.

On the other hand, the New York local-law policy that would be subordinated by giving priority to the protection of justified expectations and selecting Puerto Rican law was apparently not one to which New York was very strongly wedded. It was hardly implausible that the state's lawmakers could intend the policy to yield to another in a multistate case. As the court pointed out in the course of rejecting a public policy objection to enforcing the plaintiff's action in a New York court, "[t]he legalization of pari-mutuel betting and the operation of bingo games, as well as a strong movement for legalized off-track betting, indicate that the New York public does not consider authorized gambling a violation of 'some prevalent conception of good morals, [or] some deep-rooted tradition of the common weal.'"[30]

---

27   15 N.Y.2d 9, 254 N.Y.S.2d 527, 203 N.E.2d 210 (1964).

30   15 N.Y.2d at 15, 254 N.Y.S.2d at 531, 203 N.E.2d at 213 (*quoting* Loucks v. Standard Oil Co. of New York, 224 N.Y. 99, 111, 120 N.E. 198, 202 (1918)).

b. Serving Interstate and International Needs

As cases transcend the boundaries of a single state, important needs of the interstate and international systems may emerge as considerations warranting serious attention. One such need is ease of interstate and international commercial intercourse, and *Milliken v. Pratt,*[33] an 1878 Massachusetts case immortalized by Brainerd Currie, offers an instance in which this need warranted serious attention.

At her husband's request, Pratt, a Massachusetts resident, entered into a guaranty contract in 1870 with two partners in a Maine business. The husband, who ran a business in Massachusetts, had applied to the partners for credit, and they had conditioned granting him such credit on his securing the guaranty from his wife. Under Massachusetts law at the time the contract was made, married women lacked capacity to bind themselves by a contract of this sort. Although Massachusetts changed its law by statute in 1874 to remove this incapacity, the 1874 statute did not apply retroactively to contracts made before its enactment. The Maine legislature had removed the same type of incapacity under Maine law several years prior to the guaranty contract in question. The partners brought suit in Massachusetts on the guaranty contract, seeking payment for goods purchased on credit by the husband in 1871. Reversing a judgment below for Pratt, the Massachusetts Supreme Judicial Court held that Maine law applied.

The policy of promoting ease in interstate commercial intercourse furnished persuasive support under the circumstances for the court's choice of law. On the one hand, the policy seemed to point strongly toward a selection of Maine law. As various commentators have suggested, ease in interstate and international commercial transactions would be significantly advanced by upholding commercial contracts as long as they are valid under the law of some state reasonably connected to the transaction. Such a principle of validation would provide valuable certainty and security for transactions crossing state lines. Applied in *Milliken v. Pratt*, it would have called for a choice of the validating law of Maine.

On the other hand, Massachusetts's commitment to the policy preference expressed in its local law was rather clearly not so strong as to belie the possibility that the state could intend to subordinate the policy in a multistate case. As in *Golden*, the portion of the court's opinion in *Milliken* rejecting a public policy defense is instructive in this regard. In finding "no reason of public policy which should prevent the maintenance of this action," the Massachusetts high court in *Milliken* called attention to the fact that Massachusetts by 1870 (the time of the contract at issue) had already deviated substantially from the prevalent common-law rule that "a married woman was deemed incapable of binding herself by any contract whatever." By statute, Massachusetts by 1870 had given a married woman "a very extensive power to carry on business by herself, and to bind herself by contracts with regard to her own property, business and earnings." In addition, the high court underlined that, by virtue of the Massachusetts statute of 1874 noted above, "the power had been extended so as to include the making of all kinds of contracts, with any person but her husband, as if she were unmarried."[40]

* * * * *

---

[33]   125 Mass. 374 (1878).

[40]   *Id.* [at 383.]

Arthur T. von Mehren, *Choice of Law and the Problem of Justice*, 41 LAW & CONTEMP. PROBS. 27, 27-43, (1977)*

* * *

I

For the legal order, the problem of justice is primordial. The most basic and universal test of legal rules and institutions is that they be formally just. Rules and institutions perceived as unjust are unstable and ultimately unacceptable. Justice is a complex concept: like cases should be treated alike; the legal consequences that attach to conduct should be understandable and foreseeable. Rules and institutions must also express and advance values and purposes accepted by the community.

This conception of justice assumes that preferred values and purposes can be determined where disagreement exists or is possible. Until these preferences are authoritatively established, the justice of any given rule or institution is not formally established. A further implication is that legal rules and institutions must be known, or at least knowable, by the individuals for whose activities these rules or institutions have significance. Information must be available about the rules and institutions operative at any given time and, to the extent that the consequences of present action lie in a more or less remote future, the legal order must provide for stability and continuity. The imperatives of equal treatment, stability, and continuity require that rules be uniformly administered and that institutions operate in a coherent manner.

How can the uniform administration of rules and the coherent operation of institutions be assured? Disagreements about values and purposes can be resolved in several ways. Values and purposes may be seen as imposing themselves as a consequence of man's nature or of the culture and traditions of a given society. Alternatively, values and purposes can be determined by institutions charged with this task. The church, the monarch, the executive, the legislature, and the courts have in various degrees at different epochs discharged this function.

These values and purposes, once established, require uniform application in the administration of justice. How is this result to be achieved? Various solutions are theoretically possible but all Western legal orders, including codified systems, rely ultimately on a unified and centralized administration of justice. A single authority—the highest court—seeks to ensure the uniform application of legal rules and the coherent functioning of legal institutions. So that those whose activities are regulated by the legal order will be in a position to understand, by and large, the legal consequences of their actions, legislation and judicial decisions are published and an active and skilled legal profession is available. Legal rules are given considerable stability by the principle that legislative changes ordinarily have only prospective effect and by the proposition, expressed in various ways, that the courts, in particular the highest court, will only in exceptional circumstances change their views, once these have been stated, about the meaning and application of any given rule or principle. Finally, to ensure that legal rules and institutions remain responsive to the values and purposes held by the legal order they serve, procedures are provided through which unresponsive rules and institutions can be changed. The legislature has the primary responsibility for changing rules and institutions thought to be unwise or unjust. Comparable adjustments and determinations may, to a considerable extent, also take place judicially or administratively. Disagreement can, of course, exist within a society not only as to the justice or wisdom of a rule or an institution but also as

---

*   Reprinted with permission.

to the change that is required. To the extent that such disagreements exist, they will be authoritatively resolved for the society by the legislature, the courts, or the executive. In some societies, values and purposes that are considered basic are given special protection in the sense that they can be changed only through special procedures—in particular, constitutional amendment or, though in most legal orders to a lesser extent, decision of a court charged with deciding constitutional questions.

From the foregoing it follows that justice can be fully achieved only where the legal unit coincides with the social or economic unit within which the given problem has arisen. In the modern world, this condition is fulfilled to a considerable extent as the relevant legal, economic, and social units are typically nation states. Great difficulties have, however, been experienced in the relatively recent past with the problem of justice when the effective legal unit was smaller than the significant social and economic units. For example, France and Germany did not resolve the problem until the French Revolution of 1789 and the creation of the German Reich in 1871, respectively, made effective and centralized administration of justice possible for all of France and all of Germany. Today, to the extent that contemporary economic and social life spills across the boundaries of nation states, the problem of justice remains, as we shall see, most perplexing.

The coincidence of legal, social, and economic units is important in still another respect for the problem of justice. Where such coincidence exists, legal rules and institutions have a claim to acceptance by those affected by the rule's application or the institution's operation as they are members of the community and participate in its social, economic, and political life. They can be taken, accordingly, to accept the values and purposes that inform these rules and institutions. To the extent that the persons affected belong to different communities, the basis for such an inference disappears, at least where the respective communities do not share the same values and purposes.

II

It follows from what has been said above that neither justice nor acceptance by those affected by a rule's application or institution's operation is fully achieved where the legal, social, and economic units involved do not coincide. In the modern world, the phenomenon of non-coincidence is typically the result of economic or social activities having significant relations or connections with more than one sovereign legal order. In such situations, rules are developed and applied and institutions operate without the possibility of resolving authoritatively such disagreements as may exist with respect to values and purposes. Furthermore, to the extent that the persons affected belong to different communities and these communities do not share the same values and purposes, the sociological and political bases for acceptance of a rule's application or an institution's operation are significantly diminished. In addition, these situations frequently require a choice between two principles of justice that are not opposed in fully domestic cases. These principles are that like cases be treated alike and that rules of law advance and express values and purposes accepted by society.

These shortcomings in the handling of multistate cases when compared with wholly domestic cases inhere in the multistate situation as does the necessity, only very rarely presented in domestic cases, of choosing between the two competing principles of justice noted, that like cases be treated alike and that rules of law advance and express values and purposes accepted by society. Choice-of-law methodologies must accept these inherent shortcomings. They can seek to reduce to the greatest extent possible the number of cases in which a choice must be made between the principle of equal treatment and that of advancing the community's purposes.

Ultimately, however, each methodology faces the question of which principle to prefer where the two clash.

Having concluded that justice can rarely—if ever—be as fully achieved in multistate cases as in domestic cases, we can explore the problems of justice central to multistate cases. These are basically two: First, should one seek to avoid the choice between the principles of equal treatment and of advancing values? Second, if choice is unavoidable, which principle is to be preferred? These matters are considered seriatim.

III

Theoretically, choice between the two basic principles of justice in question—equal treatment and the advancement of values—should be avoided whenever possible. Absent other considerations, a result that satisfies both principles is more just than a result satisfying only one. Why then do not the traditional or classic approaches to the choice-of-law problem, as seen for example in the works of Beale and Savigny, address themselves in a central and sustained fashion to the problem of limiting, to the greatest extent possible, the need for such a choice?

At least two explanations can be ventured. In the first place, to the extent that traditional theories see choice of law as resulting from a kind of juristic inevitability there is nothing open for discussion. If the application of a choice-of-law rule does not advance the forum's values— or, for that matter, the values of any concerned community—that is unfortunate, but unavoidable. On the other hand, if a choice-of-law rule permits forum shopping, the responsibility rests with the other legal order's rule which is simply wrong.

Another and more satisfying explanation for the position taken by traditional theories is possible. Choice between the two competing principles of justice can be avoided where the several communities with which the case has significant connections in fact accept the same values and purposes; in such situations each can choose the same law and advance its values and purposes. But the only way to determine whether the concerned communities agree on values and purposes is to undertake a functional or instrumental analysis of the law of each community. The extensive comparative investigation thus required can be difficult and, on occasion, will face issues of great subtlety. In some cases the results will be ambiguous and engender uncertainty. Reluctance to undertake a difficult enterprise, and an understandable fear that the clarity and certainty of the solutions provided will suffer, go far to explain why, in principle, traditional methodologies make little effort to avoid the choice between the principle of equal treatment and that of advancing values.

In recent decades, especially in the United States, functional or instrumental approaches have been developed which undertake to analyze the potentially relevant laws of each concerned state. In cases of "false" or "no" conflict these approaches can avoid a choice between the principle of equal treatment and that of advancing values and purposes as neither principle need be violated if the other states concerned use the same methods. Of course, in order to achieve this advantage, functional approaches must be prepared to undertake more extensive and difficult investigations of foreign law than are normally required in traditional approaches. The practical question becomes, therefore, whether the improvement possible in the quality of justice administered in cases of "false" or "no" conflict is worth the complications and difficulties involved in determining whether a given case falls within one of these categories. One's answer to this question turns in considerable measure upon views about the feasibility and cost of the required comparative investigations.

IV

No choice-of-law methodology can harmonize the principles of equal treatment and of advancing values in all cases. Accordingly, every conflicts approach must decide which principle is ultimately to be preferred.

Theoretically, the principle of equal treatment should, where a choice must be made, perhaps be preferred to the competing principle of advancing values. In private-law contexts it is generally more important to preserve equality between the parties by regulating the controversy in the same way regardless of the forum in which the litigation proceeds than to advance the purposes of one of the concerned states particularly since, by hypothesis, those of another concerned state must be frustrated. In addition, results reached by methods that provide equal treatment have a stronger claim to acceptance by all the parties than do results reached by methods that advance instead a given state's purposes.

A theoretical preference for the principle of equal treatment may disappear, however, in the face of the difficulties encountered when one seeks to realize the principle in practice. Such treatment can be assured only if a uniform system of choice-of-law rules is accepted by all the states concerned and this system is uniformly administered. Some progress in the direction of uniform rules has been accomplished through international conventions such as those prepared by The Hague Conference on Private International Law. However, internationally accepted rules administered by an international court remain, for the most part, utopian goals. In the absence of such rules and such a court, can the principle of equal treatment be realized in practice?

Traditional theories of choice-of-law sought to achieve equal treatment by suggesting that, in the nature of the juristic universe, certain propositions and results are inevitable. Thus Beale in his vested rights analysis argued from the proposition that law is territorial in nature to the conclusion that the law of the place where the last relevant event occurred regulates the given transaction or occurrence. And Savigny, deducing from the nature of a given legal situation its *Sitz* or natural seat, asserted that the law of that jurisdiction would govern. For example, the seat of a contractual obligation is, in principle, the place of performance and that law accordingly regulates questions respecting the obligation's substantial validity. The fatal difficulty with efforts of this type to ensure uniform rules uniformly administered is that the conclusion drawn is not inevitable. The fact that a contract is signed in state A or has its *Sitz* there does not demonstrate that state A's views respecting the contract's validity must be accepted by all other states. In the legal universe, relationships of cause and effect depend significantly upon contingent and variable judgments respecting values and purposes. Appeals to juristic necessity are always misplaced.

In the absence of internationally accepted and administered rules and of juristic necessity how does the principle of equal treatment fare in practice? In theory, states may well be prepared to subordinate their particular policies if forum shopping can be avoided. But there are enormous practical difficulties in the way of achieving the required uniformity in choice-of-law rules and in their administration. In view of the difficulties and the related suspicion that in reality equality of treatment will not be secured, the alternative principle of advancing values becomes increasingly attractive. A forum proceeding on this basis can at least be sure that certain of its purposes are being served. Unlike traditional methodologies, the risk is not run that neither equality of treatment nor advancement of values will be achieved.

To the extent that the foregoing analysis is accurate, only an illusory choice exists between the two principles of conflicts justice. A preference for equal treatment cannot be realized in a systematic and coherent fashion. In practical terms, the alternative to the advancement of values is in many cases not equality of treatment but unequal treatment combined, on occasion, with non-advancement of values. Although simplicity and ease of administration may still argue for traditional methods, functional or instrumental methods may seem more attractive because they can advance in practice at least one principle of justice and sometimes both. In this perspective, the rise in recent decades of functional or instrumental analyses is entirely understandable.

In single-state cases and in cases of "false" or "no" conflict, no problem arises as to the state whose values are to be advanced. In cases of true conflict, however, the state or states must be selected. The need to select means that the results can not be as just as those reached in single-state cases or in multistate cases that do not present a true conflict. And a troublesome problem of choice is also presented. Essentially two solutions to this problem are possible. The values can be those of the forum (assuming that it is concerned on the issue) or those of another concerned state. What considerations determine the choice to be made here by a functional approach?

Several arguments can be advanced for the position that the principle of advancement should be conceived in terms of the forum's values and purposes. Considerations of simplicity and ease of administration support this solution. In particular, the problem of assessing the purposes and policies held by other communities is largely avoided and a clear rule is provided for resolving the problem of choice among conflicting values and purposes. For these reasons, among others, Professor Currie insisted that the forum's rule should be applied whenever there is "a legitimate basis for the assertion of an interest in the application" of "the governmental policy expressed in the law of the forum."[30]

Although this solution offers certain practical advantages, another approach has considerable attraction from the perspective of conflicts justice. Essentially automatic application of forum law in cases of true conflict often results in a self-serving parochialism; the views held by other states are ignored in situations where, had they been those of the forum, they would have been given effect. Cannot this self-serving parochialism, a temptation for all choice-of-law theories that are in some significant sense functional, be avoided and a higher quality of conflicts justice be assured by approaching cases of true conflict as follows: The clash of values or policies that has arisen within the ad hoc community of concerned states is to be resolved not by considering what value or policy of the forum can be advanced but rather by determining how the forum would, in general, resolve the clash in question. The most obvious and general basis for making this determination is reasoning by analogy from the results reached in wholly domestic situations involving comparable clashes. Multistate situations involving true conflicts would thus present, just as do analogous domestic situations, the problem of deciding which among conflicting policies are, in general, to be preferred.

Both the temptations of self-serving parochialism and the operation of a functional approach of the type just proposed can be illustrated in a discussion of the New York Court of Appeals decision in *Neumeier v. Kuehner*.[12] A New York resident picked up an Ontario resident in Ontario; the guest's journey ended there in a fatal accident. The guest's estate unsuccessfully sought to recover damages from the driver's estate in the New York courts. A line of decisions, beginning with *Babcock v. Jackson*,[13] had established that a New York resident, invited by a

---

[10]   [BRAINERD] CURRIE, [SELECTED ESSAYS ON THE CONFLICT OF LAWS] 183. Currie would exercise "restraint and enlightenment in the determination of what state policy is and where state interests lie." *Id.* at 186. For a general discussion of Currie's views, see von Mehren, [*Recent Trends in Choice-of-Law Methodology*, 60 CORNELL L. REV. 927,] 936-41.

[12]   31 N.Y.2d 121, 286 N.E.2d 454, 335 N.Y.S.2d 64 (1972) (6-1 decision).

[13]   12 N.Y.2d 473, 191 N.E.2d 279, 240 N.Y.S.2d 743 (1963) (5-2 decision).

New York driver in Ontario and there involved in an accident, could recover in a New York action although Ontario had a so-called "guest" statute barring, or limiting, a guest's right to recover. The *Neumeier* decision, upon one possible reading of the implicated New York and Ontario policies, squarely raises the question whether, accepting the reasoning and results of the line of cases beginning with *Babcock,* the fact alone that the victim guest is an Ontario rather than a New York resident justifies application of the Ontario statute.

From New York's perspective, the New York defendant's claim is stronger than that of the Ontario plaintiff as no New York interest in compensating a resident or his estate is present. Looking at the situation from Ontario's point of view, it is arguable that Ontario would, for the given case, wish to have its resident or his estate compensated. (The argument rests on the proposition that Ontario, in fully domestic situations, has subordinated a compensation policy to a policy of protecting insurance companies and their policyholders against possibly fraudulent claims. As this latter Ontario policy does not reach the case in question since New York insurance is involved, Ontario's domestically subordinated compensation policy should be given effect. Of course, if Ontario's guest statute has other purposes—for example, if Ontario considers it inappropriate for a guest or his estate to sue a host—the case is to be viewed as one of no conflict.) On the view that the policy which informs the Ontario guest statute does not reach to the *Neumeier* situation, the decision refuses to give effect to a relevant Ontario compensation policy benefiting an Ontario party where a comparable compensation policy, asserted by New York in favor of a New York party, would be given effect. New York thus maximizes the interests of its own residents, although this entails in the *Neumeier* case the subordination of a compensation policy, held in the event by another jurisdiction, which New York prefers over the countervailing policy of protecting insurance companies and their policyholders against possibly fraudulent claims when the clash occurs in a fully domestic context.

For those who in applying the principle of advancement do so in terms of relevant forum policies, the result reached by the New York Court of Appeals in *Neumeier* is clearly correct unless one is prepared to include among forum policies a multistate policy such as evenhandedness. However, if the principle of advancement is applied in terms of the policies held by all the concerned states and the forum is to advance the policy or policies that it prefers when a comparable clash occurs in a fully domestic case, the Ontario plaintiff prevails unless the analysis of Ontario's policies proposed above is incorrect. In resolving the problem of the host's liability to guests for fully domestic situations, New York subordinates a policy of protecting insurance companies and hosts to a compensation policy. When a multistate case presents the same policy configuration, New York accordingly should prefer the same policy even though, in the event, the policy is held by Ontario.

An approach prepared to subordinate the forum's policy in such cases meets the objection that, in practice, functional methods with their emphasis on advancing values end up applying forum law whenever there is any possible basis for doing so. In deciding which of clashing policies to prefer, decisive weight would be given not to the forum policy relevant in the particular multistate case—for example, to the protection of local insurance companies and local hosts—but rather to the forum's general view as to how the clash in policies presented should be resolved. Thus a state that allowed a guest to recover under general tort principles in domestic situations should prefer the policy of compensation over host and insurance company protection in multistate guest cases involving a clash between these policies. Had the New York Court of Appeals done so in *Neumeier*, it would have done all within its power to achieve evenhandedness and to avoid a clash between the two basic principles of conflicts justice.

V

One further aspect of conflicts justice remains to be considered. In the discussion above on the clash between the principle of equal treatment and that of advancement of values in cases of true conflict, one problem was not explored: Is there any way in which a functional or instrumental approach that does not accord an automatic preference to any relevant policy held by the forum can avoid—or minimize—this clash? Can procedures be developed to reconcile in cases of true conflict these two principles of justice?

Reconciliation is possible to the extent that true conflicts are resolved by reference to a shared, and uniformly administered, norm or standard. Again the root of the difficulty is the lack of uniform rules administered by a supra-national authority and the consequent need to find surrogates.

Three different types of procedures have been proposed. One tries to achieve agreement as to which state's position as to priorities among clashing policies should prevail in view of each state's connections with the matter in litigation; another seeks consensus as to the types of policies to be preferred; a third proposes to compromise the clashing policies. Most efforts to deal with the problem adopt either the first or the second approach. Thus priorities are established by evaluating the significance or intensity of each state's concern for the issue to which the clash of policy relates. Or appeal is made to widely held conceptions of justice, to the "better law," or to the views generally held by civilized nations. Finally, principles of choice or preference are developed on the assumption that modern societies share, for the general run of situations, certain values and are, accordingly, prepared to subordinate others that may be preferred in the particular case by a concerned state in order to advance, overall, both generally preferred values and the ideal of uniform and disinterested solutions to conflicts problems.

Each of these procedures seeks to avoid the parochialism that tempts functional methods. Each also has some potential for reconciling the principles of advancement and equality of treatment. Thus, the test of "significant relationship" used by the Second Restatement encourages a forum to yield when its concern is marginal or when not to yield would be highly disruptive for the interstate or international activities in question. Professor Cavers' principles of preference seek to contribute to equality of treatment and to decisional harmony: The forum undertakes "to adhere to a principle of preference in the hope, but not on the condition, that it will provide a mutually acceptable scheme of accommodation for laws of the same general type as are involved in the case before it."[22]

Each of the foregoing procedures could be analyzed in detail and its theoretical and practical advantages and disadvantages considered. However, in the context of efforts to reconcile the principles of advancement and of equality in cases of true conflict, the principal observation to be made is that a reasonable degree of reciprocity can not be guaranteed for those situations where another state's law is selected. The forum is asked to forego a present application of its policy in order to ensure decisional harmony and, presumably, the application by other states of its views in certain future cases of true conflict. Unfortunately, it is very difficult in practice to obtain this degree of cooperation and coordination among sovereign states. The forum is tempted to prefer a present advantage—the advancement of its policy in the instant case—to the contingent future advantage that present self-denial offers. In addition, the forum may well fear that others will engage in freeloading. Finally, even with the best will in the world, unless general agreement exists among the sovereign states as to the methods by which the principles of equality and of advancement are to be reconciled, little can be achieved. Here

---

[22]   D[AVID] CAVERS, THE CHOICE-OF-LAW PROCESS [132 (1965)].

again, the fact that in multistate situations the unit is smaller than the economic or social unit in which the problem has arisen creates difficulties that defy full solution.

A third and quite different type of procedure, which may present certain advantages, has been proposed with a view to reconciling the principles of equality and of advancement in cases of true conflict. The suggestion is that, in those cases, the values held by each concerned state should be compromised. In some cases this compromise would be on the basis of equal respect; in others, rules would be applied only to the extent that, on the actual facts, the rule's underlying policy so required. In domestic law, subordination of certain policies in favor of other policies is much more usual than is compromise of conflicting policies. However, examples of the latter can be found in domestic law. For example, workmen's compensation schemes recognize strict liability but, in return, limit compensation to scheduled amounts. And, in many legal orders, the doctrine of comparative negligence apportions loss between the parties on a sliding scale of percentages.

But traditionally Western jurists have, in principle, opposed the compromising of conflicting views or policies in the articulation of private-law rules and in the administration of these rules in discrete cases. Where the choice is inescapable, justice is ordinarily taken to require the delineation and vindication of generalized and abstract principles rather than the advancement of harmony in the human relations at stake. Accordingly, in the administration of justice full effect is to be given a party's claims if they are established; a plaintiff ordinarily receives all or nothing at all. Thus, the common law sees the plaintiff's contributory negligence as a bar to recovery rather than as a basis for reducing the damages to be awarded. Of course, as the three examples that follow illustrate, the implied rejection of compromise was never complete. The law of delict of many European countries long ago adopted the idea of comparative negligence under which fault—or loss—is apportioned according to the degree of fault. The United States Supreme Court in the 19th century accepted for admiralty matters the rule that when a collision is due to the fault of both vessels, the total damages are shared equally. Finally, the Court recently replaced the "divided-damage" rule by the degree-of-fault rule now almost universally used for admiralty matters.[28]

When judicial action is in question, the view that justice is ordinarily served by a choice among, rather than a compromise of, competing views and principles is reinforced, where the principle of separation of power obtains, by another consideration: compromising policy conflicts may be seen as a peculiarly legislative function and thus an improper task for courts.

A view of justice that in principle prefers choice among conflicting views and policies, with the consequence that some are fully vindicated and others completely subordinated, is normal—perhaps inevitable—where law is seen as ultimately emanating from one god or one nature. It is supportable—but not inevitable—where law is viewed as having its source in one sovereign. Accordingly, even though a divine or a natural source of law is no longer generally accepted, the Western view of justice derived from Greek thought and the Judaic-Christian tradition can be maintained when, as in wholly domestic situations, we are in the presence of but one sovereign. However, in multistate cases—except in an essentially formal sense (irrelevant to the issue under discussion) emphasized by such theories as Cook's "local law" analysis—several sovereigns are in the picture.

The assertion that justice in multistate situations normally requires the vindication of generalized and abstract principles implies that, in the final analysis, the law for the ad hoc community to which the multistate situation relates has, in some significant sense, its source in a

---

[28]   United States v. Reliable Transfer Co., 421 U.S. 397 (1975).

universal god or a natural order. If a unitary source is not posited, compromises—designed to take competing views and policies into account and to advance harmony within a multistate order—can hardly be viewed as necessarily or inherently unjust. On the contrary, compromise as a principle of justice becomes understandable and attractive.

The objection remains, of course, that the striking of such compromises is essentially a legislative function. But this objection loses considerable force when one bears in mind that issues which arise only occasionally and within transitory multistate orders are not likely to engage the attention of the legislative bodies of the sovereign states involved. Moreover, these bodies would presumably find both difficult and uncongenial the inquiry and analysis often required to resolve these multistate problems. Thus, when the administration of justice in multistate cases is in question, the task of adjusting and compromising conflicting views and policies is arguably one for the courts even though they will, of course, encounter difficulties in discharging it.

Compromising clashes of policy that occur in cases of true conflict involves the development of special substantive rules for these multistate situations. In its most generalized form, where two concerned states hold conflicting policies such a rule would give half a loaf to each. No shared basis for resolving the conflict being available, the disagreement is compromised with equal weight accorded the views of each state. The cause of equal treatment is thereby advanced, particularly if the resulting special substantive rules are only utilized where all the concerned states accept in principle the approach, a fact relatively easily ascertained.

Special substantive rules are not possible where the differences in values and purposes at issue are so fundamental as to make compromise unthinkable. Nor is the approach feasible where, in its nature, the issue requires a unitary solution. An example of both phenomena is furnished in some contexts by differences in views respecting monogamous and polygamous marriage. The difference in values and attitudes can be too great to permit a compromise. Thus, so far as marital relations are concerned, an on-going marriage could hardly be monogamous for one spouse and polygamous for the other, or monogamous during certain time periods and polygamous during others. (For questions of support and inheritance, on the other hand, a compromise between monogamy and polygamy is feasible.) Where a guest sues after an accident to recover from the driver of the car in which the guest was riding, a true conflict of views among the concerned legal orders could be compromised. If one concerned state denied all recovery to the guest while the other permitted normal tort recovery, it might seem fair, for example, to allow the guest to recover one-half of the damages suffered.

It is instructive to discuss the use of special substantive rules in connection with the case of *Cipolla v. Shaposka*.[32] A Delaware host, driving in Delaware a car there registered and insured, injured his guest passenger, a Pennsylvania domiciliary. Delaware had a guest statute protecting hosts while Pennsylvania permitted guests to recover under ordinary tort principles. The majority of the Pennsylvania Supreme Court found a true conflict but held the Delaware statute applicable because "Delaware's contacts are qualitatively greater than Pennsylvania's and . . . [Delaware] has the greater interest in having its law applied" and because "it seems only fair to permit a defendant to rely on his home state law when he is acting within that state."[33] The latter argument is persuasive, at least to the extent that the defendant was not protected by insurance. Where insurance coverage exists, however, the reliance-expectation argument loses some force and resolution of the true conflict is more difficult. (It is probably not feasible for

---

[32]   439 Pa. 563, 267 A.2d 854 (1970).

[33]   *Id.* at 566-67, 267 A.2d at 856.

American forums to distinguish between the handling of a case for choice-of-law purposes depending upon the existence or extent of insurance coverage; the American jury is not entitled to know whether the defendant is insured or for what amounts. Of course, this difficulty disappears in systems that do not use juries.) Justice Roberts, in dissent, agreed with the majority that the case involved a "true" conflict. However, invoking the "better rule of law approach," he would apply the Pennsylvania rule.

If the argument of fairness to the defendant is considered persuasive, *Cipolla* can be viewed as a case of no conflict; Pennsylvania is prepared to subordinate its compensatory policy to its competing policy of protecting reasonable expectations and understandings. On the other hand, if Pennsylvania rejects the fairness argument either because it is intrinsically unpersuasive on the facts of the case or because the compensation policy is considered more compelling, a true conflict is presented. Delaware will prefer its relevant policy of protecting host drivers, as it does in wholly domestic cases presenting a generally comparable clash of policies, while Pennsylvania will prefer, as it does domestically, its compensation policy. In such a situation, a compromise solution, in the form of a special substantive rule partially accommodating the divergent Delaware and Pennsylvania views, could be attractive. For example, the plaintiff might be allowed to recover one-half of what Pennsylvania law provides. Alternatively, only certain items of recovery—for example, medical expenses and lost earnings during a convalescence period—might be allowed. Finally, if the problem of jury trial does not stand in the way, distinctions could be drawn on the basis of the existence and extent of insurance coverage. Thus full or partial recovery might be given, but only up to policy limits.

Bernhard v. Harrah's Club[36] presents another situation of true conflict where the use of a special substantive rule is worth considering. A tort action was brought in California against a Nevada tavern by a California resident injured in a highway accident in California. The tavern advertised in California. A resident of California drove to the tavern, was served alcoholic beverages, and became intoxicated. Driving back to her home, she negligently collided with the plaintiff's motorcycle. The court concluded that, at least where the defendant tavern had actively solicited California business, "California has an important and abiding interest in applying its rule of decision . . . [and] that the [California] policy . . . would be more significantly impaired [than the Nevada policy] if such rule were not applied. . . ."[37] Unless Nevada is prepared to take the same position—which is not likely—the only way in which decisional harmony could be advanced is to strike a mutually acceptable compromise. This might take the form, already suggested, of allowing half the normal California recovery. Viewing the situation overall, the principle of advancement of values is as effectively served by compromise as it would be by a solution in terms of subordination; at the same time, a result is reached that might well prove acceptable to both Nevada and California and thus satisfy the principle of equal treatment.

* * * * *

What conclusions are to be reached on the issue whether, from the perspective of conflicts justice, certain choice-of-law methods are preferable to others? For reasons that have been developed above, it appears that functional or instrumental approaches can achieve a higher quality of conflicts justice than is attainable by approaches that do not proceed functionally.

---

[36]   16 Cal. 3d 313, 546 P.2d 719, 128 Cal. Rptr. 215 (1976).

[37]   *Id.* at 523, 546 P.2d at 725-26, 128 Cal. Rptr. at 221-22.

Non-functional approaches emphasize the principle of equality; however, this ideal eludes them in practice with the result that neither equal treatment nor advancement of values is achieved on a systematic basis. Functional approaches, on the other hand, in a significant class of cases—those involving "false" conflicts—advance both ideals and, in cases of "true" conflict, at least advance values on a systematic basis.

There is, as has already been observed, considerable variation in the quality of conflicts justice that different functional approaches can provide. In particular, if a priority is given in principle to the advancement of forum values, the consequences for conflicts justice are problematical. The quality of conflicts justice produced by functional approaches that do not give such a priority can, it should be remarked, be still further improved if ways are found to reconcile in some measure the principles of advancement and equal treatment.

Finally, it must be remembered that discussion of choice-of-law methodology from the perspective of justice can not demonstrate that functional approaches are necessarily preferable to more traditional approaches. Considerations of practicality, of cost, and of administrability must be taken into account before any such conclusion would be permissible. However, advantages from the perspective of the problem of justice that functional approaches offer over more traditional choice-of-law methods at least explain why these latter are today challenged by the former.

Joseph W. Singer, *Real Conflicts*, 69 B.U. L. Rev. 1, 75-78, 79-80, 80-81, 127-129 (1989)*

* * * * *

Conflicts cases raise fundamental questions about the substantive norms governing social relationships and the relations among neighboring political communities. Both courts and scholars are aware of the complexities these cases raise. As a result, most modern conflicts scholars emphasize a subtle, multi-layered policy analysis of conflicts cases.

But an awareness of these complexities is also the reason why many conflicts scholars seek to escape from these complexities by retreating to a form of analysis that effectively denies them. Some do so by rejecting analysis of substantive policies altogether, nostalgically reviving simplistic and unworkable answers based on privileging certain territorial contacts. Yet they fail to explain adequately why we should privilege certain territorial contacts over others, or why the contacts they pick are the most significant. Moreover, these scholars often presume a consensus about which contact is most significant when that consensus no longer exists. In the absence of such a consensus, we have no choice but to engage in discussion of the policy goals of conflicts law. Those who want to revive territorial approaches are so overwhelmed with the complexity of policy choices that they seek to return, at all costs, to a world where we simply ignore them. Yet the world they envision is already gone; Pandora's box can no longer be closed.

Those conflicts scholars who reject territorial analysis do so on the grounds that it formalistically defines some contact or aggregation of contracts as critical without justifying this choice by evaluating underlying policy concerns. But these same scholars have likewise for-

---

* Reprinted with permission.

malized the policy analysis. They argue that compensatory policies in both contract and tort law favor widely shared goals of compensating plaintiffs, deterring wrongful conduct, and promoting reliance on agreements. But how do they know this? They have engaged in formalism by identifying these policies as "shared" or "basic" or "emerging" or "prevalent" or "better," without confronting the conflicting values and policy arguments that are faced by those who debate the substantive content of the law. They have formalized state interests by often ignoring moral interests and interests in liberty. To figure out which law is better or which policies should prevail, we would need to engage in the kind of moral, political, and economic analysis in which torts and contracts scholars engage. These scholars recognize that the law poses choices between alternative legal rules and that each area of the law represents a patchwork of compromises between competing interests and principles. Conflicts scholars should follow their lead. Sloganeering about interests in compensation, deterrence, and party autonomy, and proclaiming these goals to be the "basic policies" of tort and contract law are inadequate and formalistic approaches to resolving conflicts problems.

From reading conflicts scholarship, one would have no idea that there are fierce battles among torts scholars on the choice between strict liability and negligence, on the efficient level of damages, and on the justice of loss-spreading. Nor would one have any idea that Grant Gilmore wrote a book entitled *The Death of Contract*, or that the goal of contract law in the twentieth century has moved steadily away from freedom of contract to the regulation of contract terms as a means of protecting the weaker party against unequal bargaining power and promoting social justice. There are no universally accepted "basic" policies underlying substantive law that can determine the outcome of every conflicts case. Conflicts scholars—if anyone—should recognize that law is an arena of conflict, of competing principles and policies, contradictory moral impulses, and wrenching dilemmas. In order to determine the "relative strength" of competing tort and contract policies and to determine which policies are better, and therefore basic, conflicts scholars need to address more fully the underlying substantive concerns of the conflicting laws at issue. After all, the fact that there is a conflict between the two laws gives us substantial evidence that the question of which law is better or more basic is not simple. It means that there is a real conflict in Amencan society about which social relationships promote justice and the general welfare.

We should also recognize the conflict among conflicts scholars about how to determine the appropriate balance between multistate policies favoring diversity and tolerance and those favoring untformity and substantive justice. We cannot resolve these conflicts by reference to a shared sense of what constitutes justified expectations or of what constitutes an illegitimate imposition of power by one state over another. We need to face the question of what kind of diversity is right for our multistate system. We also need to face our competing impulses to marginalize bad laws and to give them effect despite their extraterritorial implications.

None of the prevailing approaches to conflicts law requires us to confront these questions directly. For example, the "most significant relationship" test fails to clarify the value choices involved in evaluating the significance of different contacts. When a defendant-corporation relies on the immunizing law of the place where it acts, its relationship to the law of that place is significant. When an injured victim claims to fall under the protective umbrella of the place where she is injured or where she lives, her relationship to the law of that place is also significant. To determine which relationship is more significant, we must make hard choices between both the substantive norms of freedom of action and security and between the competing political processes and norms of separate states. We must face the conflicts among the factors we are asked to consider. How do we resolve the conflict between the policy of pursuing the (arguably) better law—what the Second Restatement calls "the basic policies underlying the particular field of law"—and the policy of promoting comity or diverse political communities—what the Second Restatement calls "the needs of the interstate system?" The Second Restatement's silence regarding the priority of these policies mystifies rather than clarifies these choices.

Recently, scholars have come much closer to confronting value choices in conflicts law by proposing choice-of-law rules that promote specific substantive policies. Scholars have explicitly stated that conflicts law should further certain values in various social contexts. Weintraub proposes choice-of-law rules to govern products liability cases that, in certain classes of cases, favor loss-spreading.[227] Reese proposes a similar rule for airplane crash cases.[228] Other scholars advise enforcing choice-of-law provisions in commercial contracts to promote the ideal of freedom of contract.[229] These developments go in the right direction. Yet, these scholars fail to give adequate justification for the value choices they make. The mere fact that these results accurately describe the choices courts make is not a sufficient reason to approve of what they are doing. Moreover, these scholars do not address the conflict between the multistate policy of applying the better law and the multistate policy of fostering diversity.

Modern policy-oriented approaches to conflicts questions, like interest or false conflict analysis, the "most significant relationship" test, comparative impairment analysis, Cavers principles of preference, or Leflar's choice-influencing considerations, take a form characteristic of legal process approaches to legal reasoning. In other words, they attempt to define the spheres of power of different government actors without directly addressing the wisdom or justice of the rules in force. Some of these approaches do this by asking us to consider the relative strength of competing substantive policies of the affected states, rather than their wisdom. For example, the comparative impairment test asks us to determine which state's policy would be most impaired if its law were not applied in the case at hand. This test assumes that the question of the extent of impairment is a question that can be answered without evaluating the content of each state's policy or determining which substantive policy should generally be preferred in a multistate system. Other approaches, like the "most significant relationship" test and Leflar'schoice-influencing considerations, simply list factors to be weighed, rather than confronting the fact that these factors identify contradictory principles, and therefore may pull us in opposite directions. Such approaches ask us to trust judges to identify an immanent social or professional consensus on these questions. Still other approaches, like Cavers' principles of preference, appeal primarily to existing practice in the courts to formulate choice-of-law rules. These approaches presume that reasoned elaboration of existing practice will reveal emerging patterns of rational consensus.

* * *

I propose an eclectic framework for analyzing conflicts cases. This framework has several important features. First, it requires us to look at particular conflicts problems from several angles. We can learn more about a conflicts problem by approaching it from many different perspectives than by utilizing only one perspective. Since we describe our moral intuitions with generalities that are often too simplistic to capture the complexities of our values, this multi-

---

[227] [RUSSEL] WEINTRAUB, [COMMENTARY ON THE CONFLICT OF LAWS § 6.29 (3d ed. 1986)].

[228] Reese, [*The Law Governing Airplane Accidents*, 39 WASH. & LEE L. REV. 1303,] 1323.

[229] *See* [WALTER WHELLER] COOK, [THE LOGICAL AND LEGAL BASES OF THE CONFLICT OF LAWS 389-432 (1942)].

plication of descriptions may help to clarify the real value choices implicated in multistate disputes. Most choice-of-law theories fail to incorporate the notion of conflict into the reasoning process itself. Conflicts reasoning, both in judicial opinions and scholarly articles, often appears one-sided. The decisionmaker or scholar often acknowledges the expectations of one of the parties and ignores the expectations of the other. Or she presents a weak version of the interests and policies of the state and the party who loses. We will make better decisions—fairer and wiser decisions—if we avoid the temptation to belittle the claims of the losing party. We will make better decisions—more knowledgeable decisions—if we recognize what we lose, as well as what we gain, by any choice of law. We will make better decisions if we recognize fully the competing forms of social justice constructed by overlapping normative communities. Finally, we will make better decisions—truer to our deep moral convictions—if we face the conflicting possible constructions of multistate policy implicated in conflicts cases.

The second important feature of this framework is that it requires the decisionmaker to focus initially on the basic considerations of substantive justice and social policy that underlie the area of law at issue, as understood by the forum. Conflicts cases present ordinary issues of tort, contract, property, family, and corporate law. Thus, the initial focus should be on the substantive goals and norms underlying the law being applied. Conflicts cases really differ from domestic disputes in only two important respects: (1) they implicate the interests of a party who may have relied on, or who claims protection under, the conflicting norms of another state; and (2) they further implicate the ability of the members of that other state to govern themselves and constitute themselves as a normative community by determining the fair contours of relationships centered there. It is my view that these unique features of conflicts cases should be folded into the initial substantive analysis of the case by asking whether these special considerations give the forum adequate reason to restrain itself from applying what it sees as the better, substantively just, forum law, in deference to the interests of those connected to the other state in governing themselves and constituting themselves as a political and normative community.

The third feature of this framework is that it identifies a paradigm for analyzing choice-of-law issues. It does not, by itself, give determinate answers to the question of how particular conflicts cases should be decided or what choice-of-law principles should be adopted. It is possible for individuals with widely differing views to use this framework to advance their proposals for adjudicating conflicts cases. For example, my framework is perfectly compatible with the possibility of rigid choice-of-law rules; and analysts could use my framework as a way to explain why certain kinds of cases are best decided by applying the law of the place where a relationship is centered, where an airline ticket was bought, or where a plane departed or arrived. An analyst could justify such rules by explaining that the place where these events are centered has the greatest interest in determining their legal consequences because those consequences are intimately connected to that community's form of social life or its ability to govern its affairs. It is also compatible with an approach that rejects choice-of-law rules entirely and relies on case-by-case adjudication. Further, different scholars and decisionmakers applying this framework may nonetheless come to radically different judgments about the circumstances under which it is appropriate for the forum to defer to the law of another state.

* * *

Here is my proposal. The decisionmaker in a conflicts case should engage in a two-step analysis. First, the decisionmaker should determine which substantive law is best as a matter of social policy and substantive justice. Ordinarily, the forum will look to forum law to answer this question. In other words, at the initial stage of the analysis, there is no reason to treat a conflicts case differently from a domestic case. The goal in both types of cases is the same: fostering substantive justice and the general welfare.

Second, the decisionmaker should further the substantive analysis by addressing the unique facts and policies presented by multistate cases. The goal of this analysis is to determine whether the forum should deviate from what it sees as the substantively correct result in deference to the ability of the members of a neighboring state to constitute themselves as a normative and political community. To answer this question, the decisionmaker should generate multiple versions of the substantive and multistate policies implicated in the case by looking at the case from the perspective of each of the parties and from the perspective of both political systems implicated in the case.* * *

* * * * *

FACING REAL CONFLICTS

Remember the story of Antigone. There has been a war, each side led by one of Antigone's brothers. The brother who attacked the city has died, and Antigone hopes to bury him. Yet Creon, king of the city and uncle of Antigone's traitorous brother, refuses to allow her to grant him this honor. The conflict between them is tragic, and they are tragic figures. Each has a vision of the world that is too simple. Antigone places a simplistic conception of duty to family above all other values; Creon similarly privileges a simplistic conception of the needs of the city. Martha Nussbaum explains that they are both "one-sided, narrow, in their pictures of what matters. The concerns of each show us important values that the other has refused to take into account."[290]

Conflicts cases present us with real conflicts among competing norms and interests, and among the social visions of separate normative and political communities.[291] To decide them, we must "constantly choose among competing and apparently incommensurable goods and [recognize] that circumstances may force [us] to a position which [we] cannot help being false to something or doing some wrong."[292] We must face these choices and then "continue with a vivid imagining of both sides of the dilemma."[293]

In several instances, I have argued that the case should be resolved by applying what the forum understands as the better law. Yet I have also argued that my views on what constitutes the better law might differ depending on the perspective from which I viewed the case. It would

---

[290]   [MARTHA] NUSSBAUM, [THE FRAGILITY OF GOODNESS 67 (1986)].

[291]   I have used the term "real conflicts" in several different senses: (1) to describe real theoretical conflicts among choice-of-law approaches, as distinguished from debates that have outlived their usefulness; (2) to describe real conflicts among the factors we consider in deciding conflicts cases, rather than understanding the factors as simply a variety of relevant considerations; (3) to describe real conflicts in actual cases between the competing substantive policies of different states; and (4) to express my view that relatively few cases can reasonably be decided by reference to the idea that they are false conflicts.

[292]   M. NUSSBAUM, *supra* note [290], at 5.

[293]   *Id.* at 42. * * * *See also* CHARLES LARMORE, PATTERNS OF MORAL COMPLEXITY (1987); JAMES WALLACE, MORAL RELEVANCE AND MORAL CONFLICT (1988) (both arguing that morality involves inevitable conflicts among moral principles that cannot be resolved by resort to a single higher-order principle).

sometimes make a difference in which court I were sitting. This difference in perspective arises from the differing institutional and communal loyalties of government actors in different governmental entities and legal systems. I have further argued that even when the forum is inclined to apply what it sees as the better, forum law, it should wrestle with the question of whether, and to what extent, application of forum law interferes with the ability of another state's residents to constitute themselves as a normative and political community. If it does, the decisionmaker must compare the interests of the two communities whose norms conflict and determine what the just relationship between the two states is in this context. Even if this exercise does not change the result—even if the forum still decides to apply forum law—it will have made a better decision by facing what is really involved in the case. It will have to recognize, as it enforces its "better" law, the injustice it is doing as it attempts to enforce justice.

Facing these real choices does not disable us from making decisions or defending them. "If we were such that we could in a crisis dissociate ourselves from one commitment because it clashed with another, we would be less good. Goodness itself, then, insists that there should be no further or more revisionary solving."[295] We differ about which contacts are more significant and what interests are real and what policies are better because we really do disagree about which kinds of social relationships are just, which market arrangements work well, and which exercises of state power illegitimately interfere with another community's power to govern its affairs. These conflicts are not false. It is only if we do not face them that we will be false to ourselves and our ideals.

Perry Dane, *Vested Rights, "Vestedness," and Choice of Law*, 96 YALE L.J. 1191, 1205-1211, 1213-1216 (1987)*

* * * * *

Vestedness

In the remainder of this Article, I will explain and defend a specific counterrevolutionary normative proposition in choice of law, which I call "vestedness." The notion of vestedness represents a reworking of the first principle in the constellation of ideas that I described in Section I as associated with the vested rights theory of Beale and Dicey. This reworking, although faithful to its forebear in many respects, differs in formulation and tone. In particular, it substitutes relatively precise operational criteria for metaphors, and it incorporates in the logic of a single proposition various notions that, in their original form, might have appeared as statements and counter-statements strung awkwardly together. More important, the part of vested rights theory with which I associate vestedness is *only* a part of that tradition, and I ignore or reject much more of what I described earlier as important to that theory. My hope is that the new label will simultaneously acknowledge the connection and let me define my own more narrow path.

---

[295] M. NUSSBAUM, *supra* note [290], at 49-50.

* Reprinted by permission of The Yale Law Journal Company and Fred B. Rothman & Company from THE YALE LAW JOURNAL, Vol. 96, pages 1191-1275.

A. *Vestedness Defined*

Subject to various interpretive glosses I will introduce shortly, vestedness can be defined as a principle of law requiring that *the court of any forum should, in selecting the criteria governing the substantive elements in an adjudication, apply choice of law criteria that could be expected to generate the same set of substantive criteria if they were applied by any other forum in an actual adjudication.* Thus, a choice of law rule requiring a court in an auto collision case to apply "the law of the place of the crash" is consistent with vestedness because any other forum, if it employed the same choice of law rule, could be expected to find the same crash-site and apply the same substantive law. On the other hand, a rule requiring a court to apply, either as a first or last resort, "the law of the forum" is not consistent with vestedness, because the application of exactly the same rule by other forums would lead each forum to apply its own, possibly very different, substantive law.

A simpler way of putting the matter might be that the principle of vestedness fundamentally rejects the notion of *lex fori* (and along with it Cook and Currie's theories of local law) and requires that a forum decide choice of law questions on the basis of second-order criteria that are in themselves forum-neutral, which is to say, based on the assumption that the merits of a case should not depend on where it happens to be brought. This alternative formulation, however, is woefully imprecise and inadequate. The opportunity to explain why this is so should allow me to explain some of the terminology used in the more formal definition of vestedness, spell out its implications, and illustrate some of the deep points of connection between vestedness and traditional vested rights theory.

Although vestedness is grounded in a rejection of *lex fori*, that rejection is complex. In some respects, vestedness is broader than a simple rule of forum-neutrality. Vestedness, for example, does more than disqualify choice of law rules that explicitly refer to the forum; it also excludes more clever efforts at referring to the law of the forum by nominally forum-neutral criteria, such as "the law of the place in whose courthouse the piece of paper that started the lawsuit happened to be lodged." Such criteria would necessarily change their reference if the identity of the forum were different, and could not therefore be expected to generate the same set of substantive criteria if they were applied by any other forum in an actual adjudication. Similarly, because vestedness applies to choice of law "criteria" at any level of abstraction, and not just isolated choice of law rules, it would also cut out, for example, a principle requiring a forum to apply "the law of the place selected by that choice of law rule—in itself consistent with vestedness—that in the aggregate of cases most often results in the application of the law of the forum."

In more important respects, however, vestedness—like the classic articulation of vested rights theory—does not, despite the strictures of the previous paragraph, require a forum to adopt choice of law criteria that will generate outcomes at trial identical or even similar to those in other forums. The most important reason for this result is that the constraint of vestedness is addressed to each forum individually. It does not assume that different forums adopt the same choice of law regime. It only requires that whatever regimes are adopted, they be such that, if they were employed by other forums, they would be expected to generate the same substantive criteria.

Even in a world in which every forum adopted the same choice of law rules, adherence to vestedness would still not guarantee identical results. Recall first that vestedness applies only to the "substantive elements" in an adjudication. By substantive elements, I mean, in a traditional sense, the criteria by which a court evaluates the primary or out-of-court conduct or status of the parties. Substantive elements, of course, should be distinguished from "adjective" issues such as procedure, evidence, and jurisdiction. They should also be distinguished from those aspects of the law of remedy that do not directly reduce to statements about substantive, out-of-court duties. And even if this brief account leaves room for debate at the margins, the determination of even undeniably non-substantive questions of law clearly can affect an outcome at trial. For that matter, vestedness is consistent with (though it does not require) the "public policy exception"—that much-maligned escape-hatch in vested rights theory—because the exception in its classic formulation is related only to a court's decision to accept or decline jurisdiction, and not to its decision on the merits once it takes a case.

In addition, recall that vestedness only requires choice of law criteria that can be "expected to" generate identical sets of substantive criteria. The phrase "expected to generate the same" is meant to be taken primarily in a formal, rather than a purely descriptive, sense. Clearly, two judges sitting in different forums could in fact look at the same accident and find two different crash sites or find the same crash site but differ over what the law of the crash site actually is. In both of these cases, though, the differences in the judges' conclusions would be the result of some disagreement between them, not of a variable uncontroversially apparent in the task of determining the crash site. Indeed, two judges sitting in the same forum might just as easily disagree about the location of the crash site or the requirements of a substantive regime. By the use of the phrase "expected to," I mean to focus on the structure of choice of law criteria rather than the vagaries of their application.

The constraint of vestedness is satisfied so long as forums can be "expected to" apply the same substantive criteria, even if they disagree about the content of the criteria they are "expected to" apply. For example, federal courts of appeals in the United States generally follow their own interpretations of federal law without feeling bound by the views of courts of appeals in other circuits. When disagreements occur, however, the issue is not framed as one of choice of law, but rather of the interpretation of the same law: Each court does not consider the other courts to have made a different choice of law, but to have adopted a mistaken view of the same law. If and when the Supreme Court decides the issue, its views are taken as an authoritative correction of one or another lower court's substantive mistake. At no point in this process would vestedness intervene.

The rather specialized way in which vestedness seeks to achieve forum-neutrality becomes even more sharply etched in light of the most important operative difference between vestedness and traditional vested rights theory: Vestedness is nothing like a full-fledged choice of law system in itself, but only a thin constraint on choice of law regimes. To construct a full-fledged choice of law system would require not only a whole set of further principles specific to the choice of law enterprise itself, but also an array of political and legal principles that go well beyond and behind that enterprise, and very likely some arbitrary conventions to fill in the details. Put another way, vestedness requires that the content of choice of law criteria should be forum-neutral, but has—as least on the surface—little to say, in itself, about a forum's selection of one set of forum-neutral choice of law criteria rather than another.

Vestedness has nothing whatsoever to say, for example, about the sort of "territorialism" that was understood by many of its adherents, as well as many of its critics, to be part and parcel of vested rights theory. Thus, although a rule requiring a court to apply the "law of the place of the crash" satisfies vestedness, so would a rule requiring a court to apply "the law of the place of the injured party's domicile," or "the law of the place in which the alleged injurer's paternal grandmother was born," or "the law of the place nearest in alphabetical order to the name of the make of the plaintiff's car." For that matter, a choice of law rule, in order to be consistent with vestedness, need not invoke the notion of place at all. Consider, for example, a rule instructing the forum to look to "the law of the parties' common religious community." Nor need it even be outcome-neutral. Consider, in this connection, a rule instructing the forum to look to "the law favoring recovery." Nor need it refer to any positive system of law at all. It would not violate vestedness, although it might pose other problems, for a choice of law rule simply to require a court to "apply natural law."

The thinness of vestedness can be illustrated with particular force by the following example: Although it would violate vestedness for a Canadian court to employ a choice of law rule that required it to look to the "law of the forum," it would not violate vestedness for the Canadian court to apply a choice of law rule that required it always to look to the "law of Canada." The difference is that the latter rule, if it were applied by any other forum, would yield the same law—namely, the law of Canada. Indeed, a choice of law rule requiring a court to apply "the law of Canada" is in this respect structurally similar to a choice of law rule requiring a court to apply "the laws of nature and of nature's God."

What renders the "law of Canada" rule implausible is not vestedness, but certain quite uncontroversial features of contemporary political theory, in particular the idea that no one nation or state has a monopoly on sovereign authority. Indeed, most choice of law analysts of any stripe would probably go further and find implausible any choice of law rule that did not, at least in formal terms, treat all legitimate sovereigns equally. On the other hand, if we put vestedness aside, and just looked to a political principle positing the equality of sovereigns, a *lex fori* rule (although not a "law of Canada" rule) would pass with flying colors. A proponent of *lex fori* is willing, after all, to grant any forum the privilege of applying its own law; a Canadian court employing *lex fori* becomes entitled to apply Canadian law because Canada is the forum, not because Canada is Canada. Only when the principle of equality of sovereigns is combined with the principle of vestedness do both "the law of the forum" and "the law of Canada" lose their plausibility.

This example suggests an even deeper point. Although the "Canada" rule itself might seem a trifle unrealistic, any choice of law criterion will limit the decisionmaker to some finite set of possibilities, with a typical such set being a list that begins with "the law of Afghanistan" and ends with "the law of Zimbabwe." In other words, the political theory needed to fill in any choice of law regime—particularly if it is constrained by vestedness—must include some conception of the nature of sovereignty and the identity of legitimate sources of law, and that conception by its nature may not admit of an infinity of legitimate sovereigns. Moreover, the political theory will have to determine what the notion of a legitimate source of law or legitimate sovereign power entails—whether, for example, it excludes choice of law rules favoring recovery in tort suits, or allowing parties to a contract to select the law by which the contract should be governed, or refusing to recognize the institution of slavery, or subordinating individual sovereign choices to certain trans-jurisdictional substantive principles, or constraining positive law as a whole by some theory of natural law.

* * * * *

B. *Vestedness (Not Quite) Defended*

* * *

To begin with, it is conceivable that vestedness could be fit into a scheme of Rules of Assimilation and Rules of Scope of the sort that I have suggested were a lasting contribution of the choice of law revolution. I do not dismiss this possibility, but it strikes me as either unlikely or unilluminating. Rules of Assimilation and Rules of Scope, after all, are not choice of law meta-principles, but rather readings of domestic law grounded in the patchwork of individual substantive and institutional concerns manifested by sovereign governments. There is no immediately apparent reason why these concerns should give rise to anything like vestedness. Even if they did, it is even harder to imagine vestedness being enshrined as a universal, overriding principle rather than one factor among many in courts' decision-making. More important, if such a result could somehow be defended, it might well only point to some deeper justification—that is, a meta-principle—that would invite examination on its own terms.

One very specific sovereign interest, which might be characterized as either within or outside the set of Rules of Assimilation and Rules of Scope, is that elusive and confused aspect of foreign relations called "comity."[76] As many traditional vested rights theorists recognized long ago, however, the problem with basing a defense of forum-neutrality on the notion of comity is that the two ideas fit together only imperfectly. First, traditional vested rights theory, as well as my reformulation of one part of it, may well require that a forum stand ready to apply the law of a jurisdiction with which it seeks no comity at all, or with which it is even at war, as long as that jurisdiction remains somehow legitimate. Second, neither theory depends on reciprocal behavior by other forums. Third, a foreign forum might well be more offended by the specific content of a choice of law regime than by its compliance with one or another abstract overarching constraint, and vestedness leaves most questions of content open. Fourth, as Currie demonstrated quite convincingly, it is not even clear why one or another version of *lex fori*—openly and unapologetically employed—would always be more damaging to friendly relations or reciprocal respect than one or another version of vested rights. Finally, even if vestedness did serve the cause of comity, it remains unclear why vestedness should be an overarching constraint on a legal regime's choice of law apparatus. After all, comity, however important, must surely give way in certain very large classes of cases to other interests of equal or greater importance.

All this is not to say that foreign (or interstate) relations are irrelevant to choice of law. Vestedness, even if it primarily manifests some other imperative, may well also serve the cause of comity or enlightened self-interest. But, on the whole, vestedness itself, to invoke the words of Dicey only somewhat out of context, "does not arise from the desire of [a] sovereign . . . to show courtesy to other states. It flows from the impossibility of otherwise determining whole classes of cases without gross inconvenience and injustice to litigants, whether natives or foreigners." So once again, we are left looking for those underlying conceptions of justice that will animate the enterprise.

One possible source of justice might be found in a body of super-jurisdictional positive law such as international law, or, in the American interstate context, federal constitutional law. The problems here, however, are similar to those already canvassed. First, even if vestedness is important and commendable, international law and constitutional law may well have good and sufficient reasons for not mandating it, unless we imagine that these bodies of law render compulsory everything that is important and commendable. Second, even if international law or constitutional law do mandate vestedness, their reasons for doing so might be too specific. International law, as relevant here, is generally concerned with the special characteristics of nation-states and transnational actors in a violent world. American constitutional law, as relevant here, is concerned with the special characteristics of a federal system within one relatively unified nation-state. Why should either of these speak in terms that would resonate with the concerns of all forums in all cases? Finally, if international law or constitutional law did res-

---

[76]   For the classic Anglo-American articulation of comity as the foundation for choice of law, see J. STORY, COMMENTARIES ON THE CONFLICT OF LAWS, FOREIGN AND DOMESTIC § 35 (1834). The rhetoric of comity has by now lost most of its cachet in choice of law scholarship and cases, although it remains important in such related areas as recognition of judgments, trans-national litigation, and the act of state doctrine.

onate in this way, that would certainly point to a more fundamental set of principles, and we would be better off looking directly to those principles in the first place. Indeed, without committing myself one way or another, I will simply assume in this Article that vestedness is not required of nation-states by public international law, or required of States of the Union by the Constitution.

In turning to more fundamental principles, one that quickly comes to mind is "equality." After all, isn't vestedness just a variation on the notion that like cases should be treated alike, or, more relevant here, that like cases should be treated alike regardless of the forum in which they happen to be heard? This sort of account begins to approach the argument I actually have in mind. Equality, however, is not the best underlying idea to serve in this case. In the first place, I have already demonstrated that vestedness does not guarantee actual equality in judicial outcomes. It guarantees only one somewhat narrow form of hypothetical equality, and it is not at all clear on the face of things why this is the sort of equality with which a legal regime should be concerned. Even more important, invoking the principle of equality provokes but does not really answer the fundamental debate within choice of law regarding exactly what is meant by equality. The norm of equality seems violated when the fortunity of where a case is brought determines the outcome. But it also seems violated when a single forum treats two cases differently simply because of the fortuity of where some event took place or where some party is domiciled. The first intuition points to something like vestedness. The second intuition leads straight to *lex fori*, and the rejection of vestedness. To choose between these two intuitions will require a set of ideas more detailed than the slogan of equality.

A similar response is evoked by a variation on the equality theme—namely, the aversion to forum-shopping. To state the obvious one more time, vestedness bears only the most attenuated connection to preventing forum-shopping, since it by no means guarantees that different forums will decide the same case the same way. Even if vestedness could eliminate forum-shopping, it is unclear why forum-shopping in the adjudicative context should strike us as inherently distasteful, while other types of jurisdiction-shopping—from the establishment of corporate residence to the flight for freedom by political refugees—give us little pause.

* * * * *

Lea Brilmayer, *Rights, Fairness, and Choice of Law*, 98 YALE L.J. 1277, 1297-1315, 1318-19 (1989)*

* * * * *

A POLITICAL RIGHTS MODEL OF CHOICE OF LAW

A political rights model of choice of law requires a state to justify its exercise of coercive authority over an individual aggrieved by the application of the state's law. This right of the individual litigant to a justification for state coercion need not have constitutional status; to claim such a right is to make a normative argument that may or may not have been recognized

---

* Reprinted with permission of The Yale Law Journal Company and Fred B. Rothman & Company from THE YALE LAW JOURNAL, Vol. 98, pages 1277-1319.

institutionally. A legal decision by the forum to recognize this right by not applying its own law resembles adoption of a state long-arm statute. A state long-arm statute might deliberately be written so as not to extend to the limits tolerated by the federal constitution, in order to respect what the state saw as nonconstitutional fairness claims of defendants. By the same token, a state might recognize claims of individual rights and fairness to a greater degree in choice of law issues than the minimal standard imposed by due process.

This model of rights requires close attention to the state's purported justification for the exercise of coercive power. The first task of a political rights model is to identify the circumstances under which the state has, or lacks, an adequate justification for coercion. Political choice of law rights derive from the limited nature of such political justifications. What sorts of justifications would satisfy our standard of fairness? Here we encounter difficult questions that have proved troublesome to political philosophers. The best that we can do here is to outline the most convincing solutions yet offered to the problem of political justification.

A. *Consent and Domicile*

The two most intuitively acceptable bases for state coercion are probably express consent and the domicile of the party burdened by the applicable law. Express consent is well recognized both by political theorists and the judges who have written choice of law and personal jurisdiction opinions, although we will see below that standing by itself, consent may not be adequate. Similarly, most political philosophers investigating the problem of the state's rights to coerce have assumed that citizenship or domicile is one of the strongest possible justifications for state authority; the paradigm case of political authority, in fact, has been the obligation of the citizen to his or her own government.

There has, of course, been substantial dispute about why, as a philosophical matter, citizenship is an adequate basis for state coercion. As a matter of choice of law, however, it seems that we cannot afford to be as concerned as professional philosophers about such scruples. Anarchism does not have a promising future as a basis for judicial decision making in choice of law cases, any more than in any other sort of substantive dispute; thus some basis for political obligation must be found. In the purely domestic arena, we seem content to point to the right to participate in political processes. If this is adequate for domestic cases, then it would seem adequate for conflicts cases as well.

What ought to be the relevant affiliating characteristics of corporations? Corporations are not automatically ineligible to be the possessors of rights, although it should not be assumed that they will necessarily have the same rights as natural persons. There would seem to be few objections, either as a matter of case law or otherwise, to subjecting the corporation to the law of its state of incorporation. As a creature of that state's laws, absent considerations of federal constitutional or statutory law objections, the corporation can have only such rights and obligations as the state's laws bestow. This does not mean that the corporation lacks relevant affiliations with other states. Perhaps most significantly, corporations often exercise considerable political clout in states other than the state of incorporation. In some instances, it might be reasonable to treat a foreign corporation as functionally analogous to an individual voter.

We can proceed on the assumption, then, that domicile, incorporation, and the right to participate politically are adequate justifications. These might loosely be referred to as domiciliary connections, and they supplement express consent as an adequate political justification for the exercise of state power. This domiciliary principle reveals an important distinguishing feature of the political rights approach to choice of law. In the historical dispute between the vested rights theorists and the interest analysts, the important dispute sometimes seemed to be between those who would base decisions upon territorial connecting factors and those who would base decisions upon domiciliary connecting factors. The Bealeans seemed to take a rule's scope as territorial unless clearly such would be unreasonable, while the interest theorists took a rule as domiciliary unless clearly proven otherwise. Our discussion of the use of domiciliary factors under a political rights model shows that these are not the only two alternatives.

The reliance upon domiciliary factors in a political rights analysis is different in the following way. Unlike the Bealean system, in a political rights analysis domiciliary connecting factors are of front-line importance, not secondary to territorial connecting factors. More important, under the political rights model, domiciliary factors function solely as a justification for the imposition of burdens; it is the party who is burdened that must have a local domicile. Under Bealean theory, domiciliary factors are not limited in this way; it is not relevant which party benefits. Traditional vested rights analysis is "jurisdiction-selecting" in that it does not require the court to ascertain the content of the law before deciding whether it is applicable. The Bealean rules on family law or validity of wills do not depend upon whether the law advantages or disadvantages the local person. By the same token, most statutory choice of law rules that rely upon domiciliary connections do so without asking whether the local person will be helped or hurt; they too are jurisdiction-selecting.

The function of domiciliary factors as burdening links in the political rights model also differentiates it from interest analysis. In interest analysis, domiciliary factors matter when they establish that application of local law will benefit one of the state's own people. For example, a guest statute is presumed to create an interest when its application would work to the benefit of a local party, namely the defendant in a tort suit. Whether application of local law would burden a local person is not directly relevant to modern choice of law approaches. There is assumed to be no reason that a state would set out to burden its own people. While there may be situations where the burdened individual is a local (in all purely domestic situations this will be true, for instance), this is not the desired goal but simply an unavoidable byproduct of the desire to help the other party to the litigation. In the modern approach, pro-plaintiff laws are only implicated when the plaintiff is a local person, and pro-defendant laws are only implicated when the defendant is a local person.

The political rights model is different from both traditional and modern choice of law theories because, while it inquires into the content of the rule, the relevant question is whether the burdened party is local. Although we will see below that some versions of a rights-based approach, taken as a whole, might be jurisdiction-selecting,—and that interest analysis itself, when applied consistently, is jurisdiction-selecting as well—the simple domiciliary principle that we have so far identified is not. It depends upon the law's content. So does the determination whether an interest exists, although the two are very different: the political rights-based approach relies upon content in a way that is the opposite of the way that policy or interest analysis does. Instead of finding a reason for the law's applicability in the fact that a local would benefit, one finds a justification for the law's applicability in the fact that a local would be burdened.

It is no coincidence that political rights analysis and policy analysis are so different. The divergence is a direct consequence of the differences between their foundations. Whenever a law is applied it will work to the advantage of one party to the litigation and to the disadvantage of the other. Choice of law at the adjudicative stage is a zero sum game; what advances the cause of the plaintiff simultaneously imposes costs on the defendant, and vice versa. This is as true in purely domestic cases as in conflicts cases. A theory of adjudication that is forward-looking focuses on one side of this balance, namely the good that can be done and how best to attain the goal that the law is designed to achieve. In the choice of law context, this approach results in a focus on whether the benefits that would be produced by the application of a law are the intended ones, that is, benefits to local persons. A theory of adjudication that is backward-looking, by contrast, focuses on whether the parties deserve their treatment, and it must therefore ask about the appropriateness of the placement of burdens. The question is not whether the benefits are intended, but whether the burdens are justified.

A model of political rights and the modern policy approach to choice of law are mirror images of one another; the rights analysis looks at *burdening* links and the policy analysis looks at *benefiting* links. Using burdening links, the rights analysis divides cases into categories that resemble the interest analysis categories of true conflicts, false conflicts, and unprovided-for cases. As with interest analysis, some cases are false problems; these occur when the parties either share a common domicile or hail from states that have the same substantive law.[81] Assume, for instance, that both parties are Connecticut domiciliaries. Connecticut law must be to the disadvantage of either the plaintiff or the defendant; whichever it is, that party has sufficient connection with Connecticut so that his or her rights are not violated by application of Connecticut law. There is no rights-based objection because whichever is the aggrieved party, he or she is a local domiciliary. This reasoning mirrors the interest analysis reasoning that where both parties are from Connecticut, then Connecticut must have an interest in having its law applied. The substance of the law need not be consulted because whether it helps the plaintiff or the defendant, Connecticut helps the local.

In cases of mixed domicile, the political rights analysis also results in a mirror image of interest analysis. Assume that New York law and Connecticut law differ and that one party is from New York and the other is from Connecticut. There are two possible configurations: Either both are relatively favored by the laws of their respective states or both are disadvantaged. Consider first the case in which each party would benefit by application of his or her home state's law.

In interest analysis terminology, this is a true conflict and therefore a hard case. Each state has a policy reason for applying its own law, because application of local law would help the local person relative to the application of the other state's law. Under a rights-based analysis, this case is indeed a hard case, but the reason is very different. The problem is not that there are two good connecting links, each of which would justify application of local law—namely, the link between Connecticut and its party and the link between New York and its party. Instead, the problem is that there are no connecting links to justify the burdensome application of either law. Connecticut lacks a link with the party that would be burdened by its local law, while New York lacks a link with the party that would be burdened if New York law were applied. Thus, from a political rights perspective, it seems that the modern theorists are correct about which cases are simple and which cases are hard; it's just that they explain their classification in what seems to the rights theorist to be precisely the wrong way.

Now consider the other possibility: cases of mixed domicile in which neither party would benefit by the application of his or her own law. Each party, in other words, would prefer the law of the other party's home state. An interest analyst would classify this situation as an unprovided-for case because no links rationalize the application of either state's law. Because policy analysts would be searching for benefiting links rather than burdening ones, they would view this case as a vacuum. A rights-based analysis, in contrast, would apply the domiciliary

---

[81]   In this and much of the discussion immediately following, I borrowed from John Ely's excellent treatment. *See* Ely, [*Chioce of Law and the State's Interest in Protecting Its Own*, 23 Wm. & Mary L. Rev. 173, 200-01 (1981)].

principle and find two adequate links which would support the application of either New York law or Connecticut law, since application of either would disadvantage only the local person. Neither the modern approach nor the rights-based domiciliary principle can provide a unique and satisfying choice of one state's law over the other.

The structure of the problem, then, appears very similar under interest analysis and a political rights approach; analysis of a case might reveal either no justifying link, one justifying link, or two justifying links. Under either approach, the hardest case is the case of mixed domicile in which each party would benefit from application of his or her own state's law. Does this mean that a rights analysis founders on the same shoals as governmental interest analysis, namely on the existence of true conflicts? Not necessarily. First, there is a default position. When there is no justification for either state's intervention, the proper solution is to remain at the status quo. Moreover, we have not yet exhausted the list of potential justifications. We must return to our original question, namely what can give a state the ability to exercise coercive power in a legitimate fashion. So far, we have investigated only one possible answer to this problem, namely that the burdened party is a domiciliary or a local corporation. Other possibilities exist.

B. *Territoriality*

Territoriality would seem to be an obvious candidate for dealing with the hard cases. It yields a compromise between giving either party the benefit of his or her home state's law. Indeed, it may supply an alternative justification for state authority, not merely a device called in to break ties. Admittedly, its association with the old-fashioned vested rights approach has given it something of a bad name, but this association is unnecessary and misleading. Territoriality need not involve an effort to single out a unique location where "the rights vest." Nor need we interpret it to require that the aggrieved party have been personally present within the state. As an initial matter, we will loosely define it as merely meaning that the location of events matters for choice of law decisions.

Despite the fact that territoriality is currently out of fashion, there can be little doubt that territoriality plays some role in a state's right to exercise coercive authority. Regulatory jurisdiction, generally, is pegged to the local occurrence of events. Criminal law and taxation depend upon a nexus with the territory of the state. In international law, application of American statutes depends upon the occurrence of conduct or impact within the United States. In resolving legal problems involving transactions between individuals from different states, the party who stayed at home seems intuitively more entitled to claim the benefit of local law than the party that ventured away from home, thereby willingly leaving the protection of his or her own home state. When in Rome, one does as the Romans do. Furthermore, one apparently subjects oneself to foreign law when one causes consequences in another state.

To describe a common intuition is not to give the arguments for why a particular rule may seem fair, however. Territoriality has not received a great deal of attention as an explicit assumption. Yet well-known treatments of the problem of political obligation rest on highly territorial assumptions, sometimes phrased in terms of implicit or "tacit" consent. The best known is probably that of Locke, who argued that one consented to the exercise of state authority when one resided or travelled upon a state's territory.[87] This argument should have

---

[87]   J. LOCKE, SECOND TREATISE OF GOVERNMENT §§ 119-21 (J. Gough ed. 1946) (3d ed. 1698).

a very familiar ring to civil procedure teachers; it reflects the same assumptions as certain well-known personal jurisdiction cases. Locke's account even matches some of these cases in detail, such as where he argued that using the state's highways amounted to consent—the precursor to modern non-resident motorist statutes!

Despite its familiarity and prestigious associations, this reasoning begs important questions. Most obviously, this "consent" is usually purely fictional. Furthermore, theories of tacit consent assume almost exactly what they set out to prove. Could England decide to infer tacit consent to English authority from an individual's French residence or use of the French highways? Presumably not. Allowing England to do so would allow it to assume authority over persons everywhere. Indeed, even if England were to notify the world in advance that it would infer tacit consent to the laws of England from entry into France, popular expectation that England would do this (if it could somehow find the means) would not make assertion of English authority legitimate.

There are limits on what the state may infer, and these limits are themselves territorial. England may infer tacit consent from the act of walking upon English soil only because England has sovereign authority over English territory. It was precisely such difficulties with theories of tacit consent that led the Supreme Court in *International Shoe Co. v. Washington*[91] to reject implied consent as a basis of adjudicative jurisdiction. Under *International Shoe*, the forum may only infer consent when doing so would be fair; the implied consent theory adds nothing to the calculus, and one is better off to proceed directly to the fairness question and skip all discussion of consent.

Another attempt to explain territoriality might focus on the benefits that an individual receives upon initiating purposeful contact with the state. Submission to state authority is then something of a quid pro quo. This argument, also, surfaces in judicial opinions: purposeful behavior and receipt of benefits have been central elements in the Supreme Court's personal jurisdiction analysis. The argument seems consistent with liberal assumptions that political obligations should be assumed by individuals voluntarily, rather than thrust upon the unwilling. But the problem of circularity is not solved. Whether phrased in terms of voluntary assumption of obligations or express or tacit consent, what remains unexplained is the fact that a state apparently may impose conditions upon some types of voluntary behavior but not others. The attachment of conditions pre-supposes that the state already has power over an individual, namely the power to attach certain conditions to the individual's actions. Furthermore, only voluntary actions that are in some way connected to the state's territory impose obligations. Behaving voluntarily towards France does not typically obligate one towards England.

Territoriality cannot be fully explained in terms of the standard arguments about consent, voluntary behavior, or receipt of benefits, because these arguments are themselves based on territorial assumptions. The problem is that the state cannot simply bootstrap itself into authority over an individual. It is almost impossible for some entity with no pre-existing authority to justify assertions of political authority over an individual. If the justification is based upon the exchange of a quid pro quo, then where does the state obtain this "quid" to exchange? How can it explain its alleged ability to withhold benefits absent the individual's assumption of political obligation when the state has not already been shown to possess some such authority? As critics of law and economics have long argued, arguments based upon the parties' consent depend upon a prior assignment of entitlements.

---

[91]   326 U.S. 310 (1945).

The modern choice of law theorists should not be too quick to celebrate the obvious difficulties of territoriality. To a certain extent, territoriality must simply be taken as axiomatic for choice of law purposes. Indeed, like the vested rights approach, modern policy analysis is permeated with territorial assumptions. Not only is it well accepted that conduct-regulating norms operate territorially, but the foundational emphasis on the welfare of local residents reflects territorial assumptions. Who else could comprise the group that (according to modern policy analysis) is to be benefited, besides those domiciled within the state? The consequences that a statute is designed to bring about or prevent, by hypothesis, are those experienced locally. Clearly there is no way to formulate a choice of law regime other than to found it upon territorial assumptions of some sort. Nor should there be, despite occasional hints to the contrary. State lines are all that distinguish one state from another, and the people of one state from another. Choice of law necessarily turns upon the contacts between the controversy and the various states.

Where the state's connection with the aggrieved individual is that the individual is domiciled in the state, this connection need not be purposeful or deliberate. Some persons take the initiative to choose their own domiciles, but others are "passively" domiciled in a state simply by having been born there. Domiciliaries are also connected, however, by their opportunity to vote. Since non-domiciliaries lack the opportunity to participate in electoral processes, some sort of purposeful action towards the territory by the individual is necessary to justify the exertion of state authority. Absent such a volitional act, there would be no way at all to influence the legal norms that governed one's behavior.

There are, in short, two ways to influence the political decisions that govern one's life, namely voice and exit. In this context, voice is ex ante influence while exit (or entrance) is ex post. Voice means input into the decision before it is made, while the exit option allows one to choose among alternative pre-existing legal schemes. The affiliation between a state and non-domiciliaries must be purposeful to assure a minimal level of individual control over the legal norms to which the individual will be subjected.

This prompts one serious criticism of the vested rights approach from a political rights-based perspective. Because it focused on particular territorial connecting factors divorced from consideration of political rights, the vested rights approach sometimes called for application of the law of a state with which the complaining party had no voluntary connection. Assume, for example, that a buyer and seller negotiate the major portion of a contract in their common home state. The contract is to be performed there as well, but before accepting the deal the buyer travels to another state (chosen for its law advantageous to buyers), and while in that state drops the acceptance into the mailbox. Under First Restatement rules, the contract would be subject to the law of that second state because that is where the acceptance was mailed.[103]

The usual criticism of this First Restatement analysis would be that this is completely arbitrary. Perhaps it is. But note that there is another objection, based upon the parties' political rights. The seller, in this scenario, has no voluntary affiliation with the second state at all; that state was chosen unilaterally by the buyer and it therefore has no right to impose its law upon the seller. Such difficulties arise in virtually every area of the First Restatement's rules, which characteristically fail to relate the chosen territorial connecting factor to the purposeful action of the party protesting application of local law.

---

[103] RESTATEMENT (FIRST) OF CONFLICT OF LAWS § 326.

For this reason, the new rights-based approach differs from the vested rights theory not only in foundation but in practice as well. Territoriality, under the aspects of the rights-based approach already described, does not mean that a state can simply assign a particular territorial factor talismanic significance, even if that factor represents the mythical "last act" of vested rights fame. The territorial factor that is chosen must reflect the aggrieved party's voluntary submission to the law that is chosen.

C. *Mutuality*

We have described at least two different theories for the fair application of state law. Even within one theory (territoriality), more than one state may have adequate connections with a dispute. A rights-based approach leaves open a wide range of permissible options. It would seem to be the rare case in which analysis of rights would narrow the range of possibilities and leave only a single fair application of one state's law. The forum is left with a choice that must be made on some other basis than the parties' negative political rights.

Does fairness have anything further to say about this choice? Is the subject exhausted once one concludes that the state whose law is applied has enough connections to fairly exercise political authority? On closer examination, there may be more to rights than simply viewing in isolation the connections between the individual and the state whose law is chosen. Different conceptions of political fairness will obviously give rise to different additional principles, but one that comes to mind involves assessing the fairness of the overall pattern of choices made by the choice of law rule (or method, or approach). This is not a simple question of a negative right to be left alone, in the sense described above, but of a right to fair treatment, even by a politically authoritative state.

An analogy will illustrate the difference between assessing the individual fairness of an action and assessing the overall pattern of results. Contrast the concerns of substantive constitutional protections such as the First Amendment with distributional provisions such as the equal protection clause. Under the requirement of equal protection, one need not argue that some benefit is unconditionally guaranteed to an individual. In isolation, the conclusion might be that the individual's rights have not been violated because the individual had no constitutional right to the benefit in the first place. This does not, however, answer the question whether the overall distribution of benefits is fair, which is the question posed by equal protection analysis. One argues instead that if the benefit is given to individual A, then it must also be given to individual B.

Similar issues arise in choice of law. Even though there may be no individual guarantee that a party not be subject to the law of state A, perhaps he or she nonetheless should not be subject to the law of state A, because this treatment would compare unfavorably either with that received by other people or with the way that same individual might be treated in other cases. If one imagines an extreme example of distributional unfairness, one can see how a choice of law rule might be unfair even though the end result was the application of a law that had adequate connections with the parties under the aspects of the rights-based approach already described. Assume that the forum adopts a choice of law rule that says, "First identify all of the state laws that could be applied without violating any of the parties' negative political rights, and then apply the one that is the most advantageous to the local person and disadvantageous to the foreign person." While objection to this rule cannot be based upon the negative claims of right that we have outlined, it certainly seems unfair nonetheless.

The problem with the hypothesized rule is that it imposes the burdens of a substantive rule on people without allowing them the corresponding benefits. In the usual domestic context, an individual would expect to experience both the benefits and the costs of a rule over the long run. Substantive rules, in other words, are actuarially fair, because an individual is eligible, in theory, to gain as much by application of the rule as he or she would lose if the tables were turned. To make a class of individuals ineligible to receive the benefits under a rule, while allowing the rule's burdens to be imposed upon them, results in an actuarial imbalance, because over the long run the rule cannot be expected to work out evenly. The point is not merely a comparison of how insiders and outsiders are treated, although these are also problems of a distributional type. Rather, the problem is that of a single individual and his or her overall expectation of benefits and burdens.

Choice of law systems that are actuarially out of balance have a redistributive effect; they cannot be explained purely in terms of corrective justice. The probability of some particular substantive rule's applicability varies according to whether the rule works to the benefit or to the detriment of the particular litigant. Under a choice of law method in which it is not legally relevant whether an individual stands to benefit, these probabilities are, formally at least, identical. Rules that are jurisdiction-selecting, in the old-fashioned sense, are actuarially balanced because whether the rule is applied does not depend upon the content of the rule, and therefore is independent of whether the content of the rule helps or hurts a particular party.

The domiciliary principle of our new rights-based approach, however, is not actuarially balanced, since it allows the application of a state's law when it burdens a local citizen but does not automatically allow application of the same law when it would work to a citizen's benefit. The only instances in which a local rule would be applied to a citizen's benefit would be when some other basis for state authority existed; e.g., the burdened party was also a citizen. The definition of state interests in interest analysis is likewise not actuarially balanced, as it takes into account whether the benefit that the substantive rule is designed to achieve will fall into the hands of a local person.

Actuarial balance is desirable, because choice of law seems an unpromising area of law in which to effect wealth redistribution. In the interstate arena, a state's authority is at its most tenuous. However, if choice of law rules are to have redistributive consequences, at least they are better directed against insiders than outsiders. This is the effect of the domiciliary principle, because the state is granted the right to coerce its own people or business entities by imposing burdens upon them. Ideally, a choice of law rule would be actuarially balanced; however, a state's choice to redistribute wealth away from its own people is not automatically illegitimate. Such a law is unnecessarily generous, but so long as the burdens are self-imposed, the state may legitimately choose to do so. The decision-maker imposing such a rule should be certain, however, that the costs are considered and found to be acceptable.

An example of such redistribution occurs in current choice between American state tort law and foreign tort law. In cases with international elements, American pro-recovery law has sometimes been applied to American defendants who injure foreigners abroad. American manufacturers are thereby held to the higher standards of liability, even though they cannot necessarily rely upon American law when it is to their advantage, since foreign individuals cannot be sued in the United States nor held to U.S. law. As one might expect, this situation is politically unpopular and has brought about calls for legislative reform. A state might understandably hesitate to adopt a choice of law rule such as the domiciliary principle because it would systematically work to the disadvantage of local persons. Arguably, a state's doing so is politically fair, in the sense discussed above, because it is imposing the costs on its own people. And whether to adopt such a substantively unfair rule is no different from the question of whether to adopt a rule of torts or contracts that is substantively unfair. But for precisely that reason, such a choice of law regime is not ideal. Adoption of such a regime should be a carefully considered choice, even if only local persons are disadvantaged.

To implement the notion of actuarial fairness, one might want to follow a general principle of mutuality. Mutuality would require that the substantive rule not be applied to an individual's detriment unless the individual would be eligible to receive the benefits if the tables were turned. This idea of "mutuality" resembles the concept of mutuality of estoppel in the context of judgments enforcement. Mutuality prohibits obviously unbalanced rules such as "choose the law that favors the local party." More subtly, it requires a judge to inquire into whether the law could fairly be applied to both parties, rather than simply whether it can fairly be applied to the aggrieved individual.

Jurisdiction-selecting rules satisfy mutuality because they do not depend upon the content of the substantive rule selected in the sense of which party will benefit. The content of the substantive rule may matter insofar as it describes relevant territorial factors, but one need not know whether it favors the plaintiff or the defendant. A jurisdiction-selecting rule will satisfy the mutuality requirement while simultaneously protecting political rights when it selects a state that has adequate connections with both parties. In such cases, one can select that state's law in the jurisdiction-selecting way—that is, without knowing what result the law, once examined, will dictate.

The ability to satisfy mutuality while respecting political rights may in fact be the distinguishing feature of the most successful applications of the old-fashioned territorial rules. Most territorial rules were adopted at a time when a greater proportion of cases, such as actions in tort or contract, involved face-to-face transactions or interactions. Under such circumstances, one could be relatively certain that the transaction could be assigned a location such that the rights "vested" in a state with which both parties had connections. That assignment might very well be arbitrary, in that other equally relevant events might have occurred in other states, yet at least a law was selected that could be applied without unfairness to either party. Today, however, it is much more common for business deals to be entered into over the phone, for products liability cases to be brought against defendants from a distant state, and for the acquisition of stock to be made through interstate tender offers. When transactions are spread out across a number of states, such a territorial assignment not only might be more arbitrary but also might be more likely to violate one or more party's rights. The arbitrariness stems from the fact that one cannot assume that the contract is negotiated, signed, and performed in the same location; to choose one factor over the others in determining a location seems hard to defend. The potential violation of rights stems from the possibility that one of the parties may have little or no contact with the state where the contract was actually formed, in the technical sense of offer and acceptance. Under modern conditions, Bealean rules are increasingly unlikely to satisfy both mutuality and negative rights.

The familiar territorial vested rights regimes would not be the only conceivable way to achieve the goal of both mutuality and protection of negative rights. Savigny pioneered a choice of law theory based on the "seat of the relationship" of the parties, which tried to assign a situs to the parties' legal transactions. While this often had consequences similar to vested-rights-style territoriality,[118] the systems were far from identical. The "center of gravity" approach[119] is similar to Savigny's. By searching for the seat of the relationship or the center of gravity, one

---

[118]   F. VON SAVIGNY, PRIVATE INTERNATIONAL LAW 27 (1869) (solution to conflicts cases turns on "ascertain[ing] for every legal relation (case) that law to which, in its proper nature, it belongs or is subject"); *id.* at 94-95 (specifying how to discover seat of legal relation).

[119]   Auten v. Auten, 308 N.Y. 155, 160-61, 124 N.E.2d 99, 101-02 (1954) (discussing 'center of gravity' or 'grouping of contacts' approach).

would with any luck find a state with which both parties were connected, because this would be a state where the parties' activities intersected. As with the vested rights approach, Savigny's system achieved the goals of political fairness and mutuality better in those days where most transactions involved at least some face-to-face dealings. Given modern communications technology, the existence of some relatively direct prior dealings between the parties can no longer be taken for granted.

D. *Interest Analysis and Fairness*

We have made mention at several points of the defects of the vested rights theory from a political rights-based perspective. We have also discussed the ways in which modern policy analysis differs from the rights-based approach at the foundational level. But as our discussion of the vested rights theory also shows, it is possible for a choice of law system to have strengths that were not deliberately planned. At this point, one might well ask how well the modern policy analysis fares in practice at the protection of political rights, however little it intends such protection.

First, and most obviously, the fact that interest analysis does not explicitly inquire into fairness allows it to apply the law of a state which has no political relationship with the aggrieved party. By focusing on the benefits bestowed by the rule's application, interest analysis fails to require justification for the burdens that it imposes. In this respect, it is in the same boat as the vested rights theory. This difficulty arises, however, only in true conflict and unprovided-for cases. It does not arise in false conflict cases because, as John Ely has demonstrated, these cases involve situations where the parties share a common domicile or hail from states with identical laws on the issue in question. False conflict cases result in no unfairness because the aggrieved party is subject to the law of his or her own home state. These conditions satisfy the domiciliary test. Surprisingly and virtually by coincidence—given its foundational differences—interest analysis thereby satisfies the political rights test on an important subset of disputes.

True conflicts and unprovided-for cases involve individuals from different states. Whether the modern approaches violate political rights in these cases depends upon whether one accepts Currie's solution to the true conflict and unprovided-for cases, or whether one seeks some other solution. Currie argued at one point that one should simply apply forum law. But it is not at all clear that the forum can fairly apply its law to any case before it. First, there are many ways of obtaining personal jurisdiction, and not all of them answer the fairness question posed by choice of law. One might be subjected to jurisdiction, for example, because one was "tagged" while simply passing through. Perhaps jurisdiction based upon mere presence should be considered fundamentally unfair and done away with as a matter of constitutional law. Arguably, once this is done the forum should automatically be allowed to apply its own law. Whether or not the wisdom of this proposal will ultimately be recognized, however, there remains the question of what we should do with choice of law in the meantime.

Moreover, there are ways of getting personal jurisdiction besides "tagging" which are less obviously unfair, yet may present the same fairness problem for a rights-sensitive choice of law theory. A defendant might consent to jurisdiction because the locale is not an inconvenient place to litigate: Perhaps it is reasonably close by and the defendant has access to good legal counsel there. Consent might occur ex ante, by contractual provision, or after the litigation is filed. Why should this consent automatically extend to choice of law as well? Alternately, one could unwittingly waive one's right to object to personal jurisdiction by failing to raise the issue at the right time. This seems eminently sensible and undoubtedly constitutional from the point of view of personal jurisdiction doctrine, but says nothing about whether the forum ought to be allowed automatically to apply its own law.

If we conclude that the mere fact that a state is the forum does not automatically give it the right to apply local law, then one must reject Currie's solution to the true conflict and unprovided-for cases on the grounds that applying forum law may violate one of the parties' rights. The other potential problem with Currie's system of interest analysis is whether it meets the requirement of actuarial fairness. It has been noted that the definition of state interests upon which Currie relied has the effect of discriminating against nonresidents because his idea of state interests did not recognize an interest in helping outsiders. This aspects of "interest" seems at first to create a possibility of loading the choice of law process against outsiders, because outsiders are held to the burdens of local law whenever the state has an interest in applying its law, but there is no corresponding interest in applying local law to their benefit.

The definition of interests that Currie prescribed does indeed have this characteristic. The method as a whole, however, avoids this consequence if consistently applied, because the concept of an interest turns out not to be necessary to the application of a state's law. It is perfectly possible to apply local law even when the state has no "interest," because forum law will apply unless both parties are from a state that has the different rule. That is, although the existence of an "interest" turns on who is benefited, application of a state's law does not turn on whether there is an interest. The probability of being benefited by local law, therefore, is the same as the probability of being burdened by it, because the probability of forum law not being applied does not depend upon whether it is helpful or harmful; all it depends upon is whether one happens to be transacting with an individual from a state with the same law. Modern policy analysis, in other words, passes the mutuality test, but only by coincidence; local law is sometimes applied even when there is no "interest." For this reason, it appears that as a method, Currie's version of policy analysis is jurisdiction-selecting—that is, whether a law applies does not depend upon its content.

* * * * *

Conclusions: Towards an Ideal Choice of Law Approach

While these observations do not dictate a unique choice of law on all occasions, they indicate that limits should be placed on what a state should feel entitled to do in pursuit of state policy. These rights-based limits are grounded in the observation that a state must be able to justify the burdens that it imposes, as well as to explain the benefits that it seeks to achieve, when it applies its law. A rights-based theory consists of two related parts. First, it must specify what rights are and why they matter. The theory of rights developed in * * * this article is different from Joseph Beale's, because the rights are not vested substantive rights but political rights. The justification for imposing burdens is not that a court must help enforce the pre-existing legal rights that the parties bring into the forum from other states, but that the state whose law is applied may fairly use this case to further local policy. Second, a rights-based theory must give some guidance about what rights exist. For Joseph Beale, this meant elaborating territorialist rules. For a political rights model, this means defining the circumstances in which interstate political authority may legitimately be applied. * * *

A state law of choice of law that took seriously the notions of political rights and fairness would address the following questions. First and foremost, what is the connection between the state and the party protesting the application of state law? There could be an adequate connection where the party is a local domiciliary, has consented to application of local law, or has voluntarily affiliated with the state by engaging in local activities or conduct with foreseeable legal consequences. Satisfaction of any of these alternatives must be gauged by reference to appropriate assumptions of territorial sovereignty. Second, what is the connection between the state and the individual who stands to benefit? Is there the sort of connection that would allow application of local law if the tables were turned and he or she thus stood to lose? If not, how can the state justify the redistributive impact? From a number of perspectives, the most attractive solution would be to select the law of a state with connections to both parties. A rule which chooses the state of common domicile satisfies the principle of mutuality; so does a rule choosing a state in which the parties have had face-to-face transactions.

What is perhaps the most surprising consequence of this analysis is the extent to which existing theories meet these standards, purely by inadvertence. Vested rights theory did not set out to meet the test of mutuality, yet because its rules are jurisdiction-selecting, they do have that characteristic. Even more surprising, interest analysis turns out to adhere to mutuality as well, because the concept of an interest turns out to be less central to the analysis than it first appears. Both theories fail most prominently in their lack of concern for the sort of purposeful conduct that makes submission to state authority fair; but often, personal jurisdiction by coincidence supplies the missing element. If it were not for these coincidences, would we have tolerated these approaches this long?

Whatever the unexpected advantages of vested rights and policy analysis, their protection of political rights is too haphazard. On some occasions, they simply fail to protect these rights at all. "Rights" is a meaningful concept for choice of law analysis, and it is important to frame choice of law analysis in these terms. Regardless of the specific contours that a rights-based analysis might take—whether it analyzes rights in territorial or in domiciliary terms— "rights" should not be allowed to slip into choice of law obscurity. The obligation to treat litigants fairly—to protect rights—is an obligation of state judges formulating state law as well as judges faced with constitutional challenges. Our jurisprudential tradition of insistence on fairness to the parties is important even in this post-realist world.

Comments

1. For additional attempts to sort out the work of recent conflicts theorists, *see* Bliesner 1994;[1] Green 1995; Sterk 1994.

2. Excerpts in Part C of this Chapter pressed for significant conflicts reform largely though the medium of state common law. In contrast, some critiques have urged changes through statutory reform. *See, e.g.,* Gottesman 1991; Kane 1991; Kramer 1991c; Stimson 1950. Other commentators have considered the possibility of conflicts reform through federal common law. *See, e.g.,* Horowitz 1967; Trautman 1977. Still others would significantly alter conflicts law by subjecting it to greater regulation under the United States Constitution. *See, e.g.,* Ely 1981; Laycock 1992.

3. Each of the contributors to Part C appeared to rest his or her reform proposal on the foundation of a pre-existing conflicts value or tradition. In this sense, Professor Kramer's "canons of construction" and Professor Simson's multi-step approach can

---

[1]   Full citations appear in the bibliography, Chapter Twelve.

be understood as different re-calibrations of unilateralism (interest analysis). The history and animating features of unilateralism in American conflicts law are the subjects of Chapter Five.

4.   Similarly, Professors von Mehren's discussion of special rules of decision for multistate cases and Professor Singer's search for the jurisprudential underpinnings of laws vying for acceptance can be seen as variations on the theme of conflicts substantivism. The basic features of substantivism are surveyed in Chapter Seven, Part B.

5.   In like manner, Professor Dane's concept of vestedness seems a partial reworking of multilateralist theory (territorialism), surveyed in Chapter Three. Multilaterist reform views also appear in Corr 1983; Ely 1981; Laycock 1992; Twerski 1981.

6.   Ties are discernable between Professor Brilmayer's political rights model and notions of party fairness found in the most expansive statements of the expectations ideal in choice of law (treated in Chapter Seven, Part A) and in policies limiting personal jurisdiction. Further examination of intersections between personal jurisdiction and choice of law appears in Chapter Ten, Part D.

7.   The contributors to Part C of this Chapter faced profound difficulties perhaps inherent in any contemporary attempt to re-conceptualize American conflicts law. As confused and complicated as conflicts theory was in the early stages of the conflicts revolution (surveyed in Chapters Three and Four), the topic has become far more difficult since. "More recently," observed one of our contributors, "choice of law has sometimes resembled the law's psychiatric ward. It is a place of odd fixations and schizophrenic visions." Dane 1996: p. 209. There is now in our conflicts literature such a disparate (and often contradictory) accretion of policies, rules, systems, catchphrases, diagnoses, and proposed cures that it seems almost impossible for critics now writing either to keep their targets in focus or to demonstrate with complete success how their ideas are new, helpful, or even intelligible.

8.   This may explain the tendency of courts not to make explicit use of the new conflicts criticism, and it may explain the fact that vigorous dialog concerning new conflicts theories occurs only within a small (if respected) academic circle. From the time of Livermore and Story, American conflicts law has taken shape and energy from legal scholarship. The writers represented in Part C are the Cavers' and Curries of our age. If they exert significantly less influence than their predecessors, does that bode ill for the future of conflicts law? How much hope exists for clarity, coherence, and reform in conflicts theory? For possible answers to this question, we can turn to Part D of this Chapter.

D. Enduring Problems of Coherence and Justice in Choice of Law

Michael H. Gottesman, *Draining the Dismal Swamp: The Case for Federal Choice of Law Statutes*, 80 GEO. L.J. 1, 11-13 (1991)*

* * * * *

Most conflict scholars decry the present chaotic state of affairs. There are ample reasons to do so. First, the system is wasteful. In the states that have adopted one of the modern choice of law approaches, the parties may litigate at length over the application of indeterminate criteria such as the "interests" that are to control under interest analysis or the combination of interests and contacts that are to be consulted under the second Restatement to determine whether the presumption in favor of a jurisdiction-selecting rule has been overcome. This is both expensive and time-consuming. What is more, after the parties have expended resources litigating the issue before the trial court, and that court has ruled that the law of State A controls, the ensuing trial may prove wholly useless if the appellate court later determines that the choice of law was error and State B's law controls. Costs are higher still if the plaintiff has chosen an incongruous forum simply to secure its choice of law rules and the case is not thereafter transferred to a more convenient forum. When that happens, the parties must bear the costs of litigating the merits in a distant and inconvenient forum.

Second, the system frustrates rational planning. Parties cannot know when they act what law governs their behavior, for that depends upon post-act events such as the plaintiff's choice of forum. Granted, not every act that gives rise to a lawsuit is planned in advance, but some are. Institutional actors, for example, must decide how much to invest in making their activities safer, and what activities to avoid because the liability risks exceed the benefits. And even acts that are not planned are often insured against in advance. There are significant costs when actors—especially risk-averse actors—are forced to make decisions without knowing what law governs their actions.

Third, it is always disturbing when the law is indeterminate, but especially so when the legal regime that will judge the propriety of conduct will be the product of events (such as forum selection) that occur *ex post*. I recognize, with the legal realists, that the law is not a mechanical science. Even when parties know the legal rules at the time they act, *ex post* considerations can upset their calculations: the quality of lawyering, the biases or intelligence of the judge or jury, mistakes in fact-finding, manipulation of precedents, and so on. But there is a quantitative, and I suggest qualitative, difference between a system in which determinate legal rules are applied (however imperfectly) and one in which the courts deliberately embrace the notion that parties will act today and find out tomorrow what was expected of them.

Finally, many observers are troubled (as I am) that the modern approaches are biased. The legal regime that will judge the past acts of the parties may differ, depending on where the lawsuit is filed. Often only one party to the dispute has the ability to choose the forum. Even where that is not so, the party who files first will, for no better reason than that it has won a race to

---

a courthouse, be able (through forum selection) to impose the legal regime most favorable to its interests.

* * * * *

Stewart E. Sterk, *The Marginal Relevance of Choice of Law Theory*, 142 U. Pa. L. Rev. 949, 951-952, 961-962, 988-989, 992-993, 1000-1001, 1030-1031 (1994)*

* * * * *

My thesis is simple. Choice of law is in disarray because conflicts scholars have not made the case that choice of law theory *should* matter in deciding a wide variety of cases. They have not persuaded judges that judges should take care to make "correct" choice of law decisions. As a result, courts often worry less about choice of law than about the other substantive implications of the decisions they reach.

This is not a correctable problem. Conflict scholars have failed to persuade courts about the importance of choice of law not because scholars are insufficiently persuasive or judges are insufficiently receptive, but because in many cases reaching the "correct" choice of law result is and should be less important to judges than other substantive law considerations. In these cases, subordinating choice of law concerns generates only one identifiable social cost—the cost of uncertainty in litigation. That loss, however, would be avoidable only if virtually all courts consistently and uniformly embraced the same choice of law approach—a possibility so unlikely that in resolving these cases courts understandably and justifiably pay little more than lip service to choice of law theory.

* * * * *

From reading judicial opinions and works of scholarship, one could easily conclude that academic theory has been far more influential in the choice of law area than in most other areas of law. Judicial opinions involving choice of law issues are frequently laced with citations to scholarly books and articles. In many jurisdictions, no conflicts discussion would be complete without a citation to the Second Restatement of Conflict of Laws. Leading casebooks are often organized not by subject matter but by academic theory, highlighting the supposed importance of theory. Leading scholars in the field make it their business to track the adoption of one theory or another by courts in different jurisdictions.

Has academic theory been as influential as the frequency of citation would indicate? The question is ultimately unanswerable, but I would suggest that, at least in many areas, citation to academic theory has served more as window dressing than as a dispositive factor in deciding choice of law cases.* * *

* * * * *

When choice of law questions reach appellate courts, fact disputes are rarely significant. If the appeal is of a judgment on the pleadings or of a summary judgment determination, the appellate court may generally assume a set of facts in considering whether the lower court's choice of law decision was legally "correct"; if the appeal comes after trial, the appellate court may well be bound by the findings of fact below. It should not be surprising, then, that many leading conflicts theorists, who have focused largely on appellate cases, have underemphasized the role of choice of law determinations in the case management process.

Typically, however, trial courts make initial choice of law determinations, and case management concerns frequently predominate. Thus, in cases involving many parties and common issues, applying different rules of law to each plaintiff or defendant would create an administrative nightmare that courts would endure only for reasons more compelling than those usually advanced in choice of law cases.

Even in cases involving fewer parties, the timing of choice of law determinations can shape much of the litigation. If a court makes a choice of law determination early in the litigation process, it may foreclose litigation about facts that would be relevant only if a particular state's law were applied to the issue at hand. Indeed, in some cases, an early choice of law determination might permit resolution of the entire case on the pleadings or on summary judgment motion.

* * * * *

Choice of law theorists have generally ignored these case management concerns, concentrating instead on how to advance state interests, protect party expectations, or enforce choice of law "rights." To judges, by contrast, case management concerns are often paramount. As we have seen, both the substance and the timing of choice of law decisions can have a significant impact on case management; when and how choice of law decisions are made may determine the duration and direction of litigation. So long as choice of law theory focuses only on what state's law should be applied to particular facts, theory cannot possibly capture the considerations that inform judicial choice of law decisions.

* * *

I have argued that the liberal citation of choice of law theory in recently decided cases overstates the significance of choice of law principles. Those principles determine case results only when courts have an intuitive sense that justice requires application of the law of a particular state. Most choice of law cases, however, do not generate that intuitive sense of conflicts justice. In the ordinary choice of law case, choice of law principles take a back seat to the substantive results that are generated by the competing rules and the effect competing rules might have on litigation complexity and settlement negotiations. Does this "failure" of choice of law theory stem from inadequacy in the approaches developed so far, or is the problem inherent to choice of law theory? In other words, are all comprehensive choice of law theories doomed to failure?

My argument is that most of the premises and principles that underlie any given choice of law theory are sufficiently unimportant to courts that any attempt to implement a comprehensive theory is doomed. In this respect, choice of law policies and principles differ from those that underlie our systems of civil, criminal, and administrative procedure. Considerations of substance often color decisions on procedural issues, just as substance informs choice of law decisions. But courts recognize that procedural requirements perform an essential function in any legal system; without a core of procedural rules, adjudication and administration is impossible. Hence, substance is not all; courts and administrators recognize that substantive results must be balanced against the harm to the system that would result if procedures were entirely ignored. By contrast, the state policies that serve as the focus of consequentialist choice of law theories rarely rise to the significance necessary to induce a judge to abandon a substantive result she might prefer; the choice of law "rights" emphasized by rights theorists are not so fundamental that they command allegiance when they seem inconvenient to a judge seeking to do justice between the competing parties.

* * * * *

Consider the difficulties in using the common-law process to institutionalize cooperation in choice of law. It is true, of course, that state courts develop state policy all the time, even in the absence of legislative action. That development, however, is generally incremental, and incrementalism is ill-suited to the problem at hand. Choice of law cases first reach trial courts. Why should any single California trial judge sacrifice forum state policy, or her own notions of justice to the parties before her, in the name of greater cooperation among states without knowing that her California colleagues will follow the same course? Unless her colleagues are committed to the same cooperative strategy, the attempt by a single California judge to pursue cooperative solutions is doomed to failure, because judges in other states have no reason to believe that a lone California trial court decision commits the California courts to a policy of reciprocity.

For a state court system to make any credible commitment to a policy of cooperation, then, the commitment must come from the state's supreme court, whose decisions bind all of the state's judges. But how can a supreme court make such a commitment? Over any reasonable time period, too few choice of law cases reach any state supreme court for the court to develop, through the common-law process, a set of comprehensive cooperative choice of law rules. The court could, of course, simply announce that it plans to adopt a cooperative approach to choice of law problems, but a statement at that level of generality will not generate confidence among judges in other states that the announcing state's conception of cooperation is similar to their own.

* * * * *

Much of modern choice of law scholarship is premised on the notion that better thinking will lead to a more coherent approach to choice of law. Even those theorists who have abandoned the notion that a comprehensive set of principles can resolve all choice of law cases continue to search for approaches that will generate unique solutions to choice of law cases.

My thesis has been that this search is misguided. In a wide range of cases, especially tort cases, no set of choice of law rules or principles will eliminate the existing regime of "choice of law chaos." In these cases, no choice of law principles are sufficiently compelling to cause judges to exalt choice of law considerations over concerns about the facts and substantive law issues involved in the individual case.

What has led choice of law scholarship astray? In part, the problem has been scholarship that starts from general principles (sometimes derived from political theory) and operates deductively to arrive at choice of law conclusions. This deductive approach to choice of law stands in sharp contrast to the common-law method, which makes real-life facts the starting point for analysis. Professionalism furnishes another explanation for the continuing quest for conflicts principles to resolve all choice of law cases. If choice of law principles are not sufficiently important to override concerns about substantive outcomes, what role is left for conflicts scholars?

The truth—that choice of law principles are often irrelevant in deciding cases with multistate conflicts—poses no real threat to the professional self-interest of conflicts scholars. Choice of law principles sometimes are and should be critically important—but only sometimes. Much work remains to be done in identifying areas where choice of law principles should influence the decision-making process. But to pretend that choice of law principles should be determinative in all multistate cases is to increase obfuscation in an area already characterized more by mud than by crystal.

James E. Westbrook, *A Survey and Evaluation of Competing Choice-of-Law Methodologies: The Case for Eclecticism*, 40 Mo. L. Rev. 407, 440-441, 442-447 (1975)*

Choice-of-Law Cases Require Courts to Reconcile the Irreconcilable

> The reconciliation of the irreconcilable, the merger of antitheses, the synthesis of opposites, these are the great problems of the law.
>
> Cardozo

Judge Cardozo was speaking of law in general when he made this statement in a lecture at Columbia University. But choice-of-law cases provide some of the more apt illustrations of the truth of his statement. It is a truism worth repeating that humans differ in their estimates of the relative importance of particular values. When important values are in conflict and one must be preferred over the other, intelligent, well-meaning persons will differ on what should be done. Moreover, the choices men make in such situations will be influenced by their institutional role. Choice-of-law problems reflect the same tensions between competing values that exist throughout law with the added complication of conflicts between the laws of different jurisdictions. The differences between the methodologies * * * derive from fundamental disagreements over the weight to be accorded values at stake in the choice-of-law process.

An examination of the choice-influencing considerations set forth in Leflar's work and in the *Restatement (Second)* will point up some of the conflicting values involved in choice-of-law. Factors (f) and (g) in section 6 of the *Restatement (Second)* emphasize certainty, predictability, uniformity of result, and ease in the determination of the law to be applied. Looking in the opposite direction are factors (b) and (c), which suggest that consideration should be given to the relevant policies and interests of the forum and other interested states. Also pointing away from such values as uniformity is Leflar's better rule of law consideration. The tension between these factors, each in itself an important value deserving consideration, corresponds to the classic tension in the law between legal certainty and equity. On the one hand, the law should be clear, foreseeable, and applicable uniformly. As Brandeis once said, ". . . in most matters it is more important that the applicable rule of law be settled than that it be settled right."[211] In stressing the importance of uniform application, Sir John Salmond argued that men's respect for law depends in large measure on their belief that "[j]ust or unjust, wise or

---

[211] Burnett v. Coronado Oil & Gas Co., 285 U.S. 393, 406 (1932) (dissenting opinion).

foolish, it is the same for all. . . ."[212] Yet there is also something in human nature that rebels at sacrificing concrete human or governmental interests to abstract goals of certainty and we recognize that these goals often are sense and decency, we want cases decided in a way that strikes us as just. This means that courts must give adequate weight to the special and unique circumstances of each case. It also means that societal changes must be accommodated by continual adjustment of the law. The authors of the first *Restatement* sacrificed the values which cluster under the umbrella of equity to those which fit under that of certainty. The functional methodologies that dominate contemporary conflicts thinking move sharply in the other direction. * * *

Varying Conceptions of How Judges Should Discharge Their Responsibilities

Different conceptions of the proper role of the judiciary are reflected in choice-of-law methodologies and in the preference of judges for particular methodologies. Not only are there differences of opinion at any one time, but the prevailing opinion changes from one period of history to another. When changes occur in the prevailing concept of the manner in which judges should discharge their responsibilities, some approaches to choice-of-law gain in popularity and others fade. Karl Llewellyn, one of the great legal realists, pointed out that there are period styles in legal writing. There are times when the climate in the legal profession and the judges' concept of their function result in opinions written in the "Formal Style," where decisions seemingly are based only on formal logic and consistency. This style is appealing to judges who are reluctant to expose their underlying social judgements to public critique. It satisfies a need to have the law appear neutral, even static. It is obvious that a classificatory approach to choice-of-law fits more comfortably into this style of opinion writing. There are times, however, when judicial opinions tend to be written in the "Grand Style," where there is an open checking of results against principle, common sense, and decency. In an age when formalism and deference to symbols is viewed with suspicion, judges earn respect by frank discussion of the actual bases of their decisions. If men no longer believe that decisions are made through sole reliance on formal conceptualism, it can be argued that the symbolic ideal of the law's certainty is better preserved by open consideration of the policies in issue.

It seems clear that the period style at present [1975] is one in which there is little tolerance of artifice and fictions. We believe that law should be a workable social tool, and we insist that law should be talked about and explained in terms of functions and policies. It is to be expected that the methodology of a Cavers, a Currie, or a Leflar, with their emphasis on the purposes which underlie laws or on choice-influencing considerations, would appeal to contemporary judges. It seems quite possible that the demise of the first *Restatement* resulted as much from the fact that its language and rationale were out of step with the current period style as from any deficiencies in the way it dealt with concrete cases. After all, judges were quite skillful in manipulating traditional concepts to achieve acceptable results. A good example of the sensitivity of an outstanding judge to such considerations is Judge Traynor's subsequent apology in the *Texas Law Review*[219] for his reliance on the substance-procedure distinction in his opinion in *Grant v. McAuliffe*.[220]

---

[212]   Salmond, *Introduction* to Science of Legal Method at lxxxi (1917).

[219]   Traynor, *Is This Conflict Really Necessary?*, 37 Tex. L. Rev. 657, 670 n. 35 (1959).

[220]   41 Cal. 2d 859, 264 P.2d 944 (1953).

The writings of Brainerd Currie provide another example of how one's view of the judiciary's proper function influences one's methodological preference. His advocacy of forum preference in a true-conflict case derived from a strongly held belief that:

> ... assessment of the respective values of the competing legitimate interests of two sovereign states, in order to determine which is to prevail, is a political function of a very high order. This is a function that should not be committed to courts in a democracy.[221]

The rejection of Currie's resort to forum preference in true-conflict cases by sympathetic scholars is in large part a result of disagreement on this view of the courts' proper function in a democracy. Most conflicts scholars believe that courts have long engaged in this weighing of competing interests and that they may be more competent than legislatures to do so. Legislatures cannot foresee all of the situations that may arise. Courts, on the other hand, can deal with problems on a case-by-case basis. If a solution fashioned in one case does not appear suitable in a slightly different case, it can be distinguished.

The Federal System

The structure of our federal system inevitably produces large numbers of conflicts problems. We have two sets of substantive law, state and federal, and two judicial systems in each state. For the most part, private law is the domain of the states. Not only are fifty states generating private law, but choice-of-law rules vary from state to state. Absent the application of the law of a state which has no substantial connection with a case, decisions of the United States Supreme Court leave a state free to make its own choice of the governing law. It would be surprising if the appellate courts and legislatures of the fifty states did not disagree frequently over the policies they think will promote the welfare of their citizens, and each such disagreement carries the potential for a conflict of laws which must be resolved by the courts. Moreover, the growing volume and complexity of statutes and decisions have caused a concomitant growth in the number of conflicts between states' laws. It is no surprise that the typical reaction of foreign observers is that our system is far too complicated. Reflecting on our legal system, Justice Jackson said that, "We have so far as I can ascertain the most localized and conflicting system of any country which presents the external appearance of nationhood."[227]

In some respects the situation in the United States is analogous to that which existed in the thirteenth century when each of the Italian city-states began developing a separate body of law. Given the fact that the citizens of those cities did not spend all of their time at home, it was natural that controversies arose between citizens of different cities. In seeking an acceptable means of choosing the applicable law, the statutists tried for six or seven hundred years to eliminate differences of opinion within their ranks. Their lack of success is sometimes explained by what are thought to have been defects in their methodology. Professor Cavers has compared them to the alchemists who sought to make gold out of other metals. It is questionable, however, whether this is a wholly satisfactory explanation of the statutists' difficulties. It is at least possible that the presence of numerous sources of law presents intractable problems which cannot

---

[221] B. CURRIE, [SELECTED ESSAYS ON THE CONFLICT OF LAWS] 113 and ch. IX.

[227] Jackson [*Full faith and Credit—The Lawyer's Clause of the Constitution*, 45 COLUM. L. REV. 1, 18 (1945)].

be completely solved through resort to choice-of-law techniques. And if six or seven centuries did not eliminate differences of opinion among the statutists, one may reasonably conclude that differences of opinion over the proper approach to choice-of-law may not disappear from our jurisprudence with the passage of time. In sum, continuing controversy over choice-of-law problems may be one of the inevitable consequences of living under a federal system such as ours.

The Large Number of Variables Presented in Choice-of-Law Cases

The almost infinite number of law-fact patterns that can arise in cases raising conflicts questions makes it extremely difficult to formulate rules of decision that will deal satisfactorily with each case that may arise. In discussing *Grant v. McAuliffe*, Brainerd Currie pointed out that there were at least 174 different fact situations involving the California statute on survival of tort actions that would give rise to choice-of-law problems. All lawyers use the technique of distinguishing cases when the facts of a case differ in some way from precedent that would otherwise govern. Because conflicts cases contain more variables than wholly domestic cases, existing precedent is more apt to be distinguishable. Since conflicts cases arise less frequently than wholly domestic cases, there are fewer reported decisions available for guidance of the court and the parties. Thus, in a field where a greater variety of questions can arise, there are fewer resources of precedent upon which one can rely.

Traditional conflicts theory dealt with this bewildering array of possible law-fact patterns by isolating only one of the relevant factors and establishing it as the key to the applicable law. It was pointed out earlier that this tendency toward oversimplification is considered to be one of the key shortcomings of the traditional system. Some contemporary conflicts scholars urge an approach that would strike a balance between the few broad rules of the first *Restatement* and an approach that would treat each case as unique. It was pointed out earlier that Professor Reese has urged the necessity of developing large numbers of relatively narrow rules. Other scholars react to the multiplicity of cases that can arise by eschewing any attempt to formulate conflicts rules and urging instead a method of analysis which can be used to decide cases on a more or less ad hoc basis. These scholars argue that such an approach is the only feasible way of dealing with the tremendous variety of cases which arise in a fashion which will give adequate weight to the varying policies brought into play by shifting law-fact patterns. The point that should be emphasized is that these differences in methodology arise because of differences of opinion as to how best to cope with the tremendous variety of problems generated by our legal system. Everyone recognizes that the creation of jurisprudential tools to deal with such complexity is very difficult. The large number of variables makes it impossible to reconcile the demands of certainty and equity in a manner that does not in itself create additional problems. The choice of a methodology is in part a decision as to which problems the legal system can best cope with and which problems are best left alone.

Societal Changes

Social and economic changes result in changes in the characteristic choice-of-law problems which confront the courts during any one period of time. Thus, even if a consensus has emerged on the most appropriate mode of analysis for dealing with a particular set of problems, the consensus may crumble if the accepted approach does not work well in dealing with the new problems generated by societal changes. Cavers has pointed out that the characteristic choice-of-law problems of nineteenth-century America were conflicts involving commercial law and the flow of funds from "the capital-rich East to the capital-poor West."[238] He notes also that conflicts problems were generated in the latter half of the nineteenth century by "the uneven emergence among the states of statutes designed to remove anachronisms in the common law, such as restraints on married women as property owners and traders, the denial of actions for wrongful death, and the fellow-servant rule. . . ." Professor Ehrenzweig has asserted that the contemporary ferment in conflicts law is concentrated in the area of tort conflicts law. Professor Juenger agrees and suggests that the rejection of the rule of *lex loci delicti* in tort cases has often been motivated by a desire to avoid the application of noxious substantive law. Seen in this light, *Babcock v. Jackson* is a product of the notorious Ontario guest statute. The emergence of no-fault statutes is now producing new choice-of-law problems.

It is true, of course, that this is a problem which exists throughout law. Social and economic changes occur continuously; the only variable from one age to another is the rate of change. Law must respond to change, and this fact of life produces one of the perennial problems of jurisprudence—the reconciliation of the claims of stability with those of progress. Yet this fundamental fact of legal life has special significance in the conflicts field. The uneven response of state courts and legislatures to societal changes provides a continuing source of conflicts problems. Although some may argue that their methodology provides a philosophy for all seasons, it seems more realistic to assert that the desirability of various choice-of-law methodologies will vary with the problems being considered. Consequently, a subject which would be difficult even if the characteristic problems remained relatively constant is periodically subjected to great stress as a result of changes in the nature of the problems which find their way into the courts.

* * * * *

Arthur T. von Mehren, *Choice of Law and the Problem of Justice*, 41 LAW & CONTEMP. PROBS. 27, 27, 42 (1977)*

Those who work in the field of choice of law are, at times, discouraged by the apparently intractable nature of the problems with which they must grapple. Intricate and subtle analyses are undertaken; ambiguities and uncertainties are painfully resolved. Ultimately, a result is reached, yet the solution is too frequently neither entirely satisfying nor fully convincing.

The process of analyzing and deciding fully domestic cases is, of course, on occasion also difficult and the results reached are at times unsatisfying. Yet, overall, one is ordinarily less dissatisfied than with multistate cases. The deeper and more pervasive malaise engendered by these latter flows only partially from the relatively greater complexity of the analysis typically required; even where wholly domestic cases present a comparable order of difficulty, the solutions given in multistate cases are more likely to trouble one's sense of justice.

* * * * *

---

[238] D. CARVERS [THE CHOICE-OF-LAW PROCESS 114-115 (1965)].

* Reprinted with permission.

[E]xcept perhaps in certain cases of "false" or "no" conflict, the standards of justice applied to fully domestic cases cannot be achieved in multistate cases. Even in cases that do not present a true conflict, the fact that the parties will ordinarily be from different states tends to reduce significantly the decision's claim to legitimacy. A further source of doubt in some cases is that lay thinking is often strongly shaped by the territorial connections of the total situation although analytically these may be largely irrelevant for a jurist deciding what law governs the issue before the court. The justice of a decision in a fully domestic case can never be challenged on such grounds and is greatly strengthened by the fact that the views of only one society need be taken into consideration. Finally, a court in a multistate case must undertake a process of analysis that is inherently more complex than that faced in a purely domestic case; to a greater or lesser degree, the court must take into account the rules and policies of foreign legal orders. Accordingly, the areas of possible doubt and ambiguity are larger. For these reasons, one who expects to achieve results in multistate cases that are as satisfying in terms of standards of justice and of party acceptability as those reached in purely domestic cases is doomed to disappointment. Perhaps the most satisfactory solution would be to render choice of law unnecessary by establishing supra-national rules administered by supra-national agencies. But this solution engenders its own difficulties and is unlikely for historical and political reasons.

Comments

1.   The attacks by Professors Gottesman and Sterk in Part D of this Chapter are not unique. Indeed, it is sobering to note the possibility that conflicts is and long has been the most unpopular subject in American law. Evidence for this may be found both in the reactions of the bench and bar and in academic writing.

2.   Negative attitudes of lawyers toward conflicts law imperiled publication of the original conflicts RESTATEMENT. An ALI insider wrote:

> The law book people with whom the Institute was associated in publishing the Restatement shook their heads dolefully at the mention of a volume in the conflict of laws. They predicted that any book bearing that title would be a financial failure because of the unpopularity of the subject. Only when marketed as part of a set of books, they said, would the Restatement volume in conflict of laws reach the shelves of lawyers and law libraries.

Goodrich 1950: p. 9.[1] There is no reason to believe that the situation has improved. Professor Joseph Singer recently reported: "Many lawyers regard modern choice-of-law analysis as a confusing morass." Singer 1990: 731.

3.   A common law subject, conflicts law could not have taken hold in American jurisprudence without active labors by the judiciary. Yet many judges have reacted to the subject with bafflement or, at times, scorn. Evidence exists as early as the 1827 case of *Saul v. His Creditors*, 5 Mart. (n.s.) 569, where a Louisiana court described conflict of laws as;

Full citations appear in the bibliography, Chapter Twelve.

a subject, the most intricate and perplexed of any that has occupied the attention of lawyers and courts: one on which scarcely any two writers are found to entirely agree, and on which, it is rare to find one consistent with himself throughout. We know of no matter in jurisprudence so unsettled, or none that should more teach men distrust for their own opinions, and charity for those of others.

Id. at 589 (quoted in Juenger 1993: p. 44). In *Erwin v. Thomas*, 506 P.2d. 494, 495 (1973), the Oregon Supreme Court observed: "It is with some trepidation that a court enters the maze of choice of law in tort cases. No two authorities agree." The court likened use of a modern choice-of-law formula "to wandering off into the jungle with a compass which everyone but its maker says is defective." *Id.* at 496. Similar sentiments appear in *In re Paris Air Crash of Mar. 3, 1974*, 399 F. Supp. 732, 739 (C.D. Cal. 1975) (finding conflicts law a "veritable jungle, which, if the law can be found out, leads not to a 'rule of action' but a reign of chaos."); and in *Paul v. National Life*, 352 S.E.2d 550, 553 (W. Va. 1986) (describing conflicts law as "cumbersome and unwieldy [creating] confusion, uncertainty and inconsistency, as well as complication of the judicial task.")

4. Scholars too have found the topic of conflicts law mysterious or worse. Benjamin Cardozo called it "one of the most baffling subjects of legal science." Cardozo 1928: p. 67. It was to Max Rheinstein the "most difficult and most confused of all branches of the law." Rheinstein 1962: p. 655. Professor Friedrich Juenger recently observed: "Alas, in spite of all the valiant intellectual efforts lavished on it, and the voluminous literature that has built up over the ages, the law of conflicts remains mired in mystery and confusion." Juenger 1993: p. 1. The best known and most severe judgment came from Professor William Prosser. Conflicts law was to Professor Prosser "a dismal swamp, filled with quaking quagmires, and inhabited by learned but eccentric professors who theorize about mysterious matters in strange and incomprehensible jargon." Prosser 1953: p. 971.

5. In their turn, law students taking the conflicts course may also experience a high level of frustration. It can take the following pattern.

> Students often enter conflicts class with an initial assumption about conflicts law. They probably share it with the community at large. The assumption is that courts simply apply their own law. To those untrained in conflicts law and analysis, the stark unilateralism of this assumption is straightforward, intelligible, and perfectly sensible. * * *. Yet conflicts professors quickly and easily demolish this assumption. We demonstrate the injustice of forum shopping, the substantive chaos, and the pernicious acts of judicial localism that would result from such law.
>
> One we have destroyed their first assumption, students shift quickly and intuitively to a second; that every jurisdiction does (or at least should) administer the same conflicts law to reach the same choice-of-

law result in a given case. For those without significant exposure to conflicts law, the pure multilateralism of this assumption can seem a simple, straightforward, and attractive idea. It comes fairly close to describing what conflicts law in this country used to be.

It takes a bit longer in the course for the second assumption to collapse. * * * However, at least by the time * * * students consider choice of law and the Constitution, it is quite clear that pure or even substantial multilateralism in American choice of law is an illusion.

About this time in the course, * * * many students start seriously to doubt the possibility of principled, coherent conflicts law. They cannot find a third successive assumption. They find instead contradiction and dissonance within courts and the scholarly community about what conflicts law is or ought to be.

Shreve 1996b: pp. 589-590.

6.   What can be said in defense of conflicts law? The excerpts concluding Part D offer two perspectives. First, as Professor Westbrook suggested, actual confusion and disarray within the subject may be less than some have suggested. In keeping with this view, Professor Willis Reese—although at times a forceful critic of conflicts law—stated:

American choice of law is not as unruly and chaotic as is generally supposed. On the basis of the actual court decisions, it appears that there is a fair measure of predictability and uniformity of result in all areas, except tort, contracts in situations where the contract does not contain a choice-of-law clause, and conveyances of interests in movables as between the parties to the conveyance.

Reese 1982a: p. 146.

7.   Second, as Professor von Mehren observed, we may simply have to live with the fact that, to a significant extent, conflicts decisions will always be more complicated and more controversial than domestic cases. In support, this author has written:

Conflicts law is far from perfect. However, particular flaws have less to do with its unpopularity than one might think. Rather, it is the innate difficulties of analysis that have made conflicts controversial and have kept it that way. It may be a sad fact of human nature that the difficulty of a legal question is demonstrated less by agreement on that score among judges and commentators than by the rising decibel level of arguments over who is obviously right and obviously wrong. The prevailing approach to resolving conflicts—whatever that approach then happens to be—will always be under attack.

Shreve 1993: pp. 911-912. Not all, however, would single out conflicts cases for such protective treatment. *See* Kramer 1991b: p. 247 (suggesting a need to "reorient choice-of-law analysis by viewing it in its ordinary procedural context," where it is merely a part of "the process of defining the elements of a claim or defense.").

CHAPTER TEN

Choice of Law and the Constitution

One of the most important and perplexing topics in conflicts commentary is choice of law and the Constitution. It is clear that conflicts decisions implicate important constitutional policies, but it is equally clear that attempts to constitutionalize any significant part of the choice-of-law process would be both controversial and difficult to implement. Thus, while the Supreme Court periodically intervenes under the Constitution to reverse a conflicts decision, these cases have proven hard to analyze and even harder to reduce to a set of regulating rules. Justice Robert Jackson observes in one of the selections appearing in this Chapter that it would be "difficult to point to any field in which the Court has more completely demonstrated or more candidly confessed the lack of guiding standards of a legal character than in trying to determine what choice of law is required by the Constitution."

The author provides an initial view of the topic in Part A of this Chapter, maintaining that parochialism in choice of law can be seen to offend a variety of interests secured under the Constitution, and contending that—despite the availability in theory of nonconstitutional means of curbing conflicts abuse—the Constitution provides the only plausible means of reform. Yet the potential breadth of constitutional policies implicated by conflicts cases may actually explain the Court's reluctance to give life to the former. The author argues that, should the Court begin to give serious weight to the Constitution in choice of law, it might be unable to find a logical stopping point short of constitutionalizing the entire subject.

Part B explores at greater length the sources traditionally used by the Supreme Court for invalidating conflicts decisions—the full-faith-and-credit and due process clauses. Justice Jackson reviews the Supreme Court's role in choice of law, with particular reference to the full-faith-and-credit clause. He concludes that the performance of the Court has been sporadic and relatively unfocused. In the next two excerpts, Professors Louise Weinberg and Robert Sedler defend the Court's failure to assign a larger role to the Constitution in choice of law. Professor Weinberg argues that the enormous costs of judicial administration that would attend any serious use of constitutional doctrine to regulate choice of law would be unjustified. Professor Sedler maintains that an understanding of the general principles that shape and limit the full-faith-and-credit and due process clauses makes clear why they have only limited application in the choice-of-law setting. Then, a selection by Professor Willis Reese offers the opposing view that the Court should give greater play to the Constitution in regulating choice of law. Part B concludes with a selection by Professor Linda Silberman, who also urges the Supreme Court to increase regulation of choice of law. But Professor Silberman advocates change through development of federal common law, as an alternative to enlargement of constitutional doctrine.

Part C of this Chapter features critics who would bring new parts of the Constitution to bear on conflicts law. In the opening selection, Professor Douglas Laycock lays groundwork for sweeping reform of conflicts law through reinterpretation of the privileges-and-immunities, commerce, and equal protection clauses of the Constitution. Professor John Ely then provides further commentary on the potential for privileges-and-immunities clause application to choice of law. Professor Harold Horowitz supports a similar use for the commerce clause. Finally, Professor Gerald Neuman adds to the case for regulating conflicts law under the equal protection clause.

Part D concludes this Chapter by comparing the respective roles of the Constitution in regulating choice of law and personal jurisdiction. The opening excerpt by the author illustrates how due process doctrine regulating personal jurisdiction obviates many choice-of-law decisions that might have been problematic under the Constitution. Next, Professor Courtland Peterson reflects on the complicated relationship between personal jurisdiction and choice of law expressed in the opinions of Supreme Court justices. He concludes that many on the Court appear to have seen the two areas as significantly overlapping. In the following excerpt, Professor Peter Hay explains why he believes that care should be taken to view separately constitutional law regulating personal jurisdiction and that regulating choice of law. Then, Professor James Martin offers a contrary position, that the best means for regulating choice of law is to borrow heavily from the features of constitutional doctrine regulating personal jurisdiction. Finally, Professor Friedrich Juenger draws a very different lesson from Supreme Court cases regulating personal jurisdiction. Professor Juenger argues that, because the Court's attempt to articulate and apply standards regulating personal jurisdiction have been unsuccessful, it should not try its hand at regulating the more difficult subject of choice of law.

A. The Constitutional Concern of Conflicts Localism

Gene R. Shreve, *Choice of Law and the Forgiving Constitution*, 71 IND. L.J. 271, 271-281, 287-289, 294-296 (1996)*

This Article confronts a paradox. Choice of law seems to have everything yet almost nothing to do with the United States Constitution. The Full Faith and Credit, Due Process, Equal Protection, Privileges and Immunities, and Commerce Clauses all can easily be read to protect nonforum state interests, or the interest of nonforum litigants, that are disrupted by parochial state conflicts decisions. Yet the Supreme Court rarely intervenes under the Constitution to protect these interests. For choice of law, ours is a forgiving Constitution.

The forgiving Constitution permits what is here termed "conflicts localism": state and federal diversity cases favoring local substantive law when the forum state's relation to the controversy is clearly less than that of the place providing conflicting law. We see that conflicts localism unfairly damages nonforum litigants, exhibits disrespect to nonforum governments, and undermines principles of order and uniformity in choice of law. This Article explains that the pernicious effects of conflicts localism are sufficiently widespread to warrant a search for some kind of cure, and why, despite many different avenues to law reform that are available in theory, nothing in fact stands in the way of conflicts localism except the Constitution.

Deeper examination of the matter reenforces this conclusion. It is striking to observe how themes appearing in the four strains of contemporary conflicts theory—substantivism, multilateralism, unilateralism, and party expectations—recur clearly in various parts of the Constitution. This Article demonstrates that, because policy inspirations for constitutional doctrine regulating conflicts are so close to those for conflicts doctrine itself, and because the Supremacy Clause grants the Supreme Court clear entry to enforce those policies as constitutional doctrine, the authority of the Court to monitor or rewrite conflicts law is unlimited. We see that the refusal of the Supreme Court to use that authority to improve the quality of conflicts justice can be defended, if at all, only as an exercise of enlightened forbearance.

Does the Supreme Court belong on the sidelines? Perhaps, the Article suggests. This answer derives from the paradox itself. The Supreme Court may have been wise to forgo a strong reaction to conflicts localism precisely because its constitutional authority over choice of law is unbounded. Constitutional justifications for Supreme Court intervention so fully partake of the mainstream values of choice of law that, should the Court begin to give serious weight to the former, it would find no logical stopping point short of constitutionalizing the entire subject. The Article confirms this idea through examination of different constitutional rules for addressing conflicts localism. It then concludes that it may be impossible for extensive constitutional and nonconstitutional components to coexist in a stable regime of American conflicts law.

---

* Reprinted with permission.

Conflicts Localism

In 1978, the Minnesota Supreme Court decided *Blamey v. Brown*[2] and *Hague v. Allstate Insurance Co.*,[3] two conflicts cases that would eventually come to the attention of the United States Supreme Court. The state court seemed in each case to go out of its way to award a local litigant the benefits of Minnesota law.

In *Blamey*, the Minnesota Supreme Court denied a Wisconsin tavern proprietor protection from dram shop liability available under Wisconsin law, although his conduct occurred in Wisconsin. Conceding that the proprietor might have failed to obtain liquor liability insurance upon the reasonable expectation that Wisconsin law would determine tort exposure from his tavern business, the Minnesota Supreme Court chose instead Minnesota dram shop law casting the defendant in liability. Its reasons for doing so were that the plaintiff in need of compensation was a Minnesotan, and that it regarded Minnesota law as more enlightened than Wisconsin law.

The Minnesota Supreme Court championed its own law again in *Hague*. Plaintiff wished to aggregate (stack) coverage on three vehicles insured by her husband at the time he died in a traffic accident. Wisconsin law did not permit stacking, however, Minnesota law did. Plaintiff therefore stood to recover three times as much under the insurance policy if Minnesota law, rather than Wisconsin law, applied. The court refused to apply Wisconsin law, notwithstanding the facts that the plaintiff and her husband lived in Wisconsin at the time of the accident, that the policy was contracted for and issued to plaintiff's husband in Wisconsin, that all of the insured vehicles were garaged in Wisconsin, and that the fatal accident occurred there. The principal reasons why the court chose Minnesota law instead were reminiscent of those it offered for choosing Minnesota law in *Blamey*. The court stressed that the plaintiff had become a Minnesotan prior to filing her case, and that Minnesota's stacking law was more just than Wisconsin's antistacking law.

The unmistakable local bias of *Blamey* and *Hague* is discernible in other choice-of-law decisions in American courts. Observers have noted this conflicts localism and the possibilities of injustice and confusion that attend it. Moreover, local bias in choice of law has not been limited to state cases. Federal diversity courts are obliged under the *Erie* doctrine to follow the conflicts decisions of the states where they are sitting. *Erie* thus denies federal judges authority to distance themselves from the most biased of state conflicts decisions.

Federal diversity judges actually seem to share much of the enthusiasm of their state colleagues for vindicating local state interests. Thus, in the well-known case of *Rosenthal v. Warren*,[12] a federal diversity court was inspired by the conflicts localism of New York state decisions to press the interests of a New York plaintiff in a case having little connection with New York. Moreover, interaction of the *Erie* doctrine and the federal transfer-of-venue law creates risks for choice of inappropriate state law that exist only in federal court.

How much of a cause for concern is conflicts localism? The answer to this question depends upon what we believe the choice-of-law process in American courts should accomplish. If we believe that results in conflicts cases should be rational, predictable, and fair; if we believe that the sovereign interests accounting for forum and nonforum law alike should be respected whenever possible; and if we believe that all jurisdictions within our system of state and federal courts should strive for uniformity in choice of law in order to promote harmony

---

2   270 N.W.2d 884 (Minn. 1978), *cert. denied*, 444 U.S. 1070 (1980).

3   289 N.W.2d 43 (Minn. 1978), *aff'd*, 449 U.S. 302 (1981).* * *

12   475 F.2d 438 (2d Cir.), *cert. denied*, 414 U.S. 856 (1973).

between jurisdictions and discourage forum shopping; then it is possible to understand the destructive effects of conflicts localism.

The Paradox of a Forgiving Constitution

The consequences of conflicts localism are, or at least could be, matters of concern under our Constitution. Aggressive but plausible readings of numerous clauses could bring the Constitution to bear. Consider some examples. The Due Process Clause[17] could protect litigants' reasonable expectations in choice of law. The Full Faith and Credit Clause[19] could prevent unwarranted refusals to apply sister-state law. The separate or combined effects of the Privileges and Immunities,[21] Equal Protection,[22] and Commerce[23] Clauses could be to secure non-resident litigants from discriminatory applications of forum state law, thereby promoting uniformity in choice of law and discouraging forum shopping.

Yet almost all of the Constitution's potential for averting the bad effects of conflicts localism is unrealized under current law. The Due Process and Full Faith and Credit Clauses exert no more than a slight influence on conflicts decisions. The Supreme Court appears to have given no role at all in conflicts to the Privileges and Immunities, Equal Protection, and Commerce Clauses. It is symptomatic of this state of affairs that, while the frustrated nonresident defendants in *Rosenthal, Hague,* and *Blamey* all petitioned the United States Supreme Court for review, the Court granted certiorari only in *Hague*—and there it affirmed the Minnesota Supreme Court's choice of its own law.

The problem is not new. Fifty years ago, Justice Robert Jackson wrote: "I think it difficult to point to any field in which the Court has more completely demonstrated or more candidly confessed the lack of guiding standards of a legal character than in trying to determine what choice of law is required by the Constitution."[30] Much later, Professors Arthur von Mehren and Donald Trautman wrote that the Supreme Court's affirmance in *Hague* was "fair warning to the profession that the Court continues to have little to contribute to the subject of constitutional control of choice of law."[31] Recently, Professor Friedrich Juenger delivered the verdict that "all attempts to induce the U.S. Supreme Court to impose limits on state court experimentation" in choice of law "have come to naught."[32]

We have now reached a series of conclusions upon which the paradox of choice of law and the forgiving Constitution rests: (1) State and lower federal courts can and do render conflicts

---

[17]   U.S. CONST. amend. V; U.S. CONST. amend. XIV, § 1.

[19]   U.S. CONST. art. IV, § 1.

[21]   U.S. CONST. art. IV, § 2.

[22]   U.S. CONST. amend. XIV, § 1.

[23]   U.S. CONST. art. I, § 8.

[30]   [Robert H.] Jackson, [*Full Faith and Credit—The Lawyer's Clause of the Constitution*, 45 COLUM. L. REV. 1, 16 (1945)].

[31]   Arthur T. von Mehren & Donald T. Trautman, *Constitutional Control of Choice of Law: Some Reflections on* Hague, 10 HOFSTRA L. REV. 35, 35 (1981).

[32]   [Freidrich K.] Juenger, [*Conflict of Laws, in* INTRODUCTION TO THE LAW OF THE UNITED STATES 411, 427 (David S. Clark & Tugrul Ansay eds., 1992)].

decisions biased against nonforum litigants and nonforum law; (2) These decisions unfairly damage nonforum litigants, exhibit disrespect to nonforum governments, and undermine principles of order and uniformity in choice of law; (3) The authority of the Supreme Court to avert these consequences seems clear under several clauses of the Constitution; (4) Yet the Supreme Court has denied the Constitution (and thus itself) a significant role in choice of law.

How Necessary Is Constitutional Reform?

These conclusions might seem to warrant immediate and more precise inquiry concerning the capacity of the Constitution to regulate choice of law. If our best understanding of the problem turns out to be that conflicts localism violates the Constitution, then, one could argue, the Supreme Court cannot refrain from announcing and acting upon that fact.

Professor Douglas Laycock seems to advocate this view, urging prompt creation of a legal regime where "[c]hoice-of-law methods that prefer local litigants, local law, or better law are unconstitutional."[33] Yet, even were we to assume that Laycock's approach or some other is preferable in theory to current law, that alone would provide an incomplete case against the Supreme Court inaction. Given the claim of so many other matters for the Court's attention, it is not enough merely to demonstrate that a different constitutional theory for conflicts would be more attractive than current law. There must also be a strong practical need for Supreme Court intervention.

To determine whether conflicts is a topic worth the Supreme Court's time, we must ask two questions. First, is conflicts localism (with its pernicious effects of injustice and uncertainty) sufficiently widespread to warrant a search for some kind of cure? Second, assuming conflicts localism does present a serious problem, is a solution other than reformation of constitutional reviewing standards readily at hand? The following discussion indicates that the answers to these successive questions are yes and no.

It is possible to argue that cases like *Blamey, Hague,* and *Rosenthal* inform more about the notoriety than the extent of conflicts localism. Certainly, decisions can be found where judges refrained from favoring local litigants with forum law, even when a plausible ground for doing so existed. Are decisions evincing principled self-denial as indicative of conflicts decisionmaking in the United States as the notorious cases? Apparently not. Empirical studies suggest a high incidence of chosen law favoring the home-state litigant, especially when that litigant is the plaintiff. It may be impossible to confirm beyond question that local bias is widespread in choice of law. Yet it takes considerable force of will to doubt that fact, and to believe instead that local judges would consistently read nonforum law as broadly and sympathetically as they would their own local law.

The conclusion that conflicts localism warrants a cure does not, however, bring us at once to the Constitution. Nonconstitutional solutions are possible through state common law, state statutes, federal common law, federal statutes, or self-executing treaties of the United States.

Through the combined effect of our separation-of-powers tradition and the Supremacy Clause of the Constitution,[40] the most authoritative nonconstitutional sources for regulating choice of law are in theory federal statutes and self-executing treaties. Yet very few conflicts cases are affected by law at this level, and, while the impact on choice of law of federal statutes

---

[33]   See [Douglas] Laycock, *Equal Citizens of Equal and Territorial States: The Constitutional Foundations of Choice of Law*, 92 COLUM. L. REV. 249, 336 (1992)].

[40]   U.S. CONST. art. VI.

and treaties may increase in the future, there is no reason to believe that the picture will soon change dramatically.

The lack of a congressional initiative leaves the way clear for the federal courts to reform state conflicts law by displacing it with a federal common law of conflicts. The Supreme Court could occupy part of the conflicts field with federal common law, either by overruling *Klaxon v. Stentor Electric Manufacturing Co.,*[46] its decision extending the *Erie* doctrine to conflicts questions, or by nationalizing choice of law for a particular category of litigation. Alternatively, the Supreme Court could nationalize the entire subject of conflict of laws.

Freeing federal diversity judges from the constraints of state conflicts law might avoid embarrassments like the *Rosenthal* case and the incongruities of federal choice of law following transfer of venue, and it might return to nonresident suitors a measure of protection from local bias that diversity jurisdiction was created to secure. At the same time, the proposition that federal diversity jurisdiction alone provides authority for a federal common law of conflicts is not free from doubt. Moreover, it would be difficult to overrule *Klaxon* without unraveling much of the *Erie* doctrine. For these reasons, and because the Supreme Court has not exhibited the slightest inclination to overrule *Klaxon*, it is doubtful that the choice-of-law picture will change for federal diversity judges.

It is ironic that, in contrast to uncertainties attending the more modest objective of overruling *Klaxon*, the authority of the federal judiciary to make conflicts law binding throughout the country is secure through the Supremacy Clause. Most agree that the federal courts may borrow the authority to regulate choice of law that lies dormant in Congress. Thus, while overruling *Klaxon* would merely create a federal common law of conflicts applicable in federal diversity cases, the same doctrine made through use of dormant congressional power would be enforceable through the Supremacy Clause in all federal and state conflicts cases.

Serious questions remain, however, concerning the wisdom or likelihood of a national common law of conflicts. Federal judges are usually reluctant to make common law. That reluctance extends to the subject of choice of law, and it is easy to understand why. Conflicts is a historically difficult and controversial legal subject; hence, the prospect of announcing, refining, and administering federal conflicts law does not attract most federal judges. They are not inclined to wrest conflicts lawmaking authority from state judges even for a limited and pressing subject like mass tort litigation. The federal judiciary is even more disinclined to nationalize conflicts law entirely. Thus, while the Justices have not spelled out their reasons for the view, there may be unanimous agreement on the Supreme Court that conflicts should not become a domain of federal law.

In the absence of federal conflicts law, state legislatures have authority to remedy conflicts localism. Yet they are not a group likely to be offended by local bias in choice of law. In fact, with a few exceptions, state legislatures seem disinterested in the subject of conflict of laws.

At the bottom of the chain of legal institutions capable of making conflicts law rests the state judiciary. Their power and obligation to make conflicts law exists by default. However, state judges appear likely for the foreseeable future to be the only lawmakers regularly on the scene, hence the only realistic source of nonconstitutional reform in choice of law. That is cold comfort to the opponents of conflicts localism. There is no reason to believe that state courts, who bear the greatest responsibility for conflicts localism, will suddenly be moved to eliminate it.

The problem may be averted without increased choice-of-law review under the Constitution if legal developments outside the conflicts field incidentally eliminate opportunities for

---

[46]   313 U.S. 487 (1941).

conflicts localism. There are two possibilities. First, the Supreme Court could significantly increase due process constraints on the personal jurisdiction of state and lower federal courts. Thus, if the Court required for personal jurisdiction a tighter relationship than exists currently between the forum and the controversy, the cases that now most clearly evince forum bias in choice of law might never reach the merits. Second, the creation of new federal substantive law would preempt the application of state law, and hence, opportunities for conflicts localism. Given the Supremacy Clause, local state law—or, for that matter, any state law conflicting with the federal law—would cease to be a legitimate choice-of-law option.

Neither of these possibilities, however, seems likely. The Supreme Court has evinced little interest of late in redrawing the boundaries of personal jurisdiction. The last important personal jurisdiction case actually supported state personal jurisdiction in a place with little connection to the controversy.[66] Similarly, the possibility of introducing federal substantive law in troubled choice-of-law areas seems unlikely to attract the interest of either Congress or the federal courts.

We have seen, that while it is difficult to measure the precise extent of damage done by conflicts localism, the problem appears serious. And we have seen, while nonconstitutional possibilities for eliminating or reducing the problem exist in theory, they depend on lawmaking initiatives that legal institutions have not taken and, in their discretion, are unlikely to take. Nothing, then, stands in the way of conflicts localism except the Constitution.

* * * * *

FIGHTING CONFLICTS LOCALISM WITH CONSTITUTIONAL LAW

* * * Attempts to understand the character and reach of constitutional policies supporting reform will be aided by the realization that these policies are virtually identical to those animating the substantive, multilateral, or unilateral approaches to choice of law, or to the concern that chosen law not unreasonably disturb party expectations.

* * *

[A]t the least, the substantive approach guides choice of law in a way offering no support to conflicts localism. At the most, it eradicates conflicts localism. The Supremacy Clause figures prominently in the second of these functions. It secures safe passage for all forms of federal substantive law when they encounter conflicting state law.

* * *

A connection between the substantive approach to choice of law and the Supremacy Clause exists, and noting it provides a certain symmetry with the more extensive discussion to follow about the connections the Constitution has with conflicts concerns of multilateralism, unilateralism, and party expectations. Yet the Supremacy Clause hardly resonates with conflicts policy. Instead, like that form of the substantive approach to which it is tied, the Supremacy Clause provides a means of obviating (rather than regulating) conflicts localism.

---

66   Burnham v. Superior Court, 495 U.S. 604 (1990).* * *

Moreover, while affinity between the substantive approach and the Supremacy Clause suggests an additional role for the latter in regulating conflicts localism, it is still a role dependent on nonconstitutional lawmaking initiatives. We cannot enlarge the meaning of the Supremacy Clause to fight conflicts localism since that clause alone secures no rights to sovereigns or to litigants in the choice-of-law process. The Supremacy Clause merely gives life to law that Congress, the executive branch, or the judiciary chooses to make in its discretion.

* * *

When we turn to the numerous conflicts policies that are capable of a second life under the Constitution, the policy that chosen law not disturb the reasonable expectations of a party seems a natural choice. Indeed, concern over unfair surprise of a party supported in part the only restrictive ruling on state choice of law the Supreme Court has made in recent years.[133]

Similarly, it follows that any strains of multilateralist conflicts policy echoed in the Constitution provide a basis for constitutional regulation of conflicts localism. Localism is an anathema to multilateralism in theory and usually in fact. Had the influence of multilateralism in this country not been weakened by inward decay and by the unilateralist challenge of interest analysis, conflicts localism would be far less of a problem.

Of the three, unilateralism might appear the least likely source of inspiration for regulating conflicts localism. Granted, unilateralism is little concerned with party fairness. Yet once we purge from interest analysis the rule requiring courts to apply the law of a truly interested forum, interest analysis can be an effective instrument for protecting nonforum sovereigns from discrimination. The Supreme Court actually toyed with this as a constitutional rule before eventually abandoning the idea.[139]

* * * * *

DOES THE SUPREME COURT BELONG ON THE SIDELINES?

* * *

An implicit assumption often found in discussions about constitutional reform in choice of law is that questions whether, when, or how the Supreme Court could implement a particular constitutional reform are subordinate to questions about the shape or coherence of new doctrine. We can sympathize with this outlook. Federal or state institutions have the discretion to decline requests for nonconstitutional reform of conflicts localism. But the Constitution is about

---

[133]   Phillips Petroleum Co. v. Shutts, 472 U.S. 797 (1985) * * *.

[139]   The standard is most often associated with Alaska Packers Ass'n v. Industrial Accident Commission, 294 U.S. 532 (1935).

> [O]nly if it appears that, in the conflict of interests which have found expression in the conflicting statutes, the interest of Alaska is superior to that of California, is there rational basis for denying to the courts of California the right to apply the laws of their own state. . . . The interest of Alaska is not shown superior to that of California.

Id. at 549-50. * * *

Four years later, the Supreme Court abandoned the *Alaska Packers* standard in Pacific Employers Insurance Co. v. Industrial Accident Commission, 306 U.S. 493 (1939).* * *

rights and authority, and the rhetoric of constitutional argument for conflicts reform * * * can easily become: Any version of the Constitution at odds with the version pressed is not merely inferior; it is illegitimate. Yet it would be a mistake to read too much into the special status of constitutional law. Even if the Justices of the Supreme Court became convinced of the doctrinal superiority of an alternative reading of the Constitution over current law, it is possible to imagine two concerns of judicial administration that could delay the Court in acting on that conviction, or lead the Justices never to act.

The first concern is about the priority of matters competing for the attention of the Court. * * * It is very difficult, of course, to determine the relative priority of conflicts localism on a complete list of social, economic, and political problems inviting revision of constitutional doctrine. However, let us assume that the place of conflicts localism on such a list would be high enough to satisfy this first concern.

The second concern is over the capacity of the Supreme Court to oversee enforcement of constitutional reforms. It is far more troublesome and may in fact eliminate the possibility of extensive Supreme Court intervention in the foreseeable future. We accept as a basic principle, grounded if necessary in Article III of the United States Constitution, that the judicial branch is reluctant to make promises it cannot keep. The Supreme Court would therefore be reluctant to declare new rights under the Constitution to be free from conflicts localism which, as a practical matter, it could not vindicate. * * *

* * *

* * * Numerous past proposals for significant but carefully limited constitutional entry into choice of law, including my own, may be in fact unworkable because of difficulties of Supreme Court administration. The subject deserves a good deal more thought and discussion. The conclusion emerging from this Article may not be inescapable. It may be, however, that there is no stopping place for significant constitutional reform of conflicts law. It may be impossible for extensive constitutional and nonconstitutional components to coexist in a stable regime of American conflicts law.

Comments

1.   General discussions of choice of law and the Constitution appear in Brilmayer 1995c: pp. 129-166;[1] Richman & Reynolds 1993: pp. 269-289; Scoles & Hay 1992: pp. 78-109; Weintraub 1986: pp. 511-572. On the effect of the constitutional law of other countries on their conflicts law, *see* Herzog 1992.

2.   The incidence of parochial conflicts decisions in state courts (what the author of this segment termed "conflicts localism") was noted by several of the sources appearing in Part A of Chapter Six. In addition, a number of commentators concur with the author's suggestion that federal courts (required under the *Erie* doctrine to apply state law) have similarly exhibited conflicts localism. *See, e.g.,* Kirgis 1976: pp. 135-136; Martin 1976: pp. 225-227; Reese 1978: pp. 1605-1606; Scoles & Hay 1992: pp. 98-99.

---

[1]   Full citations appear in the bibliography, Chapter Twelve.

3. Nonconstitutional paths to conflicts reform clearly exist in theory. For example, the interstate or international character of conflicts cases places them within the regulatory power of Congress. Currie 1963a: p. 125; Gottesman 1991: p. 1; Whitten 1982: pp. 917-918. The best known example may be the conflicts provision in the Federal Tort Claims Act, 28 U.S.C. § 1346(b), discussed in Shapiro 1992. Choice of law in cases with international contacts could easily be regulated by treaty. Burman 1995; Juenger 1995. Or conflicts cases could inspire choice-of-law rules derived from federal common law. Horowitz 1967; Silberman 1983; Trautman 1977.

4. Much commentary on choice of law and the Constitution has centered on the Supreme Court's decision in *Allstate Insurance Co. v. Hague*, summarized in the proceeding excerpt. Reactions to the case appeared in Symposium, *Choice of Law Theory After* Allstate Insurance Co. v. Hague, 10 HOFSTRA L. REV. 1 (1981) (contributions by David Cavers, Russell Weintraub, Arthur von Mehren & Donald Trautman, Robert Sedler, Linda Silberman, James Martin, Aaron Twerski, Jack Davis, Willis Reese, and Robert Leflar); Symposium, *Supreme Court Intervention in Jurisdiction and Choice of Law: From* Shaffer *to* Allstate, 14 U.C. DAVIS L. REV. 837 (1981) (contributions by Andreas Lowenfeld, Linda Silberman, Courtland Peterson, P. John Kozyris, and Friedrich Juenger); and in numerous additional articles. *See, e.g.,* Hay 1983; Hill 1981; Shreve 1982; Weinberg 1982.

B. Full Faith and Credit and Due Process—Traditional Sources for Regulating Choice of Law

Robert H. Jackson, *Full Faith and Credit—The Lawyer's Clause of the Constitution*, 45 COLUM. L. REV. 1, 16, 26-30, 33-34 (1945)*

* * * * *

* * * The Court has said that it will choose which of two contending state statutes shall apply to a controversy by appraising the governmental interests of each jurisdiction and turning the scale of decision according to their weights. The forum *prima facie*, of course, is entitled to apply its own law. "One who challenges that right, because of the force given to a conflicting statute of another state by the full faith and credit clause, assumes the burden of showing, upon some rational basis, that of the conflicting interests involved those of the foreign state are superior to those of the forum."[63]

The practical results of such standards appear in three workmen's compensation cases. In the first, the interest of the forum state was held to be "only casual," although it was the state in which a workman on public utility lines was killed. The state where he lived and was hired was held to have a superior interest which ousted the law of the forum.[64] Soon thereafter it was held that a forum state, being the place of hiring, but not of claimant's domicile, could apply its own law to compensate for an accident elsewhere, since "no persuasive reason is shown for denying" that right in favor of the law of the place of accident.[65] Somewhat later the Court held, however, that the state of accident may apply its own compensation laws and need not give faith and credit to those of a state that was the place of hiring and the domicile of both the employer and the employee.[66] But a forum state may no longer apply its laws if an award under other state law has been made.[67]

Nowhere has the Court attempted, although faith and credit opinions have been written by some of its boldest-thinking and clearest-speaking Justices, to define standards by which "superior state interests" in the subject matter of conflicting statutes are to be weighed. Nor can I discern any consistent pattern or design into which the cases fit.

Indeed, I think it difficult to point to any field in which the Court has more completely demonstrated or more candidly confessed the lack of guiding standards of a legal character than in trying to determine what choice of law is required by the Constitution.

* * * * *

---

*   This article originally appeared at 45 COLUM. L. REV. 1 (1945). Reprinted with permission.

63   Alaska Packers Ass'n. v. Industrial Accident Comm'n, 294 U.S. 532, 547-48 (1935).

64   Bradford Electric Light Co. v. Clapper, 286 U.S. 145 (1932) * * *.

65   Alaska Packers Ass'n v. Industrial Accident Comm'n, 294 U.S. 532 (1935).

66   Pacific Employers Ins. Co. v. Industrial Accident Comm'n, 306 U.S. 493 (1939).

67   Magnolia Petroleum Co. v. Hunt, 320 U.S. 430 (1943) * * *.

In the century and a half of the Court's existence, litigation as to faith and credit has concerned the recognition due to judgments. In this field the Court has built up a body of law. I do not think it departs essentially from the principles of the clause, even though it may leave it somewhat short of faultless fulfillment. While Judge Cardozo pointed out with great accuracy that the power of the precedent is only "the power of the beaten track,"[106] still the mere fact that a path is a beaten one is a persuasive reason for following it. This is especially true in this class of cases where the doctrine must in the first instance be applied chiefly in our many state courts. To be administered uniformly a rule of faith and credit must be relatively stable, certain, and of long standing.

But precedent does not offer any such well beaten path as to when a forum must accord faith and credit to the statutory and decisional law of another state. Decisions are less numerous and less consistent. As legislation becomes more complex and enters new spheres, conflicts in this field grow in number and importance. Here it is that the creative intelligence of the judicial process seems to meet its greatest challenge under the faith and credit clause. It would not be fitting to suggest how I might think particular cases should be resolved. But it has not seemed inappropriate to state some views as to the general philosophy of decision if our own time is to utilize this clause to realize its purpose as a principle of order in our federated legal systems.

That the Supreme Court should impose uniformity in choice-of-law problems is a prospect comforting to none, least of all to a member of that body. I have not paid any exaggerated tribute to its performance thus far in this complex field. But the available courses from which our choice may be made seem to me limited. One is that we will leave choice of law in all cases to the local policy of the state. This seems to me to be at odds with the implication of our federal system that the mutual limits of the states' powers are defined by the Constitution. It also seems productive of confusion, for it means that choice among conflicting substantive rules depends only upon which state happens to have the last word. And that we are not likely to accept such a principle is certainly indicated by the Court's sporadic interferences with choice of law, whether under the rubric of due process, full faith and credit, or otherwise. A second course is that we will adopt no rule, permit a good deal of overlapping and confusion, but interfere now and then, without imparting to the bar any reason by which the one or the other course is to be guided or predicted. This seems to me about where our present decisions leave us. Third, we may candidly recognize that choice-of-law questions, when properly raised, ought to and do present constitutional questions under the full faith and credit clause which the Court may properly decide and as to which it ought at least to mark out reasonably narrow limits of permissible variation in areas where there is confusion.

Always to be kept in mind in dealing with these problems is that the policy ultimately to be served in application of the clause is the federal policy of "a more perfect union" of our legal systems. No local interest and no balance of local interests can rise above this consideration. It is hard to see how the faith and credit clause has any practical meaning as to statutes if the Court should adhere to the statement that ". . . a state is not required to enforce a law obnoxious to its public policy."

The distinction between federal interest and local interest may be elusive but always it is present in these conflicts. Fundamental to every such conflict of law is that separate states consider their own interests to require inconsistent social or economic policies. The legal controversy as to whether Dred Scott's sojourn in a free state invested him with rights which must be

---

[106]   Cardozo, The Growth of the Law (1927) 62.

respected when he returned to a slave state had its roots in the two incompatible social systems. Conflicts which we face day after day are less deep and less bitter, but none the less they grow out of disagreement between states as to the policies that will promote their social welfare. One state thinks its need is to encourage industrial capital to come and exploit its latent resources and therefore is niggardly about putting the burden of industrial accidents upon industry. Another, more fully industrialized perhaps, adopts a policy of more generous workmen's compensation. Or religious convictions prevailing in one state lead to a highly restrictive policy of divorce, while another grants it on easy terms. Or one state finds actions for alienation of affections or for breach of promise to be productive of more evil than good and abolishes such causes of action; other nearby states adhere to the policy of permitting recovery. Or the state where a man dies declares him domiciled therein, and exercises its right to administer his estate. Several other states make claims based on assessment procedures for which they demand faith and credit. The state where the decedent had a summer home and the one where he spent his winters each declares itself to be a state of domicile; another claims on the ground that it is the place where certain evidences of intangible property are deposited for safe-keeping; various others, because his intangibles were shares in or obligations of corporations which they had chartered; while still others file claims showing that the issuing companies did business within their borders and some part of the value transferred was created in such state. Now of course there is no federal power over these matters, and there is no constitutional policy that one should or should not recover for alienation of affections, or be subject to strict or easy rules of divorce, or that an injured workman should proceed under one compensation system rather than another or under common law, nor is there a federal policy that one should or should not pay a particular state tax.

Certainly the personal preferences of the Justices among the conflicting state policies is not a permissible basis of determining which shall prevail in a case. But only a singularly balanced mind could weigh relative state interests in such subject matter except by resort to what are likely to be strong preferences in sociology, economics, governmental theory, and politics. There are no judicial standards of valuation of such imponderables. How can we know which is the greater interest when one state is moved by one set of considerations—economic, perhaps—to one policy, and another by different considerations—social welfare, perhaps—to a conflicting one? But, even if we could appraise or compare relative local interests, we must lift these questions above the control of local interest and must govern conflict in these cases by the wider considerations arising out of the federal order. How to determine when these require the law of the forum to give way to that of another state seems to me an unsettled question. I cannot regard the "balance of interest" test used in the compensation cases as more than a tentative and inadequate answer. It seems to assume that a state must have power to reach a matter because it has an interest in it—a power which yields only to a greater power based on a greater interest. I doubt that the position can long be maintained that the reach of a state's power is a byproduct of an interest. The ultimate answer, it seems to me, will have to be based on considerations of state relations to each other and to the federal system. What is the basis of power in a constituent state of our federation to govern a controversy, when is it exclusive of a like power asserted for another state on the same or some different basis, and when is it entitled to prevail even in the forums of another state? I leave you pretty much at large on this subject, for that is where the decisions leave me. But I could suggest no more engaging intellectual enterprise to which the scholarship of our profession might turn than to try to find the wise answers on constitutional grounds to these questions.

Even where each conflicting policy claims recognition on the same ground and the conflict proceeds from contrary findings of fact, there would seem to be a federal interest, distinct from that of either state, in its solution. Domicile is the ground which furnishes the best example. The Supreme Court still adheres, as I think it must long continue to do, to the doctrine that a domiciliary relationship of a party to the state is a sufficient basis to support various exercises of state power. But the Court has said that "Neither the Fourteenth Amendment nor the full faith and credit clause requires uniformity in the decisions of the courts of different states as to the place of domicil, where the exertion of state power is dependent upon domicil within its boundaries."[112] This seems to me to beg the real question which seeks federal decision. The real issue is not whether the court of either state must conform its decision to that of the other, but whether both must not conform their decisions in this field to some federal constitutional standard.

Of course the federal courts do not, by reason of the full faith and credit clause, have any federal interest to consider as to which of two disputed places is one's correct domicile. The Constitution is indifferent as to whether a Mr. Williams was domiciled in North Carolina or in Nevada or whether a Mr. Green was domiciled in New York, Massachusetts, or Texas. But I do think that the federal interest is concerned that a Mr. Williams and a Mr. Green have some place in our federal system where they really belong for purposes of fixing their legal status and determining by whom they shall be governed. Such a view certainly is consistent with the spirit and perhaps is required by the implications of the Fourteenth Amendment, which provides, "All persons born or naturalized in the United States, and subject to the jurisdiction thereof, are citizens of the United States and *of the State wherein they* reside." (Italics supplied.) This provision would seem to do something toward fixing one's place in our federal society. It seems to fix one standard by which to know where political rights and obligations are to be determined. Where the requisite relationship between person and place exists to warrant state exercise of power and to exclude other states from a conflicting exercise of power would seem to present, at least in connection with a faith and credit problem, a federal question on which, when properly raised, litigants would be entitled to the judgment of a federal court.

In considering claims of foreign law for faith and credit courts of course find conflict of laws a relevant and enlightening body of experience and authority to provide analogies. But while the American law of conflicts is a somewhat parallel and contemporaneous development with the law of faith and credit, they also are quite independent evolutions, are based on contrary basic assumptions, and at times support conflicting results. We must beware of transposing conflicts doctrines into the law of the Constitution. This is exactly what appears from the opinions to have been done in several of the cases where exceptions were made as to faith and credit due judgments. Private international law and the law of conflicts extend recognition to foreign statutes or judgments by rules developed by a free forum as a matter of enlightened self-interest. The constitutional provision extends recognition on the basis of the interests of the federal union which supersedes freedom of individual state action by a compulsory policy of reciprocal rights to demand and obligations to render faith and credit. States under their voluntary policy may extend recognition when they could not constitutionally be required to do so; and sometimes, of course, they have interpreted the law of conflicts to refuse credit when the constitutional mandate is held to require it.

* * * * *

* * * [A]s to extraterritorial recognition or non-recognition of state law it is doubtful if a century and a half of constitutional interpretation has advanced us much beyond where we

---

[112]   Worcester County Trust Co. v. Riley, 302 U.S. 292, 299 (1937).

would be if there had never been such a clause. Local policies and balance of local interest still dominate the application of the federal requirement. This is the more strange since the states have less to fear from a strong federalist influence in dealing with this than with most other constitutional provisions. The Federal Government stands to gain little at the expense of the states through any application of it. Anything taken from a state by way of freedom to deny faith and credit to law of others is thereby added to the state by way of a right to exact faith and credit for its own.

It seems easier for the Court to put aside parochialism and think in terms of national economy or of national social welfare than to think in terms of a truly national legal system. Perhaps that is because federalism in the field of faith and credit does not have the watchful and powerful championship of the Federal Government, to whose interests the Justices have often been made alert by prior experience in federal office. In contrast, the federalism of the faith and credit clause depends generally on private advocacy, not always supported by the best research and understanding, and often finds the perception of the Justices unsharpened and their perspective uninformed by any extensive experience or investigation of this subject.* * *

* * *

Louise Weinberg, *Choice of Law and Minimal Scrutiny*, 49 U. Chi. L. Rev. 440, 444-448, 472-474 (1982)*

* * * * *

A GENERAL ANALYTIC FRAMEWORK FOR UNDERSTANDING CONSTITUTIONAL REVIEW IN CONFLICTS CASES

Suppose we pluck up from the mass of disparate, undefined, and unseparated concepts having something to do with "limits" on choices of law the single, broad notion of lack of "interest," usually intended to convey that a state needs some rational basis for applying its laws. Let us give this concept the importance of a separate, affirmative heading and call it "power." By that we will mean the power of a state to regulate a particular controversy by its laws. The Supreme Court determines the existence of such power by considering whether the particular controversy falls within the state's legitimate sphere of interest or legislative concern.

Next, we will more narrowly define the class of remaining concepts, which includes such matters as reasonableness, fairness, and comity, as a class not simply of "limits," but of limits *on the power of an interested state.*

Finally, let us suppose that each of these two classes of concepts will be the object of its own distinct line of inquiry. On the question of "power," the inquiry will be limited to the narrow question whether the issue in controversy is within the sphere of legitimate legislative interest of the state whose law is sought to be applied. Whatever minimal degree of reasonableness, fairness, or comity the existence of a state governmental interest may imply, there is no inquiry under this heading for reasonableness, fairness, or comity as such. Our interest analysis will produce a conclusion with respect to power only. Under the second question, however, the question of "limits," the inquiry may concern itself with reasonableness, fairness, or comity beyond the minimum that the existence of acknowledged state power already implies.

---

*   Reprinted with permission.

That is because this second inquiry has to do with limits on the power of an interested state, not with limits on state power generally. This simple reorganization of the issues is not semantic juggling. It will enable us to construct a general theoretical framework for analyzing the problems of constitutional review of choices of law.

What we have done is to put interest in its correct relation to the constitutional question, as the source of state regulatory power, rather than as a disconnected concept that in some indirect way helps determine the limits upon that power. This is consonant with our understanding of the source of state lawmaking power in other contexts. The question of the existence of power can now be sorted out from the question of the wisdom or fairness of its exercise.

One consequence is that each inquiry is clarified in relation to the other. Given one inquiry about power, and a second inquiry about limits on the exercise of acknowledged power, we can now see that the second inquiry is subordinate to and dependent upon the first. If a state lacks legislative power, questions of the wisdom or fairness of the exercise of its power simply cannot arise. It will be of no constitutional consequence, then, that an application of a noninterested state's laws is also unfair: interest analysis preliminarily will have revealed the application to be arbitrary and unreasonable; thus, the application already will have been struck down.

It becomes apparent that this second inquiry, concerning limits on the power of an interested state, cannot be brought into play even where the forum has power, if the forum is the only interested state. Where the forum is the only such state, no other state's laws may be applied constitutionally, and therefore no question of want of comity or of contrary expectation can arise. Thus, this second inquiry concerning "limits" has meaning only in the so-called "true conflict" case, in which the concerned sovereigns have conflicting policies that would be advanced by application of their respective laws to the particular controversy.

We can now discern theoretical levels of constitutional scrutiny of choice of law, similar to those found in other areas of constitutional law: minimal scrutiny, which can only review as arbitrary and unreasonable the choice of a noninterested state's laws in a false conflict case and will always sustain the choice of an interested state's laws in a true conflict case; and restrictive scrutiny, which can review the choice of an interested state's laws for such deficiencies of reasonableness, fairness, or comity as the Supreme Court might further determine to control in cases of true conflict.

We now can begin to distinguish between the minimal reasonableness, fairness, or comity that minimal scrutiny requires, and the sort of reasonableness, fairness, or comity that restrictive scrutiny would require. The distinction emerges with nice clarity. Cases raising issues appropriate for restrictive review might include, for example, cases in which the defendant's conduct was authorized or protected by the laws of an interested state where the defendant acted; cases in which a party moved unilaterally and unforeseeably to the forum state after the transaction or occurrence giving rise to the litigation; cases in which the validity of a contract, trust, devise, or marriage, or the legitimacy of a birth, was called in question solely because of a contact with an interested invalidating state; cases in which the plaintiff was forced to a defendant-favoring forum; and cases in which the defendant is a state. These cases seem to be candidates for restrictive review because in them the fact of the forum's interest alone may not of itself resolve the problems of fairness or comity presented: the lack of foreseeability of the choice of law on the part of the regulated party in the first two examples, and disturbances in the functioning of the multistate system in all of them.

If in conjunction with this reformulation we refer to discerned national policies bearing upon interstate litigation and to technical considerations bearing on the feasibility of review, we will have a general theory of constitutional review of conflicts cases, with power to resolve the question whether minimal or restrictive scrutiny should furnish the level of review; and, if the former, to resolve in various contexts the question whether some exception might be made to the general rule of minimal scrutiny.

In sum, then, state governmental interest is the source of state legislative power. Minimal scrutiny of a choice of law under the Constitution will operate to strike down the application of a noninterested state's laws as arbitrary and unreasonable. Application of an *interested* state's laws can be struck down on grounds of unreasonableness, unfairness, want of comity, or other defect only through restrictive review. Policy and functional considerations relevant to the field suggest that in conflicts cases, review should be limited to minimal scrutiny for state interest alone.

THE SETTLED POSITION: MINIMAL SCRUTINY OF STATE CHOICES OF LAW

What are the constitutional limits on state choices of law? When the question is put in that capacious way, particularly if two or three unreconstructedly territorialist cases (in which a choice of law actually may have been struck down) are thrown into the hopper, it will not be wholly inaccurate to conclude, as writers tend variously to do, that the Constitution polices state choices of law for fairness or reasonableness or comity. But this conclusion will be somewhat misleading.

Once the problem is examined from the general viewpoint outlined in the previous section, one's way of stating existing law on this question will undergo a rather striking transformation. For it has been, or ought to have been, clear since the great watershed opinions of Justice Stone in *Alaska Packers*[35] and *Pacific Employers*[36] that there are, in fact, no limits whatsoever on the choice of an interested state's laws. It will, indeed, be familiar learning to toilers in these vineyards that under *Pacific Employers*, an interested state generally may apply its own laws in its own courts, just as it is understood that under the rule of *Home Insurance Co. v. Dick*,[37] a noninterested state generally may not. Under *Dick*, application of a noninterested state's laws will be struck down as arbitrary and unreasonable. Scrutiny for the minimal interest that empowers a state to regulate has become, precisely, minimal scrutiny. There is no peg beyond "arbitrary or unreasonable" on which to hang a constitutional question.

* * * * *

Of course everyone would agree that a losing party should not have been subjected to laws wholly arbitrary as applied to that party. But if a party is within a state's legitimate sphere of interest, application of that state's laws will always be nonarbitrary as they affect that party and reasonable within our understanding of the requirements of federalism. Thus, to impose further scrutiny upon the choice of an interested state's laws would put the Supreme Court in the position of having to balance what is reasonable against what is more fair or less parochial. This was the sort of challenge to its common law powers that the Court averted when *Alaska Packers* gave way to *Pacific Employers*. Just such entanglements as those would enmesh the

---

[35]   Alaska Packers Ass'n v. Industrial Accident Comm'n, 294 U.S. 532 (1935). Stone became Chief Justice in 1941.

[36]   Pacific Employers Ins. Co. v. Industrial Accident Comm'n, 306 U.S. 493 (1939).

[37]   281 U.S. 397 (1930).

Court today, if fairness or federalism were to limit the power of an interested state to apply its law to a case.

At the core of the difficulty lies the fact that the Court would have to find reasons why a state with a legitimate need to regulate a controversy should not be allowed to do so. This is precisely the sort of chore the Supreme Court has been declining all along, when it adopted, as well as when it relinquished, determinate full faith and credit, and again when it abandoned interest-weighing. There would be this difference: the Court would not turn for the content of the new federal conflicts rules to traditional choice-of-law rules; it would be forced to a higher level of creativity. The Court that has given us "purposeful availment" in the jurisdiction cases can hardly contemplate such a prospect with enthusiasm.

Of course there are some state actions that do require a more refined scrutiny than "rational basis" scrutiny or interest analysis can afford. Such state actions will generally be found to have an important characteristic not shared by choices of law. They will make inherently suspect classifications, or raise other urgent and intrinsically important challenges to fundamental rights and values. In contrast, a choice of law in a true conflict case raises only the question which of two well-meaning sister states, with equally plausible but divergent views on a point of law, should be allowed to prevail on the point in a particular case. The challenge to state action in a substantive constitutional case is based on a perceived conflict between that state action and substantive national policy. But the choice of one state's laws over another's fails to impinge upon any substantive national policy. To the extent we can discern any national policy at all concerning choices of law, it counsels us to limit, not strengthen, constitutional control. Given the expenditure of the Court's creative resources that would be entailed in fashioning law for restrictive review, a nonarbitrary but "unfair" choice of law seems inappropriate for such review, now as much as in the past.

* * * * *

Robert A. Sedler, *Constitutional Limitations on Choice of Law: The Perspective of Constitutional Generalism*, 10 HOFSTRA L. REV. 59, 59-61, 74-79, 85-86, 92, 93-94, 95-98 (1981)*

When conflict of laws commentators consider the matter of constitutional limitations on choice of law, it seems that they usually approach it from what may be called a "conflicts perspective"—a perspective that assumes constitutional limitations on choice of law are necessary to promote "conflicts justice" and to accommodate the conflicting interests of states in a federal system. They then find such limitations inhering in the due process and full faith and credit clauses of the Constitution. The debate among conflict of laws commentators concerns the extent of and the respective roles of the due process and full faith and credit clauses in imposing constitutional limitations.

Conflicts commentators do not approach the matter from a "constitutional perspective," or as I would put it, from the perspective of constitutional generalism. The perspective of constitutional generalism considers constitutional structure and doctrine and general principles of constitutional interpretation, and applies these to constitutional limitations on choice of law.

---

*   Reprinted with permission.

Under this approach, it is not assumed that the Constitution imposes limitations on the power of state courts to make choice-of-law decisions simply because such limitations are necessary to promote "conflicts justice" or to accommodate the conflicting interests of states in a federal system. Rather, the fundamental inquiry is whether such limitations properly can be found to inhere in particular provisions of the Constitution. Constitutional generalism considers the broad, organic purpose and function of the due process and full faith and credit clauses as well as the "original understanding" of the framers and the doctrines the Court has developed in applying these provisions in other contexts. Should these constitutional clauses be interpreted as placing any limitations on the power of state courts to make choice-of-law decisions, and if so, what should those limitations be? As stated above, this inquiry differs from the perspective with which conflict of laws commentators have generally approached the matter of constitutional limitations on choice of law.

Similarly, the Supreme Court's decisions in this area, including the recent decision in *Allstate Insurance Co. v. Hague*,[8] do not focus sufficiently on the analysis suggested by the perspective of constitutional generalism. The Court treats conflicts issues as if the matter of constitutional limitations on choice of law is an independent "specialized" area not to be dealt with in terms of general principles of constitutional interpretation and the consistent application of constitutional doctrine. For example, the Court's treatment of due process as a limitation on choice of law has generally taken place without regard to the Court's application of substantive due process doctrine in other areas. The Court has also assumed that the full faith and credit clause imposes limitations on the power of state courts to make choice-of-law decisions without explicitly considering whether it is properly the function of the full faith and credit clause to impose such limitations. What has happened, then, is that conceptually, and in practice, the matter of constitutional limitations on choice of law has developed as an independent "specialized" area of constitutional law rather than within the framework of constitutional generalism.

* * * * *

Although I approve of the result in *Hague* and of what will most likely be the effect of the doctrine formulated in the Brennan and Stevens opinions, I am nonetheless troubled by the failure of the Court to deal with constitutional limitations on choice of law from the perspective of constitutional generalism; that is, from a perspective emphasizing constitutional structure, doctrine and general principles of constitutional interpretation. All of the opinions in *Hague* appear to treat constitutional limitations on choice of law as a specialized area and to approach choice-of-law questions independent of general principles of constitutional doctrine. For example, all the opinions focus on due process as a limitation on choice of law, but there is no discussion whatsoever of the relationship between general due process doctrine and due process as a limitation on choice of law. Nor is there mention of the Court's application of due

---

[8]   449 U.S. 302 (1981). [This article and those by Professors Reese and Silberman that follow were occasioned in part by the *Hague* case. There, plaintiff wished to aggregate (stack) coverage on three vehicles insured by her husband at the time he died in a traffic accident. Wisconsin law did not permit stacking, however, Minnesota law did. Plaintiff therefore stood to recover three times as much under the insurance policy if Minnesota law, rather than Wisconsin law, applied. The court refused to apply Wisconsin law, notwithstanding the facts that the plaintiff and her husband lived in Wisconsin at the time of the accident, that the policy was contracted for and issued to plaintiff's husband in Wisconsin, that all of the insured vehicles were garaged in Wisconsin, and that the fatal accident occurred there. The court chose Minnesota law, stressing that the plaintiff had become a Minnesotan prior to filing her case, and that Minnesota's stacking law was more just than Wisconsin's antistacking law.]

process doctrine in other contexts. From an analytical standpoint, it seems that constitutional limitations on choice of law still remain removed from the constitutional mainstream.

Because the Court has failed to deal with constitutional limitations on choice of law from the perspective of constitutional generalism, it is likely that *Hague* will intensify rather than mute the academic debate over constitutional control of choice of law. In their search for constitutional limitations on choice of law, many of my Conflict of Law colleagues will probably scrutinize Brennan's "significant contact or significant aggregation of contacts, creating state interests"[81] language, as if it were a talismanic test for determining whether a state court's choice of law would be found unconstitutional. Similarly, there is likely to be close scrutiny of Powell's dissent in order to identify cases where the Brennan plurality and the Powell dissenters might agree that a particular choice of law is unconstitutional. Moreover, I expect there will be renewed debate over whether full faith and credit should be an independent limitation on choice of law, as contended by Justice Stevens, and if so, when a state court's choice of its own law improperly impinges on the sovereignty of another state. I believe the Court was sending out a behavioral message that there are few, if any, significant constitutional limitations on choice of law and that courts should generally abstain from considering such questions. This message is not as loud and clear as it would have been, however, had the Court dealt with constitutional limitations on choice of law from the perspective of constitutional generalism. When viewed from the perspective of constitutional generalism, the due process and full faith and credit clauses properly should be interpreted as imposing only the most minimal limitations on the power of state courts to make choice-of-law decisions.

Due Process

Structurally, the due process clause operates as a potential limitation on the power of state courts to make choice-of-law decisions, in the same manner as it operates as a limitation on the power of courts to take any action in the civil litigation process. The due process clause is applicable to any governmental action affecting property interests. In resolving private disputes in the civil litigation process, courts necessarily affect property rights. Thus, the procedural component of due process imposes limitations on the exercise of judicial jurisdiction by the courts and requires that the litigants receive fair notice of the proceedings and an opportunity to defend. Its substantive component, theoretically at least, could render a court's substantive disposition of a case violative of due process as well.

From the perspective of constitutional generalism, the most important step in the analysis of due process as a limitation on choice of law is to relate the Court's application of general due process doctrine in other contexts to due process as a limitation on choice of law. The fundamental question is whether, in light of general due process doctrine and the principles that the Court applies to determine whether governmental action is violative of due process in other contexts, due process should impose any limitations on the power of state courts to make choice-of-law decisions, and if so, what those limitations should be.

In determining the constitutionality of governmental action challenged as being violative of due process, the Court has articulated a two-tier standard of review. Where the challenged governmental action impinges on a fundamental right, such action must advance a compelling governmental interest that cannot be advanced by a less restrictive alternative than the restriction in question. Where the challenged governmental action does not impinge on a fundamental

---

[81]   449 U.S. at 313.

right, its constitutionality as a matter of due process is tested under the purportedly less restrictive rational basis standard: The restriction in question must be reasonably related to the advancement of a legitimate governmental interest. Despite the Court's articulation of a two-tier standard of review, the Court may in practice be using a sliding-scale approach, under which the degree of scrutiny of the governmental action varies depending upon the importance of the individual interest in relation to the importance of the asserted governmental interest. In any event, whether the Court actually follows a two-tier or a sliding-scale standard of review, actions taken by a state court in the civil litigation process ordinarily do not invoke a heightened degree of scrutiny. The general due process doctrine that would be applicable to determine the constitutionality of state court choice-of-law decisions, therefore, is the rational-basis test. Under that test, it must be established whether the government "has acted in an arbitrary and irrational way" so as to violate due process, or whether it has acted reasonably and fairly.[93]

The considerations in determining whether the government has acted in an arbitrary or irrational way are reasonableness and fairness. When a state has some factual connections with the underlying transaction, the choice of that state's law to govern rights and liabilities arising from that transaction would seem to be reasonable, notwithstanding that another state may have even more factual connections with that transaction. Likewise, when application of a state's law to a given factual situation advances the policy reflected in that law, it surely seems reasonable for a court to hold that that state's law should apply, again notwithstanding that another state may appear to have a "greater interest." While the consideration of fairness is more frequently involved with respect to procedural due process, it may also be involved with respect to substantive due process. A state rule of substantive law that interferes with the enjoyment of liberty or property interests in a fundamentally unfair way may be found to be violative of substantive due process. Fairness to the parties is an independent choice-of-law consideration, particularly where consensual transactions are involved. Where the choice of a state's law in the circumstances presented unfairly defeats the legitimate expectations of a party, it would be consistent with general due process doctrine to hold that the choice of law is violative of due process. It is submitted that the constitutionality of a particular choice of law should be governed by the reasonableness and fairness test. A choice of law should not be held to be violative of due process unless, under the circumstances presented, the application of the law of the chosen state is clearly unreasonable or fundamentally unfair to one of the parties.

If the constitutionality of a state court's choice-of-law decision, as a matter of due process, is tested against the arbitrary and irrational standard, neither the purported interest of the other involved state in having its law applied nor the purported multistate concerns should play any part in the constitutional analysis. Another state's apparently "greater interest" in having its own law applied, or multistate concerns dictating that the law of that state apply instead of the law of the forum, does not make the application of the forum's law unreasonable or unfair. If the application of the forum's law is not unreasonable or unfair, due process has been satisfied.

* * * * *

We may now consider under what circumstances a state court's choice-of-law decision should, under general due process doctrine, be found arbitrary and fundamentally unfair and thus violative of due process. The application of a state's law to govern liability in civil litigation should be held arbitrary for due process purposes only where that state does not have an

---

[93]   Duke Power Co. v. Carolina Envt'l Study Group, 438 U.S. 59, 83-84 (1978).* * *

interest in applying its law in order to implement the policy reflected in that law *or* where that state does not have a significant factual connection with the underlying transaction, making it reasonable to apply the law of that state on the point in issue. The application of a state's law should be held unfair only where (1) the party against whom the law is applied could not reasonably have foreseen its application to the transaction in question at the time the party entered into the transaction, and (2) the party conformed its conduct to the requirements imposed by the law of another state, in justifiable reliance that the state's law would apply to the transaction. In either of these situations, it is highly unlikely that any present-day court would *choose* to apply its own law; the forum will generally stop short of applying its own law before the permissible limits of due process have been reached. Thus, we would not expect, under this formulation, that a state court's choice-of-law decision would be found violative of due process.

* * * * *

Full Faith and Credit

* * *

The emphasis in Justice Stevens' analysis [in *Hague*] is on the federal interest in national unity. In his view, one state is required by full faith and credit in a choice-of-law case to respect the sovereignty of another state where failure to do so would significantly impair the federal interest in national unity. Under Justice Stevens' formulation, it would seem to be a rare instance where a state court's application of its own law in a conflicts case, which is valid as a matter of due process, would be held violative of full faith and credit. Where a state court's choice of its own law is neither so arbitrary nor fundamentally unfair as to be violative of due process, it is difficult to see how the federal interest in national unity ordinarily would require that another state's law be applied.

Some conflicts commentators have argued for a more expansive view of full faith and credit as a constitutional control on state court choice-of-law decisions. They believe that when a state court makes choice-of-law decisions, full faith and credit requires that the court respect the sovereignty of sister states where those states have a much greater interest in controlling the outcome of the particular litigation. Such an approach requires a weighing and balancing of the strength and legitimacy of the conflicting state interests and of the contacts that the transaction and parties have with each of the involved states. Additionally, it precludes the application of the law of a state whose interests and contacts are "relatively insignificant" in comparison with those of the other involved state. * * *

In analyzing this position from the perspective of constitutional generalism, the fundamental inquiry must be whether there is any justification for interpreting the full faith and credit clause as imposing a constitutional control on state court choice-of-law decisions. Such justification would have to be found by analyzing the broad organic purpose and function of the full faith and credit clause or by analyzing the purpose and effect of the clause as found in the original understanding of the framers.

No justification for interpreting the clause as imposing a constitutional control on choice of law can be found. First, the historical circumstances surrounding the adoption of the full faith and credit clause make it clear that the framers would not have intended that the clause operate as a limitation on state court choice-of-law decisions. Second, a significant limitation on the power of state courts to make choice-of-law decisions would seem to be inconsistent with the broad, organic purpose of the full faith and credit clause and its function in our constitutional scheme.

It is agreed that there is nothing in the language or history of the full faith and credit clause that indicates that the framers intended this clause to control state court choice-of-law decisions * * *. * * *

* * *

* * * The framers could not have intended the full faith and credit clause to operate as a limit on the power of state courts to make choice-of-law decisions, because at the time of the adoption of the Constitution, the concept of choice of law simply did not exist in this country.

At the time of the adoption of the Constitution, no common law of conflicts had been received from England, because no conflicts law existed there. In all cases coming before the English courts only English law was applied. It was not until the latter part of the eighteenth century that the English courts even considered displacing English law in such a case. Similarly, at the time of the adoption of the Constitution, differences between the laws of sister states in this country must have been exceedingly rare because of a nearly uniform common law. Thus, the framers of the Constitution were, in all likelihood, not cognizant of any concept of choice of law. If they gave any thought at all to the law that should be applied by a state court in interstate cases, they most likely would have assumed they should apply the law of the forum as the English courts had done in international cases. Whatever else the framers intended to accomplish by the promulgation of the full faith and credit clause, it is apparent that they did not intend the clause to operate to control state court choice-of-law decisions.

No justification for interpreting the full faith and credit clause as a constitutional control on state court choice-of-law decisions can be found in the clause's broad, organic purpose or in its function in our constitutional scheme. The purpose and function of a constitutional provision may be ascertained from its textual language and structural position in the Constitution, as well as from the historical circumstances surrounding its adoption. In addition to the full faith and credit clause, article IV, the "federalism" article, includes a provision prohibiting discrimination against the citizens of sister states, and one requiring the United States to guarantee to each state a "republican form of government." Read together, the provisions of article IV and the historical circumstances surrounding their adoption, seem to indicate quite clearly that the broad, organic purpose of the full faith and credit clause was to promote equality among the states and respect for the sovereignty of each state in the federal system. In light of this purpose, the Supreme Court has quite properly interpreted the full faith and credit clause as precluding one state from discriminating against the laws of another state, and requiring that each state enforce, without discrimination, claims existing under the laws of a sister state. Likewise, in light of this broad, organic purpose, the Supreme Court has again quite properly interpreted the full faith and credit clause as imposing virtually no limits on the power of state courts to make choice-of-law decisions.

An essential attribute of state sovereignty in our federal system is the authority of the states under their police power to prescribe the controlling law in civil litigation. This attribute of state sovereignty includes the power of each state to decide when its own law applies to a case containing a foreign element. Since the broad, organic purpose of the full faith and credit clause is to promote equality among the states and respect for the sovereignty of each state in the federal system, it would be anomalous and inconsistent for the Court to interpret it to require that one state yield this attribute of sovereignty to another state because the latter state had a greater interest in controlling the outcome of a particular case. To put it another way, the notion that one state can have a greater interest than another in the exercise of sovereignty reflected in the application of its substantive law in civil litigation, is inconsistent with the broad, organic purpose of the full faith and credit clause which was designed to maintain the states as sovereign equals in our federal system.

The sovereign equality of the states in our federal system properly requires the reciprocal enforcement of sister-state judgments and properly requires the non-discriminatory enforcement of claims existing under the laws of sister states. It also, however, precludes interference with the power of a state court to apply its own law simply because it is asserted that another state has a greater interest in applying its law.

* * * * *

Willis L.M. Reese, *The* Hague *Case: An Opportunity Lost*,* 10 HOFSTRA L. REV. 195, 198-200 (1981)**

* * * * *

Where the court erred, in the opinion of this writer, was in its disregard of federal-system values. One can do little but applaud Justice Stevens' statement in his concurring opinion that if there has been no unfairness to the parties, a state court's application of its own law should not be invalidated "unless that choice threatens the federal interest in national unity by unjustifiably infringing upon the legitimate interests of another State."[20]

Justice Stevens believed that there had been no such infringement because Allstate had not entered into the insurance contract in reliance upon the application of Wisconsin law. The difficulty with his reasoning arises because considerations of fairness to Allstate are quite irrelevant to the question of whether Minnesota had applied its law to matters that were beyond the proper scope of its legislative competence and in a way that was inimical to the interests of our federal system.

Justice Brennan, in his plurality opinion, took a different approach and held that application of the Minnesota stacking rule was constitutionally justified because of Minnesota's interest in the case. In large part, this interest stems from Hague's employment in the state which made "[v]indication of the rights of [his] estate" an "important state concern."[23] To a lesser degree, Minnesota's interest was also derived from Allstate's doing of business in the state and from Mrs. Hague's acquisition of a domicile there after the accident that resulted in her husband's death. Allstate's doing of business in the state seems of dubious significance because Allstate does business in every state of the United States. Therefore, if Justice Brennan is taken seriously, each of these states has an interest in regulating all of Allstate's insurance policies, including those issued in other states to residents of those states. Further, attaching weight to Mrs. Hague's acquisition of a Minnesota domicile after the death of her husband bids fair to open Pandora's box. Minnesota, to be sure, has an interest in the welfare of its domiciliaries. But the issue in this case concerned the obligations assumed by Allstate under a policy issued in Wisconsin to a resident of that state. The suggestion that the nature of these

---

*   A summary of the *Hague* case appears at the beginning of the previous excerpt by Professor Sedler.

**   Reprinted with permission.

[20]   [449 U.S.] at 324 (Stevens, J., concurring in the judgment).

[23]   *Id.* at 314-15.

obligations can be affected by a beneficiary's move to another state following an accident establishes a dangerous precedent. It will, undoubtedly, encourage forum shopping and, worse still, by taking subsequent events into consideration, will make it difficult for parties to predict with any confidence what law may ultimately be applied to determine their rights and duties under a contract. More than forty years ago, the Supreme Court held unanimously in *John Hancock Mutual Life Insurance Co. v. Yates*[27] that a state to which a widow had moved following her husband's death could not constitutionally apply its law to determine the widow's rights under a policy insuring the husband's life. The authority of this case has now been eroded.

Undoubtedly, Minnesota could be said to have an interest in Mr. Hague by reason of his employment in the state. The question is whether this interest is material to the case. This leads to the further inquiry of whether a "state interest," without further qualification, is a term that can usefully be employed in determining the propriety of a state's choice of law. The difficulty is that in most cases there will be some reason for saying that the interest of a state would be served by application of its law. Somewhat extravagantly, yet not irrationally, Minnesota, as part of our federal union, can be said to have an interest in the welfare of all persons living in the United States. Hence, when Minnesota feels that application of its own law would lead to the most just result, Minnesota might justifiably claim an interest in having this law applied even in a situation where the parties involved have no relationship whatever with the state. Less provocatively, but suggestive of the same result, Minnesota has an interest in having its courts apply Minnesota law in all cases that come before them, since it is easier for their courts to apply their own law than that of another state. Again, Minnesota can be said to be interested in the application of its law in all cases where a Minnesota domiciliary is involved. Finally, Minnesota can be said to have an interest in all corporations that do business within its territory. This interest could provide a reason why Minnesota should be permitted to apply its law to control the activities of these corporations throughout the entire world. One could go on and on. The boundaries of a state's interests can be extended as far as the imagination will permit. Surely, it is difficult to determine on any rational basis the point beyond which a state's interests do not extend.

This leads to the conclusion that "state interests" should not be employed without qualification in determining the constitutional limits on the extraterritorial reach of a state's law. Instead, the interest of a state in having a particular local law applied should be assessed in light of the policy, or policies, which the rule was designed to serve. Only if the policy (or at least one of the policies) would be served by the rule's application can the state be legitimately interested in having the rule applied. From this point of view, Minnesota's interest in the application of its stacking rule seems tenuous indeed. It is hard to believe that this policy was directed to insurance policies issued in another state to a resident of that state at least in situations where the accident in question occurred there.

* * * * *

---

[27]   299 U.S. 178 (1936).

Linda J. Silberman, *Can the State of Minnesota Bind the Nation? Federal Choice of Law Constraints After* Allstate Insurance Co. v. Hague,* 10 Hofstra L. Rev. 103, 103, 129-132 (1983)**

The Supreme Court's recent decision in *Allstate Insurance Co. v. Hague* invites the conclusion that the federal system is unable to protect itself against state parochialism in the choice-of-law process. By effectively rejecting the possibility of constitutional constraints in conflicts cases, the Court appears to have left itself and the federal system defenseless. The result is at sharp odds with the Court's recent ventures in the field of personal jurisdiction, where it has relied on the principles of fairness and the bounded reach of state sovereignty to fashion limitations on the extensions of a state's legal process.

* * * * *

One feels, however, a certain sympathy with the Court in *Hague*. Judicial second-guessing of the substantiality of state interests is uncomfortably reminiscent of the era of substantive due process. It is particularly difficult to characterize as utterly arbitrary a state's decision to apply its legal norms to litigation in its own courts when the defendant is a multistate giant which regularly does business within its borders. It is hard in a case like *Hague* to conceive of the Minnesota court's action as deeply unfair to Allstate, or as an affront to Allstate's constitutional rights. What is at stake in *Hague* is the appropriate allocation of state lawmaking authority, and the behavior of the Minnesota court clearly demonstrates the need for some restraints at the margin of state extension. The difficulty lies in translating this need into sharply edged rules whose provenance is demonstrably constitutional. Better by far would be a set of more detailed rules, clearly in service of the constitutional structure of federalism, but avowedly the product of judicial judgment and development.

But in this diagnosis there inheres a prescription for the appropriate means of restraining state excess in choice of law, namely, a set of federal common law restraints, founded upon and in service of the full faith and credit clause and the basic structure of the federal system contemplated in the Constitution. This approach is quite unlike the proposals set forth by Professors Baxter and Horowitz, calling for a full body of federal choice-of-law rules which would displace state court choice-of-law authority.[145] What is contemplated is a set of outer limits on state choice-of-law decisions, bearing to state choice of law much the same relationship as the rules developed in the negative commerce clause cases bear to state legislation which touches on interstate commerce. Like the negative commerce clause restraints developed by the federal judiciary, these choice-of-law restraints would be subject to revision and displacement at the hands of Congress, greatly reducing the threat of rigidity which the constitutionalization of the state choice-of-law process might be seen to harbor. While the negative commerce clause cases present themselves as constitutional decisions, Professor Monaghan has convincingly argued

---

*   [A summary of the *Hague* case appears at the beginning of the prior excerpt by Professor Sedler.]

**   Reprinted with permission of the Hofsta Law Review.

[145]   Baxter, [*Choice of Law and the Federal System*, 16 Stan. L. Rev. 1 (1963)]; Horowitz, *Toward a Federal Common Law of Choice of Law*, UCLA L. REV. 1191 (1967).

that they are prime examples of a tacitly developed body of federal common law rules which resonate to constitutional values.[148]

This proposal is not at war with the *Klaxon* doctrine.[149] A separate body of conflicts law for the federal courts is not contemplated. The restraints which would be developed in this constitutional common law would apply to both federal and state courts, and *Klaxon* would govern everywhere but at the extremes of state self-preference. Initially, it may well be that federal judges in diversity cases will be important actors in the application of these federal restraints, but the accommodation of the federal constitutional common law will be the responsibility of all judges who decide choice-of-law cases. The federal common law limitations would not themselves be a basis for "arising under" jurisdiction in the federal courts, so the balance of federal and state court involvement in conflicts cases would not be disturbed.

With federal restraints placed on a common law footing, reasonably broad latitude would be available to the Supreme Court to develop specific benchmarks to distinguish legitimate state court preferences for their own laws from instances where state interests have been reflexively and parochially asserted without appropriate regard for competing interests. As I have indicated, the purposefulness criteria should play a central role in the development of such benchmarks.

As to *Hague* itself, my own view is that the application of Minnesota's stacking rule transgressed these suggested limitations. Arguably, however, nationwide insurance companies might be deemed to have engaged in the kind of purposeful activity that warrants the application of a state's regulatory rule even when the rule bears no direct connection to the claim involved. As to defendants with more localized ties, such as doctors or uninsured tavern owners, a different response might be forthcoming.

Ultimately, the identification and development of basic values in this federal constitutional common law may serve to induce a greater consensus in conflicts cases. But whether or not this consensus occurs, the generation of such a body of common law restraints would serve to restore integrity to the choice-of-law process. Different melody lines may continue, but harmony ought to be assured.

---

[148]   Monaghan, *The Supreme Court 1974 Term, Foreward: Constitutional Common Law*, 89 HARV. L. REV. 1 (1975).

[149]   In Klaxon Co. v. Stentor Elec. Mfg. Co., 313 U.S. 487 (1941), the Supreme Court held that a federal court in a diversity action is bound to follow the conflict rules of the state in which it is sitting. * * *

Comments

1. Justice Jackson and Professors Weinberg and Sedler note in their selections that a state forum is basically free under the Constitution to apply its own law whenever it has a sufficient regulatory interest in the case—the basis for what commentators have termed legislative jurisdiction. *See, e.g.,* Martin 1981;[1] Reese 1978. There are obvious similarities between the concept of legislative jurisdiction and that of "interest" in interest analysis, the subject of Chapters Five and Six. Thus, beginning with Brainerd Currie, many observers have used interest analysis to describe the constitutional standard for choice of law. Currie wrote that "a state court's choice of law will be upset under the Full Faith and Credit Clause or the Due Process Clause only when the state whose law is applied has no legitimate interest in its application * * *." Currie 1963a: p. 271.

2. The Court's current reviewing standard for conflicts cases appears to be somewhat more generous than Currie's formulation. As Professor Sedler has described it:

> It is only where the application of a state's law cannot be sustained either on the basis of that state's interest in advancing the policy reflected in that law, *or* on the basis of factual connections between the underlying transaction and the state, that such application is unreasonable and hence unconstitutional.

Sedler 1985: p. 488 (emphasis added).

3. The boundaries for the second category above—factual connections making it constitutional for an uninterested forum to apply its own law—are unclear. Shreve 1987: p. 72; Weinberg 1988: p. 69. The first category of this standard—based on the concept of an interested forum—exists in sharper relief. Restated, it offers perhaps the clearest and most serviceable description of the current relation between choice of law and the Constitution: *with few if any exceptions, an interested forum may resolve true conflicts by applying its own law.*

4. Of the parts of the Constitution theoretically available to the Supreme Court to regulate choice of law, the Court has actually invoked only the full-faith-and-credit and due process clauses. Herzog 1992: pp. 285-289; Richman & Reynolds 1993: pp. 282-287. Prior to *Pacific Employers Insurance Co. v. Industrial Accident Commission*, 306 U.S. 493 (1939), the Supreme Court had on several occasions toyed with the idea of extensive regulation of choice of law. For descriptions of this earlier period, *see* Brilmayer 1995a: pp. 378-379; Ross 1931; Sedler 1981a: pp. 64-65; Shreve 1993: p. 919; Vernon, Weinberg, Reynolds & Richman 1990: p. 415. Since *Pacific Employers*, there is widespread agreement that the combined restraint of full faith and credit and due process on choice of law has been slight—that, to use Professor Weinberg's term, the Supreme Court has subjected conflicts decisions to only "minimal scrutiny."

---

[1]   Full citations appear in the bibliograpy, Chapter Twelve.

5. The Supreme Court has typically made little effort to delineate the roles of full faith and credit and due process in conflicts review. The Court seems instead to have "accepted the choice-of-law equivalence of the two clauses." Brilmayer 1995a: p. 439. In contrast, the two clauses provide sharply different functions outside the conflicts setting. They also exhibit considerably more life elsewhere. Justice Jackson noted the greater force of the full-faith-and-credit clause in the enforcement of sister-state judgments. Similar observations appear in Brilmayer 1984a: p. 95; Freund 1946: p. 1225; Reynolds 1994. The comparatively stronger role the due process clause performs in regulating personal jurisdiction is a subject of Part D of this Chapter.

6. Many commentators fault current doctrine for not focusing on the separate contributions possible from each of the two clauses, and for not using one or the other more aggressively in regulating choice of law. For example, Professor Gary Simson has urged that the Supreme Court "should recognize that the full-faith-and-credit-clause requires nationwide uniformity in choice of law and announce that this uniformity is most appropriately implemented by courts' deferring to the decisionmaking authority of the one or more jurisdictions most interested in influencing the outcome of the case under review." Simson 1978: p. 87. Possibilities for an enlarged role for the full-faith-and-credit clause are also explored in Freund 1946; Hay 1983; Martin 1976; Pielemeier 1987; Shreve 1987. Similarly, critics have examined possibilities for greater due process regulation of choice of law. *See, e.g.,* Kirgis 1976; Kozyris 1981; Leflar 1963; Reese 1978; Scoles & Hay 1992: pp. 93-103; Weintraub 1986: pp. 512-540.

7. Alternatively, Professor Silberman posed in her excerpt a federal-common-law rather than constitutional basis for conflicts reform. The late Professor Donald Trautman offered a related view:

> In the halcyon days of constitutional control, state choice-of-law practice was relatively uniform and simple; in that context, it was appropriate to identify departure from the place of wrong for tort, the place of making for contract, and the situs for property as unconstitutionally arbitrary and capricious. Choice of law has come a long way from those untroubled days, and these constitutional controls would be unthinkable today. It therefore seems to me wise to leave constitutional controls to their proper area of striking down arbitrary action and to look elsewhere for development of federal controls over choice of law.

Trautman 1992: pp. 1725-1726. He went on to state:

> Wholesale federalization of choice of law seems unattractive as a solution for the immediate future, whether through the medium of constitutional pronouncement, legislative action, or a federal common law that calls for writing on a clean slate. On the other hand, incremental federalization of choice of law—which I urge as both feasible and desirable—can be achieved by creation of a federal common law that

proceeds in the same way that federal common law develops in other areas today: as a means of modulating state law to reflect federal concerns, not addressed, or not adequately satisfied by state law.

Id. at p. 1730.

8. Controversy, which seems a perennial aspect of conflicts discourse, is much in evidence on the topic of choice of law and the Constitution. Most revolves around three issues. *First,* commentators differ over whether or to what extent reforms in conflicts law are really necessary. As discussed in Chapter Six, some doubt that local favoritism in choice of law greatly exceeds that which is inevitable under our federal system of government. Those believing that it does not reason that attempts at greater constitutional intervention are both unnecessary and unlikely to succeed. *Second,* critics believing discrimination in choice of law can and should be averted split into two groups: (1) radical theorists—who would use the Constitution to eradicate current features of conflicts law like interest analysis or the better-rule approach—and (2) traditional theorists—who do not wish to overhaul contemporary conflicts doctrine but do wish to make greater use of the Constitution to promote neutral choice-of-law results. The approach of radical theorists (discussed in the following Part) tends to rest on parts of the Constitution that currently have little if any application to choice of law: the privilege and immunities, commerce, and equal protection clauses. The approach of traditional theorists (discussed in this Part) is to rework and enlarge portions of the Constitution already associated with choice of law: the full-faith-and-credit and due process clauses. *Third* critics differ over whether the cure for real or supposed discrimination in choice of law might be worse than the disease. Concern often centers on the costs to judicial administration that might attend conflicts reform imposed by federal law. This factor was raised in the excerpt by Justice Jackson. His misgivings have been elaborated by several writers since, including this author in Part A and Professor Weinberg in Part B of this Chapter.

C. Regulatory Possibilities Under Other Parts of the Constitution

Douglas Laycock, *Equal Citizens of Equal and Territorial States, The Constitutional Foundations of Choice of Law*, 92 COLUM. L. REV. 249, 250-251, 267-270, 288-290, 336-337 (1992)*

* * * * *

One consequence of dividing a single nation into fifty quasi-sovereign states is a constant need to choose the law that governs interstate disputes. Choice of law takes on a whole new significance in such a nation. We have handled the problem badly; indeed, we have not even looked to the right sources of law. We took a fundamental wrong turn at the very beginning of modern choice-of-law scholarship.

The continuing error has been to ignore the constitutional principles that control choice-of-law questions. As Justice Jackson suggested a generation ago, choice of law within the United States is inherently constitutional law.[1] Choice-of-law questions are about the allocation of authority among the several states. Allocation of authority is what constitutions do. The essential function of constitutions is to constitute the many units of government in our federal system and define and limit the power of each. It would be an astonishing oversight if our fundamental law did not state general principles allocating authority among states and if those principles did not have implications for choice of law. This article explores the positive law bases for choosing among competing intuitions about the limits of state authority and for providing federal answers to choice-of-law questions.

I do not claim that the Constitution dictates a unique set of choice-of-law rules, but I do claim that the Constitution contains three principles from which all domestic choice-of-law rules must be derived. These three principles are:

1. The principle of equal citizens: States must treat the citizens of sister states equally with their own.
2. The principle of equal states: States must treat sister states as equal in authority to themselves.
3. The principle of territorial states: The fundamental allocation of authority among states is territorial.

The Constitution states the first two principles in operational terms, most explicitly in Article IV, in the Privileges and Immunities and Full Faith and Credit Clauses. The third principle is largely implicit, so obvious that the Founders neglected to state it. But the texts of state and federal constitutions, state organic acts, and state admission acts contain ample evidence of this allocation of authority.

The choice-of-law implications of the first two principles are negative; they state what choice of law rules cannot be. Choice-of-law rules may not prefer local citizens to citizens of

---

*   This article originally appeared at 92 COLUM. L. REV. 249 (1992). Reprinted with permission.

[1]   Robert H. Jackson, *Full Faith and Credit—The Lawyer's Clause of the Constitution*, 45 COLUM. L. REV. 1, 2, 6-7 (1945).

a sister state; that is the principle of equal citizens. And they may not prefer forum law to the law of sister states; that is the principle of equal states. Many modern choice-of-law theories violate one or both of these principles.

The implications of the third principle are affirmative: all choice-of-law rules must be consistent with, and derived from, the fundamentally territorial allocation of authority among the states. State interests are still relevant, especially in developing rules for locating relationships, intangibles, and other subjects of regulation not embodied in a single physical place. But a state's claim to regulate behavior or to govern a dispute must be based on some thing or event within its territory. And in deciding which things or events control choice of law, a state's interests in enriching local citizens and extending the territorial reach of its own law are illegitimate. They simply should not count.

A corollary proposition follows from these three principles. The constitutional principles that govern choice of law are federally enforceable like any other constitutional principle. Full enforcement requires specific federal choice-of-law rules derived from the three constitutional principles. Congress could enact such rules, but it has chosen simply to restate one of the constitutional provisions and leave the details to the courts. It therefore falls to the federal courts to derive specific choice-of-law rules in the course of adjudicating disputes under the Constitution and the implementing statute.

The three constitutional principles, plus the corollary proposition about federal enforcement, are independent in the sense that readers persuaded of any one or two or three of them can accept that much without accepting the rest. But they are interdependent in the sense that together they form a coherent and mutually supporting foundation on which to develop a system of choice-of-law rules.

* * * * *

Discrimination against citizens of sister states will sometimes be justified, but only (or almost only) when such discrimination serves federal interests and not merely the interests of the discriminating state. If a state's parochial interests can ever justify discrimination against citizens of sister states, it can only be to avoid intolerable harms. In conventional terms, the standard of review should be the compelling interest standard.

This view of the Clause derives in part from a belief that we should take the whole Constitution seriously. We cannot legitimately pick and choose the clauses we want enforced. But the Privileges and Immunities Clause is not an arguable constitutional mistake, nor is it an obsolete provision that modern Americans are stuck with; it fits neatly into modern conceptions of nondiscrimination. Discrimination against fellow Americans is intuitively unjust. Citizens of sister states are outsiders, subject to in-group/out-group bias, denied the right to vote, which is the key to power in the political process, and thus dependent on judicial protection. Faithful interpreters of the Constitution should not be seeking ways to minimize the Privileges and Immunities Clause.

* * *

Discrimination against sister-state corporations has been treated differently, because the Privileges and Immunities Clause protects only citizens. Corporations cannot be citizens, and the Court has so far been unwilling to look through the corporation and protect the sister-state investors. Instead, discrimination between local and sister-state corporations violates the Commerce Clause and the Equal Protection Clause. The Supreme Court's enforcement of these prohibitions has gradually strengthened over the years. The Court once viewed incorporation as a privilege that could be granted or withheld for any reason or no reason, and thus states were free to exclude sister-state corporations or to condition their admittance on consent to discriminatory treatment. This view was wrong even in its own time, but it became profoundly obsolete after general incorporation statutes made corporate status a right available for the asking.

Today the Court interprets the Commerce Clause to forbid all or nearly all discrimination against economic actors from sister states. It has said that discrimination against interstate commerce is "virtually *per se* invalid," without hope of justification by further inquiry into state interests. In other cases, it has said that such discrimination is subject to the "strictest scrutiny," or "more demanding scrutiny." This rule applies with equal force to discrimination against out-of-state persons and discrimination against out-of-state goods.

Discrimination against sister-state corporations violates the Equal Protection Clause as well unless it bears "a rational relation to a legitimate state purpose."[124] This rule is not so weak as it appears, because it carries the important proviso that a mere desire "to favor domestic industry within the State" is not a legitimate state purpose.[125] Rather, discrimination so motivated "constitutes the very sort of parochial discrimination that the Equal Protection Clause was intended to prevent."[126] Congress can authorize state regulation of interstate commerce that would otherwise be precluded by the Commerce Clause, but it presumably cannot authorize violations of the Equal Protection Clause.

Review of discrimination against natural persons or corporations from sister states should be equally stringent under any of these clauses. The objections to discrimination against citizens of sister states do not change when those citizens elect to do business in corporate form. The owners of a sister-state corporation are still fellow Americans exposed to the risk of local bias, and their right to do business throughout the country is still essential to national unity. The omission of corporations from the Privileges and Immunities Clause is not an element of the constitutional scheme; it is a relic from a time before general incorporation laws. The same constitutional policies of national unity and interstate equality are at work in all three clauses. The specific concerns that underlie the Privileges and Immunities Clause inform the more general right of equality in the Equal Protection Clause and the equality component of the Commerce Clause. The Court should be reluctant to imply exceptions to any of these protections.

* * * * *

The Constitution itself expressly provides for the equality of states in the context most relevant here: it provides for the equal authority of each state's law. This is the meaning of the Full Faith and Credit Clause: "Full Faith and Credit shall be given in each State to the public Acts, Records, and judicial Proceedings of every other State."

This clause is comprehensible only if one assumes a background set of choice-of-law rules. In the Full Faith and Credit Clause, and in the contemporaneous Rules of Decision Act, the Founders directed state and federal courts to apply the applicable law of other American jurisdictions. They seem not to have seen the ambiguity entailed in that instruction. Both provisions assume that it is obvious when state law applies and which state's law applies. The

---

[124]   Western & S. Life Ins. Co. v. State Bd. of Equalization, 451 U.S. 648, 668 (1981).

[125]   Metropolitan Life Ins. Co. v. Ward, 470 U.S. 869, 878 (1985).

[126]   *Id.*

Founders saw no ambiguity because they understood the instruction in light of the familiar choice-of-law rules then applied in English and American courts. They assumed that these rules would determine which state's law applied, and that the Constitution and the statute would require courts to apply the law of that state.

This is how the Full Faith and Credit Clause has always been understood with respect to judgments. Federally enforced conflict-of-law rules determine whether a state court had jurisdiction. If the first court had jurisdiction, its judgment is binding on all other states; if not, all other states are free to ignore it. As a simple matter of constitutional text, the Clause must have the same meaning with respect to rules of law.* * *

* * * * *

Choice-of-law methods that prefer local litigants, local law, or better law are unconstitutional. These unconstitutional preferences are central to some so-called modern choice-of-law methods, and infect most other methods to some extent. The choice-of-law revolution has proceeded in disregard of the Constitution.

This conclusion breaks sharply with current law and scholarship on constitutional limits to choice of law. Yet my methods of constitutional interpretation are entirely conventional. I have emphasized the constitutional text, the constitutional structure, and secondary evidence of intent.

Nor have I relied on original intentions that have become anachronistic. It is not controversial to say that all Americans are entitled to equal treatment, that the states are of equal status and authority, or that states are divided territorially. It should not be controversial to draw the choice-of-law corollaries of these propositions: that courts owe equal concern and respect to citizens of sister states, that courts owe equal respect to sister-state law, and that the boundaries separating governmental authorities are the basis for rules separating the reach of conflicting laws.

The secondary evidence of original intent supports my thesis, but the most important arguments are structural. The three constitutional principles I have identified are essential and mutually reinforcing elements of the federal structure. These three principles give simultaneous and consistent effect to the Privileges and Immunities Clause, the Full Faith and Credit Clause, and the territorial definitions of states, and they eliminate any tension with the Equal Protection Clause. Choice-of-law decisions may not be based on the forum, or on the better law, or on benefit to one litigant or the other, but they may be based on the location of the person, thing, relationship, act, or event to be regulated.

Full implementation of these constitutional provisions requires Congress or the Supreme Court to develop a determinate set of territorial choice-of-law rules. Federal responsibility for developing and enforcing these principles provides a neutral referee for interstate disputes, without displacing state authority on a single domestic issue. By contrast, leaving these matters to the states is inconsistent with the rule of law, because no person can know the law that governs his conduct until after his case has been decided.

Partial implementation requires only that the Court enforce the negative prohibitions of the Privileges and Immunities and Full Faith and Credit Clauses. The Court should reverse any choice-of-law judgment in which preference for local litigants, or a preference for forum law or better law or local public policy, played a role in the decision. States would be left free to develop their own choice-of-law rules within these restrictions. That would fall far short of the constitutional plan, but it would be a vast improvement over the status quo.

Forced to abandon the unconstitutional preferences that have dominated choice-of-law debates for a generation, courts and scholars might turn to territorial rules for lack of an alternative. We could then pursue the real task, never seriously attempted in the post-realist era, of developing determinate territorial choice-of-law rules for a modern society.

John H. Ely, *Choice of Law and the State's Interest in Protecting Its Own*, 23 WM. & MARY L. REV. 173, 183-189 (1981)*

* * * * *

In one of his early articles, Currie noted in passing that adoption of an interest analysis methodology "would give a new importance" to the Privileges and Immunities Clause.[32] It should be clear by now that that is putting it mildly. In fact few interest analysts seem prepared to take the issue seriously—the prevailing assumption seems to be that nothing so sensible could possibly be unconstitutional—but, characteristically, Currie was an exception. In two lengthy articles published in 1960 and written in collaboration with Professor Herma Kay, herself a distinguished interest analyst, Currie took the privileges and immunities attack very seriously indeed,[34] in fact so seriously as to overcomplicate it substantially.

The key device Currie and Kay recommended for coping with the constitutional problem was the so-called "intermediate solution" of extending the protection of forum law to an out-of-stater if, but only if, he or she was similarly protected by the law of his or her home state. That solution was subject to several restrictions, among them that it not be employed if it ended up generating a true conflict, and indeed the restrictions underwent significant alteration between the first article and the second. Paradoxically, however—and here the overcomplication took its toll—the intermediate solution turns out on close analysis to be a mere paper alteration, without functional significance. For if the law of a party's home state would decide the case for him, then by standard interest analysis canons that state has an interest in the application of its law. If no other state has an interest in a contrary result, the conflict is "false" and the courts of all states are instructed to find for him; no "extension" of another state's law to protect him is needed to reach that result. If on the other hand another state does have an interest in a contrary result, there exists a true conflict between the law of that state and that of the home state of the party in question. Different commentators have different ways of dealing with true conflicts, but for none will the consideration that the party is protected not only by his home state's law but also by an "extension" of another state's law make a difference. At first blush it might seem that it could make a difference for Currie, if the law whose "extension" is in issue is that of the forum. For his recommendation, not widely accepted, was that in case of a true conflict the forum, if it has an interest, apply its own law. And the "extension" of the forum's law to protect an out-of-stater will convert it from a disinterested forum into an interested one. But again, no outcome will be influenced. For Currie's recommendation was that a disinterested forum confronted with a true conflict between the interests of two other jurisdictions decide the case in accord with the law of that interested state whose law is the same

---

* Reprinted with permission. This article also appeared in John H. Ely, ON CONSTITUTIONAL GROUND 661-86 (1996).

[32] [BRAINERD] CURRIE, [SELECTED ESSAYS ON THE CONFLICT OF LAWS 185 (1963)].

[34] B. CURRIE, [*supra* note 32], chs. 10 & 11. The latter is technically about equal protection, but the authors did not significantly distinguish the two attacks: both articles are about the constitutionality of defining protective interests as running only in favor of locals.

as its own. The same result would therefore be reached whether or not the extension of the intermediate solution was made.

It may be, however, that the linchpin of that little demonstration—the realization that the party's home state has an interest in protecting him or her whether the forum does or not—provides a more direct route out of our privileges and immunities dilemma. Perhaps we have been focusing our attention too narrowly, on the recommendation that we construe a particular state's protective policies as protecting locals only. Viewed that narrowly, it's quite true that the discrimination seems just what the Privileges and Immunities Clause forbids, one between locals and nonlocals. If we widen our horizon, however, the recommendation of the interest analysts is not simply that Californians receive the protection of California's protective policies and everyone else be denied them, but rather that everyone receive the benefit of the protective policies his or her own state has seen fit to legislate. Of course that may turn out not to be possible, if two or more states wish to protect their own in ways that cannot coexist: that is the classic true conflict situation. Currie would in that event tell the forum to apply its own law. Most commentators reject that solution, however, refusing in their various processes of accommodation to discount the presumptive entitlement of an interested state to the application of law on the ground that it is not the state in which suit was brought. And if that is the approach, the system can be viewed not as one that flatly distinguishes locals from out-of-staters, but rather as one that "simply" sorts people out according to the states from which they hail. Whether or not they are accorded benefits equivalent to those accorded by local law, therefore, will depend on what their local legislators have seen fit to do for them, and that, the argument would run, is not a violation of the Privileges and Immunities Clause.

The argument does not run smooth, at least so far as the case law is concerned. For if it satisfied the Privileges and Immunities Clause to deny someone the benefits of local law so long as he is getting what his home state's law would give him, the proper course, before voiding any law under that clause, would be to inquire where the complainant is from and whether he would be entitled at home to the benefit he now seeks. If he wouldn't, his privileges and immunities challenge should be rejected (though the challenges of others from other states would succeed). Yet we know perfectly well that this is not the way the Court has proceeded under Article IV: indeed I am not aware of a single instance where it has asked what the challenger would be entitled to at home.

The Court's assumption that the content of the challenger's home state law is irrelevant to a privileges and immunities challenge was demonstrated even more forcefully, albeit still with apparent inadvertence, in its 1975 decision in *Austin v. New Hampshire*.[40] Invalidated in *Austin* was the New Hampshire Commuters Income Tax, which applied to the New Hampshire-derived income of nonresidents, but exempted the income of residents similarly earned within the state. It thus seems like a straightforward privileges and immunities case—until we add two facts, that the law imposed a ceiling on the tax rate of whatever rate would be imposed by the taxpayer's home state on income he earned there, and included a provision that in the event the home state refused to credit the taxpayer for the taxes paid to New Hampshire they would not be imposed. The net effect, therefore, was to tax an out-of-stater at the rate his home legislature had selected. Of course it can be argued that this is something other than treating him as his home legislature would, since taxes paid at home will be spent at home whereas New Hampshire will spend its revenues, understandably enough, in New Hampshire. The Court did not so much as mention this, however—unsurprisingly, I think, since New Hampshire is a place where the commuting taxpayer spends a good deal of time even if he doesn't sleep there, and as noted

---

[40]   420 U.S. 656 (1975).

the home state was given the option, which in the event was not exercised, of ensuring that the money *would* be spent at home. *Austin* thus seems to stand rather directly for the proposition that it is not sufficient under the Privileges and Immunities Clause to treat people as the laws of their home states would treat them.

The importance of this conclusion should not be underestimated. If *Austin* is right as written, the dominant contemporary choice-of-law theory is unconstitutional. The threat is by no means simply to Brainerd Currie's dictum that in cases of true conflict the forum should apply its own law; the point is much more devastating. It undercuts the entire methodology by indicating that whenever a state would claim an interest in enforcing its protective policy on the ground that the party its law would protect is a local resident—and that much is common to all "interest" or "functional" analysts—it is obligated by the United States Constitution to claim a similar interest in protecting out-of-staters, irrespective of what their home states' law provides. That, for reasons we have canvassed, spells the end of "interest analysis" in any recognizable sense of the term and insists instead that we direct our choice-of-law references to that state which will most often bear the strongest relation to the issue in question—relation, however, not being defined in terms of who lives where.

Austin was decided only six years ago, and surely the Court has cast nothing resembling explicit doubt on it. Reason to suppose its implications were not fully considered, however, is supplied by the more recent decision in *Allstate Insurance Co. v. Hague*,[43] where seven members of the Court, while they did not explicitly say that the residence of the party to be benefited could alone form the constitutional basis for the application of local law, did seem to imply that and surely indicated, as the Court had in the past, that such residence is a factor on which a state may constitutionally rely in applying its own law. The opinions in *Hague* did not even mention *Austin*.

It seems, therefore, that the one hand is not keeping up with what the other is up to, that for some reason *Austin* did not strike the Court as "a conflict of laws case" and, more surprisingly, did not even set off alarms suggesting a consideration of the implications of what the Court was saying for more run-of-the-mill conflicts cases. For if *Austin* is right as written, and it violates the Privileges and Immunities Clause to grant everyone the benefits of his or her home state's law, then interest analysis of the sort approved six years later in *Hague*—permitting states to apply local law to benefit local citizens under conditions where they would not do likewise for nonlocals—seems unconstitutional. Which should give?

* * * * *

---

[43]   101 S. Ct. 633 (1981).

Harold W. Horowitz, *The Commerce Clause as a Limitation on State Choice of Law Doctrine*, 84 HARV. L. REV. 806, 806-807, 814-816, 821-824 (1971)*

* * *

As the objectives of choice-of-law doctrine have come to be recognized as the harmonizing and reconciling of conflicting state governmental interests within the federal system, a fundamental question is whether the source of legal doctrine to resolve a conflict of state laws should be federal rather than state law. Although state law has been, and continues to be, the source of choice-of-law principles in the federal system, the Supreme Court has recognized the need for at least some minimum of federally-imposed limitations on such state law doctrine. The full faith and credit clause has occasionally been held to require that a state give effect to the law of another state, and the due process clause of the fourteenth amendment has at times been held to require that a state not give effect to its own law. However, due to the acceptance of the proposition that a state has the power to give effect to its own law if it has a legitimate interest in doing so, these constitutional provisions have not been significant limitations on state choice-of-law principles.

One constitutional provision which might limit state choice-of-law doctrine, but which has been generally ignored in this context, is the commerce clause. The commerce clause has long been held to control the application of state law in interstate contexts, and has been considered a vehicle for determining "the better and more appropriate ordering of the federal system."[8] Transactions in interstate commerce are a prime source of choice-of-law issues; and the limits imposed by the commerce clause on the effectuation of state governmental interests in order to advance national or multistate interests might also be applied to resolve conflicts among state laws.

* * * * *

The principle would be applied in at least two types of situations. One type of case would involve the legal relationships among classes of widely dispersed shareholders, creditors, or other individuals dealing with an interstate commercial enterprise, where the principle of facilitating multistate transactions would require that a single state's law, or a group of compatible state laws, should govern these relationships. Invoking the commerce clause in this type of case would minimize the possibility that a multiplicity of state laws would govern the commercial relationships of these classes and would insure that a single pattern of regulation emerged from the choice-of-law process. The second type of case would involve interstate commercial transactions between individuals who are not members of these widely dispersed classes. In such a case, a single law applicable in all forums would not be required. A conflict between two states' laws governing a contractual transaction would be resolved by selecting the state's law which would tend to facilitate interstate commercial activity.

* * *

---

[8]   Brown, *The Open Economy: Justice Frankfurter and the Position of the Judiciary*, 67 YALE L.J. 219, 237 (1957).

In several cases involving multistate commercial transactions the Supreme Court has held that the full faith and credit clause requires a specific choice-of-law decision by a state court. The cases concern the rights and obligations of members of fraternal benefit associations, and the obligations of shareholders for assessments to satisfy the claims of creditors of their corporation. In these cases the commerce clause would have provided a more convincing constitutional basis for the decisions.

* * *

These cases appear to have been decided on the ground that the rights and obligations of members should be uniform regardless of their place of residence. A more thorough analysis of the issues would have been possible under a commerce clause approach. With respect to interstate insurance functions of such associations, operations might be significantly impaired if the legal relationships among the members, their beneficiaries, and the association varied with the residence of each member.* * *

* * * * *

The preceding discussion has focused on the application of the commerce clause to limit state choice-of-law doctrine when the needs of interstate commerce require that a single uniformly applicable law be selected to govern. The general principle—that the commerce clause should be held to require a choice-of-law decision which will better facilitate multistate commercial transactions—would also be applicable to cases involving individual contractual transactions, in which the multiparty relationships found in the fraternal benefit association and corporation cases discussed above are not present. The application of the commerce clause in such cases would be far-reaching because a substantial portion of the choice-of-law issues involving contracts might then be approached as federal constitutional questions. Suggestions of this theme, although not phrased in constitutional terms, can be found in existing state choice-of-law doctrine.

One example is the principle that if a multistate commercial transaction between parties of equal bargaining power would be valid under the law of one of the interested states and invalid under the other, and if the interests of both states in having their own laws apply are of equal weight, then the court should choose that state's law which would validate the transaction. This choice-of-law principle, a "rule of validation," facilitates commerce by making the multistate transaction effective. Although the rule is said to be based on the presumption that the parties intended to enter into a binding transaction, it appears to reflect a policy of making choice-of-law decisions in a way that facilitates rather than frustrates commercial transactions. This implicit policy suggests that the "rule" could be constitutionally based in the commerce clause.

A similar illustration is found in the principle that an agreement by parties to a multistate commercial transaction as to the choice of law to govern the transaction will be given effect. Enforcement of the choice-of-law agreement enables the parties to accommodate their transaction to conflicting state laws. Again, the reason for this choice-of-law rule is that multistate commercial transactions would thereby be better facilitated. In light of the purposes of the commerce clause, this rule might also be constitutionally required.

* * *

The commerce clause decisions in cases involving state regulation and state taxation provide a starting point for application the commerce clause as a limitation on state choice-of-law doctrine. That limitation would derive from the policy of the commerce clause to protect interstate commerce from undue burdens imposed by state laws. For example, the choice-of-law doctrine of a state might impose such a burden by requiring the application of a more restrictive state law when another state, with a less restrictive law, had an equal interest in having its law applied. In such a situation, the commerce clause could be interpreted to require a state to select that law to govern which would impose the lesser burden on commerce. Or, the choice-of-law doctrines of a group of states might impose an unreasonable burden on interstate commerce when their choice-of-law rules collectively produced a disparate pattern of regulation of multistate commercial transactions. In this latter situation, the commerce clause could be interpreted to require each state to select the law of a single state, or the compatible laws of a group of states, to govern all the transactions of a particular type of commercial enterprise. Recognition of the commerce clause as a limitation on state choice-of-law doctrine would thus serve the federal interest in promoting uniform and unburdensome patterns of regulation, and would also provide a means of increasing federal control over state choice-of-law doctrine.

Gerald L. Neuman, *Territorial Discrimination, Equal Protection, and Self-Determination*, 135 U. PA. L. REV. 261, 329-331 (1987)*

* * * * *

[T]he privileges and immunities clause effectively supersedes fundamental rights equal protection in the analysis of residence classifications in choice of law, so far as claims of discrimination against citizens of sister states are concerned. The equal protection clause still has an independent role to play, however, when state residents or corporations or resident aliens are disfavored by residence classifications, because they are not protected by the privileges and immunities clause. Similarly, pure location discriminations require independent equal protection analysis.

Though out-of-state resident aliens and corporations do not vote in any state, still they are members of a self-governing community that may have a greater interest in determining their rights and duties than the forum state has. Family law for aliens and libel and shield laws for media corporations might be cited as possible examples. Once more, deference to the sovereignty of a sister state over its noncitizen residents ought to be encouraged and ought not to trigger heightened scrutiny. Because the state will still have an incentive to disfavor nonresident aliens and corporations, residence discriminations cannot simply be assumed to reflect such deference. On the other hand, the demands of national unity are not as great with regard to aliens and corporations as with regard to citizens. Thus a somewhat more deferential version of the inquiry pursued under the privileges and immunities clause should be employed: only if the forum state purports to be deferring to a state with greater interest, only if that characterization is rational, and only if the choice of law decision adopts enough of the domicile's law that it may reasonably be said to further that goal, should the forum's adoption of domicile law be excused from heightened scrutiny.

Discriminations against the state's own residents also require separate treatment, because they raise no questions under the privileges and immunities clause. A state has little incentive to disfavor its own electorate, and hostility to a fundamental right is more likely to be reflected in a restrictive substantive rule applicable to residents and nonresidents alike than in a discrimination against local residents. In the rare instances where a discrimination favoring nonresidents on its surface impairs their position of equality in the state, nonresidents can vindicate the interest in national unity by challenging the scheme. Accordingly, the same slightly more deferential test articulated for aliens and corporations should be applied to determine when a residence discrimination favoring out-of-staters escapes heightened equal protection scrutiny.

Similarly, even pure location discriminations, which never raise privileges and immunities issues, should be judged by the same standard. Choice of law decisions in which the location of a particular act becomes a decisive factor are likely to reflect a defensible choice of law methodology, though there may be instances where the chosen act is so marginal that it cannot justify the discrimination. The greater danger is that the state will abuse the method of *depecage*, for example, by denying a local defense for defamatory statements originating out of state while applying the local standard of care. As I have argued earlier, a location discrimination can have a differential impact almost as onerous on residents of the disfavored locality as an explicit residence discrimination would have. Pure location discriminations should not be excused from heightened scrutiny until the court has determined, by the inquiry outlined above, that they represent genuine deference to the interests of another state, and not a trap for an out-of-state actor.

As an illustration, consider the traditional defamation privilege for statements made in the course of judicial proceedings. Suppose that Alabama not only imposes liability for negligent defamation, but also abolishes the judicial proceedings privilege altogether. Suppose further that New York provides an absolute privilege for all statements made in judicial proceedings. Finally, suppose an Alabama resident alien sues some New York resident aliens in Alabama, alleging that they defamed her in the course of an earlier lawsuit in New York. If Alabama concludes that the rules for both liability and privilege in such cases should be dictated by the state in whose courts the prior litigation occurred, then the pure location discrimination is rational and should be upheld. First, Alabama could *rationally* conclude that the prior forum has a greater interest in striking an appropriate balance between zealous advocacy in pursuit of justice and protecting itself from being used as a vehicle for malicious defamation, even of Alabama residents; second, the adoption of the prior forum's law as to both the claim and the defense reasonably furthers the goal of deference to forum policy. Accordingly, heightened scrutiny should not be applied, and the discrimination should be upheld as rational. In contrast, if Alabama concludes that the domicile of the plaintiff dictates rules for both liability and privilege, then heightened scrutiny is required. The result of Alabama's choice of law rule is to treat all litigation between its residents and those of New York—and especially such litigation in Alabama's own courts—as an unequal contest. Alabama residents are free to defame, and New York residents are disabled from replying in kind. It is not rational to conclude that New York has an overriding interest in subjecting its residents to such an ordeal. Thus, whatever other purposes Alabama's choice of law rule might serve in this context, it does not rationally serve the purpose of deferring to the policy choices of a state with greater interest. Accordingly, it will not be excused from heightened scrutiny of its impact on first amendment rights.

* * * * *

Comments

1. In their arguments in this Part, Professors Laycock, Ely, Horowitz, and Neuman drew upon untapped sources of the Constitution. Two other commentators recently observed:

> Although the Commerce Clause has significant potential implications for choice of law, the Supreme court has never used it to decide a case in that area. * * * The Privileges and Immunities Clause has seen little use outside the area of state restrictions on access to natural resources and other state benefits (and it has never been employed by the Supreme Court in a choice-of-law case). * * * [T]he Equal Protection Clause has never been the basis of a Supreme court choice-of-law decision."

Richman and Reynolds 1993: section 96.[1] The same assessment appears in Herzog 1992: pp. 285-286, 288-289.

2. One could imagine conflicts discrimination so blatant that it would trigger one of the clauses under present law. For example:

> A choice-of-law rule that expressly required application of whichever law was most favorable to the party from the forum state would violate the privileges and immunities clause because its discrimination would be based on nothing other than a desire to prefer its own citizens. No evidence apart from the rule itself would be needed to establish its unconstitutionality.

Note 1977b: p. 286. Yet courts need not and do not make such explicit statements of discriminatory purpose. Instead, courts can mask discrimination against nonresidents or against nonforum law by utilizing two supposedly neutral features that are popular in contemporary conflicts doctrine: domicile-centered interest analysis (discussed in this Chapter and in Chapter Six) and the better-rule form of conflicts substantivism (discussed in Chapter 7, Part B). Critics interested in constitutional reform largely agree that this is the central problem; *viz.*, current conflicts law makes it difficult to expose judicial acts of discrimination. Critics do not agree, however, upon how best to bring the Constitution to bear. They are divided into traditional and radical camps.

3. Traditional theorists would base constitutional reform on the full-faith-and-credit and due process clauses (the subject of Part B of Chapter 10). In general, traditionalist reformers seek incremental improvement (greater neutrality) without working any fundamental changes in choice-of-law. Their approach does not require elimination of interest analysis or any other component of modern theory. Weight could still be given to policies that might make the forum interested in applying local law, but not disproportionate weight.

---

[1]   Full citations appear in the bibliography, Chapter Twelve.

4. Radical theorists draw anti-discrimination themes from privileges and immunities, commerce, and equal protection clauses. Their recommendations (surveyed in this Part) often appear to be frontal assaults on aspects of conflicts theory, including domicile-based interest analysis and the better-rule approach. Moreover, radical theorists are inclined to distrust the emphasis in current conflicts doctrine on method over firm rules, and to disapprove of the relatively low priority given to the value of uniformity. Thus,

> [c]onvinced that current law should be overhauled, and perhaps irritated by delay in state law reform, radical critics see a more direct route to change. They would use the U. S. Constitution as a kind of scouring pad to remove the stains of uncertainty and local bias that they find on American conflicts law.

Shreve 1993: p. 920.

D. Constitutional Intersections of Choice of Law and Personal Jurisdiction

Gene R. Shreve, *Interest Analysis as Constitutional Law*, 48 Ohio St. L.J. 51, 57-62 (1987)*

* * * * *

The Tendency of the Minimum Contacts Test to Check Conflicts Abuses—is Constitutional Review of Choice of Law Really Necessary?

The *Shutts*** Court stated that "[t]he issue of personal jurisdiction" in the case was "entirely distinct from the question of constitutional limitations on choice of law."[36] Perhaps the Court only meant to say that it has never shaped its personal (territorial) jurisdiction doctrine with the object of regulating choice of law, and that the same cannot be relied upon as a complete surrogate for constitutional supervision of conflicts decisions. But it would be a mistake to read the statement more broadly, to suggest that the two function in entirely separate spheres. The incidental effect of due process restrictions on territorial jurisdiction can be significant in checking choice-of-law abuses. The particular reach of these restrictions—contained in the Court's minimum contacts test—should be considered in order to determine whether constitutional doctrine directly addressing choice of law is even necessary.

The line between bad conflicts decisions which arguably violate the Constitution and bad decisions which are merely regrettable is not easy to draw. Without placing too much emphasis on the matter at this stage of the discussion, it is enough to say that the most suitable conflicts decisions for constitutional review usually have been cases in which the forum applied its own substantive law without justification and to the detriment of a nonresident defendant. Before courts can perform such mischief, they must be able to exercise a quality of territorial jurisdiction over the same nonresident defendant capable of satisfying due process. It follows, then, that the more stringent the due process standards for territorial jurisdiction are, the fewer opportunities will occur for conflicts decision-making so bad as to warrant constitutional intervention.

Two territorial jurisdiction cases have had the clear if incidental effect of reducing the number of constitutionally troublesome conflicts cases. *Shaffer v. Heitner*[41] and *Rush v. Savchuck*[42] eliminated the possibility of territorial jurisdiction over nonresident defendants in cases which would not satisfy the minimum contacts test. In so doing, they obviated the need for Supreme

---

*   Reprinted with permission.

** [Phillips Petroleum Co. v. Shutts, 472 U.S. 797 (1985).]

[36]   *Id.* at 821. Similar statements can be found in Allstate Insurance Co. v. Hague, 449 U.S. 302, 317 (1981); World-Wide Volkswagen Corp. v. Woodson, 444 U.S. 286, 294 (1980); Kulko v. Superior Court, 436 U.S. 84, 98 (1978); Shaffer v. Heitner, 433 U.S. 186, 215 (1978); Hanson v. Denckla, 357 U.S. 235, 254 (1958). * * *

[41]   433 U.S. 186 (1977).

[42]   444 U.S. 320 (1980).

Court intervention which occurred in *Home Insurance Co. v. Dick*,[44] long regarded as one of the Court's most significant choice-of-law cases. The Court held there that Texas had no connection with the case capable of supporting its court's application of forum law. Minimum contacts were so lacking in *Dick* that today it would not last long enough on the docket for the choice-of-law issue to materialize.

On the other hand, new opportunities for courts to render constitutinally troublesome conflicts decisions probably appeared when *International Shoe Co. v. Washington* created the possibility of personal jurisdiction over nonresident defendants when service of process could not be completed within the forum state. The period following *International Shoe* was marked by a proliferation of long-term statutes and a generally permissive trend in due process regulation of personal jurisdiction. Choice-of-law-motivated forum shopping grew in proportion to the increase in the number of courts jurisdictionally competent to hear the same case.

The Supreme Court has since curtailed some of the more freewheeling assertions of personal jurisdiction which emerged from this period. But several of the Court's recent decisions make clear that its minimum contacts test continues to permit a choice of forums in many cases with multistate contacts. The forum may have sufficient minimum contacts to entertain jurisdiction in some cases yet lack a constitutional basis for applying its own law. For example, personal jurisdiction over nonresident defendant Allstate was unquestioned in *Hague*, even though the controversy arose out of state. And there seems little doubt that Allstate's substantial—albeit unrelated—business activity in Minnesota would satisfy the minimum contacts standard recently applied in *Helicopteros Nacionales de Columbia v. Hall*.[51] Yet several distinguished commentators have questioned the constitutionality of Minnesota's choice of its own law. This suggests something about the ultimate limitations of minimum contacts as a check on choice-of-law abuses. There is a clear difference between prejudice from forcing the defendant to defend where she does not wish to defend and the greater prejudice of binding the defendant with the forum's substantive law. The minimum contacts test is only concerned with the former. Legitimate authority to force a defendant to defend in the forum does not and should not invariably connote authority for the forum to apply its own law.

The conclusion that a court may exercise territorial jurisdiction validly is likely to say even less about the court's competence to apply its own law in cases which are not subject to minimum contacts scrutiny. The Court has invoked the minimum contacts test only to protect nonresident defendants, and then only if they have neither expressly consented to jurisdiction nor cured the jurisdictional problem by their conduct in the case.

The most significant category of express consent cases involves situations in which a foreign corporation files a consent to jurisdiction with state authorities as a condition for doing business there. Depending on the wording of the consent statute, consent jurisdiction may be broad enough to cover causes of action arising outside the forum. Personal jurisdiction in such cases suggests little about the authority of the forum to apply its own law.

In addition, personal jurisdiction throws little, if any, light on the choice-of-law process when it exists only because of the acquiescence or inadvertence of a nonresident defendant. For tactical reasons, the defendant may simply decline to question jurisdiction. Or counsel may

---

[44]   281 U.S. 397 (1930). * * *

[51]   466 U.S. 408 (1984). "Even when the cause of action does not arise out of or relate to the foreign corporation's activities in the forum State, due process is not offended by a State's subjecting the corporation to its in personam jurisdiction when there are sufficient contacts between the State and the foreign corporation." *Id.* at 414.

fumble the opportunity provided by the forum to challenge it. Or a court may deem personal jurisdiction to exist as a sanction against a defendant's refusal to comply with an order compelling discovery of jurisdictional facts. It would be unreasonable to suggest that in waiving minimum contacts protection, the defendant also waives objection to the forum's substantive law. Because these cases have not run the minimum contacts gauntlet, they are even more open to unjustified choice of forum law.

There are other restrictions on the reach of the minimum contacts test. The capacity of a forum to exercise personal jurisdiction over its own citizens is well established and functions more or less independently of minimum contacts. It is possible to imagine constitutionally troublesome conflicts results when courts exercise this kind of jurisdiction. The same is true if courts can impose their jurisdiction through local service over nonresident defendants who happen to be passing through the forum state. Finally, choice of law was deprived of the salutary effect of minimum contacts in another way by the *Shutts* case itself.

For forty years the Court had administered the minimum contacts test without deciding whether it had to be satisfied to establish jurisdiction over the claims of passive, nonresident members of a plaintiff class. By the time the *Shutts* Court addressed the issue, the future of small-claim class actions depended to a considerable extent on how it was resolved. The Court took what seems to be the fairest and most sensible view in rejecting the minimum contacts test in this context. But, in refusing to dispose of the case on territorial jurisdiction grounds, the Court again demonstrated the necessity of dealing directly with the choice-of-law process.

What emerges from this discussion is that the minimum contacts test only reduces conflicts abuses. Not all assertions of territorial jurisdiction are subject to it, and some constitutionally troublesome conflicts cases are likely to pass it. A need exists, then, for conflicts review to enforce even the relatively modest constitutional guarantees the Supreme Court has so far recognized. * * *

* * * * *

Courtland H. Peterson, *Proposals of Marriage Between Jurisdiction and Choice of Law*, 14 U.C. DAVIS L. REV. 869, 872-876 (1981)*

* * * * *

That *some* relationship already exists between judicial jurisdiction and choice of law is difficult to deny. Consider the apparent anomaly arising from the situation where a state has sufficient connection with a case to justify application of its own law to a resolution of the dispute, but insufficient connection to exercise judicial jurisdiction under the rules developed from *International Shoe* [*Co. v. Washington*]. Arguments derived from that anomaly have been advanced in most of the conflicts-jurisdiction cases decided by the Supreme Court over the past twenty-five years, usually from the plaintiff's side of the case. The shorthand version of the argument is as follows: It would be appropriate on the facts of this case for the state in which

---

I brought my lawsuit to apply its own law to resolve the dispute, and this conclusion strongly supports the exercise of judicial jurisdiction by this forum over this defendant.

There is, of course, a converse paradox with its own set of arguments, which are fairly exemplified by the recent case of *Rush v. Savchuk*.[18] There the defendant argued that it would be highly inappropriate for the forum to apply its law to the case before it, but that there was some indication that it would do so therefore, the argument continued, the forum selected by plaintiff ought not to be permitted to exercise judicial jurisdiction. In the lower courts in *All-state Insurance Co. v. Hague*,[20] an unsuccessful attempt was apparently made to extend this argument to the doctrine of *forum non conveniens*. Defendant Allstate conceded that judicial jurisdiction could be asserted in Minnesota because the company was doing business there, but urged that the exercise of such jurisdiction should be declined because forum law should not be applied and because the law of Wisconsin should govern the case.

Counsel have thus persistently pressed these arguments based on a perceived relationship between jurisdictional and choice concepts. Thus far, however, the responses of the majority opinions of the Supreme Court have consistently turned the arguments aside, in dicta asserting that choice of law and jurisdiction present different issues. To the plaintiff's argument—in *Hanson v. Denckla*,[22] *Shaffer v. Heitner*[23] and *Kulko v. Superior Court*[24]—the Court has replied that the interest of the forum in the litigation may justify the application of forum law, but it does not necessarily follow that the forum can constitutionally require defendant to answer in its courts. To the defendant in *Savchuk* the Court said simply: "The constitutionality of a choice of law rule that would apply forum law in these circumstances is not before us."[25]

In every case, the Court found a violation of due process in the forum's attempt to exercise judicial jurisdiction. In those cases where the Court suggested that the law of the state might be applied, even though the state could not exercise judicial jurisdiction, the inference seems to be that a forum that could exercise such jurisdiction could permissibly also apply the law of the state lacking jurisdiction. To the extent that this may be understood as an assertion that the jurisdictional decision did not control choice of law, the assertion is clearly out of touch with reality—even in some of the cases in which the suggestions were offered.

Perhaps the clearest example is *Hanson*. The Florida court applied Florida law, invalidating the exercise of a reserved power of appointment. The Delaware court refused to recognize the Florida judgment and proceeded to apply its own law, validating the appointment. Was the Delaware court required to give full faith and credit to the Florida judgment? No, said the Court, because Florida lacked personal jurisdiction over the Delaware trustee. To suggest that Delaware could apply Florida law under these circumstances is essentially meaningless, and it is clear that the jurisdictional decision controlled the law to be applied.

Similarly, in *Kulko*, the suggestion that the obligor father's state (New York) could apply the law of the state of the dependents' residence (California), which had unsuccessfully sought to assert judicial jurisdiction in the case, is simply unrealistic. Moreover, if plaintiff had proceeded under the Uniform Reciprocal Enforcement of Support Act of 1968, as the Court sug-

---

18   444 U.S. 320 (1980).

20   449 U.S. 302 (1981).

22   357 U.S. 235, 253 (1958).

23   433 U.S. 186, 215 (1977).

24   436 U.S. 84, 98 (1978).

25   Rush v. Savchuk, 444 U.S. 320, 325 n.8 (1980).

gests, she would have found a statutory choice-of-law rule in Section 7 of the Act directing the application of New York law. In *Kulko* no less than in *Hanson,* the jurisdictional decision effectively controlled the law to be applied.

Another case demonstrating the primacy of jurisdictional over choice-of-law analysis is *Home Insurance Co. v. Dick,*[32] at least if this older decision is viewed retrospectively. There the plaintiff sued two New York insurance companies in Texas, on a garnishment theory of jurisdiction. The legislative jurisdiction question presented was whether or not Texas could apply its own law to the insurance contract since under Texas law the contractual limitations period for bringing suit would have been invalid. The Court decided that the application of Texas law was a violation of due process because Texas lacked a sufficient relation to the controversy. Although the case has generally been regarded as a landmark in the use of the due process clause as a restraint on choice of law it is clear that if the same case were now presented for decision the Court would never reach the choice-of-law issue. Instead, probably since *Shaffer* and most certainly since *Savchuk,* the Court would simply have denied that Texas had constitutional authority to exercise judicial jurisdiction in this way. As a result, the jurisdictional decision controls choice of law without examination of the choice issue.

An alternative explanation for the Court's penchant for calling attention to the possible use of a state's law, even where the state in question cannot exercise judicial jurisdiction, is that this language is intended simply to emphasize the separateness of the jurisdictional and choice concepts. If that is an appropriate interpretation, however, it raises a further question: Why is the emphasis on separateness necessary? No one asserts that judicial jurisdiction and choice of law (or legislative jurisdiction) are identical, only that they are related and that the decision of one issue may have some sensible bearing on the decision of the other. Perhaps the insistence on a clear dichotomy is a remnant of the Court's attempt in the New Deal era to redefine its own role with regard to distinctions between procedural and substantive due process. So viewed, jurisdictional decisions would seem somehow more permissible because they seem procedural, while due process restraints on choice of law might be suspect because of their substantive flavor. But if, as now seems clear, the jurisdictional decision will normally control choice of law without examination of the merits of the choice, maintenance of the dichotomy for these purposes seems irrational.

Whatever the proper understanding of the historical development may be, an overview of the more recent cases suggests that greater clarity may be forthcoming. Dissents in several cases, beginning with that of Justice Black in *Hanson,* argued that jurisdiction and choice of law, although separate inquiries, "are often closely related and to a substantial degree depend upon similar considerations."[35] In *Shaffer* Justice Brennan pointed out that "the decision that it is fair to bind a defendant by a State's laws and rules should prove to be highly relevant to the fairness of permitting that same State to accept jurisdiction for adjudicating the controversy."[36] The suggestion that forum bias in the choice process may also be relevant to the exercise of jurisdiction appears in Justice Brennan's dissent in *World-Wide Volkswagen Corp. v. Woodson* and *Rush v. Savchuk:* "One consideration that might create some unfairness [in permitting judicial jurisdiction to be exercised] would be if the choice of forum also imposed on the defendant an unfavorable substantive law which the defendant could justly have assumed would not apply."[37]

---

[32]   281 U.S. 397 (1930).

[35]   Hanson v. Denckla, 357 U.S. 235, 258 (1958) (Black, J., dissenting).

[36]   Shaffer v. Heitner, 433 U.S. 186, 225 (1977) (Brennan, J., concurring in part and dissenting in part).

[37]   444 U.S. 286, 311 n.19 (Brennan, J., dissenting).

These suggestions foreshadowed the position taken by the Court in its most recent decision in this area, *Allstate Insurance Co. v. Hague*.[38] * * *

* * *

The interesting outcome of this rather complicated state of affairs is that a majority of the members of the Court have identified themselves with the view that judicial jurisdiction and choice of law *are* related, at least in the overlapping character of the factors to be considered, and probably beyond that in the sense that there is a recognition of interplay between the concepts. The fact that this proposition must be extrapolated from several opinions obscures but does not alter the conclusion. The relationship thus recognized is rather ill-defined, and it is certainly no "marriage" at this point. Pursuing the metaphor, perhaps it would be fair to describe the relationship as falling somewhere between an illicit love affair, where the parties meet in secret, and one of the modern forms of cohabitation, in which the parties openly share their lives but make no commitments as to the future.

* * * * *

Peter Hay, *Judicial Jurisdiction and Choice of Law: Constitutional Limitations*, 59 U. COLO. L. REV. 9, 34-35 (1988)*

* * * * *

I have resisted coupling the inquiries which seek to define the constitutional limits of a court's adjudicatory jurisdiction and its freedom to apply the forum's substantive law. I would not even engage in a parallel inquiry, but would proceed *seriatim*. The reason is that different interests are involved.

The jurisdictional inquiry addresses the permissibility of requiring the defendant to litigate in the forum. The focus is on the defendant's "individual liberty interest." The source of the constitutional limitation is the Due Process Clause. The content of the limitation is "fairness:" not individualized determinations of relative convenience or inconvenience, but a standard for which there are objective guide posts.

Choice of law also involves the defendant's liberty interest: whether to be free from, or subject to liability. But it also involves competing state interests in determining the applicable law, the forum law or another. This is a federalism concern of a kind that jurisdiction is not. It derives not so much from the Due Process Clause as it does from the Full Faith and Credit Clause, as I have previously argued. In *Hague*, the plurality recognized that both provisions were the source of limitations upon choice of law.[133] In *Phillips Petroleum*, the majority took note of the *Hague* dissenter's view "that the Due Process Clause prohibit[s] the application of law which was only casually or slightly related to the litigation, while the Full Faith and Credit Clause require[s] the forum to respect the laws and judgments of other States, subject to the forum's own interest in furthering its public policy."[134]

---

[38]   449 U.S. 302 (1981).

*   Reprinted with permission of the University of Colorado Law Review.

[133]   Allstate Ins. Co. v. Hague, 449 U.S. 302, 312-13 (1981).

[134]   Phillips Petroleum Co. v. Shutts, 472 U.S. 797, 819 (1985).* * *

Coupling the inquiries blurs the analysis. It makes it possible to fudge, to support jurisdiction on the basis of the applicability of forum law, to derive the applicability of forum law from jurisdiction (without asking how it was obtained), and to apply a single and individualized standard of fairness. While I agree that the same fact pattern may support both judicial jurisdiction and the application of the substantive law of the forum, it nevertheless remains true that the *minimum* contacts of the jurisdictional case law do not, magically, constitute the required *significant* contact(s) for choice of forum law in all cases. Finally, for me and for others, it follows from the risks at stake that there ought to be such a qualitative difference in standards.

To label such an approach as "territorialist," or—Heaven forbid—as "anti-modernist," is not very helpful. The central problem still remains. It is the quest for the definition, in objective ways, of the constitutionally appropriate relationship among the defendant, the forum, and the litigation. When the relational test for adjudicatory jurisdiction has been satisfied, the forum then fashions an appropriate and permissible choice rule. Appropriateness is left to the forum, as it was upon remand in *Phillips Petroleum*; the permissible limits are set by the court. The flexibility thus left to the forum to fashion a choice rule *from among* several permissible options preserves the state-law nature of conflicts law. It permits further growth and development of choice rules, but not unfettered forum preference.

James A. Martin, *Personal Jurisdiction and Choice of Law*, 78 MICH. L. REV. 872, 872-873 (1980)*

The time has come for the Supreme Court to declare that a state may not apply its own law to a case unless it has the "minimum contacts" required by *International Shoe*[1] for the exercise of specific[2] personal jurisdiction over the defendant. Although the present state of the law is less than certain, the Supreme Court has not yet required that a state show it has minimum contacts with a defendant before applying its law. As a result, in some cases where a state has obtained personal jurisdiction because of a defendant's contacts unrelated to the case—contacts such as transaction of substantial but unrelated business within the state, or incorporation or domicile within the state—the state may apply its own law even when in conflict with the law of a state that has much greater contact with both the defendant and the events giving rise to the case. The situation fairly cries out for a standard for the application of forum law on a basis that does not depend upon the vagaries of the defendant's unrelated activities. With recent attention refocusing upon constitutional limitations on jurisdiction and choice of law, the time is ripe for examination of a "minimum contacts" limitation on choice of law. The potential rewards include greater fairness to litigants, healthier federalism, and improvements in judicial administration.

---

*   Reprinted with permission of The Michigan Law Review Association.

[1]   International Shoe Co. v. Washington, 326 U.S. 310 (1945). "Minimum contacts" is used here to indicate contacts related to the substance of the case. Thus a state's substantial but unrelated contacts would not justify application of its law under this proposal.

[2]   The term "specific" jurisdiction is used in the sense of von Mehren & Trautman, *Jurisdiction to Adjudicate: A Suggested Analysis*, 79 HARV. L. REV. 1121, 1145 (1966), to indicate jurisdiction of the type involved in *International Shoe*—based upon minimum contacts related to the plaintiff's claim and supporting only litigation related to those contacts.

The basic standard for in personam jurisdiction, despite recent elaboration, is still found in *International Shoe Co. v. Washington*: a state may not exercise in personam jurisdiction unless to do so would be consistent with "fair play and substantial justice" and unless there are either "minimum contacts" between the defendant and the forum state out of which the plaintiff's claim arises (specific personal jurisdiction), or there are substantial contacts, not necessarily related to the case, between the defendant and the state. There is no clear corresponding formula for constitutional limitations on the state's right to apply its own law to a case, but some kind of "contact" is a precondition of the state's right to apply its own law, and the Supreme Court has indicated that some contacts that may suffice for choice-of-law purposes do not suffice for jurisdiction purposes. Professor Willis Reese has recently suggested that the "same basic principles" underlie jurisdiction and choice-of-law issues, but he stops short of suggesting a minimum contacts test for constitutional limitations on choice of law.[8]

I suggest that the Supreme Court take that further step. When a state obtains jurisdiction over the defendant through substantial contacts unrelated to the case, courts should ask whether jurisdiction could have been upheld absent those substantial unrelated contacts. In other words, are there "minimum contacts" between the state and the defendant? If there are not, the forum state should not be allowed to apply its own law to the case.

* * * * *

Friedrich K. Juenger, *Supreme Court Intervention in Jurisdiction and Choice of Law: A Dismal Prospect*, 14 U.C. DAVIS L. REV. 907, 907-917 (1981)*

It is understandable that some conflicts scholars are disappointed with *Allstate Insurance Co. v. Hague*.[1] That case signals the Supreme Court's continued permissive attitude toward the "conflicts revolution" with all its excesses. The proclamation of some guidelines would have pleased those who are not "True Believers" or have become bored with "transcendental mediation over guest statutes." Moreover, the constitutionalization of choice of law might upgrade a discipline that seems mired in the attempt to derive solutions to multistate problems from analyzing what a judge once called "minor morals of expediency and debatable questions of internal policy."[4] But I, for one, question the Supreme Court's ability to improve American conflicts law.

First, let us recall that when the Court actively controlled the conflicts field by means of "first principles of legal thinking," it performed poorly. Of course, the Justices might do better next time. I doubt it. Choice of law has vexed the finest legal minds since the Middle Ages. Cardozo called it "one of the most baffling subjects of legal science"[7] and Prosser called it worse. No one maintains that jurisdiction is equally troublesome. Most law schools purport to teach that subject to first year law students, presumably because the issues are fewer and eas-

---

8   *See* [Willard] Reese, *Legislative Jurisdiction*, 78 COLUM. L. REV. 1587, 1592 (1978).

*   Copyright © 1981 by The Regents of the University of California. Reprinted with permission.

1   449 U.S. 302 (1981).

4   Mertz v. Mertz, 271 N.Y. 466, 475, 3 N.E.2d 597, 600 (1936) (Crouch, J., dissenting).

7   B. CARDOZO, THE PARADOXES OF LEGAL SCIENCES 67 (1928).

ier than those posed by choice of law. But the Supreme Court has not even done well with jurisdiction. Let us assess their work in that cognate field before we cheer on the Justices to intervene in choice of law.

Recall *Pennoyer v. Neff*,[9] where the Court shunned common sense and relied on so-called "principles of public law"[10] to slip the turf theory into the Constitution. A quarter of a century after England had followed the example of other European nations and enacted long-arm legislation, our Supreme Court reached for the ancient ingredients of sovereignty and territoriality to concoct a doctrine that could not possibly work satisfactorily in a federal system. The turf theory resembled Procrustean twin beds. It was too narrow and therefore could not cope well with such obvious practical problems as jurisdiction over foreign corporations and non-resident motorists. But it was also too broad in that it sanctioned two exorbitant practices: "tag jurisdiction" and the quasi-in-rem holdup. For almost seventy years, the Court's first misguided attempt to assess all jurisdictional assertions by a single standard forced American judges to grasp for fictions to reach decent results in interstate cases. Even now the old case still haunts us, as illustrated by the propensity of counsel and judges to say "process" when they mean jurisdiction. In fact, our current jurisdictional lore can perhaps only be understood as a reaction to the *Pennoyer* madness.

International Shoe Co. v. Washington[14] tried to set things straight. For the earlier "principles of public law" it substituted a new dogma that was but a vague policy statement with a "minimum contacts" mantra. Still, the Justices' reaction to the thirteen salesmen who roamed through Washington with one shoe apiece proved useful: it stimulated courts and legislatures to broaden unduly narrow jurisdictional bases. *McGee v. International Life Insurance Co.*[15] seemed to signal even greater freedom. But in *Hanson v. Denckla*[16] the Court reemphasized territoriality and sovereignty, the very notions that had long stunted the growth of American jurisdictional law. Beginning with *Shaffer v. Heitner*,[17] the Supreme Court became even more interventionist. With what results? After more than a century of experimentation we are still looking at dominant grays and innumerable shades. Such a chiaroscuro approach would be tolerable if it did justice. But does it?

Look at *Shaffer*. Where, in a rational legal system, should a shareholder sue the management of a Delaware corporation? The Delaware courts can best apply the law that determines the duties allegedly breached. Unless the officers and directors can be sued in one place, how can we avoid conflicting decisions? Should it really be impossible for the state of incorporation to assert jurisdiction over managerial misfeasance? Following a suggestion in Justice Marshall's opinion, Delaware passed a statute subjecting the management of Delaware corporations to local jurisdiction. Is this enactment constitutional, as the Delaware Supreme Court has held? Must California copy that statutory monstrosity, a throwback to the era of "implied consent," to collar the management of California corporations? Or are yet more potent incantations needed? Of course, the state could require officers and directors to sign a form consenting to jurisdiction as a condition of employment. Then, I suppose, even the Constitution could not break the spell cast by ink and paper.

---

[9]   95 U.S. 714 (1878).

[10]   *Id*. at 722.

[14]   326 U.S. 310 (1945).

[15]   355 U.S. 220 (1957).

[16]   357 U.S. 235 (1958).

[17]   433 U.S. 186 (1977).

Now look at *Kulko v. Superior Court.*[25] What is wrong with giving support claimants a jurisdictional preference? They have one in Europe, thanks to the Brussels Convention. Would such a preference undermine Our Federalism? Apparently in this country only the interests of illegitimate offspring are sufficiently worthy of protection to permit suits in their home state, provided that they were sired there. By giving the phrases "minimum contacts" and "fair play" a meaning the Supreme Court may never have intended, state courts have been able to help these children. Darwin and Ilsa Kulko, however, were told to try their luck with the Uniform Reciprocal Enforcement of Support Act. URESA attempts to cope with our territorialist bias against support claimants by the rubber-bands-and-matchsticks method of authorizing two concurrent actions in the claimant's and the obligor's forum. If the Supreme Court read Ann Landers as avidly as the election returns, it might have noted a recent item entitled "Fleet-foot flees." There a support claimant signed "Discouraged in Virginia Beach" said that URESA had destroyed her faith in the judicial system. As she advised others, "don't make your grocery list until you get the check!"

And what about *Rush v. Savchuk?*[30] Why should an interstate accident victim be unable to take to the local court an insurance company whose headquarters are but a few blocks away? It would be more than poetic justice to hold insurers such as Nationwide and Allstate to their suggestive names. After all, their business is to sell policies wherever they can and to litigate wherever they must. Why should such entities hide behind John Doe, the nominal defendant? And what should be the fate of all the *Seider* actions pending in the State of New York? If New York's assertion of jurisdiction was unconstitutional, the running of foreign statutes of limitation would inevitably bar numerous meritorious claims. How can it be squared with common sense and social justice to penalize tort victims for their counsels' strategy? And what about counsel? Are *Seider* attorneys liable for malpractice even though they were misled by the Supreme Court?

Finally, there is *World-Wide Volkswagen Corp. v. Woodson.*[33] Only Justice Blackmun wondered "why the plaintiffs . . . are so insistent that the regional distributor and the retail dealer . . . be named defendants." If his brethren had asked themselves this simple question they might not have granted the petition for certiorari. The real reason for importuning the Court was intrastate forum shopping: by joining the regional distributor and the retailer as defendants, plaintiffs' counsel sought to destroy diversity. Defendants, however, preferred to litigate in the federal district court in Tulsa, rather than face a jury from Creek County, Oklahoma, a blue-collar neighborhood renowned for lavish awards. The Court's failure to grasp that venue-shopping, rather than sovereignty and comity, was at issue may explain its decision. That decision, in countless products cases, will thwart the policy which calls for liability of every link in the distributive chain. And, like *Shaffer, Volkswagen* is bound to impede the rational disposition of multiple-defendant cases.

We would be better off if the Court had just denied the petitions for review in all of these cases. Only Mr. Kulko was truly aggrieved, though the requested increase in child support was dwarfed by the cost of taking the matter to the Supreme Court. If the Justices sought an opportunity to refine their jurisdictional thinking, they should have chosen more appealing cases. But the merits of a case may no longer concern the Court. *Volkswagen* tells us that the plaintiff's interest, the effective resolution of interstate controversies, and fundamental sub-

---

25   436 U.S. 84 (1978).

30   444 U.S. 320 (1980).

33   444 U.S. 286 (1980).

stantive policies shared by all states, are but secondary considerations. Nothing matters unless the defendant has "contacts, ties, or relations" with the forum state. Thus

> [e]ven if the defendant would suffer minimal or no inconvenience from being forced to litigate before the tribunals of another State; even if the forum State has a strong interest in applying its law to the controversy; even if the forum State is the most convenient location for litigation, the Due Process Clause, acting as an instrument of interstate federalism, may . . . act to divest the State of its power to render a valid judgment.[37]

In other words, we are asked to believe that something in the Constitution blocks rational interstate procedure. But the due process clause does not refer to "contacts, ties, or relations"; the Court added this gloss. As in *Pennoyer*, the Justices are again prepared to sacrifice sane multistate procedural rules for doctrinal purity.

But what dogma could be so powerful as to outweigh fairness and common sense? Behind the catchphrase "contacts, ties, or relations" there lurks a thought which Justice Douglas, in *Milliken v. Meyer*, expressed as follows:

> The state which accords . . . [a citizen] privileges and affords protection to him and his property by virtue of his domicile may also exact reciprocal duties.[39]

While *Milliken* used the tit-for-tat theory to support a state court's jurisdiction over an absent domiciliary, *Hanson v. Denckla* employed it to defeat a jurisdictional assertion over nonresidents. Chief Justice Warren, who wrote the majority opinion in *Hanson*, reformulated the pertinent test to require

> some act by which the defendant purposefully avails itself of the privilege of conducting activities within the forum State, thus invoking the benefits and protection of its laws.[41]

The "purposeful availment" formula, today's conventional wisdom, is of course but a reincarnation of the old implied consent fiction. Yet the underlying notion of reciprocity, or retaliation, is even older. It inheres in the phrases "tacit submission" and "temporary allegiance" that have afflicted the conflicts vocabulary for centuries. These verbalizations are but variants of the thought that jurisdiction is the price for imposing upon a sovereign. This simplistic quid-pro-quo idea has now become the touchstone of American jurisdictional law. Of the entire bench only Justice Brennan questions it.

Pennoyer should have taught the Supreme Court to beware of self-evident truths. Yet, once again the Justices, mesmerized by conceptual symmetry, embrace a "single standard"[46] premised on sovereignty. To be sure, rationalizations such as the tit-for-tat theory can serve a valid purpose. Like fictions, they can help adapt the law to changed realities. This, of course, was the function the stock phrase "minimum contacts" served in *International Shoe*. But the

---

[37]   World Wide Volkswagen Corp. v. Woodson, 444 U.S. 286, 294 (1980).

[39]   [311 U.S. 457 463 (1940)].

[41]   [347 U.S. 235, 253 (1958)].

[46]   Shaffer v. Heitner, 433 U.S. 186, 209 (1977).

Court should not allow such constructs to frustrate what Holmes called "felt necessities and intuitions of public policy."[47] As the recent cases show, "purposeful availment" causes problems. It may not work, for instance, in multiparty cases such as *Shaffer, World-Wide Volkswagen* and *Mullane v. Central Hanover Bank & Trust Co.*[48] It will cause hardship for accident victims and support claimants, as *Savchuk* and *Kulko* demonstrate. It will also leave the law of jurisdiction quite confused.

The spate of recent Supreme Court decisions has not infused the law of jurisdiction with greater certainty and predictability. Commenting on *Shaffer*, a distinguished scholar has noted that the case's "implications and ramifications remain quite nebulous and are bound to necessitate further clarification."[49] As shown by the many jurisdictional cases that continue to grace the advance sheets, *Kulko, Savchuck* and *World-Wide Volkswagen* have hardly dispelled the "doubts and perplexity in the lower courts"[50] that *Shaffer* introduced. On the highest echelon, if the Justices continue playing the role of a court of error and appeals, they will have to parse "every variant in the myriad of motor vehicle fact situations that present themselves."[52] All in all, the Court's intervention has made our jurisdictional law more cluttered than ever.

And this, finally, brings me back to choice of law. Clearly, *Allstate* could have wrought havoc with that field. As in the jurisdictional cases, a common sense determination by a state supreme court was attacked on grounds that had but little to do with the parties' squabble. At issue was the grievance of an insurance company which had sold a poorly drafted policy that covered three cars. Although the insurer had collected a separate premium for each automobile, it took the position that it had to pay off on only one uninsured motorist coverage. To save thirty thousand dollars, the insurer converted the dispute into a vicarious fight between sovereigns who quarrel about state interests and federalism. The authors of the plurality and the dissenting opinons readily accepted this transmogrification. By anthropomorphizing the states of Minnesota and Wisconsin, and making them the real parties in interest, the Justices were able to train the heavy guns of due process and full faith and credit on a rather piddling controversy between private parties. They thus failed to heed the statement of one of the Court's most distinguished members who had said, many years ago, that conflicts law "is chiefly seen and felt in its application to the common business of private persons, and rarely rises to the dignity of national negotiations, or of national controversies."[54]

However, the petitioner's ploy, one that had worked so well in the jurisdictional cases, fell flat: a majority decided to leave well enough alone. The plurality opinion written by Justice Brennan adopted a much broader, less defendant-oriented test than purposeful availment to determine the constitutional propriety of applying forum law. Although there must be contacts, what counts is not solely the relationship of the defendant with the forum. Rather, in Justice Brennan's words, the application of forum law is improper only if the forum has "no significant contact or significant aggregation of contacts, creating state interests, with the parties and

---

[47]   O. Holmes, The Common Law 5 (1881).

[48]   339 U.S. 306 (1950).

[49]   Riesenfeld, Shaffer v. Heitner, *Holding, Implications, Forebodings*, 30 Hastings Law Rev. 1183, 1203 (1979).

[50]   *Id.* at 1183.

[52]   World-Wide Volkswagen Corp. v. Woodson, 444 U.S. 286, 319 (1980) (Blackmun, J., dissenting).

[54]   J. Story, [Commentaries on the Conflict of Laws 9 (7th ed. 1872).

the occurrence or transaction."[55] Even the dissenters agreed that the forum may apply its own law unless there are "no significant contacts between the State and *the litigation*."[56]

This broad language leaves lower courts ample leeway in multistate cases. Moreover, *Allstate* allows state courts to premise their choice-of-law decisions on any rationale, including the preference for the forum rule as the one best suited to do justice. Unlike jurisdictional assertions, the power of state courts to apply forum law does not depend on their proffering some "particularized interest."[58] Rather, the Court will supply its own constitutional analysis after the fact. This frees inferior judges from the need to simulate the Supreme Court's mock arbitration of sovereign grievances; they need not count contacts or divine interests. Nor do state judges need to short-circuit the problem by invoking public policy, by specious characterizations or by presuming (or guessing) that a foreign rule is identical to forum law. In other words, after *Allstate* neither modern gimmickry nor old-fashioned escape devices are needed to make choice-of-law determinations certiorari-proof.

This is not to say that all is well. Although most of the Justices agreed on principle, they differed on price. In counting the contacts of this borderline case Justice Brennan came up with three, Justice Stevens with one, and Justice Powell with none that mattered. Inevitably, the Justices' disagreement on its application cast doubt on the test they purported to establish. Nor are any of their opinions particularly persuasive. Justice Brennan's enumeration of sundry connections of the parties and the deceased bi-state employee with Minnesota amounts to a strained and implausible lumping technique. Justice Powell's dissenting opinion, on the other hand, draws a distinction between trivial or irrelevant and policy-related contacts that may be more helpful to conflicts professors than to trial judges. Only Justice Stevens realized that the Constitution was not in danger, because application of the Minnesota stacking rule could hardly threaten the "federal interest in national unity by unjustifiably infringing upon the legitimate interests of another state."[62] His concurring opinion is, however, marred by a confusing reference to "normal conflicts law" and the gratuitous slap on the wrist of the Minnesota Supreme Court, whose decision he calls "plainly unsound."[64]

Yet, these deficiencies are minor if one considers what the Court might have done with *Allstate*. The opinions in the case merely confirm what should be obvious from watching the Justices' labors in the jurisdictional vineyard, namely that there is little reason to trust their ability to cultivate the conflicts jungle. If *Shaffer* and its progeny are any indication, Supreme Court intervention in choice of law would hardly improve interstate justice. The Court's devotion to dogma could only further frustrate interstate support claimants, accident victims and policyholders. Any attempt to correct some imaginary evil by setting aside the Minnesota court's supremely sensible decision in *Allstate* would have been the first step down the wrong road.

---

[55] Allstate Ins. Co. v. Hague, 449 U.S. 302, 308 (1981).

[56] *Id.* at 332 (Powell, J., dissenting) (emphasis added).

[58] *See* Kulko v. Superior Court, 436 U.S. 84, 98 (1978); Shaffer v. Heitner, 433 U.S. 186, 214 (1977).

[62] [*Hague*, 449 U.S. 302,] 323 (concurring opinion).

[64] *Id.* [at 324].

Comments

1. Conflicts and civil procedure professors alike lay claim to the subject of personal jurisdiction. General surveys of the subject include Casad 1991;[1] Richman & Reynolds 1993: pp. 13-133; Scoles & Hay 1992: pp. 215-359; Shreve & Raven-Hansen 1994: pp. 23-88.

2. It is not easy to entirely separate constitutional standards for regulating personal jurisdiction from those applicable to choice of law. The excerpt of the author suggested that, while much of the effect on conflicts law of the Supreme Court's personal jurisdiction rulings may be incidental rather than intended, those rulings have nonetheless eliminated much of the need for constitutional intervention in choice of law.

3. Several of the excerpts in this Part suggested that the Court is at a fork in the road. One direction is represented by Professor Peterson and the late Professor Martin, who maintained in different ways that the Supreme Court should explicitly merge personal jurisdiction and conflicts-reviewing doctrine into a single, consolidated body of constitutional law. The other direction is represented by Professor Hay, who urged the Court to take greater pains to delineate and preserve different roles for the Constitution in regulating personal jurisdiction and choice of law.

4. Others have commented on the anomaly noted in the excerpt by Professor Peterson that the Constitution often seems to pose more restrictions on the exercise of personal jurisdiction than upon choice of law. Professor Linda Silberman wrote: "To believe that a defendant's contacts with the forum state should be stronger under the due process clause for jurisdictional purposes than for choice of law is to believe that an accused is more concerned with where he will be hanged than whether." Silberman 1978: p. 88. Agreeing, Professor John Kozyris observed that "how to decide a case is more important than where to decide it." Kozyris 1981: p. 892. Professor Earl Maltz took an opposing view. He wrote that

> the dissonance between the Court's respective approaches to the two problems is more apparent than real. Accordingly, the decision to impose substantial constraints on the reach of personal jurisdiction while leaving choice of law virtually unconstrained is not only plausible, but entirely within the mainstream approach of constitutional analysis.

Maltz 1988: p. 768.

---

[1]   Full citations appear in the bibliography, Chapter Twelve.

CHAPTER ELEVEN

A Glimpse at the Literature on Additional Conflicts Topics

Many more conflicts topics have been the subject of illuminating commentary, enough to fill a second volume of this anthology. This Chapter notes some of the writing available on these topics.

A. CONFLICTS WRITING IN SUBSTANTIVE AREAS

1. Torts

De Boer, Theodore M. (1987) BEYOND LEX LOCI DELICTI: CONFLICTS, METHODOLOGY AND MULTISTATE TORTS IN AMERICAN CASE LAW, Boston: Kluwer. Goodrich, Herbert F. (1924) *Tort Obligations and the Conflict of Laws*, 73 U. PA. L. REV. 19. Juenger, Friedrich K. (1989) *Mass Disasters and the Conflict of Laws*, 1989 U. ILL. L. REV. 105. Juenger, Friedrich (1989) *Choice of Law in Interstate Torts*, 118 U. PA L. REV. 202. Leflar, Robert A. (1972) *The Torts Provisions of the* Restatement (Second), 72 COLUM. L. REV. 267. Lorenzen, Ernest G. (1931) *Tort Liability and the Conflict of Laws*, 47 L.Q. REV. 483. Lowenfeld, Andreas F. (1989) *Mass Torts and the Conflict of Laws: The Airline Disaster*, 1989 U. ILL. L. REV. 157. Dougal, Luther L., III, (1979) *Comprehensive Interest Analysis Versus Reformulated Governmental Interest Analysis: An Appraisal in the Context of Choice-of-Law Problems Concerning Contributory and Comparative Negligence*, 26 UCLA. L. REV. 439. Morris, J. H. C. (1951) *The Proper Law of a Tort*, 64 HARV. L. REV. 881. Morse, C. G. J. (1984) *Choice of Law in Tort: A Comparative Survey*, 32 AM. J. COMP. L. 51. Mullenix, Linda S. (1992) *Federalizing Choice of Law of Mass-Tort Litigation*, 70 TEX. L. REV. 1623. Nafziger, James A. R. (1994) *Choice of Law in Air Disaster Cases: Complex Litigation Rules and the Common Law*, 54 LA. L. REV. 1001. Note (1929) *Tort Obligations: Liability for Injury in One State under Statute of Another State*, 27 MICH. L. REV. 462. Note (1969) *Post Transaction or Occurrence Events in Conflict of Laws*, 69 COLUM. L. REV. 843. O'Brien, Bernard (1990) *Choice of Law in Torts*, 12 ADEL. L. REV. 449. Reese, Willis L. M. (1982) *The Law Governing Airplane Accidents*, 39 WASH. & LEE L. REV. 1303. Sedler, Robert A. (1971) *The Territorial Imperative: Automobile Accidents and the Significance of a State Line*, 9 DUQ. L. REV. 394. Symeonides, Symeon C. (1990) *Problems and Dilemmas in Codifying Choice of Law for Torts: The Louisiana Experience in Comparative Perspective*, 38 AM. J. COMP. L. 431. Van Couter, (1995) Barkanic: *The New York Choice-of-Law Method and Recovery for Air Crashes Abroad*, 60 J. AIR L. & COM. 759. Weintraub, Russell J. (1977) *The Future of Choice of Law for Torts: What Principles Should be Preferred?*, 41 LAW & CONTEMP. PROBS. 146.

2. Contracts

Borchers, Patrick J. (1995) *The Internationalization of Contractual Conflicts Law*, 28 VAND. J. OF TRANSNAT'L L. 421. Burman, Harold S. (1995) *International Conflict of Laws, The 1992 Inter-American Convention on the Law Applicable to International Contracts, and Trends for the 1990s*, 28 VAND. J. OF TRANSNAT'L L. 367. Cook, Walter W. (1936) *Contracts and the Conflict of Laws*, 31 ILL. L. REV. 143. Falconbridge, John D. (1933) *Contract and Conveyance in the Conflict of Laws*, 81 U. PA. L. REV. 661. Friedler, Edith (1989) *Party Autonomy Revisited: A Statutory Solution to a Choice-of-Law Problem*, 37 KANS. L. REV. 471. Ingrim, Christopher L. (1995) *Choice-of-Law Clauses: Their Effect on Extraterritorial Analysis—A Scholar's Dream, A Practitioner's Nightmare*, 28 CREIGHTON L. REV. 663. James, Louis C. (1972) *The Effects of the Commerce-Clause Constitutional Limitations on Parties' Intent Choice of Law in the Conflict-of-Laws of Commercial Contracts*, 21 AM. U. L. REV. 543. Johnston, Robert (1966) *Party Autonomy in Contracts Specifying Foreign Law*, 7 WM. & MARY L. REV. 37. Juenger, Friedrich K. (1994) *The Inter-American Convention on the Law Applicable to Inter-*

national Contracts: Some Highlights and Comparisons, 42 AM. J. COMP. L. 381. Juenger, Friedrich K. (1995) *American Conflicts Scholarship and the New Law Merchant*, 28 VAND. J. OF TRANSNAT'L L. 487. Lando, Ole (1982) *New American Choice-of-Law Principles and the European Conflict of Laws of Contracts*, 30 AM. J. COMP. L. 19. Leflar, Robert A. (1981) *Conflict of Laws Under the U.C.C.*, 35 ARK. L. REV. 87. Lorenzen, Ernest G. (1921) *Validity and Effects of Contracts in the Conflict of Laws*, 30 YALE L.J. 565; 31 YALE L.J. 53. Lorenzen, Ernest G. (1923) *The Statute of Frauds and the Conflict of Laws*, 32 YALE L.J. 311. Morris, J. H. C. and Cheshire, G. C. (1940) *The Proper Law of a Contract in the Conflict of Laws*, 56 L.Q. REV. 320. Note (1982) *Effectiveness of Choice of Law Clauses in Contract Conflict of Law: Party Autonomy or Objective Determination?*, 82 COLUM. L. REV. 1659. Note (1985) *New York Choice of Law Rule for Contractual Disputes: Avoiding the Unreasonable Results*, 71 CORNELL L. REV. 227. Note (1985) *Title 14, New York Choice of Law Rule for Contractual Disputes: Avoiding the Unreasonable Results*, 71 CORNELL. L. REV. 227. Nussbaum, Arthur (1942) *Conflict Theories of Contracts; Cases Versus Restatement*, 51 YALE L.J. 893. Sedler, Robert A. (1972) *The Contracts Provisions of the* Restatement (Second)*: An Analysis and a Critique*, 72 COLUM. L. REV. 279. Talyor, E. Hunter (1978) *Uniformity of Commercial Law and State-by-State Enactment: A Confluence of Contradictions*, 30 HASTINGS L.J. 337. Trautman, Donald T. (1984) *Some Notes on the Theory of Choice of Law Clauses*, 35 MERCER L. REV. 535. United Nations (May, 1980) *Conference on Contracts for the International Sale of Goods*, XIX INT'L LEGAL MATERIALS, No. 3, p. 668. Weintraub, Russell J. (1961) *The Contracts Proposals of the Second Restatement of Laws—A Critique*, 46 IOWA L. REV. 713.

3. Insurance and Products Liability

Hay, Peter (1992) *Conflicts of Law and State Competition in the Product Liability System*, 80 GEO. L.J. 617. Kozyris, P. John (1972) *No-Fault Automobile Insurance and the Conflict of Laws—Cutting the Gordian Knot Home-Style*, 1972 DUKE L.J. 331. Kozyris, P. John (1973) *No-Fault Insurance and the Conflict of Laws—An Interim Update*, 1973 DUKE L.J. 1009. Kozyris, P. John (1990) *Values and Methods in Choice of Law for Products Liability: A Comparative Comment on Statutory Solutions*, 38 AM. J. COMP. L. 475. McConnell, Michael W. (1988) *A Choice-of-Law Approach to Products-Liability Reform*, pp. 90-101 from Walter Olson, ed., NEW DIRECTIONS IN LIABILITY LAW.

4. Property

Carnahan, Wendell (1935) *Tangible Property and the Conflict of Laws*, 2 U. CHI. L. REV. 345. Falconbridge, John D. (1942) *Immovables in the Conflict of Laws*, 20 CAN. BAR REV. 1. Goodrich, Herbert F. (1924) *Matrimonial Property and the Conflict of Laws*, 30 W. VA. L.Q. 61. Juenger, Friedrich K. (1981) *Marital Property and the Conflict of Laws: A Tale of Two Countries*, 81 COLUM. L. REV. 1061. Leflar, Robert A. (1933) *Community Property and the Conflict of Laws*, 21 CALIF. L. REV. 221. Lowenfeld, Andreas F. (1972) *"Tempora Mutantu."— Wills and Trusts in the Conflicts Restatement*, 72 COLUM. L. REV. 382. Merriman and Nafziger, James A. R. (1994) *The Private International Law of Cultural Property in the United States*, 42 AM. J. COMP. L. 221. Note (1966) *Marital Property and the Conflict of Laws: The Constitutionality of the "Quasi-Community Property" Legislation*, 54 CALIF. L. REV. 252. Note (1987) *Modernizing the Situs Rule for Real Property Conflicts*, 65 TEX. L. REV. 585. Oldham, J. Thomas (1987) *Conflict of Laws and Marital Property Rights*, 39 BAYLOR B. REV. 1255. Stumberg, George W. (1932) *Marital Property and Conflict of Laws*, 11 TEX. L. REV. 53. Weisberger (1987) *Selected Conflict of Laws Issues in Wisconsin's New Marital (Community) Property Act*, 35 AM. J. COMP. L. 295.

5. Trusts and Estates

Beale, Joseph H. (1932) *Living Trusts of Movables in the Conflict of Laws*, 45 HARV. L. REV. 969. Comment (1929) *What Governs the Validity and Administration of Trusts of Personal Property*, 39 YALE L.J. 100. Comment (1969) *Choice of Law: The Validity of Trusts and Movables-Intention and Validation*, 64 NW. L. REV. 388. Falconbridge, John D. (1931) *Renvoi and Succession to Movables*, 46 L.Q. REV. 465 (1930); 47 L.Q. REV. 271. Gaillard, Emmanuel and Trautman, Donald T. (1987) *Trusts in Non-Trust Countries: Conflict of Laws and the Hague Convention on Trusts*, 35 AM. J. COMP. L. 307. Goodrich, Herbert F. (1926) *Inheritance Problems in the Conflict of Laws*, 24 MICH. L. REV. 558. Hopkins, Bert E. (1943) *Conflict of Laws in Administration of Decedents' Intangibles*, 28 IOWA L. REV. 422. Moore, James A. (1949) *Estate Administration and the Conflict of Laws*, 35 VA. L. REV. 316. Mulford, John (1939) *Conflict of Laws and Powers of Appointment*, 87 U. PA. L. REV. 403. Scoles, Eugene F. (1955) *Conflict of Laws and Elections in the Administration of Decedents' Estates*, 30 IND. L.J. 293. Scoles, Eugene F. (1957) *Conflict of Laws and Creditor's Rights in Decedents' Estates*, 42 IOWA L. REV. 341. Scoles, Eugene F. (1955) *Conflict of Laws and Nonbarrable Interests in Administration of Decedents' Estates*, 8 U. FLA. L. REV. 151. Scott, Austin W. (1964) *Spendthrift Trusts and the Conflict of Laws*, 77 HARV. L. REV. 845. Swabenland, Walter W. (Land) (1938) *The Conflict of Laws in Administration of Express Trusts of Personal Property*, 45 YALE L.J. 438.

6. Family Law

Baade, Hans W. (1972) *Marriage and Divorce in American Conflicts Law: Governmental-Interests Analysis and the* Restatement (Second), 72 COLUM. L. REV. 329. Bailey-Harris, Rebecca (1991) *Madame Butterfly and the Conflict of Laws*, 39 AM. J. COMP. L. 157. Baty, Thomas (1917) *Capacity and Form of Marriage in the Conflict of Laws*, 26 YALE L.J. 444. Fentiman, Richard (1985) *The Validity of Marriage and the Proper Law*, 44 CAMB. L.J. 256. Fine, J. David (1980) *The Application of Issue-Analysis to Choice of Law Involving Family Law Matters in the United States*, 26 LOYOLA L. REV. 31. Hernanz, Francisca (1990) *Recognition—Exequatur—Of Foreign Judgments, Especially of U.S. Divorce Judgments in Spain*, 38 AM. J. COMP. L. 567. Hovermill, Joseph W. (1994) *A Conflict of Laws and Morals: The Choice of Law Implications of Hawaii's Recognition of Same-Sex Marriages*, 53 MD. L. REV. 450. Lorenzen, Ernest G. (1923) *Polygamy and the Conflict of Laws*, 32 YALE L.J. 471. Reese, Willis L. M. (1977) *Marriage in American Conflict of Laws*, 26 INT'L & COMP. L.Q. 952. Siehr, Kurt G. (1982) *Domestic Relations in Europe: European Equivalents to American Evolutions*, 30 AM. J. COMP. L. 37. Stimson, Edward S. (1942) *Law Applicable to Marriage*, 16 U. CINN. L. REV. 81. Storke, Frederic P. (1959) *Annulment in the Conflict of Laws*, 43 MINN. L. REV. 849. Symeonides, Symeon C. (1987) *Louisiana's Draft on Successions and Marital Property*, 35 AM. J. COMP. L. 259.

7. Business Law

Coleman, William T., Jr. (1950) *Corporate Dividends and the Conflict of Laws*, 63 HARV. L. REV. 433. Comment (1962) *Limited Liability of Shareholders in Real Estate Investment Trusts and the Conflict of Laws*, 50 CALIF. L. REV. 696. Demott, Deborah A. (1985) *Perspectives on*

Choice of Law for Corporate Internal Affairs, 48 LAW & CONTEMP. PROBS. 161. Foley, Henry E. (1929) *Incorporation, Multiple Incorporation, and the Conflict of Laws*, 42 HARV. L. REV. 516. Hay, Peter and Muller-Freienfels, Wolfram (1979) *Agency in the Conflict of Laws and the 1978 Hague Convention*, 27 AM. J. COMP. L. 1. Kaplan, Stanley A. (1968) *Foreign Corporations and Local Corporate Policy*, 21 VAND. L. REV. 433. Kozyris, P. John (1985) *Corporate Wars and Choice of Law*, 1985 DUKE L.J. 1. Kozyris, P. John (1989) *Some Observations on State Regulation of Multistate Takeovers—Controlling Choice of Law Through the Commerce Clause*, 14 DEL. J. CORP. L. 499. McNulty, John K. (1967) *Corporations and the Intertemporal Conflict of Laws*, 55 CALIF. L. REV. 12. Note (1989) *Interest Analysis Applied to Corporations: The Unprincipled Use of Choice of Law Method*, 98 YALE L.J. 597. Reese, Willis L. M. and Kaufman, Edmund M. (1958) *The Law Governing Corporate Affairs: Choice of Law and the Impact of Full Faith and Credit*, 58 COLUM. L. REV. 1118. Reese, Willis L. M. and Flesch, Alma Suzin (1960) *Agency and Vicarious Liability in Conflict of Laws*, 60 COLUM. L. REV. 764.

B. ASSORTED RULES AND CONCEPTUAL DEVICES FOR CONFLICTS CASES

1. Domicile

Beale, Joseph H. (1926) *Proof of Domicil*, 74 U. PA. L. REV. 552. Cavers, David F. (1972) *"Habitual Residence": A Useful Concept?*, 21 AM. U. L. REV. 475. Corr, John B. (1983) *Interest Analysis and Choice of Law: The Dubious Dominance of Domicile*, 1983 UTAH L. REV. 651. Coudert, Frederic R. (1927) *Some Considerations in the Law of Domicil*, 36 YALE L.J. 949. Ely, John H. (1981) *Choice of Law and the State's Interest in Protecting Its Own*, 23 WM. & MARY L. REV. 173. Falconbridge, John D. (1941) *Renvoi and the Law of the Domicile*, 19 CAN. BAR REV. 311. Reese, Willis L. M. (1955) *Does Domicil Bear a Single Meaning?*, 55 COLUM. L. REV. 589. Wade, J. A. (1983) *Domicile: A Re-Examination of Certain Rules*, 32 INT'L & COMP. L.Q. 1. Weintraub, Russell J. (1965) *An Inquiry into the Utility of "Domicile" as a Concept in Conflicts Analysis*, 63 MICH. L. REV. 961. Wurfel, Seymour W. (1975) *Jet Age Domicil: The Semi-Demise of Durational Residence Requirements*, 11 WAKE FOREST L. REV. 349.

2. Renvoi[1]

Abbott, Edwin H., Jr. (1908) *Is the* Renvoi *a Part of the Common Law?*, 24 L.Q. REV. 133. Briggs, Edwin W. (1954) *"Renvoi" in the Succession to Tangibles: A False Issue Based on Faulty Analysis*, 64 YALE L.J. 195. Cormack, Joseph M. (1941) Renvoi, *Characterization, Localization, and Preliminary Question in the Conflict of Laws*, 14 S. CAL. L. REV. 221. Falconbridge, John D. (1931) Renvoi *and Succession to Movables*, 46 L.Q. REV. 465; (1930) 47 L.Q. REV. 271. Falconbridge, John D. (1941) *The* Renvoi *and the Privy Council*, 19 CAN. BAR REV. 682. Falconbridge, John D. (1941) Renvoi *and the Law of the Domicile*, 19 CAN. BAR REV. 311 (1941). Griswold, Erwin N. (1939) Renvoi *Revisited*, 51 HARV. L. REV. 1165. Griswold, Erwin N. (1939) *In Reply to Mr. Cowan's Views on* Renvoi, 87 U. OF PA. L. REV. 257. Kramer, Larry (1991) *Return of the* Renvoi, 66 N.Y.U. L. REV. 979. Lorenzen, Ernest G. (1910) *The* Renvoi *Theory and the Application of Foreign Law*, 10 COLUM. L. REV. 190. Lorenzen, Ernest G. (1918) *The* Renvoi *Doctrine in the Conflict of Laws—Meaning of "The Law of a Country,"* 27 YALE L.J. 509. Schreiber, Ernst O. (1918) *The Doctrine of the* Renvoi *in Anglo-American Law*, 31 HARV. L. REV. 523. Shapiro, James A. (1992) *Choice of Law Under the Federal Tort Claims Act:* Richards *and* Renvoi *Revisited*, 70 N.C. L. REV. 641. Von Mehren, Arthur T. (1961) *The* Renvoi *and Its Relation to Various Approaches to the Choice-of-Law Problem*, pp. 395-408 in K. Nadelmann, et al., eds., XXTH CENTURY COMPARATIVE AND CONFLICTS LAW: LEGAL ESSAYS IN HONOR OF HESSELL E. YNTEMA, Leyden: A. W. Sythoff.

3. Depecage[2]

Reese, Willis L. M. (1973) *Depecage: A Common Phenomenon in Choice of Law*, 73 COLUM. L. REV. 58. Weintraub, Russell J. (1974) *Beyond Depecage: A "New Rule" Approach to Choice of Law in Consumer Credit Transactions and a Critique of the Territorial Application*

---

[1]   Discussed in the commentary following Chapter Three, Part A.

[2]   The technique of applying laws of different jurisdictions to the same case.

of the Uniform Consumer Credit Code, 25 CASE WESTERN RES. L. REV. 16. Wilde, Christian L. (1968) *Depecage in the Choice of Tort Law*, 41 So. CAL. L. REV. 329.

4. Characterization[3]

Cook, Walter W. (1941) *Characterization in the Conflict of Laws*, 51 YALE L.J. 191. Cormack, Joseph M. (1941) *Renvoi, Characterization, Localization, and Preliminary Question in the Conflict of Laws*, 14 S. CAL. L. REV. 221. Ehrenzweig, Albert A. (1961) *Characterization in the Conflict of Laws: An Unwelcome Addition to American Doctrine* , pp. 395-408 in K. Nadelmann, et al., eds., XXTH CENTURY COMPARATIVE AND CONFLICTS LAW: LEGAL ESSAYS IN HONOR OF HESSELL E. YNTEMA, LEYDEN: A. W. Sythoff. Falconbridge, John D. (1937) *Conflict of Laws: Examples of Characterization*, 15 CAN. B. REV. 215. Falconbridge, John D. (1937) *Characterization in the Conflict of Laws*, 53 L.Q. REV. 235. Lorenzen, Ernest G. (1941) *The Qualification, Classification, or Characterization Problem in the Conflict of Laws*, 50 YALE L.J. 743. Morse, Joseph (1949) *Characterization: Shadow or Substance*, 49 COLUM. L. REV. 1027. Pascal, Robert A. (1940) *Characterization as an Approach to the Conflict of Laws*, 2 LA. L. REV. 715. Robertson, A. H. (1940) CHARACTERIZATION IN THE CONFLICT OF LAWS, Cambridge: Harvard Univ. Press.

5. Public Policy[4]

Corr, John B. (1985) *Modern Choice of Law and Public Policy: The Emperor Has the Same Old Clothes*, 39 U. MIAMI L. REV. 647. Greenberg, Herbert W. (1977) *Extrastate Enforcement of Tax Claims and Administrative Tax Determinations Under the Full Faith and Credit Clause*, 43 BKLYN. L. REV. 630. Goodrich, Herbert F. (1930) *Public Policy in the Conflict of Laws*, 36 W. VA. L.Q. 156. Leflar, Robert A. (1932) *Extrastate Enforcement of Penal and Government Claims*, 46 HARV. L. REV. 193. Lorenzen, Ernest G. (1924) *Territoriality, Public Policy and the Conflict of Laws*, 33 YALE L.J. 736. Nussbaum, Arthur (1940) *Public Policy and the Political Crisis in the Conflict of Laws*, 49 YALE L.J. 1027. Nutting, Charles B. (1935) *Suggested Limitations of the Public Policy Doctrine*, 19 MINN. L. REV. 196. Paulsen, Conrad G. and Sovren, Michael I. (1956) *"Public Policy" in Conflict of Laws*, 56 COLUM. L. REV. 969. Reese, Willis L. M. (1952) *Full Faith and Credit to Statutes: The Defense of Public Policy*, 19 U. CHI. L. REV. 339 (1952). Sack, A. N. (1933) *Non-Enforcement of Foreign Revenue Laws*, 81 U. PA. L. REV. 559.

6. Substance-Procedure Distinctions in Choice of Law

Bradford, Steven (1991) *Conflict of Laws and the Attorney-Client Privilege: A Territorial Solution*, 52 U. PITT. L. REV. 909. Cook, Walter W. (1933) *"Substance" and "Procedure" in the Conflict of Laws*, 42 YALE L.J. 333. Cooper, Laura (1986) *Statutes of Limitations in Minnesota Choice of Law: The Problematic Return of the Substance-Procedure Distinction*, 71 MINN. L. REV. 363. Grossman, Margaret ROSSO, (1980) *Statutes of Limitations and the Conflict of Laws: Modern Analysis*, 1980 ARIZ. ST. L.J. 1. Leflar, Robert A. (1983) *The New Conflict-Lim-*

---

[3]   Discussed in the commentary following Chapter Three, Part A.

[4]   Discussed in the commentary following Chapter Three, Part A.

itations Act, 35 MERCER L. REV. 461. Lorenzen, Ernest G. (1919) *The Statute of Limitations and the Conflict of Laws*, 28 YALE L.J. 492. Martin, James A. (1980) *Statutes of Limitations and Rationality in the Conflict of Laws*, 19 WASHBURN L.J. 405. McClintock, H. L. (1930) *Distinguishing Substance and Procedure in the Conflict of Laws*, 78 U. PA. L. REV. 933. Milhollin, Gary L. (1975) *Interest Analysis and Conflicts Between Statutes of Limitations*, 27 HASTINGS L.J. 1. Note (1989) *Shopping for a Statute of Limitation—Sun Oil Co. v. Wortman*, 37 U. KAN. L. REV. 423. Reese, Willis L. M. and Leiwant, Barry D. (1977) *Testimonial Privileges and Conflict of Laws*, 41 LAW & CONTEMP. PROB. 85. Risinger, D. Michael (1982) *"Substance" and "Procedure" Revisited with Some Afterthoughts on the Constitutional Problem of Irrebuttable Presumptions*, 30 UCLA L. REV. 189. Sterk, Stewert E. (1977) *Testimonial Privileges: An Analysis of Horizontal Choice of Law Problems*, 61 MINN. L. REV. 461. Twerski, Aaron D. and Mayer, Renee G. (1979) *Toward a Pragmatic Solution of Choice-of-Law Problems—At the Interface of Substance and Procedure*, 74 Nw. U. L. REV. 781. Weinberg, Louise (1991) *Choosing Law: The Limitations Debate*, 1991 U. ILL. L. REV. 683.

7. Pleading and Proving Foreign Law

Baade, Hans W. (1978) *Proving Foreign and International Law in Domestic Tribunals*, 18 VA. J. INT'L L. 609. Fentiman, Richard (1992) *Foreign Law in English Courts*, 108 L.Q. REV. 142. Pollack, Milton (1978) *Proof of Foreign Law*, 26 AM. J. COMP. L. 470. Sass, Stephen L. (1981) *Foreign Law in Federal Courts*, 29 AM. J. COMP. L. 97. Schlesinger, Rudolf B. (1973) *A Recurrent Problem in Transnational Litigation: The Effect of a Failure to Invoke or Prove the Applicable Foreign Law*, 59 CORNELL. L. REV. 1. Sprankling, John G. and Lanyi, George R. (1983) *Pleading and Proof of Foreign Law in American Courts*, 19 STAN. J. INT'L L. 3. Szladits, Charles (1984) *Foreign Law in English*, 32 AM. J. COMP. L. 213. Wing, Adrien K. (1983) *Pleading and Proof of Foreign Law in American Courts, A Selected Annotated Bibliography*, 19 STAN. J. INT'L L. 175. Yates, George T., III (1978) *Foreign Law Before Domestic Tribunals*, 18 VA. J. INT'L L. 725.

C. CODIFYING CONFLICTS LAW

Bayitch, S. A. (1954) *Conflict Law in United States Treaties*, 8 MIAMI L.Q. 501; 9 MIAMI L. Q. 9, 125. B, Harold S. (1995) *International Conflict of Laws, The 1992 Inter-American Convention on the Law Applicable to International Contracts, and Trends for the 1990s*, 28 VAND. J. OF TRANSNAT'L L. 367. Friedler, Edith (1989) *Party Autonomy Revisited: A Statutory Solution to a Choice-of-Law Problem*, 37 KANS. L. REV. 471. Gottesman, Michael H. (1991) *Draining the Dismal Swamp: The Case for Federal Choice of Law Statutes*, 80 GEO. L.J. 1. Kozyris, P. John (1990) *Values and Methods in Choice of Law for Products Liability: A Comparative Comment on Statutory Solutions*, 38 AM. J. COMP. L. 475. Kramer, Larry (1991) *On the Need for a Uniform Choice of Law Code*, 89 MICH. L. REV. 2134. Leflar, Robert A. (1977) *Choice-of-Law Statutes*, 44 TENN. L. REV. 951. Leflar, Robert A. (1981) *Conflict of Laws Under the U.C.C.*, 35 ARK. L. REV. 87. Morris, J. H. C. (1946) *The Choice of Law Clause in Statutes*, 62 L.Q. REV. 170. Peterson, Courtland H. (1990) *New Openness to Statutory Choice of Law Solutions*, 38 AM. J. COMP. L. 423. Rheinstein, Max (1951) *Conflict of Laws in the Uniform Commercial Code*, 16 LAW & CONTEMP. PROB. 114. Stimson, Edward S. (1950) *Simplifying the Conflict of Laws: A Bill Proposed for Enactment by the Congress*, 36 A.B.A. J. 1003. Symeonides, Symeon C. (1987) *Louisiana's Draft on Successions and Marital Property*, 35 AM. J. COMP. L. 259. Symeonides, Symeon C. (1989) *The New Swiss Conflicts Codification: An Introduction*, 37 AM. J. COMP. L. 187. Symeonides, Symeon C. (1990) *Problems and Dilemmas in Codifying Choice of Law for Torts: The Louisiana Experience in Comparative Perspective*, 38 AM. J. COMP. L. 431. Symeonides, Symeon C. (1990) *Revising Puerto Rico's Conflicts Law: A Preview*, 28 COLUM. J. TRANSNAT'L L. 413. Symeonides, Symeon C. (1992) *Louisiana's New Law of Choice of Law for Torts Conflicts: An Exegesis*, 66 TUL. L. REV. 677 (1992). Symeonides, Symeon C. (1993) *Private International Codification in a Mixed Jurisdiction: The Louisiana Experience*, RABELS ZEITSCHRIFT pp. 460-507, Max-Planck Institut. Talyor, E. Hunter (1978) *Uniformity of Commercial Law and State-by-State Enactment: A Confluence of Contradictions*, 30 HASTINGS L.J. 337. United Nations (May, 1980) *Conference on Contracts for the International Sale of Goods*, XIX INT'L LEGAL MATERIALS, No. 3, p. 668. Weisberger, June Miller (1987) *Selected Conflict of Laws Issues in Wisconsin's New Marital (Community) Property Act*, 35 AM. J. COMP. L. 295.

D. INTERSECTIONS OF CONFLICTS LAW WITH OTHER FORMS OF PROCEDURE

1. Personal Jurisdiction

[See Chapter 10, Part D]

2. Intersystem Preclusion

Brand, Ronald A. (1991) *Enforcement of Foreign Money-Judgments in the United States: In Search of Uniformity and International Acceptance*, 67 NOTRE DAME L. REV. 253. Brand, Ronald A. (1994) *Enforcement of Judgments in the United States and Europe*, 13 J.L. & COM. 193. Caust-Ellenbogen, Sanford N. (1990) *False Conflicts and Interstate Preclusion: Moving Beyond a Wooden Reading of the Full Faith and Credit Clause*, 58 FORDHAM L. REV. 593. Hay, Peter (1992) *The Recognition and Enforcement of American Money—Judgments in Germany— The 1992 Decision of the German Supreme Court*, 40 AM. J. COMP. L. 1001. Hernanz, Francisca (1990) *Recognition—Exequatur—Of Foreign Judgments, Especially of U.S. Divorce Judgments in Spain*, 38 AM. J. COMP. L. 567. Homburger, Adolf (1970) *Recognition and Enforcement of Foreign Judgments*, 18 AM. J. COMP. L. 367. Lewis, Jeffrey E. (1974) *Mutuality in Conflict— Flexibility and Full Faith and Credit*, 23 DRAKE L. REV. 364. Note (1981) *Power to Reverse Foreign Judgments: The British Clawback Statute Under International Law*, 81 COLUM. L. REV. 1097. Peterson, Courtland H. (1972) *Foreign Country Judgments and the Second Restatement of Conflict of Laws*, 72 COLUM. L. REV. 220. Pryles, Michael Charles (1971) *Impeachment of Sister State Judgments for Fraud*, 25 SW. L.J. 697. Reynolds, William L. (1994) *The Iron Law of Full Faith and Credit*, 53 MD. L. REV. 412. Shreve, Gene R. (1986) *Preclusion and Federal Choice of Law*, 64 TEX. L. REV. 1209. Shreve, Gene R. (1992) *Judgments from a Choice of Law Perspective*, 40 AM. J. COMP. L. 985. Von Mehren, Arthur T. (1981) *Recognition and Enforcement of Sister-State Judgments: Reflections on General Theory and Current Practice in the European Economic Community and the United States*, 81 COLUM. L. REV. 1044. Wurfel, Seymour W. (1971) *Recognition of Foreign Judgments*, 50 N. CAR. L. REV. 21.

3. Complex Litigation

(a) Issues Under Current Law

Juenger, Friedrich K. (1989) *Mass Disasters and the Conflict of Laws*, 1989 U. ILL. L. REV. 105. Lowenfeld, Andreas F. (1989) *Mass Torts and the Conflict of Laws: The Airline Disaster*, 1989 U. ILL. L. REV. 157. Miller, Arthur R. and Crump, David (1986) *Jurisdiction and Choice of Law in Multistate Class Actions After* Phillips Petroleum Co. v. Shutts, 96 YALE L.J. 1. Mullenix, Linda S. (1992) *Federalising Choice of Law of Mass-Tort Litigation*, 70 TEX. L. REV. 1623. Mullenix, Linda S. (1996) MASS TORT LITIGATION: CASES AND MATERIALS, St. Paul: West Publishing Co. Van Couter, (1995) Barkanic: *The New York Choice-of-Law Method and Recovery for Air Crashes Abroad*, 60 J. AIR L. & COM. 759. Weintraub, Russell J. (1989) *Methods for Resolving Conflict-of-Laws Problems in Mass Tort Litigation*, 1989 U. ILL. L. REV. 129.

(b) Proposals for Reform—Mass Tort Cases

Carson, Lynn D. (1990) *Choice of Law Issues in Mass Tort Litigation*, 56 J. AIR L. & COM. 199. Juenger, Friedrich K. (1994) *The Complex Litigation Project's Tort Choice-of-Law Rules*, 54 LA. L. REV. 907. Kalis, Peter J., Segerdahl, James R., and Waldron, John T., III (1994) *The Choice-of-Law Dispute in Comprehensive Environmental Coverage Litigation: Has Help Arrived from the American Law Institute Complex Litigation Project?*, 54 LA. L. REV. 925. Kane, Mary Kay (1991) *Drafting Choice of Law Rules for Complex Litigation: Some Preliminary Thoughts*, 10 REV. LITIG. 309. Kozyris, P. John (1994) *The Conflicts Provisions of the ALI's Complex Litigation Project: A Glass Half Full?*, 54 LA. L. REV. 953. Sedler, Robert A. (1994) *The Complex Litigation Project's Proposal for Federally-Mandated Choice of Law in Mass Tort Cases: Another Assault on State Sovereignty*, 54 LA. L. REV. 1085. Sedler, Robert A. and Twerski, Aaron D. (1989) *The Case Against All Encompassing Federal Mass Tort Legislation: Sacrifice Without Gain*, 73 MARQ. L. REV. 76. Sedler, Robert A. and Twerski, Aaron D. (1990) *State Choice of Law in Mass Tort Cases: A Response to "A View from the Legislature,"* 73 MARQ. L. REV. 625. Seidelson, David E. (1994) *Section 6.01 of the ALI's Complex Litigation Project: Function Follows Form*, 54 LA. L. REV. 1111. Shreve, Gene R. (1994) *Reform Aspirations of the Complex Litigation Project*, 54 LA. L. REV. 1139. Symeonides, Symeon C. (1994) *The ALI's Complex Litigation Project: Commencing the National Debate*, 54 LA. L. REV. 843. Trautman, Donald T. (1994) *Some Thoughts on Choice of Law, Judicial Discretion, and the ALI's Complex Litigation Project*, 54 LA. L. REV. 835. Weinberg, Louise (1993) *Mass Torts at the Neutral Forum: A Critical Analysis of the ALI's Proposed Choice Rule*, 56 ALBANY L. REV. 807.

E. CHOICE OF LAW IN THE FEDERAL SYSTEM

1. Conflicts Law and the *Erie* Doctrine

Atwood, Barbara A. (1986) *The Choice-of-Law Dilemma in Mass Tort Litigation: Kicking Around* Erie, Klaxon, *and* Van Dusen, 19 CONN. L. REV. 9. Borchers, Patrick J. (1993) *The Origins of Diversity Jurisdiction, the Rise of Legal Positivism, and a Brave New World for* Erie *and* Klaxon, 72 TEX. L. REV. 79. Cardozo, Michael H. (1960) *Choosing and Declaring State Law: Deference to State Courts Versus Federal Responsibility,* 55 NW. U. L. REV. 419. Cavers, David F. (1963) *The Changing Choice-of-Law Process and the Federal Courts,* 28 LAW & CONTEMP. PROBS. 732. Clark, Charles E. (1946) *State Law in the Federal Courts: The Brooding Omnipresence of* Erie v. Tompkins, 55 YALE L.J. 267. Corr, John B. and Robbins, Ira P. (1988) *Interjurisdictional Certification and Choice of Law,* 41 VAND. L. REV. 411. Corr, John B. (1995) *State Searches, Federal Cases, and Choice of Law: Just a Little Respect,* 23 PEPPERDINE L. REV. 31. Friendly, Henry J. (1964) *In Praise of* Erie—*and of the New Federal Common Law,* 39 N.Y.U. L. REV. 383. Maltz, Earl M. (1991) *Choice of Forum and Choice of Law in the Federal Courts: A Reconsideration of* Erie *Principles,* 79 KY. L. J. 231. Marcus, Richard L. (1984) *Conflicts Among Circuits and Transfers Within the Federal Judicial System,* 93 YALE L. J. 677. Note (1955) *Applicability of State Conflicts Rules When Issues of State Law Arise in Federal Question Cases,* 68 HARV. L. REV. 1212. Note (1977) *Choice of Law in Federal Court after Transfer of Venue,* 63 CORNELL L. REV. 149. Ragazzo, Robert A. (1995) *Transfer and Choice of Federal Law: The Apellate Model,* 93 MICH. L. REV. 703. Ratner, James R. (1989) *Using Currie's Interest Analysis to Resolve Conflicts Between State Regulation and the Sherman Act,* 30 WM. & MARY L. REV. 705. Seidelson, David E. (1991) *1 (*Wortman*) + 1 (*Ferens*) = 6 (Years): That Can't be Right—Can It? Statutes of Limitations and Supreme Court Inconsistency,* 57 BROOK. L. REV. 787. Shapiro, James A. (1992) *Choice of Law Under the Federal Tort Claims Act:* Richards *and Renvoi Revisited,* 70 N.C. L. REV. 641. Shreve, Gene R. (1993) *Conflicts Law—State or Federal?,* 68 IND. L.J. 907. Trautman, Donald T. (1992) *Towards Federalizing Choice of Law,* 70 TEX. L. REV. 1715. Weinberg, Louise (1992) *The Federal-State Conflict of Laws: "Actual" Conflicts,* 70 TEX. L. REV. 1743. Weintraub, Russell J. (1964) *The* Erie *Doctrine and State Conflict of Laws Rules,* 39 IND. L.J. 228.

2. Federal Common Law for Conflicts?

Henkin, Louis (1964) *The Foreign Affairs Power of the Federal Courts:* Sabbatino, 64 COLUM. L. REV. 805. Horowitz, Harold W. (1967) *Toward a Federal Common Law of Choice of Law,* 14 UCLA L. REV. 1191. Paul, Roland A. (1965) *The Act of State Doctrine: Revived But Suspended,* 113 U. PA. L. REV. 691. Redish, Martin H. (1989) *Federal Common Law, Political Legitimacy, and the Interpretive Process: An Institutionalist Perspective,* 83 NW. U. L. REV. 761. Shreve, Gene R. (1982) *In Search of a Choice-of-Law Reviewing Standard—Reflections on* Allstate Insurance Co. v. Hague, 66 MINN. L. REV. 327. Shreve, Gene R. (1991) *Pragmatism Without Politics—A Half Measure of Authority for Jurisdictional Common Law,* 1991 B.Y.U. L. REV. 767. Shreve, Gene R. (1996) *Choice of Law and the Forgiving Constitution,* 71 IND. L.J. 271. Silberman, Linda J. (1983) *Can the State of Minnesota Bind the Nation? Federal Choice of Law Constraints After* Allstate Insurance Co. v. Hague, 10 HOFSTRA L. REV. 103. Trautman, Donald T. (1977) *The Relation Between American Choice of Law and Federal Common Law,* 41 LAW & CONTEMP. PROBS. 105. Trautman, Donald T. (1992) *Towards Federalizing Choice of Law,* 70 TEX. L. REV. 1715. Weinberg, Louise (1989) *Federal Common Law,* 83

Nw. U. L. Rev. 805. Weinberg, Louise (1989) *The Curious Notion that the Rules of Decision Act Blocks Supreme Federal Common Law*, 83 Nw. U. L. Rev. 860.

F. INTERNATIONAL PERSPECTIVES

1. Extraterritorial Application of American Law

Born, Gary B. (1992) *A Reappraisal of the Extraterritorial Reach of U.S. Law*, 24 LAW & POL-ICY IN INT'L BUSINESS 1. Burman, Harold S. (1995) *International Conflict of Laws, The 1992 Inter-American Convention on the Law Applicable to International Contracts, and Trends for the 1990s*, 28 VAND. J. OF TRANSNAT'L L. 367. Kramer, Larry (1991) *Vestiges of Beale: Extraterritorial Application of American Law*, 1991 SUP. CT. REV. 179. Kramer, Larry (1995) *Extraterritorial Application of American Law After the Insurance Antitrust Case: A Reply to Professors Lowenfeld and Trimble*, 89 AM. J. OF INT'L L. 750. Symposium (1995) *Conference on Jurisdiction, Justice, and Choice of Law for the Twenty-First Century—Case Two: Extraterritorial Application of United States Law Against United States and Alien Defendants*, 29 NEW ENG. L. REV. 577. Van Couter (1995) Barkanic: *The New York Choice-of-Law Method and Recovery for Air Crashes Abroad*, 60 J. AIR L. & COM. 759. Weintraub, Russell J. (1992) *The Extraterritorial Application of Antitrust & Security Laws: An Inquiry into the Utility of a "Choice-of-Law" Approach*, 70 TEX. L. REV. 1799. Weintraub, Russell J. (1994) Hartford Fire Insurance Co., *Comity and the Extraterritoral Reach of United States Antitrust Law*, 29 TEX. INT'L L.J. 427.

2. Choice of Law Abroad

(a) Africa

Bankas, Ernest K. (1992) *Problems of Intestate Succession and the Conflict of Laws in Ghana*, 26 INT'L LAW. 433. Tier, Akolda M. (1990) *Conflict of Laws and Leqal Pluralism in the Sudan*, 39 INT'L & COMP. L.Q. 611.

(b) Asia and Australia

Bailey-Harris, Rebecca (1991) *Madame Butterfly and the Conflict of Laws*, 39 AM. J. COMP. L. 157. Huang, Jin and QIAN, Andrew X. (1995) *"One Country, Two Systems," Three Law Families, and Four Legal Regions: The Emerging Inter-Regional Conflicts of Law in China*, 5 DUKE J. COMP. & INT'L L. 289. Nygh, Peter (1995) *Choice-of-Law Rules and Forum Shoppinq in Australia*, 46 S.C. L. REV. 899. O'Brien, Bernard (1990) *Choice of Law in Torts*, 12 ADEL. L. REV. 449. Sykes, Edward I. and Pryles, Michael C. (1991) AUSTRALIAN PRIVATE INTERNATIONAL LAW, 3rd ed., Sydney: The Law Book Co., Ltd.

(c) Canada

Maslechko, William S. (1986) *Revolution and Counter-revolution: "Interest Analysis" in the United States and its Relevance to Canadian Conflict of Laws*, 44 U. TORONTO FAC. L. REV. 57. Swan, John (1995) *Federalism and the Conflict of Laws: The Curious Position of the Supreme Court of Canada*, 46 S.C. L. REV. 923.

(d) England

Opeskin, Brian R. (1992) *Choice of Law in Torts and Limitation Statutes,* 108 L. Q. REV. 398. Fawcett, J. J. (1982) *Is American Governmental Interest Analysis the Solution to English Tort Choice of Law Problems?*, 31 INT'L & COMP. L. Q. 150. Fentiman, Richard (1992) *Foreign Law in English Courts,* 108 L. Q. REV. 142. Lowenfeld, Andreas F. (1989) *Conflict of Laws English Style—Review Essay,* 37 AM. J. COMP. L. 353. North, Peter M. and Fawcett, J. J. (1992) CHESHIRE AND NORTH'S PRIVATE INTERNATIONAL LAW, London: Butterworths, 12th ed. Prebble, John (1973) *Choice of Law to Determine the Validity and Effect of Contracts: A Comparison of English and American Approaches to the Conflict of Laws,* 58 CORNELL L. REV. 433.

(e) Europe

Borchers, Patrick J. (1992) *Comparing Personal Jurisdiction in the United States and the European Community: Lessons for American Reform,* 40 AM. J. COMP. L. 121. Comment (1972) *International Commercial Arbitration Under the United Nations Convention and the Amended Federal Arbitration Statute,* 47 WASH. L. REV. 441. Hanotiau, Bernard (1982) *The American Conflicts Revolution and European Tort Choice-of-Law Thinking,* 30 AM. J. COMP. L. 73. Hernanz, Francisca (1990) *Recognition—Exequatur—Of Foreign Judgments Especially of U.S. Divorce Judgments in Spain,* 38 AM. J. COMP. L. 567. Juenger, Friedrich K. (1981) *Marital Property and the Conflict of Laws: A Tale of Two Countries,* 81 COLUM. L. REV. 1061. Juenger, Friedrich K. (1982) *American and European Conflicts Law,* 30 AM. J. COMP. L. 117. Lando, Ole (1982) *New American Choice-of-Law Principles and the European Conflict of Laws of Contracts,* 30 AM. J. COMP. L. 19. Lowenfeld, Andreas F. (1982) *Renvoi Among the Law Professors: An American's View of the European View of American Conflict of Laws,* 30 AM. J. COMP. L. 99. Reimann, Mathais (1995) CONFLICT OF LAWS IN WESTERN EUROPE: A GUIDE THROUGH THE JUNGLE, Transnational Publishers, Inc. Irvington, New York. Siehr, Kurt G. (1982) *Domestic Relations in Europe: European Equivalents to American Evolutions,* 30 AM. J. COMP. L. 37. Symeonides, Symeon C. (1989) *The New Swiss Conflicts Codification: An Introduction,* 37 AM. J. COMP. L. 187. Vitta, Edoardo (1982) *The Impact in Europe of the American "Conflicts Revolution",* 30 AM. J. COMP. L. 1. Von Mehren, Arthur T. (1981) *Recognition and Enforcement of Sister-State Judgments: Reflections on General Theory and Current Practice in the European Economic Community and the United States,* 81 COLUM. L. REV. 1044.

(f) Latin America

Juenger, Friedrich K. (1994) *The Inter-American Convention on the Law Applicable to International Contracts: Some Highlights and Comparisons,* 42 AM. J. COMP. L. 381. Valladao, Haroldo (1954) *The Influence of Joseph Story on Latin American Rules of Conflict Laws,* 3 AM.J. COMP. L. 27. Vargas, Jorge A. (1994) *Conflict of Laws in Mexico: The New Rules Introduced by the 1988 Amendments,* 28 Int'l Law. 659.

(g) Other Studies

Gaillard, Emmanuel and Trautman, Donald T. (1987) *Trusts in NonTrust Countries: Conflict of Laws and the Hague Convention on Trusts*, 35 AM. J. COMP. L. 307. Guedj, Thomas G. (1991) *The Theory of the Lois de Police, A Functional Trend in Continental Private International Law—A Comparative Analysis With Modern American Theories*, 39 AM. J. COMP. L. 661. Herzog, Peter E. (1992) *Constitutional Limits on Choice of Law*, 234 RECUEIL DES COURS 239. Jaffrey, A.J.E. (1982) *The Foundations of Rules for the Choice of Law*, 2 OXFORD J. OF LEG. STUD. 368. Jayme, Erik (1989) *The American Conflicts Revolution and its Impact on European Private International Law,* pp. 15-27 in FORTY YEARS ON: THE EVOLUTION OF POSTWAR PRIVATE INTERNATIONAL LAW IN EUROPE (Deventer: Kluwer). Juenger, Friedrich K. (1995) *American Conflicts Scholarship and the New Law Merchant*, 28 VAND. J. TRANSNAT'L L. 487. Symeonides, Symeon C. (1990) *Problems and Dilemmas in Codifying Choice of Law for Torts: The Louisiana Experience in Comparative Perspective*, 38 AM. J. COMP. L. 431. Zaphiriou, George A. (1985) *State or Country Interest as Analytical Framework for Choice of Law*, 46 OHIO ST.L.J. 537.

CHAPTER TWELVE

BIBLIOGRAPHY

This bibliography is arranged alphabetically by author. Multiple entries for the same author appear chronologically. There are many uses for the bibliography. It facilitates the short form of citation used in my comments throughout the book. By listing additional works of authors represented in the anthology, the bibliography allows readers to discover more about their views. The bibliography is not exhaustive; nonetheless, it gives a sense of the richness and breadth of conflicts literature. Finally, it may provide a useful data base for those beginning research projects in conflict of laws.

The bibliography corresponds to the topic of the anthology: conflicts law and theory. Additional topics that might be taken up in a Conflicts course (including personal jurisdiction, res judicata, federal common law, and the *Erie* doctrine) receive only incidental treatment. That is to say, listings on these topics appear only when the works inform thinking about conflicts law in some way.

Coverage of conflicts writing prior to 1960 is restricted. More bibliographical material from this period is available in Culp 1956. Foreign-language materials on conflicts (private international law) are important but inaccessible to most of us in America who study or follow the subject. Therefore, I have not included them. Foreign-language materials have received bibliographical coverage elsewhere. *See, e.g.*, Juenger 1993: pp. 238-249; Lowenfeld 1994: pp. 314-319; Mosconi 1989: pp. 203-214; North 1990: pp. 283-288.

Abbott, Edwin H., Jr. (1908) *Is the Renvoi a Part of the Common Law?*, 24 L.Q. REV. 133.

Alexander, Gregory S. (1975) *The Application and Avoidance of Foreign Law in the Law of Conflicts*, 70 Nw. U. L. REV. 602.

Alexander, Gregory S. (1979) *The Concept of Function and the Basis of Regulatory Interests Under Functional Choice of Law Theory: The Significance of Benefit and the Insignificance of Intention*, 65 VA. L. REV. 1063.

American Law Institute (1934) RESTATEMENT OF THE LAW OF CONFLICT OF LAWS, St. Paul: ALI Publishers.

American Law Institute (1969) STUDY OF THE DIVISION OF JURISDICTION BETWEEN STATE AND FEDERAL COURTS, Philadelphia: The Institute.

American Law Institute (1982) RESTATEMENT OF THE LAW, SECOND, OF JUDGMENTS, St. Paul: ALI Publishers.

American Law Institute (1987) RESTATEMENT OF THE LAW, THIRD, OF THE FOREIGN RELATIONS LAW OF THE UNITED STATES, St. Paul: ALI Publishers.

American Law Institute (1994) COMPLEX LITIGATION: STATUTORY RECOMMENDATIONS AND ANALYSIS, Philadelphia: ALI.

Atiyah, P. S. and Summers, Robert S. (1987) FORM AND SUBSTANCE IN ANGLO-AMERICAN LAW, Oxford: Clarendon Press.

Atwood, Barbara A. (1986) *The Choice-of-Law Dilemma in Mass Tort Litigation: Kicking Around Erie, Klaxon, and Van Dusen*, 19 CONN. L. REV. 9.

Baade, Hans W. (1967) *Counter-Revolution or Alliance for Progress? Reflections on Reading Cavers,* The Choice-of-Law Process, 46 TEX. L. REV. 141.

Baade, Hans W. (1972) *Marriage and Divorce in American Conflicts Law: Governmental-Interests Analysis and the* Restatement (Second), 72 COLUM. L. REV. 329.

Baade, Hans W. (1973) *The Case of the Disinterested Two States:* Neumeier v. Kuehner, 1 HOFSTRA L. REV. 150.

Baade, Hans W. (1978) *Proving Foreign and International Law in Domestic Tribunals*, 18 VA. J. INT'L L. 609.

Bailey-Harris, Rebecca (1991) *Madame Butterfly and the Conflict of Laws*, 39 AM. J. COMP. L. 157.

Bankas, Ernest K. (1992) *Problems of Intestate Succession and the Conflict of Laws in Ghana*, 26 INT'L LAW. 433.

Basedow, Jurgen (1994) *Conflicts of Economic Regulation*, 42 AM. J. COMP. L. 423.

Baty, Thomas (1917) *Capacity and Form of Marriage in the Conflict of Laws*, 26 YALE L.J. 444.

Baxter, William F. (1963) *Choice of Law and the Federal System*, 16 STAN. L. REV. 1.

Bayitch, S. A. (1954) *Conflict Law in United States Treaties*, 8 MIAMI L.Q. 501; 9 MIAMI L. Q. 9, 125.

Beach, John K. (1918) *Uniform Interstate Enforcement of Vested Rights*, 27 YALE L.J. 656.

Beale, Joseph H. (1902) *Summary of the Conflict of Laws*, in SELECTION OF CASES ON THE CONFLICT OF LAWS, vol. III, pp. 501, Cambridge, Mass: Harv. L. Rev. Pub. Ass'n.

Beale, Joseph H. (1909) *What Law Governs the Validity of a Contract*, 23 HARV. L. REV. 1.

Beale, Joseph H. (1920) *The Progress of the Law, 1919-1920*, 34 HARV. L. REV. 50.

Beale, Joseph H. (1926) *Proof of Domicil*, 74 U. PA. L. REV. 552.

Beale, Joseph H. (1935) *History and Doctrines of the Conflict of Laws*, in A TREATISE ON THE CONFLICT OF LAWS, vol. III, Appendix: pp. 1879, New York: Baker, Voorhis & Co.

Beale, Joseph H. (1937) *The Conflict of Laws, 1886-1936*, 50 HARV. L. REV. 887.

Berman, Donald H. (1985) *To Brainerd Currie: A Fallen Giant*, 46 OHIO ST. L.J. 529.

Bickel, Alexander M. (1957) THE LEAST DANGEROUS BRANCH: THE SUPREME COURT AT THE BAR OF POLITICS, Indianapolis: Bobbs-Merril.

Bliesener, Dirk H. (1994) *Fairness and Choice of Law: A Critique of the Political Rights-Based Approach to the Conflict of Laws*, 42 AM. J. COMP. L. 687.

Borchers, Patrick J. (1991) *Professor Brilmayer and the Holy Grail*, 1991 WIS. L. REV. 465.

Borchers, Patrick J. (1992a) *The Choice of Law Revolution: An Empirical Study*, 49 WASH. & LEE L. REV. 357.

Borchers, Patrick J. (1992b) *Choice of Law in American Courts in 1992: Observations and Reflections*, 42 AM. J. COMP. L. 125.

Borchers, Patrick J. (1992c) *Comparing Personal Jurisdiction in the United States and the European Community: Lessons for American Reform*, 40 AM. J. COMP. L. 121.

Borchers, Patrick J. (1993a) *Conflicts Pragmatism*, 56 ALB. L. REV. 883.

Borchers, Patrick J. (1993b) *The Origins of Diversity Jurisdiction, the Rise of Legal Positivism, and a Brave New World for* Erie *and* Klaxon, 72 TEX. L. REV. 79.

Borchers, Patrick J. (1993c) *New York Choice of Law: Weaving the Tangled Strands*, 56 ALBANY L. REV. 93.

Borchers, Patrick J. (1995a) *The Return of Territorialism to New York's Conflicts Law:* Padula v. Lilarn Properties Corp., 58 ALB. L. REV. 775.

Borchers, Patrick J. (1995b) *The Internationalization of Contractual Conflicts Law*, 28 VAND. J. TRANSNAT'L L. 421.

Born, Gary B. (1987) *Reflections on Judicial Jurisdiction in International Cases*, 17 GA. J. INT'L & COMP. L. 1.

Born, Gary B. (1992) *A Reappraisal of the Extraterritorial Reach of U.S. Law*, 24 LAW & POLICY IN INT'L BUSINESS 1.

Born, Gary B. and Westin, David (1992) INTERNATIONAL CIVIL LITIGATION IN UNITED STATES COURTS: COMMENTARY AND MATERIALS, 2nd ed. Boston: Kluwer.

Bourne, Richard W. (1993) *Modern Maryland Conflicts: Backing into the Twentieth Century One* Haunch *at a Time*, 23 U. BALT. L. REV. 71.

Bradford, Steven (1991) *Conflict of Laws and the Attorney-Client Privilege: A Territorial Solution*, 52 U. PITT. L. REV. 909.

Brand, Ronald A. (1991) *Enforcement of Foreign Money-Judgments in the United States: In Search of Uniformity and International Acceptance*, 67 NOTRE DAME L. REV. 253.

Brand, Ronald A. (1994) *Enforcement of Judgments in the United States and Europe*, 13 JOURNAL OF LAW AND COMMERCE 193.

Briggs, Edwin W. (1954) *"Renvoi" in the Succession to Tangibles: A False Issue Based on Faulty Analysis*, 64 YALE L.J. 195.

Brilmayer, Lea (1980) *Interest Analysis and the Myth of Legislative Intent*, 78 MICH. L. REV. 392.

Brilmayer, Lea (1981) *Legitimate Interests in Multistate Problems: As Between State and Federal Law*, 79 MICH. L. REV. 1315.

Brilmayer, Lea (1984a) *Credit Due Judgments and Credit Due Laws: The Respective Roles of Due Process and Full Faith and Credit in the Interstate Context*, 70 IOWA L. REV. 95.

Brilmayer, Lea (1984b) *Methods and Objectives in the Conflict of Laws: A Challenge*, 35 MERCER L. REV. 555.

Brilmayer, Lea (1985) *Governmental Interest Analysis: A House Without Foundations*, 46 OHIO ST. L.J. 459.

Brilmayer, Lea (1989a) *Consent, Contract, and Territory*, 74 MINN. L. REV. 1.

Brilmayer, Lea (1989b) *Rights, Fairness, and Choice of Law*, 98 YALE L.J. 1277.

Brilmayer, Lea (1991) *The Other State's Interests*, 24 CORNELL INT'L L.J. 233.

Brilmayer, Lea (1992) *Conflict of Laws: Foundation and Future Directions*, 90 MICH. L. REV. 1682.

Brilmayer, Lea (1993) *Interstate Preemption: The Right to Travel, the Right to Life, and the Right to Die*, 91 MICH. L. REV. 873.

Brilmayer, Lea (1995a) CONFLICT OF LAWS: CASES AND MATERIALS, 3rd ed. Boston: Little, Brown.

Brilmayer, Lea (1995b) *The Role of Substantive and Choice of Law Policies in the Formation and Application of Choice of Law Rules*, 252 RECUEIL DES COURS 11.

Brilmayer, Lea (1995c) CONFLICT OF LAWS, 2nd ed Boston: Little, Brown.

Burman, Harold S. (1995) *International Conflict of Laws, The 1992 Inter-American Convention on the Law Applicable to International Contracts, and Trends for the 1990s*, 28 VAND. J. TRANSNAT'L L. 367.

Cardozo, Benjamin N. (1928) THE PARADOXES OF LEGAL SCIENCE.

Cardozo, Michael H. (1960) *Choosing and Declaring State Law: Deference to State Courts Versus Federal Responsibility*, 55 NW. U. L. REV. 419.

Carnahan, Wendell (1935) *Tangible Property and the Conflict of Laws*, 2 U. CHI. L. REV. 345.

Carson, Lynn D. (1990) *Choice of Law Issues in Mass Tort Litigation*, 56 J. AIR L. & COM. 199.

Casad, Robert C. (1991) JURISDICTION IN CIVIL ACTIONS, 2nd ed. Salem, New Hampshire: Butterworth Legal Publishers.

Caust-Ellenbogen, Sanford N. (1990) *False Conflicts and Interstate Preclusion: Moving Beyond a Wooden Reading of the Full Faith and Credit Statute*, 58 FORDHAM L. REV. 593.

Cavers, David F. (1933) *A Critique of the Choice of Law Problem*, 47 HARV. L. REV. 173.

Cavers, David F. (1963) *The Changing Choice-of-Law Process and the Federal Courts*, 28 LAW & CONTEMP. PROBS. 732.

Cavers, David F. (1965a) THE CHOICE-OF-LAW PROCESS, Ann Arbor: Univ. Michigan Press.

Cavers, David F. (1965b) *Some of Ehrenzweig's Choice-of-Law Generalizations*, 18 OKLA. L. REV. 357.

Cavers, David F. (1970) *Contemporary Conflicts Law in American Perspective*, 131 RECUEIL DES COURS 75.

Cavers, David F. (1971) Cipolla *and Conflicts Justice*, 9 DUQUESNE L. REV. 360.

Cavers, David F. (1972) *"Habitual Residence": A Useful Concept?*, 21 AM. U. L. REV. 475.

Cavers, David F. (1981) *International Enforcement of Family Support*, 81 COLUM. L. REV. 994.

Cavers, David F. (1933-1983) THE CHOICE OF LAW: SELECTED ESSAYS, Durham: Duke Univ. Press.

Chafee, Zachariah, Jr. (1943) *Joseph Henry Beale*, 56 HARV. L. REV. 699.

Cheatham, Elliott E. (1941) *Sources of Rules for Conflict of Laws*, 89 U. PA. L. REV. 430.

Cheatham, Elliott E. (1945) *American Theories of Conflict of Laws: Their Role and Utility*, 58 HARV. L. REV. 361.

Cheatham, Elliott E. (1946) *Stone on Conflict of Laws*, 46 COLUM. L. REV. 719.

Cheatham, Elliott E. and Reese, Willis L. M. (1952) *Choice of the Applicable Law*, 52 COLUM. L. REV. 959.

Cheatham, Elliott E. and Maier, Harold G. (1968) *Private International Law and Its Sources*, 22 VAND. L. REV. 27.

Clark, Charles E. (1933) *The Restatement of the Law of Contract*, 42 YALE L.J. 643.

Clark, Charles E. (1946) *State Law in the Federal Courts: The Brooding Omnipresence of* Erie v. Tompkins, 55 YALE L.J. 267.

Coleman, William T., Jr. (1950) *Corporate Dividends and the Conflict of Laws*, 63 HARV. L. REV. 433.

Comment (1929) *What Governs the Validity and Administration of Trusts of Personal Property*, 39 YALE L.J. 100.

Comment (1962) *Limited Liability of Shareholders in Real Estate Investment Trusts and the Conflict of Laws*, 50 CALIF. L. REV. 696.

Comment (1969) *Choice of Law: The Validity of Trusts and Movables—Intention and Validation*, 64 NW. L. REV. 388.

Comment (1972) *International Commercial Arbitration Under the United Nations Convention and the Amended Federal Arbitration Statute*, 47 WASH. L. REV. 441.

Cook, Walter W. (1924) *Logical and Legal Bases in the Conflict of Law*, 33 Yale L.J. 457.

Cook, Walter W. (1933) *"Substance" and "Procedure" in the Conflict of Laws*, 42 YALE L.J. 333.

Cook, Walter W. (1936) *Contracts and the Conflict of Laws*, 31 ILL. L. REV. 143.

Cook, Walter W. (1941) *Characterization in the Conflict of Laws*, 51 YALE L.J. 191.

Cook, Walter W. (1942) THE LOGICAL AND LEGAL BASES OF THE CONFLICT OF LAW, Cambridge: Harvard Univ. Press.

Cook, Walter W. (1943) *An Unpublished Chapter of* The Logical and Legal Bases of the Conflict of Laws, 37 ILL. L. REV. 418.

Cooper, Laura (1986) *Statutes of Limitations in Minnesota Choice of Law: The Problematic Return of the Substance-Procedure Distinction*, 71 MINN. L. REV. 363.

Cormack, Joseph M. (1941) *Renvoi, Characterization, Localization, and Preliminary Question in the Conflict of Laws*, 14 S. CAL. L. REV. 221.

Corr, John B. (1983) *Interest Analysis and Choice of Law: The Dubious Dominance of Domicile*, 1983 UTAH L. REV. 651.

Corr, John B. (1985a) *Criminal Procedure and the Conflict of Laws*, 73 GEO. L.J. 1217.

Corr, John B. (1985b) *Modern Choice of Law and Public Policy: The Emperor Has the Same Old Clothes*, 39 U. MIAMI L. REV. 647.

Corr, John B. and Robbins, Ira P. (1988) *Interjurisdictional Certification and Choice of Law*, 41 VAND. L. REV. 411.

Corr, John B. (1995) *State Searches, Federal Cases, and Choice of Law: Just a Little Respect*, 23 PEPPERDINE L. REV. 31.

Coudert, Frederic R. (1927) *Some Considerations in the Law of Domicil*, 36 YALE L.J. 949.

Cox, Stanley E. (1987) *The Interrelationship of Personal Jurisdiction and Choice of Law: Forging New Theory Through* Asahi Metal Industry Co. v. Superior Court, 49 U. PITT. L. REV. 189.

Cox, Stanley E. (1993) *Razing Conflicts Facades to Build Better Jurisdiction Theory: The Foundation—There is No Law but Forum Law*, 28 VAL. U. L. REV. 1.

Cox, Stanley E. (1995) *Back to Conflicts Basics*, 44 CATHOLIC U. L. REV. 525.

Cramton, Roger C., Currie, David P., Kay, Herma Hill, and Kramer, Larry A. (1993) CONFLICT OF LAWS: CASES—COMMENTS—QUESTIONS, 5th ed. St. Paul, Minn.: West Pub. Co.

Culp, Maurice S., ed. (1956) SELECTED READINGS ON CONFLICT OF LAWS, St. Paul: West Publishing Co.

Currie, Brainerd (1959) *Notes on Methods and Objectives in the Conflict of Laws*, 1959 DUKE L.J. 171.

Currie, Brainerd (1963a) SELECTED ESSAYS ON THE CONFLICT OF LAWS, Durham: Duke Univ. Press.

Currie, Brainerd (1963b) *The Disinterested Third State*, 28 Law & Contemp. Probs. 754.

Damrosch, Lori F. (1987) *Foreign States and the Constitution*, 73 Va. L. Rev. 483.

Dane, Perry (1987) *Vested Rights, "Vestedness," and Choice of Law*, 96 Yale L.J. 1191.

Dane, Perry (1996) *Conflict of Laws*, Ch. 13, pp. 209-220, in D. Patterson ed., A Companion to Philosophy of Law and Legal Theory: Blackwell Pub. Co.

De Boer, Theodore M. (1987) Beyond *Lex Loci Delicti*: Conflicts, Methodology and Multistate Torts in American Case Law, Boston: Kluwer.

DeMott, Deborah A. (1985) *Perspectives on Choice of Law for Corporate Internal Affairs*, 48 Law & Contemp. Probs. 161.

De Sloovere, Frederick J. (1928) *The Local Law Theory and its Implications in the Conflict of Laws*, 41 Harv. L. Rev. 421.

Dorf, Michael C. (1995) *Prediction and the Rule of Law*, 42 UCLA L. Rev. 651.

Easley, Allen K. (1988) *An Examination of Choice-of-Law Theory and Practice in the Kansas Supreme Court: A Historical Perspective on Rules and Reasons*, 27 Washburn L.J. 407.

Ehrenzweig, Albert A. (1954) *American Conflicts Law in Its Historical Perspective*, 103 U. Pa. L. Rev. 133.

Ehrenzweig, Albert A. (1960) *The Lex Fori—Basic Rule in the Conflict of Laws*, 58 Mich. L. Rev. 637.

Ehrenzweig, Albert A. (1961) *Characterization in the Conflict of Laws: An Unwelcome Addition to American Doctrine*, pp. 395-408 in K. Nadelmann, et al., eds., XXth Century Comparative and Conflicts Law: Legal Essays in Honor of Hessell e. Yntema, Leyden: A. W. Sythoff.

Ehrenzweig, Albert A. (1963) *The "Most Significant Relationship" in the Conflicts of Law of Torts*, 28 Law & Contemp. Probs. 700.

Ehrenzweig, Albert A. (1965a) *A Proper Law in a Proper Forum: A "Restatement" of the "Lex Fori Approach,"* 18 Okla. L. Rev. 340.

Ehrenzweig, Albert A. (1965b) *The Second Conflicts Restatement: A Last Appeal for Its Withdrawal*, 113 U. Pa. L. Rev. 1230.

Ehrenzweig, Albert A. (1966) *A Counter-Revolution in Conflict Law? From Beale to Cavers*, 80 Harv. L. Rev. 377.

Ehrenzweig, Albert A. (1967, 1973, 1977) Private International Law, Dobbs Ferry, NY: Oceana.

Ehrenzweig, Albert A. (1971) *Conflict, Crisis and Confusion in Pennsylvania*, 9 Duquesne L. Rev. 459.

Ely, John H. (1981) *Choice of Law and the State's Interest in Protecting Its Own*, 23 Wm. & Mary L. Rev. 173.

Falconbridge, John D. (1931) *Renvoi and Succession to Movables*, 46 L.Q. Rev. 465; 47 L.Q. Rev. 271.

Falconbridge, John D. (1933) *Contract and Conveyance in the Conflict of Laws*, 81 U. PA. L. REV. 661.

Falconbridge, John D. (1937a) *Conflict of Laws: Examples of Characterization*, 15 CAN. B. REV. 215.

Falconbridge, John D. (1937b) *Characterization in the Conflict of Laws*, 53 L.Q. REV. 235.

Falconbridge, John D. (1941a) *The Renvoi and the Privy Council*, 19 CAN. BAR REV. 682.

Falconbridge, John D. (1941b) *Renvoi and the Law of the Domicile*, 19 CAN. BAR REV. 311.

Falconbridge, John D. (1942) *Immovables in the Conflict of Laws*, 20 CAN. BAR REV. 1.

Fawcett, J. J. (1982) *Is American Governmental Interest Analysis the Solution to English Tort Choice of Law Problems?*, 31 INT'L & COMP. L.Q. 150.

Felix, Robert L. (1971) *The Choice-of-Law Process at a Crossroads*, 9 DUQUESNE L. REV. 413.

Felix, Robert L. (1980) *American Conflicts Law:* American Conflicts Law, 31 S.C. L. REV. 423.

Fentiman, Richard (1985) *The Validity of Marriage and the Proper Law*, 44 CAMB. L.J. 256.

Fentiman, Richard (1992) *Foreign Law in English Courts*, 108 L.Q. REV. 142.

Finch, Michael S. (1995) *Choice-of-Law Problems in Florida Courts: A Retrospective on the* Restatement (Second), 24 STETSON L. REV. 653.

Fine, J. David (1980) *The Application of Issue-Analysis to Choice of Law Involving Family Law Matters in the United States*, 26 LOYOLA L. REV. 31.

Foley, Henry E. (1929) *Incorporation, Multiple Incorporation, and the Conflict of Laws*, 42 HARV. L. REV. 516.

Foley, Ridgway K., Jr. (1968) *Fragmentation in the Conflict of Laws*, 47 ORE. L. REV. 377.

Frankfurter, Felix (1943) *Joseph Henry Beale*, 56 HARV. L. REV. 701.

Franklin, Mitchell (1934) *The Historic Function of the American Law Institute: Restatement as Transitional to Codification*, 47 HARV. L. REV. 1367.

Freund, Paul A. (1946) *Chief Justice Stone and the Conflict of Laws*, 59 HARV. L. REV. 1210.

Friedler, Edith (1989) *Party Autonomy Revisited: A Statutory Solution to a Choice-of-Law Problem*, 37 KANS. L. REV. 471.

Friendly, Henry J. (1964) *In Praise of* Erie—*and of the New Federal Common Law*, 39 N.Y.U. L. REV. 383.

Gaillard, Emmanuel and Trautman, Donald T. (1987) *Trusts in Non-Trust Countries: Conflict of Laws and the Hague Convention on Trusts*, 35 AM. J. COMP. L. 307.

Gergen, Mark P. (1988a) *Equality and the Conflict of Laws*, 73 IOWA L. REV. 893.

Gergen, Mark P. (1988b) *Territoriality and the Perils of Formalism*, 86 MICH. L. REV. 1735.

Gilmore, Grant (1977) THE AGES OF AMERICAN LAW, New Haven: Yale University Press.

Goodrich, Herbert F. (1924) *Matrimonial Property and the Conflict of Laws*, 30 W. VA. L.Q. 61.

Goodrich, Herbert F. (1926) *Inheritance Problems in the Conflict of Laws*, 24 MICH. L. REV. 558.

Goodrich, Herbert F. (1930) *Public Policy in the Conflict of Laws*, 36 W. VA. L.Q. 156.

Goodrich, Herbert F. (1937) *Conflict of Laws Since the Restatement*, 23 A.B.A. J. 119.

Goodrich, Herbert F. (1938) HANDBOOK ON THE CONFLICT OF LAWS, 2nd ed. St. Paul: West Publishing Co.

Goodrich, Herbert F. (1941) *Five Years of Conflict of Laws*, 32 VA. L. REV. 295.

Goodrich, Herbert F. (1950) YIELDING PLACE TO NEW: REST VERSUS MOTION IN THE CONFLICT OF LAWS, New York: The Ass'n of the Bar of the City of New York.

Goodrich, Herbert F. (1951) *The Story of the American Law Institute*, 1951 WASH. U. L.Q. 283.

Gottesman, Michael H. (1991) *Draining the Dismal Swamp: The Case for Federal Choice of Law Statutes*, 80 GEO. L.J. 1.

Green, Michael S. (1995) *Legal Realism, Lex Fori, and the Choice-of-Law Revolution*, 104 YALE L.J. 967.

Greenberg, Herbert W. (1977) *Extrastate Enforcement of Tax Claims and Administrative Tax Determinations Under the Full Faith and Credit Clause*, 43 BKLYN. L. REV. 630.

Griswold, Erwin N. (1939a) *In Reply to Mr. Cowan's Views on Renvoi*, 87 U. PA. L. REV. 257.

Griswold, Erwin N. (1939b) Renvoi *Revisited*, 51 HARV. L. REV. 1165.

Griswold, Erwin N. (1943) *Mr. Beale and the Conflict of Laws*, 56 HARV. L. REV. 690.

Grossman, Margaret Rosso (1980) *Statutes of Limitations and the Conflict of Laws: Modern Analysis*, 1980 ARIZ. ST. L.J. 1.

Guedj, Thomas G. (1991) *The Theory of the* Lois de Police*, A Functional Trend in Continental Private International Law—A Comparative Analysis With Modern American Theories*, 39 AM. J. COMP. L. 661.

Hancock, Moffatt (1975) *Some Choice-of-Law Problems Posed by Antiguest Statutes: Realism in Wisconsin and Rule-Fetishism in New York*, 27 STAN. L. REV. 775.

Hancock, Moffatt (1984) STUDIES IN MODERN CHOICE-OF-LAW: TORTS, INSURANCE, LAND TITLES, Buffalo: Hein.

Hanotiau, Bernard (1982) *The American Conflicts Revolution and European Tort Choice-of-Law Thinking*, 30 AM. J. COMP. L. 73.

Harding, Arthur Leon (1937) *Joseph Henry Beale: Pioneer*, 2 MO. L. REV. 131.

Harper, Fowler (1947) *Policy Bases of the Conflict of Laws: Reflections on Rereading Professor Lorenzen's Essays*, 56 YALE L.J. 1155.

Haworth, Charles R. (1974) *The Mirror Image Conflicts Case*, 1974 WASH. U. L.Q. 1.

Hay, Peter (1983) *Full Faith and Credit and Federalism in Choice of Law*, 34 MERCER L. REV. 709.

Hay, Peter (1988) *Judicial Jurisdiction and Choice of Law: Constitutional Limitations*, 59 U. COLO. L. REV. 9.

Hay, Peter (1991) *Flexibility versus Predictability and Uniformity in Choice of Law*, 226 RECUEIL DES COURS 281.

Hay, Peter (1992a) *Conflicts of Law and State Competition in the Product Liability System*, 80 GEO. L.J. 617.

Hay, Peter (1992b) *The Recognition and Enforcement of American Money-Judgments in Germany—The 1992 Decision of the German Supreme Court*, 40 AM. J. COMP. L. 1001.

Hay, Peter and Muller-Freienfels, Wolfram (1979) *Agency in the Conflict of Laws and the 1978 Hague Convention*, 27 AM. J. COMP. L. 1.

Hay, Peter and Ellis, Robert B. (1993) *Bridging the Gap Between Rules and Approaches in Tort Choice of Law in the United States: A Survey of Current Case Law*, 27 INT'L LAW. 369.

Henkin, Louis (1964) *The Foreign Affairs Power of the Federal Courts:* Sabbatino, 64 COLUM. L. REV. 805.

Henkin, Louis (1972) FOREIGN AFFAIRS AND THE CONSTITUTION, Mineola, NY: Foundation Press.

Hernanz, Francisca (1990) *Recognition*—Exequatur:—*Of Foreign Judgments, Especially of U.S. Divorce Judgments in Spain*, 38 AM. J. COMP. L. 567.

Herzog, Peter E. (1992) *Constitutional Limits on Choice of Law*, 234 RECUEIL DES COURS 239.

Hill, Alfred (1981) *Choice of Law and Jurisdiction in the Supreme Court*, 81 COLUM. L. REV. 960.

Hill, Alfred (1985) *The Judicial Function in Choice of Law*, 85 COLUM. L. REV. 1585.

Hill, Alfred (1992) *After the Big Bang: Professor Sedler's Remaining Dilemma*, 38 WAYNE L. REV. 1471.

Holland, Maurice J. (1980) *Modernizing Res Judicata: Reflections on the* Parklane *Doctrine*, 55 IND. L.J. 615.

Homburger, Adolf (1970) *Recognition and Enforcement of Foreign Judgments*, 18 AM. J. COMP. L. 367.

Hopkins, Bert E. (1943) *Conflict of Laws in Administration of Decedents' Intangibles*, 28 IOWA L. REV. 422.

Horowitz, Harold W. (1967) *Toward a Federal Common Law of Choice of Law*, 14 UCLA L. REV. 1191.

Horowitz, Harold W. (1971) *The Commerce Clause as a Limitation on State Choice of Law Doctrine*, 84 HARV. L. REV. 806.

Horowitz, Harold W. (1974) *The Choice of Law in California—A Restatement*, 21 UCLA L. REV. 719.

Horowitz, Harold W. (1975) *Choice-of-Law Decisions Involving Slavery: "Interest Analysis" in the Early Nineteenth Century*, 17 UCLA L. REV. 587.

Hovermill, Joseph W. (1994) *A Conflict of Laws and Morals: The Choice of Law Implications of Hawaii's Recognition of Same-Sex Marriages*, 53 MD. L. REV. 450.

Huang, Jin and Qian, Andrew X. (1995) *"One Country, Two Systems," Three Law Families, and Four Legal Regions: The Emerging Inter-Regional Conflicts of Law in China*, 5 DUKE J. COMP. & INT'L LAW 289.

Hull, N. E. H. (1990) *Restatement and Reform: A New Perspective on the Origins of the American Law Institute*, 8 LAW & HISTORY REV. 55.

Ingrim, Christopher L. (1995) *Choice-of-Law Clauses: Their Effect on Extraterritorial Analysis—A Scholar's Dream, A Practitioner's Nightmare*, 28 CREIGHTON L. REV. 663.

Jackson, Robert H. (1945) *Full Faith and Credit—The Lawyer's Clause of the Constitution*, 45 COLUM. L. REV. 1.

Jaffrey, A. J. E. (1982) *The Foundations of Rules for the Choice of Law*, 2 OXFORD J. LEG. STUD. 368.

James, Louis C. (1972) *The Effects of the Commerce-Clause Constitutional Limitations on Parties' Intent Choice of Law in the Conflict-of-Laws of Commercial Contracts*, 21 AM. U. L. REV. 543.

Jayme (1989) *The American Conflicts Revolution and its Impact on European Private International Law*, pp. 15-27 in FORTY YEARS ON: THE EVOLUTION OF POSTWAR PRIVATE INTERNATIONAL LAW IN EUROPE, Deventer: Kluwer.

Johnston, Robert (1966) *Party Autonomy in Contracts Specifying Foreign Law*, 7 WM. & MARY L. REV. 37.

Juenger, Freidrich K. (1975) *Lessons Comparison Might Teach*, 23 AM. J. COMP. L. 742.

Juenger, Friedrich K. (1980) *Leflar's Contributions to American Conflicts Law*, 31 S.C. L. REV. 413.

Juenger, Friedrich K. (1981a) *Marital Property and the Conflict of Laws: A Tale of Two Countries*, 81 COLUM. L. REV. 1061.

Juenger, Friedrich K. (1981b) *Supreme Court Intervention in Jurisdiction and Choice of Law: A Dismal Prospect*, 14 U.C. DAVIS L. REV. 907.

Juenger, Friedrich K. (1982) *American and European Conflicts Law*, 30 AM. J. COMP. L. 117.

Juenger, Friedrich K. (1983) *A Page of History*, 35 MERCER L. REV. 419.

Juenger, Friedrich K. (1984) *Conflict of Law: A Critique of Interest Analysis*, 32 AM. J. COMP. L. 1.

Juenger, Friedrich K. (1985a) *General Course on Private International Law*, 193 RECUEIL DES COURS 9.

Juenger, Friedrich K. (1985b) *What Now?*, 46 OHIO ST. L.J. 509.

Juenger, Friedrich K. (1989a) *Mass Disasters and the Conflict of Laws*, 1989 U. ILL. L. REV. 105.

Juenger, Friedrich (1989b) *Choice of Law in Interstate Torts*, 118 U. PA. L. REV. 202.

Juenger, Friedrich K. (1992) *Conflict of Laws*, Ch. 17, pp. 411-37 in D. Clark and T. Ansay eds., INTRODUCTION TO THE LAW OF THE UNITED STATES.

Juenger, Friedrich K. (1993) CHOICE OF LAW AND MULTISTATE JUSTICE, Boston: Nijhoff.

Juenger, Friedrich K. (1994a) *The Complex Litigation Project's Tort Choice-of-Law Rules*, 54 LA. L. REV. 907.

Juenger, Friedrich K. (1994b) *The Inter-American Convention on the Law Applicable to International Contracts: Some Highlights and Comparisons*, 42 AM. J. COMP. L. 381.

Juenger, Friedrich K. (1995) *American Conflicts Scholarship and the New Law Merchant*, 28 VAND. J. TRANSNAT'L L. 487.

Kahn-Freund, O. (1968) *Delictual Liability and the Conflict of Laws*, 124 RECUEIL DES COURS 1.

Kalis, Peter J., Segerdahl, James R., and Waldron, John T., III (1994) *The Choice-of-Law Dispute in Comprehensive Environmental Coverage Litigation: Has Help Arrived from the American Law Institute Complex Litigation Project?*, 54 LA. L. REV. 925.

Kalman, Laura (1986) LEGAL REALISM AT YALE: 1927-1960, Chapel Hill: University of North Carolina Press.

Kane, Mary Kay (1991) *Drafting Choice of Law Rules for Complex Litigation: Some Preliminary Thoughts*, 10 REV. LITIG. 309.

Kanowitz, Leo (1978) *Comparative Impairment and Better Law: Grand Illusion in the Conflict of Laws*, 30 HASTINGS L.J. 255.

Kaplan, Stanley A. (1968) *Foreign Corporations and Local Corporate Policy*, 21 VAND. L. REV. 433.

Katzenbach, Nicholas de Belleville (1956) *Conflicts on an Unruly Horse: Reciprocal Claims and Tolerances in Interstate and International Law*, 65 YALE L.J. 1087.

Kay, Herma Hill (1980) *The Use of Comparative Impairment to Resolve True Conflicts: An Evaluation of the California Experience*, 68 CAL. L. REV. 577.

Kay, Herma Hill (1982) *Theory into Practice: Choice of Law in the Courts*, 34 MERCER L. REV. 521.

Kay, Herma Hill (1989) *A Defense of Currie's Governmental Interest Analysis*, 215 RECUEIL DES COURS 19.

Kirgis, Frederic L. (1976) *The Roles of Due Process and Full Faith and Credit in Choice of Law*, 62 CORNELL L. REV. 94.

Kogan, Terry S. (1987) *Toward a Jurisprudence of Choice of Law: The Priority of Fairness over Comity*, 62 N.Y.U. L. REV. 651.

Korn, Harold L. (1983) *The Choice Of Law Revolution: A Critique*, 83 COLUM. L. REV. 772.

Kozyris, P. John (1972) *No-Fault Automobile Insurance and the Conflict of Laws—Cutting the Gordian Knot Home-Style*, 1972 DUKE L.J. 331.

Kozyris, P. John (1973) *No-Fault Insurance and the Conflict of Laws—An Interim Update*, 1973 DUKE L.J. 1009.

Kozyris, P. John (1981) *Reflections on* Allstate—*The Lessening of Due Process in Choice of Law*, 14 U.C. DAVIS L. REV. 889.

Kozyris, P. John (1985a) *Corporate Wars and Choice of Law*, 1985 DUKE L.J. 1.

Kozyris, P. John (1985b) *Postscript: Interest Analysis Facing Its Critics—And, Incidentally, What Should Be Done About Choice of Law for Products Liability?*, 46 OHIO ST. L.J. 569.

Kozyris, John P. (1988) *Choice of Law in the American Courts in 1987: An Overview*, 36 AM. J. COMP. L. 547.

Kozyris, P. John (1989) *Some Observations on State Regulation of Multistate Takeovers—Controlling Choice of Law Through the Commerce Clause*, 14 DEL. J. CORP. L. 499.

Kozyris, P. John (1990) *Values and Methods in Choice of Law for Products Liability: A Comparative Comment on Statutory Solutions*, 38 AM. J. COMP. L. 475.

Kozyris, P. John (1994) *The Conflicts Provisions of the ALI's Complex Litigation Project: A Glass Half Full?*, 54 LA. L. REV. 953.

Kozyris, P. John and Symeonides, Symeon C. (1990) *Choice of Law in the American Courts in 1989: An Overview*, 38 AM. J. COMP. L. 601.

Kramer, Larry (1989a) *Interest Analysis and the Presumption of Forum Law*, 56 U. CHI. L. REV. 1301.

Kramer, Larry (1989b) *The Myth of the "Unprovided-For Case,"* 75 VA. L. REV. 1045.

Kramer, Larry (1990) *Rethinking Choice of Law*, 90 COLUM. L. REV. 277.

Kramer, Larry (1991a) *Choice of Law in the American Courts in 1990: Trends and Developments*, 39 AM. J. COMP. L. 465.

Kramer, Larry (1991b) *More Notes on Methods and Objectives in the Conflict of Laws*, 24 CORNELL INT'L L.J. 245.

Kramer, Larry (1991c) *On the Need for a Uniform Choice of Law Code*, 89 MICH. L. REV. 2134.

Kramer, Larry (1991d) *Return of the* Renvoi, 66 N.Y.U. L. REV. 979.

Kramer, Larry (1991e) *Vestiges of Beale: Extraterritorial Application of American Law*, 1991 SUP. CT. REV. 179.

Kramer, Larry (1995) *Extraterritorial Application of American Law After the Insurance Antitrust Case: A Reply to Professors Lowenfeld and Trimble*, 89 AM. J. INT'L. L. 750.

Kreimer, Seth F. (1992) *The Law of Choice and Choice of Law: Abortion, the Right to Travel and Extraterritorial Regulation in American Federalism*, 67 N.Y.U. L. REV. 451.

Kreimer, Seth F. (1993) *"But Whoever Treasures Freedom. . .": The Right to Travel and Extraterritorial Abortions*, 91 MICH. L. REV. 907.

Lando, Ole (1982) *New American Choice-of-Law Principles and the European Conflict of Laws of Contracts*, 30 AM. J. COMP. L. 19.

Laycock, Douglas (1987) *Equality and the Citizens of Sister States*, 15 FLA. ST. U. L. REV. 431.

Laycock, Douglas (1992) *Equal Citizens of Equal and Territorial States: The Constitutional Foundations of Choice of Law*, 92 COLUM. L. REV. 249.

Leach, W. Barton (1937) *The Restatements as They Were in the Beginning, Are Now, and Perhaps Henceforth Shall Be*, 23 A.B.A. J. 517.

Leflar, Robert A. (1932) *Extrastate Enforcement of Penal and Government Claims*, 46 HARV. L. REV. 193.

Leflar, Robert A. (1933) *Community Property and the Conflict of Laws*, 21 CALIF. L. REV. 221.

Leflar, Robert A. (1963) *Constitutional Limits on Free Choice of Law*, 28 LAW & CONTEMP. PROBS. 706.

Leflar, Robert A. (1966a) *Choice-Influencing Considerations in Conflicts Law*, 41 N.Y.U. L. REV. 267.

Leflar, Robert A. (1966b) *Conflicts Law: More on Choice-Influencing Considerations*, 54 CAL. L. REV. 1584.

Leflar, Robert A. (1972a) *The Torts Provisions of the* Restatement (Second), 72 COLUM. L. REV. 267.

Leflar, Robert A. (1972b) *The "New" Choice of Law*, 21 AM. U. L. REV. 457.

Leflar, Robert A. (1977a) *Choice-of-Law Statutes*, 44 TENN. L. REV. 951.

Leflar, Robert A. (1977b) *Choice of Law: A Well-Watered Plateau*, 41 LAW & CONTEMP. PROBS. 10.

LeflaR, Robert A. (1980) *A Response from the Author*, 31 S.C. REV. 457.

Leflar, Robert A. (1981a) *Choice of Law: State's Rights*, 10 HOFSTRA L. REV. 203.

Leflar, Robert A. (1981b) *Conflict of Laws Under the U.C.C.*, 35 ARK. L. REV. 87.

Leflar, Robert A. (1981c) *The Nature of Conflicts Law*, 81 COLUM. L. REV. 1080.

Leflar, Robert A. (1983) *The New Conflict-Limitations Act*, 35 MERCER L. REV. 461.

Leflar, Robert A., McDougal, Luther L., and Felix, Robert L. (1986) AMERICAN CONFLICTS LAW, 4th ed. Charlottesville, VA: Michie Co.

Lewis, Jeffrey E. (1974) *Mutuality in Conflict—Flexibility and Full Faith and Credit*, 23 DRAKE L. REV. 364.

Livermore, Samuel (1828) DISSERTATIONS ON THE QUESTIONS WHICH ARISE FROM THE CONTRARIETY OF THE POSITIVE LAWS OF DIFFERENT STATES AND NATIONS.

Lorenzen, Ernest G. (1910) *The* Renvoi *Theory and the Application of Foreign Law*, 10 COLUM. L. REV. 190.

Lorenzen, Ernest G. (1918) *The* Renvoi *Doctrine in the Conflict of Laws—Meaning of "The Law of a Country,"* 27 YALE L.J. 509.

Lorenzen, Ernest G. (1919) *The Statute of Limitations and the Conflict of Laws*, 28 YALE L.J. 492.

Lorenzen, Ernest G. (1921) *Validity and Effects of Contracts in the Conflict of Laws*, 30 Yale L.J. 565; 31 YALE L.J. 53.

Lorenzen, Ernest G. (1923a) *The Statute of Frauds and the Conflict of Laws*, 32 YALE L.J. 311.

Lorenzen, Ernest G. (1923b) *Polygamy and the Conflict of Laws*, 32 YALE L.J. 471.

Lorenzen, Ernest G. (1924) *Territoriality, Public Policy and the Conflict of Laws*, 33 YALE L. J. 736.

Lorenzen, Ernest G. (1931) *Tort Liability and the Conflict of Laws*, 47 L.Q. REV. 483.

Lorenzen, Ernest G. (1934) *Story's Commentaries on the Conflict of Laws—One Hundred Years After*, 48 HARV. L. REV. 15.

Lorenzen, Ernest G. (1941) *The Qualification, Classification, or Characterization Problem in the Conflict of Laws*, 50 YALE L.J. 743.

Lorenzen, Ernest G. (1947) SELECTED ARTICLES ON THE CONFLICT OF LAWS, New Haven: Yale Univ. Press.

Lowenfeld, Andreas F. (1972) *"Tempora Mutantur . . ."—Wills and Trusts in the Conflicts Restatement*, 72 COLUM. L. REV. 382.

Lowenfeld, Andreas F. (1982) Renvoi *Among the Law Professors: An American's View of the European View of American Conflict of Laws*, 30 AM. J. COMP. L. 99.

Lowenfeld, Andreas F. (1989a) *Conflict of Laws English Style—Review Essay*, 37 AM. J. COMP. L. 353.

Lowenfeld, Andreas F. (1989b) *Mass Torts and the Conflict of Laws: The Airline Disaster*, 1989 U. ILL. L. REV. 157.

Luneburg, William V. (1985) *Interest Analysis, Substantive Law-Making, and the Multistate Case*, 46 OHIO ST. L.J. 545.

Maier, Harold G. (1991) *Baseball and Chicken Salad: A Realistic Look at Choice of Law*, 44 VAND. L. REV. 827.

Maier, Harold G. (1993) *Finding the Trees in Spite of the Metaphorist: The Problem of State Interests in Choice of Law*, 56 ALB. L. REV. 753.

Maier, Harold G. and McCoy, Thomas R. (1991) *A Unifying Theory for Judicial Jurisdiction and Choice of Law*, 39 AM. J. COMP. L. 249.

Maltz, Earl M. (1988) *Visions of Fairness—The Relationship Between Jurisdiction and Choice of Law*, 30 ARIZ. L. REV. 751.

Maltz, Earl M. (1991) *Choice of Forum and Choice of Law in the Federal Courts: A Reconsideration of Erie Principles*, 79 KY. L.J. 231.

Marcus, Richard L. (1984) *Conflicts Among Circuits and Transfers Within the Federal Judicial System*, 93 YALE L.J. 677.

Martin, James A. (1976) *Constitutional Limitations on Choice of Law*, 61 CORNELL L. REV. 185.

Martin, James A. (1980a) *Personal Jurisdiction and Choice of Law*, 78 MICH. L. REV. 872.

Martin, James A., ed. (1980b) PERSPECTIVES ON CONFLICT OF LAWS: CHOICE OF LAW, Boston: Little Brown.

Martin, James A. (1980c) *Statutes of Limitations and Rationality in the Conflict of Laws*, 19 WASHBURN L.J. 405.

Martin, James A. (1981) *The Constitution and Legislative Jurisdiction*, 10 HOFSTRA L. REV. 133.

Martin, James A. (1983) *An Approach to the Choice of Law Problem*, 35 MERCER L. REV. 583.

Maslechko, William S. (1986) *Revolution and Counter-Revolution: "Interest Analysis" in the United States and its Relevance to Canadian Conflict of Laws*, 44 U. TORONTO FAC. L. REV. 57.

McClintock, H. L. (1930) *Distinguishing Substance and Procedure in the Conflict of Laws*, 78 U. PA. L. REV. 933.

McConnell, Michael W. (1988) *A Choice-of-Law Approach to Products-Liability Reform*, pp. 90-101 from Olson, Walter, ed. NEW DIRECTIONS IN LIABILITY LAW.

McDougal, Luther L., III (1979) *Comprehensive Interest Analysis Versus Reformulated Governmental Interest Analysis: An Appraisal in the Context of Choice-of-Law Problems Concerning Contributory and Comparative Negligence*, 26 UCLA L. REV. 439.

McDougal, Luther L., III (1984) *Toward Application of the Best Rule of Law in Choice of Law Cases*, 35 MERCER L. REV. 483.

McDougal, Luther L., III (1990) *"Private" International Law:* Ius Gentium *Versus Choice of Law Rules or Approaches*, 38 AM. J. COMP. L. 521.

McDougal, Luther L., III (1996) *Toward the Increased Use of Interstate and International Policies in Choice-of-Law Analysis in Tort Cases under the Second Restatement and Leflar's Choice-Influencing Considerations*, 70 TULANE L. REV. 2465.

McNulty, John K. (1967) *Corporations and the Intertemporal Conflict of Laws*, 55 CALIF. L. REV. 12.

McLaughlin, James Audley (1991a) *Conflict of Laws: The Choice of Law* Lex Loci *Doctrine, the Beguiling Appeal of a Dead Tradition, Part One*, 93 W. VA. L. REV. 957.

McLaughlin, James Audley (1991b) *Conflict of Laws: The New Approach to Choice of Law: Justice in Search of Certainty, Part Two*, 94 W. VA. L. REV. 73.

Merriman, John H. and Nafziger, James A. R. (1994) *The Private International Law of Cultural Property in the United States*, 42 AM. J. COMP. L. 221.

Miller, Arthur R. and Crump, David (1986) *Jurisdiction and Choice of Law in Multistate Class Actions After* Phillips Petroleum Co. v. Shutts, 96 YALE L.J. 1.

Milhollin, Gary L. (1975) *Interest Analysis and Conflicts Between Statutes of Limitations*, 27 HASTINGS L.J. 1.

Milner, Alan (1959) *Restatement: The Failure of a Legal Experiment*, 20 U. PITT. L. REV. 795.

Moore, James A. (1949) *Estate Administration and the Conflict of Laws*, 35 VA. L. REV. 316.

Morris, J. H. C. (1946) *The Choice of Law Clause in Statutes*, 62 L.Q. REV. 170.

Morris, J. H. C. (1951) *The Proper Law of a Tort*, 64 HARV. L. REV. 881.

Morris, J. H. C. (1953) *The Eclipse of the* Lex Loci *Solutions—A Fallacy Exploded*, 6 VAND. L. REV. 505.

Morris, J. H. C. (1973) *Law and Reason Triumphant: How Not to Review a Restatement*, 21 AM. J. COMP. L. 322.

Morris, J. H. C. and Cheshire, G. C. (1940) *The Proper Law of a Contract in the Conflict of Laws*, 56 L.Q. REV. 320.

Morrison, Mary Jane (1984) *Death of Conflicts*, 29 VILL. L. REV. 313.

Morse, C. G. J. (1984) *Choice of Law in Tort: A Comparative Survey*, 32 AM. J. COMP. L. 51.

Morse, Joseph (1949) *Characterization: Shadow or Substance*, 49 COLUM. L. REV. 1027.

Mosconi, Franco (1989) *Exceptions to the Operation of Choice of Law Rules*, 217 RECUEIL DES COURS 9.

Mulford, John (1939) *Conflict of Laws and Powers of Appointment*, 87 U. PA. L. REV. 403.

Mullenix, Linda S. (1992) *Federalizing Choice of Law of Mass-Tort Litigation*, 70 TEX. L. REV. 1623.

Mullenix, Linda S. (1996) MASS TORT LITIGATION: CASES AND MATERIALS, St. Paul: West Publishing Co.

Nadelmann, Kurt H. (1957) *Full Faith and Credit to Judgments and Public Acts*, 56 MICH. L. REV. 33.

Nadelmann, Kurt H. (1961) *Joseph Story's Contribution to American Conflicts Law: A Comment*, 5 AM. J. LEGAL HIST. 230.

Nadelmann, Kurt H. (1963) *Marginal Remarks on the New Trends in American Conflicts Law*, 28 LAW & CONTEMP. PROBS. 860.

Nadelmann, Kurt H. (1972) CONFLICT OF LAWS: INTERNATIONAL AND INTERSTATE, The Hague: Nijhoff.

Nafziger, James A. R. (1994) *Choice of Law in Air Disaster Cases: Complex Litigation Rules and the Common Law*, 54 LA. L. REV. 1001.

Neuhaus, Paul Heinrich (1963) *Legal Certainty Versus Equality in the Conflict of Laws*, 28 LAW & CONTEMP. PROPS. 795.

Neuman, Gerald L. (1987) *Territorial Discrimination, Equal Protection, and Self-Determination*, 135 U. PA. L. REV. 261.

Neuner, Robert (1942) *Policy Considerations in the Conflict of Laws*, 20 CAN. BAR REV. 479.

North, Peter M. (1990) *Reform But Not Revolution: General Course on Private International Law*, 220 RECUEIL DES COURS 9.

North, Peter M. and Fawcett, J. J. (1992) CHESHIRE AND NORTH'S PRIVATE INTERNATIONAL LAW, 12th ed. London: Butterworths.

Note (1929) *Tort Obligations: Liability for Injury in one State under Statute of Another State*, 27 MICH. L. REV. 462.

Note (1955a) *Applicability of State Conflicts Rules When Issues of State Law Arise in Federal Question Cases*, 68 HARV. L. REV. 1212.

Note (1955b) *Enforcement of Fair-Trade Laws in Non-Fair Trade Jurisdictions*, 22 U. CHI. L. REV. 525.

Note (1963) *Comments on* Babcock v. Jackson, *A Recent Development in Conflict of Laws (Cavers, Cheatham, Currie, Ehrenzweig, Leflar, Reese)*, 63 COLUM. L. REV. 1212.

Note (1966) *Marital Property and the Conflict of Laws: The Constitutionality of the "Quasi-Community Property" Legislation*, 54 CALIF. L. REV. 252.

Note (1967) *False Conflicts*, 55 Calif. L. Rev. 74.

Note (1969) *Post Transaction or Occurrence Events in Conflict of Laws*, 69 Colum. L. Rev. 843.

Note (1971) *American Slavery and the Conflict of Laws*, 71 Colum. L. Rev. 74.

Note (1977a) *Choice of Law in Federal Court after Transfer of Venue*, 63 Cornell L. Rev. 149.

Note (1977b) *Unconstitutional Discrimination in Choice of Law*, 77 Colum. L. Rev. 272.

Note (1980) *Sovereign Immunity in Sister-State Courts: Full Faith and Credit and Common Law Solutions*, 80 Colum. L. Rev. 1493.

Note (1981) *Power to Reverse Foreign Judgments: The British Clawback Statute Under International Law*, 81 Colum. L. Rev. 1097.

Note (1982a) *Comparative Impairment Reformed: Rethinking State Interests in the Conflict of Laws*, 95 Harv. L. Rev. 1079.

Note (1982b) *Effectiveness of Choice of Law Clauses in Contract Conflict of Law: Party Autonomy or Objective Determination?*, 82 Colum. L. Rev. 1659.

Note (1985) *New York Choice of Law Rule for Contractual Disputes: Avoiding the Unreasonable Results*, 71 Cornell L. Rev. 227.

Note (1987) *Modernizing the Situs Rule for Real Property Conflicts*, 65 Tex. L. Rev. 585.

Note (1989a) *Interest Analysis Applied to Corporations: The Unprincipled Use of Choice of Law Method*, 98 Yale L.J. 597.

Note (1989b) *Shopping for a Statute of Limitation*—Sun Oil Co. v. Wortman, 37 U. Kan. L. Rev. 423.

Note (1996) *Conflicts on the Net: Choice of Law in Transnational Cyperspace*, 29 Vand. J. Transnat'l L. 75.

Nussbaum, Arthur (1940) *Public Policy and the Political Crisis in the Conflict of Laws*, 49 Yale L.J. 1027.

Nussbaum, Arthur (1942) *Conflict Theories of Contracts; Cases Versus Restatement*, 51 Yale L.J. 893.

Nutting, Charles B. (1935) *Suggested Limitations of the Public Policy Doctrine*, 19 Minn. L. Rev. 196.

Nygh, Peter (1991) Conflict of Laws in Australia, 5th ed. Salem, NH: Butterworths.

Nygh, Peter (1995) *Choice-of-Law Rules and Forum Shopping in Australia*, 46 S.C. L. Rev. 899.

O'Brien, Bernard (1990) *Choice of Law in Torts*, 12 Adel. L. Rev. 449.

Oldham, J. Thomas (1987) *Conflict of Laws and Marital Property Rights*, 39 Baylor L. Rev. 1255.

Opeskin, Brian R. (1992) *Choice of Law in Torts and Limitation Statutes*, 108 L.Q. Rev. 398.

Organization of American States, Inter-American Convention on the Law Applicable to International Contracts, March 17, 1994, 33 reproduced in International Legal Materials, pp. 733-39.

Overton, Elvin Ellis (1943) *State Decisions in Conflict of Laws and Review by the United States Supreme Court under the Due Process Clause*, 22 ORE. L. REV. 109.

Owens, Edwin J. (1946) *The Judicial Process, Stare Decisis and the Restatements*, 21 CALIF. ST. B. J. 116.

Pascal, Robert A. (1940) *Characterization as an Approach to the Conflict of Laws*, 2 LA. L. REV. 715.

Paul, Roland A. (1965) *The Act of State Doctrine: Revived but Suspended*, 113 U. PA. L. REV. 691.

Paulsen, Monrad G. and Sovren, Michael I. (1956) *"Public Policy" in Conflict of Laws*, 56 COLUM. L. REV. 969.

Pelaez, Alfred S. (1971) *Interest Analysis—The Sands of Confusion*, 9 DUQUESNE L. REV. 446.

Peterson, Courtland H. (1972) *Foreign Country Judgments and the Second Restatement of Conflict of Laws*, 72 COLUM. L. REV. 220.

Peterson, Courtland H. (1981) *Proposals of Marriage Between Jurisdiction and Choice of Law*, 14 U.C. DAVIS L. REV. 869.

Peterson, Courtland H. (1988) *Jurisdiction and Choice of Law Revisited*, 59 U. COLO. L. REV. 37.

Peterson, Courtland H. (1990) *New Openness to Statutory Choice of Law Solutions*, 38 AM. J. COMP. L. 423.

Pielemeier, James R. (1987) *Why We Should Worry About Full Faith and Credit to Laws*, 60 S. CAL. L. REV. 1299.

Pielemeier, James R. (1994) *Some Hope for Choice of Law in Minnesota*, 18 HAMLINE L. REV. 8.

Pollack, Milton (1978) *Proof of Foreign Law*, 26 AM. J. COMP. L. 470.

Posnak, Bruce (1982) *Choice of Law: A Very-Well Curried Leflar Approach*, 34 MERCER L. REV. 731.

Posnak, Bruce (1988) *Choice of Law: Interest Analysis and Its "New Critics."* 36 AM. J. COMP. L. 681.

Posnak, Bruce (1989) *Choice of Law Rules v. Analysis: A More Workable Marriage Than the (Second) Restatement; A Very Well Curried Leflar Over Reese Approach*, 40 MERCER L. REV. 869.

Posnak, Bruce (1990) *The Court Doesn't Know Its* Asahi *From Its* Wortman: *A Critical View of the Constitutional Constraints of Jurisdiction and Choice of Law*, 41 Syracuse L. Rev. 875.

Posnak, Bruce (1994) *Choice of Law—Interest Analysis: They Still Don't Get It*, 40 WAYNE L. REV. 1121.

Posner, Richard A. (1985) THE FEDERAL COURTS: CRISIS AND REFORM, Cambridge: Harvard University Press.

Posner, Richard A. (1987) *The Decline of Law as an Autonomous Discipline: 1962-1987*, 100 HARV. L. REV. 761.

Posner, Richard A. (1992) ECONOMIC ANALYSIS OF LAW 4th ed. Boston: Little Brown.

Pound, Roscoe (1943) *Joseph Henry Beale*, 56 HARV. L. REV. 695.

Powers, William C., Jr. (1976) *Formalism and Nonformalism in Choice of Law Methodology*, 52 WASH. L. REV. 27.

Prebble, John (1973) *Choice of Law to Determine the Validity and Effect of Contracts: A Comparison of English and American Approaches to the Conflict of Laws*, 58 CORNELL L. REV. 433.

Prosser, William (1953) *Interstate Publication*, 51 MICH. L. REV. 959.

Pryles, Michael Charles (1971) *Impeachment of Sister State Judgments for Fraud*, 25 SW. L. J. 697.

Ragazzo, Robert A. (1995) *Transfer and Choice of Federal Law: The Appellate Model*, 93 MICH. L. REV. 703.

Ratner, James R. (1989) *Using Currie's Interest Analysis to Resolve Conflicts Between State Regulation and the Sherman Act*, 30 WM. & MARY L. REV. 705.

Redish, Martin H. (1989) *Federal Common Law, Political Legitimacy, and the Interpretive Process: An Institutionalist Perspective*, 83 NW. U. L. REV. 761.

Rees, John B. (1960) *American Wills Statutes: II*, 46 VA. L. REV. 856.

Reese, Willis L. M. (1952) *Full Faith and Credit to Statutes: The Defense of Public Policy*, 19 U. CHI. L. REV. 339.

Reese, Willis L. M. (1955) *Does Domicil Bear a Single Meaning?*, 55 COLUM. L. REV. 589.

Reese, Willis L. M. (1963) *Conflict of Laws and the* Restatement Second, 28 LAW & CONTEMP. PROBS. 679.

Reese, Willis L. M. (1971) *Chief Judge Fuld and Choice of Law*, 71 COLUM. L. REV. 548.

Reese, Willis L. M. (1972) *Choice of Law: Rules or Approach*, 57 CORNELL L. REV. 315.

Reese, Willis L. M. (1973) *Depecage: A Common Phenomenon in Choice of Law*, 73 COLUM. L. REV. 58.

Reese, Willis L. M. (1976) *General Course on Private International Law*, 150 RECUEIL DES COURS 1.

Reese, Willis L. M. (1977) *Marriage in American Conflict of Laws*, 26 INT'L & COMP. L.Q. 952.

Reese, Willis L. M. (1978) *Legislative Jurisdiction*, 78 COLUM. L. REV. 1587.

Reese, Willis L. M. (1981) *The* Hague *Case: An Opportunity Lost*, 10 HOFSTRA L. REV. 195.

Reese, Willis L. M. (1982a) *American Choice of Law*, 30 AM. J. COMP. L. 135.

Reese, Willis L. M. (1982b) The Second Restatement of Conflict of Laws Revisited, 34 MERCER L. REV. 501.

Reese, Willis L. M. (1982c) *The Law Governing Airplane Accidents*, 39 WASH. & LEE L. REV. 1303.

Reese, Willis L. M. (1986) *Substantive Policies and Choice of Law*, 2 TOURO L. REV. 1.

Reese, Willis L. M. and Kaufman, Edmund M. (1958) *The Law Governing Corporate Affairs: Choice of Law and the Impact of Full Faith and Credit*, 58 COLUM. L. REV. 1118.

Reese, Willis L. M. and Flesch, Alma Suzin (1960) *Agency and Vicarious Liability in Conflict of Laws*, 60 COLUM. L. REV. 764.

Reese, Willis L. M. and Leiwant, Barry D. (1977) *Testimonial Privileges and Conflict of Laws*, 41 LAW & CONTEMP. PROB. 85.

Reese, Willis L. M., Rosenberg, Maurice, and Hay, Peter (1995) CONFLICT OF LAWS—CASES AND MATERIALS: 1995 Supplement.

Reiblich, G. Kenneth (1938) *The Conflict of Laws Philosophy of Mr. Justice Holmes*, 28 GEORGETOWN L.J. 1.

Reimann, Mathais (1995) CONFLICT OF LAWS IN WESTERN EUROPE: A GUIDE THROUGH THE JUNGLE, Irvington, New York: Transnational Publishers, Inc.

Rendleman, Doug (1981) McMillan v. McMillan: *Choice of Law in a Sinkhole*, 67 VA. L. REV. 315.

Reppy, William A. (1983) *Eclecticism in Choice of Law: Hybrid Method or Mishmash?*, 34 MERCER L. REV. 645.

Reynolds, William L. (1994) *The Iron Law of Full Faith and Credit*, 53 MD. L. REV. 412.

Rheinstein, Max (1944) *The Place of Wrong: A Study in the Method of Case Law*, 19 TULANE L. REV. 4.

Rheinstein, Max (1951) *Conflict of Laws in the Uniform Commercial Code*, 16 LAW & CONTEMP. PROB. 114.

Rheinstein, Max (1962) *How to Review a Festschrift*, 11 AM. J. COMP. L. 632.

Rheinstein, Max (1965) *Ehrenzweig on the Law of Conflict of Laws*, 18 OKLA. L. REV. 238.

Richman, William M. (1982) *Diagramming Conflicts: A Graphic Understanding of Interest Analysis*, 43 OHIO ST. L.J. 317.

Richman, William M. and Reynolds, William L. (1993) UNDERSTANDING CONFLICT OF LAWS, 2nd ed. New York: Bender.

Risinger, D. Michael (1982) *"Substance" and "Procedure" Revisited with Some Afterthoughts on the Constitutional Problem of Irrebuttable Presumptions*, 30 UCLA L. REV. 189.

Robertson, A. H. (1940) CHARACTERIZATION IN THE CONFLICT OF LAWS, Cambridge: Harvard Univ. Press.

Rosenberg, Maurice (1967a) *Two Views on* Kell v. Henderson: *A Comment*, 67 COLUM. L. REV. 459.

Rosenberg, Maurice (1967b) *Comments on* Reich v. Purcell, 15 UCLA L. REV. 551.

Rosenberg, Maurice (1980) *A Comment on* Neumeier, 31 S.C. L. REV. 443.

Rosenberg, Maurice (1981) *The Comeback of Choice of Law Rules*, 81 COLUM. L. REV. 946.

Ross, G. W. C. (1931) *Has the Conflict of Laws Become a Branch of Constitutional Law?*, 15 MINN. L. REV. 161.

Sack, A. N. (1933) *Non-Enforcement of Foreign Revenue Laws*, 81 U. Pa. L. Rev. 559.

Sass, Stephen L. (1981) *Foreign Law in Federal Courts*, 29 Am. J. Comp. L. 97.

Scheffler, Samuel, ed. (1988) Consequentialism and its Critics, New York: Oxford Univ. Press.

Schlesinger, Rudolf B. (1973) *A Recurrent Problem in Transnational Litigation: The Effect of a Failure to Invoke or Prove the Applicable Foreign Law*, 59 Cornell. L. Rev. 1.

Schmertz (1978) *The Establishment of Foreign and International Law in American Courts: A Procedural Overview*, 18 Va. J. Int'l L. 665.

Schreiber, Ernst O. (1918) *The Doctrine of the* Renvoi *in Anglo-American Law*, 31 Harv. L. Rev. 523.

Scoles, Eugene F. (1955a) *Conflict of Laws and Elections in the Administration of Decedents' Estates*, 30 Ind. L.J. 293.

Scoles, Eugene F. (1955b) *Conflict of Laws and Nonbarrable Interests in Administration of Decedents' Estates*, 8 U. Fla. L. Rev. 151.

Scoles, Eugene F. (1957) *Conflict of Laws and Creditors' Rights in Decedents' Estates*, 42 Iowa L. Rev. 341.

Scoles, Eugene F. and Hay, Peter (1992) Conflict of Laws, 2nd ed. St. Paul: West Publishing Co.

Scott, Austin W. (1964) *Spendthrift Trusts and the Conflict of Laws*, 77 Harv. L. Rev. 845.

Sedler, Robert A. (1971) *The Territorial Imperative: Automobile Accidents and the Significance of a State Line*, 9 Duquesne. L. Rev. 394.

Sedler, Robert A. (1972) *The Contracts Provisions of the* Restatement (Second)*: An Analysis and a Critique*, 72 Colum. L. Rev. 279.

Sedler, Robert A. (1973) *Interstate Accidents and the Unprovided for Case: Reflections on* Neumeier v. Kuehner, 1 Hofstra L. Rev. 125.

Sedler, Robert A. (1977) *Rules of Choice of Law Versus Choice-of-Law Rules: Judicial Method in Conflicts Torts Cases*, 44 Tenn. L. Rev. 975.

Sedler, Robert A. (1981a) *Constitutional Limitations on Choice of Law: The Perspective of Constitutional Generalism*, 10 Hofstra L. Rev. 59.

Sedler, Robert A. (1981b) *Reflections on Conflict of Laws Methodology*, 32 Hastings L.J. 1628.

Sedler, Robert A. (1982) *Interest Analysis and Forum Preference in the Conflict of Laws: A Response to the "New Critics,"* 34 Mercer L. Rev. 593.

Sedler, Robert A. (1985) *Interest Analysis as the Preferred Approach to Choice of Law: A Response to Professor Brilmayer's "Foundational Attack,"* 46 Ohio St. L.J. 483.

Sedler, Robert A. (1989) Across State Lines: Applying the Conflict of Laws to Your Practice, Chicago: ABA.

Sedler, Robert A. (1990) *Professor Juenger's Challenge to the Interest Analysis Approach to Choice of Law: An Appreciation and a Response*, 23 U.C. Davis L. Rev. 865.

Sedler, Robert A. (1992) *Continuity, Precedent, and Choice of Law: A Reflective Response to Professor Hill*, 38 WAYNE L. REV. 1419.

Sedler, Robert A. (1994a) *Interest Analysis, Party Expectations and Judicial Method in Conflicts Torts Cases: Reflections on* Cooney v. Osgood Machinery, 59 BROOK. L. REV. 1323.

Sedler, Robert A. (1994b) *The Complex Litigation Project's Proposal for Federally-Mandated Choice of Law in Mass Tort Cases: Another Assault on State Sovereignty*, 54 LA. L. REV. 1085.

Sedler, Robert A. and Twerski, Aaron D. (1989) *The Case Against All-Encompassing Federal Mass Tort Legislation: Sacrifice Without Gain*, 73 MARQ. L. REV. 76.

Sedler, Robert A. and Twerski, Aaron D. (1990) *State Choice of Law in Mass Tort Cases: A Response to "A View from the Legislature,"* 73 MARQ. L. REV. 625.

Seidelson, David E. (1971) *Comment on* Cipolla v. Shaposka, 9 DUQUESNE L. REV. 423.

Seidelson, David E. (1981) *Interest Analysis: The Quest for Perfection and the Frailties of Man*, 19 DUQUESNE. L. REV. 207.

Seidelson, David E. (1988) *Interest Analysis or the* Restatement Second *of Conflicts: Which is the Preferable Approach to Resolving Choice-of-Law Problems?*, 27 DUQUESNE L. REV. 73.

Seidelson, David E. (1991) *1 (*Wortman*) + 1 (*Ferens*) = 6 (Years): That Can't be Right—Can It? Statutes of Limitations and Supreme Court Inconsistency*, 57 BROOK. L. REV. 787.

Seidelson, David E. (1992) *Resolving Choice-of-Law Problems Through Interest Analysis in Personal Injury Actions: A Suggested Order of Priority Among Competing State Interests and Among Available Techniques for Weighing Those Interests*, 30 DUQUESNE. L. REV. 869.

Seidelson, David E. (1994) *Section 6.01 of the ALI's Complex Litigation Project: Function Follows Form*, 54 LA. L. REV. 1111.

Shaman, Jeffrey M. (1980) *The Choice of Law Process: Territorialism and Functionalism*, 22 WM. & MARY L. REV. 227.

Shapira, Amos (1970) THE INTEREST APPROACH TO CHOICE OF LAW, The Hague: Nijhoff.

Shapira, Amos (1973) *"Manna for the Entire World" or "Thou Shalt Love Thy Neighbor as Thyself"—Comment on* Neumeier v. Kuehner, 1 HOFSTRA L. REV. 168.

Shapira, Amos (1977) *"Grasp All, Lose All": On Restraint and Moderation in the Reformulation of Choice of Law Policy*, 77 COLUM. L. REV. 248.

Shapiro, James A. (1992) *Choice of Law Under the Federal Tort Claims Act:* Richards *and* Renvoi *Revisited*, 70 N.C. L. REV. 641.

Shreve, Gene R. (1982) *In Search of Choice-of-Law Reviewing Standard—Reflections on* Allstate Insurance Co. v. Hague, 66 MINN. L. REV. 327.

Shreve, Gene R. (1985) *Currie's Governmental Interest Analysis—Has It Become a Paper Tiger?*, 46 OHIO ST. L.J. 541.

Shreve, Gene R. (1986) *Preclusion and Federal Choice of Law*, 64 TEX. L. REV. 1209.

Shreve, Gene R. (1987) *Interest Analysis as Constitutional Law*, 48 OHIO ST. L.J. 51.

Shreve, Gene R. (1991) *Pragmatism Without Politics—A Half Measure of Authority for Jurisdictional Common Law*, 1991 B.Y.U. L. REV. 767.

Shreve, Gene R. (1992a) *Judgments from a Choice of Law Perspective*, 40 AM. J. COMP. L. 985.

Shreve, Gene R. (1992b) *Teaching Conflicts, Improving the Odds*, 90 MICH. L. REV. 1672.

Shreve, Gene R. (1993) *Conflicts Law—State or Federal?*, 68 IND. L.J. 907.

Shreve, Gene R. (1994) *Reform Aspirations of the Complex Litigation Project*, 54 LA. L. REV. 1139.

Shreve, Gene R. (1996a) *Choice of Law and the Forgiving Constitution*, 71 IND. L.J. 271.

Shreve, Gene R. (1996b) *The Odds Against Teaching Conflicts*, 27 U. TOLEDO L. REV. 587.

Shreve, Gene R. and Raven-Hansen, Peter (1994) UNDERSTANDING CIVIL PROCEDURE, 2nd ed. New York: Bender.

Siehr, Kurt G. (1982) *Domestic Relations in Europe: European Equivalents to American Evolutions*, 30 AM. J. COMP. L. 37.

Silberman, Linda J. (1978) Shafffer v. Heitner: *End of an Era*, 53 N.Y.U. L. REV. 33.

Silberman, Linda J. (1983) *Can the State of Minnesota Bind the Nation? Federal Choice of Law Constraints After* Allstate Insurance Co. v. Hague, 10 HOFSTRA L. REV. 103.

Silberman, Linda J. (1994) Cooney v. Osgood Machinery, Inc.: *A Less than Complete "Contribution."* 59 BROOK. L. REV. 1367.

Silberman, Linda J. (1995) *Judicial Jurisdiction in the Conflict of Laws Course: Adding a Comparative Dimension*, 28 VAND. J. TRANSNAT'L L. 389.

Simson, Gary J. (1978) *State Autonomy in Choice of Law: A Suggested Approach*, 52 S. CAL. L. REV. 61.

Simson, Gary J. (1991) *Plotting the Next "Revolution" in Choice of Law: A Proposed Approach*, 24 CORNELL INT'L L.J. 279.

Simson, Gary J. (1993) *The* Neumeier-Schultz *Rules: How Logical A "Next Stage in the Evolution of the Law" After* Babcock?, 56 ALBANY L. REV. 913.

Singer, Joseph W. (1989) *Real Conflicts*, 69 B.U. L. REV. 1.

Singer, Joseph W. (1990) *A Pragmatic Guide to Conflicts*, 70 B.U. L. REV. 731.

Singer, Joseph W. (1991) *Facing Real Conflicts*, 24 CORNELL INT'L. L.J. 197.

Smith (1987) *Choice of Law in the United States*, 38 HASTINGS L.J. 1041.

Solimine, Michael E. (1989) *An Economic and Empirical Analysis of Choice of Law*, 24 GA. L. REV. 49.

Solimine, Michael E. (1992) *Choice of Law in the American Courts in 1991*, 40 AM. J. COMP. L. 951.

Sprankling, John G. and Lanyi, George R. (1983) *Pleading and Proof of Foreign Law in American Courts*, 19 STAN. J. INT'L L. 3.

Stephan, Paul B., Wallace, Don, Jr., and Roin, Julie A. (1993) INTERNATIONAL BUSINESS AND ECONOMICS: LAW AND POLICY, Charlottesville, VA: Michie Co.

Sterk, Stewert E. (1977) *Testimonial Privileges: An Analysis of Horizontal Choice of Law Problems*, 61 MINN. L. REV. 461.

Sterk, Stewart E. (1994) *The Marginal Relevance of Choice of Law Theory*, 142 U. PA. L. REV. 949.

Stimson, Edward S. (1942) *Law Applicable to Marriage*, 16 U. CINN. L. REV. 81.

Stimson, Edward S. (1950) *Simplifying the Conflict of Laws: A Bill Proposed for Enactment by the Congress*, 36 A.B.A. J. 1003.

Stone, O. M. (1955) *Reciprocity and Common Form in the Conflict of Laws*, 18 MOD. L. REV. 177.

Storke, Frederic P. (1959) *Annulment in the Conflict of Laws*, 43 MINN. L. REV. 849.

Story, Joseph (1834) COMMENTARIES ON THE CONFLICT OF LAWS, Boston: Hilliard, Gray & Co.

Stumberg, George W. (1932) *Marital Property and Conflict of Laws*, 11 TEX. L. REV. 53.

Stumberg, George W. (1963) PRINCIPLES OF CONFLICT OF LAWS, 3rd ed. Brooklyn: Foundation Press.

Swabenland, Walter W. (Land) (1938) *The Conflict of Laws in Administration of Express Trusts of Personal Property*, 45 YALE L.J. 438.

Swan, John (1991) *Choice of Law in Contracts*, 19 CAN. BUS. L.J. 213.

Swan, John (1995) *Federalism and the Conflict of Laws: The Curious Position of the Supreme Court of Canada*, 46 S.C. L. REV. 923.

Sykes, Edward I. and Pryles, Michael C. (1991) AUSTRALIAN PRIVATE INTERNATIONAL LAW, 3rd ed. Sydney: The Law Book Co., Ltd.

Symeonides, Symeon C. (1985) *Revolution and Counter-Revolution in American Conflicts Law: Is There a Middle Ground?*, 46 OHIO ST. L.J. 549.

Symeonides, Symeon C. (1987) *Louisiana's Draft on Successions and Marital Property*, 35 AM. J. COMP. L. 259.

Symeonides, Symeon (1989a) *Choice of Law in the American Courts in 1988*, 37 AM. J. COMP. L. 457.

Symeonides, Symeon C. (1989b) *The New Swiss Conflicts Codification: An Introduction*, 37 AM. J. COMP. L. 187.

Symeonides, Symeon C. (1990a) *Problems and Dilemmas in Codifying Choice of Law for Torts: The Louisiana Experience in Comparative Perspective*, 38 AM. J. COMP. L. 431.

Symeonides, Symeon C. (1990b) *Revising Puerto Rico's Conflicts Law: A Preview*, 28 COLUM. J. TRANSNAT'L L. 413.

Symeonides, Symeon C. (1992) *Louisiana's New Law of Choice of Law for Torts Conflicts: An Exegesis*, 66 TUL. L. REV. 677.

Symeonides, Symeon C. (1993) *Private International Codification in a Mixed Jurisdiction: The Louisiana Experience*, RABEL ZEITSCHRIFT pp. 460-507, Max-Planck Institut.

Symeonides, Symeon C. (1994a) *Choice of Law in the American Courts in 1993 (and in the Six Previous Years)*, 42 AM. J. COMP. L. 599.

Symeonides, Symeon C. (1994b) *Exception Clauses in American Conflicts Law*, 42 AM J. COMP. L. (SUPPLEMENTS) 813.

Symeonides, Symeon C. (1994c) *The ALI's Complex Litigation Project: Commencing the National Debate*, 54 LA. L. REV. 843.

Symeonides, Symeon C. (1995) *Choice of Law in the American Courts in 1994: A View "From the Trenches,"* 43 AM. J. COMP. L. 1.

Symeonides, Symeon C. (1996) *Choice of Law in the American Courts in 1995: A Year in Review*, 44 AM. J. COMP. L. 181.

Symposium (1968) *Comments on* Reich v. Purcell, 15 UCLA L. REV. 552.

Symposium (1973) Neumeier v. Kuehner: *A Conflicts Conflict*, 1 HOFSTRA L. REV. 93.

Symposium (1985) *Interest Analysis in Conflicts of Laws: An Inquiry into Fundamentals with a Side Glance at Products Liability*, 46 OHIO ST. L.J. 457.

Symposium (1995a) *Conference on Jurisdiction, Justice, and Choice of Law for the Twenty-First Century—Case One: Choice of Forum Clauses*, 29 NEW ENG. L. REV. 517.

Symposium (1995b) *Conference on Jurisdiction, Justice, and Choice of Law for the Twenty-First Century—Case Two: Extraterritorial Application of United States Law Against United States and Alien Defendants*, 29 NEW ENG. L. REV. 577.

Symposium (1995c) *Conference on Jurisdiction, Justice, and Choice of Law for the Twenty-First Century—Case Four: Choice of Law Theory*, 29 NEW ENG. L. REV. 669.

Symposium (1997) *Twenty-Fifth Anniversary of the Restatment (Second)*, 56 MD. L. REV. (No. 4, forthcoming).

Symposium (1997) *Conflict of Laws*, 48 MERCER. L. REV. (No. 2, forthcoming).

Szladits, Charles (1984) *Foreign Law in English*, 32 AM. J. COMP. L. 213.

Talyor, E. Hunter (1978) *Uniformity of Commercial Law and State-by-State Enactment: A Confluence of Contradictions*, 30 HASTINGS L.J. 337.

Thatcher, Charles M. (1990) *Choice of Law in Multi-State Tort Actions After* Owen v. Owen: *The Less Things Change . . .*, 35 S.D. L. REV. 372 (1990).

Tier, Akolda M. (1990) *Conflict of Laws and Legal Pluralism in the Sudan*, 39 INT'L & COMP. L.Q. 611.

Todd, John J. (1980) *A Judge's View*, 31 S.C. L. REV. 435.

Trautman, Donald T. (1967) *Two Views on* Kell v. Henderson: *A Comment*, 67 COLUM. L. REV. 465.

Trautman, Donald T. (1977) *The Relation Between American Choice of Law and Federal Common Law*, 41 LAW & CONTEMP. PROBS. 105.

Trautman, Donald T. (1984) *Some Notes on the Theory of Choice of Law Clauses*, 35 MERCER L. REV. 535.

Trautman, Donald T. (1992) *Towards Federalizing Choice of Law*, 70 TEX. L. REV. 1715.

Trautman, Donald T. (1994) *Some Thoughts on Choice of Law, Judicial Discretion, and the ALI's Complex Litigation Project*, 54 LA. L. REV. 835.

Twerski, Aaron D. (1971) *Enlightened Territorialism and Professor Cavers—The Pennsylvania Method*, 9 DUQUESNE. L. REV. 373.

Twerski, Aaron D. (1973) Neumeier v. Kuehner: *Where are the Emperor's Clothes?*, 1 HOFSTRA L. REV. 104.

Twerski, Aaron D. (1981) *On Territoriality and Sovereignty: System Shock and Constitutional Choice of Law*, 10 HOFSTRA L. REV. 149.

Twerski, Aaron D. (1994) *A Sheep in Wolf's Clothing: Territorialism in the Guise of Interest Analysis in* Cooney v. Osgood Machinery, Inc., 59 BROOK. L. REV. 1351.

Twerski, Aaron D. and Mayer, Renee G. (1979) *Toward a Pragmatic Solution of Choice-of-Law Problems—At the Interface of Substance and Procedure*, 74 NW. U. L. REV. 781.

United Nations (May, 1980) *Conference on Contracts for the International Sale of Goods*, XIX INT'L LEGAL MATERIALS, No. 3, p. 668.

Valladao, Haroldo (1954) *The Influence of Joseph Story on Latin American Rules of Conflict Laws*, 3 AM. J. COMP. L. 27.

Van Couter, (1995) Barkanic: *The New York Choice-of-Law Method and Recovery for Air Crashes Abroad*, 60 J. AIR L. & COM. 759.

Vargas, Jorge A. (1994) *Conflict of Laws in Mexico: The New Rules Introduced by the 1988 Amendments*, 28 INT'L LAWYER 659.

Vazquez, Carlos Manuel (1995) *The Four Doctrines of Self-Executing Treaties*, 89 AM. J. INT'L L. 695.

Vernon, David H., Weinberg, Louise, Reynolds, William L. and Richman, William M. (1990) CONFLICT OF LAWS: CASES, MATERIALS AND PROBLEMS, New York: Bender.

Vitta, Edoardo (1982) *The Impact in Europe of the American "Conflicts Revolution"*, 30 AM. J. COMP. L. 1.

Von Mehren, Arthur T. (1961) *The* Renvoi *and Its Relation to Various Approaches to the Choice-of-Law Problem*, pp. 395-408 in K. Nadelmann, et al., eds. XXTH CENTURY COMPARATIVE AND CONFLICTS LAW: LEGAL ESSAYS IN HONOR OF HESSELL E. YNTEMA, Leyden: A. W. Sythoff.

Von Mehren, Arthur T. (1974) *Special Substantive Rules for Multistate Problems: Their Role and Significance in Contemporary Choice of Law Methodology*, 88 HARV. L. REV. 347.

Von Mehren, Arthur T. (1975) *Recent Trends in Choice of Law Methodology*, 60 CORNELL L. REV. 927.

Von Mehren, Arthur T. (1977) *Choice of Law and the Problem of Justice*, 41 LAW & CONTEMP. PROBS. 27.

Von Mehren, Arthur T. (1981) *Recognition and Enforcement of Sister-State Judgments: Reflections on General Theory and Current Practice in the European Economic Community and the United States*, 81 COLUM. L. REV. 1044.

Von Mehren, Arthur T. (1993) *Recognition of United States Judgments Abroad and Foreign Judgments in the United States: Would an International Convention Be Useful?*, RABEL ZEITSCHRIFt, pp. 450-59 Max-Planck-Institut.

Von Mehren, Arthur T. and Trautman, Donald T. (1965) THE LAW OF MULTISTATE PROBLEMS: CASES AND MATERIALS ON CONFLICT OF LAWS, Boston: Little, Brown.

Von Mehren, Arthur T. and Trautman, Donald T. (1966) *Jurisdiction to Adjudicate: A Suggested Analysis*, 79 HARV. L. REV. 1121.

Von Mehren, Arthur T. and Trautman, Donald T. (1981) *Constitutional Control of Choice of Law: Some Reflections on* Hague, 10 HOFSTRA L. REV. 35.

Wade, J. A. (1983) *Domicile: A Re-Examination of Certain Rules*, 32 INT'L & COMP. L.Q. 1.

Watson, Alan (1992) JOSEPH STORY AND THE COMITY OF ERRORS: A CASE STUDY IN CONFLICT OF LAWS, Athens: Univ. Georgia Press.

Wechsler, Herbert (1969) *The Course of the Restatements*, 55 A.B.A. J. 147.

Weinberg, Louise (1982) *Choice of Law and Minimal Scrutiny*, 49 U. CHI. L. REV. 440.

Weinberg, Louise (1983) *On Departing From Forum Law*, 35 MERCER L. REV. 595.

Weinberg, Louise (1988) *The Place of Trial and the Law Applied: Overhauling Constitutional Theory*, 59 U. COLO. L. REV. 67.

Weinberg, Louise (1989a) *Federal Common Law*, 83 NW. U. L. REV. 805.

Weinberg, Louise (1989b) *The Curious Notion that the Rules of Decision Act Blocks Supreme Federal Common Law*, 83 NW. U. L. REV. 860.

Weinberg, Louise (1991a) *Against Comity*, 80 GEO. L.J. 53.

Weinberg, Louise (1991b) *Choosing Law: The Limitations Debate*, 1991 U. ILL. L. REV. 683.

Weinberg, Louise (1992) *The Federal-State Conflict of Laws: "Actual" Conflicts*, 70 TEX. L. REV. 1743.

Weinberg, Louise (1993) *Mass Torts at the Neutral Forum: A Critical Analysis of the ALI's Proposed Choice Rule*, 56 ALBANY L. REV. 807.

Weinberger, Alan D. (1976) *Party Autonomy and Choice-of- Law: The Restatement (Second), Interest Analysis, and the Search for Methodological Synthesis*, 4 HOFSTRA L. REV. 605.

Weintraub, Russell J. (1961) *The Contracts Proposals of the Second Restatement of Laws — A Critique*, 46 IOWA L. REV. 713.

Weintraub, Russell J. (1964) *The* Erie *Doctrine and State Conflict of Laws Rules*, 39 IND. L.J. 228.

Weintraub, Russell J. (1965) *An Inquiry into the Utility of "Domicile" as a Concept in Conflicts Analysis*, 63 MICH. L. REV. 961.

Weintraub, Russell J. (1966) *An Inquiry into the Utility of "Situs" As a Concept in Conflicts Analysis*, 52 CORNELL L.Q. 1.

Weintraub, Russell J. (1974) *Beyond Depecage: A "New Rule" Approach to Choice of Law in Consumer Credit Transactions and a Critique of the Territorial Application of the Uniform Consumer Credit Code*, 25 CASE WESTERN RES. L. REV. 16.

Weintraub, Russell J. (1977) *The Future of Choice of Law for Torts: What Principles Should be Preferred?*, 41 LAW & CONTEMP. PROBS. 146.

Weintraub, Russell J. (1981) *Who's Afraid of Constitutional Limitations on Choice of Law?*, 10 HOFSTRA L. REV. 17.

Weintraub, Russell J. (1984a) *Due Process Limitations on the Personal Jurisdiction of State Courts: Time for a Change*, 63 OR. L. REV. 485.

Weintraub, Russell J. (1984b) *Interest Analysis in the Conflict of Laws as an Application of Sound Legal Reasoning*, 35 MERCER L. REV. 629.

Weintraub, Russell J. (1985) *A Defense of Interest Analysis in the Conflict of Laws and the Use of that Analysis in Products Liability*, 46 OHIO ST. L.J. 493.

Weintraub, Russell J. (1986) COMMENTARY ON THE CONFLICT OF LAWS, 3rd ed. Mineola, NY: Foundation Press.

Weintraub, Russell J. (1989) *Methods for Resolving Conflict-of-Laws Problems in Mass Tort Litigation*, 1989 U. ILL. L. REV. 129.

Weintraub, Russell J. (1990) *The Contributions of Symeonides and Kozyris to Making Choice of Law Predictable and Just: An Appreciation and Critique*, 38 AM. J. COMP. L. 511.

Weintraub, Russell J. (1992) *The Extraterritorial Application of Antitrust & Security Laws: An Inquiry into the Utility of a "Choice-of-Law" Approach*, 70 TEX. L. REV. 1799.

Weintraub, Russell J. (1993) *An Approach to Choice of Law that Focuses on Consequences*, 56 ALB. L. REV. 701.

Weintraub, Russell J. (1994a) *Choosing Law with an Eye on the Prize*, 15 MICH. J. INT'L L. 705 (1994).

Weintraub, Russell J. (1994b) Hartford Fire Insurance Co., *Comity and the Extraterritorial Reach of United States Antitrust Law*, 29 TEX. INT'L L.J. 427.

Weisberger (1987) *Selected Conflict of Laws Issues in Wisconsin's New Marital (Community) Property Act*, 35 AM. J. COMP. L. 295.

Wengler, Wilhelm (1963) *The Significance of the Principle of Equality in the Conflict of Laws*, 28 LAW & CONTEMP. PROBS. 822.

Westbrook, James E. (1975) *A Survey and Evaluation of Competing Choice-of-Law Methodologies: The Case for Eclecticism*, 40 MO. L. REV. 407.

Whitten, Ralph U. (1981a) *The Constitutional Limitation on State Court Jurisdiction: A Historical Interpretive Reexamination of the Full Faith and Credit and Due Process Clauses*, 14 CREIGHTON L. REV. 499.

Whitten, Ralph U. (1981b) *The Constitutional Limitations on State Choice of Law: Full Faith and Credit*, 12 MEM. ST. U. L. REV. 1.

Whitten, Ralph U. (1982) *The Constitutional Limitations on State Choice of Law: Due Process*, 9 HASTINGS CONST. L.Q. 851.

Wickersham, George W. (1927) *The American Law Institute and the Projected Restatement of the Common Law in America*, 43 L.Q. REV. 449.

Wilde, Christian L. (1968) *Depecage in the Choice of Tort Law*, 41 SO. CAL. L. REV. 329.

Williston, Samuel (1943) *Joseph Henry Beale—A Biographical Sketch*, 56 HARV. L. REV. 685.

Wing, Adrien K. (1983) *Pleading and Proof of Foreign Law in American Courts, A Selected Annotated Bibliography*, 19 STAN. J. INT'L L. 175.

Wurfel, Seymour W. (1971) *Recognition of Foreign Judgments*, 50 N.C. L. REV. 21.

Wurfel, Seymour W. (1975) *Jet Age Domicil: The Semi-Demise of Durational Residence Requirements*, 11 WAKE FOREST L. REV. 349.

Yates, George T., III (1978) *Foreign Law Before Domestic Tribunals*, 18 VA. J. INT'L L. 725.

Yntema, Hessell E. (1928) *The Hornbook Method and the Conflict of Laws*, 37 YALE L.J. 468.

Yntema, Hessell E. (1934) *The American Law Institute*, 12 CAN. BAR REV. 317.

Yntema, Hessell E. (1936) *What Should the American Law Institute Do?*, 34 MICH. L. REV. 461.

Yntema, Hessell E. (1953) *The Historic Bases of Private International Law*, 2 AM. J. COMP. L. 297.

Yntema, Hassell E. (1957) *The Objectives of Private International Law*, 35 CAN. BAR REV. 721.

Yntema, Hessell E. (1966) *The Comity Doctrine*, 65 MICH. L. REV. 9.

Zaphiriou, George A. (1985) *State or Country Interest as Analytical Framework for Choice of Law*, 46 OHIO ST. L.J. 537.

Zweigert, Konrad (1973) *Some Reflections on the Sociological Dimensions of Private International Law or What Is Justice in Conflict of Laws*, 44 COLO. L. REV. 283.

TABLE OF CASES

INDEX

Choice-of-law discussions in the book touch upon the topics listed below. References are to chapter, chapter section, or page.